BULLS, BEARS, BOOM, AND BUST

BULLS, BEARS, BOOM, AND BUST

A Historical Encyclopedia of American Business Concepts

John Dobson

A B C CLIO
Santa Barbara, California   Denver, Colorado   Oxford, England

Library of Congress Cataloging-in-Publication Data
Dobson, John M.
Bulls, bears, boom, and bust : a historical encyclopedia of American business concepts / John Dobson.
p. cm.
Includes bibliographical references and index.
ISBN 1-85109-553-5 (hard cover : alk. paper) 1. United States—Commerce—History—Encyclopedias. 2. Business enterprises—United States—History—Encyclopedias. 3. Industries—United States—History—Encyclopedias. 4. Businesspeople—United States—Biography. 5. Businesspeople—United States—History—Encyclopedias. I. Title. II. Title: Historical encyclopedia of American business concepts.

HF3021.D59 2006
330.973003—dc22

2006027499

11 10 09 08 07 10 9 8 7 6 5 4 3 2 1

ISBN-13: 978-1-85109-553-7 (ebook) 978-1-85109-558-2
ISBN-10: 1-85109-553-5 (ebook) 1-85109-558-6

Production Editor: Kristine Swift
Editorial Assistant: Alisha Martinez
Production Manager: Don Schmidt
Media Resources Manager: Caroline Price
File Manager: Paula Gerard

This book is also available on the World Wide Web as an ebook. Visit http://www.abc-clio.com for details.

ABC-CLIO, Inc.
130 Cremona Drive, P.O. Box 1911
Santa Barbara, California 93116-1911

This book is printed on acid-free paper ∞

Manufactured in the United States of America

Contents

Preface

As with all major writing projects, the scope of this book evolved and expanded over time. Initially I intended to define and describe the origins of a relatively limited set of concepts important to the history of American business. It quickly became apparent that certain people played vital roles in inventing or innovating devices, mechanisms, or processes that profoundly shaped how business was and is conducted in the United States. That led me to include biographical entries on key inventors, entrepreneurs, and industrial and business leaders. I have paid particular attention to those like Goodyear, Woolworth, Hilton, Maytag, and Westinghouse, whose names remain actively associated with major ongoing business ventures.

My understanding and appreciation of what constituted important business-related concepts expanded in other directions as well. For example, government restrictions, encouragement, and regulations have exercised critical influence on business activities throughout American history, so government decisions and policies appear among the topical entries. Similarly economic theories, industrial organizational structures, marketing and merchandising strategies, and the availability of capital resources including various types of money, all helped mold the American business environment. Many other concepts also demanded attention as I explored the development of business from the nation's colonial origins to the present day.

As a historian, I found a chronological approach appropriate and appealing. It allowed me to distribute the 210 topical entries and 160 biographical sketches into five sections, each covering a relatively limited span of years. A brief historical review introduces each section, explaining where and how each topical entry fits into the overall picture. Each chronological section also includes biographical entries describing people who played active roles in American business during the appropriate frame of years. A user interested in a particular period will therefore find relevant associated information in the entries assembled within the same section.

Innovations and developments often have long-term consequences, however, and the influence of some of the topics and people extended well beyond the chronological limits of the individual sections. To assist readers in pursuing connections and consequences, most of the entries contain references to related topics or people included elsewhere in the book.

Reference Aids

In addition to a standard index, the book contains three appendixes. The first provides an alphabetical listing of all the entries included in the book and notes the section in which each can be found.

The second sorts the topical entries into the following groupings: agriculture, antitrust, banking, business cycles, capital, electronics, entertainment, government, industry, intellectual property, international, labor, merchandising, money, organization, railroads, regulation, speculation, strategy, theory, and transportation.

The third identifies common characteristics or fields of endeavor of the individuals included in the biographical entries. These groupings include: agriculture, aircraft, automobiles, banking, business, clothing, conglomerates, cosmetics, electronics, entertainment, food, government, industry, inventions, merchandising, publishing, railroads, service, speculation, and theory.

As some of the people discussed obviously have direct links with one or more of the topics discussed in the general entries, readers interested in information on a particular subject may find it useful to compare one list with the other to identify these commonalities.

ACKNOWLEDGMENTS

No project of this type could have been completed without extensive support and encouragement. I owe a debt of gratitude to my extraordinarily congenial colleagues in the Department of History at Oklahoma State University where most of the research and writing took place. No matter how obscure or detailed the information I sought, the university's library collection unfailingly provided me with appropriate references and in-depth sources. I was also fortunate in being invited to teach at the University of Glasgow while working on major aspects of this book. Here again, the history faculty proved to be an agreeable group who welcomed me with respect and friendship. I was equally pleased to discover a quite comprehensive library collection on campus. As one of Britain's "ancient" institutions, the University of Glasgow appears to have retained every book it acquired since its founding in 1451, providing a historian with a delightful treasure trove of sources to explore.

I am also indebted to the capable staff at ABC-CLIO, beginning with Alicia Merritt, whose enthusiasm for my work proved especially encouraging. Three others who made major contributions in helping refine the final text are Alex Mikaberidze, Kristine Swift, and Anne Friedman. Last but certainly in no way the least, I wish to thank my wife Cindy for her support. She not only helped me conceive of this project, but showed remarkable tolerance as I became distracted by and absorbed in the research and writing it involved.

JMD

Section 1

Colonial America, 1607–1760

The first permanent English settlement in North America began in 1607 with the founding of Jamestown in Virginia. Over the next century and a half, the population of British North America grew to over 3 million people living in thirteen distinct colonies. Many economic and business developments that emerged in this period set precedents that still affect current events.

Conditions and ambitions in England stimulated colonial expansion. The **enclosure** movement forced farm families into cities long before an industrial revolution provided jobs for them. Trading opportunities and international rivalries attracted financial investment and fueled imperial ambitions. The royal government remained strapped for funding and was absorbed in internal controversies and conflicts. The shaky hold exercised by Stuart kings broke down in the mid-1600s, only to be restored after an eleven-year experiment with the Puritan Commonwealth. Twenty-five years later, the Glorious Revolution of 1688 brought William and Mary over to England from Holland. The internal political situation finally became more stable under the Georges in the eighteenth century.

In the early years the distracted monarchy relied almost exclusively on private enterprise to plant its colonies. To initiate such a grand endeavor, however, royal permission was needed in the form of either a **charter** or a **proprietary** grant. While a few wealthy individuals could finance their own expeditions, a **joint-stock company** of investors and adventurers established the first successful colony. When its initial capital dried up, the Virginia Company supplemented its finances with national **lotteries**. Occasionally, optimism got out of hand, creating a speculative **bubble** that soon collapsed, inflicting devastating costs on the unwary.

Disappointed in their search for gold and other quick riches, English investors and proprietors realized that land and its products offered alternative pathways to wealth. While many proprietors retained substantial land holdings, they also handed off or sold tracts to others. To encourage immigration, many colonies offered **head rights**, grants of fifty acres or more to anyone who would settle in America.

The colonies exploited a number of methods to meet their constant need for labor in a hand-built world. Young people routinely signed **apprenticeship** contracts hoping to learn a trade that would improve their chances of employment. Penniless people in the British Isles signed similar labor agreements called **indentures** in return for transport to opportunities in the New World. When the supply of indentured servants waned in the late 1600s, landowners increasingly relied on **slave labor** to work their fields.

Agriculture was consistently the most important economic activity in the land-rich colonies. **Staples** like **tobacco**, sugar, **naval stores**, and grain were shipped all over the world. The bounty of American fields created periodic gluts of some commodities and depressed prices. To lower production costs, farmers sought to expand their operations into large-scale **plantations** capable of exploiting economies of scale. **Factors** acted as purchasing and supply agents for the larger plantation owners.

In the Northeast, where farming was less rewarding, alternatives like **fishing** and **shipbuilding** became major industries. A lively and expanding **fur trade** thrived throughout the colonies as well. In urban centers, wage workers and artisans experimented with primitive organizational efforts in the form of **guilds**. Although colonial governments repeatedly attempted to impose **wage codes** to control costs and maintain social control, the persistent labor shortage in North America undermined such regulatory efforts. Meanwhile, speculators in the busy port of New York laid the groundwork for its future prominence by congregating along **Wall Street** to conduct their business.

As the colonial population expanded, the British government took greater interest in controlling commerce among the colonies, and between them and the rest of the world. The conceptual basis for these moves became known as **mercantilism**. Beginning with the restoration of the monarchy in 1660, a series of **navigation acts** attempted to channel colonial trade. Parliament subsequently passed **manufacturing acts** designed to protect industrial activities in the home islands by discouraging manufacturing in the colonies.

Many Americans viewed these rules and restrictions as detrimental to their development. They also suffered from a lack of sound currency. Barter was the most common method for exchanging goods and services in the early days, and it continued to prevail right through the colonial period. As merchants became more prosperous and influential, however, they took bartering to a higher level by recording debts and assets in ledgers and thereby creating **book credit** for their clients and customers. Hoping to provide a sounder basis for trade, the Massachusetts Colony issued silver coins called **pine tree shillings** until the royal government shut down the mint in 1684. But up to the eve of the American Revolution, British coins remained so scarce that many Americans were often more familiar with foreign **dollars** than with pounds sterling.

As these factors suggest, tension between the royal government and the colonists waxed and waned over the years. In general the colonists thought of themselves as English people and of the colonies as overseas extensions of the home islands. British authorities increasingly tried to rationalize the structure and improve the overall efficiencies of their expanding empire. But the imperial connection also drew American settlers into a series of international wars that often seemed to have no relevance or benefit to their lives and livelihoods. Their positions within the imperial system thus became less comfortable by the end of the French and Indian War in 1763. In the next few years disaffection with imperial rules, taxes, and perceived arrogance would lead to the American Revolution.

KEY CONCEPTS

Apprenticeship

To learn a craft or trade in colonial America, children served apprenticeships with master craftsmen. An apprentice signed an indenture, or labor contract, that included an obligation to work for a set period of years. In return the master agreed to provide shelter, food, and clothing, as well as training and experience in his craft or profession.

Apprenticeships were common throughout medieval Europe. Skilled craftsmen and artisans usually enjoyed higher social and economic standing than did unskilled laborers or peasants. Consequently, parents were eager to apprentice out their children, sometimes even paying the potential master to do so. In other cases, a master might pay a small sum to a potential apprentice's family to obtain a good worker.

In the British North American colonies, apprenticeships were less common in the early years in part because so few skilled masters were in residence. As the New England economy developed, however, with its poor farmlands and growing cities, the prospect of learning a trade was increasingly attractive. Common schooling was scarce throughout the colonies, and higher education scarcer still. Children therefore entered apprenticeships at early ages, staying on with a master for six to eight years. Masters charged from £2 to £6 to take on a new trainee.

As in any system, the quality of apprentices' experiences varied widely, depending on the relative wealth, skill, and personality of their masters. Some apprentices were consigned to heavy labor and failed to develop skills, while others who had more benevolent masters were taught how to read and write and some basic business skills along with training in a craft or profession. Carpenters, shipwrights, tailors, and blacksmiths were typical products of craft apprenticeships, while other young people learned from merchants and ship captains.

At the conclusion of an apprenticeship, the master was expected to provide "freedom dues" in the form of clothing and money to help the new craftsman become established. Many who had completed their apprenticeships spent several years in transition as journeymen. The expression came from the French word *jour,* or day, signifying that these people worked on a day-to-day basis for others. The ultimate goal was to be recognized as a master craftsman who could establish an independent, profitable shop or business and, in due course, train a new generation of apprentices.

Apprenticeships enabled energetic and resourceful young people to greatly improve their prospects. Probably the most famous early American apprentice was Benjamin Franklin. He was fortunate enough to have obtained some grammar school education in his native Boston before being apprenticed at the age of twelve to his older brother, a printer. Five years later, young Benjamin abandoned his apprenticeship and moved to Philadelphia, where he established himself as a successful newspaper publisher on the basis of the skills he had learned as an apprentice.

Formal or informal apprenticeships continued to train young people well into the nineteenth century. They remained an attractive option for children who might otherwise never have learned a trade or been able to become independent businessmen.

See also Franklin, Benjamin; Indenture.

References and Further Reading

Barck, Oscar Theodore Jr., and Hugh Talmage Lefler. *Colonial America.* New York: Macmillan, 1968.

Boorstin, Daniel J. *Americans: The Colonial Experience.* New York: Random House, 1958.

Book Credit

Colonial merchants who dealt with a number of buyers and sellers often kept track of their accounts with bookkeeping techniques. Book credit became an essential substitute for other financial instruments in a cash-poor economy.

During the seventeenth and eighteenth centuries, the British colonists in North America continually experienced an unfavorable balance of trade, always importing more than they were able to export. As a result, very little specie or other European currency remained in circulation in the colonies. Instead, it was quickly sent back to England to pay for new imports. The colonists therefore had to rely on barter, commodity money, or book credit to conduct business in America.

Merchants could keep track of exchanges of goods and services without cash simply by recording the value of the items or activities in their ledgers. An individual customer might be ahead or behind at any given time. For example, a farmer might "borrow" tools to produce a crop and then "pay" the merchant back with the grain he harvested. The merchant would record the value of the tools in the spring and then offset that indebtedness in his books with the value of the commodities he received in the fall.

An individual merchant might have similar arrangements with dozens of clients, some of whom would be in debt while others maintained positive balances. In addition to recording the ebb and flow of transactions for an individual, the merchant could transfer book credit from one customer to another. In this way, the merchant was essentially operating as a banker for his clients but often without ever handling any currency or coins at all.

Many merchants also relied on book credit to handle transactions with and among clients in other colonies and even with contacts in the home country. The book credit system provided considerable flexibility in the valuation of goods and services and allowed people with limited financial resources to trade whatever they had for items they needed. Of course, a merchant often had to be creative in disposing of some of the items that people presented for payment, such as chickens, beaver pelts, firewood, grain, whiskey, and homespun cloth.

Book credit continued to facilitate trade in America long after the Revolution because specie continued to be scarce and the questionable value of paper currency issued by private banks, state governments, and, from time to time, even the U.S. Treasury.

See also Commodity Money; Dollar; Trade Balance.

References and Further Reading

Bailyn, Bernard. *The New England Merchants in the Seventeenth Century.* New York: Harper and Row, 1955.

Bruchey, Stuart. *The Colonial Merchant.* New York: Harcourt, Brace and World, 1966.

Bubble

When prices for a commodity rise far beyond the intrinsic value of that commodity, a *bubble* can occur. Speculators continue bidding the price up until, quite abruptly, demand or interest in the commodity evaporates. When the bubble bursts, overextended speculators can lose significant sums.

Although it had only marginal impact on the recently founded British American colonies, a bubble in tulip prices in the early 1630s rocked the international trading community in Holland and other European countries. Over several centuries, tulip cultivation migrated from Central Asia to Western Europe. Dutch gardeners became particularly intrigued with tulips, cross-breeding various strains and producing more colorful varieties.

Early in the seventeenth century, Holland began to profit handsomely from its international trade, causing a corresponding rise in the standard of living in the Netherlands. At first only the wealthiest individuals could dabble in the tulip trade, bidding up the prices for rare bulbs with desirable or fashionable characteristics. And, for a time, the resulting inflation in prices affected only small circles of knowledgeable growers, gardeners, and buyers.

By the 1630s, however, the number of Dutchmen with funds available for discretionary investment had grown quite large. People with little or no knowledge of horticulture began speculating on individual bulbs or one-pound batches, often putting down only minimal deposits in the range of 10 percent of the bid price. Their goal was to resell their options quickly at higher prices. These speculators were essentially working within an early sort of futures trading system. The lure of quick profits encouraged the spread of buying and selling throughout Holland. Some buying and selling occurred in more structured exchanges, but much of it occured in unregulated saloons.

By late 1636, a full-scale boom was evident, with prices advancing weekly or more often, even for the most mundane bulbs. An exponential frenzy of buying activity peaked in December 1636 and spilled over into Janu-

Frenzied speculators like these bought and sold shares in the South Sea Company, contributing to the bubble that ruined many when it burst. (Library of Congress)

ary 1637. In early February, the boom ran out of buyers. No one seemed willing to bid at any price, leaving thousands of speculators holding bulbs or paper receipts they could not sell. As the boom collapsed, aggrieved parties sought legal remedies. After reviewing the tangled financial mess for two months, the Court of Holland at the Hague suggested a temporary moratorium on all tulip buy-and-sell contracts. This measure evolved into a more permanent resolution, leaving individuals to work out solutions on a one-to-one basis. The Tulip Bubble had burst.

This tulip-buying fiasco occurred in one of the most stable, well-educated, and prosperous countries in the world, demonstrating that a bubble could occur anywhere, anytime. Great Britain experienced an even more pervasive and destructive financial catastrophe eighty years later when the infamous South Sea Bubble developed.

The legitimate, if unrealistic, premise for founding the South Sea Company was the prospect of profitable British trade with Spain's South American colonies. The company obtained a royal charter in 1711 granting it a monopoly of this trade, even though England and Spain were at war. The Treaty of Utrecht in 1713 ended that phase of the conflict, but it authorized only very limited British commerce with South America. Other than a restricted and ultimately unprofitable trade in African slaves, Spain permitted just one British ship to enter its colonial ports. To make matters worse, the two rivals again went to war in 1718.

The company had meanwhile offered to assume Great Britain's war-swollen national debt. After winning out over a similar offer from the Bank of England, the South Sea Company began exchanging company shares for government loan notes. By 1720 the company had become almost exclusively a financial and banking concern, managing the enormous debt and issuing additional lots of stock to attract new investors. Its association with the government helped encourage sales and, through both legitimate and fraudulent manipulation, its share prices continued to rise.

The South Sea Company generated a speculative frenzy that stimulated dozens of other joint-stock ventures for all sorts of real or imagined purposes. For example, one company was founded ostensibly to import walnut trees from Virginia; another announced its sole purpose to be importing "pitch and tar, and other naval stores, from north Britain and America." Regardless of the listed purpose, the real goal was to sell shares to credulous buyers. These schemes became so outrageous that Parliament passed the Bubble Act in June 1720 requiring any joint-stock enterprise to obtain a royal charter.

Ironically, this legislation momentarily boosted public confidence in the South Sea Company because it had possessed a royal charter for nearly a decade. The company's share price briefly topped £1,000 a share at the end of the month. However, the bubble expanded well beyond its ability to sustain itself. By September, the asking price had fallen to £135 and speculators, investors, company officials, and government supporters of the company were all blamed. Thousands lost life savings to speculation, others lost everything to confiscation. But, as is often the case in business turmoil, a few of those shrewd or lucky enough to have sold out early gained substantial fortunes. The South Sea Bubble so traumatized the British people that for decades afterward even legitimate organizations seeking investment capital could not rely on public subscriptions.

A similar speculative binge took place in France at about the same time. The architect of the debacle was Scottish-born John Law, an articulate and plausible exponent of novel economic concepts. Law moved to Paris in 1715 and befriended the Duc D'Orleans who was serving as the regent of France for the five-year-old Louis XV. Law founded a bank in 1716 and, a year later, used his political connections to obtain control of the Mississippi Company, which had exclusive rights to trade in Louisiana, but had fallen on hard times. Within a couple of years, Law had used this company, renamed Compagnie d'Occident, as a platform to obtain control of all of France's non-European trade.

Law simultaneously took on the task of reorganizing the war-ravaged French financial system, using massive distributions of paper currency as a major tool. Speculators eagerly bid up the price of shares in the Compagnie d'Occident, from an initial level of 500 French livres to over 10,000. Unrealistic expectations, countervailing moves by the government, and disappointing returns from the company's overseas trading ventures combined to undermine the stock's value. In a matter of months it fell back to its original level, dragging down or completely destroying the wealth of countless investors and speculators. The stunning rise and collapse of the Mississippi Company Bubble proved so traumatic that the French government avoided issuing paper currency for more than half a century.

The United States has experienced bubbles of its own. The most famous was the Florida Land Bubble in the 1920s. More recently, the frenzy of speculation in high-tech or "dot.com" stocks in the 1990s had many similarities to the earlier historical bubbles.

See also Charter, Royal; Florida Land Bubble; Joint-Stock Company.

References and Further Reading

Dash, Mike. *Tulipomania.* New York: Crown, 1999.

Garber, Peter M. *Famous First Bubbles: The Fundamentals of Early Manias.* Cambridge, MA: MIT Press, 2000.

Charter, Royal

In colonial America, ultimate authority resided with the royal government in London. One way it exercised its authority was through issuing charters to various individuals, groups, or enterprises that legitimated their business activities.

Royal charters were essential elements in the British settlement of North America. Both the Virginia Company of London and its rival, the Virginia Company of Plymouth, obtained charters from the government of King James I authorizing them to establish plantations or colonies in America. Considerable politicking and influence peddling were involved in obtaining a royal charter. Only by obtaining charters could the investors and adventurers begin operating their companies as recognized business entities.

Official permission to do business was only part of the benefit the Virginia companies gained with their charters. The royal government maintained claims to lands adjacent to the northeast coast of North America dating back to John Cabot's exploratory voyages in the late 1490s. A royal charter transferred ownership of such lands to companies and proprietors, thus providing the essential real estate for a colonizing effort.

The charters for the Virginia companies contained overlapping land grants, designating the area between 40° and 48° north latitude in both documents. The Plymouth group's claims stretched well north of the overlapping area, however, so it rushed ahead with plans to send over a colonizing group in 1607. The goal was a permanent settlement along the Kennebec River in what is present-day Maine. This area proved inhospitable, so the potential settlers quickly abandoned the effort. The London company was therefore able to mount its more successful Jamestown Plantation on the Chesapeake Bay without competition from the Plymouth company.

A royal council exercised considerable influence under the Virginia Company of London's original charter. To insulate itself from direct royal oversight, the company negotiated a new charter in 1609 that established it as a joint-stock company. The company never managed to generate the anticipated financial returns, and that, combined with organizational problems and strife in Virginia, led to its collapse in 1624. The charter privileges reverted to the government at that point, and Virginia remained a "royal colony" directly answerable to the monarchy until the American Revolution.

Meanwhile the Council for New England had inherited the Plymouth company's claims to the northern coastal area. The council encouraged the formation of the Massachusetts Bay Colony. The Puritan leaders who formed a company to settle in that area obtained their own royal charter that allowed the whole organization, including its charter, to move to the New World. The theocracy that subsequently ruled Massachusetts thus did so with royal authorization. In the late seventeenth century, the British government withdrew this favorable charter, and the colony was managed like most of the other royal colonies in the eighteenth century.

Many other colonizing efforts involved royal charters, but two colonies operated quite differently than the rest. Connecticut and Rhode Island were settled by discontented or ambitious people who moved south and west from the rigidly controlled society in Massachusetts. The leaders of these offshoots worked with agents in London to obtain independent charters from the royal government. When King Charles II was restored to the throne after the English Civil War in 1660, he wanted to reward these two colonies for their expressions of loyalty to him. He did so by issuing each of them a very liberal charter. They were allowed to elect their own governors and otherwise function as semi-independent republics.

While many provisions of the royal charters dealt with political issues and organization, these documents were also crucial to business and economic development. They granted royal permission for individuals and groups to create and operate a broad variety of enterprises. The latter aspect of the royal charters remained important after the Revolution. The governments that succeeded the colonial administrations continued the process of issuing charters to promote and regulate business activities. In this way state charters took the place of the royal charters that had encouraged enterprise in the earlier period.

See also Calvert, George; Charter, State; Joint-Stock Company; Proprietary Colonies.

References and Further Reading

Andrews, Charles M. *Our Earliest Colonial Settlements.* New York: New York University Press, 1933.

Barbour, Philip. *The Three Worlds of Captain John Smith.* Boston: Houghton Mifflin, 1964.

Vaughn, Alden T. *Captain John Smith and the Founding of Virginia.* Boston: Little, Brown, 1975.

Commodity Money

A chronic shortage of coins and specie forced American colonists to find alternatives to hard currency. Commodity money served that purpose throughout the colonies, ranging from tobacco in the Tidewater area to wampum in New England. In several instances, colonial governments officially sanctioned the use of such commodities for taxes and trade.

The perennial trade deficit that plagued Britain's North American colonies caused most hard currency to be exported to England to buy items not available locally. As in most primitive agrarian societies, barter was the most common means of exchange. A desire for more predictable valuation of basic commodities quickly developed, however, and local authorities enacted various laws to do so.

The predominance of tobacco cultivation in the Tidewater Colonies of Virginia and Maryland made tobacco a natural choice as commodity money. Taxes, rent, wages, and even clergymen's salaries were often contracted in pounds of tobacco. Cured and rolled tobacco was far less perishable than other farm produce, so it could be transferred and stored appropriately. Those who did not want to contend with bulk goods could accept receipts for up to 90 percent of the value of the tobacco they owned and use these receipts like paper currency. As with all types of commodity money, quality control was virtually impossible to enforce, and debtors often tried to pass off their worst produce to pay their obligations.

European settlers in the northeast used the Native American practice of stringing shells or glass beads into strands called wampum. New Netherlands accepted wampum as legal tender as early as 1634; Massachusetts followed suit six years later. Some of the legal definitions were quite explicit. A 1664 New York law, for example, decreed that a string of eight white and four black beads had the value of a penny.

Many other commodities served as money. At one point, North Carolina laws recognized twenty different items as legal tender. Sometimes referred to as "country pay," tender included products as diverse as corn, hides, rum, sheep, and whale oil. Leonard Hoar, a future president of Harvard College, paid his student tuition bill in 1649 with what he described as "an old cow." As late as the Revolutionary period, Paul Revere was accepting chickens and other produce in exchange for his fine silver pieces.

Commodity money was never a good means of exchange due to its fluctuating quality and price, perishability, bulk, and the need for appropriate storage. A number of alternatives appeared including book credit, foreign coins, promissory notes, and other paper pledges. But throughout the colonial period, governments arbitrarily set commodity values in pounds, shillings, and pence. Ironically, in 1933, the United States government used the opposite strategy, arbitrarily defining the dollar's value in comparison to set measures of agricultural and other products, a technique that was called the "commodity dollar."

See also Book Credit; Commodity Dollar; Trade Balance.

References and Further Reading

Moore, Carl H., and Alvin E. Russell. *Money: Its Origin, Development and Modern Use.* Jefferson, NC: McFarland, 1987.

Weatherford, Jack. *The History of Money.* New York: Crown, 1997.

Dollar

Relatively few British coins either reached or stayed in the colonies, so American colonists became far more familiar with other kinds of currency. Silver coins minted in the Spanish colony of Mexico circulated so widely that the "Spanish dollar" became a commonly recognized coin. When the colonies reformulated themselves into the United States, they adopted the dollar as the basis for the new nation's currency.

The word *dollar* originated in a Bohemian valley that is located in the present day Czech Republic. Early in the sixteenth century, the Holy Roman Empire extended its control over Bohemia. Shortly afterward in 1516, extensive silver deposits were discovered in the nearby mountains, and the local count began minting it into silver coins called *groschen.* The German name for the valley was Joachimsthal, so the coins produced there were called *joachimsthalergroschen.* This awkward name was quickly shortened to *thalergroschen* and, later, simply to thalers. During the succeeding hundred years, this region put over 12 million thalers into circulation, and they became so common that the word *thaler* came to be applied to any large silver coin.

The name found its way to Scotland in the 1560s. King James VI minted a coin valued at thirty shillings similar in size to the German thalers. The Scots transliterated the name into *dollar,* a term they stubbornly adhered to even after their monarch became James I of England in 1603. Dollars remained symbolic of Scottish nationalism, and Scotch-Irish immigrants brought the term with them when they traveled by the thousands to the American colonies in the early 1700s.

These immigrants did not, however, bring very much cash with them. Throughout the colonial period, American settlers maintained an unfavorable trade balance with the mother country. Far more wealth was transported from the British Isles to the New World than was transported from the New World to the British Isles, so the colonies generally remained deeply in debt. That meant that any British coins that somehow made the transatlantic passage were almost immediately shipped back across the ocean to offset new purchases of goods and services. Moreover, in 1695 the British government passed legislation that forbid the export of specie to the colonies. Consequently, few average Americans ever possessed or even saw British coins.

Trade relationships with other regions tended to be less one-sided. The Spanish authorities in Mexico had access to very rich silver mines, so they minted silver peso coins that quickly began to circulate all over the world. The British colonies ended up collecting rather substantial numbers of these coins, which the Americans usually referred to as Spanish dollars. In the Mexican system, eight *reals* made up one *peso,* but the Americans referred to these minor divisions as *bits* with a dollar being worth eight bits.

Even though merchants kept their books and recorded prices in the official British systems of pounds, shillings, and pence, cash-paying customers often bought their wares with dollar coins. By the time of the Revolution, Americans had become quite used to figuring their wealth in dollars rather than pounds. Like the nationalistic Scots, the American revolutionaries adopted the dollar in part to distinguish their new nation from the British Empire.

See also Book Credit; Commodity Money; Trade Balance.

References and Further Reading

Moore, Carl H., and Alvin E. Russell. *Money: Its Origin, Development and Modern Use.* Jefferson, NC: McFarland, 1987.

Weatherford, Jack. *The History of Money.* New York: Crown, 1997.

Enclosure

During the sixteenth century, much agricultural land in the British Isles was "enclosed" and converted from farmland to pastures for sheep. This enclosure phenomenon forced thousands of farm families off the land and into poverty.

As it emerged from the Middle Ages, England's economy and society followed the classic feudal pattern. The population was primarily agrarian, dispersed throughout the countryside either on tiny holdings or as tenant farmers. The primary landowners prospered in proportion to the success of the efforts of those who worked the land and paid their feudal dues.

When King Henry VII emerged victorious from the Wars of the Roses in 1485, he was able to consolidate authority and power in the Tudor monarchy. His reign also ushered in economic changes including a significant rise in international trade, much of it stimulated by the export of British woolen goods. It was only natural, then, that landowners increasingly saw the raising of sheep as the most rewarding agricultural pursuit.

To run sheep effectively, croplands had to be converted to pasture, and, equally important, competing livestock had to be excluded from common pasturage. As ambitious landowners enclosed fields and commons, they drove poorer farmers and tenants off the land. Cut off from their traditional livelihoods, substantial numbers of men, women, and children migrated to London and other cities. Most found little relief in the cities where they often became absorbed in a large, destitute mob that relied on petty crime or badly overtaxed charities.

As the seventeenth century dawned, both the dispossessed people and government authorities were seeking ways to ameliorate their plight. The prospect of free land in the New World, particularly after the establishment of the head right system, encouraged many of these people to undertake the grueling voyage to the American colonies. Thus the enclosure movement helped stimulate the populating of Britain's overseas possessions.

See also Head Rights; Indenture.

References and Further Reading

Seebohm, M. D. *The Evolution of the English Farm.* Cambridge, MA: Harvard University Press, 1927.

Thirsk, Joan, ed. *Agrarian History of England and Wales, 1500–1640.* Cambridge: Cambridge University Press, 1967.

Factor

Factors conducted much of the commercial activity in the American colonies. They were independent businessmen who acted as commission agents. Factors handled the marketing of agricultural commodities often collected from a number of farms or plantations. They also served as bankers, creditors, and suppliers to their place-bound clients. These entrepreneurs provided invaluable service as middlemen for the colonies being carved out of the American wilderness, remote from major commercial centers.

The factorage system had its roots in the late Middle Ages, developing when larger-scale trade in commodities became more prevalent. Farmers and craftsmen were far too busy with their own productive activities to handle distribution and sales in an expanding economy. Middlemen with resources and contacts both at home and abroad were better positioned to identify markets and locate needed supplies. The word *factor* was based on roots that signified a "doer" or a "maker," and it came into use to describe these versatile businessmen as early as the sixteenth century.

The conditions that created the factorage system in Europe were even more prevalent in colonial settings. For some time, the sugar islands of the West Indies were the most profitable overseas enterprises, but the day-to-day management of a large plantation with a sizable slave labor force left its owner with little time or energy to market his produce or buy supplies. Agents of established merchant houses in England or prosperous shipowners could provide some of the marketing and logistical needs of these planters. Very quickly, however, individuals who specialized in being middlemen began to compete.

Factors seldom bought sugar or tobacco from a particular planter, being content to collect a commission for serving as marketing agents. Throughout the colonial period, the standard commission charged was 2.5 percent of the commodities' value. Factors who arranged for the shipment of supplies or other goods to their agrarian clients charged a similar commission for their services.

Factors in the Tidewater South often operated on a very intimate basis with their clients. The region's slow-moving navigable rivers and streams permitted the shipment of goods by boat or barge, and facilitated personal travel. Further south, barrier islands and adverse currents encouraged the development of coastal ports where factors handled rice, indigo, and other products. Many of these colonial factors were either English or Scottish people whose contacts with merchants and buyers in the British Isles gave them easy access to the importers of American products. The sugar, tobacco, and rice factors of the eighteenth century served as models and precedents for the much more substantial cotton factorage system that prevailed in the cotton kingdom after 1800.

See also Cotton Factorage; Plantation; Staples.

References and Further Reading

Bruchey, Stuart. *The Colonial Merchant*. New York: Harcourt Brace, 1966.

Woodman, Harold D. *King Cotton and His Retainers*. Lexington, KY: University of Kentucky Press, 1968.

Fisheries

Fishing was one of the most important economic activities in the New England colonies. Hundreds of vessels and thousands of men participated in this industry, and dried and cured fish from New England were shipped literally all over the world by the time of the Revolution. Profits from fishing stimulated the shipbuilding industry and provided the basis for an enterprising merchant class.

Fishing along the northeast coast of North America and the Grand Banks adjacent to Newfoundland began long before the founding of the British colonies. In the late 1490s John Cabot reported a plentiful fish population in that area, and European fishing vessels began sailing west on annual voyages to tap these valuable resources. The fishing fleet included ships from several countries, and international negotiations and rivalries persisted well into the eighteenth century.

English fishermen were already quite familiar with and continuously exploiting the bounty of the region by the time the Pilgrims established their settlement at Plymouth Colony in 1620. Although they had come to America expecting to farm, the new settlers quickly began harvesting the sea and the coastal inlets. The Council for New England made sure that its royal charter included exclusive rights to fish off the New England coast. By 1630 shipments of salted fish were routinely sailing back to the mother country, and the establishment of the Puritan settlements at Boston and Salem that year only served to increase the trade.

The scope and size of the fishing industry entered a new phase in 1641 when Massachusetts-based ships began trolling Newfoundland's Grand Banks. Though they lacked the exclusive rights they enjoyed further south, the New Englanders soon came to dominate this rich resource. But the English were hardly alone in exploiting the fishing bonanza. The most persistent competitors were the French, whose settlements along the Canadian coastline also served as convenient bases for fishing fleets. The series of conflicts between England and France kept the area in turmoil until 1763. Under the terms of the Treaty of Paris that ended the French and Indian War that year, France ceded all its Canadian possessions to Great Britain, insuring better protected access to these fishing grounds for English and colonial vessels.

Cod was the industry's mainstay. Cod could easily be dried or salt cured, and the preserved fish could be shipped long distances. The catch was separated into three grades: merchantable, middling, and the refuse. Spain and Portugal were major buyers of the merchantable grade, in part because of the Catholic Church's injunction against meat consumption on Fridays and holy days. The middling catch usually found its way to the Canaries and Madeiras or Jamaica. The refuse, the lowest quality, was mostly consigned to the West Indies to feed slaves laboring on sugar plantations. In addition to cod, the New Englanders also caught and shipped haddock, herring, hake, halibut, mackerel, and flounder.

The financial returns from the fishing industry were substantial. In 1700 New Englanders shipped ten million pounds of cured fish, and the output had tripled by the middle of the century. An official estimate shows Massachusetts alone sold £243,000 worth of seafood in 1763. Crew members typically received a share of the catch in return for their labor, but most of the profit from the fisheries ended up in the pockets of ship captains and the merchants who funded the voyages. Even so, literally thousands of men captained their own small craft to and from the fishing grounds during the colonial period, and the industry continued to support individual enterprise long after the Revolution.

See also Shipbuilding.

References and Further Reading

McFarland, Raymond. *A History of the New England Fisheries.* Philadelphia, PA: University of Pennsylvania Press, 1911.

Santos, Michael Wayne. *Caught in Irons: North Atlantic Fishermen in the Last Days of Sail.* Selinsgrove, PA: Susquehanna University Press, 2002.

Steele, Ian K. *The English Atlantic, 1675–1740.* New York: Oxford University Press, 1986.

Fur Trade

The fur trade began in North America long before the English established their settlements. European demand for furs, leather, and animal products remained strong throughout the colonial period, and every colony had trappers, traders, merchants, and shippers. In time competition over the sources of fur contributed to military conflict and rivalry between England and France.

At first, the French were the most energetic in exploiting the wildlife resources of North America. Their explorers used the St. Lawrence River route to penetrate all the way to the Great Lakes. While most of the trade involved the region's Native population, many Frenchmen shucked off their European ways in pursuit of furs. Hardy frontiersmen called *coureurs de bois* loaded canoes with trade goods and disappeared into the interior for months or years at a time. The French also established permanent posts, laying the foundations for communities like Quebec and Montreal.

The Dutch arrived early as well. The trading post they established on Manhattan Island flourished from handling furs ferried from the interior down the Mohawk and the Hudson rivers. Gaining access to the profitable fur trade was a major motivation for the British takeover of New Amsterdam, and by 1672 the hinterland stretched all the way to Niagara Falls.

From the very beginning, British settlers in New England hunted and trapped wildlife and traded goods for furs with the Indian population. Complementing their focus on fishing and farming, New Englanders moved west and north in search of furs. Trading posts were stationed on the upper Connecticut River in the 1630s, and the Maine woods were seen as a vital resource as well.

The southern colonies also engaged in a profitable fur trade. Virginia pioneers pushed far west into the Appalachians in search of animals and trading opportunities. For many years, South Carolina's survival depended on an expanding trade in furs and, more important, deerskins. Charleston's profits from leather exports exceeded those from rice cultivation into the 1720s.

Several different business organizations exploited or even tried to monopolize the fur trade. The Dutch West India Company supposedly controlled all trade in Nieu Netherland, the early name for present day New York State, and the proprietors in Pennsylvania and the Carolinas also attempted to assert exclusive trading rights. Individual initiative easily undermined any centralized attempt at control, however, because almost anyone could make a profit trading low-cost trade goods for furs. Large-scale organizations such as the Hudson's Bay Company and the British Northwest Company, which exploited truly remote areas, were more successful in later years.

As the South Carolina example suggests, a number of different animal products entered the trade. The most valuable mink and otter furs could be worn by fashionable Europeans as clothing or accessories. The value in beaver pelts came from the fur that was scraped off and pressed into felt for cloaks and hats. Bearskins, deer hides, and other types of leather also found markets abroad.

Indian trappers and traders obtained a great variety of products in return for their furs. Woolen cloth and blankets were popular. Metal items ranging from steel knives and utensils, iron and brass cooking pots, buttons, needles, and trinkets were also highly desired. More dangerous were muskets, gunpowder, and lead shot. Perhaps the most detrimental trade goods of all were the alcoholic beverages like rum and whisky that white settlers exchanged for Native goods.

The expansion of the harvest of fur-bearing animals in size and scope throughout the colonial period strained the source of supply. Trappers and traders pushed ever further into the wilderness, putting pressure on the Indian population, and the members of some tribes encroached on other tribes' traditional hunting grounds. Simultaneously, this aggressive search for new sources brought French and British settlers into contact and conflict. By the mid-eighteenth century, the French were attempting to seal off the regions that lay between the Ohio Valley and the Mississippi River, an area the British colonies claimed as their own. The fur trade thus contributed to the growing hostility between these rivals, culminating in the French and Indian War (1754–1763). The British victory in that conflict effectively ended French occupation and claims in North America.

See also Mercantilism.

References and Further Reading

Morris, Michael P. *The Bringing of Wonder: Trade and the Indians of the Southeast, 1700–1783.* Westport, CN: Greenwood, 1999.

Norton, Thomas Eliot. *Fur Trade in Colonial New York: 1686–1776.* Madison, WI: University of Wisconsin Press, 1974.

Volo, James M., and Dorothy Denneen Volo. *Daily Life on the Old Colonial Frontier.* Westport, CT: Greenwood, 2002.

Guilds

Throughout medieval Europe craftsmen and merchants in many areas established guilds, voluntary associations to enhance their economic power and to control markets. Although guilds had become widespread in England by the time of the settlement of the colonies, they were far less common in America. Instead, a mix of trade associations and primitive versions of labor unions came into being with different economic and social goals.

The Tudor Industrial Code that had developed in England to regulate an increasingly urban and industrializing economy permitted the formation of guilds. Artisans with particular skills or merchants dealing in specific product lines coalesced into groups that attempted to impose standards of behavior and control wages and prices. Some of the guilds became very influential in London, and they played an important role in the mercantilist system.

Conditions in the American colonies discouraged such a development. The chronic shortage of skilled or even semiskilled labor meant that competent artisans or tradesmen could exercise considerable economic bargaining power as individuals. The colonial governments were always less powerful and authoritative than the royal government at home, and many skilled craftsmen sailed across the Atlantic in anticipation of higher wages and greater individual freedom.

Those few who did attempt to form guilds were quickly discouraged. Massachusetts chartered guilds for shoemakers and coopers; Pennsylvania did the same for shoemakers and tailors; and New York sanctioned a weaver's guild. From the government's perspective, it made sense to protect and encourage skilled laborers to remain in their jurisdictions. None of these guilds survived, however, largely because there were so many opportunities in America.

The failure of American craftsmen to form guilds carried with it other consequences. Master craftsmen, for example, found it difficult to control their apprentices. Individuals with only partial training or limited experience could set up shop and compete with those who had completed the standard apprenticeship and journeyman experience. Free entry and exit undermined government and trade association efforts to limit the number of establishments or the number of workers in a particular field. By the eighteenth century, laissez faire attitudes and opportunities generally prevailed for free workers in the New England and middle colonies of New York, Pennsylvania, and New Jersey.

In some instances mechanics' societies took the place of guilds. In colonial America, the term *mechanic* was applied to any skilled worker in any field. Unlike guilds, mechanics' societies tended to be less focused on economic and more on social issues. Instead of attempting to dictate wage levels or working conditions, they were more likely to serve as benevolent societies. Some went so far as to provide charity for members who were injured or temporarily out of work.

Some of these societies also engaged in politics. Perhaps the best known examples were the urban workingmen who either converted their own organizations or joined companion groupings that became known as patriotic societies. The most famous of these, the Boston-based Sons of Liberty, took the lead in fomenting anti-British sentiments. These patriotic societies contained merchants, wage laborers, lawyers, shopkeepers, and artisans, all of whom recognized the benefits they enjoyed in the freer economic environment of the colonies. They naturally became even more active and outspoken when they concluded that the royal government was intent on enforcing old regulations and imposing new restrictions on their behavior after 1763. To that extent, workers organizations were key factors in fomenting the American Revolution.

See also Navigation Acts; Wage Codes.

References and Further Reading

Rayback, Joseph G. *A History of American Labor.* New York: Macmillan, 1961.

Taft, Philip. *Organized Labor in American History.* New York: Harper and Row, 1964.

Head Rights

To stimulate productivity and attract new settlers, many British colonies in America offered tracts of land called head rights. The prospect of land ownership proved to be an effective incentive for impoverished, landless people in England, and the distribution of head rights led to the establishment of much more widely distributed property ownership than was common in Europe.

The Virginia Company of London was the first to offer head rights to encourage settlement in its Jamestown Colony. The decision to distribute land privately was a significant change. Up to that point, the company had owned all the land it had obtained through its charter from the royal government. For the first several years, in fact, food, structures, and even tools were supplied by or built for the company. If a settler survived and worked for the company for seven years, he was granted a tract of 100 acres, but relatively few people qualified for that distribution.

By 1616 the company recognized that individuals were likely to labor more intensively if they owned the land they worked. Consequently, the company offered tracts of land of various sizes to individuals and groups willing to settle in Virginia. In a labor-intensive economy, however, there were never enough hands to accomplish the work available.

The company went through many reorganizations in its relatively short existence, but none was more comprehensive than the restructuring that occurred in 1618. It included the drafting of the "great charter" of grants and liberties. This revised charter authorized the distribution of a head right to anyone who came to the colony with the intention of settling.

Under the new system, fifty acres of land was made available on a per head basis, so that any man, woman, or child could qualify for a head-right grant. People unable to fund their own travel to Virginia could sign indentures with agents, ship captains, or others who paid for their passage. The head right went to whoever paid for the trip, so middlemen often received substantial tracts of land.

The company's fundamental goal, however, was to distribute land to people who would put it into production. Therefore, as indentured servants already in America worked out their contracts, they could apply for and receive head rights for themselves and their families. Over time, tens of thousands of head-right grants were made. Many people who had lived in abject poverty in England became small landholders and, in a few cases, managed to build on that base to accumulate large estates. Some of the so-called First Families of Virginia can trace their roots to indentured servants who obtained head rights to begin their rise.

The head-right system was well established in Virginia early enough to serve as a model for other colonization efforts. Head rights were distributed up and down the Atlantic coast as a continuing inducement for people to settle. They were offered by colonial proprietors like William Penn as well as by the royal colonies, north and south, which were eager to encourage population growth. Some early immigrants from Africa received head rights in America, but this became very rare when the slave system was institutionalized in the late seventeenth century.

An interesting consequence of the head-right system was that it fostered much more broadly based democratic government in American than was the norm in the mother country. Landownership had traditionally qualified Englishmen to participate in government through representatives in the House of Commons. When private landownership spread in the Virginia colony, that democratic principle spread as well. The Virginia Company established a new governing structure that included the House of Burgesses to represent the growing number of people who owned land. Thus head rights and representative government went hand in hand in fundamentally shaping the economic and political character of the American colonies.

See also Indenture; Joint-Stock Company; Penn, William; Proprietary Colonies.

References and Further Reading

Bailyn, Bernard. *The Peopling of British North America.* New York: Knopf, 1986.

Kim, Sung Bok. *Landlord and Tenant in Colonial New York.* Chapel Hill, NC: University of North Carolina Press, 1978.

Indenture

An indenture is a labor contract that obligates an individual to work for a fixed period of time. In colonial America those who signed indentures often received no wages in return for their labor. But the holder of the indenture was normally obligated to provide clothing, food, and shelter, as well as some sort of compensation at the end of the contract's term.

Verbindniß eines Lehrjungen.

THIS INDENTURE witneſseth, that JOHN NEMO, by the Conſent of . . . . . . hath put himſelf, and by theſe Preſents, with the Conſent aforeſaid, doth Voluntarily, and of his own free Will and Accord, put himſelf Apprentice to Philip Sharp of Briſtol, to learn his Art, Trade and Myſtery, and after the Manner of an Apprentice to ſerve him, his Executors and Aſsigns from the Day of the Date hereof, for, & during, & to the full End & Term, of (die Jahre) next enſuing: During all which Term, the ſaid Apprentice his ſaid Maſter faithfully ſhall ſerve, his Secrets keep, his lawful Commands every where readily obey. He ſhall do no Damage to his ſaid Maſter nor ſee it to be done by others, without letting or giving Notice thereof to his ſaid Maſter, he ſhall not waſte his ſaid Maſters Goods, nor lend them unlawfully to any. He ſhall not commit Fornication, nor contract Matrimony, within the ſaid Term: At Cards, Dice, or any other unlawful Games he ſhall not play, whereby his ſaid Maſter may have Damage. With his own Goods, nor the Goods of others, without Licence from his ſaid Maſter, he ſhall neither buy nor ſell. He ſhall not abſent himſelf Day nor Night from his ſaid Maſters Service without his Leave: Nor haunt Ale-houſes, Taverns, or Play-houſes; but in all Things behave himſelf as a faithful Apprentice ought to do, during the ſaid Term. And the ſaid Maſter ſhall uſe the utmoſt of his Endeavour to teach, or cauſe to be taught and inſtructed the ſaid Apprentice in the Trade or Myſtery of a Taylor, and procure and provide for him ſufficient Meat, Drink, Apparel, Lodging and Waſhing, fitting for an Apprentice, during the ſaid Term of . . .
YEARS

As late as 1776, Europeans were signing indentures like this, promising to work in exchange for passage to Britain's North American colonies. (Library of Congress)

Indentures were quite common in England and other countries in the seventeenth and eighteenth centuries. Master craftsmen frequently signed indentures with young people interested in becoming apprentices. Other indentures were signed to offset indebtedness or for other purposes. In addition to those formally indentured, a substantial number of people were "in service" in Europe, spending their whole lives in positions that kept them under the authority of a master.

Indentures were also quite common in the British colonies. Tens of thousands of people came to the colonies as indentured servants. Some historians estimate that half of the white people who migrated to the colonies before the American Revolution came in some sort of indentured status.

The first wave of indentured servants came directly from England. Economic and social conditions in the British Isles were distinctly unfavorable for poorer people. Enclosure had driven peasants off their small holdings; industrialization would not begin creating alternative employment opportunities for another century. Many of the first settlers in the colonies were servants of adventurers or investors who expected their charges to do the heavy work of colonizing for them.

Through the 1670s, indentured servants flowed from the British Isles across the Atlantic in a constant stream, sometimes by their own volition, sometimes almost by accident. Some individuals negotiated contracts prior to leaving home to get to the New World. Other jobless people who roamed around England looking for work ended up in British ports. With no other prospect in view, they took passage on ships heading west. When they arrived in America, they paid for their travel expenses by indenturing themselves to a planter, merchant, or ship captain. Many vagabonds, debtors, and petty criminals were forced to sign indentures and were then transported to the colonies.

While the basic terms of the indentures varied widely, they had some common characteristics. In America, the labor contracts usually extended for at least four years but seldom beyond seven years. The owner of an indenture could sell or trade it to someone else without consulting the indentured servant. Custom and colonial legal codes usually required that the contract holder provide reasonable food, shelter, and adequate clothing for those in service. Monetary wages were seldom paid, but most contracts included a provision for "freedom dues" to be provided at the contract's termination. These might include a modest monetary payment, new clothing, tools, or other items to assist the transition to independent status. In some colonies, the freedom dues included a grant of land or head right of fifty acres either from the former master or the colonial government.

As with any large population, indentured servants came in all sorts. Some were dedicated, efficient, and industrious, looking ahead to independence and personal betterment. Others were lazy, resentful of their status, and lacking in ambition. Those who had come to America only as a last resort were often less interested in making a place for themselves.

Complicating their plight was the fact that establishing a settlement in the wilderness required constant, strenuous, often boring, and repetitive hard work. Most English indentured servants went to America before 1680, during the years when life was unstintingly hard and unrewarding in general. Disease was ever present; many indentured servants failed to survive their contracts. And, given the difficulties that they, too, endured, owners, masters, and planters often used harsh means to enforce their will on their servants. The legal system permitted masters to whip recalcitrant servants and to extend the terms of their contracts as punishment for failure to work or attempted escape.

Some of these characteristics sound quite similar to those embodied in the slave codes that developed prior to the Civil War. Indeed, slavery was another factor that added complexity to the plight of indentured servants. By 1700 slaves constituted only about 10 percent of the population in the British North American colonies. In many areas, however, particularly in the plantation South, they were regarded as much more reliable and tractable than indentured servants.

The types of people who served out indentures in Colonial America changed over time. The gender ratio was quite skewed, with some sources estimating that as many as 80 percent of indentured servants were male. Young, strong men were seen as most desirable for the heavy manual labor the wilderness demanded. But the relative shortage of women stifled population growth until the eighteenth century when the gender imbalance among immigrants lessened. The British Isles supplied the majority of indentured servants, with nearly 200,000 arriving between 1607 and 1700. In the eighteenth century, England declined as a source, but substantial numbers continued to arrive from Ireland and Scotland. They were joined by tens of thousands of German indentured servants and many others from different European countries. For these later immigrants, opportunities in Maryland, Pennsylvania, and other northern colonies were more attractive than in the South with its growing reliance of slave labor.

Fortunately, thousands of indentured servants lived to work out their contracts and establish themselves as independent citizens. Those who received head rights could begin subsistence farming and, with diligence and luck, expand their holdings and become commercial farmers in time. A few even managed to join the planter class in the South or, by pursuing crafts, become independent business owners or merchants in the North.

See also Enclosure; Head Right; Slavery.

References and Further Reading

Dunn, Richard S. "The Recruitment and Employment of Labor," in *Colonial British America,* ed. Jack P. Greene and J. R. Pole. Baltimore, MD: Johns Hopkins University Press, 1984.

Galenson, David W. *White Servitude in Colonial America.* New York: Cambridge University Press, 1981.

Morgan, Kenneth. *Slavery and Servitude in Colonial North America.* New York: New York University Press, 2001.

Joint-Stock Company

A joint-stock company is a business enterprise that distributes shares of stock to those who invest in it. The rise of foreign trade in the sixteenth century helped concentrate wealth in the hands of a merchant class. Meanwhile, the enclosure movement began to lock up ownership of virtually all of the arable land, the traditional measure and means of wealth in the British Isles. Unable to purchase land, entrepreneurial merchants looked for an alternative investment for their money. A joint-stock company provided a convenient mechanism for individuals who had accumulated some capital but were not individually capable of financing a major enterprise.

The most significant joint-stock company in early American history was the one that established the Virginia colony at Jamestown in 1607, the first successful British settlement in North America. While the Spanish and Portuguese monarchs had provided much of the financing for their colonies in the New World, British imperial adventures drew substantially from private funds. In the late Elizabethan era, Sir Walter Raleigh spent some £40,000 of his personal fortune in three unsuccessful attempts to establish a colony on Roanoke Island off the coast of present-day North Carolina. When King James I ascended the throne in 1603, his government looked favorably on British colonization but lacked the resources to finance it. Consequently, bands of adventurers undertook the task, the most prominent group being the Virginia Company of London. This company obtained its first charter from the king in 1604, but control was lodged in a royal council, answering directly to the monarch, not the English investors or those who embarked for the New World.

Acknowledging the difficulties inherent in this framework, the company negotiated a new charter in 1609 that gave it much greater control over its affairs. The charter also authorized the company to issue stock representing shares of ownership of the company. Such an organization was known as a joint-stock company. Like a modern corporation, the company was able to amass a substantial pool of money. Each share sold for 12 pounds 10 shillings, and a number of investors bought blocks of three or more shares at a slight discount. Still other shares were apparently distributed at no cost to the investor simply as bribes or to draw influential people into the enterprise.

With the money it collected, the company rounded up potential settlers, bought needed supplies, and booked ships to carry them to Virginia. A few of those called planters who sailed on the early voyages owned shares in the company, but most of its stockholders remained in England, anticipating profits on their investments. Thus the very first business venture in what is now the United States was a stock-issuing company with multiple shareholders, a format that persists to the present day as the most common form of large-scale business enterprise.

From 1607 to 1624 the company experimented with a variety of organizational structures. Tension persisted between the company officials in London and those who were coping with disease, hunger, and other tribulations in America. The company initially attempted to dictate all policies and procedures. For example, with the first shiploads of colonists, it sent a sealed box containing the names of seven men whom the company intended to act as a sort of board of directors for the colonizing effort. One of the designated leaders was a fractious military veteran named Captain John Smith, who arrived at Jamestown in the ship's brig. Within a few months Smith emerged as the most prominent leader in the colony, and he is generally credited with ensuring the colony's survival during its first two difficult years.

The company failed to generate the hoped-for profits even as the struggling colony required continuing shipments of men and supplies. Running short of invested capital by 1612, the company petitioned the royal government for permission to raise additional money through a lottery. The basis for a tangible economic return finally developed when colonist John Rolfe imported Caribbean tobacco plants to Virginia in 1612. The colony soon began shipping surplus tobacco back to Europe, but production failed to reach a level sufficient to compensate the stockholders. In 1618 the company attempted to encourage individual effort by distributing land to new settlers through a head-right system. Even this change could not keep the company from collapsing in 1624. At that point ownership and management of the colony reverted to the control of the chartering agent, King James. Virginia thus became Great Britain's first royal colony because the joint-stock company that had founded the colony failed to return adequate profits to its investors.

See also Head Right; Lottery; Raleigh, Sir Walter; Rolfe, John.

References and Further Reading

Andrews, Charles M. *Our Earliest Colonial Settlements.* New York: New York University Press, 1933.

Craven, Wesley F. 1957. *Virginia Company of London.* Williamsburg, VA : Virginia 350th Anniversary Celebration Corporation, 1957.

Morton, Richard L. *Colonial Virginia.* Chapel Hill, NC: University of North Carolina Press, 1960.

Lottery

A lottery is a gambling arrangement in which individuals buy tickets, usually containing a number or combination of numbers. Winning entries are determined in a drawing of numbers by lot. The administering agency keeps some of the money and distributes the rest to the winners. Governments often sanction legal lotteries to raise money for special projects or to supplement tax revenues or bond sales. An illegal lottery is known as a numbers game.

Lotteries have been a part of America's history from the earliest days of British colonization. The first major lottery affecting what is now the United States appeared in 1612. The Virginia Company of London had been organized in 1609 as a joint-stock enterprise. Even though it managed to sell shares to hundreds of investors, the costs of establishing a colony on the untamed coast of North America rose well beyond anyone's expectations. In 1612 the company tried to resolve some of its problems by obtaining a new royal charter, the third issued to the group.

In addition to approving some organizational changes, the charter permitted the company to hold one or more lotteries each year in several English cities. The king then issued a royal proclamation authorizing these activities. The money collected enabled the company to continue pouring money into the colonization effort long enough for the settlers to identify tobacco as a cash crop.

Meanwhile, the company continued to be poorly managed, and it went through additional restructuring. In 1621 it suffered a major blow when the royal government cancelled its lottery authority. The House of Commons had urged this action, responding to complaints from local business and political leaders that popular excitement about the Virginia lottery was a distraction from normal trade and industry. And so, "for the public good," the king issued another proclamation, prohibiting the lottery.

This early experience with lotteries has been repeated throughout American history, often with similar consequences. A lottery looks like an ideal way to raise money voluntarily, but it often rouses strident opposition. Some critics view the system as gambling, which they consider inherently immoral. On a more practical basis, it may well distract attention from more essential matters, and some people do become compulsive buyers.

Still, a majority of the states currently sponsor local or interstate lotteries, collecting billions of dollars and redistributing some of the take to the owners of lucky tickets. Today's Power Ball players can comfort themselves with the thought that they are carrying on an American tradition of participation in government-sanctioned lotteries that dates back almost four centuries.

See also Joint-Stock Company.

References and Further Reading

Andrews, Charles M. *Our Earliest Colonial Settlements.* New York: New York University Press, 1933.

Andrews, Matthew Page. *The Soul of a Nation.* New York: Scribner, 1944.

Manufacturing Acts

Britain's mercantilist strategy expected its colonists in America to be major customers for the goods it produced. To encourage that dependency, Parliament approved manufacturing acts that prohibited the colonial manufacture of certain types of goods for sale to people in other colonies or countries.

The Woolen Act of 1699 was the first manufacturing act. Throughout the fifteenth and sixteenth centuries, British woolens were highly prized around the world. Wool yarn and finished wool cloth constituted the preeminent British export in this era, helping support the empire's favorable balance of trade. Although full-scale industrialization of spinning and weaving would not take place until the mid-1700s, wool processing employed tens of thousands of English workers of all ages.

As key figures in such a vital economic activity, wool merchants and manufacturers exercised considerable influence in Parliament. The Woolen Act permitted colonial households to fabricate wool cloth for local consumption but prohibited it from being sold on a commercial basis. The law discouraged development of a more sophisticated industry in the New England and middle colonies.

The Hat Act of 1732 applied similar restrictions. No hat maker in America could export his products outside of the colony in which he resided. Moreover, the law forbade any individual hat maker from employing more than two apprentices at any given moment, a measure designed to limit the growth of the industry. Meanwhile, beaver pelts were added to the list of enumeration. They could only be exported to England, where English workers scraped off the fur, pressed it into felt, and fashioned hats for sale at home and abroad.

For years, English ironmongers and iron manufacturers disagreed over whether colonial iron should be admitted duty-free. The ironmongers in the home islands favored high protective tariffs that would raise the price of imported iron and guarantee them higher profits. But the Iron Act of 1750 represented a victory for the manufacturers who saw the advantages of importing less expensive pig and bar iron from the colonies. Duties on the imported raw material were removed, but the act prohibited the construction of new rolling and slitting mills in America. A substantial number of nails, sheet iron products, and tools were fashioned out of colonial pig iron and sent back across the Atlantic for sale.

While these restrictions discouraged the evolution of colonial manufacturing, their effects were not necessarily all negative. The colonies fit comfortably within the expectations of a mercantile empire, producing raw materials for export and buying manufactured or processed goods from the home country. The economic dependency that these restrictions helped reinforce persisted long after the American Revolution. As late as the 1810s, British textile merchants swamped wharfs in New York and Boston with bolts of cloth manufactured at extraordinarily low prices in factories far more advanced and efficient than their American counterparts. Until well into the nineteenth century, agricultural pursuits prevailed over industry in the United States.

See also Mercantilism; Navigation Acts.

References and Further Reading

Barrow, Thomas C. *Trade and Empire.* Cambridge, MA: Harvard University Press, 1967.

Steele, Ian Kenneth. *Politics of Colonial Policy.* Oxford: Clarendon Press, 1968.

Mercantilism

To establish a mercantile empire in British North America, the English government attempted to regulate and control imports and exports between its colonies and the home country. The ultimate objective was to create an economically self-sufficient empire in which the colonies' primary role was to supply raw materials that could be sold or processed in the British Isles. Finished goods were then shipped back to the colonies or reexported to other countries in pursuit of a favorable trade balance.

The historic roots of mercantilism lay in medieval Europe. The emergence of several unified and substantial nation–states was a key factor in bringing an end to the feudal system. Portugal and Spain achieved this goal in the late 1400s; France, Holland, and England joined them in the following century.

These nation–states shared similar goals: political stability and economic growth. The most straightforward way to evaluate success was to count up the amount of gold and silver or bullion that the nation accumulated. Of course a few isolated locations in Spain's American colonies did produce bullion directly. English sea dogs like Sir Francis Drake captured a number of Spanish galleons carrying cargoes of precious metals and diverted them to England. But bullion was only one measure of economic success.

No European nation had the ability to achieve economic self-sufficiency within its borders. Spices, furs, naval stores, and other raw materials were considered exotic luxuries in medieval Europe. By the seventeenth century, however, these items had become everyday necessities, and America produced abundant supplies of them. One way to tap this resource was to develop a favorable trade balance with the nations that already had colonies producing exotic goods. A European nation could more safely and reliably gain access to these same commodities, however, by establishing its own colonies in America and ensuring that their products were traded within that nation's expanded empire.

The earliest British colonies in America were founded somewhat haphazardly, often motivated by gold fever or resentment against Spain. By the mid-seventeenth century, thoughtful people in London were developing plans for a better articulated and more regimented economic relationship between mother country and colonies. Their primary goal was to establish a mercantile empire in which the colonies' chief responsibility would be to produce raw materials either unavailable or too costly in England. There industrialists and merchants could process and distribute American products within the home country and its colonies or resell them abroad at higher prices. Either way, the result encouraged self-sufficiency within the empire.

Formal implementation of this strategy began when Parliament passed a series of navigation acts to impose a structure for the mercantile empire. These acts regulated both imports to and exports from the American colonies. One set of laws listed or enumerated specific colonial products that could only be shipped to England, including sugar, tobacco, cotton, and indigo. Other items were added over time, guaranteeing British merchants and shippers monopoly control over vital commodities. To a large extent, these products were already being funneled to the British Isles, so the regulations acted primarily to reinforce the colonists' natural dependence on the mother country as a market for their products.

Other legislation regulated trade to the colonies. The Staple Act of 1663, for example, dictated that goods being shipped to America either had to originate in or be transshipped through ports in the British Isles. That ensured that the royal government would benefit from the customs duties, license fees, and other charges levied on merchants and shippers. It also exercised some control over the types of commodities the colonists could buy.

Even before the restoration of King Charles II in 1660, shipping regulations had dictated that all trade with the British American colonies must be conducted on British-owned vessels. At least three-quarters of the crew members had to be British citizens. With minor modifications, similar restrictions persisted up to the time of the American Revolution. They were quite advantageous to the colonists, however, because the ships they owned were considered British. These regulations stimulated an already vibrant shipbuilding industry in New England.

Colonists who served as crew members on these ships were considered British as well, giving them an advantage in hiring. The disadvantage was that they could also be pressed into service on Royal Navy vessels during wartime. Indeed, the shipping restrictions to and from the colonies served a double purpose. They guaranteed that the profits from such shipping would stay within the empire—a mercantilist objective—at the same time they provided a reliable, renewable supply of ships and trained seamen to be drawn into naval service as needed.

As the seventeenth century drew to a close, another mercantilist strategy was imposed on the colonists. In addition to supplying raw materials, colonies in an ideal mercantile empire were increasingly viewed as important markets for goods produced in the home country. Responding to considerable domestic pressure from both landowners and merchants, Parliament passed the Woolen Act in 1699. It prohibited people in one colony from selling finished woolen cloth to customers outside of that colony. All imported woolen goods had to come from English spinners and weavers, who thus enjoyed a protected market for their output. The Woolen Act was the first of several manufacturing acts that limited colonial production of processed or manufactured goods that might compete with those produced in the British Isles.

Through the first half of the eighteenth century, the North American colonies fit comfortably within the British mercantile empire. Their farms and plantations produced raw materials for export, usually to the home country. The industries that did spring up tended to be small, serving a local clientele. The colonists depended on British sources for most processed goods, and the colonies served as the most important market for English manufacturers. This symbiotic relationship appeared beneficial to both parties as it seemed to play to the strengths that each region's economy possessed.

Not everyone was satisfied. Many colonists resented being consigned to a dependent role in the empire. Meanwhile, the royal government faced mounting costs in defending its expansive empire. At the end of the French and Indian War in 1763, the British government tried to impose taxes on the colonists at the same time that it tightened imperial controls. Americans gradually concluded that independence was the only way to avoid both of these unpopular royal policies. The American Revolution thus represented a violent dismemberment of the Britain's mercantilist empire.

See also Manufacturing Acts; Molasses Act; Navigation Acts; Trade Balance.

References and Further Reading

Kammen, Michael. *Empire and Interest: The American Colonies and the Politics of Mercantilism.* Philadelphia: Lippincott, 1970.

McCusker, John J., and Russell R. Menard, *The Economy of British America, 1607–1812.* Chapel Hill, NC: University of North Carolina Press, 1985.

Molasses Act

In 1733 Parliament imposed a tax of six pence on each pound of molasses imported from non-British sources. Most colonial shippers ignored or avoided paying this levy, and the act had little immediate impact. It was modified in 1763 as the Sugar Act.

As the British mercantile empire developed, special interest groups put pressure on the government to provide protection for or to ensure the profitability of particular activities. Sugar plantations dominated several English colonies in the West Indies, but many owners of these properties continued to live in England. Some of these absentee landowners were themselves members of Parliament or influential friends of other members. The sugar growers were therefore far more successful than their colleagues in the North American colonies in lobbying for favorable legislation.

Meanwhile, rum distilling had become particularly important in Rhode Island and other New England colonies, creating a large and persistent demand for imported sugar and molasses. Indeed, the American demand coupled with that of the home islands was greater than the British West Indies could supply.

A third factor underlying the passage of the Molasses Act was that production costs in the British possessions were considerably higher than in the neighboring Dutch, French, and Spanish West Indies. As a result, "foreign" sugar could be obtained at much lower prices than the British product. North American importers were naturally inclined to buy wherever the price was lowest, leaving British producers with a smaller share of the colonial market.

The Molasses Act was designed to ensure that British growers would be able to sell all of their output at higher prices than those of their competitors. A six-pence import duty added to the normally lower market price pushed the foreign product's price well above that of molasses from the British West Indies. Had the levy been strictly enforced, it would have guaranteed sale of all the British output. In practice, little changed. The price difference and the demand for imports encouraged shippers and merchants to smuggle foreign sugar and molasses into New England.

Thirty years later, the British government was much more interested in generating revenue to offset its debts from the French and Indian War than it was in protecting the market for West Indies planters. Therefore, Parliament passed the Sugar Act, which dropped the duty from six to three pence and encouraged much stricter enforcement. This legislation fueled the rising protest from Americans regarding "taxation without representation."

See also Mercantilism; Sugar Act.

References and Further Reading

Barrow, Thomas C. *Trade and Empire.* Cambridge, MA: Harvard University Press, 1967.

Steele, Ian Kenneth. *Politics of Colonial Policy.* Oxford: Clarendon Press, 1968.

Naval Stores

In the colonial period, the term *naval stores* was applied to pitch, turpentine, hemp, and tar as well as to the masts and yardarms needed to build and maintain a wooden-hulled sailing fleet. Because the North American colonies were heavily forested, they were well positioned to supply naval stores to American and British customers. By the time of the Revolution, the Carolinas and Georgia had become the major sources of naval stores for the British Empire.

Although the British were a seafaring people who sailed on hundreds of commercial, fishing, and naval vessels, they depended on external sources for key supplies. For example, the Swedish Tar Company had a virtual monopoly, forcing the British to pay high prices for this critical commodity. It was only natural, then, for them to look to America for naval stores and, simultaneously, promote the development of industries that would generate export commodities for the trade-dependent colonies.

Some traffic in these items sprang up as soon as the first English settlers arrived in America. The forests ran right down to the waterline, and those who planned to farm the land had to cut down the trees. Some of the resulting lumber went into shipbuilding. Roasting pine knots in kilns liquefied the natural tar, allowing it to be collected into barrels. Tar could be distilled into turpentine and pitch, and both these products were more valuable than the original ingredient. Hemp could be spun into rope and lines. Naval stores were used locally in New England shipyards or sold to British captains and merchants.

An intermittent but recurring series of wars put strains on the Royal Navy and its maintenance. In 1705, therefore, Parliament passed an act to encourage New Englanders to focus more attention on naval stores. It included provision for bounties to be paid to individual producers. The Board of Trade was responsible for managing this aspect of the empire. It dispatched an agent to America to implement the plan, but he found the locals quite hostile to any government interference with their activities. In 1710 the Board of Trade shifted its attention to New York, where it sent some three thousand German refugees specifically charged with boosting that colony's output of naval stores. That effort was equally unsuccessful.

Instead, the industry developed naturally in the Carolinas and Georgia. The pine woods that covered the hinterland in these colonies were particularly well suited to producing naval stores of all kinds. Agriculture was less profitable there than in Virginia and the middle colonies, and shipbuilding never took off in the South. Encouraged by New England merchants who collected the parliamentary bounty and shipped their output, southerners developed an extensive and profitable export trade in naval stores. The total value of the bounties paid through 1774 was just under £1.5 million. In 1770 alone, the American colonies shipped 82,000 barrels of tar and 17,000 barrels of turpentine. The Revolution temporarily halted this business, but it recovered after the war ended and Anglo-American trade revived.

See also Proprietary Colonies.

References and Further Reading

Albion, Robert G. *Forests and Sea Power.* Hamdon, CT: Archon, 1965.

Barck Jr., Oscar Theodore, and Hugh Talmage Lefler. *Colonial America.* New York: Macmillan, 1968.

Navigation Acts

A series of Parliamentary actions aimed at regulating trade and shipping within the British Empire between 1650 and 1673 made up the core of the Navigation Acts. These actions represented some of the earliest conscious efforts to develop a coherent mercantile system, and they influenced colonial development for the next century.

In the first half of the 1600s, British settlers established colonies in America in a fairly haphazard manner. Royal authorities in London had no consistent policies for approving colonizing ventures or for regulating the resulting settlements. The earliest serious attempt at control was 1621 legislation that directed that colonial tobacco must be sold only to British merchants and shippers.

Growing conflict between the king's supporters and the Puritan opposition distracted people in the mother country from the trade and development of its colonies. The Puritans prevailed in 1649, executing King Charles and establishing their Commonwealth under the leadership of Oliver Cromwell. At that point, the most serious external threat was Dutch predominance in international trade. Both to encourage trade and to improve its navy, the Commonwealth government issued regulations in 1649 and 1651 that decreed that all trade to and from the British Isles should be handled by English-owned and commanded ships, with crews predominantly made up of English citizens. Included among the English in this legislation were those colonists who were living in British North America.

In 1660 King Charles II was restored to the throne and Parliament immediately reconfirmed the earlier rules in an "Act for the Encouraging and Increasing of Shipping and Navigation." In addition to insisting on the use of English ships and crews for imperial trade, the 1660 Navigation Act enumerated several colonial products. Like the earlier tobacco stricture, enumerated items could only be sold to English buyers and exported to English ports. Tobacco, sugar, cotton-wool (i.e., cotton), indigo, ginger, fustic, and other dying woods were subject to these restrictions. Subsequent legislation added naval stores, rice, molasses, beaver pelts, copper, and even whale fins to the list of goods.

Recognizing that trade was a two-way proposition, Parliament passed the so-called Staple Act in 1663. It ordered that goods shipped to the colonies from any source must be transported on English vessels. Moreover, with a few minor exceptions like salt from Spain for the New England fisheries and wine from the Azores, all colony-bound goods had to be transshipped through ports in the British Isles.

Evasion of the Navigation Acts began immediately. A popular tactic to avoid the 1660 fleet rules was to ship cargo from one colony to another colonial port instead of to England. The goods were then transshipped to non-English ports in Europe. In 1673, Parliament attempted to close that loophole by imposing a plantation duty. This tax was collected in colonial ports to offset the lost port fees and associated revenue from ships that failed to stop in England proper. To enforce this law, English customs collectors were stationed in colonial ports, an unpopular move, but one that had relatively little impact at that point.

The 1696 Board of Trade Act reconfirmed and somewhat systematized the administration of the earlier navigation acts. For the first hundred years or so, these regulations worked reasonably well. A key factor in their acceptance was that the system tended to either create or protect markets for goods that the colonies were well equipped to produce. The enumeration of tobacco, for example, created a monopoly for American produce in England because very high customs duties on tobacco from other nations or their colonies discouraged their importation. Besides, enforcement tended to be lax enough to allow alternative trade paths to develop and flourish. An increasingly strict interpretation and enforcement of the Navigation Acts beginning around 1760 provoked anti-British and anti-imperial sentiments in the American colonies, the first step toward revolution.

See also Manufacturing Acts; Mercantilism; Shipbuilding.

References and Further Reading

Harper, Lawrence A. *The English Navigation Laws.* New York: Columbia University Press, 1939.

Steele, I. K. 1968. *Politics of Colonial Policy: The Board of Trade in Colonial Administration.* Oxford: Clarendon Press, 1968.

Paper Currency

As early as 1690, various colonial governments began issuing paper currency for a variety of purposes. Some of these experiments were quite successful; others produced floods of unbacked, depreciated paper that undermined the economy. The mixed experience with government-issued paper currency provided historical precedents for the appearance of Continental bills in the Revolutionary War and a plethora of state paper as well.

The Massachusetts Bay Colony was the first to issue paper currency. Like many other pre-Revolutionary experiments, these bills were designed to compensate soldiers.

They were essentially promissory notes given to those who volunteered to mount an attack on Quebec. The expectation was that they would be redeemed with booty seized in the raid. Even though the military action failed to achieve its goal, Massachusetts bills continued to circulate at nearly par value against gold and silver for another twenty years.

Jurisdictions in the middle colonies prudently distributed paper currency for a variety of purposes, most importantly to supplement scarce hard currency. A perennial shortage of coins limited the money supply in the rapidly growing colonies, pushing down prices and depressing the economy. Pennsylvania and New York issued paper notes to expand the money supply and shore up prices, leading to both a psychological boost and an actual healthy inflation that encouraged production. Nineteenth century advocates of greenbacks and free silver called for expansion of the money supply for exactly the same expected benefit. Benjamin Franklin was an avid supporter of paper currency as an economic instrument and, not incidentally, as a profitable sideline in his printing business in Philadelphia.

Reckless behavior on the part of South Carolina and Rhode Island more than offset the positive record of the middle colonies. Both governments issued far more paper currency than they had any possibility of redeeming with specie or other sound monetary instruments. Not surprisingly, this currency rapidly lost all value whatsoever, a circumstance that undermined the credibility of the practice in more prudent colonies.

In 1751 the British government outlawed the issuance of colonial paper money in Massachusetts and eventually extended that prohibition to all the American colonies by 1764. This policy was quite shortsighted, however, given the persistent shortage of hard money, a shortage that Britain's mercantilist policies made inevitable. As they gradually threw off other Parliamentary restraints during the Revolution, many a colony-turned state issued paper notes to fund military activities.

See also Banknotes; Continental Currency.

References and Further Reading

Galbraith, John Kenneth. *Money.* Boston: Houghton Mifflin, 1995.

Shaw, William Arthur. *The History of Currency.* New York: Kelley, 1967.

Pine Tree Shilling

Between 1652 and 1684, the Massachusetts Bay Colony operated a mint that produced silver coins modeled after the British shilling. Rather than a portrait of a monarch, the heads side of the coin displayed a pine tree, symbolic of the New England forests.

No one disputed the need for circulating coinage in North America. What few English coins managed to make their way to the colonies immediately went back across the Atlantic to buy needed supplies. Spanish, French, and Dutch coins were more common, but no one could ever be certain of their current value. And, like their English cousins, these foreign coins were very likely to be exported from the colonies to pay for imported goods.

Massachusetts asserted its right to establish an independent mint because its charter granted the colonial government more latitude than was the case in other colonies. Moreover, the mint began operating only after the execution of King Charles I and the installation of the Puritan Commonwealth in England. This change undermined the tradition that only the monarchy could coin money. To discourage the export of pine tree shillings, the coins contained only 72 grains of silver instead of the 93 grains in British shillings. It was assumed that these pre-devalued coins would be far less attractive to overseas merchants.

This assumption proved false. Instead, the price of imported goods in pine tree shillings quickly rose sufficiently to offset the lower intrinsic value of the American coin. Essentially, English merchants simply demanded the same amount of silver for their wares, and a two-price structure developed. Meanwhile, prices for locally produced goods tended to remain unchanged. In effect, the colonial coins ended up overvaluing imports and undervaluing exports, hardly a positive outcome for the cash-hungry colonists.

Rather than promoting trade, the experiment actually complicated transactions. By 1684 the monarchy had firmly reestablished itself in England and the royal government was increasingly annoyed with the arrogant and insular Massachusetts government. It went so far as to revoke the colony's charter, in part because of its unauthorized experiment with the pine tree shilling. No other mint was ever established in the colonies, and the settlers were forced to rely on commodity money, book credit, or straightforward bartering for most business transactions.

See also Book Credit; Commodity Money; Dollar; Trade Balance.

References and Further Reading

Morgan, E. Victor. *A History of Money.* Baltimore, MD: Penguin, 1965.

Plantation

The first colonial settlements were called plantations because they represented a "planting" of English settlers in the New World. Very quickly the term took on a second, more persistent meaning: a large-scale farming operation, particularly one in the southern colonies. A southern plantation was a complex business organization with many workers and diversified products.

When English companies or proprietors began to send people to America in the early 1600s, the settlements were called plantations. That usage has persisted down to the present time in the name of Plimoth Plantation, a living history exhibit located in Massachusetts where the Pilgrims established their settlement in 1620. Early writings and legislation about the British colonies in North America frequently refer to plantations, and one must be careful to recognize that the word was used to describe settlements or colonies, not agricultural units.

A variant use of the term became common in both the Caribbean and the Tidewater regions. When the Virginia Company began transferring land to private ownership, certain settlers emerged as major landowners. And, because their primary objective was to plant crops in this land, they were called planters. No fixed rule dictated how much land was qualified to be called a plantation and, here again, the early writings apply the term rather freely. More than a dozen Virginians held contracts for at least ten servants by the mid-1620s, suggesting that larger farming operations were underway at a very early stage.

Ambitious farmers recognized they could benefit from economies of scale if they cultivated larger tracts of land with a low cost labor force. Even in the early years, a colonial tobacco plantation was a highly diversified business operation. It produced food, fuel, and shelter for the workforce. A constant interest in clearing new lands kept workers busy year round, even when they were not needed to cultivate and harvest both the food and staple crops.

Beginning in the 1680s, slaves began to replace indentured servants on plantations. This change partly stemmed from the depressed price for tobacco that undermined profits for everyone except those with the lowest production costs. At the same time, the number of people able and willing to move to America as servants declined, leaving those desiring to run large operations with an added incentive to buy a permanent enslaved labor force.

Over the years, some individuals became very substantial landowners, and land speculation consumed large amounts of their time and capital. The cycle included buying undeveloped lands to exploit and selling worn out tobacco lands to farmers who would plant other crops. By 1700 Robert Beverly owned nearly 40,000 acres. Four years later, William Byrd II inherited 26,000 acres from his father and namesake. When he died in 1744, he left an estate of 179,000 acres.

Because a 500 acre plantation generally required a labor force of twenty to thirty slaves, these planters were obviously major slave holders as well. Plantation ownership on this scale also supported an aristocratic lifestyle, and many planters devoted their time to politics, military service, and social activities. Indeed, it could be said that a farmer crossed the threshold to the planter class when he no longer had to do heavy manual labor in his farming operation.

Plantations also developed in other areas. The Calvert family proprietorship in Maryland was originally conceived as a sort of feudal system in which the proprietor would grant huge tracts or manors to favored individuals. There were never enough people willing to serve as tenants on such manors, so most of them reverted to plantations in the Virginia image. Charleston in South Carolina became the home of many very wealthy absentee plantation owners whose profits came from rice grown in the coastal region and offshore islands. Some farms qualified as plantations in southern Pennsylvania, but agriculture in the northern colonies tended to follow a freeholding pattern with farms on a much smaller scale.

Despite the chronically depressed prices for tobacco and other plantation staples, the system, once established, became the norm. It provided a template for cotton production introduced on a large scale in the late eighteenth century. In the decades leading up to the Civil War, plantation agriculture became even more entrenched and with it, the slave labor system that had taken root in the region two centuries earlier.

See also Byrd, William, II; Indenture; Proprietary Colonies; Slavery; Staples; Tobacco.

References and Further Reading

Carr, Lois Green, et al. *Colonial Chesapeake Society.* Chapel Hill, NC: University of North Carolina Press, 1988.

Rhys, Isaac. *The Transformation of Virginia, 1740–1790.* Chapel Hill, NC: University of North Carolina Press, 1982.

Tate, Thad. *The Chesapeake in the Seventeenth Century.* New York: Norton, 1979.

Proprietary Colonies

To stimulate settlement in the New World, British monarchs granted land to a number of proprietors or groups of proprietors. Lord Baltimore received the first of these in 1633, and his sons used the grant to create Maryland, the first proprietary colony. Several other individuals and groups received proprietary grants over the next hundred years, laying the basis for the colonies of North and South Carolina, New York, New Jersey, Pennsylvania, Delaware, New Hampshire, and Georgia.

In the seventeenth century, the royal government was land-rich and capital-poor. Early explorations by English agents such as John Cabot established a British claim to the east coast of North America, a claim that asserted the monarchy's dominion over the land. As the colonization spirit rose, the royal government lacked the resources to implement a colony-building effort. Private joint-stock companies sent settlers to Virginia and New England with variable success, so the government of King Charles I decided to try a different tactic: transferring land directly to wealthy or influential people who would take on the responsibility of establishing settlements in America. These were known as proprietors and the entities they established became known as proprietary colonies.

The first major proprietor was George Calvert, 1st Baron Baltimore. Calvert was a member of the Virginia Company of London and, on his own, attempted to establish a permanent colony called Avalon in Newfoundland in the early 1620s. Later in that same decade he became interested in the land adjacent to the increasingly successful Virginia Colony. Charles I agreed to issue a proprietary grant, and Lord Baltimore apparently wrote the documents that the king eventually approved. Based on feudal precedents, they gave the proprietor full ownership of the land and almost unlimited governing authority.

George Calvert died shortly before the grant was finalized, so his son, Cecilius, 2nd Baron Baltimore, inherited the proprietorship. He, in turn, chose his brother Leonard to lead a group of settlers who established the first outpost in 1634. They set up a capital for the colony named St. Mary's on the southeastern shore of the Chesapeake Bay. Well supplied from England and able to reprovision from Virginia sources, the colonists had a relatively easy time establishing their farms. The grant required the proprietor to remit to the king one-fifth of all gold and silver found in the colony and a token payment of two Indian arrowheads a year. Maryland never produced any precious metals, but the Calvert family dutifully dispatched the requisite arrowheads to London every year, thus preserving its right to retain control.

George Calvert originally conceived of the colony as a refuge for English Catholics who suffered considerable persecution from both Anglican and Puritan factions at home. His sons, however, could not establish a Catholic government or prevent the settlement of non-Catholics. The colony quickly boasted a Protestant majority that carped at the feudal controls the proprietor and his agents maintained. The Calvert family retained ownership of the bulk of the land, collecting rents from tenants and otherwise tried to behave like members of a medieval nobility. They also unsuccessfully attempted to install a stratified ruling system run by other landed nobility they created.

The Maryland colony suffered internal turmoil throughout the seventeenth century. During the latter stages of the Commonwealth period, Puritans briefly seized control of the government, but the restoration of the British monarchy in 1660 also restored the Baltimore line's control of the colony. This control lapsed again after the Glorious Revolution of 1688, and the area was governed as a royal colony for over twenty years. It then reverted to the control of the proprietor and remained quite literally a fiefdom of the Calvert family until the eve of the American Revolution. Maryland thus survived as the longest held and, in many ways, the most restrictive of all of the proprietary colonies.

Two other proprietary endeavors began in this early period as well. John Mason received a grant from the Council for New England in 1635 for what became the colony of New Hampshire. Four years later Ferdinando Gorges received a similar proprietary grant for what is now the State of Maine. Neither area prospered, however. The Mason grant lapsed in 1679, making New Hampshire a royal colony, and Maine ultimately functioned as a satellite of Massachusetts.

The same dynamic that motivated the early experiments underlay subsequent proprietary grants. When Charles II was restored to the throne in 1660, he lacked the financial resources to expand the empire. He was therefore willing to grant substantial tracts of land to wealthy or influential individuals who would take up the challenge. A group of eight such men banded together to develop Carolina, a colony named after the Latin spelling of the king's name.

One of the leaders of the group, Sir John Colleton, hoped to provide new opportunities for a group of independent sugar planters in Barbados whose livelihood was being undermined by imported slave labor. Anthony Ashley Cooper was the Chancellor of the Exchequer, a position that put him in the innermost circle of the king's government. Sir William Berkeley was governor of Virginia and his brother, John, Lord Berkeley was a staunch retainer of the exiled monarchy. The other four proprietors were the Earl of Clarendon, the Earl of Craven, the Duke of Albemarle, and Sir George Carteret.

The proprietary grant assigned this group ownership of all of the land lying between

31° north latitude on the south and 36°30′ on the north. A preliminary settlement already existed at a location later named Albemarle Sound in present day North Carolina. The proprietors' main effort came to fruition in 1670 with the founding of Charles Town, the community that would develop into Charleston in present day South Carolina.

In addition to possessing substantial wealth, the proprietors also had considerable experience in colonization attempts. Following the lead of the Calverts in Maryland, they asked political philosopher John Stuart Mill to develop plans for a complex feudal landholding and governance scheme. The proprietors would profit from quitrents collected from those actually working the land. The wilderness proved inhospitable to such elaborate plans, however, and the two regions developed along quite different paths. Charleston became a major fur-trading port until 1685 when the introduction of rice cultivation on low-lying coastal islands began to build substantial fortunes. Slaves provided the labor for these unhealthy plantations whose owners absented themselves in Charleston or even back in England.

Coastal reefs and outer banks made sail-driven shipping treacherous in North Carolina, therefore, the colony was slow to prosper. It eventually began to resemble the southern counties of Virginia with tobacco, grain, and naval stores harvested from the forested regions, providing some economic return. Political controversy ebbed and flowed in both colonies until 1719 when the citizens of Charleston seized control from the proprietors' government and successfully petitioned the king to take over. Ten years later, North Carolina became a royal colony as well.

A year after the Carolina proprietors received their grant, King Charles II gave an even more valuable gift to his brother, James, Duke of York. The Duke was named proprietor of the region between Maryland and New England, but it was under Dutch administration. Henry Hudson explored the river named for himself in the early 1600s, and his sponsors in the Netherlands followed up by establishing a trading outpost on Manhattan Island. By 1664 the colony of Nieu Netherland was well established, and the outpost had become the bustling port of Nieu Amsterdam.

Since relatively few Dutchmen were willing to leave their prosperous homes in Holland for distant lands, Nieu Netherland encompassed a substantial English population. Many of these settlers disliked the political structure of the colony. Consequently, they welcomed the fleet of four ships and 400 Englishmen that the duke dispatched to take control of his proprietorship. A peaceful transition from Dutch to English control occurred, and both the town and the colony were renamed New York in honor of their new proprietor.

Political conditions improved somewhat, but the duke was unwilling to permit the establishment of a popular assembly, preferring to rule arbitrarily through a series of governors. The colonists particularly objected to the levying of taxes without representation. After temporarily losing control of the colony in the early 1670s, the duke's government reluctantly agreed to create a popularly selected legislative body. It was slated to go into action just when King Charles II died in 1685 without an heir. The throne passed to his brother, the Duke of York, who became King James II. Overnight the colony switched from proprietary to royal status, and the newly crowned king cancelled the legislative plans. The Glorious Revolution ousted James II three years later, but New York remained a royal colony under William and Mary and their successors until the War for Independence.

The proprietary grant Charles gave James included present-day New Jersey. James had little interest in the area, however, and he quickly transferred it to Sir John Carteret and Lord John Berkeley, two of the Carolina proprietors. They issued a document in

1665 called the "Concessions and Agreement," which offered land, religious freedom, and a representative government to potential settlers. Several communities were established, though they developed more slowly than the thriving port of New York.

Internal squabbles, disputes between the proprietors, and poor relations with their neighbors complicated life in New Jersey. In 1675 the colony was split down the middle, and Berkeley abandoned his share, now called West New Jersey, to a group of Quakers who were interested in establishing a religious refuge. The creation of Pennsylvania just to the west soon eclipsed this effort. The situation became even more confused when Carteret's widow turned her inheritance over to twenty-four disputatious proprietors. In 1702, the whole colony reverted to royal control.

William Penn was clearly the most successful colonial proprietor. Well aware of the failure of the Quaker group in West New Jersey, Penn petitioned King Charles II for a grant of his own. The king owed Penn's father a great debt, and, despite his nonconformist religious views, young William was popular and respected in court circles. The proprietary grant issued in 1681 was slightly more restrictive than earlier grants, but Penn managed to make the most of his opportunity.

He personally sailed to America to found Philadelphia, literally the "city of brotherly love." Penn planned to conduct a "holy experiment" in which a self-governing colony would offer freedom of political and religious thought and action. While his fellow Quakers dominated the governing structure well into the seventeenth century, swarms of settlers poured into the colony. Many of them were attracted by Penn's extensive advertising campaigns in the British Isles and Europe. In the early 1700s, a huge wave of Scotch-Irish immigrants crested, to be followed by an influx of thousands of Germans, Dutch, and other European settlers in the 1720s.

The Penn family retained its proprietary interest right up to the American Revolution, in large part because of the benevolence of its administration and the remarkable economic prosperity of the colony. Shortly after Penn's arrival in America, he convinced the Duke of York to cede to him the three "lower counties" clustered along the west bank of the Delaware River estuary. This area was incorporated into the Pennsylvania colony for the next twenty years, but it petitioned for separate status in 1704. Penn acceded to this request, but retained proprietary control of the Delaware colony for himself and his heirs.

The final proprietary colony, Georgia, owed its existence to philanthropy and international politics. General James Oglethorpe embodied both motivations. As a member of Parliament, he had toured debtors' prisons and slums. As a military man, he was well aware of the threat that Spain's colony of Florida presented to British settlers in the Carolinas. In 1732 Parliament granted Oglethorpe and nineteen other people a proprietorship over the area south of the Savannah River.

The proprietors advertised the colony widely and carefully selected debtors and other unfortunates to send to America. Oglethorpe led the first group, laying the foundations of the city of Savannah. He also led military expeditions in the colony. But the proprietary grant was much more restrictive than earlier ones, and it had a fixed termination date. Progress was so disappointing under the proprietors, however, that they relinquished control two years early in 1751. Georgia prospered much more as a royal colony.

As a group, the colonial proprietors had many similarities. They had to be wealthy and politically well-connected to lobby successfully for their grants. In all cases except Georgia, the proprietors expected to draw considerable wealth from quitrents, personal land holdings, and other colonial enterprises. Several of the proprietors engaged in extensive advertising of their colonies to encourage settlement.

In the end, the success of these enterprises stemmed not so much from the nature of the proprietors but from the character of those who actually settled in America. Except for the Calverts and the Penns, the proprietors failed to sustain their control or influence over time. Attempting to impose feudal, social, and economic structures in the wilderness were bound to fail. Even so, the proprietary activities did provide important bridging support for expanding the area and scope of the British North American empire.

See also Calvert, George; Charter, Royal; Franklin, Benjamin; Penn, William.

References and Further Reading

Craven, Wesley F. *New Jersey and the English Colonization of North America.* Princeton, NJ: Van Nostrand, 1964.

Dunn, Mary Maples. *William Penn: Politics and Conscience.* Princeton, NJ: Princeton University Press, 1967.

Ettinger, A. A. *James Edward Oglethorpe, Imperial Idealist.* Oxford: Clarendon Press, 1936.

Kammen, Michael. *Colonial New York: A History.* New York: Scribner, 1975.

Peare, Catherine O. *William Penn: A Biography.* Philadelphia: Lippincott, 1956.

Sirmans, M. E. *Colonial South Carolina: A Political History, 1663–1763.* Chapel Hill, NC: University of North Carolina Press, 1966.

Shipbuilding

Shipbuilding was a major colonial industry. While vessels were constructed up and down the Atlantic Coast, New Englanders developed the most prominence in the industry. Many vessels were built for local use in fishing and coastal trade, but others were designed for oceangoing trade and even warfare. By the time of the American Revolution, one-third of all the vessels flying the British flag had been built in America.

Shipbuilding skills were essential as soon as Europeans attempted to settle in North America. Shipwrecks were common, and they stimulated emergency construction all along the North American coastline. Perhaps the most famous early disaster occurred when two Virginia-bound ships became lost in a storm and wrecked on an unchartered island later named Bermuda. News of this event provided the inspiration for Shakespeare's play *The Tempest.* The stranded crew cobbled together replacement vessels that enabled them to complete their voyage to Jamestown in 1610.

As early as 1640 Boston had become a major shipbuilding center. Local merchants needed ships to trade along the coast, the fishing fleet constantly needed new boats, and transatlantic and intercolonial commerce were growing rapidly. Satellite shipyards sprang up in Massachusetts towns like Salem and Marblehead to the north and in the neighboring colonies of Rhode Island, Connecticut, and New Hampshire. New England remained a very successful shipbuilding center up to the time of the Revolution.

Dutch settlers had built ships in Nieu Netherland long before the British seized this colony in 1664. The activity continued in New York and New Jersey. Pennsylvania became an even more formidable rival to New England. The Delaware River estuary was ideally suited to the industry, and its many shipyards had made Philadelphia a major source of new vessels by the 1730s. Further south, other economic opportunities drew resources and attention away from shipbuilding but, even so, workers in the Chesapeake colonies and the Carolinas continued to construct smaller vessels in the eighteenth century.

Shipbuilding thrived in America for several reasons. The thick forests that grew down the waterline contained pine, oak, locust, and other trees, each of which contributed special qualities to ships. In this preindustrial era, all ships were handcrafted, and many of the settlers and the crew members who sailed to America came equipped with the skills needed to construct a vessel. Until well into the nineteenth century when roads and railroads became more common, coastal trade was the most efficient and least expensive means of transportation in America. Finally, several key colonial industries such as fishing, export of staple crops, and coastal shipping all used vessels of various sizes.

To be called a ship, a colonial vessel usually had a displacement of at least 40 tons with some eventually exceeding 400 tons. These ships were square rigged with two or more masts. Smaller, lighter-draft vessels called pinnaces were popular choices for coastal shipping and exploration. A pinnace might have one or two masts and a variety of sail configurations. Barks and ketches were similar in size to pinnaces, but tended to be much more solidly and heavily constructed. The smallest vessel capable of engaging in coastal trade was the shallop, a sturdy open boat with a single mast, ranging in length up to 30 feet.

American shipbuilders were heavily reliant on imports of all sorts. They deliberately recruited English carpenters and shipwrights to come to the colonies. The iron components on American-built ships were almost exclusively fashioned from metal forged in Great Britain. Colonial designs and rigging schemes largely copied European models as well, although the Americans eventually did develop the sloop as an effective coasting vessel.

Lower construction costs gave the colonies their major competitive advantage. In the 1670s, a ship built in New England could cost less than £4 a ton, approximately half that of an English shipyard. Plentiful local timber and naval stores provided some of the cost advantage, but Americans also tended to build simpler, utilitarian craft lacking the decorations and frills that British shipwrights included in their vessels. The less complex colonial ships often required smaller crews, however, and the resulting lower operating costs made them attractive not only to American but to European buyers.

Merchants in the colonies provided the primary financing for the shipbuilding industry. Not only did the investors reap profits from the ships that were sold, but the merchant class needed the shipping capacity new vessels provided to expand their own activities. The British government never imposed restrictions on American shipbuilding. In fact, Americans benefited from the Navigation Acts that attempted to control colonial economic development. These regulations insisted that colonial trade be conducted on British ships, and colonial vessels were specifically included in that designation.

See also Navigation Acts.

References and Further Reading

Baker, William A. *The Mayflower and Other Colonial Vessels.* Annapolis, MD: Naval Institute Press, 1983.

Goldenberg, Joseph A. *Shipbuilding in Colonial America.* Charlottesville, VA: University Press of Virginia, 1976.

Heyrman, Christine. *Commerce and Culture: The Maritime Communities of Colonial Massachusetts, 1690–1750.* New York: Norton, 1984.

Slavery

By the time of the American Revolution, slaves resided in all of the British American colonies. They constituted a substantial percentage of the population in the Chesapeake region and were in the majority in several Carolina counties laboring on tobacco and rice plantations. Slavery had generally replaced indentured servitude as the primary source of labor by the mid-eighteenth century. The institution was thus well established prior to the rise of the cotton kingdom in the nineteenth century.

When Europeans first began to settle in the Americas, the area had a substantial indigenous population. Attempts to either coerce or enslave the Native American population were seldom successful. The newcomers were impatient, however, to promote economic development and exploit the resources of the New World. Almost all of the work had to be done by hand in that preindustrial era, and there were never enough workers available to match the Europeans' ambitions. Very quickly established settlers began to import a workforce. In the early years of British North America, the primary dependent labor force came over as indentured servants.

In other areas a well-developed slave trade already existed. It had flourished within Africa for centuries before a ship brought African slaves to Portugal in 1444. This was the first step in what was to become a very active Atlantic slave trade. Over the next four centuries an estimated 12 million enslaved Africans were transported west across the Atlantic.

The first shipment of African workers in British North America arrived at the Jamestown colony in 1619. Between 1662 and 1807, when Parliament halted the slave trade, about 3.4 million slaves traveled to different parts of the British Empire. Most of these went first to Britain's Caribbean possessions. Living and working conditions there tended to be much harsher than on the mainland, so the labor force required constant resupply. While some slaves were shipped to North American locations from the islands, thousands came directly from Africa. If they survived the rigors of the "middle passage" they would most likely end up working in Virginia or the Carolinas.

The formalization of slavery as a legal system came sometime after 1619. Some of the earliest arrivals held term contracts as indentured servants. By the time of the English Restoration in 1660, however, such contracts had mostly given way to lifetime status as slaves for African workers. Over the next century, laws and regulations drew ever more distinct lines between free and slave people and, in the process, between whites and blacks.

Depressed tobacco prices in the 1670s encouraged the expansion of plantations as a way of reducing production costs. This development in turn stimulated demand for more labor at a time when fewer British people were willing to sign indentures. Slaves were a logical alternative, and the slave population in the Chesapeake region rose from around 2,500 in 1670 to over 30,000 in 1720. A similar rise began somewhat later in the Carolinas, particularly associated with an expansion in the growing of rice on the coastal islands and lowlands. Only about 1,800 slaves labored in the lower south in 1690, but that population had ballooned to 14,800 by 1720.

Local conditions played a major role in how the slave population expanded as the eighteenth century wore on. The Chesapeake area, for example, became much less dependent on the slave trade than the Carolinas. Better living conditions and an increase in the birth rate in Virginia meant that natural increase produced sufficient growth in the slave population. By 1770 only one-tenth of black people in Virginia had been born in Africa, the rest had lived in America all of their lives. Harsher working conditions in the rice country further south caused South Carolina planters to rely more heavily on new arrivals to replace or expand their work forces.

The nature of the work slaves performed also varied enormously. In New England, slaves worked as sailmakers, dock workers, ironmongers, and artisans, while many female slaves served as personal servants. In the middle colonies some slaves were craftsmen, others worked as farmhands. Along the southern coast, many plantation slaves labored anonymously in gangs rather than as individual workers. To the west, in the Piedmont region, however, slaves were much more likely to do general farmwork. North or south, slavery in colonial America was seen as a relatively inexpensive way to deal with the chronic labor shortage.

Few questioned the morality of a system that was so widespread and apparently profitable. In the 1750s a few Pennsylvania Quakers began to raise concerns. At that point, slaves constituted about one-sixth of the population in the colonies, and as many as 70 percent of the wealthier craftsmen in Philadelphia owned slaves. As revolutionary fervor arose, however, the existence of slavery seemed increasingly incompatible with the rights of man doctrine that served as a justification for the war for independence. Even so, several states north of the Mason-Dixon Line took some time to outlaw slavery within their borders. Abolitionist sentiments were almost unknown further south, however, so the United States entered the nineteenth century with its "peculiar institution" well ingrained.

See also Cotton; Plantation; Staples; Tobacco.

References and Further Reading

Johnson, Charles, Patricia Smith, et al. *Africans in America: America's Journey through Slavery.* New York: Harcourt, Brace, 1998.

Kulikoff, Allan. *Tobacco and Slaves: The Development of Southern Cultures in the Chesapeake, 1680–1800.* Chapel Hill, NC: University of North Carolina Press, 1986.

Morgan, Edmund S. *American Slavery, American Freedom: The Ordeal of Colonial Virginia.* New York: Norton, 1975.

Morgan, Kenneth. *Slavery and Servitude in Colonial North America.* Washington Square, NY: New York University Press, 2001.

Staples

A staple is a commodity that is more or less in constant demand. Because people can usually find a market for such commodities, they are likely to focus their attention on producing staples. Merchants and shippers also exploit the staple trade.

Tobacco is the most prominent early staple product of the British North American colonies. The cultivation of tobacco spread from Jamestown throughout Virginia and Maryland, and the Chesapeake Bay's Tidewater emerged as the most productive region. Low market prices encouraged the development of plantation agriculture. This became even more essential when an international glut of tobacco beginning in the 1680s reduced prices so that only the most efficient growers could prosper.

Other colonies produced their own staples. Sugar was so important a staple that Europeans often considered their Caribbean colonies far more valuable than those on the mainland. Rice and furs brought from the hinterland stimulated the growth of Charleston in South Carolina. New Englanders fishing off the Grand Banks produced enormous stocks of fish that were exported to England and the Catholic countries of southern Europe. Indigo grew well in North Carolina, and it became a major staple export for use in dying. Over time even such mundane crops as wheat and corn became recognized as staples, highly useful in feeding the hungry population concentrated in the British Isles.

The staple trade was seen as essential to an imperial nation's prosperity. Beginning in 1660, the British government began passing its Navigation Acts. The Act of Enumeration required that key colonial staples like sugar, tobacco, and indigo be shipped directly to ports in the home islands. The goal was not only to control the trade but to prevent other nations from siphoning off the wealth that these staples represented.

The staple trade was a mainstay of the British American colonies. To the extent that they produced desirable commodities that were relatively scarce in England, the colonists were fulfilling a mercantilist function. And, to the extent that the staple trade prospered, it tended to discourage investment in and attention to colonial manufacturing and other enterprises. Long after the Revolution, the United States remained a major exporter of staples to overseas markets. The rapidly rising demand for another staple, cotton, had enormous social and political ramifications for the South and the nation as a whole.

See also Mercantilism; Navigation Acts; Tobacco.

References and Further Reading

Gipson, Lawrence Henry. *The British Empire before the American Revolution.* Vol. 2. New York: Knopf, 1960.
Waterhouse, Richard. *A New World Gentry.* New York: Garland, 1989.

Tobacco

First exported in bulk in 1617, tobacco became the leading staple of the Virginia Colony. For the next century and a half, tobacco cultivation, curing, and exporting remained the principal economic activities of the Tidewater region.

Tobacco imported from the Spanish West Indies began to attract attention in England in the late 1500s. Sir Walter Raleigh helped popularize tobacco smoking, even though the product remained quite expensive. Almost immediately, tobacco provoked criticism. The most prominent opponent was none other than King James I, who anonymously published a pamphlet entitled *Counter-blast to Tobacco* in 1604. He continued to oppose its importation and usage, and like successor authorities, his government imposed stiff taxes on the commodity.

None of this did much to discourage a rapidly increasing demand for the addictive weed. The local Indian population grew and used tobacco in Virginia for social and religious purposes, but Europeans found the Native strain unappealing. John Rolfe is credited with introducing tobacco from the West Indies into the Virginia Colony, and two years later, he arranged the shipment of several barrels of cured leaves to England.

The relatively low priced Virginia product stimulated increasing use. Aware of the growing demand, a substantial number of colonists abandoned or reduced their planting of other crops in favor of tobacco. A substantial shipment of 20,000 pounds left Virginia for England in 1617. Ten years later, the colony exported half a million pounds, and output rose to 23 million pounds of tobacco by 1662. Tobacco became so pervasive a product that it was adopted as a form of commodity money in the cash-poor colonial economy.

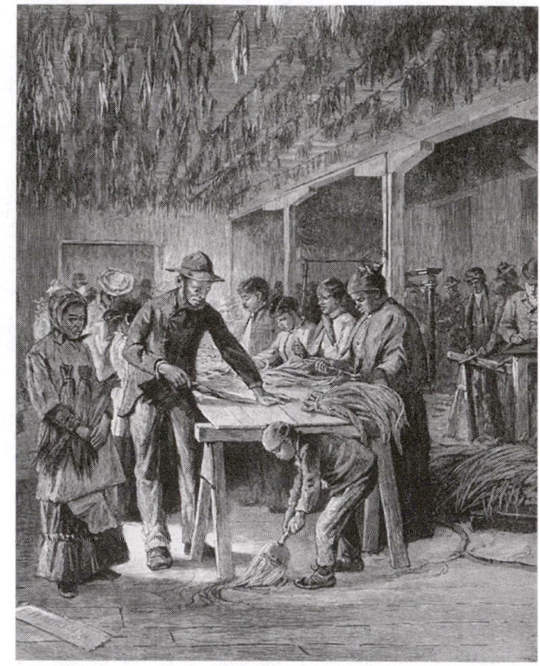

Tobacco, the leading colonial export from the North American colonies, encouraged the plantation system and the use of slaves like these in a Virginia tobacco warehouse. (North Wind Picture Archives)

The American colonists' ability to produce tobacco increased much more quickly than did the English market's ability to absorb it. For a time, British reexports to Europe helped shore up demand for the very popular Virginia variety. In 1621 the royal government imposed a tobacco contract on importers. It required that all tobacco grown in America be shipped directly to England where it might be sold or reshipped elsewhere. Meanwhile, the Virginia Company attempted to limit production. One tactic was to insist that food crops be planted in conjunction with tobacco plots. Broader-reaching attempts to limit overall production to a fixed maximum were largely unsuccessful.

Prices continued to fluctuate in subsequent years, as tobacco cultivation spread, becoming the major staple crop in neighboring Maryland and North Carolina. On several occasions supply so exceeded demand that the price for tobacco fell below the cost of production. In the years 1680 to 1720 a persistent production glut and correspondingly low prices severely depressed the colonial economy. One consequence was diversification to other agricultural crops like wheat and corn. Another was that the amount of tobacco exported from America remained relatively constant right up to the time of the Revolution (see fig. 1.1 showing tobacco exports from 1700 to 1770).

The tobacco glut also encouraged the growth of plantations. By bringing together a relatively larger, diversified workforce, a plantation owner could exploit economies of scale to reduce substantially the costs of producing a staple crop. Low prices favored large landowners over small holders. It also encouraged planters to invest in the cheapest labor system available. The number of black slaves in Virginia grew substantially after 1680, in large measure because of their attractiveness to tobacco planters.

Tobacco thus significantly influenced early colonial development. It was a valuable staple product that could be exported. It thrived in the rich, humid Tidewater soil, so settlers quickly focused their efforts on growing tobacco for market. The depressed prices encouraged plantation growth and the spread of slavery. In many ways, therefore, tobacco deserves to be considered the reigning southern monarch that preceded the enthronement of king cotton in the nineteenth century.

See also Joint-Stock Company; Plantation; Raleigh, Sir Walter; Rolfe, John; Staples.

References and Further Reading

Breen, T. H. *Tobacco Culture.* Princeton, NJ: Princeton University Press, 1985.

Machines, Clarke M. *The Early English Tobacco Trade.* London: Paul, Trench, Trubner, 1926.

Main, Gloria L. *Tobacco Colony: Life in Early Maryland, 1650–1720.* Princeton, NJ: Princeton University Press, 1982.

Trade Balance

The value of exports compared to the value of imports determines a nation's or an area's trade balance. If these values are equal, the trade balance is zero. However, if more is exported than imported, a *trade surplus* occurs, and the nation is said to have a favorable or

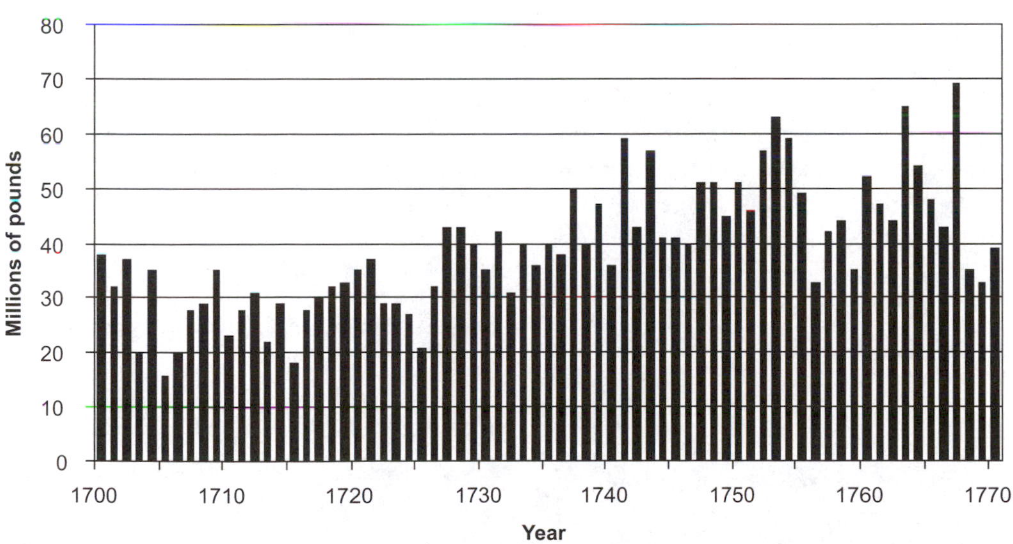

Figure 1.1 American tobacco exports to England, 1700–1770. (Data from Historical Statistics of the United States, Colonial Times to 1970. *Washington, DC: U.S. Bureau of the Census, 1975.)*

positive trade balance. Similarly, a *trade deficit* occurs if imports exceed exports, causing an unfavorable or negative trade balance. Throughout the seventeenth and eighteenth centuries, the American colonies perennially ran up trade deficits, importing far more than they collectively exported to Great Britain and other areas.

It was only natural that a trade deficit would characterize the early stages of British settlement in North America. English ports collected ships, people, and supplies for transport to the New World. Several years might pass before a colony's population could produce enough even to feed itself, much less think about exports. Disease and starvation killed thousands of settlers; Indian attacks decimated others. A constant resupply of people and goods was necessary to maintain a settlement. The colonies were thus heavily dependent on imports from the mother country, imports of both human and material resources.

The whole endeavor would never have occurred, however, had not optimistic investors and adventurers expected profitable enterprises to develop in America. Prospects of quick and bountiful riches failed to materialize. The exportable resources of the British colonies tended to be relatively bulky and inexpensive. Dried and salted fish, lumber, and clapboards were primary exports from the New England colonies. People in the middle colonies shipped grain and furs, while staples like tobacco and rice were the major exports from the southern colonies. A local trade surplus might develop from one or another of these common exports, but collectively their value never matched or exceeded that of the goods, services, and immigrants that flowed from the home islands.

The traditional method of paying for a surplus of imports was to balance the books with shipments of gold or other precious metals. As late as the 1930s, the world operated on a gold standard, with ownership of gold switching hands to offset trade deficits. But the North American colonies did not produce gold. Any coins or specie that managed to find their way there almost immediately went back to England either to pay for earlier imports or to purchase additional goods and services. The perennial trade deficit meant that the colonists had to rely on alternatives like commodity money and book credit for their own commercial transactions.

The unfavorable trade balance had other negative consequences. Many of the apparently wealthiest Virginia planters, those with huge estates and multiple plantations, were actually indebted to overseas merchants. Like most farmers, they borrowed to finance the current crop year or to expand their operations. The generally depressed price of tobacco meant that even a bumper crop might barely offset expenses. At the time of the American Revolution, many substantial southern planters owed millions of pounds to British creditors. Some of these leading patriots may well have supported revolution in the hope that independence might clear their balance sheets.

The unfavorable trade balance did not, however, end with the Revolution. The United States continued to run annual trade deficits into the 1870s. Remarkably, the nation was able to maintain positive trade balances in almost every one of the subsequent forty years, essentially paying back all of its accumulated indebtedness. At the outbreak of the First World War, the United States became a creditor nation, owed more by others than it owed to them. Favorable trade balances continued to accrue until well after World War II.

See also Book Credit; Commodity Money; Mercantilism; Staples.

References and Further Reading

Bryant, Samuel Wood. *The Sea and the States.* New York: Crowell, 1947.

Buck, Norman S. *The Development of Anglo American Trade.* New Haven, CT: Yale University Press, 1925.

Gipson, Lawrence Henry. *The British Empire before the American Revolution.* Vol. 3. New York, Knopf, 1960.

Triangular Trade

Earlier history books often stated that colonial merchants sent their trading ships on three-way voyages, picking up locally available cargo and selling it at the next port. A classic triangular trade route had American-distilled rum carried to West Africa and traded for slaves, the slaves then transported to the West Indies and sold for sugar, and the sugar carried home to New England to be manufactured into more rum.

More recent scholarship has undermined this concept. A key factor is that American merchants were not heavily engaged in the slave trade during the colonial period. Fewer than 3 percent of all American voyages included an African stop, and not all of those involved slaves. Compared to their English competitors, American ships sailed with smaller crews, lacked established contacts in West Africa, and had little access to domestically manufactured goods that were much more popular than American staples in purchasing slaves.

Even more important, however, was that American-based shippers tended to specialize in particular commodities or markets. They relied on correspondents at overseas ports to keep them informed of local trade conditions, and shaped their sailing schedules to maximize profit. The more successful merchants were those who established reliable contacts and solid reputations through repeat service.

Obviously, miscalculations were unavoidable due to poor communication, so an individual captain might have to improvise, following current rumors if the anticipated market conditions did not exist. In such a case, the pattern of trade might involve three or more stops in search of cargo. But there is no evidence of deliberate or consistent pursuit of triangular trade.

See also Shipbuilding.

References and Further Reading

Matson, Cathy D. *Merchants and Empire.* Baltimore, MD: Johns Hopkins University Press, 1998.

Liss, Peggy K. *Atlantic Empires.* Baltimore, MD: Johns Hopkins University Press, 1993.

Wage Codes

Colonial governments frequently passed laws that stipulated wage rates for certain activities. These wage codes were designed both as economic and social control mechanisms. Enforcing the codes was very difficult so colonial governments shifted the responsibility to local authorities whose efforts were seldom more effective.

The concept of wage codes was imported from Great Britain where the Tudor Industrial Code had been in place for some time. Its goals were to ensure that agricultural and industrial enterprises would be profitable and, simultaneously, to provide hired workers with protections against exploitation.

Massachusetts established a wage code in 1630 that imposed strict limitations on the compensation of wage workers. In addition to controlling prices and costs, the code was also designed to keep labor in its relatively low status as compared to those who engaged in business or intellectual pursuits. The colony's Puritan leadership was hardly alone in believing that hard work was a virtue and that working class people should not have access to wealth that might encourage them either to idleness or social climbing.

Several other colonial administrations followed this example by creating wage codes of their own, but they rather quickly proved to be unenforceable and were abandoned. A chief cause for this failure was the extreme shortage of free labor of any kind in the colonies that enabled a worker with even a modest degree of skill to set his own price. Local authorities interested in social and economic control attempted to enforce wage codes in their own areas once the colonial governments had abandoned their efforts, but they failed for the same economic reasons.

Throughout the colonial and early national periods, various public and private groups attempted to dictate wage and price levels for particular activities. In some cases these efforts arose from the workers themselves, acting through primitive trade associations. The early American economy remained so fluid and labor-deficient, however, that any attempts at price control or labor regulation tended to be short-lived. These early efforts thus had little relationship to later legislation like the imposition of the federal minimum wage in the late 1930s.

See also Guilds; Indenture.

References and Further Reading

Rayback, Joseph G. *A History of American Labor.* New York: Macmillan, 1961.

Dubofsky, Melvyn, and Foster Rhea Dulles. *Labor in American: A History.* Wheeling, IL: Harlan Davidson, 1999.

Wall Street

Conveniently located on lower Manhattan Island in one of the busiest ports in the New World, Wall Street quickly became a meeting place for commercial interests. Long before the establishment of the New York Stock Exchange, merchants and speculators met informally along the street to buy and sell commodities and property, as well as to share business information. This informal venue for negotiations and trade later developed into the financial and business center of the newly formed United States.

The street got its name from the wall erected across Manhattan Island in the early 1650s. The Dutch governor of Nieu Amsterdam, Peter Stuyvesant, was well aware that British farmers and merchants were envious of the excellent location of his port city. Anticipating the possibility of a land invasion from the north, the governor ordered a tall, wooden palisade to be constructed most of the way across the southern tip of the island. To buttress the defensive position, the land north of the palisade was kept clear of any structures.

An English invasion finally did occur in 1664 when four armed ships and 400 men sailed into the harbor under orders from James, Duke of York, the brother of King Charles II. The soldiers and sailors landed well below the wall, rendering it irrelevant. The Dutch residents and settlers of other nationalities in Nieu Amsterdam convinced Stuyvesant to surrender without a fight, and the city and colony immediately became known as New York.

The palisade was torn down in the 1690s, but the open area that had been left along it remained an attractive cross-island thoroughfare. Wall Street quickly became a major commercial venue and gathering place for merchants and shippers. A lively trade in slaves, furs, and grain developed at the eastern end of the street where it connected with Pearl Street along the wharfs. By the time of the American Revolution, Wall Street had become a familiar trading venue, setting the stage for its development into the new nation's leading financial center.

See also New York Stock and Exchange Board; Proprietary Colonies.

References and Further Reading

Geisst, Charles R. *Wall Street: A History.* New York: Oxford University Press, 1997.

Gordon, John Steele. *The Great Game.* New York: Scribner, 1999.

BIOGRAPHIES

Byrd, William, II (1674–1744)

The son of a wealthy Virginia planter, young William Byrd II was shipped off at the age of seven to be educated in England. He completed his schooling there and spent some time in a commercial apprenticeship in Holland. In 1704 he inherited 26,000 acres in Virginia as well as a post on the governor's council and some government offices his father had held. Although he spent most of his time in England until the 1720s, he remained actively involved in operating and expanding his land holdings in America. His marriage added substantial lands from his wife's family. For the last twenty years of his life, he resided in his Virginia mansion at Westover and remained very active in the management of his many plantations, and the buying and selling of land. He participated as an aristocrat in the colony's governing structure and left a debt-free estate of 179,000 acres to his heirs.

See also Plantation.

References and Further Reading

Beatty, R. C. *William Byrd of Westover.* Boston: Houghton, Mifflin, 1932.

Calvert, George (1580?–1632)

A quintessential adventurer and promoter of American expansion, George Calvert participated in a number of colonizing efforts. As a young man, he earned two degrees at Oxford and cultivated a personal friendship with King James I. The king reciprocated by awarding him a knighthood in 1617 and naming him secretary of state. When Calvert converted to Catholicism, he had to relinquish his position in the Anglican government, so the king compensated him by naming him Baron Baltimore in the Irish peerage. Calvert was a founding member of the Virginia Company of London, and he also participated in the Council for New England. He won a proprietary grant from King James I in 1620 and eventually spent £200,000 of his own money on an unsuccessful attempt to establish a colony called Avalon in Newfoundland. Hoping to provide an American refuge for his fellow Catholics, he then sought a proprietary grant for lands adjacent to Virginia. King Charles I was willing to oblige his father's great friend, but Calvert died shortly before the grant was issued. His first son, Cecilius, 2nd Baron Baltimore, inherited the proprietorship, and his second son, Leonard, led the first colonizing expedition to what became the Maryland colony.

See also Proprietary Colonies.

References and Further Reading

Browne, William H. *George Calvert and Cecilius Calvert.* New York: Dodd, Mead, 1890.

Franklin, Benjamin (1706–1790)

Although Benjamin Franklin is most remembered as a scientist, writer, diplomat, and patriot, he began his career as a shrewd and ambitious businessman. The fifteenth child of a Boston soap maker, young Benjamin received somewhat limited schooling before being apprenticed at the age of twelve to his brother James, a printer. In addition to learning the printing trade, Franklin read voraciously and began writing witty, often barbed political commentary while still in his teens. When James and Benjamin fell out, Benjamin sailed south, ending up in Philadelphia. There he worked in Samuel Keimer's printing establishment but wanted to strike out on his own. In 1729 he and a partner purchased Keimer's failing *Pennsylvania Gazette,* which they printed in their own shop and turned into the city's leading newspaper. They also obtained a contract from the Pennsylvania assembly to serve as the colony's official printers, work that eventually included printing paper currency. In 1732 Franklin wrote and published his first edition of *Poor Richard's Almanac,* which sold 10,000 copies. Each subsequent annual edition was a bestseller as well. With some of his profits Franklin formed partnerships with printers in other areas, essentially creating a modest publishing chain. The busy entrepreneur supplemented his income by serving as Philadelphia's postmaster, experience that led to later appointments to colony-wide postal positions. Along the way, Franklin invented useful devices such as an efficient heating stove, bifocal lenses, and lightning rods. By 1748 Franklin was wealthy enough to retire from active participation in the printing business, though he continued to write the bulk of the almanac for another decade. He spent the last half of his eventful life focused on politics and scientific research, but these pursuits were only possible because of his earlier success as an apprentice-turned-businessman.

See also Apprenticeship; Paper Currency; Proprietary Colonies.

References and Further Reading

Isaacson, Walter. *Benjamin Franklin.* New York: Simon and Schuster, 2003.

Morgan, Edmund S. *Benjamin Franklin.* New Haven, CT: Yale University Press, 2002.

Penn, William (1644–1718)

William Penn was the son of a British admiral to whom King Charles II owed some £16,000. William inherited this obligation as well as considerable real estate and money in 1670. A Quaker convert, he set out to use this fortune to create a colonial refuge for other members of the Society of Friends. To cancel his debt, the king granted William Penn the region that constitutes the present state of Pennsylvania, the most valuable royal land grant ever issued. Penn sold smaller tracts of land in the colony to wealthy Quakers and ultimately offered head rights to thousands of settlers. He wrote enthusiastically about the colony, encouraging large numbers of English, Irish, Scottish, and Welsh to settle there. He also produced foreign language publications to attract German, Dutch, Swedish, and Finnish immigrants. William Penn can thus be credited with mounting the most successful advertising campaign in colonial America.

See also Proprietary Colonies.

References and Further Reading

Wildes, Harry Emerson. *William Penn.* New York: Macmillan, 1974.

Raleigh, Sir Walter (1554–1618)

In a sense, Sir Walter Raleigh can be considered the first American entrepreneur because of his investment in a colony in America. In 1578 he was captain of one of the ships in his half-brother Humphrey Gilbert's unsuccessful expedition to colonize what is now Newfoundland. Back in England, Raleigh became a prominent courtier under Queen Elizabeth I. She officially sanctioned his own plans for colonizing Virginia, and Raleigh spent an estimated £40,000 of his own resources on three expeditions to Roanoke Island. This investment evaporated along with the famous "lost colony." Later Raleigh explored the Orinoco River basin seeking gold mines. During the reign of James I, Raleigh was accused of treason for working for Spain, England's commercial and political rival. He was imprisoned in the Tower of London for many years and was eventually executed.

See also Joint-Stock Company.

References and Further Reading

Carter, W. Horace. *A Man Called Raleigh.* Tabor City, NC: Atlantic, 1988.

Rolfe, John (1585–1622)

English-born John Rolfe sailed to Virginia in 1610, but was among a group washed ashore by a storm on an undiscovered island, later named Bermuda. By 1612 Rolfe was established at Henrico in the Virginia Colony, and he, along with several other farmers, began planting tobacco imported from the Spanish West Indies. Rolfe's main innovation was a new technique for curing tobacco leaves, and he is generally credited with introducing tobacco as the major staple crop in the Chesapeake Tidewater region. In 1613 a British ship captain captured the Powhatan Indian princess Pocahontas and brought her to Henrico. Rolfe and the captive were married in 1614, and they traveled to England in 1616. Pocahontas died seven months later. Rolfe returned to Virginia where he served as the colony's recorder until his death in 1622.

See also Joint-Stock Company; Tobacco.

References and Further Reading

Barbour, Philip L. *Pocahontas and Her World.* Boston: Houghton, Mifflin, 1969.

Section 2

The New Nation, 1760–1860

After the French and Indian War, the Parliament in London took several steps that disillusioned many people living in the North American colonies. Immediately after the war ended in 1763, the British government issued the Proclamation Act that restricted westward expansion and stymied the **land companies** eager to exploit the area beyond the Appalachians. At the same time Parliament began imposing taxes on the colonists to offset the costs of the recent conflict. The **Sugar Act**, the **Stamp Act**, and the Tea Act that created a **monopoly** for the East India Company, all triggered outrage and even violence. The Declaration of Independence in 1776 was something of an afterthought; the war for independence had begun more than a year earlier.

The conflict tested the resolve and creativity of the Founding Fathers. The newly independent states jealously guarded the right to tax their citizens, so Congress issued unbacked **Continental currency** in massive amounts to pay its war expenses. Lacking a large navy, both Congress and individual states issued letters of mark and reprisal to **privateers**, shipowners, and captains now legally authorized to capture and sell enemy vessels. French loans aided the American war effort but left the new nation deeply in debt.

During the troubled postwar Confederation period, disputes over **interstate commerce** and concern over the accumulated national indebtedness encouraged American leaders to write and adopt the Constitution. When the first Congress convened in 1789, it immediately levied customs duties to create a revenue stream. This early legislation also included **protective tariffs** aimed at promoting domestic enterprises. Treasury Secretary Alexander Hamilton then produced major reports on the **public credit** offering plans to promote financial stability. He also proposed the creation of a **Bank of the United States**, one of whose major functions was to issue **banknotes** backed by interest-bearing federal bonds. Although many Americans opposed the establishment of such an institution, the ***McCulloch v. Maryland*** decision in 1819 confirmed its constitutionality. Hamilton was also charged with defining the **American dollar**, and his decisions affected all future American commerce.

Hamilton's assertion of federal authority ran counter to the popularity of a **laissez-faire** approach. The views of Hamilton's bitter political rival, Thomas Jefferson, were much more in line with the prevailing sentiment that a limited government was preferable. As President Jefferson resorted to extraordinary and unpopular measures like **nonimportation** and an **embargo** to protect the United States from involvement in the Napoleonic wars. The measures failed to protect his successor, James Madison, from going to war against Great Britain in 1812.

Coinciding with the political revolution and stimulated by domestic shortages during the War of 1812, an **industrial revolution** began to alter fundamentally the lives and occupations of the American people. One of its key aspects was a deliberate **division of**

labor that greatly increased workers' productivity. Even at this early stage, some workers attempted to improve their situation by organizing primitive **labor unions**. Other changes stemmed from mechanical innovations like the **cotton gin.** Novel production methods also spurred industrialization such as the development of **integrated mills**, the use of **interchangeable parts**, and other advances in mass production.

These innovations, in turn, required modifications or innovations in business practices. Entrepreneurs needed capital, so brokers began selling bonds and other investments through organizations like the **New York Stock Exchange**. **State charters** legitimized new enterprises, but the number and variety of state governments led to highly varied sets of rules and procedures for establishing **corporations**. Federal **patent** laws encouraged inventors, and some entrepreneurs collected the rights of several inventors into **patent pools** to enhance their market prospects.

The **Panic of 1819** sent shock waves through the new nation and encouraged Kentucky's leading politician, Henry Clay, to devise a comprehensive framework for economic development. In his 1824 presidential campaign, Clay proposed an **American System** that would link the nation's businesses together with federal banks, canals, protective tariffs, and exploitation of land. But strict constructionists objected to federal intrusion in the laissez-faire system, so private or state financed companies built the **canals** and **railroads** that broke down the physical isolation of the interior. Meanwhile the development of powerful **steamboats** made two-way river travel possible. The transportation revolution enabled some manufacturers to establish national **dealership** networks to handle their products.

Like Hamilton in the previous generation, Clay provoked formidable opposition, this time in the person of Andrew Jackson. During his two terms as president, Jackson systematically dismantled or weakened all the elements of the American System, most dramatically in a confrontation over the **tariff of abominations**, during the **bank war**, and with the issuance of the **specie circular**. The latter move alienated the substantial number of Americans who favored **soft money**. Fortunately the growing use of personal **checks** provided a substitute for purchases, and many of them were written on accounts in new institutions organized under **free banking** laws.

To a large degree, Jackson reflected the views of the anti-industrial South devoted to growing **cotton**. Southern planters seldom formed corporations, but they did become dependent on another business mechanism, **cotton factorage**, which bought, shipped, and marketed the world's most important raw material in the nineteenth century.

More than any other product, cotton came to symbolize the United States abroad and it encouraged enlargement of the nation's **carrying trade**. The **packet ships** of the 1820s established regular, more or less reliable shipping routes between the New World and the Old. In the 1840s **clipper ships** extended American merchants' reach around the world. They carried prospectors to the California **gold rush** and made globe-girdling voyages that included calls aimed at exploiting the **China market**. Far Eastern trade expanded still further in 1854 when Commodore Matthew Calbraith Perry's expedition opened **Japan** to international contact. In England the abandonment of the **Corn Law** gave productive American farmers additional market outlets for their surpluses.

The vibrant, energetic, growing, productive nation seemed virtually unstoppable at mid-century. But slavery was increasingly seen as an immoral and life-sapping institution. Neither politicians nor moralists could find a peaceful way to bridge the growing gulf between the slave states and the free states. In the end, a protracted, bloody, and costly civil war took place to resolve that dilemma.

KEY CONCEPTS

Abominations, Tariff of

In 1828 Congress passed and President John Quincy Adams signed legislation setting the highest import duties the United States imposed before the Civil War. Opponents of high tariffs and of Adams reveled in calling this the Tariff of Abominations. It remained in force for four years, however, before a compromise plan replaced it in 1833.

The passage of the Tariff of Abominations completed one political cycle and set off another that triggered the nullification controversy. Underlying the raw politics were profound philosophical differences between northerners and southerners over whether industrialism or agrarianism promised the brightest future for the United States.

In the 1790s Alexander Hamilton had proposed levying relatively high, protective tariffs on items that Americans were beginning to manufacture, and the nation's first tariff act included some modestly protective features. By 1816 the industrial revolution was invigorating the economy of the Northeast, and President James Madison called for additional protectionism. The industrialization process continued, but it was most apparent in cities and the northeastern states in general. Manufacturers urged their government representatives to impose ever higher customs duties on imported products to protect their domestic industries from lower-cost foreign imports. A new tariff act in 1824 acknowledged these attitudes by raising customs duties on several products.

Meanwhile agriculture continued to dominate the southern and western states. Plantations in the old Southeast in particular produced bumper crops that would only be profitable if the surplus was exported to overseas buyers. Spokesmen for this region naturally opposed international trade barriers like tariffs that might limit the foreign market for American commodities. To generate popular support for their position, they pointed out that protective tariffs tended to raise prices for manufactured goods whether they were produced at home or abroad.

Beyond these quite reasonable but differing economic attitudes were the ambitions of politicians. Four men began the race for the presidency in 1824, but the race devolved into a bitter two-person confrontation between Andrew Jackson of Tennessee and John Quincy Adams of Massachusetts. Jackson won a plurality of both the popular and electoral vote, but Adams ultimately locked up a clear majority when the members of the House of Representatives decided the outcome. Jackson vowed to oust his rival in 1828 and seemed willing to use almost any means to achieve that revenge.

Jackson's handlers concocted a tariff campaign that was far too clever. They urged individual congressmen to approve sometimes ridiculously higher rates on a large number of items, expecting that the resulting bill would be too high even for the protectionists in Adams's political retinue. Instead, his fellow northeasterners simply added even more protectionism to the bill. Because so many individuals had supported one amendment or another, they felt obliged to vote for the final bill, presenting the president with a measure that included truly exorbitant rates. As a strict constructionist of the Constitution, Adams felt he lacked the authority to veto the bill and it became law in 1828.

The Jackson camp immediately dubbed it the Tariff of Abominations and blamed Adams for failing to stop it. It proved to be a popular campaign issue with Jackson's Democratic Party cronies in the South and the West, but the widely admired military hero would probably have won the election of 1828 in any case. In fact, President Jackson cared very little about the tariff issue, and he largely ignored it for several years.

By 1832, however, the 1828 law's high rates were annually producing far more revenue than the government could justify spending. An old Jeffersonian who favored a limited central government, Jackson finally felt he had to urge Congress to modify the 1828 tariff schedules to reduce the embarrassing federal surpluses. None of that discouraged special interest groups from being just as active as they had been earlier, so responsive representatives and senators ended up producing a new tariff bill that, overall, looked just about as protectionist as the 1828 law. Like his predecessor, Jackson saw no reason not to sign the bill, so it was slated to go into operation in February 1833.

All of this political maneuvering deeply disturbed a third prominent politician. South Carolinian John Calhoun had been vice president under Adams and was reelected in 1828 to serve a second term, this time as a member of the Jackson administration. An outspoken enemy of protectionism in all its forms, Calhoun became frustrated when Jackson failed to act. When the Tariff of 1832 that Calhoun considered unacceptable finally emerged, he was apoplectic.

Meanwhile Calhoun had developed an innovative political doctrine called *nullification* to protect his fellow southerners from what he saw as an unfriendly national government. The underlying concept was that if enough states protested, the federal government would never be able to impose an unpopular policy on the nation. And that number was quite small, because one-fourth plus one state in the union could prevent the Constitution from being amended. Although his immediate focus was on protective tariffs, Calhoun was looking ahead to a time when the federal government might pass legislation inimical to slavery.

In the fall of 1832, he resigned from the vice presidency and returned to his home in Charleston to help state leaders craft a nullification policy. It would have state authorities prevent the collection of nullified customs duties in South Carolina. Calhoun expected other southern states to follow his lead in nullifying the protective tariff law and thus prevent it from being implemented.

But South Carolina stood alone. Jackson issued an outspoken rebuttal in his *Nullification Proclamation*. It rejected the states' rights concept. The president then asked for and obtained from Congress authority to use force to collect the duties in Charleston if any attempt was made to prevent federal customs officers from doing so. An armed confrontation seemed likely.

At that point, cooler heads prevailed. Kentucky Senator Henry Clay began working on a compromise plan called the Verplanck Bill that would gradually lower the protective rates of the 1832 law. The South Carolina legislature appointed Calhoun to the U.S. Senate, and he returned to Washington to assist Clay in hammering out the compromise. Their new bill cleared both houses of Congress early in 1833, prior to the starting date for the 1832 law. The compromise thus staved off the potential armed confrontation and it effectively terminated the Tariff of Abominations. Perhaps the most important consequence of the whole affair, however, was that it fatally undermined Calhoun's nullification doctrine.

See also American System; Clay, Henry; Jackson, Andrew; Protective Tariff.

References and Further Reading

Dobson, John. *Two Centuries of Tariffs.* Washington, DC: U.S. International Trade Commission, 1976.

Freehling, William. *Prelude to Civil War: The Nullification Controversy in South Carolina.* New York: Harper and Row, 1966.

Hargreaves, Mary W. M. *The Presidency of John Quincy Adams.* Lawrence, KS: University Press of Kansas, 1985.

Schlesinger, Jr., Arthur. *The Age of Jackson.* Boston: Little, Brown, 1945.

American System

While running for the presidency in 1824, Henry Clay developed a platform that became known as the American System. It called for supporting the central bank, high protective tariffs, federally funded internal improvements, and higher land prices.

Kentucky Representative Henry Clay faced stiff competition from three other popular candidates with regional appeal: John Quincy Adams from Massachusetts, Andrew Jackson from Tennessee, and William Crawford from Virginia. Clay developed his American System platform to appeal to people in all regions, assuming that nationalism would transcend localism.

The American System would draw on each region's strengths. An industrial revolution was already underway in the Northeast, so Clay's plan was designed to promote that development. Meanwhile, southeasterners were devoting their land and labor to the cultivation of cotton, the nineteenth century's preeminent industrial raw material. This staple was so marketable that some southern planters failed to grow enough food for their labor forces. Western settlers quickly established farms more than capable of feeding themselves and their families. Western farm surpluses could thus feed both southern agricultural workers and northeastern factory hands.

Clay wanted the federal government to actively promote these interrelated developments. He was a strong advocate of the Second Bank of the United States, seeing it as an ideal institution to link all sections of the country financially and commercially. To promote industrialization, he advocated protective tariffs so high they would discourage imports and encourage domestic manufacturing. His nationalistic scheme required the transfer of commodities from one region to another on a massive scale. Therefore, he urged the federal government to finance internal improvements like canals and wagon roads and, later, railroads.

Clay's ambitious plans would be costly, and a truly effective protective tariff system would not generate much revenue. To finance the internal improvements he advocated, Clay favored selling the federal government's major asset, its public lands, at relatively high prices.

Clay placed third in the 1824 popular vote but became secretary of state when Adams finally won the disputed election on the basis of a vote in the House of Representatives. Four years later Andrew Jackson mounted a successful grassroots campaign to defeat Adams's reelection bid. As President, Jackson rejected all four of the American System's planks, most dramatically in the Bank War. His behavior encouraged the evolution of an opposition coalition that came to be known as the Whig Party. Henry Clay remained a perennial Whig presidential hopeful, but he suffered a final defeat in the election of 1844 when he lost to Democrat James K. Polk.

While it failed to elect Clay, his platform proposals continued to have appeal in certain quarters. In the late 1850s, the newly formed Republican Party included a central banking plan, protective tariffs to promote industrialization, and federal funding for transcontinental railroads. Thus the American System's concepts survived and were implemented long after Clay's death in 1852.

See also Abominations, Tariff of; Bank War; Clay, Henry.

References and Further Reading

Baxter, Maurice G. *Henry Clay and the American System.* Lexington, KY: University of Kentucky Press, 1995.

Remini, Robert V. *Henry Clay: Statesman for the Union.* New York: Norton, 1995.

Bank of the United States

Chartered by Congress in 1791, the Bank of the United States functioned effectively for two decades. With a capital base of $10 million, it was the largest enterprise in the United States by far. The Philadelphia-based bank generated investment capital, circulated banknotes, collected and disbursed federal funds, and returned a solid profit to its stockholders. Its charter lapsed in 1811, but Congress chartered a successor five year later.

The Bank of the United States was a multifaceted anomaly. No other banking institution received a federal charter during its existence; no other corporation enjoyed such extensive federal investment; and no other institution exercised such a strong influence on economic and business developments in the early national period. Despite its success at carrying out its chartered duties, the bank generated considerable opposition before and during its existence.

The United States had experimented with other central banking institutions prior to 1791. The Confederation Congress had created the Bank of North America in 1781, but it barely survived the Revolutionary War. Neither of the other institutions the central government chartered was nearly as successful as the one Treasury Secretary Alexander Hamilton deliberately modeled after the Bank of England. That British institution was privately owned but very much subject to government regulation and control. It provided the United Kingdom with a sound paper currency and other benefits that Hamilton thought would be equally advantageous to the United States.

He faced an uphill battle trying to convince Americans who had only recently thrown off British rule that an English-style institution was desirable. In December 1790 Hamilton sent Congress his *Report on a National Bank.* While he advocated private control of the bank, he suggested that the federal government put up one-fifth of the $10 million in capital he considered reasonable for the new institution. His report listed several functions for the bank including issuing a sound paper currency, handling all federal deposits, collecting taxes, paying government debts, and selling bonds when the government needed to borrow. In its private capacity, he expected the bank to concentrate capital for investment in enterprises like manufacturing that would promote economic development.

Strict constructionists complained that the Constitution did not explicitly grant Congress authority to charter a bank or any other enterprise. Hamilton countered that the Constitution implied that Congress could create an entity like a bank to carry out the financial and fiscal actions the document explicitly mandated. This concept of implied powers was acceptable to Hamilton's northern, Federalist colleagues who tended to favor a strong central government. But these attitudes worried southerners and states' rights advocates who wanted careful limits on central authority. Hamilton's persuasiveness carried the day even though the bank chartering bill got very few votes from members of Congress who represented southern constituencies.

The legislation, approved on February 25, 1791, specified a twenty-year charter. The federal government was responsible for providing $2 million of the $10 million capitalization and for appointing five of its twenty-five directors. Private investors would be offered stock representing the other $8 million, with at least $2 million in specie and no more than $6 million in federal bonds. Sale of the stock was delayed until the summer to allow as many people as possible to become shareholders, and the full capitalization was obtained just one hour after the bidding opened. Clearly, Americans saw the bank as an excellent investment opportunity.

The Bank of the United States opened its doors on Chestnut Street in Philadelphia, the nation's financial center. Thomas Willing, a prominent and respected Pennsylvania businessman, became the first president of the bank, and he served in that capacity for the next sixteen years. In its first year, the bank established branches in Boston, New York, Baltimore, and Charleston. Norfolk, Washington, Savannah, and New Orleans got their own branches shortly afterward.

As the federal government's fiscal agent, the bank collected tariff revenue at its coastal branches. It transferred money among them at no cost to the government, ensuring that federal funds would be available where needed. In one sense, the bank was a great bargain for the government, which never actually had to put real money up for its initial stock purchases. Moreover, it was later able to sell its shares for a profit of $700,000. Another benefit was the annual dividend of over 8 percent that the bank paid to its stockholders. The federal share added up to over a million dollars during the time that it owned stock.

The bank also provided some of the public benefits Hamilton had anticipated. It acted as a magnet for investors, collecting and concentrating capital to be available for reinvestment. Equally important it issued paper currency, something the federal government was reluctant to do in the aftermath of the Continental currency fiasco. The bank distributed notes in a variety of denominations to facilitate both large and small transactions. It adhered to a conservative approach, keeping the total value of the currency it issued well below its capitalization. One estimate is that it never allowed more than $6 million in banknotes to circulate at any given point.

The bank also acted as a redemption agent for banknotes that state chartered or private banks issued. Through the normal course of business, the Bank of the United States and its branches accumulated large numbers of notes from other institutions. The central bank routinely presented them to the issuing banks for redemption in either specie, federal bonds, or other sound money. These subordinate banks therefore had to carefully monitor the number of notes they issued, with the positive result that individuals could accept notes from most American banks with some assurance that they were sound.

Not everyone saw that as an advantage. Southern and western banks tended to be undercapitalized and have overly optimistic policies. Their managers and supporters carped at the constraints that the central bank's redemption activities appeared to be imposing on their ambitious plans. These people often lived in the same districts where Hamilton's Federalist Party was unpopular for other reasons. When Thomas Jefferson and James Madison brought the Democratic-Republican Party into existence, it drew strong support from those districts. The party leaders generally favored a limited role for all aspects of the central government that included outspoken opposition to the Bank of the United States.

Albert Gallatin served both Presidents Jefferson and Madison as secretary of the treasury. Although he differed with many of Hamilton's attitudes, Gallatin recognized the solid value that the Bank of the United States provided. That led him to endorse rechartering the bank in 1811. Despite his support, critics of the bank managed to kill the rechartering bill with a single vote. The bank had to close almost immediately.

The timing could hardly have been worse. Within a year, the United States had become embroiled in the War of 1812. Lacking a central bank, President Madison's administration encountered a series of crises in financing its war effort. It was hardly surprising, then, that Madison strongly advocated chartering a new central bank in 1816. The Second Bank of the United States came into existence with virtually the same authority and role as its predecessor.

See also Banknotes; Bank War; Hamilton, Alexander; Public Credit, Report on the.

References and Further Reading

Cowen, David Jack. *The Origins and Economic Impact of the First Bank of the United States.* New York: Garland, 2000.

Hammond, Bray. *Banks and Politics in America.* Princeton, NJ: Princeton University Press, 1957.

McDonald, Forrest. *Alexander Hamilton: A Biography.* New York: Norton, 1979.

Sharp, James Rogers. *American Politics in the Early Republic.* New Haven, CT: Yale University Press, 1993.

Bank War

The Bank War was the popular term applied to the political battle that President Andrew Jackson provoked when he determined to kill the Second Bank of the United States. An experienced general, Jackson won the war and the bank closed its doors in 1837.

The nation's first treasury secretary, Alexander Hamilton had popularized the concept of a national bank as a means for handling the federal government's financial affairs. Established in 1791 over strenuous objections from the advocates of a limited central government, the Bank of the United States operated much as Hamilton had hoped. Even so, his political rivals considered the bank a Federalist institution that primarily benefited relatively few wealthy investors. Congress failed to extend its twenty-year charter, so the bank closed in 1811.

The troubled economic times that developed during and persisted after the War of 1812 fostered support for reviving a central bank. Jefferson's successor, President James Madison advocated reestablishing a bank in his Seventh Annual message, and Congress authorized a new charter with a twenty-year term. Although the Second Bank of the United States (B.U.S.) was primarily a private entity, the federal government owned one-fifth of its stock and appointed 20 percent of its board of directors.

The bank's early years were troubled. Mismanaged by its first president, William Jones, the bank's policies fueled inflation, and it was popularly viewed as a major contributor to the Panic of 1819. When conservative South Carolinian Langdon Cheeves replaced Jones, he ran a tight ship during the ensuing depression. The bank's stringent policies did little to foster economic recovery. Its poorly conceived policies roused widespread criticism, disappointing even some of its most enthusiastic supporters.

When Nicholas Biddle became the bank's president in 1823, he discovered that Cheeves' conservative policies had corralled half of all the gold in the United States in B.U.S. vaults. An energetic and intelligent Philadelphia aristocrat, Biddle understood the positive influence the institution could exercise. It served as the government's bank, collecting all federal income from tariffs and other sources and paying the government's obligations. It provided this service at no cost because, like any other bank, it could earn income off the investment of its holdings.

Like other private banks in the era, the B.U.S. issued banknotes, paper currency backed by the funds on deposit and its invested capital. These notes almost always circulated at face value because anyone could obtain gold in exchange for the notes either at the bank's headquarters in Philadelphia or at one of its many branches located throughout the United States. By judiciously monitoring the bank's capital and specie holdings and simultaneously taking advantage of the inherent soundness of its circulating banknotes, Biddle exercised enormous control over the nation's money supply, adjusting it to what he perceived to be an ideal level.

The more effective the bank appeared to be at managing the economy, the more enemies it made. Many of those who owned or operated the hundreds of other private banks in the United States were particularly annoyed. Their institutions also issued banknotes, sometimes in amounts well in excess of their ability to redeem them. B.U.S. branches throughout the nation accumulated large numbers of private banknotes and periodically presented them to the issuing institutions for redemption. Poorly managed or overextended private banks that could not redeem their notes with specie or federal notes were forced to close.

Soft money advocates also disliked the B.U.S.'s redemption policies. This group favored expansion of the money supply, hoping it would raise prices and promote business. In the process, the soft money faction tended to ignore the sloppy or outright criminal behavior of some private bankers. This attitude was particularly prevalent in rural areas where specie and sound money were harder to obtain. Those same districts tended to favor candidates in what was emerging as Andrew Jackson's Democratic Party.

When Jackson became president, the bank's supporters recognized that he and his constituency might be enemies. In the spring of 1832, therefore, the pro-bank faction urged Congress to recharter the institution for an additional period, even though its original charter had another five years to run. Jackson vetoed the rechartering bill, claiming among other reasons that the bank as Biddle had configured it was unconstitutional. Jackson's landslide reelection in the fall of 1832 suggested that a majority of the American people agreed with his opposition to the bank.

But the Bank War had only begun. Biddle mounted both a public relations campaign and an economic drive to convince everyone that the bank was essential. Critics perceived his actions as high-handed and further evidence that the bank had grown too powerful. Not content to wait for the original charter to lapse, Jackson countered Biddle's campaign with definitive actions of his own. He ordered the treasury secretary to stop depositing federal funds in the bank. When the incumbent refused, Jackson replaced him with a man of his own persuasion, Roger Taney. The change in policy eroded the bank's reserves so severely that Biddle had to reduce its circulating currency. That, in turn, reduced the nation's overall money supply, the very consequence that soft money men opposed.

Jackson didn't care. In 1837 he issued the Specie Circular, revealing himself to be a hard money man through and through. He distrusted all banks, regardless of their affiliation, and favored a solid gold standard instead. Not surprisingly, he expressed no remorse when the Second Bank of the United States closed its doors for good in 1837. The bank war ended with a victory for those opposed to a strong federal influence in the economy and related money matters. That victory was so profound that nearly eighty years passed before the United States reinstituted an effective central banking structure in the form of the Federal Reserve System in 1914.

See also Banknotes; Biddle, Nicholas; Clay, Henry; Jackson, Andrew; *McCulloch v. Maryland;* Soft Money; Specie Circular.

References and Further Reading

McFaul, John. *The Politics of Jacksonian Finance.* Ithaca, NY: Cornell University Press, 1972.

Remini, Robert V. *Andrew Jackson and the Bank War.* New York: Norton, 1967.

Taylor, George Rogers. *Jackson v. Biddle's Bank.* Boston: Heath, 1972.

Watson, Harry L. *Andrew Jackson v. Henry Clay.* Boston: Bedford/St. Martin's, 1998.

Banknotes

Beginning in the 1790s, a growing number of state-chartered and private banks issued banknotes, based on their specie or other capital holdings. Because the central government failed to create a federal currency system, these private banknotes ended up serving as a major element in the nation's money supply. Relatively unregulated, many banknotes were of dubious value, however, and were discounted substantially or even rejected for payments. From time to time federal, state, and private mechanisms developed to systematically redeem banknotes and thus stabilize their value. This proved to be a challenging task since the number of banks grew rapidly, and they had issued an estimated 30,000 different types and denominations of banknotes by the time of the Civil War.

At the simplest level, a banknote was a receipt for funds deposited in the issuing institution. The language used varied widely, but the notes often included a promise that the bank would redeem the note with some other type of money. While specie was always the most desirable form of money, a great many banks hedged their pledge so that other paper currency, bonds, or deposit notices might be substituted for the persistently scarce gold and silver. The value of the note's pledge depended on the credibility and reputation of the issuing bank. In general, a bank that was perceived to be sound was far less likely to see its notes presented for redemption than a less respected institution.

While some state charters included specific restrictions, classical economic theory held that a bank could safely issue notes worth more than its capital holdings. This was feasible because many people held onto banknotes for long periods or traded them for goods and services from other people. Notes from reputable banks might circulate through dozens of private hands before being presented for redemption. The father of classical economic theory, Adam Smith contended that, in a well functioning market economy, the ratio of notes issued to reserves could reach as high as five to one.

The stunning proliferation of notes issued caused many contemporary and later commentators to presume that American banks in the early nineteenth century must certainly have exceeded that theoretical level. While there were particularly blatant examples of unscrupulous banks running their printing presses night and day, most institutions adhered to quite conservative policies. A well-managed bank generally restricted its note issue to no more than twice or three times its actual specie holdings. And, because specie normally represented only a small percentage of a bank's capitalization, such a bank could count on being able to redeem its outstanding notes quite easily.

That did not always occur. The many other demands on a bank's capital for loans and other investments caused many institutions to be reluctant to redeem their notes. Some bankers went to extraordinary lengths to avoid redemption. One strategy was to situate the redemption office in a remote location with limited hours of operation. Other institutions collected notes issued by small or distant banks and forced these on customers requesting an alternative to their own notes. Some banks subjected those presenting notes to complex questioning and arcane rules to discourage redemption. In blatant cases, bank rules insisted on an elaborate procedure for redemption of each individual note, with the whole process being repeated for each subsequent note presented.

From time to time, various state governments passed laws aimed at curbing or discouraging this sort of behavior. One of the most successful was the New York State Safety Fund Law. Passed in 1829, it required state-chartered banks to contribute half of 1 percent of their capital to a government managed fund that gave customers of failed banks some relief. Several other states created safety funds modeled after the New York system. Private action proved even more successful in New England. Leading citizens in Massachusetts established the Suffolk Bank and managed it as a central clearing house for the redemption of notes. It collected paper currency from local and regional banks on a regular basis and presented the notes for redemption at issuing institutions. The Suffolk System quickly rooted out poorly or unscrupulously managed banks and ensured a stable, reliable currency system in the years prior to the Civil War.

The federal government played a changing role in redemption. Though both were based in Philadelphia, the First and the Second Banks of the United States established branches in other cities. These branches collected private banknotes in large numbers and presented them for redemption on a regular basis. Particularly under the leadership of Nicholas Biddle in the 1820s, the Second Bank of the United States (B.U.S.) maintained such effective control over private banking that the country as a whole enjoyed remarkable financial stability. This collapsed when President Andrew Jackson initiated his war against the bank in 1832, undermining Biddle's ability to serve as a national redemption agent.

Even during relatively stable periods, a substantial number and variety of undervalued or outright counterfeit banknotes circulated. This was hardly surprising since the nation boasted over 1,300 independent banking institutions by 1862, almost all of which issued notes in a proliferation of sizes, denominations, and colors. As early as 1805, a Boston newspaper began issuing descriptions of counterfeit notes in circulation. Other journals followed suit, some eventually printing daily reports on bogus bills. Periodic publications also appeared listing the current value of literally thousands of valid banknotes. Depending on a bank's reputation or its remoteness from commercial centers, its notes might be subject to substantial discounts. Banks paid close attention to these constantly changing values, and the unwary or naive individual who accepted payment in unusual notes at face value could suffer severe financial loss when he tried to exchange them for more reputable notes.

Hard times forced all institutions including the most respectable ones to suspend payments from time to time. The Panic of 1837 set off a period of general insolvency that persisted into the next decade. A less severe panic in 1857 also led to widespread suspension. The most protracted period of suspension, however, began in 1861 and continued well beyond the end of the Reconstruction period. At that point, the federal government and the national banks that Civil War exigencies had created were operating on a more reliable basis.

Banknotes issued by privately owned institutions provided a currency system that encouraged industrialization in the Northeast, agricultural expansion in the West, and capital growth in the Southeast. Except for the occasional monitoring that the Banks of the United States provided, the federal government remained largely on the sidelines. Memories of the disastrous consequences of the Continental bills during the Revolutionary War served as a major disincentive to Congress and the Treasury Department for taking an active part in developing a paper money supply. Although the state charters and banking laws imposed serious constraints on private enterprise, the merchants, investors, and capitalists who engaged in private banking played an essential part in providing the United States with the monetary flexibility it needed to grow in the antebellum era.

See also Bank of the United States; Checks; Continental Currency; Free Banking; Soft Money.

References and Further Reading

Hammond, Bray. *Banks and Politics in America.* Princeton, NJ: Princeton University Press, 1957.

Klebaner, Benjamin J. *American Commercial Banking: A History.* Boston: Twayne Publisher, 1990.

Wright, Robert E. The *Origins of Commercial Banking in America, 1750–1800.* New York: Rowman and Littlefield, 2001.

Canal Era

In 1817 the State of New York authorized and financed construction of a canal that linked the Hudson River with Lake Erie. The Erie Canal took nearly nine years to complete, but it was so successful that it stimulated interest in dozens of other canal projects. Although no other waterway ever matched the Erie's success, the canal building craze continued into the early 1850s. Canal enthusiasm waned at that point. Most of the feasible routes had been exploited and stiff competition from railroads discouraged further investment in canals.

Despite its fame, the Erie was not the first such project in the United States. Two shorter canals were opened shortly after the American Revolution, both constructed to connect local hinterlands to major port cities. In Massachusetts, the Merrimac Canal facilitated transportation of bulk goods like timber and granite from New Hampshire and central Massachusetts to Boston. In South Carolina, the Santee Canal created a water route from rural regions to Charleston.

Private investors played major roles in financing these early state-chartered enterprises, but the magnitude of subsequent projects proposed argued for government support. President James Madison urged the nation to improve its internal transportation system after the close of the War of 1812. When Congress responded with a bill to use the federal government's profits from the Second Bank of the United States to finance internal improvements, Madison vetoed it. As a strict constructionist, he did not believe that the Constitution gave the U.S. government authority for such activities.

DeWitt Clinton, long an advocate of an east-west canal, was serving as governor of New York when he learned that federal funding would not be available. He immediately called on his state's legislators to step in, and the New York Assembly responded with an agreement to provide $7 million to finance the canal. It was a great bargain for the state because the tolls often exceeded a million dollars a year, providing plenty of money to more than pay off the construction and operating costs of the waterway.

The canal opened in sections. The first segment was ready for traffic in 1820 in large part because it traversed a relatively level, well-populated area. Three years later, the eastern segment opened, allowing boats to travel between Rochester and New York City. In October 1825, huge celebrations greeted the opening of the final segment extending all the way to Buffalo and Lake Erie. It was the first major civil engineering project in the United States, a waterway 4 feet deep and 40 feet wide stretching over 380 miles across the center of the state. A series of 83 locks raised and lowered boats over a maximum rise of 568 feet. Projects over the next several years widened and deepened the waterway and added a network of feeder canals to serve other markets within the state.

One of the most interesting aspects of this and other canal projects was that, though primarily funded by government resources, they created all sorts of opportunities for private enterprise. Unlike a railroad that owned and operated its own rolling stock, canal administrators did not run their own boats. Instead, literally thousands of individuals took advantage of the new inland waterways. Building a canal boat in the 1820s cost somewhere between $1,000 and $1,500 so that with relatively few round-trips, a vessel could make enough of a profit to pay for itself. Moving the boats was relatively inexpensive as well. Teams consisting of a couple of horses or mules harnessed to the prows of canal boats walked along adjacent towpaths. A strong team in good weather could plod along at 4 miles an hour, tugging a boat that on average had a 30-ton capacity.

Country carpenters could knock together a cargo carrier out of inexpensive materials. Very soon, however, brilliantly decorated and elegantly furnished passenger vessels began plying the canals. Some of these were owned by partnerships or other companies. Copying the success of their oceangoing cousins, a few organizations offered the equivalent of packet service. Their boats departed and arrived on set, dependable schedules, providing their paying passengers with reliable, comfortable transportation.

The economic benefits of the canal more than matched Clinton's optimistic expectations. The canal carried over 200,000 tons in its first year of operation, a figure that rose every year until it exceeded 4 million tons in the mid-1850s. Bulk cargoes from western New York and, ultimately Ohio, Indiana, Illinois, and points north stimulated settlement and growth not only of New York City but of the vast agricultural hinterland the canal served. At the same time, it provided an inexpensive way to ship desirable manufactured goods from the industrializing East to the agrarian West.

In one sense, the Erie Canal was too successful. Publicity about its profitability encouraged promoters in other states to lobby energetically for either parallel, competing canals or, in the case of Ohio and Indiana, canals that would complement the Erie route. Pennsylvania mounted the most ambitious project of them all, eventually investing tens of millions of dollars in its Mainline Canal that linked Philadelphia and Pittsburgh. The route included far more substantial geographic obstacles than the one along the Mohawk River Valley. Hundreds of locks were required and, where the mountain passes were just too steep, engineers installed complex systems of winches and inclined planes to drag canal boats from one side to the other. It was hardly surprising that the Pennsylvania Canal never paid for its costs.

Further south, the Chesapeake and Ohio Canal slowly carved its way to Cumberland in Maryland but never managed to cross the Appalachian Chain and complete a connection to the Ohio River. In Virginia, the James River and Kanawha Canal also failed to penetrate into the Midwest. Ohio had more success with the Ohio and Erie Canal in the east and the Miami and Ohio Canal linking Toledo with Cincinnati in the west. A branch of that canal also headed southwest through Indiana as the Wabash and Erie Canal, connecting with the Ohio River at Evansville, Indiana. Another major north-south canal connected Chicago with the Illinois River and, thence, on to the Mississippi.

These canal projects, most of them begun in the 1830s and constructed through the next two decades, quickly encountered stiff competition from railroads. The cost of a mile of almost any canal exceeded that of the similar outlay for a mile of track. Moreover, rails could be laid over grades impossible for canals to surmount, and they had the added advantage of neither freezing in the winter nor running dry in the summer. More than any other factor, railroads brought the canal era to a close.

It probably would have ended in any case due to the huge costs and very long-term return on investment that a canal project involved. One estimate is that nearly $190 million was invested in canals between 1815 and 1860, of which $136 million or approximately 73 percent represented government funds from various state, municipal, and, rarely, federal sources. An enormous amount of foreign investment went into the American canal systems as well, either in the form of private investment in construction companies or because European speculators eagerly bought state bonds. Several states suffered severe financial strains in attempting to build and finance their canals, and from time to time states like Ohio and Indiana were driven to insolvency. Meanwhile periodic business downturns punctuated the era, further undermining the progress on and value of the overextended canal system.

The canal craze lasted only one generation, but it affected an enormous number of Americans. Some built and ran boats, many more rode on them as passengers, and countless more benefited from the low-cost transportation they provided. They definitely helped stimulate settlement in the upper Midwest. Perhaps even more significantly, the mainline canals strengthened east-west ties. By the 1850s, the major sectional division in the country was between north and south, and it was this division that ultimately tore apart during the Civil War.

See also American System; Railroads.

References and Further Reading

Albion, Robert Greenhalgh. *The Rise of New York Port.* New York: Scribners, 1939.

Goodrich, Carter, ed. *Canals and American Economic Development.* New York: Columbia University Press, 1961.

Scheiber, Harry N. *Ohio Canal Era.* Athens, OH: Ohio University Press, 1969.

Carrying Trade

The series of international wars that began in 1793 disrupted trade between European nations and their Western Hemisphere colonies. As citizens of a neutral country, U.S. shipowners took advantage of this turmoil by hauling cargo between colonies and home countries. Known as the *carrying trade,* this activity proved to be remarkably profitable for American merchants and sea captains, and it stimulated a major economic growth spurt in the United States in general. It only flourished for a dozen years, but the carrying trade created the first American millionaires and generally raised the nation's standard of living.

The French Revolution that established a republican government was anathema to the traditional monarchies in Europe. Even in Great Britain, where the government had evolved into a constitutional monarchy, the events in France appeared to be extremely subversive. By 1793 Britain was at war with France, the opening skirmish in a conflict that lasted for more than two decades with only brief periods of peace. In each phase, the major combatants received assistance from a changing panoply of allies, although Spain was most frequently linked with France.

Each of these nations had managed its American colonies in a closed, mercantilist system. Trade between the colonies and the home countries was strictly controlled and, except for a few minor exceptions, handled by ships flying the home country's flag. These exclusive trading policies were detrimental to the newly independent United States in the Confederation period. This was especially so because the American break from England denied the United States access to the carrying trade within the British Empire on which the colonies had relied throughout the eighteenth century.

The world war changed all that. Britain's Royal Navy held such a dominant position that it could routinely prevent French and Spanish ships from carrying goods between Europe and the Caribbean. France and Spain therefore temporarily shelved their mercantilist rules and opened their colonial ports to outsiders. Plenty of American vessels were available to handle this carrying trade. Simultaneously, the wartime disturbances created shortages of all sorts of goods around the world so that virtually any ship's cargo could be sold at premium prices.

President Washington issued his Neutrality Proclamation in 1793 to avoid a military commitment to either side. But the neutrality concept gave New England shipowners a rationale for moving full sail into the colonial carrying trade. International law remained a controversial concept in this era, with each nation tending to interpret it in a way that would be most advantageous. In the American view, naval vessels from one of the warring parties should not molest or seize a ship from a neutral nation. They might make an exception if the neutral ship was carrying contraband goods, but contraband was generally limited to weapons, gunpowder, and other armaments, not agricultural commodities like sugar and tobacco that the Caribbean Islands produced.

The British rejected such a narrowly defined prohibition. Well aware that colonies contributed to the general wealth of European nations, they were eager to close off all trade that did not directly benefit the United Kingdom. They cited as a precedent the Rule of 1756, a reference to an earlier policy that stated that trade prohibited during peacetime could not be carried out during wartime either. Applied to the situation prevailing in the 1790s, it meant that Britain objected to American ships carrying cargo from French or Spanish ports that the European countries' peacetime restrictions would have forbidden.

American negotiator John Jay reconfirmed the Rule of 1756 in the treaty he hammered out with the United Kingdom in 1794, but a British order-in-council that same year undermined the rule's impact. This new policy allowed American ships to load colonial cargo from any of the West Indies and take it back to the United States. In this way, Americans presumably would not directly be supporting either France or Spain. Hundreds of American-owned ships began visiting Caribbean ports and sailing unmolested back home. There the cargo could be unloaded and either sold for local consumption or reshipped as American rather than foreign goods.

In practice, many ships simply dropped anchor briefly in a U.S. port and then sailed on to Europe without ever unloading the colonial cargo. The British nevertheless accepted this as a broken voyage that accorded with the technical definition of its order-in-council. In 1800, in fact, a British admiralty court issued a landmark decision involving a ship named *Polly* that confirmed the legality of this practice. For the next several years, the *Polly* decision allowed American ships to participate in the carrying trade without fear of British interference.

By 1807, however, European tensions had escalated, and British naval vessels began seizing American-owned ships and impressing American citizens off merchant ships into service in the Royal Navy. A particularly outrageous case of impressment, this time off the U.S. Navy vessel *Chesapeake,* spurred anti-British sentiments to new heights. President Thomas Jefferson responded with a full-scale embargo that officially halted all shipping in or out of American ports.

Even so, Americans had profited enormously from the carrying trade. The United States had reexported only about $2 million worth of goods in 1793, but that figure had risen to $26 million just three years later. With only a couple of exceptions, the value of the carrying trade exceeded that of direct American foreign trade every year between 1797 and 1807. This highly remunerative activity created the first millionaires in the United States. The most successful was Stephen Girard who amassed somewhere between $7 and $9 million largely from his trading activities based in Philadelphia. His wealth earned primarily from the carrying trade made him the richest man in America.

When the Embargo halted both carrying and domestic trade possibilities, many newly wealthy merchants and shipowners looked for other investment opportunities. Between 1807 and 1815, much of their money flowed into building domestic manufacturing operations. In this way, the carrying trade was a key element in financing the industrial revolution that took hold in the Northeast in the early nineteenth century.

See also Clipper Ships; Embargo; Girard, Stephen; Industrial Revolution; Lowell, Francis Cabot.

References and Further Reading

Bruchey, Stuart. *Enterprise.* Cambridge, MA: Harvard University Press, 1990.

Morison, Samuel Eliot. *Maritime History of Massachusetts: 1783–1860.* Boston: Houghton Mifflin, 1961.

Charter, State

When they declared their political independence from British rule, the states also achieved economic autonomy. Individual state governments immediately exercised their authority to promote and regulate business activities within their borders. A common method for doing so was by issuing a charter. State charters permitted and encouraged individuals, partnerships, and corporations to engage in all sorts of business and industrial activities until they were largely supplanted by the passage of general incorporation laws in the late nineteenth century.

Many colonial enterprises had benefited from possession of a grant or charter from the royal government. Both in America and in the United Kingdom itself, chartering authority resided with the monarch, and obtaining a charter often involved currying favor with highly placed officials. Colonial governors exercised the king's authority on the American side of the Atlantic, so they and their councils and counselors often dictated the terms and extent of any royal charter granted.

To a degree, then, the situation after independence was not as revolutionary as it might have been. Now-independent state governments rather than dependent colonial administrations asserted that they possessed the authority to grant and enforce charters within their boundaries. Entrepreneurs found themselves lobbying legislators and other state officials for special favors much as they had in pre-Revolutionary times.

As a general rule, this process involved far fewer bureaucratic hurdles than had prevailed in the colonial era. State legislatures were more accessible to the people, the size of the political units were smaller and more manageable, and extraneous factors such as which party currently held the king's favor ceased to matter. Americans took advantage of the comparatively easier process of obtaining a charter to develop literally thousands of ambitious schemes. Interestingly enough, the federal government offered very little competition in this arena. With a few exceptions like those it granted to the First and Second Banks of the U.S., the central government did not grant charters.

Most state governments were eager to promote enterprises. Canal, bridge, highway, and other internal improvement projects were particularly popular with cash-strapped legislatures. Chartering a group of investors who proposed to build a toll bridge or toll road could benefit the citizens without putting a strain on state resources. Added inducements for individual legislators were monetary bribes or shares they received in return for their help in passing a law granting a charter. Sometimes this sort of behavior went well beyond petty corruption as it did in 1794 when all but one of the Georgia legislators reputedly took a bribe before granting a charter to the Yazoo Land Company.

In the early years, a state typically prohibited the holders of one of its charters from operating outside of its borders. Such provisions exerted a degree of control and oversight over the corporation's activities and discouraged it from becoming too large. Depending on the state and the nature of the activity proposed, the charter might contain any number of other restrictions. It could specify exactly how the company's directors would be selected, how many of them there should be, and what authority they would have. In some instances, the charters prohibited its grantees from engaging in activities not specified in the charter itself. To evade such restrictions, some entrepreneurs obtained banking charters and then poured their banking investments and capital into other enterprises.

Charter-seekers often demanded and received monopoly rights that protected them from competition. The Supreme Court decision in the *Gibbons v. Oregon* case in 1824 discouraged the issuance of monopoly grants, however, when it invalidated the Robert Fulton group's exclusive right to operate steamboats in New York's inland waters. This policy was confirmed in the 1837 *Charles River Bridge* decision that stated that a corporate charter did not and could not create a monopoly.

Early in the nineteenth century, some states acknowledged that the chartering process was too cumbersome and fraught with opportunities for corruption. Hoping to encourage economic development, their legislatures passed general incorporation laws. To go into business, a corporation need only meet the law's standards for capitalization and management. This proved to be a popular development, and so general incorporation laws became increasingly common throughout the country.

They did not completely replace charters, however. Perhaps one of the most notorious state charters in American history was the one John D. Rockefeller used to consolidate his hold over oil refineries in Cleveland in 1870. Some years earlier the State of Ohio issued a charter for the innocuously and ambiguously named South Improvement Co. The charter was vague as to what activities it countenanced as well, so Rockefeller and his partners used it to convince the owners of competing refineries that the South Improvement Company already held majority control over the local refining business, and that they had better sell out to this company. It was only a sham, however, quickly replaced by other organizing structures once the desired consolidation had taken place. Rockefeller personally stonewalled Ohio officials when they held hearings to try to determine just how the state's charter might have been misused.

Despite the many problems they caused and the invitation to corruption they presented, state charters were an important element in the growth of American business. They were relatively easy to obtain, enabling individuals, partnerships, and corporations to operate with state authority throughout the United States. By the close of the nineteenth century, however, many enterprises had spilled across state lines, and a state-chartered firm often found itself hamstrung in trying to compete in that larger, national market. General incorporation laws allowing and, indeed, encouraging companies to operate both within and outside of state boundaries became the key to promoting business activity.

See also Corporations; Industrial Revolution.

References and Further Reading

Lamoreaux, Naomi R. Entrepreneurship, Business Organization, and Economic Concentration. Vol. 2 of *The Cambridge Economic History of the United States,* ed. Stanley L. Engerman and Robert E. Gallman. New York: Cambridge University Press, 2000.

Checks

Checks and checking accounts came into general use in Great Britain in the mid-1700s. In their simplest form they were receipts for specie deposited in a bank. While a check might be written to a specific person for a specific purpose, some checks changed hands many times, serving as substitutes for specie or paper currency.

The ultimate origin of checks is unknown. People had received paper acknowledgments for valuables placed in the custody of others for centuries. The appearance of banks or of substantial merchants with reputations for honesty encouraged the expansion of this practice. A depositor would essentially store his specie or other valuables in the vaults of the bank or merchant house. He could then write a "bill" for any amount up to the full value of the deposit, and use it to pay debts or buy other goods. The recipient of the bill could redeem it at the bank or merchant house.

Checks as such were less common in the early United States where any state-chartered bank could issue banknotes. In Great Britain, however, the royal government permitted only the Bank of England to issue notes. Private banks therefore relied on checking accounts to expand their operations and scope.

The convenience of checking accounts led to their popularity, however. An individual check could be written for the exact amount of a transaction. Checks also offered security because they eliminated the need to carry wads of cash or bags of coins to conduct business. But unregulated checking accounts could inflate the amount of money in circulation, an aspect that eventually encouraged government control of the banking system.

Checking accounts had several advantages for bankers. For example a bank could advertise its existence by printing elaborate blank checks with the institution's name in bold letters. Because checks might be held uncashed for days or even months, the bank had full use of its customers' deposits during that period. And, in early America, checks often circulated from one person to another. When they finally came back to the bank, they might have a dozen or more names endorsed on the back.

The use of checks became so widespread in the United States by the mid-nineteenth century that some sort of centralized clearing apparatus was needed. New York City had become the nation's banking center, so it was not surprising that the New York

Clearing House Association was established in 1853. In the next few years regional clearing arrangements appeared in other major financial centers including Boston, Philadelphia, Baltimore, and Cleveland.

By the mid-twentieth century clearing houses with nationwide scope were handling millions of checks written every day. This demand stimulated the invention of machines that could read carefully designed numbers along the bottom edge of the check. These peculiarly shaped digits are still printed in magnetic ink on blank checks and clearing machines add additional numbers to indicate the amount of the check. Meanwhile, the federal government began issuing checks with rectangular holes punched in them so a Hollerith card-sorting machinery could tabulate them. Thus the processing of checks was already highly automated long before the development of personal and business computers.

At one point checks were used in about 90 percent of all financial transactions in the United States. In recent years, however, credit cards and electronic or computerized accounts have made checks much less important.

See also Banknotes; Book Credit; Free Banking; Hollerith, Herman.

References and Further Reading

Moore, Carl H., and Alvin E. Russell. *Money: Its Origin, Development and Modern Use.* Jefferson, NC: McFarland, 1987.

China Market

Even before the United States had won its independence, American traders were attempting to expand their operations to include China. Throughout the nineteenth century the China market remained far more important as a concept and a goal than it did as a reality. Even so, China was a constant topic in diplomatic, business, and expansionist discussions. American traders remained minor players in this arena until official treaty relations were established in the 1840s.

In 1781 an American trading vessel aptly named *Empress of China* reached the port of Hong Kong, the only access the Chinese empire allowed to foreign traders. Other adventurous ships seeking trade opportunities followed, and some of them carried *supercargoes,* business agents for the merchants who had sent out the ships. Many of these supercargoes were younger sons of major merchants and one of them, Samuel Shaw, established a trading house in China. John Jay was the Confederation government's secretary of foreign affairs, and he recognized Shaw's importance by naming him American consul in Hong Kong.

For the next several decades, however, Shaw and his successor consular officers possessed little power and exercised only minor influence, mostly focusing their efforts on their companies' trading activities. Customers in the United States eagerly snapped up whatever silk, porcelain, and exotic herbs American ships brought home. But the trade was strictly limited to Hong Kong because foreigners were denied access to the interior.

The British were far more entrepreneurial than Americans, and a major element of their trade consisted of shipping opium to China. Chinese imperial officials objected to this trade and the rowdy behavior of British sailors in general. The result was a confrontation called the Opium War that began in 1839. The British won an easy and decisive victory and were able to dictate the Treaty of Nanking that gave them access to four additional ports and greatly expanded the opportunities for foreign penetration of all of China.

American diplomats quickly capitalized on this development by negotiating a most-favored-nation treaty with a Chinese government anxious to dilute British influence. The agreement gave Americans access privileges identical to those in the Treaty of Nanking, and interest in the China trade expanded correspondingly in the United States. Asa Whitney, for example, proposed building a transcontinental railroad to bring American trading opportunities closer to Asia by eliminating the long ocean passage around Cape Horn. Simultaneously, the growing fleet of clipper ships substantially reduced the length of such voyages. But these ships' limited cargo capacity meant that trade with China continued to be only a minor part of America's overseas commerce.

The Chinese remained generally hostile to all foreigners, however, and xenophobia definitely played a part in triggering the fifteen-year-long Taiping Revolt against the imperial government. Even while contending with this major internal disturbance, imperial officials became increasingly confrontational with outsiders and deliberately failed to honor their treaty commitments. By 1857 the French and the British had become so frustrated that they decided to resort to armed intervention. Their success in the resulting Anglo-French war significantly undermined the empire's ability to limit foreign exploitation of its territory. Although it had taken no part in the conflict, the United States joined with the victors in negotiating the 1858 Treaty of Tientsin that significantly broadened trade and missionary opportunities in China. Shortly afterward, however, the Civil War and Reconstruction distracted Americans from overseas expansionism, and Far Eastern trade continued to be more a concept than a reality. The potential of the China market once again assumed greater importance when a new era of expansionist attitudes developed in the 1890s. The famous Open Door Policy promulgated in 1900 represented the high point of American diplomacy and defined U.S.-Chinese relations well into the 1930s.

See also Carrying Trade; Clipper Ships; Japan, Opening of.

References and Further Reading

Cohen, Warren I. *America's Response to China,* 4th ed. New York: Columbia University Press, 2000.

Fay, Peter W. *The Opium War.* Chapel Hill, NC: University of North Carolina Press, 1975.

Van Alstyne, Richard W. *The United States and East Asia.* New York: Norton, 1973.

Clipper Ships

Between 1843 and 1860, American yards built longer, relatively narrow-hulled sailing ships that were much faster than other ocean-going vessels. They were called clipper ships, a name derived from the verb *clip,* one meaning of which is "to travel or pass by rapidly." Their speed made them very popular for long-distance voyages, but their streamlined shape limited cargo capacity. Consequently, they were mostly used on high-profit routes like the China trade or to link East Coast American ports with gold-rich California.

In the 1830s even an expertly captained ship could average no more than 5 knots on a voyage from New York to San Francisco, so a round trip could take a year or more. The earliest experiments with a more refined hull configuration with a sharper bow and concave sides occurred in England. These early clippers were quickly pressed into service in the opium trade, carrying goods from India to Chinese ports. American shipbuilders adopted and greatly advanced the design principles, building still larger and faster vessels. For a time, many of these also focused on Far Eastern trade.

The discovery of gold in California in 1848 boosted interest in clipper ships. Many of those built in the early 1850s could sail from New York around Cape Horn and to San Francisco in less than a hundred days. While passengers were a major source of revenue, commodities, tools, and other manufactured products could be sold for anywhere from double to ten times their cost on the remote and underdeveloped West Coast. After marketing their initial cargo in California, many clipper ships continued sailing west, eventually loading up with tea in China or India for the English market before arriving back in their home ports. So profitable was this trade that many ships earned more than the entire cost of their construction and operation in one globe-circling voyage that took less than a year.

Shipyards in New England, New York, and other American ports rushed to build more clipper ships. In general, American-built and captained vessels far outperformed those constructed in Great Britain or elsewhere. The most prominent American builder was Donald McKay whose shipyards in East Boston turned out some of the largest, fastest, and most graceful clipper ships. In 1854 his *Flying Cloud* made the Boston to San Francisco run in eighty-nine days, a record that no other commercial sailing vessel has ever beaten.

As with so many other fads, too many clipper ships were built in the 1850s and the market became glutted. They always sacrificed cargo space for speed, and by 1860 improvements in steam power nullified that advantage. In retrospect, the clipper ship era was an exciting but rather brief transition point between sail and steam, but one that brought the art of shipbuilding to an admirable pinnacle.

See also China Market; Gold Rush; Packet Ships.

References and Further Reading

Cosgrave, II, John O'Hara. *Clipper Ship; America's Famous and Fast Sailing Queens of the Sea.* New York: Macmillan, 1963.

Cutler, Carl. *Greyhounds of the Sea; the Story of the American Clipper Ship.* New York: Putnam, 1930.

Lyon, Jane D. *Clipper Ships and Captains.* New York: American Heritage, 1962.

Continental Currency

Even before the signing of the Declaration of Independence, the Continental Congress began issuing paper currency to pay for its own and its army's operations. Over the next four years, *Continentals* with a paper value of over $200 million were issued, stimulating rampant price inflation. These controversial notes undermined faith in the central government and created a major financial problem for the newly independent United States to solve.

Taxation, or rather, a lack thereof was its primary cause. Revolutionaries throughout the colonies who adopted the slogan "no taxation without representation" had helped provoke the outbreak of the war, and no one wanted to accord the power to levy taxes to a nonrepresentative political body. The Continental Congress was not popularly elected; instead the various state governments sent delegates to speak for their interests. Moreover, the states themselves were caught up in the heady experience of learning how to make their own adjustments to political independence.

Pressures from the war effort left no time to work out a better political system. Congress named George Washington commander-in-chief of a Continental Army in 1775. Troops had to be paid, supplies requisitioned, weapons and ammunition purchased. Lacking hard currency or any other type of funds, Congress authorized the issuance of bills of credit. These were essentially IOUs from the Continental Congress, printed and distributed to pay for goods or services. Hypothetically, the states stood behind them, but there was no direct linkage between them and the state governments.

The first $2 million worth of Continental currency appeared in June 1775. When Congress abandoned the practice some four years later, $241,552,780 had been printed and circulated, none of it with any concrete backing. Not surprisingly, the Continentals immediately began to depreciate in value. They had fallen to around eight to one compared to Mexican silver dollars in January 1779; by November of that year, the ratio had deteriorated to forty to one. It only got worse in the years to come, and the expression "not worth a Continental" came into general use.

To make matters worse, the states were issuing their own bills of credit, contributing substantially to the flood of unbacked, devalued paper currency. After 1780 the Continental Congress collaborated with the states in issuing what were called *new tenor* notes in an attempt to consolidate efforts. Joint sponsorship of these bills did prevent them from depreciating as fast or as far as the *old tenor* notes issued earlier, but they in no way solved the financial crisis.

The only really bright aspect in this dismal financial picture came after 1778 when foreign money began flowing into the United States as a result of the signing of the military alliance with France. Both the French and Spanish governments provided outright grants, and other funds were loaned from those two countries and Holland. While these sources brought hard currency into circulation and helped establish some financial sanity, they contributed to the further depreciation of Continental and state-issued notes.

During and after the war, speculators purchased Continentals at bargain prices from those who had lost faith in the central government's ability to make good on its debts. These speculators became targets of criticism in the early 1790s when Treasury Secretary Alexander Hamilton proposed a funding scheme that would compensate the current holders of the discredited currency. All in all, the experiment with unbacked bills of credit was so traumatic that the federal government refused to issue unbacked paper currency until the exigencies of the Civil War forced it to resort to using greenbacks.

See also Banknotes; Greenbacks; Specie Circular.

References and Further Reading

Dewey, Davis Rich. *Financial History of the United States.* New York: Longmans, Green, 1936.

Myers, Margaret G. *A Financial History of the United States.* New York: Columbia University Press, 1970.

Corn Law

Although the Corn Law was a British tariff, it profoundly influenced American international trade. The repeal of the Corn Law in 1846 signaled Great Britain's conversion to a free trade policy that opened its markets to American agricultural exports.

In Great Britain, the word *corn* stood for all cereal grains whether English wheat, Scottish oats, or American maize. Consequently, the Corn Law primarily dealt with the regulation of wheat. As early as 1660, responding to lobbying from farming interests, Parliament imposed duties on wheat imported from abroad. The purpose was to protect English growers from overseas competition. These restrictions were associated with the seventeenth century Navigation Acts and supported the mercantilist policies of the British Empire.

Revised and renewed in subsequent years, these protective measures maintained a price support for domestically grown wheat. Meanwhile grain production in the American colonies and later the United States expanded enormously, creating a surplus for which merchants and shippers sought overseas markets. Protectionist sentiments held sway in Great Britain, however, with the security of domestic producers cited as the major goal of the tariff policy.

By the dawn of the nineteenth century, the enclosure process and the industrial revolution had reoriented much of Great Britain's economy away from growing field crops. Domestic grain production had become so restricted, in fact, that it could not meet the demand for food. Even so, representatives of the landowners maintained their traditional influence in Parliament and insisted on the retention of the tariffs on agricultural imports. The duties on imported grain raised the price of food for everyone and generated distress and opposition.

That opposition coalesced in 1838 with the formation of the Anti-Corn Law League. Richard Cobden and John Bright led this group, opposing not just the protective tariffs on food but on all imports. They argued that free trade would benefit everyone and especially the government because effective protective tariffs discouraged imports and actually decreased government tax revenue. These arguments began to influence the Conservative government of Robert Peel who was grappling with persistent budget shortfalls.

Two natural disasters nudged Peel further toward free trade. Blight destroyed the Irish potato crop in 1845 and, shortly afterward, torrential rains drowned the English wheat crop. Faced with the prospect of massive starvation, the government authorized free importation of food through Irish ports. Early in 1846, Parliament went further, canceling the Corn Law for all of Great Britain and setting in motion a complete abandonment of protectionism. By 1849 free trade had become the British policy and it remained so well into the twentieth century.

The repeal of the Corn Law had two important consequences for the United States. It gave American farmers unrestricted access to a major market for their food exports. At the same time, the conversion of the main U.S. trading partner to free trade put pressure on American politicians to do the same. Despite the fact that the British economy boomed as never before under its new policy, Americans continued to hide behind protective tariff walls.

See also Enclosure; Mercantilism; Navigation Acts; Protective Tariff.

References and Further Reading

Gash, Norman. *Sir Robert Peel.* Totowa, NJ: Rowman and Littlefield, 1972.

Kitson Clark, G. S. R. *Peel and the Conservative Party.* Hamden, CT: Archon, 1964.

McCord, Norman. *The Anti-Corn Law League: 1838–1846.* London: Allen and Unwin, 1958.

Corporations

After the American Revolution, states chartered hundreds of corporations, most of them relatively small. These business entities were privately owned and managed but often enjoyed monopoly or other special privileges outlined in their charters. Most of these early corporations were devoted to internal improvements, banking, and insurance. Only later in the nineteenth century would manufacturing and other industrial corporations become common.

A few corporations traced their roots back to the colonial period. In those years, authority to grant corporate charters stemmed ultimately from the royal government, but many of the colonial governments were allowed to charter organizations for particular purposes. Most of these were small, localized operations focused on municipal and other public purposes with only a scant half dozen specifically created for manufacturing. Colonial charters tended to be very restrictive, granted for very specific activities and usually only to a few influential citizens.

The American Revolution swept away all royal restrictions and neither the Confederation nor the Constitutional Congress stepped in to replace Britain's central authority over corporate activities. The states jealously guarded their authority to promote and regulate activities within their borders, and their legislatures were eager to encourage enterprises of all sorts. The legislators themselves were eager as well to benefit from their positions, so a good deal of influence peddling took place to move a charter proposal through the legislative process.

Like their colonial predecessors, early state charters tended to be explicit and restrictive. They spelled out precisely what activities a corporation could engage in, how its management should be structured, and even what reports it must publish. In return, many of the early charters conveyed state authority to the proposed enterprise, in some cases creating a monopoly for the corporation within the state's boundaries.

Awarding local monopolies made some sense because a large percentage of them were for internal improvement projects. Corporations agreed to build toll roads; river improvements like bridges and, later, canals; and railroads to promote economic development. In such instances, the charter protected these enterprises from competing groups. Inherent in them, however, was an expectation that the corporation would operate only within the state's boundaries. The goal was to keep the enterprise under the supervision of and answerable to state authorities.

Over the years, the real or perceived monopolistic aspects as well as the restrictiveness of these charters became increasingly unpopular. By the 1830s, many states had passed general incorporation laws that permitted much wider competition and flexibility. These laws specified limited requirements and low filing fees for any group wishing to form a corporation. Over time, the stipulations in general incorporation laws became fewer, encouraging more widespread use of the mechanism. By the late nineteenth century, in fact, some states had even abandoned the restrictions against a corporation crossing the state's boundaries, opening the way for the creation of nationwide holding companies.

A number of advantages encouraged enterprising people to seek corporate status. Unlike individual businesses and partnerships, a corporation could continue to exist and operate even if one or more of its principal owners decided to withdraw from the organization. When a partner died, on the other hand, a partnership often had to be dismantled or completely restructured from the ground up, but a corporation could redistribute or sell shares and continue operating virtually unchanged. This flexibility of ownership also provided an easy way to raise capital from outside investors. It should be noted, however, that most early corporations were of modest size, not requiring the massive amounts of capital that later industrial corporations would consume.

Another key advantage of the corporate structure was that it limited the liability of its owners. In partnerships, each participant was responsible for all the debts that other partners might incur, and all of one's wealth could be devoured in coping with adversity. In a corporation, the investor or shareholder was only liable to lose the funds he had actually invested in the corporation's stock. If the corporation ran up excessive debts or became insolvent, it did not necessarily bankrupt those who participated in it.

Two major Supreme Court decisions affected the status of corporations in this early period. In 1819 the state of New Hampshire arbitrarily altered the charter it had earlier granted to Dartmouth College. The new arrangement would turn what had been a private corporation into a public institution, answerable to the government rather than to its independent board of trustees. Daniel Webster won renown for his brilliant defense of his alma mater, maintaining that the original charter was a contract the state could not change. Chief Justice John Marshall's opinion favored the college, confirming the charter as an inviolable contract. One unexpected consequence of this ruling, however, was that state legislatures tended to be much more careful in drafting charter legislation, often including a provision that specifically authorized subsequent amendments to the original structure.

The second judicial ruling was a victory for those interested in exploiting new opportunities. The Charles River Bridge Co. in Massachusetts planned to build a toll bridge, and it obtained a charter in 1775 that implied it would be the only corporation permitted to span the river. When the state authorized another company to build a toll-free bridge, the original corporation sued. In 1837 Chief Justice Roger Taney wrote the opinion in the *Charles River Bridge Co.* decision, ruling that the free bridge would be in the public interest and rejected the claim that the original charter had implied a monopoly grant.

By the mid-nineteenth century, corporations of all sorts had become quite common. General incorporation laws made them easier to form and court decisions had weakened the restrictiveness of earlier charters. As railroads and manufacturing concerns proliferated, the benefits and flexibility of the corporate format were increasingly appreciated.

See also Charter, Royal; Charter, State; General Incorporation Laws.

References and Further Reading

Bruchey, Stuart. *Enterprise.* Cambridge: Harvard University Press, 1990.

Lamoreaux, Naomi R. "Entrepreneurship, Business Organization, and Economic Concentration." Vol. 2 of *The Cambridge Economic History of the United States,* ed. Stanley L. Engerman and Robert E. Gallman. New York: Cambridge University Press, 1990.

Cotton

Throughout the first half of the nineteenth century, the value of the U.S. cotton shipped overseas exceeded that of all other American exports combined. Cotton was the most reliable cash crop for southern farmers whether they were smallholders or substantial planters. Its influence became so pervasive that much of the South became known as the *Cotton Kingdom.* Slavery was inextricably associated with the production of cotton in the period before that institution helped trigger the Civil War. Cotton production was clearly big business in the United States and it had profound consequences on life, labor, and wealth.

To rise to such prominence, cotton had to be considered a valuable product. In the 1700s a series of English inventions and innovations sped up the various stages of textile production. The machines and power applied to carding raw fiber, spinning thread, and weaving finished cloth set off the British industrial revolution, and it, in turn, needed an ever-growing supply of raw material. Historic sources of cotton like India and Egypt simply could not fulfill the demand, so armies of American growers stepped in.

The demand for cotton appeared to be virtually insatiable. In 1800 the United States exported some 92,000 bales of cotton, each weighing an average of 228 pounds. In 1860, the average bale weighed more than twice as much, 461 pounds, and the United States shipped nearly 3.8 million bales overseas, more than 80 times as much fiber as had been sent abroad at the beginning of the century. In that same year, domestic factories processed another million bales. At that point, the United States was producing around 70 percent of the world's supply of raw cotton, and no one anticipated that global demand would decline. Figure 2.1 illustrates the almost exponential increase in cotton production and exports prior to the Civil War.

Production of such an enormous cash crop had profound consequences for all Americans living in the cotton-growing region. The Cotton Kingdom stretched from South Carolina all the way to eastern Texas, and from the Gulf Coast north to Kentucky. Overplanting had depleted much of the land in South Carolina and Georgia by midcentury, but even there cotton could still be profitably cultivated in smaller patches or on newly cleared lands. The most productive areas were the bottomlands of Alabama, Mississippi, and Louisiana where rich alluvial soil, a long growing season, and plentiful rainfall combined to create ideal conditions for the crop.

No farm was too small to grow a little cotton. A backwoods homesteader could sow an acre or two of cotton, reasonably sure he could market it for cash at the end of the season. At the other end of the scale, entrepreneurial planters with dozens of slave laborers could farm hundreds or even thousands of acres. Land changed hands frequently in the antebellum South as smallholders earned premiums selling land they had cleared to planters eager to extend their holdings. Some of the wealthiest planters skipped this step altogether, taking advantage instead of cheap prices for federal land and leapfrogging settled areas to establish plantations in virgin lands to the west. The Cotton Kingdom remained a patchwork of very small, medium-size, and huge tracts of land, but all of these plots could produce cotton.

Growing the crop effectively required year-round hand labor. Throughout much of the pre–Civil War period, farmers consid-

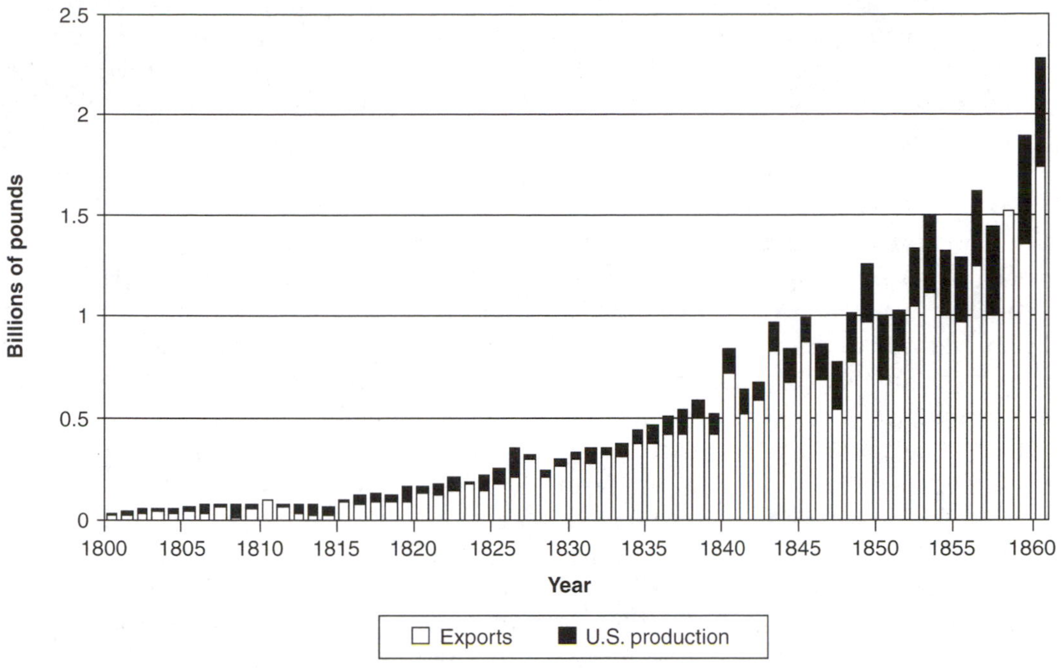

Figure 2.1 Cotton production and exports, 1800–1860. (Data from Historical Statistics of the United States, Colonial Times to 1970. *Washington, DC: U.S. Bureau of the Census, 1975.)*

ered cotton seeds a useless by-product of the ginning process, so they planted dozens or even hundreds at a time. When the seeds germinated, the fields had to be *scraped*, a process involving a hoer chopping down weaker seedlings and leaving behind rows of strong, healthy plants. Painstaking hand cultivation continued through the summer, as weeds and grass were just as likely to thrive as cotton plants.

The real bottleneck developed in August when some of the cotton bolls ripened. Picking crews conscripted everyone available regardless of age, gender, or race to roam through the fields harvesting cotton. The seed stock was of such variable quality that the plants matured over a long period, so the same field had to be harvested several times, sometimes delaying the final harvest until well into December. Within a few weeks, the hands returned to the fields to clear last year's crop and prepare to plant a new one.

This labor-intensive enterprise encouraged the continuation of and substantial growth of the slave system. By 1860 over 3 million people lived in bondage, one-third of the South's population. Some 10,000 families each owned 50 or more slaves, and these people were the ones who tended to live in plantation settings. The larger the group, the more likely there was to be a complex division of labor within it. In addition to field hands, a plantation could support carpenters, blacksmiths, cooks, drovers, laundresses, and nurses as well as a bevy of specialists who worked as household servants.

While plantations with huge mansions and hundreds of cultivated acres were symbolic of the Cotton Kingdom, the vast majority of slaves were owned in smaller lots. Many yeoman farmers worked hard to put aside enough to buy a slave, or two or three. Slave ownership was a sign of prestige in the South, so purchasing a slave represented a social as well as a financial investment. On smaller farms with relatively few slaves, bondsmen often worked at a variety of tasks, freely intermixing with the farmer and his family members. They might sleep in the barn, but many ate communal meals with their owners. Even so, life in these circumstances was often as hard and debilitating as on larger operations, given the unrelenting, year-round demand for hand labor on any nineteenth century farm.

The social and personal costs of slavery were equally harsh. Owners could sell slaves individually at any time, making family relationships difficult to maintain. Southern state legislatures reinforced the system by enacting ever tougher slave codes in response to perceived rebelliousness among the enslaved population. These codes prohibited slaves from learning to read, from owning property, even from legally marrying. Worse still, they granted owners literal control over life and limb. Whipping was a common punishment and many slaves died at the hands of their masters. But the law generally protected the rights of owners to deal with their property pretty much as they saw fit.

Most of the slaves who labored in the Cotton Kingdom had been born in the United States. Despite the hardships, the black population expanded primarily from natural increase throughout the nineteenth century. Yeoman farming had largely supplanted plantations in states like Virginia, so it had more slaves than it could profitably employ. Although there is little evidence that it was deliberately encouraged, the Upper South ended up exporting thousands of slaves to the Cotton Kingdom. And, despite the best efforts of abolitionists, relatively few blacks managed to escape to the free states.

Both contemporary and some more recent commentators insisted that there was a natural limit to the area and size of the slave system. Some of the more optimistic went so far as to claim that slavery would have collapsed within a few years even if Abraham Lincoln had never issued his Emancipation Proclamation. Critics of this view contend that the social control mechanisms underlying the slave codes would not simply fade away. Moreover, cotton continued to be the major cash crop in the South until well into the twentieth century, and machinery for planting, cultivating, and harvesting the crop were very slow to develop. Even after being freed, black people living in the South in the late nineteenth century remained trapped in a cotton-dominated sharecropping status that kept them just as impoverished as they had been before the Civil War.

Others have taken the position that the whole system was inherently unprofitable and, therefore, it was bound to collapse for purely economic reasons. They cite as evidence fluctuations in the price of cotton prior to the Civil War. As a rule, a New York market price of ten cents a pound was considered essential to offset the costs of production. The average price hovered around that figure through most of the 1820s and rose slightly in the next decade, but the 1840s were particularly hard on cotton growers. In all but two years, the average price remained below the critical ten-cent level, and it dropped below six cents in 1845. Prices recovered in the 1850s with the decade average standing at 11.3 cents a pound.

A related economic consideration was the cost of the slaves themselves. By 1860, southern whites had around $2 billion invested in slave property. This was capital that could not be redirected to other purposes, and it left the South with limited resources to pay for industrialization or improved transportation. Indeed, the trend was going in the opposite direction. The market price for a prime field hand rose markedly in the 1850s, from under $1,000 to almost $1,800. Clearly, southern whites remained eager to invest in human capital in pursuit of a greater share in the apparently unending cotton bonanza.

The benefits of that bonanza spread well beyond the farmers and planters of Cotton Kingdom. Factors located throughout the South earned solid incomes buying and exporting the raw product. New York became the leading cotton market in the United States, handling sales and transshipments both for the New England and European markets. Northern shipowners made good money in the carrying trade since so much of the crop was exported. When the southern states seceded, New Yorkers involved in the cotton trade were outraged, and a good deal of dissent against the Union war effort centered in their city when the Civil War cut off access to southern supplies of cotton.

Even if an exhaustive economic cost analysis had conclusively demonstrated the inefficiencies of cotton cultivation, it probably would have had little effect. The cotton culture had become too ingrained and interwoven into southern life in general. It had strengthened a slave labor system that had long traditional roots; it was not likely to fade away on its own. Indeed, even after the painful process of Civil War and Reconstruction, cotton remained king throughout much of the South, and it continues to be one of the region's chief cash crops even today.

See also Cotton Factorage; Cotton Gin; Plantation.

References and Further Reading

Franklin, John Hope. *From Slavery to Freedom.* New York: Knopf, 1947.

Munro, John M. *Cotton.* Harlow, UK: Longman Scientific and Technical, 1987.

Stampp, Kenneth M. *The Peculiar Institution.* New York: Knopf, 1956.

Volo, James M., and Dorothy Denneen Volo. *The Antebellum Period.* Westport, CT: Greenwood, 2004.

Watkins, James Lawrence. *King Cotton.* New York: Negro Universities Press, 1969.

Woodman, Harold D. *Slavery and the Southern Economy.* New York: Harcourt Brace and World, 1966.

Wright, Gavin. *The Political Economy of the Cotton South.* New York: Norton, 1978.

Cotton Factorage

Agents called *factors* handled many of the business details associated with the shipping and sale of cotton in the pre-Civil War South. Most factors operated out of ports along the Atlantic and Gulf coasts, but they maintained close and durable relationships with inland planters. The factorage system thrived due to the lack of urbanization in the region and because most cotton was shipped north or overseas. Factors provided essential commercial linkages between remote rural areas and the outside world.

While many of the colonial factors who had handled tobacco and other products represented particular English shippers or merchant houses, nineteenth-century cotton factors tended to be homegrown and self-employed. Planters who lived in coastal areas might get into the business by combining their own produce with that of less-advantageously located growers. In other instances, a local factor became successful by establishing strong links with New York or London merchants and mill owners. With cotton production booming and a seemingly insatiable demand for the product, the opportunities for factors continued to develop.

Cotton's natural advantages encouraged the factorage system. Ginned on individual plantations, it could be stored in the bale for relatively long periods without major deterioration. Moreover, cotton grown on a single plantation might include a number of varieties and qualities. Factors could exploit these differences to bargain for better prices. Factors who accumulated large inventories of cotton could sell or hold depending on market conditions. The larger the operator, the more an individual factor could influence prices and supplies.

Busy planters willingly forged long-term relations with trusted factors whose prosperity and profitability depended on reliable supplies. Cotton was rafted in bulk quantities down interior streams and rivers to coastal outlets where factors took control of the product. They might dispose of it locally or arrange shipping to northeastern or British ports and market the cotton there. At either location, factors might use the services of a cotton broker, a businessman who specialized in facilitating buying and selling.

Factors provided many services to their clients beyond simply buying their cotton.

Planters in remote areas depended on factors to be their purchasing agents as well. In any given year a factor might be called on to furnish supplies, furniture, housewares, and building materials to a back country plantation. Factors also extended credit to their clients, providing them with the capital they needed to plant and produce their crops. To an extent, then, many factors functioned as commission agents, providing a wealth of goods and services in return for the right to buy and market cotton.

While some of the factors' profits came directly from buying low and selling high, they also benefited from commissions and fees. As had been the case during the colonial period, the standard commission for selling an agricultural commodity was 2.5 percent of the gross price, which seldom varied throughout the antebellum period. Factors also charged interest on cash or commodity loans. An interest rate of 8 percent per year was common, but it could rise much higher in times of economic boom or monetary shortage. Finally, factors might charge a commission or fee for supplies provided even when the planter could pay cash.

Cotton growers and textile mills were the vital starting and end points to the thriving cotton industry. Factors provided the essential link between remote or isolated plantations and the distant mills in New England or Great Britain. Factors became correspondingly less important after the Civil War when much of the American textile industry moved south with the erection of mills close to the source of supply. By 1900 more sophisticated financial and marketing apparatuses and more accessible transportation facilities had all but eliminated the need for the nineteenth century cotton factorage system.

See also Cotton; Factor.

References and Further Reading

Jones, Fred Mitchell. *Middlemen in the Domestic Trade of the United States.* Urbana, IL: University of Illinois Press, 1937.

Shore, Laurence. *Southern Capitalists.* Chapel Hill, NC: University of North Carolina Press, 1986.

Woodman, Harold D. *King Cotton and His Retainers.* Lexington, KY: University of Kentucky Press, 1968.

Wright, Gavin. *The Political Economy of the Cotton South.* New York: Norton, 1978.

Cotton Gin

In 1792 Eli Whitney fashioned a crude machine that mechanically separated cotton fibers from seed. Almost immediately planters all over the southeast adopted versions of Whitney's cotton gin, and their usage stimulated intensive cotton cultivation prior to the Civil War.

Although it was a simple technological advance, the introduction of the cotton gin had a profound social and economic impact. The worldwide demand for tobacco had never kept up with the productive capabilities of the Old Southeast's plantation economy, and that region's economy was faltering after the American Revolution. Some planters were experimenting with cotton, but only long-staple or *sea island* cotton was truly cost efficient and it fared poorly on the mainland.

Short-staple or *green seed* cotton, however, flourished in the Tidewater, the Piedmont, and the bottomlands of the Deep South. Where sea island cotton had small seeds and long, luxurious fibers, the green seed variety had large sticky seeds and relatively shorter fibers. Pulling the fibers off the seeds by hand was time and labor intensive and extraordinarily debilitating.

After graduating from Yale in 1792, Eli Whitney boarded a ship, planning to take a position as a tutor in South Carolina. On board, he met Catherine Greene, a plantation owner and widow of General Nathaniel Greene. When the tutoring job failed to meet Whitney's expectations, he accepted an invitation to stay temporarily at Mrs. Greene's Georgia plantation. There he observed the frustration and tedium associated with cleaning short-staple cotton.

As a youth, Whitney had tinkered with all sorts of mechanical devices, and, working with crude tools, he assembled a very simple device for ginning cotton. It consisted of a rotating drum with bent nails that caught the cotton fibers as they passed. A comb lined up with the nails then swept the fibers off the spikes, leaving the cleaned seeds in a hopper. Whitney's design was simple and easy to construct, far better than the many other experimental methods others had attempted.

To exploit his invention, Whitney entered a partnership with the widow Greene's second husband, Phineas Miller. Using Miller's and his wife's financial resources, Whitney obtained a federal patent for his technology in 1794. The partners planned to establish ginning operations throughout the South and collect 20 percent of the cotton recovered as a fee for their services.

But if Whitney could construct a successful device in a matter of days with the tools available in a plantation workshop, so could many other people. Very quickly hundreds of cotton gins sprang up, many of them built and maintained on individual plantations. The Whitney-Miller partnership spent years and substantial amounts of money in a futile effort to control or at least reap some profit from the spread of the timely innovation.

The economic opportunity that cotton cultivation presented to the American South was far too compelling for any individual or partnership to constrain. Overnight the cotton gin had eliminated the production bottleneck, freeing farmers and slaves for other essential work. At the same time, it breathed new life into the deteriorating slave system, and some historians consider the cotton gin ultimately responsible for the persistence of slavery into the nineteenth century.

See also Cotton; Cotton Factorage.

References and Further Reading

Green, Constance McLaughlin. *Eli Whitney and the Birth of American Technology.* Boston: Little, Brown, 1956.

Huff, Regan A. *Eli Whitney.* New York: PowerPlus Books, 2004.

Lakwete, Angela. *Inventing the Cotton Gin.* Baltimore, MD: Johns Hopkins University Press, 2003.

Lewton, Frederick L. *Historical Notes on the Cotton Gin.* Washington: U.S. Government Printing Office, 1938.

Meltzer, Milton. *The Cotton Gin.* New York: Benchmark Books, 2004.

Dealership

Cyrus McCormick created the first major nationwide dealership system when he began to market his mass-produced patented reaper prior to the Civil War. Because it was a complex mechanical device subject to frequent breakdowns, McCormick contracted with local mechanics to provide service, parts, repairs, and even financing for customers. Many other manufacturers and distributors followed this example in establishing local dealers for their products. Tinkerers all over the United States developed their own devices or modified those of other inventors to speed the process of harvesting field crops. Planting and cultivating wheat could be spread out over weeks or even months, but when the crop ripened, it had to be harvested within a span of a few days. A man with a scythe could, at best, barely reap an acre or so working sunup to sundown; thus a ready market existed for a mechanical reaper that could harvest whole fields in a single day.

Robert McCormick was a tinkerer who built a mechanical reaper to use on his farm in western Virginia. His son, Cyrus vastly improved on his father's design and constructed his own prototype in 1831. He patented the device three years later but then pursued other interests until the early 1840s. Operating out of his Virginia home Cyrus McCormick began building and selling reapers to local customers. In 1847 he acknowledged that the market for his product had migrated west by building a huge, modern factory in Illinois that used the latest mass-production techniques and interchangeable parts. He sold 1,500 machines in 1850 and his output increased steadily throughout the decade. It expanded even more rapidly during the Civil War when farm laborers by the thousands joined the army.

To sell and service these complex machines, McCormick sought out local mechanics willing to handle his product. Within a few years the arrangement became much more formalized, with individuals in various locations signing on as franchised dealers. The franchise involved an agreement that the dealer would market, sell, and repair reapers as well as maintain an inventory of parts for those capable of handling repairs themselves.

In addition to these product services, the dealers extended credit to buyers unable to pay cash for what were, after all, quite expensive machines. In 1850 McCormick priced his basic model at $130, substantially more than most independent farmers earned in a year. The dealers, in turn, often relied on McCormick to provide them with credit, so he ended up serving as a lender of last resort. From time to time, customers who had purchased his machines on time owed him more than a million dollars.

The sales, service, parts, and financing aspects of the McCormick dealership network became models for other manufacturers. The precedent he established became especially important after the turn of the twentieth century when automobile manufacturers adopted similar dealership arrangements to market and service their products.

See also Interchangeable Parts; McCormick, Cyrus Hall.

References and Further Reading

Judson, Clara Ingram. *Reaper Man: The Story of Cyrus Hall McCormick.* Boston: Houghton Mifflin, 1948.

Lyons, Norbert. *The McCormick Reaper Legend.* New York: Exposition Press, 1955.

Division of Labor

To increase productivity, particularly in manufacturing, it is common to break the enterprise into a number of simpler steps. The division of labor follows this breakdown, with each worker being assigned a particular, usually repetitive task. The expectation is that workers will become increasingly efficient at their differentiated tasks, thus increasing the overall productivity of the labor force.

A division of labor developed naturally in many primitive societies, with some individuals becoming expert in particular activities and essentially selling their expertise to their family or community. The industrial revolution called for a much more self-conscious division of labor. It became a cornerstone of classical economics, brilliantly articulated in Adam Smith's *The Wealth of Nations.* Published in 1776, Smith's book analyzed all sorts of human enterprises and provided suggestions for maximizing individual productivity and national wealth.

Smith found many existing instances of a division of labor to illustrate his point. For example, he described the rather mundane production of pins, noting that even small groups found it profitable to break the production down into simpler, repetitive steps. One man might draw out the wire, another cut it to the right length, a third sharpen the point, and still others focus on attaching heads to the pins. None of these individuals needed any significant amount of training, and an important consequence of a division of labor was that unskilled laborers could replace skilled craftsmen and work in larger concerns.

Some increase in productivity arose from workers honing their skills on simple tasks, but Smith also noted that the division of labor encouraged the invention of specialized machines and tools to further enhance output. Unlike a modern, computerized assembly line with robotic machines and electronic process controls, early manufacturing tended to be human-labor intensive. Therefore, it paid entrepreneurs to encourage their workers to invent or use existing labor-saving devices in their work.

While *The Wealth of Nations* won international recognition as a seminal work, its true success came from the practicality of its conclusions. Even illiterate people could grasp the concepts like the division of labor that were universally adopted in the nineteenth century. When Eli Whitney developed jigs to fashion interchangeable musket parts, he was implementing concepts Smith had outlined a quarter century earlier. When Francis Cabot Lowell established his integrated textile mill at Waltham in 1815, he divided the work among carders, spinners, and weavers, all equipped with the latest state-of-the-art machinery that he had borrowed from England.

As long as the United States economy remained primarily agrarian, however, the system could only be so productive. Smith's book noted that the opportunities for an effective division of labor in farming were limited by seasonal changes, the complexity of many farm tasks, and the versatility labor had to exhibit to complete these tasks. Even so, a division of labor greatly enhanced productivity on large farming operations. Prosperous cotton growers in the South, for example, often developed very sophisticated and detailed sets of responsibilities for their slave labor forces. Certain slaves were assigned to serve as field hands, cooks, laundresses, herders, carpenters, masons, house servants, and dozens of other specialized jobs. And, like factory workers, they could become very productive with minimal training.

As the industrial revolution spread throughout the United States, the benefits of a division of labor became increasingly apparent. The larger the factory, the more likely it was to subdivide the work into smaller and simpler repetitive tasks. That allowed managers to hire unskilled, illiterate, and/or non-English speaking workers and incorporate them into their workforces. Wages could be kept low, and advancement within a given factory was often limited. Although automation did not become a widespread concept until much later, progressive manufacturers early recognized the advantages of replacing humans with machine power, further limiting the need for skilled or educated workers.

The division of labor reached a new level of sophistication when Henry Ford introduced his moving assembly line in 1913 to speed the production of Model T cars. *Scientific Management* or Taylorism came into vogue, with time-and-motion experts examining every facet of the manufacturing process to reduce wasted motion and increase worker productivity. The speed of the assembly process continually rose as an increasingly detailed division of labor took place.

The division of labor has become so commonplace that we scarcely notice it in today's world. Adam Smith's contribution, however, was more than simply to describe what was already occurring. By pointing out its advantages, he and his fellow classical economists popularized the concept of a division of labor and made manufacturers much more conscious of how it could be used to their advantage.

See also Integrated Mill; Interchangeable Parts; Moving Assembly Line; Scientific Management.

References and Further Reading

Muller, Jerry Z. *Adam Smith in His Time and Ours.* New York: Oxford University Press, 1995.

Smith, Adam. *An Inquiry into the Nature and Causes of the Wealth of Nations.* New York: Macmillan, 1985. First published 1776.

Smith, Roy C. *Adam Smith and the Origins of American Enterprise.* New York: St. Martin's Press, 2002.

Dollar, American

The Continental Congress selected the dollar to be the American medium of exchange, but

Alexander Hamilton was left to define it in the early 1790s. As the nation's treasury secretary, Hamilton not only stipulated the specie content of the dollar but he also set the specie ratio between gold and silver. With only minor variations, the values he established remained in force until the United States abandoned the gold standard in 1934.

To the extent that Americans in the Revolutionary Era were familiar with a dollar, it was a Spanish or Mexican coin containing about one ounce of silver. These coins circulated throughout North America during the colonial period at varying exchange rates compared to British sterling. In 1774, for example, Maryland printed paper dollar notes that listed an exchange rate of four shillings and a sixpence to the dollar. During the Revolutionary War, however, no one could be certain of the value of a paper dollar due to the massive oversupply of Continental bills issued to fund the American war effort.

During its first session under the Constitution, Congress created three executive departments: state, war, and treasury. President George Washington appointed Hamilton to serve as secretary of the treasury, and Congress assigned him the task of straightening out the nation's finances. His duties included setting the value of the dollar in relation to specie and authorizing the minting of coins.

Hamilton carefully considered the question before decreeing that a dollar should contain 24.75 grains of gold. That would mean that the value of an ounce of gold would stand at $19.39. And, because the British pound sterling was also pegged to specie, Hamilton's action simultaneously set an international exchange ratio of $4.44 for each pound sterling. Not incidentally, this valuation was almost identical to the one printed on Maryland's colonial paper bills. Moreover, this valuation of the dollar at approximately $20 for one ounce of gold remained the American standard well into the twentieth century.

Having assessed the domestic supplies of both gold and silver, Hamilton also set a fixed value of 371.25 grains of silver for one dollar. This created an official government exchange rate of 15 ounces of silver to 1 ounce of gold. This, too, remained relatively unchanged until it was adjusted to 16 to 1 in the 1830s when the nation's supply of silver increased relative to that of gold. This adjustment provided the basis for the Silverites who campaigned in the late nineteenth century, calling for "the free and unlimited coinage of silver at 16 to 1."

Hamilton also saw to it that a mint in Philadelphia was established to produce coins with the appropriate specie content. Congress initially ordered the minting of a ten-dollar gold piece, popularly known as an eagle because of the symbol embossed on its reverse side. Over time the mint also produced five-dollar half eagles and twenty-dollar double eagles as well as gold coins in smaller denominations. Because the government's official rate for an ounce of gold remained below the world market price, a great many U.S. gold coins were exported. The undervaluing of gold also meant that no eagles were produced between 1805 and 1837. By the latter date, the 16 to 1 adjustment made specie more likely to flow into rather than away from the U.S. Treasury.

The minor coins included silver dollars, half-dollars, quarters, dimes, nickels, and copper pennies. The number of such coins in circulation fluctuated widely over the next several decades. As with gold, the market value of silver itself fluctuated and the supply of specie varied due to internal economic business cycles and international trade relationships. During the Civil War, for example, silver and copper coins disappeared from circulation almost completely because the metal in them was much more valuable for other purposes. The federal government partially met this shortage of minor coins by issuing paper bills (shinplasters) and ungummed postage stamps in various denominations.

After the war, controversy over the money supply included calls for such diverse strategies as devaluing the dollar, printing greenbacks, and coining more silver, which was now in abundant supply. The election of a staunch fiscal conservative, William McKinley, as president and a Republican-controlled Congress in 1896 effectively scotched these more radical schemes. In 1900 Congress approved and McKinley signed a Gold Standard Act that reconfirmed the connection of the dollar to gold at the traditional ratio of $20 for 1 ounce of gold. It remained that way until 1934 when the Depression crisis forced President Franklin Roosevelt to abandon the gold standard and institute an abrupt devaluation that changed the ratio to $35 per ounce of gold. President Richard Nixon took the final step in the 1970s when he floated the dollar. Gold prices quickly rose to hundreds of dollars an ounce where they have remained ever since.

Silver dollars began to disappear about the same time. Silver certificates remained in circulation as small denomination bills as late as the 1960s, but Federal Reserve Notes eventually took their place. People who still had silver certificates were allowed to redeem them for silver, however. If one so desired, he could present a $1 bill and receive in exchange an envelop containing 0.77 ounces of silver powder—the same 371.25 grains of silver that Hamilton had stipulated for a dollar more than a century and a half earlier.

See also Commodity Dollar; Dollar, American; Free Silver; Greenbacks; Hamilton, Alexander.

References and Further Reading

Dewey, Davis Rich. *Financial History of the United States.* New York: Longmans, Green, 1936.

Moore, Carl H., and Alvin E. Russell. *Money: Its Origin, Development and Modern Use.* Jefferson, NC: McFarland, 1987.

Myers, Margaret G. *A Financial History of the United States.* New York: Columbia University Press, 1970.

Embargo

An embargo is a government policy that prohibits trade. An embargo can be imposed against a particular foreign country as was the case with Iraq in the 1990s. Or an embargo can also involve a general prohibition of commercial trade with all nations like the American Embargo of 1807. In all cases, an embargo is an instrument of economic coercion, designed to force other countries to make either trade or diplomatic concessions.

The United States developed an interest in international trade regulation because of its economy's continuing dependent situation. Under Great Britain's prevailing mercantilist policy, its colonies were seen primarily as suppliers to and markets for English goods. The Revolutionary War temporarily interrupted that American dependency. For many years afterward, however, the new nation's economy remained colonial in nature, exchanging raw agricultural produce for processed or manufactured goods from more industrially advanced European economies.

When England and France became mired in a long-term conflict, the United States found itself increasingly affected by the rivalry between its two major trading partners. Neither of the European combatants wanted the other to benefit from American trade, so both of them announced policies designed to limit U.S. commercial freedom.

President George Washington tried to clarify the American position by issuing his Proclamation of Neutrality in 1793. Within a matter of months both England and France had issued their own decrees that would force Americans to support one or the other. Instead, Congress chose to impose an embargo on all shipping out of American harbors. It was extended briefly but then abandoned in favor of John Jay's diplomatic mission to Great Britain. Jay's Treaty was ultimately ratified by the U.S. Senate, but it solved little and stimulated emotional partisan criticism.

The Anglo-French conflict persisted for another twenty years, and the United States continued to find itself boxed in by the demands of one side or the other. In 1806 and 1807, Napoleon's government issued imperial decrees and the British government issued orders-in-council that forbade trade with the enemy. Thus any American ship trading with either England or France was subject to seizure by the navy of the other country. At that point the continuing warfare had driven world prices up so high that even if only one American ship in three reached its European destination, profits on that single voyage offset the costs of the lost vessels.

British impressments of American seamen added pressure on President Thomas Jefferson's administration to take action on these maritime problems. At his urging, Congress approved a full-scale embargo in December 1807. Jefferson believed that American trade, both imports and exports, was so crucial to the European economies that cutting it off would force one or the other antagonist to withdraw its edicts.

Instead, the embargo's primary damage came at home. Ships lay idle in American ports; goods rotted on the wharves. At this point many who had made their livelihoods in shipping redirected their resources to manufacturing, laying the seeds for what would become a major industrial revolution in the New England and mid-Atlantic states. A lively cross-border land trade with Canada flourished. Some ships slipped out illegally; other American vessels simply failed to return to their home ports so they would remain outside of the embargo's reach. An economic depression settled in, affecting not only northeastern shippers but also southern and western farmers who were denied access to overseas markets for their surplus produce.

The embargo also had dramatic political consequences, breathing life into the nearly moribund Federalist Party and undermining the influence and reputation of Jefferson's Democratic-Republicans. But the trade cutoff apparently had no effect on European determination. Unable to ignore its negative consequences in the United States, Jefferson urged Congress to terminate the embargo just days before he surrendered the presidency to James Madison.

Because he had been secretary of state in the previous administration, President Madison was well aware of the diplomatic issues involved. He urged Congress to take an alternative approach in the Non-Intercourse Act of 1809. This legislation forbade the United States from trading directly with England and France but reopened American commerce with all other nations. Still neither of the major powers was willing to alter its policies—in part because both could now obtain some essential American goods indirectly.

The final, foolish piece of this increasingly desperate American policy was to replace the 1809 legislation with Macon's Bill Number 2 early in 1810. It opened trade with all nations, but promised to impose a unilateral embargo on England if France revoked its hated decrees. France would be targeted if England cancelled its orders-in-council. France took advantage of the opportunity by claiming to have altered its policy even though its navy continued seizing American vessels. A frustrated Madison nevertheless imposed nonimportation on England, setting the stage for a declaration of war in June 1812.

Ironically, at almost the same moment, Jefferson's goal of using economic coercion to force a change in Britain's policies bore fruit. British merchants, traders, and, most important, manufacturers who depended on American raw materials like cotton had long suffered from the effects of the 1807 embargo and its successors. The royal government responded to their pleas for relief by revoking its orders-in-council. It was too late. News arrived shortly on a transatlantic ship that the U.S. Congress had declared war.

The American experience during the Napoleonic Wars is hardly unique. Historically there have been few instances where an embargo has worked effectively. Inevitably, the country imposing the embargo suffers negative economic consequences, sometimes even more devastating than those inflicted on its enemies. Nevertheless, the declaration of an embargo continues to be a policy that is considered in times of stress.

See also Carrying Trade; Nonimportation; Privateering; Protective Tariff.

References and Further Reading

McDonald, Forrest. *The Presidency of Thomas Jefferson.* Lawrence, KS: University Press of Kansas, 1976.

Perkins, Bradford. *Prologue to War: England and the United States, 1805–1812.* Berkeley, CA: University of California Press, 1961.

Spivak, Burton. *Jefferson's English Crisis.* Charlottesville, VA: University of Virginia Press, 1974.

Free Banking

On the heels of the Panic of 1837, several states approved free banking legislation. These new laws permitted individuals or groups of individuals to establish a bank without obtaining a state charter. Instead, they simply had to meet certain prescribed financial conditions. Free banking quickly became popular in many states, providing competition for chartered banking institutions until the 1860s when the federally chartered National Banks became predominant.

With few exceptions, early banks in the United States operated under some form of federal or state charter. Obtaining a state charter involved extensive and often expensive lobbying, and the charter itself imposed restrictions and conditions on the successful applicants. Criticism of both charter restrictions and government regulation of banking in general blossomed during President Andrew Jackson's assault on the Second Bank of the United States. By 1837 many Americans were convinced that a more liberal, unregulated system was preferable.

The State of Michigan passed the nation's first free banking legislation in that year, and it was a colossal failure. The forty banks that took advantage of it all fell into receivership within a year, and new legislation in 1839 ended the state's free banking experiment for nearly twenty years. Fortunately, the experience of other states was more favorable.

One of the major reasons that state legislators favored the free banking initiative was that the law insisted that those who intended to establish a bank must buy and retain state bonds as major elements in their capitalization. Whereas state governments had profited from chartering fees in the earlier years, they now viewed the free banking system as an excellent way to boost and maintain the value of their state debt notices.

In those states that approved free banking legislation, anyone could set up a bank provided minimum capital requirements were met. The resulting institutions could issue banknotes just like those of chartered banks, with similar expectations regarding redemption and limitations on the number of notes issued. These provisions were so attractive that by 1860 over 1,100 free banks were operating in the United States, constituting about 40 percent of the total number of financial institutions.

In addition to the predictable human factors such as greed and skullduggery that could undermine a particular institution's soundness, the free banks had an additional burden. In states where the government ran on a sound basis, state bond backing proved to be a solid foundation for success. But the creditworthiness of other states could collapse due to mismanagement or broader economic problems, undermining the value of a free bank's capital holdings. The State of Indiana defaulted on its bonds in 1841, for example, an event that inevitably caused the collapse of many of the free banks in its jurisdiction.

Once the Civil War began, the free banking system provided a model for the Union government to follow as it attempted to float loans to pay for war expenditures. The

National Banking Act provided federal charters to banks that agreed to purchase substantial blocs of federal bonds to serve as part of their capitalization. When the owners of state chartered and free banks proved slow to take up these charters, Congress imposed a 10 percent levy on all notes issued by nonnational banks. This encouraged a substantial increase in the number of national banks after the Civil War, and a corresponding decline in the number of state chartered and free banks.

See also Bank War; Charter, State; National Bank Notes.

References and Further Reading

Dowd, Kevin. "Money and Banking: The American Experience," in *Money and Banking: The American Experience.* Fairfax, VA: George Mason University Press, 1995.

Klebaner, Benjamin J. *American Commercial Banking: A History.* Boston: Twayne Publisher, 1990.

Gold Rush

The California gold rush began with the discovery of traces of gold in a stream bed in Coloma early in 1848. Before the year was out 10,000 people had abandoned their normal pursuits to become miners. That number jumped tenfold in the next year as "Forty-Niners" poured in from the United States and countries around the world. California miners extracted more than a billion dollar's worth of gold in the next couple of decades, adding significantly to the world's supply of bullion and laying the basis for the development of a rich and diversified economy on the Pacific Coast.

As a remote northern province of Mexico, California had received relatively little attention from the Mexican central government until war broke out with the United States in 1846. U.S. President James K. Polk authorized the dispatch of both army and navy units to the province. American forces quickly occupied key points in both California and the intervening New Mexico Territory. As part of the Treaty of Guadalupe Hidalgo that ended the war in 1848, Mexico ceded both California and New Mexico to the United States in return for $20 million. From a strictly financial perspective, that turned out to be a tremendous bargain for the Americans.

Even before the treaty won ratification, James Marshall stumbled across traces of gold in a ditch he was digging along the American River. It was part of a project to provide water power for a lumber mill on the property of a Swiss immigrant, John Sutter. The news of the discovery at Sutter's Fort quickly leaked out, attracting local treasure hunters from as far away as San Francisco. Additional finds along the nearby Feather River and elsewhere extended the range of potential claims. In the first year, the average take for a miner working the rich river and stream beds was around one pound of gold a day.

Thousands of people streamed in from around the world, rapidly expanding the number of working claims. The simplest approach was to use a pan to scoop sand and gravel up from a waterway and find the gold nuggets or dust that settled to the bottom. Pick and shovel work unearthed other deposits. More ambitious operators built wooden sluices down which they directed streams of mineral-laden water. Here again, the heavier gold grains settled out and accumulated along the bottom of the sluice. Regardless of the specific method used, all involved relatively simple tools or structures that easily allowed anyone to get into the business. The gold rush thus involved thousands of independent operators who did not need much capital to exploit the resources.

One immediate economic effect was dramatic price inflation. The huge influx of people required food, clothing, and other goods that were in relatively short supply. Moreover there was little coordination of supplies shipped to California. More than 500 ships called at San Francisco in 1849, unloading whatever someone 3,000 miles

Nathan Currier (of Currier and Ives fame) drew this editorial cartoon in 1849 to illustrate how eager Americans were to reach California in search of gold. (Library of Congress)

away thought might find a market. By the mid-1850s, however, the average miner's take had dropped to around 1 ounce a day from working poorer claims, and prices fell to more reasonable levels.

In the early days, stories spread of crowded mining camps, claim jumping, and general rowdiness, suggesting that the rush had attracted only the dregs of society. But passage from the East to the West Coast by sea cost nearly an average worker's annual pay, and the overland trek could require a similar outlay. Many of those attracted by the prospect of instant wealth were middle class, respectable, hardworking people intent on seizing a chance to improve themselves. Thousands of men left wives and families back east as they pursued their dreams, but thousands of other families accompanied gold seekers heading west.

Those who went by sea had the choice of two major routes. The most popular, most expensive, and slowest was a cruise all the way around the tip of South America. This involved spending several months at sea but it avoided the complications of the alternative. Some entrepreneurs had already been sending ships down to both sides of the Isthmus of Panama, and this route gained popularity with gold seekers. It only took half as long to sail from New York to Central America, hike across the isthmus, and then board another ship for San Francisco. Cornelius Vanderbilt constructed a railroad across the isthmus to ease what had been a disease-ridden and difficult passage. Tens of thousands of others plodded along the overland route of the Santa Fe Trail or an alternative route that traversed Nebraska, Colorado, Utah, and Nevada.

California's huge influx of population had important political consequences. The 1787 Northwest Ordinance stipulated that a territory with 60,000 inhabitants could apply for statehood. As early as 1850 California's population had risen to nearly double that minimum, encouraging the area to seek statehood. The North-South sectional controversy threatened to derail this move until Henry Clay and others cobbled together the Compromise of 1850. San Francisco had been a sleepy town with fewer than 1,000 inhabitants in 1848, but it quickly grew into the major West Coast port, hosting the 40,000 people who arrived in the next year. Many of these never went to the gold country, content to settle in the city and provide much needed services and support for the men toiling in the hills.

The impact of the gold rush extended well beyond those directly involved. Between 1850 and 1865, California annually produced an average of $50 million in gold. This contributed significantly to the whole world's stock of bullion, affecting price levels and stimulating growth not only in the United States but in Europe and beyond. California continued to produce gold throughout the rest of the nineteenth century, although by the close of the Civil War, mining no longer ranked as its most important occupation.

Other major finds set off rushes of their own including the discovery of the Comstock Lode in Nevada and subsequent deposits in Colorado and Montana. In the 1890s thousands of hardy adventurers responded to the lure of gold in Alaska and Canada's adjacent Northwest Territories. None of these matched the long-term impact of the 1849 rush, however. In addition to producing thousands of individual fortunes, it created the basis for a permanent, well-settled, and highly productive population in what had previously been a remote backwater.

See also Dollar; Dollar, American; Gold Corner; Specie Circular; Strauss, Levi.

References and Further Reading

Caughey, John Walton. *California.* New York: Prentice Hall, 1946.

Roberts, Brian. *American Alchemy.* Chapel Hill, NC: University of North Carolina Press, 2000.

Industrial Revolution

Shortly after completing its political revolution, the United States began to experience an industrial revolution. This phenomenon did not occur all at once, nor was it uniformly experienced in all regions of the country. The chief characteristic of the revolution—the replacement or enhancement of worker productivity with nonhuman power and machinery—was most evident in northeastern cities. The development of inexpensive transportation systems beginning in the 1820s helped spread centers of production and distribute manufactured products themselves to a much broader market. By the late 1840s, the benefits and consequences of increasing industrialization affected virtually all Americans.

The economic changes that occurred were first characterized as revolutionary as a complement and a contrast to the political revolution that occurred in France in the 1790s. The industrial revolution was slower paced and certainly a much less chaotic event than its political model. Many people whose lives encompassed these economic changes remained largely unaware of its broader impact. The changes in the worldly goods they used came slowly enough to justify calling it an evolution rather than a revolution.

An increase in the productivity of individual workers is a key characteristic of an industrial revolution. One way to improve productivity is to assemble a workforce in a factory setting, use a division of labor, simplify the workers' tasks, and equip them with labor-saving machines. Efficiencies of mass production will promote productivity for the workforce as a whole. The theories expressed in Adam Smith's *The Wealth of Nations* provided a sort of blueprint for this approach.

Treasury Secretary Alexander Hamilton was eager to sponsor mass-production. In 1791 he sent a *Report on Manufactures* to Congress urging the government to promote such a change by imposing high protective tariffs, encouraging manufacturers with government bounties, and facilitating the creation of investment capital. He was also a leading supporter of the Society for Useful Manufactures, a group dedicated to copying the success of England's industrialization. But Hamilton and his colleagues were too far in advance of events. Neither the nation nor its people were ready to abandon farming and shipping as their major money-making enterprises.

Some theorists maintain that a surplus of labor is essential for industrialization. No such surplus existed among the hardworking western farmers or in the South where slaves as well as freemen had more than enough to do growing and harvesting field crops. Only in the Northeast did circumstances conspire to produce a labor surplus. When the War of 1812 shuttered the shipping industry, it threw sailors and longshoremen out of work. At the same time, depleted soil and low prices in rural New England were forcing thousands of people off their farms. A growing number of people were seeking alternative employment.

The war also idled shipowners and merchants, forcing them to turn to other enterprises. Replicating the success of the English textile industry offered these people a profitable investment opportunity and a way to supply the continuing domestic demand for cotton cloth that could not be imported because of the war. Francis Cabot Lowell and his Boston Associates took the lead in creating a state-of-the-art integrated textile mill at Waltham, Massachusetts. Dozens of other groups copied it as a model for their own factories. They all faced hard times after peace returned in 1815 when British merchants dumped their stockpiled textiles on the American market at prices even below their already low manufacturing costs. But the wartime experience proved valuable as future investors sought other industrial investment opportunities.

Easy access to natural resources was another advantage for the United States in its industrial revolution. The New England area in particular was laced with streams capable of producing power, and factories sprang up wherever a millrace could be established. Waterpower would remain the predominant energy source in the United States into the 1870s, and it helped reinforce New England's leading position in industrialization.

Philadelphia also thrived as a major industrial center due to its proximity to natural resources. As early as 1820, two-thirds of its workers were engaged in either manufacturing or trade. Nearby coal deposits encouraged the construction of steam-powered factories. The Pennsylvania iron industry had received a boost in the 1780s from the development of reliable smelting methods for ridding ore of carbon and other impurities. Using iron and steel, Americans became particularly adept at inventing and innovating machine tools to adapt to factory settings.

Equally important in stimulating industrialism is access to a broad market. The completion of the Erie Canal in 1825 set off a craze of canal building that ultimately exploited all reasonable and many unreasonable canal routes. Steam locomotives appeared in the 1830s, and rails began to link towns and villages in the hinterland with industrializing cities. The ever-expanding market in the United States called for larger factories, more detailed divisions of labor, and, ultimately, lower costs and higher profits.

Prosperity remained unpredictable. Major financial panics in 1819 and 1837 plunged the United States into long depressions. Less efficient factories closed, workers lost their jobs, and investment capital became scarce. With each recovery, however, the nation advanced further along the industrializing path. By 1840 northeastern cities had assumed a truly industrial character, complete with urban woes like air and water pollution, clogged streets, and overcrowded housing. But industrial workers' productivity continued to rise at a remarkable 2 percent a year on average, ensuring that the industrial revolution would continue to progress.

Despite these urban developments, it is important to remember that during the period from 1790 to 1840, the vast majority of Americans continued to live and work in farm rather than factory settings. Interestingly enough, the productivity of the rural workforce generally rose throughout this period at rates only slightly lower than those of industrial workers.

A good deal of that rise in agricultural productivity was essentially home-grown. Hardworking farmers and their families were always ready to adopt new techniques that would reduce their own labor efforts and increase their output. As the farms in a particular area evolved from subsistence farms into mature, commercial operations, economies of scale and specialization in crops enhanced the agricultural profits.

Industrialization played a key role in this rural development due to the increasing use of tools and goods manufactured elsewhere. Cheaper transportation made it far easier for farmers to obtain and benefit from factory-made products. Textiles are an excellent example. If a farm wife spent all of her spare time carding and spinning thread, after a year she might have produced enough to weave a single change of clothes for her family. The burgeoning cotton and wool textile mills on the East Coast and overseas could produce better quality cloth at affordable costs, freeing the farmstead from this exhausting and relatively unproductive labor.

In this and countless other ways, the industrial revolution expanded and influenced all Americans. The direct benefits were most evident in the Northeast and less so in the West. Even in the traditional agrarian regions of the South, industrialization altered lives and lifestyles. After all, the industrialized textile industry both in the United States and in Great Britain created the demand for an ever-increasing supply of the world's most important industrial raw material—cotton.

And the industrialization process had only begun. Exciting changes were set to take place in the 1840s and 1850s when railroads became the nation's leading industrial sector. For the next sixty years, railroads absorbed more capital, more iron, and more importance than any other industrial development. But to do so, they had to rely on the experience of earlier enterprises as well as the coal, iron, and machine resources that had bloomed during the first half century of the U.S. industrial revolution.

See also Division of Labor; Integrated Mill; Lowell, Francis Cabot.

References and Further Reading

Bruchey, Stuart. *Enterprise.* Cambridge, MA: Harvard University Press, 1990.

Meyer, David T. *The Roots of American Industrialization.* Baltimore, MD: Johns Hopkins University Press, 2003.

Integrated Mill

An integrated mill is one in which several manufacturing and processing steps take place under one roof. The result can be a very efficient self-contained factory that takes in raw materials and produces finished marketable goods.

While many present-day factories fit this pattern, none existed anywhere in the world in 1800. Raw-material processing and manufacturing activities took place independently, often in quite diverse locations. Textile milling in the British Isles triggered the world's first industrial revolution in the mid-eighteenth century. It stemmed from inventions and innovations in carding and spinning machinery. The spinning jenny patented by James Hargreaves in 1770 was a key innovation, using waterpower to spin woolen and later cotton fibers onto multiple spindles. Spinning mills sprang up wherever fast-moving waterways could be found to turn waterwheels.

For some time, weaving the spun yarn and thread into cloth remained a cottage industry, with individual weavers or families of weavers working in their own homes. In 1785 Edmund Cartwright successfully constructed a loom that applied external power to the weaving process. This development encouraged the consolidation of weaving into a mass-production effort just as spinning had become.

Integrating the distinct steps of the textile-making process was the brilliant concept of a wealthy New England merchant. Profits from the shipping trade had created Francis Cabot Lowell's fortune, but the Embargo of 1807 all but destroyed the New England shipping business. Seeking an alternative business opportunity, Lowell took an extended trip in 1810 to Great Britain, where he observed the disaggregated elements that constituted the world's premier textile industry. He returned home committed to constructing a single facility that would combine carding, spinning, and weaving under one roof.

Such an ambitious undertaking required considerable capital, more than Lowell personally had to invest. His first step, then, was to obtain a charter from the State of Massachusetts for the Boston Associates. This organization issued 100 shares of stock in 1813, and Lowell and his friends purchased them for $400 per share. Lowell thus gained control of what was for the time an enormous amount of capital.

In Waltham, Massachusetts, the Associates purchased an operating paper mill that they converted to textiles. One building served as a workshop where mechanics and craftsmen built improved versions of textile machinery. In an adjacent structure they installed water-powered spinning jennies and weaving frames as well as other equipment essential for self-contained textile production. The factory opened in 1815, just as the War of 1812 ended and British merchants began dumping huge surpluses of textiles in American seaports at bargain prices. Even so the efficiencies of scale in Lowell's integrated mill enabled him and his associates to market finished cloth at very low, competitive prices.

The Waltham mill's machinery was so sophisticated and efficient that people with no prior mechanical training or skills could operate it. New England was overpopulated with farm families unable to make ends meet on the unforgiving stony and forested hills. Lowell and his associates therefore had their pick of potential employees. The majority of their workforce consisted of unmarried women in their late teens or early twenties. These factory workers came to Waltham and lived in dormitories near the mill. The company provided the equivalent of housemothers and tutors for their workers, ensuring safe living conditions, educational opportunities, and, most important, wages that could be saved for use as doweries.

The so-called *Waltham System* attracted visitors from nearby communities and states as well as foreigners interested in learning about the efficiencies of the new factory system. Similar integrated textile mills were quickly erected, stimulating a regional industrial revolution in New England as well as a growing domestic market for raw cotton from the southern states. Although the textile industry suffered hard times off and on over the next century, mill owners who emulated Francis Cabot Lowell's model were better able to survive economic downturns with less damage. And the straightforward concept of a factory dedicated to producing a single product or related products from scratch became a standard for the United States and the world in subsequent years.

See also Division of Labor; Industrial Revolution; Lowell, Francis Cabot.

References and Further Reading

Dalzell, Robert F. *The Boston Associates and the World They Made.* Cambridge, MA: Harvard University Press, 1987.

Jeremy, David J. *Transatlantic Industrial Revolution.* Cambridge, MA: MIT Press, 1981.

Selden, Bernice. *The Mill Girls.* New York: Atheneum, 1983.

Interchangeable Parts

Most modern factories use mass production systems, churning out thousands of interchangeable parts that are assembled into finished products. This system, sometimes referred to as the American system of manufacturing gradually took hold in the United States before the Civil War. Inventor Eli Whitney played a vital role in popularizing the concept, though many others helped perfect the technique.

In the eighteenth century, manufacturing was just what the word originally meant: fabrication or *facturing* by hand from the Latin root *manus*. Craftsmen handmade the machines, tools, and implements that were used, improved, or invented. A few early attempts at more standardized production were made, but they had little long-term effects. For example, the American minister to France, Thomas Jefferson, observed a gentleman named Le Blanc demonstrate the assembly of carefully made interchangeable parts into musket firing mechanisms in Paris in 1785.

Ironically, the outbreak of the so-called *Quasi War* with France in 1798 encouraged American experimentation with this concept. The United States government was ill-prepared for war, short on ships for the navy and muskets for the army. Eli Whitney had become famous for developing a successful cotton gin earlier in the decade, so he received a positive response from the federal government when he proposed to manufacture 10,000 muskets in two years.

Like many other government contractors, Whitney failed to fulfill his promise. He delivered only 500 muskets in the first year because he had spent most of his time building machinery to build gun components. He used patterns or *jigs* to guide water-powered machine tools in the cutting and shaping of both wooden and metal parts.

Impatient government authorities inquired after the muskets in 1801 (the same year, incidentally, that the United States and France signed a peace treaty). Whitney brought the parts for ten muskets to Washington, D.C., for a demonstration. The panel that included both President John Adams and Vice President Thomas Jefferson saw him select parts at random and quickly assemble them into a completed weapon. But, like other contractor demonstrations, this one was rigged. The parts he brought had been machined at his plant in Connecticut, but he made sure that they were hand polished and finished sufficiently to be truly interchangeable. Not until 1809 did he complete delivery of the 10,000 muskets—just in time for them to be used against the British in the War of 1812.

An avid self-promoter, Eli Whitney took credit for this new manufacturing process, but several other individuals did as much or more than he did to actually make it work. Muskets were sufficiently complex and remained constantly in demand, so most of the early successes came in gun-manufacturing plants. Simeon North began manufacturing weapons for the government in 1799, and he was far more effective in achieving the results Whitney desired. Rather than rely solely on private entrepreneurs, the government had also established arsenals at Springfield, Massachusetts, and at Harper's Ferry in what was then part of the state of Virginia. It was at the Harper's Ferry arsenal in 1826 that John H. Hall finally achieved the level of efficiency and precision that qualified as the first successful implementation of the interchangeable parts process.

Although the method was slow to catch on overseas, the use of jigs to produce interchangeable parts spread to the manufacture of other products in the United States. Eli and Seth Thomas used it in their wooden clock factory as early as 1815. It was a logical step to extend the technique to the manufacture of brass clocks. By the time Elias Howe was ready to mass produce sewing machines in 1846, the American machine tool industry and the interchangeable parts system were sufficiently mature to produce thousands of machines quickly and relatively inexpensively. Cyrus McCormick applied the technique to his mass-produced reapers, and farmers found them much easier to repair than handmade implements.

The switch from handcrafting to machine production had important social consequences. Because the machines and their jigs did most of the precision work, an aspiring factory worker no longer had to endure a long apprenticeship. In fact, unskilled or semiskilled laborers were often far more likely to function effectively in a mechanized factory system than were highly skilled craftsmen. Factory owners could pay these laborers far less and exploit untrained immigrants who flocked to the United States as well as the children of farmers who found their way to the growing industrialized cities. Thus the interchangeable parts system created an interchangeable labor system that would fundamentally change the industrial workplace in America.

See also Cotton Gin; Industrial Revolution; McCormick, Cyrus Hall; Thomas, Seth; Whitney, Eli.

References and Further Reading

Green, Constance McLaughlin. *Eli Whitney and the Birth of American Technology.* Boston: Little, Brown, 1956.

Fuller, Claud E. *Whitney Firearms.* Huntington, WV: Standard Publications, 1946.

Pursell, Jr., Carroll W. *Technology in America: A History of Individuals and Ideas.* Cambridge, MA: MIT Press, 1990.

Interstate Commerce Clause

The delegates to the Constitutional Convention were well aware that trading disputes had arisen among various states. To deal with the issue, they assigned Congress authority over interstate commerce. Because the extent and nature of that commerce changed markedly over the years, the interstate commerce clause was the subject of frequent debate and judicial reinterpretation. By the end of the nineteenth century it had emerged as a far more significant and greatly expanded authority for federal involvement in and regulation of all sorts of commercial activities in the United States.

To a degree, disputes over interstate trade played a major role in the decision to call a Constitutional Convention. Marylanders used the Chesapeake Bay as a commercial waterway, but the State of Virginia controlled the land on both sides of the bay's mouth. Virginia therefore could impose taxes or otherwise interfere with Maryland citizens' access to the Atlantic Ocean. George Washington invited representatives from both states to his home at Mount Vernon in 1785 to discuss this situation. Recognizing that similar issues could arise between other states, the Mt. Vernon conferees called for a second meeting in 1786 at Annapolis and invited spokesmen from other states.

Delegates from six states convened at the Annapolis gathering, and they discussed various problems related to control of trade on rivers and in harbors. Meanwhile, New York, New Jersey, and Connecticut had become locked in a tariff war. New York was taxing goods shipped in from neighboring states, and they, in turn, were taking steps to tax or regulate imports from New York City. Aware that these and similar trade disputes threatened the fragile unity of the newly independent nation, the delegates at Annapolis called for a general conference in Philadelphia to meet the following year.

Representatives from every state attended the Philadelphia Convention in the summer of 1787, expecting it to draft a new provision or two to supplement the Articles of Confederation. But the assemblage quickly fell under the influence of nationalists like James Madison and Alexander Hamilton who advocated a completely new document and organizational structure. Negotiating behind closed doors, the Convention produced the Constitution.

Tucked away in Article 1, Section 8 the document assigns Congress the power "To regulate commerce with foreign nations, and among the several States, and with the Indian tribes." This clause grants the federal government authority over imports and exports including tariffs as well as commerce between states. Congress immediately exercised some of this power by imposing customs duties or tariffs on overseas imports. This federal action effectively ended differential taxes that some states were levying on goods transferred from other states.

For many years, however, other aspects of the clause remained largely unused. Commerce within the new nation tended to be very local. Transportation costs were high relative to the value of the available farm produce and rough-hewn products, which discouraged land-based shipments between neighboring states. It was far more likely that American products would be carted to the nearest ocean port and shipped overseas. Congress did not perceive much need to regulate or control the relatively minor interstate commerce that occurred.

The first major legal test of the interstate commerce clause came in the 1820s in the *Gibbons v. Ogden* case. New York had granted the group headed by Robert Fulton and Robert Livingston an exclusive right to operate steamboats within the state's boundaries that included New York Harbor. Cornelius Vanderbilt and his associates objected, and the matter ultimately arrived at the Supreme Court. Chief Justice John Marshall's majority opinion noted that New York's laws prohibiting duly registered U.S. vessels from operating within its jurisdiction were "repugnant" to the U.S. Constitution and therefore void. In his opinion, the interstate commerce clause gave the federal government, not any state, the authority to determine who could operate commercially within the United States.

One interesting aspect of the decision was that it declared state legislation unconstitutional even though Congress had not itself enacted any specific laws regarding steamboats. For Marshall, the key factor was that the Constitution had assigned authority to the federal government, even if that entity failed to exercise it. He was also aware that both Connecticut and New Jersey were developing their own legislative responses to New York's action because its monopoly grant clearly infringed on their ability to transport goods in adjacent waters. This was reminiscent of the Confederation Era trade wars that had helped stimulate the drafting of the Constitution in the first place.

Marshall's decision was hardly popular. It appeared contrary to the tradition of states' rights and gave the federal government responsibility that many associated with that government did not desire. It was quite clear, however, that Marshall was acting against a strict construction of the Constitution and was sensitive to any state's attempt to limit or interfere with the powers and authority of the central government. To that extent, his actions in this case and others were consistent in asserting and strengthening federal authority.

It was inevitable that interstate commerce would become more significant and more controversial in succeeding decades. The construction of railroads both within and across state lines facilitated inexpensive transportation throughout the nation. Even so, Congress was very slow to exert its authority over these developments. The states took the lead in chartering and incorporating railroads, in setting standards and issuing regulations for their operations, and in serving as public watchdogs over their behavior.

The absence of congressional action left the courts to mediate disputes. Chief Justice Roger Taney is perhaps most famous for his role in drafting the *Dred Scott* decision, but he was responsible for a number of other cases that tested the limits of the interstate commerce clause. While he could not ignore the federal authority Marshall had established, Taney tended to support state regulation of commerce as long as Congress had failed to act.

This encouraged the belief that Taney was an old-line states' rights advocate, but his views were far more subtle. Competition between railroad promoters over rights of way, fares, operating procedures, and the like needed some governmental oversight. To the extent that he considered various states' regulatory procedures to be in the public interest, Taney was willing to allow them to continue. If Congress did not exert its authority, he believed the states had every right to manage these commercial enterprises in ways that suited their citizens.

By mid-century, the interstate commerce clause remained more a potential than active factor. The Marshall precedent had called attention to its importance, the Taney Court continually noted its existence, but Congress remained disinterested in its potential. Only after the Civil War did the commerce clause begin to exert a more pervasive influence on American life.

See also Interstate Commerce Commission; Laissez-Faire.

Reference and Further Reading

Frankfurter, Felix. *The Commerce Clause.* Chapel Hill, NC: University of North Carolina Press, 1937.

Japan, Opening of

American merchants and shippers developed a strong interest in Far Eastern trade as early as the Revolutionary War. While they were able to develop a modest trade with China, Japan remained almost completely closed to outside influences until U.S. Navy Commodore Perry sailed his squadron into Tokyo Bay in the 1850s. This event signaled the opening of Japan, and both American and European merchants were quick to exploit this access to Japanese trade.

The earliest Western contact with Japan came in the form of Portuguese and Dutch ships that arrived in the 1600s. Concurrently, the Japanese emperor became subordinate to the shogun, a hereditary military leader. The Shogunate maintained its authority largely by clamping down on any form of dissent. Europeans who brought with them a strong Christian missionary impulse seemed particularly subversive to a regime that relied on ancient traditions. Therefore, the Shogunate prohibited virtually all outside contact and Japan remained a closed society well into the nineteenth century.

For many years, the only official link to the outside world was a single Dutch ship allowed to visit the remote island of Deshima once a year. When the Napoleonic Wars engulfed Holland in the early 1800s, American ships stepped in to make these annual trips. Subsequently, New England whaling vessels hunted in the fertile waters off Japan's east coast, and American seamen occasionally ended up stranded on shore. Despite several American attempts, Japanese authorities refused to establish regular procedures for repatriating these unfortunate men.

Calls for U.S. government action motivated President Franklin Pierce to authorize Matthew Calbraith Perry to take a four-ship navy squadron to Japan in 1853. Perry's ships boldly sailed into Edo Bay adjacent to present-day Tokyo. The commodore delivered a letter to the authorities and promised to return shortly with more ships. This event coincided with the growth of strong pressures within Japan to open relations with the outside world. When Perry's fleet returned in 1854, the government agreed to open negotiations. The result is sometimes called the Wood and Water Treaty because its main provision was to permit American vessels in need to obtain fuel and water along the Japanese coast.

Perry's agreement also established limited consular relations with Japan. Townsend Harris served as the first U.S. consul, and by exercising great tact and patience, he eventually worked out a much broader trading treaty with a still reluctant Japanese government. British and other European diplomats quickly moved in, demanding most-favored-nation status for their officials and traders. Thus Perry's successful venture opened Japan not only to U.S. trade but also to much broader relations with the rest of the world.

As with the China market, Americans never became major trading partners with

Japan. Even so, because of this country's leading role in opening the doors, American statesmen and merchants continued to believe that the United States had a special relationship with Japan. To an extent, Japan held similar views, in part because Americans appeared less obtrusive than other Europeans whose way was paved by Perry's diplomacy.

See also China Market; Clipper Ships.

References and Further Reading

Dulles, Foster Rhea. *Yankees and Samurai.* New York: Harper and Row, 1965.

Morison, Samuel Eliot. *"Old Bruin": Commodore Matthew C. Perry, 1894–1858.* Boston: Little, Brown, 1967.

Wiley, Peter Booth, and Korogi Ichiro. *Yankees in the Land of the Gods.* New York: Viking, 1900.

Labor Unions, Early

Craftsmen and artisans created the first unions in the United States. While these tended to be very localized and specialized, they employed many of the tactics that later and larger labor organizations used—strikes, collective bargaining, and calls for a closed shop. Early labor unions exercised some influence in periods of prosperity, but the depressions that followed the Panics of 1819 and 1837 severely undermined their influence.

Labor unions came into existence as a consequence of major changes in the U.S. economy. In the colonial period, most craftsmen and artisans worked in small shops producing goods on order. Masters, journeymen, and apprentices worked side by side on a commission basis. By the 1790s, however, merchant capitalists in cities and towns had become more common, running small factories to supply their stores. Products were produced ahead of orders, and price competition forced these entrepreneurs to seek ways to reduce their production costs. This, in turn, led to pressure to reduce workers' wages and to extend their working hours.

Skilled workers who failed to become independent merchants ended up working for wages. As the number of such employees grew, they began to realize that collective efforts might be more effective than individual pleas to improve their working conditions. Building on the model of pre-Revolutionary mechanics' societies, local organizers called for more broad-reaching groupings to protect and improve their plight.

After a couple of short-lived attempts, the shoemakers in Philadelphia formed the Federal Society of Cordwainers in 1794. Acknowledged as the first labor union in American history, this group persisted for a dozen years and used strikes and collective bargaining to promote the livelihoods of its members. Another notable early union was the Franklin Typographical Society of Journeymen Printers, a New York City organization that developed a comprehensive wage scale and then fomented strikes to force employers to abide by it.

Craftsmen in other lines of work formed similar organizations with greater or lesser success through the early years of the nineteenth century. In almost every case these were small, local organizations devoted to particular trades. Their goals included establishing and maintaining minimum wage levels for their members, discouraging employers from hiring apprentices or "halfway" journeymen who had not completed their training, and giving support to members suffering from adversity. They used collective bargaining, publicity, boycotts, and *turnouts* or short-term work stoppages to encourage employers to conform to their desires.

Employers fought back by hiring scabs (nonunion workers) and filing legal challenges. The Philadelphia cordwainers were the target of the first major conspiracy trial in 1806, and the court cases in subsequent years almost always went against the unions. The key issue was whether turnouts and collective action violated a common law prohibition against conspiracies. The courts often concluded that union tactics encouraged people to engage in criminal actions and therefore that the unions themselves could be construed as criminal conspiracies.

Even without legal challenges, early union efforts were rather feeble. In prosperous times, the persistent nationwide shortage of skilled labor forced employers to pay relatively higher wages for their workforce than they would have preferred, thus undermining the justification for collective action. When depressions hit as they did in the 1820s and late 1830s, widespread unemployment was a more critical problem for all workers, skilled or unskilled, than wage levels. Support for unions evaporated quickly when hard times settled in.

As the industrial economy continued to develop, however, labor organizers gained influence through political action and emerging national craft unions.

See also Guilds.

References and Further Reading

Dubofsky, Melvyn, and Foster Rhea Dulles. *Labor in American: A History.* Wheeling, IL: Harlan Davidson, 1999.

Rayback, Joseph G. *A History of American Labor.* New York: Macmillan, 1961.

Taft, Philip. *Organized Labor in American History.* New York: Harper, 1964.

Laissez-Faire

The French term *laissez faire* literally means "to let do." As applied in the American context, the term means that individuals should be allowed to do whatever they wish without major governmental interference or restrictions. A laissez-faire economy, then, is one in which government functions are minimized or restricted as far as possible to encourage individual initiative. To a large degree, the federal government, especially under presidents Jefferson and Jackson, subscribed to the laissez-faire principle, and they limited governmental initiatives and restrictions on the business community.

Although laissez-faire first emerged as a popular doctrine among liberals, by the end of the nineteenth century, political conservatives had become its staunchest champions. One reason for the early liberal support was that the monarchical nation–states that emerged from the medieval period often exercised autocratic, centralized control. Critics of such restrictive systems were therefore attracted to the laissez-faire approach and its emphasis on individual liberty and responsibility rather than royal prerogative. As more liberal regimes became established, those who benefited from the lack of central constraints became committed defenders of the laissez-faire concept.

The so-called *Ancien Regime* in France was the birthplace of laissez-faire. A group of philosophers generally known as Physiocrats objected to the restrictiveness of the French Empire's mercantilist system. They articulated the concept of a higher law; a natural order that superceded the power of the monarch. Fundamental to this natural order was the precept that individuals had inherent rights to pursue their own best interests. While these novel ideas took some time to percolate in France, the American colonists were quicker to adopt them, especially those who increasingly found British mercantile policies repugnant.

Adam Smith's book, *The Wealth of Nations,* was published in 1776, the same year as the signing of the American Declaration of Independence, and it made a convincing case for limited government. In Smith's view, a nation's wealth arose from the individual activities of countless citizens, not the royal government. He insisted that if everyone was free to maximize his own personal prosperity, the nation as a whole would prosper far more than if it was constricted by central laws and regulations.

This view naturally appealed to the American revolutionaries who became engaged in a war to free themselves from what they considered a repressive imperial government. The Declaration of Independence stated as a fundamental principle that all people have an "inalienable right to life, liberty and the pursuit of happiness." Additional natural rights were articulated and confirmed in the Bill of Rights added to the U.S. Constitution and incorporated into the newly formed states' governing instruments.

The American Revolution thus rejected external controls and promised individual freedom. As it turned out, the revolution went too far, so the states and the American people had to endure the hardships of the Confederation period before they adopted a replacement for the British government they had rejected. But the U.S. Constitution was a brief document that assigned very limited authority to Congress. To that extent, it created a system closer to laissez-faire than a strong central government.

The controversy had only begun. The energetic Alexander Hamilton headed a faction that immediately attempted to expand the powers of the central government. He proposed protective tariffs, a central bank, internal taxation, and a host of other controls on the economy. He also urged Congress to consider bounties and subsidies to encourage industrialization. These federalist ideas encouraged the formation of another major faction whose chief spokesmen were Thomas Jefferson and James Madison. They had chafed under British mercantile controls and had little interest in replacing them with dictates from an intrusive American government. With their friends, they coalesced into the Democratic-Republican Party dedicated to limiting government regimentation.

Under presidents Washington and Adams, Federalism scored some early victories, but laissez-faire proved to be far more popular and enduring. With few exceptions, the limited-government advocates in the Democratic-Republican coalition and its successor, the Democratic Party, controlled the U.S. government prior to the Civil War. They opposed high protective tariffs and generally refused to allocate federal funds for internal improvements like highways, canals, and railroads. They let the first Bank of the United States wither away, and President Andrew Jackson destroyed its successor.

This left ample opportunity for individual initiative. People established farms, built factories, ran banks, and pursued a thousand other enterprises without significant federal oversight or involvement at all. State governments took advantage of the weakness of the central government, actively promoting business by issuing charters, providing bounties, funding roads and canals, and even setting up factories. Because of this state-level activity, the American economy was far from a purely laissez-faire arrangement.

By the 1840s, however, some of the ambitious state enterprises had failed dramatically. State bonds issued for canals and railroads lost their worth, and several state governments essentially operated in a deficit or even bankrupt status. Purely private enterprise seemed more successful. Corporations sold bonds and actually built railroads. Private capital financed factories that employed thousands of workers. Individual farmers transformed their pioneer, subsistence homesteads into commercial farms.

Many Americans attributed these successes to laissez-faire, and they were reluctant to consider any change. Social problems, urbanization, congestion, and unpredictable business cycles became more evident as the nation grew, however, and a few voices called for panaceas that only a stronger state or federal government could provide. But the political realities were such that even the Whig coalition that attempted to counter the Democratic dynasty failed to propose major changes. Henry Clay's American System concepts received considerable attention, but they fell far short of proposing a strong, intrusive central government. The United States in the first half of the nineteenth century came closer to achieving an ideal laissez-faire environment than at any other time.

The Civil War only reinforced the appeal of laissez-faire. High taxes, suspension of civil rights, and massive government spending were only some of the intrusions that occurred. As quickly as possible after the Union victory, the federal government closed down its emergency activities, demobilized its huge army, and cancelled the economic restraints it had imposed as wartime measures. The trend toward a return to laissez-faire was clearly evident despite the Republican Party's support of land grants for railroads and education.

A whole new generation of proponents of laissez-faire emerged in the late nineteenth century. Herbert Spencer, William Graham Sumner, and other Social Darwinists published trenchant defenses of the doctrine. The judicial system systematically knocked down legislative initiatives that might increase the authority of the central government. It was only toward the close of the century that alternative economic philosophies began to weaken the laissez-faire orientation of the United States.

See also American System; Bank War; Social Darwinism.

References and Further Reading

Faulkner, Harold U. *The Decline of Laissez Fare.* New York: Rinehart, 1951.

Fine, Sidney. *Laissez Faire and the General-Welfare State.* Ann Arbor, MI: University of Michigan Press, 1956.

Fried, Barbara H. *The Progressive Assault on Laissez Fair.* Cambridge, MA: Harvard University Press, 1998.

Kanth, Rajani K. *Political Economy and Laissez-Faire.* Totowa, NJ: Rowman and Littlefield, 1986.

Smith, Roy C. *Adam Smith and the Origins of American Enterprise.* New York: Truman Talley Books, 2003.

West, Edwin G. *Adam Smith and Modern Economics.* Aldershot, UK: Edward Elgar, 1990.

Land Companies

The vast expanse of sparsely populated land west of the Appalachian Mountains encouraged the formation of companies hoping to profit from land sales beyond the frontier. The Ohio Company appeared in Virginia as early as 1750, and the transfer of colonial and state claims to the federal government after the American Revolution stimulated even more activity. While these organized efforts created few actual settlements, land speculation continued to be a popular activity well into the nineteenth century.

Despite being called companies, these organizations typically were partnerships of men capable of influencing governments. The Ohio Company of Virginia, for example, included prominent planters who lobbied the House of Burgesses for access to western lands. At that point Virginia's claims stretched from north of the Ohio River as far west as Alaska. Eventually the Board of Trade in London approved a grant to the Ohio Company, but title to the land remained unclear due to competing Indian, French, British, and rival colonies' claims. Some members of the company continued to put forward optimistic plans even after the Revolution, but nothing substantial ever came of them.

With the adoption of the Articles of Confederation, most states surrendered western land claims to the central government. Congress set some public land aside to compensate soldiers, and both Virginia and Connecticut were assigned large tracts in the Northwest Territory. These areas, including Connecticut's Western Reserve, lost their distinctive character once individual settlers began to carve homesteads out of the wilderness.

Meanwhile, ambitious individuals convinced members of the Confederation Congress to grant them substantial lands. The Ohio Company of Associates, John Cleves Symmes, and the Scioto Company each obtained access to more than a million acres north and west of the Ohio River. Many participants in these schemes also lobbied to be named to federal posts in the territories. Even with this added influence, their efforts produced little actual settlement.

Symmes' experience was typical. He led a group in establishing a settlement that later developed into the river port of Cincinnati. Even so, he was unable to sell much of the land he had arranged to buy from Congress. Symmes eventually reduced his asking price to a dollar an acre, just slightly more than his agreed price from the federal government, but he found few takers. Many frontiersmen simply squatted on wilderness lands, hoping to pay nothing at all. Worse yet, the federal government also offered very similar tracts at low prices. To generate revenue Congress was eager to make money from the public domain, its only tangible asset, so it continued to reduce both the parcel size and the price of the land it hoped to sell in the Northwest Territory. Symmes did obtain appointment as a federal judge in the territory, but his land speculation failed to produce a profit.

The land company approach failed for several reasons. Clearly, there was far more land available than willing settlers, so price competition was always intense. Moreover, unlike the railroad companies that energetically advertised their lands after the Civil War, these early companies generally failed to develop publicity campaigns to attract buyers. Perhaps most important, the character of the people who struck out for the West worked against the company model. Many were poor or even destitute and financially unable to buy land from any seller. Others were deliberately setting off for the frontier to carve out an independent life incompatible with any company plan.

The most celebrated land speculation scandals involved the Yazoo lands in what was to become the states of Alabama and Mississippi. Unlike the northern states after the Revolution, Georgia did not cede its claims to western lands to the federal government. A varied group of claimants including companies with very prominent citizens obtained numerous grants from the Georgia legislature. The activity was so intense that many of these grants either overlapped other claims, were occupied by powerful Indian tribes or, worse yet, lay in areas still under Spanish domination.

Rumors circulated that all but one of the Georgia legislators accepted bribes in 1794 before approving the sale of 35 million acres to four Yazoo companies. This act was so blatant that a subsequent legislature repealed the sale two years later and ordered the statute that had approved it burned and all mention of the sale expunged from official records. This hardly ended the matter, however, as the participants in the companies insisted that they had acted in good faith. The matter of the Yazoo frauds eventually reached the Supreme Court. In 1810 Chief Justice John Marshall wrote the prevailing opinion in the case of *Fletcher v. Peck* that supported the speculators' claims. In essence, the ruling denied the state's right to rescind a valid contract.

The Yazoo land speculation schemes had no significant success in promoting settlement along the Gulf Coast, but they did produce a landmark constitutional decision. It endorsed the sanctity of contracts, ensuring that future business dealings among individuals and between them and governmental agencies would be subject to legal enforcement. Because the disputed land had subsequently fallen under federal jurisdiction, the claimants appealed to the U.S. Congress for restitution. Congress approved a compensation bill in 1814, and by 1820, had distributed millions of dollars to claimants. In that sense, then, the speculators who had formed the Yazoo land companies ultimately obtained some return on their investment.

Congress continued to modify its land distribution policies in the nineteenth century, almost always in the direction of encouraging actual settlers rather than company structures. By 1832 an individual could pay as little as $50 to obtain clear title to a 40 acre parcel from the public domain. In addition, the government offered credit arrangements that further eased the process of setting up a farm. Thirty years later, the

Homestead Act reduced the price to nothing, allowing an individual to stake a claim to 160 acres for a modest filing fee. There simply was no profit possible for companies in such circumstances, so speculators directed their money to other investments.

See also Symmes, John Cleves.

References and Further Reading

Hinderaker, Eric. *Elusive Empires.* New York: Cambridge University Press, 1997.

Magrath, C. Peter. *Yazoo: Law and Politics in the New Republic.* Providence, RI: Brown University Press, 1966.

Philbrook, Francis S. *The Rise of the West, 1754–1830.* New York: Harper and Row, 1965.

McCulloch v. Maryland

In 1819 Supreme Court Chief Justice John Marshall issued a decision that confirmed the federal government's right to create a national bank and insulate it from state taxation. While the immediate impact of the *McCulloch v. Maryland* decision was to preserve the Second Bank of the United States, it set a major precedent for a much more dynamic federal government presence in, and regulation of, the nation's business.

A deep-seated mistrust of and hatred for the Second Bank of the United States fueled the controversy that led to the *McCulloch v. Maryland* case. Chartered in 1816, the bank had been poorly managed under its first president, William Jones. He was a weak, unsophisticated administrator, who allowed the bank's nineteen branches to operate without any serious central control. In the South and West, the branches behaved like private institutions in their regions, extending enormous amounts of credit to land speculators. The eastern branches were more restrained in their fiscal policies but found their resources being drained due to system rules that allowed obligations of less solvent branches to be redeemed at any branch.

Even a better managed system would have been unpopular with those who favored states' rights in opposition to a strong central government. Adding to the problem was the outrageous behavior of the Baltimore branch. Its cashier, James McCulloch, was personally involved in dubious schemes, and the branch's general mismanagement encouraged state officials to attempt to regulate it. Maryland legislation dictated that all banks buy special, stamped paper for printing notes and specified substantial fines for those that failed to do so.

Convinced that his federally chartered institution was not subject to state laws, McCulloch sued for protection. The case quickly made its way through the appeal process to the Supreme Court. John Adams, the last Federalist president, had appointed John Marshall to serve as chief justice late in his term in 1801. Marshall continued to espouse the Federalist belief that the U.S. government had independent and even superior powers compared to the states.

The decision he drafted confirmed the supremacy of federal law and rejected the state's right to tax or otherwise regulate a federal institution. Equally important, Marshall's opinion confirmed that the so-called necessary and proper clause of the U.S. Constitution gave broad powers to the federal government to create agencies and procedures it considered essential to carrying out duties the Constitution specified.

The decision was generally unpopular, given the widespread dismay with the poorly functioning bank. But *McCulloch v. Maryland* was a strong statement of federal supremacy, and it served as a precedent for future actions of the central government. By the end of the nineteenth century, federal authority over business matters stretched well beyond what the Constitution specifically mentioned. Regulatory legislation like the Sherman Antitrust Act and agencies like the Interstate Commerce Commission gained some of their legitimacy and acceptance from this 1819 court case.

See also Bank War; Interstate Commerce Clause; Panic of 1819.

References and Further Reading

Dangerfield, George. *The Era of Good Feelings*. New York: Harcourt, Brace, 1952.

Hammond, Bray. *Banks and Politics in America*. Princeton, NJ: Princeton University Press, 1957.

Monopoly

A *monopoly* exists when a company or other agency can exercise complete control of a particular economic or business segment. Some monopolies develop from successful marketing or production strategies; others arise from deliberate legislative action. In a free-enterprise system, governments and the public tend to object to monopoly control, but the early history of the American colonies contains a number of examples of government-sponsored or condoned monopolies.

One of these, a Parliamentary grant to the English East India Company aroused particular outrage. The grant gave the company a monopoly of the legitimate trade in tea to the American colonies after 1750. This represented an evolutionary step, however, as this same company had enjoyed monopoly status from its very origins a century and a half earlier.

To capitalize on the spirit of adventure pervading the British Isles in 1600, Queen Elizabeth's government issued a charter to some 218 people who called themselves "The Company of Merchants of London Trading into the East Indies." It was not entirely clear at that point just what constituted the East Indies, especially since Portuguese and then Dutch merchants had established trading relationships with a number of different jurisdictions and locations throughout southern and eastern Asia. Even so, the royal charter gave the London Company monopoly authority to conduct all British trade within this undefined area.

Operating as a joint-stock enterprise, the company gathered capital and sent ships around the Cape of Good Hope. In the early years, some of the company's captains made quick profits by capturing valuable cargoes from other European or local trading vessels. Over time, British agents established trading outposts and expanded their influence in particular regions to guarantee more reliable sources of supply. Trade involving Chinese products and ports proved quite profitable in the 1600s.

By the eighteenth century, the organization had become known as the English East India Company, a name that appropriately acknowledged the growing importance of its relations with people on the Indian subcontinent. While ostensibly a business venture, with Parliament's blessings the company exercised civil and military control over a growing number of Indian districts. It maintained its own army and, under Robert Clive's leadership in the mid-1750s, it began the process of bringing virtually the entire area of present-day India and Pakistan under British authority.

The company prospered to the extent that it could market desirable and often exotic goods from its far-flung holdings. By the 1760s, tea from India and China had become its most important commodity. Tea was highly desired by both Europeans and those who had settled in America. The market demand was so strong, in fact, that growers, traders, and distributors from a number of countries gave the English company stiff competition. To guarantee its market access, it successfully petitioned Parliament to give the company monopoly control of the distribution of tea in both the British Isles and the North American colonies.

That arrangement came with heavy costs. The company had to pay an assessment of £400,000 to the royal government in any year that its dividends exceeded 6 percent. In addition, a 25 percent import tax and a similar 25 percent inland duty were levied on any tea the company brought into British jurisdiction. These charges significantly raised the price of the company's tea. For many years merchants had been selling tea smuggled in from Dutch and other sources at half the price of the company's product or for even less.

By 1772 the English East India Company was in a crisis. It had 18 million pounds of tea in storage, on all of which it had already paid the mandated duties. Its product simply could not compete in price with the tea illegally being distributed. As much as half of all the tea consumed in England came from foreign sources that evaded paying any duties. At the same time, prominent American merchants like John Hancock were profiting handsomely from their own trade in tax-free smuggled tea.

Well aware of the company's straits, British authorities tried to level the playing field by passing a new bill in 1773. The resulting Tea Act exempted the company from paying hefty dividends to the government, and it cancelled the domestic duties on tea shipped directly to the American market. Significantly, however, the Tea Act specifically referred to the Declaratory Act of 1766 in which Parliament had asserted its right to collect taxes in the colonies. To reconfirm that right, the Tea Act insisted that American buyers continue paying a small import duty on East India Company tea.

The new royal policies appeared to be a step in the right direction to solve the company's economic problems because they reduced the price for its tea to equal or even undercut the cost of foreign supplies. But they failed to address the more fundamental issue of who had the right to tax the colonists. The slogan "no taxation without representation" became a byword in colonial patriotic societies. By 1773 resentment against Parliamentary rule had spread throughout the colonies. Rebellious Americans simply refused to buy East India Company tea—even though it was now cheaper than the smuggled variety—if in doing so they would also be paying a tax to the British government.

Boycotts and protests erupted up and down the Atlantic Coast. The royal governor of Massachusetts, Thomas Hutchinson, was determined to force the local population in Boston to adhere to the new law. Eventually three ships loaded with East India Company tea docked in Boston Harbor. Militant opponents of Parliamentary rule dressed up as Mohawk Indians, boarded these vessels, and dumped 340 chests of tea overboard to prevent anyone from paying the tax.

News of this "Boston Tea Party" quickly spread to other colonies and back to England. In short order, the king's ministers had convinced Parliament to pass the Coercive Acts to stifle the growing rebelliousness in America. The colonists referred to martial rule in Massachusetts and related actions as the Intolerable Acts. The train of events that would lead to open confrontation and ultimately the battle for independence had begun. Ironically, in 1776, rebels took other stocks of East India Company tea out of storage and sold them to finance their revolution.

The East India Company's involvement in triggering the American revolt was only one in a series of adventures and misadventures in its long history. In the 1850s, there was another bloody revolt that involved its native military units in India. The so-called Sepoy Mutiny undermined the company's authority and led to much more direct British government participation in the administration of the Jewel of the Crown (i.e., India). Even so, the monopoly status accorded the company had been effective in focusing British economic and trade relationships in pursuit of imperial designs for over two hundred years.

See also Joint-Stock Company; Nonimportation; Sugar Act.

References and Further Reading

Edney, Matthew H. *Mapping and Empire.* Chicago: University of Chicago Press, 1990.

Ekelund, Jr., Robert B., and Robert D. Tollison. *Politicized Economies: Monarchy, Monopoly, and Mercantilism.* College Station, TX: Texas A&M University Press, 1997.

Keay, John. *The Honourable Company: A History of the English East India Company.* New York: Macmillan, 1991.

New York Stock and Exchange Board

Formally organized in 1817, the New York Stock and Exchange Board was the successor to a loose organization that had begun with the signing of the Buttonwood Agreement on Wall Street in 1792. It created an exclusive mechanism for brokers to meet on a regular basis and charge set commissions for trades. Members had to pay a fee to belong to the Buttonwood Group and, later, the stock exchange, but other traders continued to operate outside these organizations.

Buyers and sellers of bonds had been meeting informally along Wall Street for some time before the establishment of structured operations. The precedents and models for the American organizations were the European *bourses* that emerged in the eighteenth century. Both London and Antwerp established more carefully regulated exchanges in the wake of the Tulip and South Sea Bubbles. As long as they remained under British control, however, American colonists failed to take any major independent initiatives.

Even after the Revolution, the chaotic money system and the lack of major private investment opportunities delayed the development of an American exchange. In the early 1790s, Treasury Secretary Alexander Hamilton's ambitious federal financial plans stimulated more interest. The U.S. government issued some $80 million in bonds, and private individuals agreed to try to sell large blocs of these bonds. New York State also issued bonds, and soon a lively trade developed in marketing government obligations.

Until 1792 many speculators did their buying and selling outdoors at various points along Wall Street. Some acted as auctioneers, deliberately attempting to raise selling prices. In part to avoid such price-fixing tactics several traders signed an agreement under a buttonwood (or sycamore) tree located at what is now 68 Wall Street. A total of twenty-one individuals and three firms became parties to the agreement, announcing themselves as "brokers for the purchase and sale of public stocks."

The Buttonwood Agreement included several characteristics that are still part of the New York Stock Exchange structure. To join the group, members had to pay a fee initially set at $25. They also agreed to charge a fixed commission amounting to less than $^{1}/_{4}$ percent for buying and selling bonds. Within a year, the group had begun meeting on a regular basis in the board room of the Tontine Coffee House for a set amount of time each day to facilitate trades.

At the same time, this nascent exchange was very different from its modern successor. It dealt exclusively in government bonds in the early years and only gradually began handling privately issued securities. Before 1820 these were almost all bonds rather than shares of stock. The operations of the exchange were kept strictly confidential as well, with no public reporting of prices or number of securities bought and sold.

After surviving troubled economic times during the War of 1812, brokers were motivated to establish a more formal system. In 1817 a group including many original signers of the Buttonwood Agreement formed the New York Stock and Exchange Board, named for the coffeehouse's boardroom. By the early 1820s, the board had established a regular list and a free list. Each day securities on the regular list were announced in order to open trading. Securities on the free list would only be opened for bidding on request.

The absolute number of issues handled remained limited. In 1827, ten years after it had been founded, the board's list consisted of only forty-two issues that included bank stocks, government bonds, and insurance company securities. Canal company stocks attracted increasing interest, however, and in succeeding decades, railroad shares proliferated. The New York Board was the most prestigious trading organization by this time, but other cities had their own exchanges and many speculators in Manhattan continued to trade "on the curb" (outside the formal exchange, often outdoors on the street) or in relatively short-lived rival trading venues.

Even as the public came to identify Wall Street as the center of speculation in the 1830s, the New York Stock and Exchange Board moved from one location to another. A huge fire that destroyed 700 buildings in lower Manhattan in 1835 precipitated an emergency relocation, but the exchange was in operation the day after the fire in temporary quarters.

By the mid-1850s, the board was handling almost all major railroad securities. It therefore bore the brunt of the so-called western blizzard. A bad crop year, too many western rails laid with borrowed funds, and shaky banking practices combined to set off the financial Panic of 1857. The outbreak of the Civil War brought some relief by ushering in a flurry of new opportunities for both financial and industrial speculation. In 1863, the organization formally changed its name to the New York Stock Exchange, and ever since it has been the major forum for buying and selling securities in the United States.

See also Bulls and Bears; Wall Street.

References and Further Reading

Geisst, Charles R. *Wall Street: A History.* New York: Oxford University Press, 1997.

Gordon, John Steele. *The Great Game.* New York: Scribner, 1999.

Wyckoff, Peter. *Wall Street and the Stock Markets.* Philadelphia: Chilton Book Co., 1972.

Nonimportation

One of the most successful strategies American colonists used to protest royal policies was simply to stop importing goods from the British Isles. Nonimportation was first widely employed during the Stamp Act crisis in 1765; it undermined the effect of the Townshend Acts in 1770; and it was one of the first actions the Continental Congress advocated in 1774. Americans resorted to this powerful economic weapon in subsequent confrontations as well.

Obviously, for nonimportation to have any effect a substantial amount of trade must exist between two political entities. A strong trading relationship certainly did bind Great Britain to its American colonies in the 1760s and the 1770s. The British Isles were the source of the vast majority of goods that Americans imported from overseas. Indeed, by the mid-eighteenth century, substantial economic sectors in the British home islands had become focused on producing goods for the colonies and relied on sales in America for their continued prosperity.

Parliament's attempt to stiffen its enforcement of existing trade regulations and, more to the point, collect tax revenue from the colonies spurred strong resistance. Protests and mob violence greeted the passage of the 1764 Sugar Act and the 1765 Stamp Act, but these dramatic incidents were far less effective than a colony-wide call for Americans to stop buying taxed goods or conducting business that would require the purchase of revenue stamps. Sons of Liberty organizations throughout the colonies specifically touted nonimportation as the best means of forcing a reversal of Parliamentary policy.

These protests succeeded in getting the stamp tax cancelled, but they also left an impression in Great Britain that the colonies mainly objected to Parliament's imposing internal taxes like the stamp levy. External taxes like the import duties that had existed in various forms for over a century seemed less controversial. Chancellor of the Exchequer Robert Townshend therefore proposed, and Parliament approved, a new set of import taxes in the Revenue Act of 1767. Popularly known as the Townshend Duties, they applied to common items like paper, glass, tea, paint, and paint pigments like lead, all of which Americans had typically purchased in quantity from English producers.

No one had more to do with spurring nonimportation than Boston radical Samuel Adams. In addition to organizing local resistance to the British policy, he also drafted a circular letter that aroused sympathy and support in other colonies. But nonimportation also appealed to many Americans who had not previously been considered radicals. John Dickinson, a moderate from Pennsylvania, wrote eloquent letters that rejected as irrelevant Townshend's attempt to distinguish between internal and external taxes. The key factor was a growing American resolve against any taxation whatsoever from a body like Parliament where they were not represented.

Dickinson's thoughtful comments were widely read throughout the colonies, and they helped individuals unwilling to engage in more violent or dangerous actions to support nonimportation. The decision not to import or purchase English products with taxes on them began in Boston but quickly spread throughout the colonies in 1768. The economic impact of this strategy was profound. The revenue actually collected from the Townshend Duties amounted to only £3,500 by 1769. During that same period, nonimportation inflicted over £7 million worth of losses on British businesses.

Parliament had to act, and so it did by repealing the Revenue Act early in 1770. Unfortunately, news of the repeal failed to reach Boston until after a bloody confrontation had taken place outside the local customs house. Five Americans were killed in what Sam Adams and his cronies immediately publicized as the Boston Massacre. But that incident was the last major agitation for three years. The colonists dropped their nonimportation policy since all of the taxes on British products except a token levy on tea had been rescinded.

When the imposition of a new Tea Act in 1773 set off another round of protests, Americans quickly resorted to nonimportation. Directed first against tea imports, the policy was quickly adopted in many jurisdictions as a peaceful but very effective economic weapon. The First Continental Congress called for colony-wide nonimportation of British goods when it met in 1774, recognizing the power it had to influence merchants and traders in the home country. Nonimportation was far more damaging to the British economy than all of the military costs of the Revolutionary War combined. Indeed, British merchants and traders with groaning warehouses stuffed full of export goods created specifically for the American market played a key role in convincing Parliament to stop sending troops across the Atlantic after British General Lord Cornwallis surrendered at Yorktown in 1781.

With its respectability assured by its Revolutionary roots, nonimportation remained a major element in American diplomacy in the years to come. Perhaps the most dramatic use occurred prior to and during the War of 1812. And it was almost as successful in that case as it had been in the earlier conflict. Here again, frustrated British agents were eager to see an end to the conflict so they could dump their backlogged inventories on an American market starved of consumer goods.

More recently, the United States has imposed nonimportation on particular countries or commodities from time to time. The nation has also seen its economy suffer when other countries use nonimportation for their own purposes. In every instance, however, the effectiveness of the policy depends very much on the importance of the trading relationship as well as the ability of the authorities to enforce the policy. It is never a popular alternative, and public support for nonimportation tends to degrade quickly over time.

See also Embargo; Monopoly; Stamp Act.

References and Further Reading

Maier, Pauline R. *From Resistance to Revolution.* New York: Knopf, 1972.

Thomas, P. D. G. *The Townshend Duties Crisis.* New York: Oxford University Press, 1987.

Zobel, Hiller B. *The Boston Massacre.* New York: Norton, 1970.

Packet Ships

Early in the nineteenth century, some merchants and shipowners began sending their vessels out on a regular schedule. Called packet ships, they left port on specified days, empty or full. Because of their predictability, packet lines quickly became the major transporters of passengers, high-value cargo, and mail in the transatlantic trade. In the 1840s, steam-powered ships replaced the sailing packets, further improving the predictability of scheduled shipping.

The introduction of packet ships was a major innovation in the already well-developed American shipping industry. In the colonial period, most ships behaved as transients or *tramps,* carrying whatever cargo they could find in one port to a likely market. They typically left port only when fully laden, and the vagaries of the world's markets discouraged careful preplanning.

The next step was the development of *regular traders,* ships that called at a predefined set of ports. Departure times for the regular traders remained unpredictable, however, because few were willing to sail without a full load. After the War of 1812, some of those plying the U.S. coastal trade became sufficiently aware of market conditions to preschedule sailings, confident of finding adequate cargo to make the voyage pay.

The next bold step was to apply that same strategy to transatlantic voyages. In late 1817 a group of New York merchants assembled a fleet of four ships and promised regular departures throughout the year from New York and Liverpool. To distinguish their vessels from others, they painted a large black circle on the forward mainsail, causing the fleet to be dubbed the Black Ball Line. The first transatlantic packet left Liverpool on January 4, 1818, and a day later another Black Ball ship hoisted anchor in New York Harbor.

The line fared poorly at first due to the Panic of 1819 and the depression that followed. By the early 1820s, however, the packet ship concept had proven to be very successful, and other lines followed the Black Ball lead. The vessels engaged in this service tended to be rather stubby, full-masted sailing ships of anywhere between 400 and 1,000 tons displacement. They had to be very well constructed to weather the inevitable winter gales and high seas if they were to meet their year-round schedules. Prevailing winds meant that the eastward crossing was almost always faster than the westward voyage.

Very quickly, the quality of the passenger accommodations on the packet ships improved dramatically. The predictable departure times convinced wealthier people to abandon the regular traders, and competition among competing packet lines encouraged them to upgrade their cabins and amenities. By the 1830s, packet ships carried most of the paying passengers on the transatlantic routes as well as specie, mail, and high-value, low-bulk cargo often referred to as *fine freight.*

In 1848 Englishman Samuel Cunard inaugurated the first packet steamship service. Because they were not as affected by wind direction and intensity, steamships added much more predictability to arrival times as well as departure times. They quickly siphoned off a lot of the mail and fine freight cargo, but passengers preferred the more comfortable and supposedly safer sailing ships well into the 1850s. After the Civil War, sailing packet ships were consigned to bulky cargoes and, occasionally, impoverished steerage passengers. The last Black Ball sailing ship made its final run in 1878.

Throughout the packet ships' heyday, New York remained the American port of choice, in large part because it always offered valuable cargos to be shipped to European destinations. Boston, Philadelphia, and even Baltimore entrepreneurs experimented with packet lines, but they simply could not make the guaranteed profits typical of the New York companies. At the same time, the packet lines played a key role in the enormous growth in importance that characterized the port of New York in the early nineteenth century.

See also Carrying Trade; Clipper Ships; Panic of 1819.

References and Further Reading

Albion, Robert Greenhalgh. 1938. *Square Riggers on Schedule.* Hamden, CT: Archon Books, 1965.

———. 1939. *The Rise of New York Port, 1815–1860.* New York: South Street Seaport Museum, 1984.

Lubbock, Basil. 1925. *The Western Ocean Packets.* Glasgow, UK: J. Brown and Son, 1925.

Panic of 1819

Westward expansion and industrialization boomed after the end of the War of 1812. But overoptimism and risky financing plagued both activities. By 1819, the unregulated banking system essentially collapsed, setting off the United States' first nationwide financial panic. Settlers lost their land, factories closed and created unemployment, and general gloom settled in. The ensuing depression lasted for several years, finally easing in 1823.

The War of 1812 cut Americans off from their usual agricultural markets in Europe and from their main suppliers of manufactured goods in the British Isles. Enterprising traders and merchants responded to this circumstance by investing in domestic manufacturing. Francis Cabot Lowell, for example, pulled together substantial capital resources to build his highly profitable integrated textile mill near Boston. His success encouraged others to follow his lead. By 1815 a fairly sizable textile industry had developed in the Northeast.

The Treaty of Ghent reopened trade between the United States and Great Britain on essentially the same terms as had existed prior to the conflict. British manufacturers had suffered enormously from being denied access to their traditional American customers, and huge stockpiles of manufactured and processed goods crammed English warehouses. Eager to dispose of these surplus goods at any cost, British exporters dumped them on the American market at remarkably low prices. The United States imposed a protective tariff on textile imports in 1816, but its average rate of 20 percent was far too low to offset the higher costs American mills experienced. British traders easily reestablished their supremacy in the textile trade, forcing many American industrialists out of business.

If the end of the war encouraged an economic revival for British industry, it also stimulated an enormous boom in westward expansion. Hailing their victory in the conflict, Americans saw it as permanently ending a British threat to control of the Mississippi Valley. Prospective farmers poured into western districts both north and south of the Ohio River, creating new states and buying large tracts of land. To do so, they borrowed freely from a very accommodating group of hastily created banks. These institutions flourished under either lax or nonexistent state regulations, and the branches the Second Bank of the United States established in western districts were virtually unregulated as well.

The American agricultural products that had managed to reach European markets during the Napoleonic Era had drawn high prices. Optimistic Americans believed that this premium on their produce would continue unabated, but war-weary Europeans rather quickly reestablished their own productive farms. Within a couple of years of the Battle of Waterloo, the world market for some agricultural products had become glutted, discouraging American farmers and making them less able to keep up with their mortgage payments.

Simultaneously, the global production of specie dropped, undermining the ability of banks and financiers to expand their loans. The financial Panic of 1819 thus stemmed from three major sources: a decline in domestic industrial production in the Northeast, overexpansion in the agrarian South and West, and sloppy and even criminal behavior on the part of the unregulated banking community. To protect themselves, banks ceased redeeming their notes with specie, causing an immediate and drastic deflation in the nation's money supply. In some areas, paper money suffered a devaluation of 50 percent or more virtually overnight. By year's end there were land foreclosures by the thousands.

Because of its central role, the Second Bank of the United States became a popular scapegoat. Its branches had flooded the market with banknotes it could not now redeem. William Jones, the bank's first president, tardily realized how serious this error was and he reversed course, attempting to reduce the bank's outstanding obligations. Langdon Cheeves replaced Jones in 1819 and was even more dedicated to restoring the fiscal institution's soundness. He did save the bank, but its strategy of sharply limiting its contribution to the nation's money supply in a time of depression only exacerbated the fiscal crisis.

The Northeast recovered sooner than the South and West. Manufacturing slowly became more competitive, and new enterprises like canal building stimulated the economy. The worldwide market for cotton also stabilized in the early 1820s, allowing the most efficient producers to earn reasonable returns. Nevertheless, the Panic of 1819 had been a frightening phenomenon, one that few contemporaries truly understood. Unfortunately, it proved to be only the first of a series of distressing downturns. Some of the factors that triggered the Panics of 1837 and 1857 were remarkably similar to those that had torn the economy apart in 1819.

See also Bank War; Integrated Mill; *McCulloch v. Maryland;* Protective Tariff.

References and Further Reading

Dangerfield, George. *The Era of Good Feelings.* New York: Harcourt, Brace, 1952.

Hammond, Bray. *Banks and Politics in America.* Princeton, NJ: Princeton University Press, 1957.

Rothbard, Murray Newton. *The Panic of 1819: Reactions and Policies.* New York: Columbia University Press, 1962.

Patent Pool

A series of patent lawsuits developed in the sewing machine industry in the 1850s. To curb these destructive assaults, the major manufacturers agreed to assign their individual patent rights to the Sewing-Machine Combination. The combination then issued licenses that required companies to pay royalties on all the machines they sold. This patent pool opened the way for a huge increase in output, but it also raised concerns about potential monopolistic control of the industry.

Elias Howe's business plan was a major factor in triggering the need for a patent pool. A Yankee tinkerer, Howe experimented with a machine that used two threads. One fed through an eye in the point of a needle, which punched through the cloth and created a loop. His device passed a second thread through that loop, creating a lock stitch. His invention won the fifth U.S. patent issued for a sewing machine in 1846, and his innovations were incorporated in all subsequent sewing machines regardless of manufacturer. Although Howe actually built and sold a number of machines, he became much more interested in collecting patent royalties from those who quickly adapted his system into their own sewing machines.

Among the literally hundreds of innovations that appeared in the next few years, a few stand out. Allen Benjamin Wilson obtained a patent on a tiny shuttle that sent the bottom thread back and forth, a much more efficient method than the one-way movement earlier models had employed. He then developed a rotating bobbin that was even more efficient. Another inventor, Isaac Merritt Singer created a horizontal sewing platform with a presser foot to hold cloth in place while the needle did its work. Singer and his associates also developed a simple but effective toothed device that moved the cloth forward as well, and they added flywheels and treadles to their models. All of these innovations became common elements in sewing machines.

Although Singer claimed his later patents were based on a primitive design he had registered in 1834, Elias Howe sued Singer for infringement. Singer took on a lawyer named Edward Clark as a partner to help him fight this action. Meanwhile, several other companies bought licenses from Howe, and they assured potential customers it would be safer to buy one of their machines because it did not involve the risk of a patent suit. Singer and Clark eventually acceded as well, paying Howe $15,000 for a license.

At that point, Elias Howe was receiving $25 on every machine made under his license, but when he attempted to sell his own machines, rivals sued him for infringing on their patents. In 1856 Orlando B. Potter, president of the Grover and Baker Company, proposed a method to end this destructive storm of lawsuits. He suggested that the companies he, Howe, Singer, and Wilson headed should create a *combination* that would pool their patents. For each machine sold, a manufacturer would be expected to pay a $15 fee to the Sewing-Machine Combination, which would allocate the resulting income proportionally to individual patent holders.

While the other companies eagerly accepted Potter's suggestion, Elias Howe insisted on a couple of key provisions. To prevent any one manufacturer from monopolizing the industry, he forced the combination to agree to license at least twenty-four manufacturers. And, because he believed his patent was the preeminent one, he demanded a flat $5 before the rest of the royalty payments were distributed.

The patent pool promoted rapid expansion in the industry. U.S. makers turned out over 100,000 sewing machines in 1860 and more than half a million fifteen years later. Singer's firm made the most of its opportunities, building industrial as well as domestic models at many different price levels. Singer also introduced installment payment plans to help individual customers purchase his machines. Orders for millions of uniforms during the Civil War created enormous demand for both basic and specialized sewing machines. The industry continued to thrive after the fighting ended because the wartime experience made Americans familiar with and comfortable wearing ready-made clothing of all types.

The industry's pioneering patent pool became a model for other sectors where rapid technological advances stimulated numerous patents. Pooling the rights to major developments allowed manufacturers to avoid costly lawsuits and high royalty charges. Inventors liked the pools because they saved the cost of pursuing infringement cases and guaranteed respectable, regular income. Elias Howe, for example, earned more than $2 million from his initial patent, most of it the result of money remitted to him from the Sewing-Machine Combination. By 1900 patent pooling had become common in dozens of industries and remains a familiar practice to this day.

Not everyone was pleased. Critics included those who were left out of or continued to object to combinations that asserted exclusive rights. The control that a relatively small number of manufacturers operating a patent pool could exert also stimulated concerns about unfair competition. Some even see patent pooling as a major stimulus to the passage of antitrust legislation in the late nineteenth century.

See also Antitrust Laws; Patents; Selden Patent.

References and Further Reading

Brandon, Ruth. *Singer and the Sewing Machine.* New York: Kodansha International, 1996.

Burlingame, Roger. *March of the Iron Men.* New York: Grosset and Dunlap, 1938.

Cooper, Grace Rogers. *The Sewing Machine: Its Invention and Development*. Washington, DC: Smithsonian Institution Press, 1968.

Patents

To encourage inventiveness and economic growth, the Framers of the Constitution included a provision for individual patents. Congress drew up relatively simple rules and specified low costs for those who wished to register their inventions. A patent assigned property rights to individuals and protected them from those who might infringe on them. Like many of the inventions they protected, the U.S. patent law proved to be very effective in promoting economic development.

It was relatively easy to establish a new property rights system in a new nation. In England, royal patents and privileges were carefully controlled and often restricted to those with political influence or social stature. In the United States, no such traditional factors prevented widespread access to federal protections. The Revolution, after all, had been rationalized as a democratic one designed to maximize the rights of individuals. It was only natural that the patents in the new nation would be available to everyone.

Article 1, Section 8 of the Constitution gives Congress the power "To promote the Progress of Science and useful Arts, by securing for limited Times to Authors and Inventors the exclusive Right to their respective Writings and Discoveries." The clause creates the basis for both patent and copyright protection. The underlying premise was that inventive people had a natural right to their creations, and that the government should recognize and defend that right.

In addition to assuring benefits to individuals, those who drafted the patent laws were keenly aware that the nation as a whole stood to benefit from them. Inventors would be more likely to perfect their concepts if they stood to make money from their efforts. To the extent that they trusted the government to stand behind their claims, they would be more likely to publicize their ideas and make them accessible to all.

Encouraging inventiveness was the primary goal, so Congress created a system that was easy to use. The registration fees were modest. To assure clarity in the process, the government did insist on detailed drawings and designs and, where appropriate, an actual working model of an invention. These served not only to define the inventors' rights in detail, but they also allowed for rapid and efficient publicity of new methods and machines.

The process was not without flaws. Eli Whitney's experience in the 1790s was anything but encouraging. His patented cotton gin was, after all, an extraordinarily simple machine, easily constructed in a farm workshop, and subject to countless modifications. He expended much of his time, energy, and wealth in a fruitless endeavor to ensure his property rights and, more to the point, his right to profit from his invention.

As the system became more familiar and refined, however, the government's role in defending inventors became stronger. By the 1820s, court decisions and legal procedures had emerged that much more effectively protected patentees and punished infringers. Paralleling these legal changes was the rise of patent experts or agents who, for a fee, would assist clients through the necessary steps and help them defend their patents.

The trickle of patents that began in the 1790s grew to a substantial stream. By the 1820s, the government was issuing an average of about 500 patents annually, a figure that had risen fivefold by the 1850s. In that decade, the yearly average was 2,525, reflecting the rapidly advancing industrial revolution that was sweeping the country.

Some inventors exploited their ideas personally. Cyrus McCormick, for example, patented his mechanical reaper in 1831. After selling as many as he could make on a small scale, he built a huge plant in Chicago to mass produce them. Others inventors were content either to sell or license their ideas to others. Here again, they often turned to patent experts for advice and assistance in assuring that licensees made appropriate royalty payments. Samuel Finley Breeze Morse also patented his telegraph system in the 1830s, but he made his fortune from shares in the American Telegraph Company. Licensed by Morse, Cyrus Field and Peter Cooper created the company to build a nationwide communication network.

However a patented concept was used, it stood a good chance of promoting efficiency or productivity. The new nation boasted a large population of self-employed people who worked with their hands every day. This army of potential inventors was always interested in a new device or a refinement in a tool that would ease their workload. To that extent, then, the drafters of the Constitution had created a useful invention of their own in calling forth a liberal patenting process.

See also Goodyear, Charles; McCormick, Cyrus Hall; Patent Pool; Whitney, Eli.

References and Further Reading

Burlingame, Roger. *March of the Iron Men.* New York: Scribners, 1938.

Engerman, Stanley L., and Kenneth L. Sokoloff. "Technology and Industrialization, 1790–1914," in Stanley L. Engerman and Robert E. Gallman, *The Cambridge Economic History of the United States.* Vol. 2. New York: Cambridge University Press, 2000.

The Story of the U.S. Patent and Trademark Office. Washington, DC: U.S. Department of Commerce, 1988.

Privateering

During wartime some governments issued privateering commissions to individuals authorizing them to capture enemy ships. The privateer would outfit a ship, hire a crew, and begin patrolling the sea lanes. Commercial ships, often unarmed but carrying valuable cargo, were the prey. Captured vessels were sailed into friendly ports to be sold, with the proceeds going to the privateer's owners and crew. American privateering flourished during the Revolution.

Privateering had a long history, and it was often confused with outright piracy. Pirates also captured ships and sold them and their cargoes, but they did so without official sanction. Privateers, on the other hand, could claim to be engaged in a legitimate enterprise. When England was at war during the colonial period, American merchants and ship captains had acted as privateers, interfering with the trade of Britain's enemies like Spain and France. The practice was thus well established by 1775 when the War for Independence began.

Because it offered a low-cost method for interfering with enemy commerce, privateering was especially popular in nations that lacked strong conventional naval forces. The U.S. Continental Congress did commission a number of navy vessels and sent officers like John Paul Jones to harass the Royal Navy in its home waters. But this tiny force was no match for the world's largest navy. It was a natural step, therefore, for the United States to send out privateers.

An American privateer could obtain a commission either from one of the newly independent states or the Continental Congress itself. The legal arrangements varied among these jurisdictions, but those interested in mounting a privateering expedition usually had to swear that they would abide by the relevant law. Several states established prize courts to legitimize the capture and arrange the auction or sale of captured ships and cargoes. Congress issued its first commissions in 1776 and, four years later, created a court to handle appeals from state prize courts. The alliance France signed with the United States in 1778 opened French ports to American privateers as well.

The costs of obtaining a privateering commission were minimal. The profit from the enterprise came from the sale of prizes. Typically the merchant or group of merchants who owned one of the marauding vessels received a share representing half or even two-thirds of the return. The crew split the remainder, and captains and prize masters received larger shares than ordinary crew members. The fact that all participants shared in the spoils served as a major motivating factor.

Because the existence of the war had cut off conventional trade, Americans had all sizes and sorts of ships available to fit out as privateers. Vessels as small as 15 tons and as large as 350 participated. Because the objective was to capture, not sink, the prize, privateers tended to display an intimidating show of force that would avoid bloodshed and unnecessary damage. Privateers also usually carried large crews because some of them would be needed to sail any vessels captured back to friendly harbors.

Literally thousands of vessels sailed as privateers during the conflict, with as many as 550 carrying Continental commissions in 1781 alone. Massachusetts and Pennsylvania together accounted for two-thirds of the state-commissioned privateers, with other jurisdictions sending out smaller fleets. These ships ranged all along the Atlantic coastline, terrorized the Caribbean, interfered with transatlantic commerce, and operated as far away as the English Channel and the North Sea. This irregular armada captured over 2,000 British ships and some 12,000 British seamen during the war. The total cost to Great Britain is estimated at £18 million.

The privateering enterprise had two major long-term consequences. First, it provided profitable employment for ships and crews previously engaged in trade. Therefore, even though British warships blockaded or interdicted American commerce during the war, some shipowners and sailors continued to prosper. Equally important, a lucky or skillful privateer could capture a new fortune literally overnight, so some individuals accrued substantial wealth that they could use to finance post-war enterprises. Several influential families like the Cabots of Massachusetts can trace their fortunes back to successful Revolutionary privateering adventures.

Privateering continued around the world, playing a major part in the Napoleonic Wars that ended in 1815. By 1856, however, the powers concluded that it was too open to abuse. The Declaration of Paris signed in that year outlawed privateering.

See also Carrying Trade; Embargo.

References and Further Reading

Fowler, Jr., William M. *Rebels Under Sail.* New York: Scribners, 1976.

Lydon, James G. *Pirates, Privateers, and Profits.* Upper Saddle River, NJ: Gregg Press, 1970.

Jamesŏn, J. Franklin, ed. *Privateering and Piracy in the Colonial Period.* New York: A. M. Kelly, 1923.

Protective Tariff

With the rationalization that it will encourage investment in domestic manufacturing, a government may levy import duties so high they discourage imports. These protective tariffs differ from other levies because they are deliberately designed to act as barriers to international trade. Highly charged political debates often arise over which home industries should be protected and, indeed, whether protectionism in general is advisable.

With the exception of slavery, no other issue generated more political controversy in the nineteenth century United States than did tariff legislation. And, because import duties and land sales together generated the vast bulk of income for the federal government, tariff decisions could markedly affect the government's ability to carry out its responsibilities.

On July 4, 1789, the First Session of the First Congress passed the first tariff legislation for the United States. Although it was primarily designed as a revenue measure, it contained mildly protectionist rates on a few imported items. Protectionism quickly became a major political issue. In his 1791 *Report on Manufactures,* Treasury Secretary

Alexander Hamilton called for higher protective tariffs to stimulate industrialization. His proposal attracted some support primarily among northeasterners interested in promoting manufacturing. But merchants and importers from the same region opposed raising trade barriers that might interfere with their international commerce.

Support for higher protective tariffs was slow to develop in the South and West. Industrious producers in those regions were more interested in access to overseas markets for their agrarian surpluses than they were in promoting industrialization. This concern for market access played a key role in triggering the War of 1812, and that conflict, in turn, stimulated interest in national self-sufficiency.

Keenly aware of the U.S. economy's vulnerability to outside forces, President James Madison urged Congress to raise tariff rates after the war hoping to protect the nascent industries the conflict had spawned. Interestingly enough, many of the former War Hawks from the South and West patriotically acted on Madison's proposal. The merchant class in New England still dominated that region's politics, however, and protectionism was not universally popular in the industrializing Northeast.

The Tariff Act of 1816 contained many more protective measures than previous legislation. For example, it stipulated a levy of 25 percent of the value of most finished cotton goods. This tax would correspondingly raise the price to consumers. That, in turn, allowed American textile manufacturers to charge higher prices that would help offset their relatively higher production costs. In the long run, a better strategy was to reduce American production costs by adopting the integrated mill approach Francis Cabot Lowell had pioneered.

Whatever the wisdom of pursuing a protectionist policy, it was not sufficient to prevent the Panic of 1819 and a subsequent depression. Nevertheless, the protective tariffs had become a persistent political issue. In the next few years, northeastern shippers lost political clout to the rising manufacturing class. By the mid-1820s, politicians like Massachusetts Senator Daniel Webster had become outspoken proponents of using higher tariff rates to protect their region's industrial expansion. Simultaneously, the export-oriented southern and western populations urged their representatives in Washington to oppose protective tariffs. This set the stage for the dramatic and divisive debates that resulted in the passage of the so-called Tariff of Abominations in 1828.

Subsequent generations of American politicians continued to grapple with what became an increasingly emotional division between proponents of protection and opponents to it, some of whom went so far as to advocate the opposite extreme of free trade. Indeed, every major debate over tariff policy right through the passage of the Smoot-Hawley Act in 1930 involved widely differing viewpoints and positions on protectionism. Some people even today favor protective tariffs, but the adoption of a reciprocity policy in the mid-1930s has lessened considerably the controversy and emotionalism that characterized earlier tariff debates.

See also Abominations, Tariff of; American System; Panic of 1819; Reciprocity.

References and Further Reading

Dobson, John M. *Two Centuries of Tariffs.* Washington, DC: U.S. International Trade Commission, 1976.

Lenner, Andrews C. *Federal Principles in American Politics, 1790–1833.* Lanham, MD: Rowman and Middlefield, 2001.

Remini, Robert V. *John Quincy Adams.* New York: Time Books, 2001.

Public Credit, Report on the

In 1790 Treasury Secretary Alexander Hamilton delivered to Congress his "Report on the Public Credit." It outlined a plan to create a funding scheme for the federal and state debts that had accumulated during the Revolutionary War and afterward. Hamilton would use the funded debt as the basis for a national currency to promote interstate trade and industrialization. Congress ultimately implemented most of his plan.

Financial uncertainty, economic depression, and an unreliable money system had helped spur the drafting of the Constitution. Therefore, it was hardly surprising that the First Congress immediately began considering financial matters. Its first major legislation imposed customs duties on some sixty-five imported commodities. Congress subsequently created the Treasury Department and asked that the Secretary of the Treasury prepare a report on the public credit that included a plan for using the tariff revenues.

President George Washington appointed Alexander Hamilton to the newly created post, and he immediately set about developing a broad-ranging financial plan. He sent his *Report on the Public Credit* to Congress on January 9, 1790. It discussed three different types of indebtedness that had arisen during the Revolutionary War. First was the federal obligation to foreign investors from France, Spain, and Holland who had lent money to the American cause. All agreed that these foreign debts must be paid if the United States was to have any credibility with other nations.

The Continental Congress had also borrowed money from many Americans by issuing promissory notes and selling bonds throughout the conflict. By 1790 many of the original holders of the bonds and notes had long since sold them to speculators, sometimes at enormous discounts. Nevertheless, Hamilton insisted that the current holders should be paid at the notes' face value, again to establish full faith in the credit of the United States. Critics charged that Hamilton and his speculator associates would unduly benefit from this plan, but no alternative seemed workable. Tracing the notes back to their original recipients and assessing how much of a discount they had suffered was simply impossible.

The third major category of indebtedness involved state borrowing. Some state governments had already made substantial progress in paying off their wartime obligations; others had not only failed to redeem war debts but had issued additional promissory notes in the intervening years. Consequently, representatives of the prudent states opposed a plan to have the federal government bail out impecunious states. Hamilton won crucial support for his plan to assume responsibility for the state debts by agreeing with Secretary of State Thomas Jefferson that the nation's capital should be moved to the Potomac River.

Congress eventually agreed to all provisions of the plan, giving Hamilton responsibility for funding a huge debt. Foreign loans amounted to just under $12 million, U.S. domestic obligations added another $40 million, and federal assumption of state debts brought in some $25 million in additional debts. Because federal tax receipts during the early 1790s never exceeded $5 million annually, the Treasury could not possibly pay off the national debt. Instead, Hamilton directed a substantial stream of tax revenue into a sinking fund sufficient to pay the annual interest on the debt as well as slightly reducing the principal. This arrangement is referred to as *funding the debt.*

To implement the new scheme, the Treasury issued millions of dollars worth of new interest-bearing federal bonds to be exchanged for existing Continental and state notes. Because the fund guaranteed that federal bondholders would receive up to 6 percent interest each year, the new bonds represented excellent investments. Relatively few bondholders insisted on redeeming them, and they circulated throughout the country pretty much at face value. In this way Hamilton had converted a huge debt liability into a remarkably flexible and reliable circulating money system for the United States.

Not surprisingly, funding a debt of this size required more revenue than the modest tariff collections could provide. Hamilton issued a *Second Report on the Public Credit* in December 1790, calling on Congress to authorize excise taxes. These were internal as opposed to external taxes, and they were primarily levied on liquor and tobacco. Western farmers converted a lot of their surplus grain into whiskey because it was easier to transport to market. In 1794 opposition to these new excise taxes among corn and tobacco growers coalesced into what was overdramatized as the Whiskey Rebellion. But as long as the debt load remained large, excise taxes were needed to help fund it.

Although it alienated and angered many Americans, Hamilton's plan for handling the debt problem was a rational one for the period. It accomplished his primary goal: establishing sound public credit for the United States at a time when the new nation's credibility was still very much in question. Even more important, the basic concept of funding the national debt that lay at the heart of his plan still characterizes the handling of current deficits.

See also Bank of the United States; Continental Currency; Hamilton, Alexander; Protective Tariff.

References and Further Reading

McDonald, Forrest. *Alexander Hamilton: A Biography.* New York: Norton, 1979.

Sharp, James Rogers. *American Politics in the Early Republic.* New Haven, CT: Yale University Press, 1993.

Stourzh, Gerald. *Alexander Hamilton and the Idea of Republican Government.* Stanford, CA: Stanford University Press, 1970.

Railroads

Not until 1829 did experimentation in England demonstrate the feasibility of a steam-powered railroad. Americans eagerly adopted this new technology, laying twice as many miles of track as all of the European countries combined in the next ten years. The pace of expansion increased in subsequent years, and railroads became a dominant force in American life in the 1850s, operating over 30,000 miles of track and absorbing one-quarter of the nation's investment capital. The surge of interest in railroads profoundly altered transportation, engineering, commerce, finance, and business in the United States.

The development of railroads required a convergence of several technical innovations. Horse-drawn trams had been carrying passengers and other cargo over short distances for some time, but the introduction of the steam locomotive revolutionized rail transportation. These increasingly powerful engines could pull a whole string of cars more efficiently and far more rapidly than any animals could. The first locomotive imported from England was too heavy for the existing tracks. Very quickly, American factories began building their own locomotives and gradually expanding their size and power. This in turn forced Americans to build heavier, more durable tracks.

In the late eighteenth century, mines experimented with grooved granite blocks, but these were too hard on the rolling stock. Surrounded by abundant forests, Americans exhibited a good deal of interest in wooden rails, many of which had iron slats laid along the surface to add strength and prolong life. An American engineer developed a much better alternative in the 1830s, an all metal T-shaped rail design that was strong and durable. Until 1860 the American iron and steel industry was not advanced enough to supply such rails, however, so imports from England remained essential.

Americans also imported the standard gauge of 4 feet 8 1/2 inches, a throwback to the width of traditional English wagon axles. Many U.S. railroads went their own way, however, laying both narrow and wider gauge tracks. The Erie Railroad was at one extreme, with a 6-foot gauge, and 5 feet was common throughout the South. The standard gauge did not become the national norm until well after the Civil War.

The first American railroads tended to be quite short, linking neighboring towns or a port city with its nearby hinterland. In the 1830s the success of the Erie and Pennsylvania canal systems stimulated competitive railroad construction elsewhere. Massachusetts promoters designed a network of lines reaching out in all directions from Boston. Marylanders installed tracks along the route of the old National Road. In South Carolina, Charlestonians saw the advantages of linking their city with the Savannah River and built a road into the interior that ran for 136 miles, the longest railroad under single management operating in the 1830s.

Both the New York and Pennsylvania state governments had invested so much money in canal systems that they were slower to acknowledge the superiority of railroads. Completion of trunk lines connecting New York City and Philadelphia with the Midwest was delayed until the 1850s. The Erie Railroad running along a southern route through the Empire State was the first to offer through service in 1851. Three years later, the New York Central system linked together a chain of seven intercity railroads to create an alternative rail route paralleling the Erie Canal.

The Pennsylvania Railroad followed a similar pattern to create what became the most successful of all the trunk lines. It tied Philadelphia to Pittsburgh on the Ohio River. Wheeling, another river port, became the western terminus of the Baltimore and Ohio Railroad, the last of the four major east-west trunk lines completed in the 1850s. By 1860 these railroads had arranged onward linkages that enabled them to route passengers and traffic all the way to Chicago.

The first burst of railroad growth in the 1830s saw the construction of over 3,000 miles of track, almost all of it in the Northeast. Twice as much was added to the nation's rail network in the next decade, and again, most of it appeared in the Northeast with links to the Midwest. In the 1850s the pace of construction rose dramatically, with some 21,000 miles of track put into operation.

The vast bulk of these new rails were in western states with Illinois, Indiana, and Ohio being the leaders. Chicago became the most popular destination. By 1860 fifteen different railroad companies offered service radiating out in all directions from the Windy City. While some expansion took place in the southern states as well, they never came close to matching the enthusiasm for railroading that northerners exhibited.

A lack of capital was one factor limiting southern railroad construction. Building a railroad was a very expensive enterprise. The Erie Railroad cost an estimated $25 million and its companion, the New York Central, required $30 million to complete. Even constructing the shorter Baltimore and Ohio Railroad ran up a $15 million bill. Clearly, financing such projects was well beyond the means of any individual or group of partners. To raise funds, railroad companies sold stock and issued bonds. By 1860 the U.S. railroad network had absorbed some $1.5 billion, a figure that dwarfed any other industrial investment.

Raising such huge sums required a whole new set of financial mechanisms. Exchanges in several cities sprang up to deal in railroad stocks and bonds. Indeed some banks were founded primarily for the purpose of amassing sufficient funds to build or invest in railroads. Thousands of Americans participated in this exciting business. The Pennsylvania Railroad, for example, had over 2,600 individual stockholders in the early 1850s, and other roads had proportionate numbers of investors. Enterprising brokers peddled American stocks and bonds abroad so successfully that foreigner's owned one-quarter of all U.S. railroad bonds in the 1850s.

The federal government played a limited role in promoting the railroad business in this period. It approved a couple of land grants, the most important of which went to the Illinois Central Railroad in 1850. Other federal policies had less direct but quite important impacts. The government maintained remarkably low prices for publicly owned lands, often a dollar or less for an acre. Moreover, Congress set low tariff rates on imported rails prior to the Civil War. Both of these policies reduced railroad construction costs.

By contrast, local and state governments considered rail service so important that they contributed generously. By 1860 state governments had borrowed some $90 million for the express purpose of promoting railroad construction. They also granted generous charters that gave companies eminent domain rights to their routes, provided land grants, allowed banking privileges, and added other inducements.

A few states went all the way and actually built railroads themselves. Massachusetts, Georgia, and Virginia were early entrants in this field; Michigan, Indiana, and Illinois joined later. In almost every case, however, the states quickly divested themselves of the responsibility for operating the railroads by turning them over to private companies. That was, in fact, the crux of the problem: simply laying tracks was not enough; ongoing operations required constant attention.

To that extent, railroads differed significantly from canals. There, continual maintenance might be necessary, but the boats and commerce on the canal remained strictly independent operations. Some railroad companies initially expected railroads to function the same way, particularly when teams of horses provided the pulling power. But the introduction of powerful steam locomotives capable of hauling both freight cars or passenger carriages ruled out private traffic on the rails.

Many railroad entrepreneurs recognized the dual nature of their enterprises by establishing separate construction and operating companies. Once the tracks had been laid, the construction company's work was done. The operating company took over, buying locomotives and rolling stock, building stations, establishing freight depots, and setting traffic schedules. The company collected fares and freight charges to pay for its operations and to generate profits for its stockholders.

The larger the system, the more complex the organization had to be. Large railroads like the Pennsylvania created regional divisions, each with its own superintendent to handle traffic and operations on a local basis. The introduction of telegraphic communication in the 1850s greatly improved the quality and predictability of rail service, allowing agents and managers up and down the line to coordinate their activities.

Operating the nation's first truly big businesses, railroad companies had to develop novel management and organizational structures. David McCallum, for example, designed a detailed and comprehensive management scheme for the Erie Railroad that served as a model for many other operating companies. Railroads were also major employers, hiring skilled workers like engineers and telegraph operators, as well as laborers to maintain and repair tracks. As a result, railroads had to develop methods for handling their human resources as well as their tracks and rolling stock.

Railroads enjoyed great popularity in this period. They were seen as providing essential services and spurring economic development. To a degree, then, they were functioning as the leading sector in the industrial revolution that continued to evolve in the nineteenth century. They provided an alternative opportunity for investment and were capable of generating substantial profits for their shareholders. They created a sustained demand for rails, machinery, and fuel (both wood and coal) that stimulated growth in secondary industries. Finally, and perhaps most important, they were creating a truly national market for products of all types.

Unfortunately, the optimism that accompanied the railroad boom in the 1850s generated a false sense of security. Internal stresses and international crises like the Crimean War put strains on the American economy. The flurry of rapid railroad expansion further stretched the nation's ability to provide needed capital. By 1857 railroad stock prices had dropped over 40 percent from their 1853 high point. Overenthusiasm for railroading thus became a leading cause for the financial Panic of 1857, which forced several roads into bankruptcy. The Civil War broke out before the effects of this economic crisis had receded.

Irreversible progress had been made, however, in establishing a nationwide rail network. It provided cheap and widely available opportunities for passenger travel and freight movement. Once the disruptions of the war ended, the boom in railroad building reappeared, and it played a dominant role in the nation's achievement of a mature industrial economy by 1900.

See also Canal Era; Corning, Erastus; Land Grant Railroads; Vanderbilt, Cornelius.

References and Further Reading

Cochran, Thomas C., and William Miller. *The Age of Enterprise.* New York: Harper, 1961.

Stover, John F. *American Railroads.* Chicago: University of Chicago Press, 1997.

Taylor, George Rogers. *The Transportation Revolution: 1815–1860.* New York: Rinehart, 1957.

Ward, James Arthur. *Railroads and the Character of America, 1820–1887.* Knoxville, TN: University of Tennessee Press, 1986.

Soft Money

Soft money was a term used to distinguish paper currency from *hard money* in the form of gold and silver. The nineteenth century saw the production and abandonment of many forms of soft money including federal issues like the Revolutionary War's Continental bills, state bonds and notes, and private banknotes. While hard money advocates insisted that specie alone represented the only reliable basis for a monetary system, soft money remained popular with debtors, farmers, and others interested in increasing the money supply.

Government agencies resorted to issuing paper currency for a variety of quite logical reasons. The Continental Congress issued millions of dollars worth of Continental bills to pay its obligations. State governments simultaneously issued their own notes for similar purposes, creating a huge supply of soft money. In the 1790s Treasury Secretary Alexander Hamilton developed a plan whereby the federal government would assume the state obligations and then erect a mechanism for funding both this and the federal debt. He used the Bank of the United States effectively to stabilize the value of these combined debts. While his policies made good sense from a central financial perspective, they in no way satisfied the advocates of soft money.

Among the motivations for increasing the amount of soft money in circulation, three stand out. First, debtors tended to favor an expansion of the money supply in general, hoping it would deflate the cost of a dollar. Debtors could then repay their loans with "cheaper" money. To discourage this sort of behavior, some lenders wrote gold clauses into their loan contracts, forcing borrowers to repay with specie rather than devalued paper currency.

A good many farmers borrowed heavily not only to clear land and establish farmsteads but also to finance annual operating costs. They, in turn, hoped to sell their produce at high prices. If the money supply increased and brought more dollars into circulation, prices would tend to inflate and give the farmer a higher dollar yield for his efforts. For this reason, people in agrarian districts tended to favor soft money throughout the nineteenth century.

A third bloc that favored soft money were those who invested in or formed banks. The absence of a strong federal currency system encouraged a proliferation of state chartered and private banks all over the country. These institutions typically issued bank notes in large numbers and bankers objected to any restrictions on their ability to do so. This diversified banking community was rife with dishonest or overly optimistic operators, leading to a general suspicion of all banks and their banknotes. Hard money advocates could easily cite numerous instances of insolvency and chicanery as arguments against the use or expansion of soft money.

In the early nineteenth century, the Bank of the United States (B.U.S.), and its successor, the Second B.U.S. did creditable service as redemption centers for the nation's many banknotes. But President Andrew Jackson hated all banks and distrusted banknotes so intensely that he killed the B.U.S. and then promulgated the Specie Circular to put federal land sales on a more secure basis. From the late 1830s until the Civil War, a constant strain prevailed between hard and soft money advocates. This was all the more acute because the federal government generally stayed on the sidelines, handling its financial dealings through subtreasuries that operated more like strongboxes than like banks.

Civil War military expenses rose far higher than the government's ability to meet them through its normal revenue sources. The Confederacy cranked out a blizzard of paper money, all of which became completely worthless when Lee surrendered to Grant in 1865. The Union government, too, issued soft money in the form of greenbacks and national banknotes. In this case, however, the stimulus of the war that persisted into the postwar period substantially increased the size of the national economy, allowing the federal government eventually to make good on its obligations.

Many Americans, however, felt that the nation's money supply was not growing fast enough to match the needs of its expanding economy. Calls for soft money grew even more insistent after the Panic of 1873 and the so-called Crime of '73 in which the federal government effectively demonetized silver. The Greenback Party became powerful enough in rural areas to force the ruling Republican Party to modify its plans for strengthening the nation's adherence to the international gold standard.

The Resumption Act, passed in 1875, stabilized the value of the greenbacks sufficiently to lessen their appeal to the soft money faction. Still convinced that the money supply needed to grow, the impetus from the debtor and agrarian groups switched to support for the free and unlimited coinage of silver. Although technically hard money, silver's value compared to gold remained deflated in the 1880s and 1890s. Coining more silver would have an inflationary effect on the money supply similar to issuing more greenbacks. The Republican Party's decisive victory in the elections of 1896 ensured that the nation would adhere to a gold standard.

The generally prosperous times that prevailed in the first three decades after the passage of the Gold Standard Act of 1900 muted agitation for soft money. It rose again, however, when the Great Depression drove prices down to unprecedented low levels. President Franklin Roosevelt chose to pursue other financial strategies to deal with the crisis, including abandoning the gold standard. By that point, the Federal Reserve System had assumed responsibility for balancing the money supply to the economy's needs, and simplistic support for soft money lost its appeal.

See also Banknotes; Bank War; Free Silver; Greenbacks; Specie Circular.

References and Further Reading

Dewey, Davis Rich. *Financial History of the United States.* New York: Longmans, Green, 1918.

Friedman, Milton. *Money Mischief: Episodes in Monetary History.* New York: Harcourt Brace Jovanovich, 1992.

Nugent, Walter T. K. *Money and American Society, 1865–1880.* New York: Free Press, 1968.

Ritter, Gretchen. *Goldbugs and Greenbacks.* New York: Cambridge University Press, 1997.

Specie Circular

President Andrew Jackson issued an executive order in July 1836 stipulating that all large-scale purchases of public land must be made in specie. He intended this insistence

President Andrew Jackson's imposition of the specie circular in 1837 provoked considerable negative publicity like this political cartoon. (Library of Congress)

on the use of either gold or silver rather than paper currency to subdue the boom in land sales that a free flow of unregulated banknotes appeared to have stimulated. The Specie Circular was highly unpopular in many quarters, and it is often cited as a cause for the Panic of 1837.

The Specie Circular was an unexpected but logical final act in the Jackson Administration's attempt to reshape the U.S. financial system. During Jackson's assault on the Second Bank of the United States, many Americans believed his primary objection was to what he considered high-handed behavior on the part of the bank's president, Nicholas Biddle. Under Biddle's control, the bank maintained a substantial circulation of banknotes that could always be redeemed in specie. Moreover, the bank and its branches collected and presented for redemption the notes of unregulated private banks, forcing them to maintain reasonable reserves of specie as well.

Many of the bank's critics were soft money men who wanted private banks to issue even more notes, inflating the nation's money supply, and making credit easier to obtain. The president seemed sympathetic to this approach when he ordered surplus federal funds to be deposited in what came to be called *pet banks,* private institutions that Jackson and his advisors selected. Fortified with these federal funds, the pet banks increased their banknote circulation substantially. Meanwhile, other private banks did the same, no longer having to be concerned over the B.U.S.'s rigorous redemption policies.

This extra supply of money stimulated a boom in the sale of western lands. Legislation passed in 1832 stipulated a fixed price of $1.25 per acre for unsold federal land. This bargain price attracted individuals and groups of speculators who purchased large tracts of land, often using easily obtainable banknotes or loans. The speculators assumed they could resell the land at much higher prices once settlers began farming operations. The land boom was dramatic. Whereas federal land sales had brought in a little over $4 million in 1833, government receipts jumped to almost $25 million three years later in 1836.

Jackson considered this boom unhealthy, and he attributed it to the fact that paper currency was too easily available. Moreover, he had long nursed resentment against all banks, fortified by a belief that hard money was vastly preferable to soft money. On July 11, 1836, he issued an executive order that future land payments had to be made in gold or silver. While there were some exceptions like the one for an individual buying fewer than 320 acres, the Specie Circular had the desired effect. Revenue from federal land sales averaged only $5 million in each of the next four years.

Unfortunately, this was not the only economic consequence of the Panic of 1837 that followed hard on the heels of the Specie Circular. Hundreds of private banks closed their doors, unemployment soared in urban areas, and prices for both industrial and agricultural products fell. Equally disturbing, American bankers suspended specie payments to those attempting to redeem their banknotes. The value of their notes fell as much as 10 percent in a matter of months, putting further deflationary pressure on prices.

Although many of Jackson's contemporaries blamed the Specie Circular for wreaking this economic havoc, historical analysts have concluded that other factors were much more responsible for plunging the nation into hard times in the late 1830s. Poor crops in the United States, overextended British merchants who reduced their purchases of American cotton, and sloppy or even criminal conduct of private bankers were just some of the causes of the collapse. Even so, the Specie Circular is remembered as one of the most controversial federal financial policies instituted in the nineteenth century.

See also Bank War; Soft Money.

References and Further Reading

Schlesinger, Jr., Arthur M. *The Age of Jackson.* Boston: Little, Brown, 1945.

Temin, Peter. *The Jacksonian Economy.* New York: Norton, 1969.

Stamp Act

In 1765 Parliament passed the Stamp Act, extending a common form of British taxation to America. There it provoked protest and riots throughout the colonies. The issue of taxation without representation led to a successful call for a Stamp Act Congress, the first major cooperative effort in the colonies. The royal government quickly rescinded the measure and replaced it with a series of less controversial import duties.

The French and Indian War and a subsequent decision to maintain a substantial military presence in British North America levied high costs on the British government. Prime Minister George Grenville's government attempted to address the issue with a series of trade regulations and import duties, promulgated in the 1764 Sugar Act. Even before the full extent of that law's unpopularity had become apparent, Parliament approved another set of measures that included the 1765 Stamp Act.

Stamp taxes had been collected throughout the British Isles for over a century, so it seemed reasonable to extend the practice to the American colonies. Moreover, the total revenue anticipated was a mere £60,000 per year from a population of 1.2 million people. This amounted to a charge of one shilling per person per year, or approximately one-third of a day's pay for a common workman. So modest a levy hardly seemed likely to provoke calls for revolution.

By 1765, however, many American colonists were well beyond rational economic

The TIMES are Dreadful, Dismal Doleful Dolorous, and DOLLAR-LESS.

An Emblem of the Effects of the STAMP
O! the fatal Stamp

Thursday, October 31, 1765. THE NUMB 1195.

PENNSYLVANIA JOURNAL;
AND
WEEKLY ADVERTISER.

EXPIRING: In Hopes of a Resurrection to LIFE again.

I AM sorry to be obliged to acquaint my Readers, that as The STAMP-ACT, is fear'd to be obligatory upon us after the *First of November* ensuing, (the *fatal To morrow*) the Publisher of this Paper unable to bear the Burthen, has thought it expedient TO STOP awhile, in order to deliberate, whether any Methods can be found to elude the Chains forged for us, and escape the insupportable Slavery, which it is hoped, from the last Representations now made against that Act, may be effected. Mean while, I must earnestly Request every Individual of my Subscribers many of whom have been long behind Hand, that they would immediately Discharge their respective Arrears that I may be able, not only to support myself during the Interval, but be better prepared to proceed again with this Paper, whenever an opening for that Purpose appears, which I hope will be soon. WILLIAM BRADFORD

This colonial newspaper warns that it may have to cease publication if the hated stamp tax is enforced. (Library of Congress)

behavior. First of all, the taxation process itself was highly intrusive. A stamp distributor was designated in each of the colonies, and he was responsible for ensuring that all public documents were stamped. Newspaper pages had to have a half-penny stamp affixed or impressed; an attorney's license required a £10 tax payment. Wedding licenses, death certificates, shipping documents, even playing cards had to carry valid stamps of various denominations. Virtually no one in the colonies could escape confronting a tax levy that reached down to some of the most mundane transactions of everyday life.

Opponents of the Stamp Act therefore had no trouble drawing a crowd. The most prominent agitator was Samuel Adams, a founding member of the Sons of Liberty. This group began as a relatively small radical faction in Boston but, by the end of the year, almost every colony had its own active group or groups of Sons of Liberty. Mobs hung effigies of tax distributors, attacked and burned their offices and houses, and, on some occasions, even threatened to injure or kill those officials whom they captured. In short order the prominent citizens who had volunteered or been appointed to be stamp distributors resigned from their positions. When the law officially went into force on November 1, 1765, no one was left to distribute the stamps.

Meanwhile legislative meetings and committees of correspondence circulated a call for a colony-wide protest meeting. The Stamp Act Congress met in New York in early October and eventually sent separate protest declarations to the House of Commons, the House of Lords, and King George himself. All asserted that the British government had no right to tax the American colonists directly because they had no representatives in Parliament. Taxation without representation had been a rallying cry against the 1764 Sugar Act, and it found much broader support in the protest against the stamp tax.

Not surprisingly, the king, his ministers, and the legislators disagreed. Meeting early in 1766, Parliament drafted what became known as the Declaratory Act. It specifically rejected the Americans' claims and reconfirmed Parliament's right to tax citizens anywhere within the British Empire.

Simultaneously, the government made a major, fateful concession by rescinding the Stamp Act. Far more persuasive and crucial to the Empire's prosperity was a rising tide of complaint from English merchants, manufacturers, and traders whose commerce with the colonies had declined sharply even before the Stamp Act Congress met. After November 1, no ship could legally enter or leave an American port without stamped documents; yet no one was available to supply the required stamps. The already weak English and American economies seemed fated to plunge further into depression as long as this stand-off persisted.

Once it had cancelled the stamp tax in America, the British government sought a less controversial way to confirm its right to tax and to generate much needed revenue from the colonies. Chancellor of the Exchequer Robert Townshend proposed a series of import duties, external taxes that would not be so blatantly obvious to all Americans. Although many Americans tried to evade the Townshend acts through a policy of nonimportation, the question of taxation with or without representation receded from prominence until the passage of the Tea Act revived it again in 1773.

See also Monopoly; Nonimportation; Sugar Act.

References and Further Reading

Bullion, John L. *A Great and Necessary Measure: George Grenville and the Genesis of the Stamp Act.* Columbia, MO: University of Missouri Press, 1982.

Morgan, Edmund S., and Helen M. Morgan. *The Stamp Act Crisis.* Chapel Hill, NC: University of North Carolina Press, 1953.

Thomas, P. D. G. *British Politics and the Stamp Act Crisis.* Oxford: Clarendon Press, 1987.

Steamboats

Although early experiments had occurred prior to the War of 1812, steam-powered navigation really began blossoming in the 1820s and 1830s. Steamboating flourished in bays, estuaries, lakes, and rivers through the mid-nineteenth century. The switch from sail to steam on ocean routes was delayed until the 1850s. At about the same time, railroad competition began to reduce the importance of inland steamboats. They had, however, proved vital to the settlement and economic development of the nation during their heyday, and they pioneered a number of key business developments.

While Robert Fulton is generally credited with inventing the steamboat, his 1807 experiment with the *Clermont* was mainly important as a publicity event. John Fitch had built several different steam-powered vessels in the 1780s, including both paddle wheel and mechanical oar mechanisms. John Stevens had successfully experimented with screw-propulsion prior to the Fulton paddle wheeler's famous round trip voyage between New York and Albany.

Equally important in establishing Fulton's prominence was the exclusive license he and his partner, Robert Livingston, obtained from the State of New York. This allowed the Fulton-Livingston partnership to dominate steam navigation in the most important harbor and river system for some time. They also encouraged Nicholas Roosevelt to construct a steamboat in Pittsburgh, which made the first long-distance river voyage to New Orleans in 1811–1812.

Like Eli Whitney's cotton gin, the concept of placing a steam engine on a boat was so simple and attractive that hundreds of competitors quickly developed their own versions. Some operated in other states to avoid the New York license, but others like Cornelius Vanderbilt chose to confront the monopolists head on. Fulton and Livingston squandered much of their profits on legal maneuvers. This wrangling finally reached the Supreme Court in the case of *Gibbons v. Ogden* in 1824. Chief Justice John Marshall's opinion reasserted the federal government's right to regulate interstate commerce, forcing New York and other states to revoke their exclusive licenses and monopoly legislation.

Steamboat ownership was a classic example of the free enterprise system. Individuals or partnerships built almost all of the boats. Private investment and entrepreneurship were the keys to the proliferation of these vessels along the East Coast, in the Great Lakes, and along the Mississippi River system. Building a boat in the 1830s or 1840s required only about $20,000 in capital, an investment well within the reach of individuals or small groups of individuals. The waterways were freely available to all comers. Profits tended to be high, so literally hundreds of people and groups entered the business.

Along the East Coast, a substantial intercity traffic developed. Boats employed in this trade resembled sailing ships with narrow hulls and sharp prows. Side-wheelers predominated, giving the boats remarkable maneuverability. Low-pressure, wood-fired boilers were the norm, and the walking beam mechanism typically transmitted power from the engines to the wheels. Because sailing ships could service many Atlantic ports, eastern steamboats tended to emphasize higher-value passengers as opposed to freight. That focus, in turn, led proprietors to provide increasingly luxurious accommodations and fixtures.

Boats operating on the inland waterways tended to be more utilitarian. They were necessarily more broad-beamed and shallow-drafted than their oceangoing counterparts. The most common cause of accidents were river snags—uprooted trees that became lodged in a riverbed—so the delicate paddle-wheels were placed on the sterns of the vessels rather than the sides to prevent damage to the paddles. Because they were far less likely to encounter waves and wind, these river boats could carry tall, lightweight superstructures, often reaching three or four floors in height.

Steam power turned rivers into two-way transportation systems. Even so, the flatboat and keelboat traffic along the Ohio and Mississippi route continued to increase substantially in the 1830s and 1840s. Bulk produce from western farms could be cheaply transported down river on vessels propelled by the current. Steamboats were reserved for higher-value perishable goods and for people. Most important, they provided upstream transportation for manufactured goods and scarce commodities as well as for farmers who had ridden with their produce when it had floated downstream.

A few proprietors attempted to run a packet service with fixed sailing schedules, but the vagaries of the water and the weather undermined those plans. In the winter, ice was a constant threat, closing some channels completely for several months and creating floating hazards even after the thaw had begun. In the summer, low water might develop at any moment and then persist for weeks or even months. Most steamboats therefore functioned essentially as tramps, calling at ports on an unpredictable basis whenever they could or if their captains learned of cargo that needed movement. Here again, the variability of schedules encouraged individual initiative.

Steamboating could be dangerous. The river boats quickly adopted high-pressure steam engines both for greater power but also because they could function with muddy water drawn from the river. This increased the chance of an explosion—especially when rival boats challenged each other in races. Snags, ice, bars, underwater ledges, and floating wreckage could damage or even sink a steamboat. One estimate is that the average life span of a nineteenth century river boat was no more than five years. That caused constant uncertainty among owners, with huge, unexpected losses always a possibility.

The dangers from both human and natural conditions put pressure on governmental authorities. States and municipalities set aside large sums of money for snag removal, dredging shallows, and other improvements that barely kept ahead of natural deterioration. Several states also attempted to legislate the human element with little success. The number of fatal accidents, many of them the result of racing, eventually led Congress to draft the first federal regulations for any industry. A weak regulatory act appeared in 1838, foreshadowing the passage of the 1852 Steamboat Act that set out effective rules and regulations along with some enforcement measures including hiring federal inspectors.

See also Canal Era; Evans, Oliver; Fulton, Robert; Packet Ships.

References and Further Reading

Burlingame, Roger. *March of the Iron Men.* New York: Scribner's, 1938.

Taylor, George Rogers. *The Transportation Revolution, 1815–1860.* New York: Holt, Rinehart and Winston, 1951.

Sugar Act

In 1764 Parliament approved a multipart revenue act. It quickly became known as the Sugar Act because it simultaneously raised import taxes on foreign sugar imports and reduced the duty on imported molasses. This legislation provoked widespread objections to taxation without representation that grew more strident when the Stamp Act was approved in the following year.

George Grenville inherited a serious financial crisis when he became prime minister in 1763. Due in part to its involvement in the French and Indian War or Seven Years War (1756–1763) Great Britain doubled its national debt to almost £130 million. To prevent further foreign inroads and to protect its North American holdings, the royal government maintained some 10,000 troops in America at an annual cost of £350,000. The new prime minister felt he had to explore alternatives for generating revenue from the colonies that had contributed so much to this financial crisis.

One possibility was to modify the 1733 Molasses Act. It had imposed a six pence a gallon duty on molasses imported to the North American colonies from French, Dutch, Spanish, or other sources. Over the next three decades, the act only generated about £20,000 because the duty was so high and the enforcement apparatus so weak. These factors encouraged rampant smuggling that had made some American merchants like John Hancock extremely wealthy.

The Sugar Act of 1764 addressed both of these flaws. First it cut the duty in half to three pence per gallon, a level that would match or even undercut the costs smugglers ran up when they brought in foreign products. The legislation also outlined a much more ambitious customs collection process that would significantly increase the number of British government agents in America and transfer jurisdiction for violators to a vice-admiralty court in Halifax, Nova Scotia. While smugglers were upset at the economic blow this policy dealt their affairs, the Sugar Act also generated widespread popular objection to what they saw as an enhancement of external (Canadian) authority over the colonists.

The most important issue, however, was the Sugar Act's explicit statement that its purpose was to raise revenue in the American colonies. Up to that point, colonists had been relatively tolerant of legislation they could view as having as a primary purpose trade regulation within the empire. But they objected strenuously to being taxed specifically to raise revenue for the British government. Throughout the colonies, speeches, meetings, and letters protested this development that appeared inconsistent with the long-standing English tradition that the people themselves had to agree to any imposition of taxes. The colonists had no representatives in Parliament, they argued, so they should not suffer from taxation without representation.

Agitation over the Sugar Act set the stage for even greater protests in the following year when Parliament introduced a stamp tax on all colonists. The sugar and molasses duties were modified over the next several years, but they remained a sore point with many Americans. This residual sensitivity contributed substantially to later agitation over the Tea Act and other Parliamentary actions, agitation that ultimately resulted in the signing of the Declaration of Independence.

See also Molasses Act; Navigation Acts; Stamp Act.

References and Further Reading

Jensen, Merrill. *The Founding of a Nation.* New York: Oxford University Press, 1968.

Tyler, John W. *Smugglers and Patriots.* Boston: Northeastern University Press, 1968.

Ward, Henry M. *The American Revolution.* New York : St. Martin's Press, 1995.

BIOGRAPHIES

Adams, Samuel (1722–1803)

Although he was born into a prominent Boston family, earned both a bachelor's and a master's degree at Harvard College, and received a substantial inheritance, Samuel Adams spent most of his life near or in poverty. He was a terrible businessman, losing money through bad loans or mismanagement. But he did have extraordinary skill at explaining political issues and stimulating others to take radical action. He found his voice in 1764 protesting the Sugar Act; he found a following in 1765 when he successfully advocated nonimportation in response to the Stamp Act. He relished engaging in political controversy and was one of the chief proponents of the Boston Tea Party in 1773. Before the Revolution he served in various government posts, always pursuing the goal of defending Americans' rights up to and including sponsoring independence from Great Britain. He continued in public life as a member of the Continental Congress, the U.S. Congress, and, late in life, as governor of Massachusetts, but his influence never again reached the pinnacle he had achieved as a radical in the 1760s and 1770s.

See also Stamp Act; Sugar Act.

References and Further Reading

Fowler, William M. *Samuel Adams.* New York: Longman, 1997.

Astor, John Jacob (1763–1848)

Born into a poor family in Germany, John Jacob Astor moved to London as a teenager to work in his brother's music company. After four years in the business, he headed to New York with $25 and seven flutes. He continued to buy and sell musical instruments for many years, long after he had become a prominent fur trader. Astor personally toured upper New York State, Ohio, and even Canada, leaving his wife, Sara, to run his affairs in New York City. In 1794 Jay's Treaty cancelled all British claims to the Northwest Territory, and Astor quickly exploited this development to become the leading fur trader in the United States. In 1800 he sent a shipload of furs to China and made a huge profit. That success encouraged him to establish Astoria, a fur-trading post located in the Oregon Territory in 1811. It was difficult to manage, especially during the War of 1812, but after the hostilities ended, Astor extended his activities throughout the far west. By 1820 his American Fur Company controlled virtually all of the trade in the United States and it was the nation's largest company of any kind when he sold it in 1834. Meanwhile he had been amassing valuable real estate parcels on Manhattan Island. The $20 million he left his heirs when he died at the age of eighty-five was the largest personal fortune in the history of the United States up to that time.

References and Further Reading

Madsen, Axel. *John Jacob Astor: America's First Multimillionaire.* New York: Wiley, 2001.

Belmont, August (1816–1890)

Although his family was well-off, German-born August Belmont chose to go to work in his early teens at the Frankfurt branch of the House of Rothschild. Over the years this prestigious firm had provided substantial financing for various enterprises including major European governments. The firm recognized August Belmont's energy and acumen by sending him to work at its branch in Naples when he was only seventeen. He prospered there and was dispatched to Cuba in 1837, but he left his ship when it stopped in New York City. He found the metropolis reeling in the aftermath of the Panic of 1837, a crisis that had brought down the local Rothschild branch as well. Without prior authorization, Belmont began buying and selling securities, using the Rothschild name as collateral. He was so successful that the European firm hired him at a handsome salary to handle its American interests, and Belmont used his connections to build a sizable personal fortune. As an established and wealthy private banker, Belmont became a naturalized U.S. citizen in 1844 and a preeminent supporter of Democratic politicians. The party rewarded him with an appointment as American minister to the Netherlands, and Belmont played a major role in maintaining good relations between Europeans and the Union cause during the Civil War. He retired from politics in 1872, but devoted his attention to other interests like horse racing, where his name lives on in the Belmont Stakes.

References and Further Reading

Katz, Irving. *August Belmont.* New York: Columbia University Press, 1968.

Biddle, Nicholas (1786–1844)

Member of a prominent Philadelphia family, Nicholas Biddle became president of the Second Bank of the United States in 1823. An able, articulate, and energetic financier, he turned the bank into a model central banking institution. A private organization with some public stockholders and directors, the bank handled all federal financial affairs. It established branches throughout the nation and issued its own banknotes as well as serving as a clearing house for the banknotes that other private banks issued. President Andrew Jackson and Biddle became engaged in a bank war in the early 1830s. Jackson vetoed the bill to recharter the bank, forcing Biddle into a financially untenable position. The bank closed in 1837 even though Biddle had tried to keep it operating under a state charter from Pennsylvania.

See also Bank War; Jackson, Andrew.

References and Further Reading

Govan, Thomas P. *Nicholas Biddle.* Chicago: University of Chicago Press, 1959.

Borden, Gail (1801–1874)

Gail Borden was in his mid-fifties when he obtained a patent for a milk-condensing process, and it proved to be the most profitable enterprise in his busy life. Born in Norwich, New York, he traveled extensively as a child and teenager, training as a surveyor in Indiana. He pursued his trade in Mississippi before heading west to Texas in 1829. His interests there included ranching, surveying, newspaper publishing, and politics. He served as customs collector for the port of Galveston for a time, but left Texas for good in 1851. He settled in New York City to pursue experimentation in food preservation, producing a "meat biscuit" that had a very long shelf life. While trying to develop a market for this unappetizing product, he obtained a patent for condensing milk with a vacuum process. By the late 1850s, he and a partner had formed the New York Condensed Milk Co., and it thrived as a supplier to Union soldiers in the Civil War. Renamed the Borden Condensed Milk Co., it grew into a major food processing enterprise after the war ended.

References and Further Reading

Wharton, Clarence R. *Gail Borden, Pioneer.* San Antonio, TX: Naylor, 1941.

Clay, Henry (1777–1852)

A Virginia native who established a law practice in Kentucky as a young man, Henry Clay was an accomplished orator and politician. As a U.S. congressman he was one of the war hawks who advocated war against Great Britain in 1812. He furthered his national reputation by superintending the passage of the Missouri Compromise of 1820. He repeatedly ran for the presidency touting the American System plan he had first developed in 1824. Many of the policies Clay advocated were later adopted by the Republican Party. He served as secretary of state and in the U.S. Senate where, in 1850, he once again was instrumental in the passage of another compromise that forestalled a North-South conflict over the extension of slavery.

See also American System; Bank War.

References and Further Reading

Baxter, Maurice G. *Henry Clay and the American System.* Lexington, KY: University of Kentucky Press, 1995.

Colt, Samuel (1814–1862)

A Yankee tinkerer, Samuel Colt was born in Hartford, Connecticut, where his childhood work in his father's textile mill encouraged his interest in machinery. At the age of fifteen he went to sea on a ship bound for India. During his travels, he is reputed to have whittled a wooden model of a pistol with a revolving cylinder to hold cartridges. He patented his design first in England and then in the United States in the mid-1830s. His efforts to capitalize on his invention failed until he won an army contract for his revolvers in 1847. Like Eli Whitney before him, to fill this large order, Colt fashioned equipment to make precise interchangeable parts. In 1855 he opened the largest private arms factory in the world in Hartford and perfected his mass-production methods. His wife carried on the business after his death, and the Colt model nicknamed The Peacemaker truly became legendary in the frontier West.

See also Remington, Philo; Winchester, Oliver Fisher.

References and Further Reading

Hosley, William. *Colt: The Making of an American Legend.* Amherst, MA: University of Massachusetts Press, 1996.

Corning, Erastus (1794–1872)

Although his name is most frequently associated with glass manufacturing, Erastus Corning engaged in an extraordinarily diverse set of enterprises. Born in Connecticut, Corning moved with his family to the Albany, New York, area in 1805. There he clerked for a local mercantile company, became a partner, and ended up owning the company in 1824. A couple of years later he purchased the Albany Iron Works, which, by the late 1830s, was well-positioned to profit from the railroad building boom. Corning contributed to this boom by buying shares in new railroads and purchasing acreage in Michigan and elsewhere to sell to railroad companies or to the settlers they served. In the mid-1830s, he founded the town of Corning to house his glassworks. When a string of shorter lines managed to provide rail service between Albany and Buffalo, Corning and his associates decided to consolidate them into a system. That required action by the New York State Legislature where Corning had extensive political influence because of his association with Martin Van Buren's Regency group. In 1853 legislation approving the merger passed, and Erastus Corning became the first president of the New York Central Railroad. Corning's ironworks profited by selling rails and equipment to the New York Central as it upgraded and expanded its service. The Albany Ironworks went on to become a major supplier of war material in the Civil War, and Corning himself served a couple of terms in the U.S. House of Representatives before and during the conflict. In the late 1860s, he was directly involved in the management of a dozen railroads as well as the New York Central.

See also Railroads.

References and Further Reading

Neu, Irene D. *Erastus Corning*. Ithaca, NY: Cornell University Press, 1960.

Deere, John (1804–1886)

John Deere was born and raised in Vermont, where he spent four years apprenticed to a blacksmith. Driven west by the persistent agricultural depression in rural Vermont, Deere established a forge in New Detour, Illinois, in 1836. Within a year, he had developed the world's first self-scouring steel plow out of a broken steel saw blade. This innovation enabled farmers to cultivate the thick, rich prairie soil throughout the upper Midwest, and Deere easily found buyers for every plow he could produce. He was somewhat limited because his innovation required rolled steel imported from England. In 1846 a Pittsburgh mill finally became advanced enough to supply his needs. Two years later Deere established a factory in Moline capable of mass producing his popular product. Always a step ahead of his competition, Deere continually improved his designs, waiting until 1864 to obtain his first patent. In 1858 John Deere turned business control over to his son, Charles Deere, who developed a dealer network and expanded the product line for his father's company. John Deere continued tinkering and engaged in philanthropy and local politics until his death.

See also McCormick, Cyrus Hall.

References and Further Reading

Clark, Neil McCullough. *John Deere: He Gave to the World the Steel Plow.* Moline, IL: Desaulniers and Co., 1937.

du Pont de Nemours, Éleuthère Irénée (1771–1834)

As one might expect, Éleuthère Irénée (E. I.) du Pont de Nemours was a member of an aristocratic French family. Even as a child, Irénée was fascinated by gunpowder, and he served something of an apprenticeship with world famous chemist Antoine-Laurent Lavoisier. Irénée devoted much of his early business attention to publishing, a profession that became increasingly dangerous as France passed through a series of revolutionary phases. By 1800 most of the extended Du Pont family had relocated to the United States intending to pursue a variety of business ventures. Irénée found his calling when he discovered that American gunpowder was quite inferior to the European product he was fully capable of producing. He rounded up financing from family and other investors to build what came to be called the Eleutherian Mills south of Wilmington, Delaware. Du Pont gunpowder was crucial to the American economy during the years of the Embargo of 1807 and even more essential during the subsequent War of 1812. The Hagley Mills were added to the complex during that conflict, and the E. I. du Pont de Nemours and Company remained the nation's leading producer of gunpowder throughout the nineteenth century. Diversification into dyes and chemical products eventually made the enterprise Irénée had founded into one of the world's leading chemical companies.

References and Further Reading

Dorian, Max. *The du Ponts: From Gunpowder to Nylon*. Boston: Little, Brown, 1962.

Duer, William (1747–1799)

William Duer was the son of a successful West Indian planter who sent young William to Eton College in England. Later he served with General Clive in India and returned to help manage his father's sugar plantations before moving to the colony of New York in 1768. Exploiting a Royal Navy contract to supply masts, Duer bought stands of timber and other land in upstate New York and became a prominent member of the community. This led to a political career that included membership in the Continental Congress and many other posts, culminating in his appointment as assistant secretary of the Treasury under Alexander Hamilton. Along the way, Duer's currency and land speculation had made him extremely wealthy. Unlike Hamilton, Duer had no compunction about acting on insider information. He resigned from his federal post in 1791 and joined forces with Alexander Macomb. They hatched a complex plot to buy and sell stock in the Bank of New York, profiting from rumors it would be taken over by the Bank of the United States. The collapse of their scheme helped trigger the Panic of 1792 and encouraged the development of an open and more respectable stock exchange along Wall Street. Once one of the richest men in American, Duer died penniless in prison.

See also New York Stock and Exchange Board.

References and Further Reading

Davis, Joseph Stancliffe. *Essays in the Earlier History of American Corporations.* Cambridge, MA: Harvard University Press, 1917.

Evans, Oliver (1755–1819)

Delaware-born Oliver Evans was an inveterate tinkerer. At the age of twenty-two he built an efficient machine to install pins into wool carding blocks. In 1787 he patented a plan for a fully automated mill. It relied on gravity to pull grain down through a complex water-powered apparatus and deliver refined flour on the ground floor. His most noteworthy project was a steam-powered amphibious dredge he completed in Philadelphia 1805. The Evans dredge had a novel high-pressure steam engine whose water pipes ran right through the fire box. This technological innovation eventually became common in locomotives and other steam engines. Some consider his contraption to be the first American steamboat since it appeared two years before Robert Fulton's *Clermont.* Like other American inventors, Evans spent a lot of time and money defending his intellectual property rights.

See also Integrated Mill; Steamboats.

References and Further Reading

Evans, Harold. *They Made America.* New York: Little, Brown, 2004

Fulton, Robert (1765–1815)

Pennsylvania-born Robert Fulton dabbled in many fields. He was a successful artist who studied with Benjamin West in England. While there he also became interested in mechanical engineering and canal navigation. He obtained English patents for a variety of concepts including a marble-cutting machine, a dredge, an inclined-plane system for canal boats, a flax-spinning machine, and several kinds of boats. He built and tested unsuccessfully both a submarine and undersea torpedoes. The American minister to France, Robert Livingston, encouraged Fulton to return to the United States and construct a steam-powered vessel. In 1807 his lightweight boat, the *Clermont,* powered by a small imported steam engine, traveled from New York City to Albany in thirty-two hours against the current on the Hudson River. Fulton and Livingston patented their concept and obtained a monopoly charter for steam navigation on New York rivers. For the next several years they also sponsored the introduction of steamboats into the Ohio-Mississippi River region. Controversy dogged Fulton throughout his life and long afterward. Many other inventors had cobbled together steam-powered vessels before he built the *Clermont,* and his New York monopoly was successfully broken in the *Gibbons v. Ogden* case. Nevertheless, Robert Fulton deserves recognition for his innovations and for popularizing steamboat travel.

See also Evans, Oliver; Steamboats.

References and Further Reading

Sale, Kirkpatrick. *The Fire of His Genius: Robert Fulton and the American Dream.* New York: Free Press, 2001.

Girard, Stephen (1750–1831)

Like so many successful American businessmen, Stephen Girard came to the country as an immigrant. Born in Bordeaux, France, he ran away to sea as a cabin boy at the age of fourteen. Within a few years he had qualified as a licensed sea captain and traded on his own account while sailing other people's ships. He profited from a number of mercantile enterprises both before and during the American Revolution, finally settling in Philadelphia. He was a major investor in the Bank of the United States and was outraged when the Madison administration allowed its charter to expire in 1811. He bought the bank's building and assets and operated them as a private enterprise called the Bank of Stephan Girard. He enthusiastically welcomed the establishment of the Second Bank of the United States and personally provided $3 million of its $20 million initial capitalization. He retired to a farm in the 1820s and contributed large sums to various charitable activities.

See also Bank of the United States.

References and Further Reading

Adams, Jr., Donald R. *Finance and Enterprise in Early America: A Study of Stephen Girard's Bank.* Philadelphia: University of Pennsylvania Press, 1978.

Goodyear, Charles (1800–1860)

Many American inventors became enmeshed in lengthy and costly patent infringement battles, but Charles Goodyear may well have suffered the most from this process. A native of New Haven, Connecticut, Goodyear belonged to a family that included a number of inventors. A failure at the hardware business and other retail ventures, Charles Goodyear repeatedly served time in prison for failing to pay his debts. When he could, he devoted all his attention to his passion: rubber. By the late 1830s he had managed to buy the Eagle India Rubber Co. in Massachusetts. After numerous experimental failures, Goodyear mistakenly allowed a combination of rubber and sulfur to overheat, only to discover that the result was a stable, durable, and very useful form of rubber. Patented in 1844, Goodyear's so-called vulcanization process invigorated the struggling rubber industry. Unfortunately, his process was so simple it encouraged others to use it without paying royalties. Although Goodyear's famous lawyer, Daniel Webster, won a dramatic victory in a patent infringement case in 1852, Goodyear continued to suffer financial and business reverses and died deeply in debt. Franklin Sieberling immortalized this inventive pioneer by naming his very successful enterprise the Goodyear Tire and Rubber Company.

See also Patents.

References and Further Reading

Korman, Richard. *The Goodyear Story.* San Francisco: Encounter Books, 2002.

Hamilton, Alexander (1757–1804)

Alexander Hamilton could never be president because he was born in the West Indies, but he had more political influence in the 1790s than anyone but George Washington himself. Hamilton obtained a smattering of education in his native Nevis, then moved to New York City and eventually attended Kings College (now Columbia University). During the Revolutionary War he

Alexander Hamilton, the nation's first treasury secretary, established the Bank of the United States. (Library of Congress)

volunteered for military service, rose to the rank of lieutenant colonel, and served as General Washington's aide-de-camp. After the war Hamilton passed the bar in New York and worked as a lawyer when not engaged in politics. A committed Federalist, he was a delegate to the Continental Congress and later advocated and then served in the Constitutional Convention in 1787. After Washington became president, he chose his former military aide to head the Treasury Department. Secretary Hamilton produced reports on the public credit, banking, manufacturing, and coinage, as well as establishing the department's administrative offices and procedures. He resigned from his cabinet post in 1795 but remained very active in national and local politics while pursuing his legal career. He vigorously opposed Vice President Aaron Burr's run for the New York governorship in 1804, and the unsuccessful candidate killed Hamilton in a duel shortly afterward.

See also Bank of the United States; Dollar, American; Public Credit, Report on the.

References and Further Reading

Randall, William Sterne. *Alexander Hamilton.* New York: HarperCollins, 2003.

Hancock, John (1737–1793)

The son of an impoverished clergyman, John Hancock was adopted at an early age by his uncle Thomas Hancock, the wealthiest merchant in Massachusetts. Having no children of his own, Thomas gave young John every advantage including a Harvard education, training as a merchant in England, and a partnership in his firm. When he died in 1764, he left John an inheritance of £70,000. Always more interested in politics than business, John Hancock became a confirmed and prominent revolutionary in 1768 when the Royal Navy seized his merchant ship *Liberty,* charging Hancock with smuggling Madeira wine into the colonies. Hancock was a major financial supporter of the Revolution, and he served as president of both the Continental Congress and the Constitutional Convention. Although he was repeatedly reelected governor of Massachusetts, he never achieved his ambition of becoming president of the United States.

See also Stamp Act.

References and Further Reading

Unger, Harlow G. *John Hancock.* New York: Wiley, 2000.

Howe, Elias (1819–1867)

Elias Howe's father was a Massachusetts farmer who dabbled in milling and manufacturing to make ends meet. This environment gave young Elias plenty of opportunity to learn about and experiment with mechanical processes. Shortly after he moved to Boston in 1837 to work as a machinist, he hatched the idea of creating a mechanical sewing machine. After eight years of poverty and disappointment, he completed his first two machines. He submitted one to the U.S. Patent Office with his successful application and demonstrated the other in various settings. When no Americans seemed interested, he grasped at an opportunity to take it to England, only to encounter similar indifference. On returning to the United States in 1849, he discovered that a number of people were manufacturing machines similar to his own. Over the next several years he requested and received royalty payments from many and successfully sued others. He was reluctant to join the patent pool that the Sewing Machine Combination created in 1856, but it proved a wise move. Royalties from the combination made him a millionaire even though he never became a major sewing machine manufacturer.

See also Patent Pool; Singer, Isaac Merritt.

References and Further Reading

Cooper, Grace Rogers. *The Sewing Machine: Its Invention and Development.* Washington, DC: Smithsonian Institution Press, 1968.

Jackson, Andrew (1767–1845)

Born in the backwoods on the border between North and South Carolina, Andrew Jackson had little formal education. Like many of his contemporaries, however, he read law for a couple of years and practiced as a lawyer and a politician. The capstone of his distinguished military career was his stunning victory over a superior British force attempting to invade New Orleans in 1815. He accumulated sufficient wealth to buy land and slaves and build a substantial plantation house he called The Hermitage near Nashville. He is the first westerner elected president and was extraordinarily popular with the common people. During his two terms in the White House (1829–1837) he was a strong chief executive who defended the nation's tariff policy from nullifiers, led a successful fight against the Second Bank of the United States, and spearheaded the removal of the Five Civilized Nations to Oklahoma. While he favored low land prices to encourage western settlement, he became convinced that the banknotes used for these purchases created unhealthy inflation. To cancel that effect he issued the Specie Circular in 1836, revealing himself to be a confirmed hard money man, distrustful of all paper currency. It is truly ironic, therefore, that his portrait appears on all twenty-dollar federal reserve notes.

See also Bank War; Specie Circular.

References and Further Reading

Ellis, Richard. *Andrew Jackson.* Washington, DC: Congressional Quarterly Press, 2003.

Lowell, Francis Cabot (1775–1817)

A prominent Boston merchant and shipping magnate, Francis Cabot Lowell suffered financial losses during the 1807 embargo. Seeking an alternative, Lowell made an extended visit to the British Isles to learn about the highly profitable textile industry there. In 1813 he and his associates formed the Boston Manufacturing Co. with an unprecedented $400,000 in capital. The company bought an existing paper mill at Waltham, Massachusetts, and poured substantial funds into renovations. The result was the world's first integrated mill that took raw cotton in one door and shipped finished bolts of cloth out another. The company paid very good wages for the time to the hundreds of young women it hired as unskilled laborers. Lowell's success helped spur a regional industrial revolution in New England.

See also Integrated Mill.

References and Further Reading

Evans, Harold. *They Made America.* New York: Little, Brown, 2004.

McCormick, Cyrus Hall (1809–1884)

Born on a farm in Virginia's Shenandoah Valley, Cyrus Hall McCormick grew up well aware of the problems associated with farming in an age of hand labor. His father built a crude wheat reaper, but young Cyrus improved on it substantially, reputedly doing all of the major work in a period of six weeks to assist in the harvest of 1831. He patented his design and began building and selling reapers in Virginia. In 1847 he moved his operation to the Midwest, building a large, modern factory in Chicago. His reaper won a gold medal at the Crystal Palace Exposition in London in 1851, giving him and his machines an international reputation. In the 1850s his company was selling thousands of reapers every year through an elaborate dealer network. He continued to improve his machines and to fight competition with aggressive sales and efficient manufacturing strategies. McCormick's firm became the International Harvester Company in 1902.

See also Dealership; Deere, John; Interchangeable Parts.

References and Further Reading

Lyons, Norbert. *The McCormick Reaper Legend.* New York: Exposition Press, 1955.

Morse, Samuel Finley Breese (1791–1872)

Son of a prominent Massachusetts clergyman, Samuel Finley Breese Morse enjoyed an elite education at Phillips Andover Academy and Yale University. An artist, he painted miniature portraits for a living and helped found the National Academy of Design in New York where he also taught. He was well aware of the electromagnetism discoveries that Michael Faraday reported in 1831. Morse turned these scientific findings into practical use by sending electromagnetic pulses along a wire. To enhance his invention's applicability, he also devised a code system with combinations of long and short pulses to designate letters and numbers. Morse completed his first successful demonstration in 1835, but it was not until 1843 that he obtained congressional support to lay a line between Baltimore and Washington. In the following year his system transmitted the message "What hath God wrought" between the cities. The next year, 1844, was an election year, and his telegraph system became famous literally overnight by transmitting convention and election news instantaneously. Like many other American inventors, he spent years defending his patent, No. 1,647. Much of Morse's ultimate wealth came from the stock he owned in the American Telegraph Company that Cyrus Field and Peter Cooper formed to exploit and, ultimately, dominate U.S. telegraphy.

References and Further Reading

Silverman, Kenneth. *Lightning Man: The Accursed Life of Samuel F. B. Morse.* New York: Knopf, 2003.

Otis, Elisha Graves (1811–1861)

The ingenuity of Elisha Graves Otis enables people to ride confidently on elevators all around the world. A classic tinkerer and jack-of-all trades, Vermonter Otis worked as a builder, a bedstead manufacturer, a machine-shop operator, a sawyer, and a general mechanic before settling in New Jersey. Contracted to move a bedstead manufacturing plant from one location to another, Otis constructed a hoist that included a ratchet device to prevent the load from falling even if the hoist's main support broke. By 1853 he had adapted this safety system to passenger and freight elevators that he offered for sale at $300. As business picked up, Otis added other improvements to his basic design including steam power. Otis's elevator helped transform the shape and skyline of cities by encouraging the construction of high-rise buildings. His sons carried on and expanded the business, forming the Otis Brothers Elevator Co. in 1861. The company remained a world leader of innovation and is currently an element of United Technologies Corporation.

References and Further Reading

Goodwin, Jason. *Otis: Giving Rise to the Modern City.* Chicago: Ivan R. Dee, 2001.

Remington, Philo (1816–1889)

Growing up in rural New York State, Philo Remington had plenty of opportunity to tinker in his family farm's machine shop. His father, Eliphalet Remington, developed a high-quality rifle barrel and eventually received government contracts for his rifles. Young Philo assumed responsibility for manufacturing in the family's gunsmithing company and became its president in 1861. The Civil War vastly expanded his business, but the end of the conflict left him with excess capacity. Over the next decade, his company sought international contracts and delivered a million weapons to foreign governments. At home Remington's diversification into farm implements proved unsatisfactory as did a spin-off sewing machine company. In 1873 he struck gold, however, when he obtained patent rights from James Densmore and G. W. N. Yost to manufacture typewriters. Remington moved well beyond their primitive design, introducing both uppercase and lowercase type in 1878. Remington's personal finances deteriorated badly in the depression years of the late nineteenth century, forcing him to sell off both his typewriter business, and eventually his firearms operation as well shortly before his death. The Remington Standard Typewriter Co. went on to become a major supplier of office machines, and the Remington Arms Co. thrived as well, fitting tributes to the innovate and creative Philo Remington.

See also Office Appliances; Winchester, Oliver Fisher.

References and Further Reading

Current, Richard N. *The Typewriter and the Men Who Made It.* Urbana: University of Illinois Press, 1954.

Singer, Isaac Merritt (1811–1875)

Born and raised in upper New York State, Isaac Merritt Singer dabbled as a cabinetmaker and mechanic before appearing on stage as Isaac Merritt. He sold the patent to his first invention, a mechanical rock drill, and used the $2,000 he obtained to finance his own theater troupe called the Merritt Players. When the troupe ran out of money, he found work in a plant that produced wooden type. There Singer invented an improved system for carving type but never found solid financial backing or customer interest. Hoping to interest New Yorkers in his invention in 1850, Singer rented display space from Orson C. Phelps, a man who was manufacturing sewing machines for other companies. Singer studied these and suggested many improvements that Phelps and others encouraged him to incorporate into a product line of his own. The Singer Sewing Machine Co. was a founding member of the Sewing Machine Combination's patent pool, and it quickly became an industry leader. Singer retired from the business in 1863, spending much of his later years in France and England. He left an estate valued at around $15 million.

See also Howe, Elias; Patent Pool.

References and Further Reading

Brandon, Ruth. *Singer and the Sewing Machine.* New York: Kodansha International, 1977.

Slater, Samuel (1768–1835)

Although he came from a middle-class family in rural England, young Samuel Slater signed on as an apprentice with one of Richard Arkwright's partners. Arkwright had recently perfected a water-powered machine that carded and spun fiber into yarn in a single operation. The Arkwright water frame was a key factor in the British industrial revolution, and the royal government forbid anyone with knowledge of its textile milling techniques to leave the country. Having completed his seven-year apprenticeship, Slater dressed himself as an agricultural laborer and boarded a boat for America. In New York, he learned that Rhode Island entrepreneur Moses Brown was doing poorly in his effort to build modern textile machinery. Based on his remarkably clear memories, Slater constructed the first successful water-powered spinning device in America in 1793. He became a partner in the milling firm of Almy and Brown, and his designs were adopted widely, helping to cut costs in the burgeoning American textile industry. For that reason, Slater is credited with helping trigger the U.S. industrial revolution.

See also Industrial Revolution.

References and Further Reading

Tucker, Barbara M. *Samuel Slater and the Origins of the American Textile Industry.* Ithaca, NY: Cornell University Press, 1984.

Smith, Adam (1723–1790)

Son of a government official, Adam Smith was born in Scotland and attended the University of Glasgow as well as Oxford. He taught at both Edinburgh and Glasgow where he published his first noteworthy book *Theory of Moral Sentiment* in 1759. He devoted a whole decade of study to the preparation of his most important work, *The Wealth of Nations* which appeared in 1776. It discussed such concepts as the division of labor, the nature of mercantilism, and the invisible hand. He is recognized as the first of the so-called classical economists, and his ideas profoundly influenced other key figures like David Ricardo, Thomas Malthus, and John Stuart Mill. Perhaps in part because the publication of his book coincided with the signing of the Declaration of Independence and the fact that it was quite critical of the British mercantilist system, his ideas enjoyed widespread popularity in the United States. Shortly after the publication of his seminal work, he became a commissioner of customs for Scotland, a position he held until his death.

See also Laissez-Faire; Mercantilism.

References and Further Reading

Simpson Ross, Ian. *The Life of Adam Smith.* New York: Oxford University Press, 1995.

Strauss, Levi (1829?–1902)

The fire associated with the 1906 San Francisco earthquake burned up all records of Levi Strauss and the company he founded, so much of what is written about him cannot be proven. Lob Strauss was born in Bavaria but he moved to the United States in 1847 to join family members already residing there. A skillful tailor and a persuasive peddler, the man who now called himself Levi Strauss sailed for San Francisco in 1850 where he planned to sell cloth and clothing to the burgeoning gold-mining community. Legend has it that he sold his finer grade cloth to fellow passengers on the long sea voyage and only had a roll of tent canvas left. A miner suggested that he fashion it into work pants, and these tough, long-wearing trousers were an instant success. Strauss established a factory in San Francisco and began importing cotton twill fabric called *serge de Nimes* from France. In the United States this became shortened into "denim" and Strauss further Americanized the fabric by dying it a deep indigo blue. In 1873 Strauss and a partner, Jacob Davis, patented the use of copper rivets to strengthen pocket seams. He had thus created an enduring classic. Levi Strauss and Co. prospered throughout its founder's life, and the lifelong bachelor devoted much of the wealth it generated for him to charities.

See also Gold Rush.

References and Further Reading

Cray, Ed. *Levi Strauss and Company.* Boston: Houghton Mifflin, 1978.

Symmes, John Cleves (1742–1814)

John Cleves Symmes' overoptimistic settlement efforts in Ohio illustrate the many problems involved in early land promotion schemes. Born on Long Island, Symmes trained as a surveyor before moving his family to New Jersey. Caught up in the Revolutionary fervor, he served as a colonel in a militia regiment for three years and then entered politics. Over the next few years he served as a provincial delegate, helped draft the New Jersey Constitution, became an associate justice of the New Jersey Supreme Court, and won election to the Continental Congress. There he succumbed to the lure of western expansion and convinced his fellow delegates in Congress to grant him a contract to buy 2 million acres of public land in the West. The following year Symmes led a group of thirty to establish an outpost along the Miami River in what became the Ohio Territory. His goal was to resell the land at a profit to incoming settlers but too few arrived and his grants were often too ill-defined to be enforceable. Despite his financial troubles, he remained a visionary to the end of his life. He even managed to convince Congress to appropriate funding for an exploratory mission to find the "holes at the poles." He believed that the earth was hollow, and if access through these polar pathways could be achieved, vast tracts of empty land inside the earth could be opened to settlement. The Lewis and Clark Expedition distracted attention from Symmes' scheme, but in 1838 Charles Wilkes began a four-year naval exploratory voyage that revived interest in the polar regions. He never located any holes at the poles, but he did fulfill Symmes' ultimate goal of finding new lands by discovering the continent of Antarctica.

See also Land Companies.

References and Further Reading

Barnhart, John D. *Valley of Democracy.* Bloomington, IN: Indiana University Press, 1953.

Thomas, Seth (1785–1859)

After a smattering of schooling, young Seth Thomas was apprenticed to a carpenter and later built houses. In 1807 he went into partnership with Eli Terry and Silas Hoadley to mass produce inexpensive wooden clocks. In 1812 Thomas left the partnership to establish his own factory at Plymouth Hollow, Connecticut. From Terry he bought the rights to make and sell a shelf clock with a brass mechanism. Using interchangeable parts technology, his company eventually became the nation's leading clock manufacturer. His son and namesake inherited control of the company, and he ran an expanding business enterprise until his death in 1888. The Seth Thomas Clock Company still contains a version of the original shelf clock in its current product line.

See also Interchangeable Parts.

References and Further Reading

Taylor, Snowden. *The Developmental Era of Eli Terry and Seth Thomas Shelf Clocks.* Fitzwilliam, NH: K. Roberts, 1985.

Vanderbilt, Cornelius (1794–1877)

Because he was born on Staten Island, it was natural that Cornelius Vanderbilt would begin his career operating a ferry boat in New York Harbor at the age of sixteen. His low fares beat out his competition, and he earned the nickname "Commodore" by operating a fleet of harbor craft during the War of 1812. In 1819 he began working for Thomas Gibbons, a bitter rival of the Fulton-Livingston steamboat monopoly on the Hudson River. The monopolists sued to prevent Vanderbilt from undercutting their operation, but the Supreme Court struck down the monopoly legislation in its 1824 *Gibbons v. Ogden* decision. In the late 1820s Vanderbilt struck out on his own again and, for two decades, dominated the Atlantic coastal trade. During the gold rush, he established a railroad through Central America thus substantially reducing the time and cost of reaching California by sea. At the age of seventy, he began buying control of shorter railroad properties and eventually linked them together into the New York Central Railroad that came to dominate east-west trade from New York

Cornelius Vanderbilt was a pioneer in the steamship industry during the early 1800s, who then went on to build a railroad empire. (Library of Congress)

City to the Midwest. A crusty, aggressive, unlettered man, he kept most of his vast fortune except for a million-dollar grant to a college in Tennessee that became Vanderbilt University. His $100 million estate was the largest accumulated by any American up to that point, and he left virtually all of it to his son William Vanderbilt. Within a matter of a few years, William had more than doubled his inheritance largely through successful acquisition of railroad shares.

See also Railroads; Steamboats.

References and Further Reading

Vanderbilt, Arthur T., III. *Fortune's Children, The Fall of the House of Vanderbilt.* New York: William Morrow, 1989.

Whitney, Eli (1765–1825)

The most famous of the New England inventors, Eli Whitney honed his creativity at Yale University. Shortly after graduating, he decided to travel south, seeking a position as a tutor. No suitable position was available, so he ended up staying as a guest on a Georgia plantation owned by Catherine Greene, widow of the famous Revolutionary War general, Nathaniel Greene. There Whitney experimented with methods for separating cotton fiber from seed. He built a successful prototype in 1792 and obtained a patent for his cotton gin in 1794. He spent much of the rest of his life in a largely fruitless effort to profit from his intellectual property claims. In part to obtain money to pursue this legal fight, he contracted in 1798 to produce 10,000 muskets for the U.S. government. This led to his experimentation with interchangeable parts and the use of jigs and machine tools. He was far better at claiming success than actually accomplishing it, but his energetic self-promotion convinced

Eli Whitney made two major contributions: the invention of the cotton gin and the popularization of the use of interchangeable parts in manufacturing. (Library of Congress)

many others to use and often improve the technologies he touted.

See also Cotton Gin; Interchangeable Parts; Patents.

References and Further Reading

McLaughlin, Constance Green. *Eli Whitney and the Birth of American Technology.* Boston: Little, Brown, 1956.

Winchester, Oliver Fisher (1810–1880)

Boston native Oliver Fisher Winchester experienced extreme poverty as a child and tried farming, carpentry, construction, and clerking before opening a successful men's clothing store in Baltimore. He patented a technique for manufacturing shirts and formed a partnership to produce them in New Haven, Connecticut, in 1850. With the profits from his shirt factory, Winchester invested in the Volcanic Repeating Arms Company, becoming its chief stockholder and executive in the late 1850s. One of the company's employees, Tyler Henry, added many improvements to the firm's rifles. Although the company never won a government contract, many soldiers purchased Henry rifles in preference to the Springfield rifles produced at the federal arsenal in Massachusetts. Additional technological advances enabled the company to produce the extraordinarily popular Winchester rifle in 1866. By 1870 Oliver Winchester had reorganized and expanded the enterprise into the Winchester Repeating Arms Co. with plants in New Haven and Bridgeport. Winchester continued to purchase or encourage improvements for his rifles, and the company he left behind remained a major arms manufacturer for many years.

See also Remington, Philo.

References and Further Reading

Houze, Herbert G. *Winchester Repeating Arms Company.* Iola, WI: Krause, 2004.

SECTION 3

INDUSTRIALIZING AMERICA, 1860–1900

During the late nineteenth century the American people grappled with the impact of industrialization on a grand scale. The Civil War had provided an enormous stimulus to the adoption of new manufacturing methods, it generated capital to assist in the organization of ever larger business combines, and it had dislocated individuals and families. Strident advocates of **Social Darwinism** reinforced the prevailing belief in the wisdom of a laissez-faire approach.

Aggressive and creative businessmen took advantage of this conventional wisdom to construct new, large, and sometimes amazing enterprises. Many copied the **trust** format that John D. Rockefeller had created to administer his holdings that represented more than 90 percent of the nation's oil industry. His Standard Oil empire used **horizontal integration** and generous **rebates** to control refining and transportation. Meanwhile, Andrew Carnegie pursued a **vertical integration** approach to achieve his dominant position in the steel industry. Some rivals attempted to use **pools** to compete, and some of these arrangements in turn gave them **oligopoly** control of other industries. By 1890 several states had passed new **general incorporation laws** that encouraged entrepreneurs to form holding companies within their borders. These companies were often capable of operating nationwide enterprises.

Simultaneously, public concern over the sheer size and dominance of some of these giant enterprises led to new interpretations of the **interstate commerce clause**. In 1890 Congress responded with an **antitrust law** that temporarily slowed the business consolidation drive. But the Supreme Court's ruling in favor of the **E. C. Knight Co.** reassured those interested in assembling ever larger industrial combinations.

Nowhere was this trend more evident than in the nation's leading sector—railroads. **Railroad consolidation** occurred on a grand scale throughout the postwar years. The **land grant railroads** were swept into these combinations just as effectively as those funded through private investments. Optimists and scoundrels were not averse to using **watered stock** to promote their objectives. Perhaps the most notorious scandal involved the **Credit Mobilier**, a construction company that built the Union Pacific Railroad. It managed to siphon off tens of millions of dollars, much of it from federal government land grants and loans using a process of creative bookkeeping and strategic bribes of politicians.

While some entrepreneurs used new technologies, aggressive capitalization, and novel organizational structures to fashion industrial empires, the economy in general remained unpredictable. Both **bulls and bears** could make or lose fortunes in this largely unregulated speculative age. The economy stumbled badly in the **Panic of 1873**, which punctured business optimism and heralded the onset of a protracted depression. The 1880s seemed better on the whole, but the **Panic of 1893** once again sent recession shock waves through the nation.

Americans developed a number of ideas about how they could lessen the impact of these periodic downturns. As with previous generations, monetary policy and the money supply received plenty of attention. The Union government had taken two key steps to increase its ability to borrow and pay its Civil War expenses. The U.S. Treasury issued unbacked **greenbacks** that some considered no better than the discredited continental currency distributed during the Revolution. Their value fluctuated compared to gold, and Jay Gould's attempted **gold corner** in 1869 further undermined confidence in greenbacks. The Lincoln administration made a more prudent decision when it began issuing federal charters to institutions that authorized them to issue **national bank notes** based on their holdings of federal bonds. Paper alternatives to hard currency were hardly universally popular, but low specie reserves forced the Union government to issue low-denomination **shinplasters** at the height of the conflict. The gold supply rebounded after the war but not enough to satisfy debtors and rural citizens. They urged the government to issue more greenbacks or, as an alternative, to exploit the nation's plentiful supply of silver to increase the money supply. Calls for **free silver** persisted through the presidential election of 1896.

This futile rural challenge reflected widespread frustration among the nation's farmers. In the South, tenant farming kept both white and black families mired in poverty. **Sharecropping** and **crop liens** locked them into debt and stripped them of their dignity. In the North, many farmers objected to high property taxes and swung behind the **single tax** movement designed to limit unearned income for landlords. Agrarians also complained about the persistence of high protective tariffs even though many commodities appeared on the **free list**. A major experiment that applied modern industrial techniques to traditional farming activities peaked in the **bonanza farm** phenomenon, but it proved unpopular and ultimately unprofitable as well.

Those who worked in the factories and mines spawned by the industrial revolution often mirrored rural discontent. Labor union organization provided some hope. The **National Labor Union** tried but failed to create an effective strategy for organizing all sorts of workers. In the 1870s and into the 1880s, the **Knights of Labor** appeared to be much stronger but it collapsed before the end of the decade. About the same time Samuel Gompers and his associates formed the **American Federation of Labor (AFL)**, which drew its strength from skilled workers and craftsmen. Judicious use of collective bargaining, **boycotts**, and other tactics helped the AFL survive, even as more radical groups like the American Railway Union staged dramatic but futile protests like the 1894 **Pullman Strike**.

Despite the pessimism and rancor that existed at some levels of society, the era did produce a remarkable cornucopia of technological advances. **Office appliances** like typewriters, adding machines, and cash registers facilitated record keeping and commercial transactions. Strides in **tabulating** data occurred as well, laying the foundation for an explosion in statistical and business analyses in the years to come. Thomas Edison and George Westinghouse used their inventive talents to perfect **electric power**. Frank Sprague applied it to streetcars and William C. Whitney to an ultimately failed attempt to build an **electric car**.

Meanwhile swelling urban populations encouraged innovative merchandising. **Department stores** sprang up in city centers, encouraging Americans to engage in **shopping** for business and pleasure. **Chain stores** proliferated as well, exploiting the efficiencies of volume buying to lower prices. **Catalog sales** gave rural residents access to unprecedented varieties of products. All these developments underlined the growing importance of consumers in the U.S. economy. As the nation entered the twentieth century it was already well along the path to the modern age of mass consumption.

KEY CONCEPTS

American Federation of Labor

The American Federation of Labor (AFL) coalesced in the late 1880s as an alternative to the Knights of Labor. Unlike the Knights, the AFL, under the leadership of Samuel Gompers, focused on basic, practical issues like wages and hours. As a federation of craft unions, it pursued a conservative course and allowed its member unions considerable independence but provided advice and support. This approach proved so successful that the AFL ultimately grew into the nation's largest labor organization.

A number of strategies for creating a national labor union were proposed and some were actually attempted prior to 1880. In most instances, however, these earlier attempts veered away from bread and butter issues to emphasize broader social or political reforms. The National Labor Union in the 1860s and the Knights of Labor in later years hoped to influence government or other interest groups in more generalized programs to ameliorate or improve the lot of working Americans.

Meanwhile a number of relatively strong and effective craft unions developed and operated either independent of or in conjunction with these overarching movements. One example was the International Cigar Makers' Union, which enjoyed a revival in the 1870s. Adolph Strasser and Samuel Gompers were key figures in its resurrection. They charged members comparatively high dues, but that made it more capable of supporting its initiatives and easing the plight of striking workers. Through carefully planned and executed campaigns, the union achieved many of its goals such as better wages, shorter hours, and union benefits.

The first attempt at a broader craft union structure came with the establishment of the Federation of Organized Trades and Labor Unions in 1881. It remained weak and poorly administered, and it suffered from the rivalry of the much more powerful and growing Knights of Labor. Unlike the craft unions that restricted membership to skilled and trained workers, the Knights also encouraged enrollment of unskilled workers. The explosive growth this strategy encouraged undermined the more conservative craft union movement.

Determined to create an alternate national organization more sensitive to their desires, representatives of the craft unions met at Columbus, Ohio, in December 1886. They formed the American Federation of Labor and installed Samuel Gompers as its first president, a position he was to hold with one minor lapse until 1924. While the AFL continued to vie for membership with the Knights into the early 1890s, the new formulation proved much more effective in the long run.

As he had in the cigar makers' union, Gompers focused his coordinating efforts on practical issues at the local level. The AFL was a true federation in the sense that each constituent union managed its own affairs, membership rolls, and strategies. The central organization remained underfunded and small, but it served as an effective clearinghouse for ideas and encouragement. If a member union called a strike, the AFL could direct resources from its treasury to supplement local strike funds. The central organization also provided publicity through its journal, *The American Federationist,* as well as occasionally urging its members to support embattled members or boycott some companies.

To a large degree, the major events in labor history during these early years resulted from individual craft union initiatives. The AFL served a relatively nondirective but supportive function, one that helped protect it from frontal assault. While its boycotting policies had negative consequences in the early 1900s, the federation's practical, non-radical approach enabled it to survive and outlast more flamboyant or doctrinaire organizations such as the Knights of Labor and the Industrial Workers of the World.

See also Boycott; Gompers, Samuel; Knights of Labor; National Labor Union.

References and Further Reading

Dulles, Foster Rhea. *Labor in America.* New York: Crowell, 1966.

Livesay, Roger. *Samuel Gompers and Organized Labor in America.* New York: Little, Brown, 1978.

Taft, Philip. *The A. F. of L. in the Time of Gompers.* New York: Harper, 1957.

Antitrust Laws

A number of major business consolidations in the 1880s used the trust mechanism that Standard Oil had pioneered. These consolidations triggered rising concern over potential monopolistic control of major business sectors and led to the passage of antitrust laws in several states. The U.S. Congress weighed in with the Sherman Antitrust Act of 1890, creating the basis for federal prosecution of large business combines.

The United States inherited a British common law prohibition against monopolies. Occasionally a state charter might grant a canal or bridge company exclusive control over a transportation route, but a laissez-faire approach prevailed in most business activities. The building of interstate railroads and the rise of multistate manufacturing and trading enterprises, however, led to calls for legislation to reinforce the common-law prohibition.

Two political splinter groups, the Greenback-Labor Party in the 1870s and the Anti-Monopoly Party in the 1880s, promoted legislation to control or eliminate the negative effects of large-scale enterprises. Beginning in the 1880s, several state legislatures responded to these and other political pressures by approving laws aimed at regulating business consolidation within their jurisdictions.

The Standard Oil Trust was a wide-ranging business combination created in the early 1880s to facilitate operations that crossed many state lines. As it and similar interstate operations became more prominent, those interested in regulating big business threw their support behind federal initiatives. For the presidential election of 1888 both major political parties adopted platform planks that called for some form of national legislation to control monopolistic tendencies.

After Republican Benjamin Harrison won the election, he urged Congress to take action. Ohio Senator John Sherman's name became associated with the resulting bill, although he was only a tepid supporter of the concept. Even so, the Sherman Antitrust Act received virtually unanimous support in both houses of Congress, and President Harrison signed it in July 1890.

The legislation's first section seemed clear in stating its purpose: "Every contract, combination in the form of trust or otherwise, or conspiracy, in restraint of trade or commerce among the several states or with foreign nations, is hereby declared to be illegal. . . ." Participating in such activities was defined as a misdemeanor that could lead to fines or imprisonment. It was left to the U.S. attorney general to bring suit against violators.

Several factors conspired against rapid and decisive action. Republicans were traditionally friendly toward big business. When Democrat Grover Cleveland was inaugurated for his second term as president in 1893, he appointed Richard Olney, a railroad corporation lawyer in private practice, to be attorney general. Moreover, the Panic of 1893 discouraged further business consolidation of any type and lessened fears of monopolies.

The first attempt at enforcing the Sherman Act only served to weaken its scope. Attorney General Olney pursued a case against the E. C. Knight Co. that his Republican predecessor had begun in 1892. The Supreme Court's 1895 opinion drew a distinction between manufacturing and commerce, ruling that the sugar refining company was engaged in the former and not the latter. Consequently, it could not be guilty of restraining commerce. Four years later, in its opinion on the Addyston Pipe case, the Supreme Court cancelled that distinction, finding a manufacturing company in violation of the Sherman Antitrust Act. The company involved was a small one, though, so this decision had only limited consequences.

As the economy recovered after the depression of the mid-1890s, dozens of new business combinations came into being. The merger frenzy ended abruptly in 1902 when President Theodore Roosevelt's Attorney General Philander Knox instituted an antitrust case against a railroad holding company, the Northern Securities Co. The court's decision two years later instituted the first federally mandated dissolution of a major interstate business combination. To do so it had to reject a key defense argument that the exchange of stock across state lines was a financial transaction unrelated to commerce or trade.

This case earned President Roosevelt the nickname "trustbuster," and his administration instituted over forty additional litigations, including one directed at the granddaddy of all trusts, Standard Oil. The Supreme Court ordered the dissolution of that trust in 1911. Tucked away in the ruling, however, was a key reinterpretation of the original Sherman Act that came to be known as "the rule of reason."

The nuance added here was the necessity of deciding whether a particular combination unreasonably restrained trade or commerce. Standard Oil met this revised criterion, as did the American Tobacco Co., which the court ordered dissolved shortly afterward. When the case against United States Steel finally reached the justices in 1920, however, they concluded that the holding company did not at that point unreasonably restrain trade even though it had earlier controlled 80 percent of all steel production in the United States.

The ambiguities inherent in the Sherman Antitrust Act and the subsequent promulgation of the rule of reason led to calls for more specific legislation that would define precisely what corporations could and could not do. This was the motivation behind the passage of the Clayton Antitrust Act in 1914. It listed four major prohibitions: (1) price discrimination, (2) *tying* agreements that prohibited dealers from handling competing product lines, (3) interlocking directorates, and (4) certain corporate mergers. However, these activities were only unlawful if they substantially lessened competition or tended to create a monopoly. This language left broad latitude to the courts, so the Clayton Act ultimately proved almost as open to interpretation as the Sherman Act.

Both the Sherman and Clayton acts remain on the books, and antitrust cases involving corporations like American Telephone and Telegraph and Microsoft have been initiated in recent years. AT&T was ordered dissolved in 1984, but Microsoft appears to have successfully weathered the litigation.

The creation of a group of federal regulatory agencies has proven to be a far more effective strategy than trust-busting in controlling corporate behavior. The Interstate Commerce Commission (1887), Federal Trade Commission (1914), and the Securities and Exchanges Commission (1934) represent efforts to encourage reasonable corporate behavior and to police corporate activities so that entrepreneurs can avoid antitrust litigation.

See also Dodd, Samuel Calvin Tate; E. C. Knight and Co. Case; General Incorporation Laws; Holding Company; Northern Securities Co. Case; Rockefeller, John Davison; Trust.

References and Further Reading

Handler, Milton. *Antitrust in Perspective.* New York: Foundation Press, 1937.

Shenefield, John H. *The Antitrust Laws: A Primer.* Washington, DC: AEI Press, 2001.

Thorelli, Hans B. *Federal Antitrust Policy.* Baltimore, MD: Johns Hopkins Press, 1955.

Bonanza Farms

In the late nineteenth century, large-scale farming operations developed in the upper Midwest. Referred to as bonanza farms, they involved large acreage, corporate ownership and management, and a hired labor force. In the mid-1890s adverse weather and low prices contributed to the collapse of the bonanza farm phenomenon.

Those involved in building transcontinental railroads across the northern tier of states were naturally interested in developing the lands along their routes. Although some individuals and families were willing to settle in the vast plains of the Dakota Territories, that area was less attractive than more conventional farming opportunities further south. A collapse in the value of Northern Pacific Railroad stock set off the Panic of 1873 and halted laying rails in western North Dakota. A federal land grant had encouraged construction of the railroad, and some investors traded their devalued railroad bonds for large tracts of vacant lands in the Red River Valley.

The newly endowed landlords hired Oliver Dalrymple, a wheat-growing expert from nearby Minnesota to manage an eighteen-section parcel. The investors supplied additional capital for buildings and equipment and guaranteed Dalrymple ownership of half of the farmland once these capital costs had been recouped. He harvested his first wheat crop in 1875, and the success of the experiment encouraged other entrepreneurs to establish bonanza farms of their own.

Dalrymple's operation became the model. He divided the holdings into 2,000-acre units, each with its own superintendent, buildings, and equipment. The farms relied on an army of migrant labor, employing more people in planting and reaping seasons and cutting the labor force back at other times. Expensive, large-capacity farm machinery enhanced the productivity of these wage laborers. The deliberate use of industrial techniques caused the bonanza farms to be characterized as factory farms.

Economies of scale and the division of labor definitely promoted efficiency in the bonanza farms. They tended to specialize, sometimes exclusively, in wheat production, and the larger operations produced so much grain that the managers could bargain successfully for low shipping rates or even rebates from the railroads.

In the mid-1880s, however, the Great Plains entered a decade-long dry spell. Low yields combined with low prices in the nationwide depression that struck after the Panic of 1893. Even with their operational efficiencies, the bonanza farms could not survive in such discouraging conditions. Dalrymple's pioneering effort ended in 1896, and much of the land was distributed to smallholders. The Red River Valley reverted to more conventional agricultural production where crop diversification and intensive cultivation replaced the factory farm.

See also Panic of 1873; Panic of 1893.

References and Further Reading

Drache, Hiram M. *Day of the Bonanza.* Fargo, ND: North Dakota Institute for Regional Studies, 1964.

Murray, Stanley N. *Valley Comes of Age.* Fargo, ND: North Dakota Institute for Regional Studies, 1967.

Boycott

This protest tactic is named for Charles C. Boycott, an English land agent in western Ireland. A boycott can take many forms including refusals to work for an employer, buy products of a particular manufacturer, or deal with family members of hated individuals.

Charles Boycott's name became famous overnight in the summer of 1880. He was the agent for absentee landlords in County Mayo. To bring in the harvest, he relied on local tenants, but he offered wages so low that summer that they refused to work. A series of confrontations ensued, culminating in the aggrieved tenants calling on everyone to have no any dealings with Boycott or the members of his family. An American newsman first publicized the use of the term *boycott* to describe this activity. Local merchants joined in the boycott, refusing to buy or sell goods to Boycott or his family, and some of Boycott's personal servants abandoned their posts.

This first boycott drew attention to the harsh conditions under which landless Irish farm laborers worked, but it also simply popularized the term. Refusing to work for or buy goods from someone was, of course, a tactic with a long history. Stirring a community or interest group to collaborate in economic ostracism was a common tactic. The radical calls for nonimportation of British goods that culminated in the Boston Tea Party in 1773 are famous examples from an earlier century.

Once the term boycott gained circulation, however, it was applied to a number of activities. Perhaps the most famous early example occurred in 1894 during the Pullman Strike, which is often referred to as the Pullman boycott. In this labor action, members of or sympathizers with the American Railway Union refused to handle trains that included cars built by the Pullman company. It had systematically reduced wages in its factories while continuing to charge high rents to the workers it employed. The boycott grew into a nationwide protest directed against the company workers considered to be heartless.

Labor unions increasingly used boycotts to pressure companies that maintained bad working conditions. One landmark case of this type involved the Buck Stove and Range Company. The American Federation of Labor (AFL) placed the manufacturer on its "We Don't Patronize" list in 1907 because it refused to shorten work hours in its unhealthy metals polishing shop. The resulting national boycott inflicted severe losses on the company. Three leaders of the AFL, including Samuel Gompers, eventually served short prison terms for violating an injunction against the boycott.

The Danbury Hatters' case began in 1902 when Connecticut-based D. E. Loewe and Co. refused to agree to a closed shop, one in which all workers had to join the Brotherhood of United Hatters of America. Because hats were a popular consumer product with a substantial number of competing manufacturers, the boycott was very effective, reducing Loewe's sales by a factor of five. Here again, a lengthy court battle ensued, with the manufacturers seeking triple damages from the boycotters for their profit losses. The aggressive prosecution of cases like these illustrates how very effective a local or nationwide boycott could be. It remained a popular union tactic, despite the legal costs involved.

Sometimes boycotts seem to occur almost spontaneously. In the 1970s, labor organizer Cesar Chavez called attention to the harsh working conditions that migrant laborers endured in California vineyards. A grape boycott spread across the United States, supported by many people who had no direct connection to the laborers or even to unions. More recently athletic shoe companies, fast-food chains, and hotels have been boycotted. It is a tactic that is likely to persist, because in a consumer economy, individuals' decisions are subject to an enormous number of factors.

See also American Federation of Labor; Gompers, Samuel; Pullman Strike.

References and Further Reading

Karson, Marc. *American Labor Unions and Politics, 1900–1918.* Carbondale, IL: Southern Illinois University Press, 1958.

Taft, Philip. *The A. F. of L. in the Time of Gompers.* New York: Harper, 1959.

Warne, Colston, ed. 1955. *Pullman Boycott of 1894: Problem of Federal Intervention.* Boston: Heath, 1955.

Bulls and Bears

The terms *bull* and *bear* came into common usage much earlier, but Charles Francis Adams, Jr., succinctly defined them in *A Chapter of Erie,* his 1869 expose of railroad stock manipulation: "A bull, in the slang of the stock exchange, is one who endeavors to increase the market price of stocks, as a bear endeavors to depress it. The bull is supposed to toss the thing up with his horns, and the bear to drag it down with his claws."

When a speculator buys low in hopes of selling high, he or she is acting as a bull. Bulls buy shares at a current market price they consider well below the real or ultimate value of the security. It may take months, years, or only a day or two for other buyers to realize how undervalued it is and bid the price up. The bull can then sell his or her holdings at a profit.

In a bull market like the one that existed in the 1920s, such expectations were easily fulfilled. Sometimes less scrupulous individuals spread rumors boosting a company's prospects, hint at an imminent new product, or simply encourage friends and associates to buy shares in the companies they hold. Bulls depend on both real or imagined improvements in the corporations they speculate in to produce the rising in stock price they need to realize profits.

Bears have quite a different perspective. They believe or hope stock prices will fall. In anticipation of such a change they negotiate a futures contract or option for a particular stock at a higher price level. For a bear to succeed, the stock price must indeed fall below the contracted price. He or she can then buy shares at this reduced price and sell them to whoever has granted the bear an option at a higher price. The bear profits from the difference between the two prices.

Here again skulduggery can influence the value of a stock. Sometimes, as in the case of the attempted Gold Corner in 1869, a bear pool coalesces that includes speculators determined to lower prices artificially if natural forces fail to cause a reduction. Inside information, unflattering rumors, and negative news reports play into the hands of bears by weakening faith in a company's future prospects and therefore causing a reduction in the market price of its shares. During the 1920s, far fewer bears roamed the stock exchange than bulls. But some of those who adopted bear positions in 1929 profited enormously when the market crashed and stock prices were dragged down across the board.

Bulls are often seen as romantic optimists and bears are criticized as disgruntled pessimists. In fact both types of speculators can prove useful. Bulls anticipate good news and generally encourage positive attitudes about the economy's prospects. Meanwhile, bears provide a healthy dose of skepticism and their actions can bring inflated or unrealistic prices down to more reasonable levels that better match actual asset values. In a well-functioning stock exchange, both bulls and bears can profit handsomely even when the exchange records only minor ups or downs.

See also Bull Market; Gold Corner; New York Stock and Exchange Board; Stock Options.

References and Further Reading

Adams, Jr., Charles Francis, and Henry Adams. *Chapters of Erie.* Ithaca, NY: Cornell University Press, 1956.

Catalog Sales

In the late nineteenth century, several firms published extensive catalogs designed to sell goods by mail throughout the United States. Montgomery Ward and Co. was the leading innovator, but Sears, Roebuck grew even more quickly, and its annual sales outstripped Wards by 1900. Both companies initially focused on serving an expanding rural population, but the size and diversity of their operations won them recognition as major retailers nationwide. Though catalog sales became less prominent in the mid-twentieth century, credit-card and Internet technology has stimulated a revival of catalog sales from hundreds of mass-market vendors.

Rural America prior to the Civil War was predominantly a handmade environment. Farmers constructed their own cabins or houses and fashioned many of their own tools and housewares. Farmwives wove and sewed homespun fabrics and preserved fruits and vegetables from their gardens. To the extent possible, self-sufficient farmers tried to avoid purchasing relatively expensive hardware, foodstuffs, clothing, or linens from the local general or country stores that sprang up to serve them. An incessant demand for uniforms, shoes, canned goods, and other products during the Civil War stimulated mass-production of many items that had previously been made by hand. After the war, frenetic railroad construction and lenient federal land policies triggered a massive migration of new farm families into the upper Midwest and onto the Great Plains.

Living in Chicago, Aaron Montgomery Ward recognized that expanded rail service and low-cost mass-production presented an attractive opportunity to someone interested in serving rural customers. Moreover, he was well acquainted with the rapidly growing Patrons of Husbandry, familiarly known as the Grange. In 1872 Ward printed a one-page flyer listing 163 items for sale and used Grange contacts to help distribute it to potential customers throughout the agricultural hinterland. Simultaneously, he began placing large orders with suppliers. Bulk buying reduced his costs, enabling him to offer products for sale at prices much lower than country stores could afford. Even when shipment costs were added, Ward's products were very attractively priced.

His business flourished from the start. By 1875 his catalog had grown to seventy-two pages and, for the first time, it included a money-back guarantee. While some big city merchants had previously offered such assurance, Ward's was the first to be made available to rural customers. In the next year, the catalog had doubled in size and listed nearly 4,000 items. In many instances potential customers could select from a range of sizes, types, and prices for each product listed. Throughout these early years, Ward continued to focus his marketing on struggling farmers and pioneers.

Montgomery Ward joined forces with Charles Thorne in 1873, and Thorne's five sons eventually joined the rapidly expanding firm as well. Montgomery Ward and Co. repeatedly had to move into larger quarters to handle its vast increases in orders and inventory. In response to demands from the still very significant bloc of rural voters, Congress approved the initiation of Rural Free Delivery in 1893, and Ward's company benefited enormously from this system that dispatched his shipments literally to the doors of his far-flung clientele. By 1900 the company was doing almost $10 million worth of business a year. Montgomery Ward stepped down three years later, but the company continued to flourish under Charles Thorne's leadership.

Nearly a decade and a half after Ward distributed his first product list, Richard Sears took the initial step toward creating a mail-order empire that would surpass Montgomery Wards. As a 22-year-old shipping clerk for a railroad in Minnesota, Sears ended up with a consignment of watches that the intended recipient refused to collect. The resourceful young man obtained permission from the shipper to sell the watches on his own. He contacted acquaintances up and down the line and managed to dispose of the entire shipment at a handsome profit. He immediately ordered additional watches and, within a matter of months, abandoned his railroad position to establish the R. W. Sears Watch Co.

After relocating to the nation's rail hub in Chicago, Sears exploited his formidable talents as a persuasive salesman to expand his business. Like Ward, he distributed lists of attractively priced goods to a broad audience. And because he bought in bulk, he made a good profit on each sale even though his prices undercut those of local jewelers. Looking for a reliable person to repair his watches, he hired Alvah Roebuck. This expert watchmaker proved so talented that he and his team could assemble watches from surplus parts Sears obtained at close-out costs. After several attempts at organization, Sears, Roebuck and Co. was formed in 1893. The business expanded well beyond jewelry as Sears sniffed out bargain deals on other items, and the company's catalog grew larger and much more diverse.

Despite the success of the enterprise, Sears was a poor businessman and Roebuck decided to get out. In what would prove to be a monumentally poor financial decision, he sold his interest to Sears for $20,000 in 1895. Sears teamed up with Julius Rosenwald shortly afterward, and it was Rosenwald who solved the management problems that had plagued the company. Aping Ward's strategy, the company advertised itself as the "buyer for the American farmer," and by the end of the decade its revenues had outstripped its rival. The company never lost its leadership position in the catalog sales business.

Sears resigned from the company in 1909, leaving Rosenwald to guide it through even more profitable times during the First World War. Both the Sears and Wards customer bases shrank when an agricultural depression set in early in the 1920s and severely limited the ability of their rural customers to continue buying. Both companies acknowledged the importance of the automobile revolution and the growth of suburbia by opening retail outlets in the mid-1920s. By the 1950s Sears and Wards were prominent anchor tenants in suburban malls all across the country. Even so, they continued to publish catalogs, thus honoring their roots as pioneering mail-order houses.

The success of these mail-order powerhouses encouraged other firms like J. C. Penney's to issue catalogs as well. While no other contemporary operation ever surpassed the success of the industry leaders, catalog sales remain a significant source of revenue. Major department store chains like Bloomingdales and Marshall Fields distribute catalogs on a regular basis, and specialty retailers like Talbots, Eddie Bauer, and L. L. Bean earn substantial percentages of their income from catalog operations. The concept of selecting products from an attractive and diversified catalog and having them delivered to your door continues to be a very profitable retail strategy.

See also Chain Stores; Department Store; Sears, Richard Warren (R. W.).; Ward, Aaron Montgomery.

References and Further Reading

Emmett, Boris, and John E. Jeuck. *Catalogs and Counters.* Chicago: University of Chicago Press. 1950.

Werner, M. R. *Julius Rosenwald.* New York: Harper Brothers, 1939.

Worth, James C. *Shaping an American Institution: Robert E. Wood and Sears, Roebuck.* New York: New American Library, 1986.

Chain Stores

In the late nineteenth century, many an ambitious local retailer chose to expand his market reach by opening similar stores in other communities. Some of these groups of stores developed into chains with dozens or even hundreds of links. Chain stores benefited from common advertising, low wholesale costs because of their ability to place large orders, and growing brand-name recognition. The A&P grocery chain was the nation's early pioneer in this area, and similar chains developed to market drugs, clothing, hardware, and inexpensive items, the latter in variety or five-and-dime stores. Chains grew even more explosively in the twentieth century, engulfing a huge share of consumer purchases.

The concept of a single proprietorship with multiple outlets had developed much earlier. A pre-Revolutionary example was the line of frontier outposts that the Hudson's Bay Co. established in the late 1600s throughout its vast Canadian holdings. Small chains consisting of a few stores in adjacent communities also served Americans in the antebellum period. None of these, however, experienced the rapid growth and geographic spread of the chains founded just before and after the Civil War.

Many of these chains had humble beginnings. In 1859 George F. Gilman and George Huntington Hartford opened a shop in New York City to sell tea they imported directly from the Far East at very low cost. Their profit margin was so great that they were able to open additional tea shops. Their Great American Tea Co. was operating twenty-five outlets in 1865. As the company expanded westward, the founders adopted a more grandiose name, founding the Great Atlantic and Pacific Tea Co. in 1869. The system also extended its product line to include all sorts of food items, and some 200 A&P grocery stores were operating by the turn of the century.

That was just the beginning. The chain doubled to 400 members 10 years later and exploded to over 4,600 by 1920. In the succeeding decade, A&P opened relatively small grocery stores all over the country, expanding the chain to a high of nearly 16,000 units by 1930. The Great Depression dampened the drive for continued expansion, but even more important was the development in the 1930s of the grocery supermarket. To compete with these new, much larger retailers, A&P closed thousands of its smaller stores and concentrated in the next few years on expanding the size and offerings of its own supermarkets. By the 1950s, the chain had reached something of an equilibrium, operating just over 4,000 stores right through the decade. These stores collectively generated over $5 billion in sales each year.

The success of the A&P strategy encouraged imitators. The Brooklyn-based Jones Brothers Tea Co. established in 1872 grew into the Grand Union Chain. Ten years later Bernard H. Kroger opened the Great Western Tea Co. in Cincinnati, the forerunner of today's Kroger chain.

Frank W. Woolworth used a chain-store approach to create a whole new retailing field. As a young clerk in a dry goods store, he set up a table with odds and ends under a sign offering "Anything on this table, 5¢." When it sold out in a day, he bought other goods to market on the cheap. By 1881 he was operating several five-and-dime variety stores in Pennsylvania, the basis of what would eventually become a worldwide chain including thousands of outlets. S. H. Kress and S. S. Kresge modeled their stores after Woolworth's successful endeavor, building nationwide chains of variety stores in the early twentieth century.

In most cases, the founders of retail chains used the profits from their first store or group of stores to finance expansion. Outside capital was neither sought nor essential in the early years, and many of these huge enterprises remained in the hands of one or a few private owners. The very success of the expanding chains, however, eventually attracted investment capital that enabled further growth.

Another common characteristic of early chains was the modest size of the individual stores. Like the A&P, the strategy was to reach as many customers as possible but with a fairly specialized or limited inventory. During the same period urban department stores were growing much larger and offering a vastly more diverse array of goods. The chains' small, dispersed specialty shops competed only to the extent that they were sprinkled throughout cities and even smaller towns, easily accessible to local customers.

The huge growth potential for chain stores in the twentieth century attracted many other entrepreneurs. The appropriately named James Cash Penney began his hugely successful chain with a single small dry goods store in Kemmerer, Wyoming, in 1902. Two years later he opened a second store in a nearby mining community. By 1920 his chain had grown to over 300 stores with annual sales that matched those of the Macy's Company. Penney's eventually became one of the nation's most ubiquitous chains, adopting both a successful department store format as well as a broad-ranging catalog sales operation. Other major chains founded just after the turn of the century were Walgreens

Drugs (1901), Peoples Drug Stores (1905), W. T. Grant and G. C. Murphy (1906), and Western Auto Supply (1909).

Local merchants and homegrown businesses often objected strenuously to the appearance of what were essentially absentee-owned commercial ventures. In the 1930s, for example, Congress conducted intensive investigations into the question of whether and what legislative restraints should be imposed on chain-store expansion. This phenomenon has by no means abated. Many citizens and local businessmen currently oppose construction of Wal-Mart stores in their communities for many of the same reasons. Nevertheless, the chain-store phenomenon has only seemed to grow more powerful and pervasive in American retailing.

See also Department Store; Penney, James Cash (J. C.); Woolworth, Frank Winfield (F. W.).

References and Further Reading

Beasley, Norman. *Main Street Merchant.* New York: McGraw-Hill, 1948.

Lebhar, Godfrey M. *Chain Stores in America: 1859–1962.* New York: Chain Store Publ. Co., 1963.

Nichols, John P. *The Chain Store Tells Its Story.* New York: Institute of Distribution, 1940.

Credit Mobilier

A major political and financial scandal developed in the early 1870s over the Credit Mobilier, a construction company that had built the Union Pacific Railroad, the eastern link of the nation's first transcontinental railroad. In addition to generating huge profits for its shareholders, the company distributed shares of its stock to prominent politicians to curry their favor. The scandal rocked the administration of President Ulysses Grant and added to its reputation for corruption.

Borrowing a format used in France, the organizers of the Union Pacific Railroad created a parallel company to perform the actual construction. Named the Credit Mobilier, it operated in some ways like an early version of a holding company, distributing shares and issuing stock on its own but depending on contracts from the railroad's operating company to finance its activities. The construction company raised capital in both the United States and abroad where many investors eagerly bought into the dream of building a railroad all across the country.

The company began laying tracks in 1867, heading west from Omaha, Nebraska. The enterprise benefited from federal land grants as well as generous federally supported loans. For every mile of track the company laid through level country, the loan subsidy was $16,000. In hilly areas, the subsidy doubled to $32,000 per mile and jumped up to $48,000 a mile for construction in mountainous terrain. Creative surveyors defined flat lands as hill country and hilly country as mountains to increase the size of the railroad's subsidies. Enormous popularity and interest in the project caused stock prices for both the railroad and the associated construction company to rise dramatically.

The Credit Mobilier did spend considerable sums on the actual laying of track. By the time the Union Pacific linked up with the California-based Central Pacific at Promontory Point in Utah Territory in 1869, the construction company claimed to have run up expenses totaling $94 million. Later estimates, however, concluded that the actual costs of construction could not have amounted to more than $50 million, so the additional $44 million must have been distributed to shareholders as profits. That was consistent with one report that the Credit Mobilier declared a total of 341 percent in dividends over a period of one and a half years.

To encourage congressional support for the enterprise, agents like Massachusetts Representative Oakes Ames offered small blocs of Credit Mobilier stock to his fellow legislators at very low prices. A typical package would be ten shares at $100 a share even though the open market price for those same shares might already be twice as high.

And if the potential buyer could not come up with $1,000, Ames loaned him the money. The congressman could then turn around and sell his shares for $2,000, pay off the loan, and end up with $1,000 free and clear.

The scandal broke in the fall of 1872, just as President Ulysses Grant was winning reelection with huge majorities. A congressional investigation began in 1873, and it eventually disclosed that two vice presidents and several senators and representatives including future president James A. Garfield had accepted lucrative stock deals from the Credit Mobilier. From one perspective, only $65,000, a tiny portion of the company's capitalization, actually ended up in the hands of these politicians. But a congressman's salary stood at $5,000 in that era, so public perceptions that the company had provided substantial bribes to politicians to guarantee support for its project were quite damaging.

Despite the controversy that the Credit Mobilier scandal generated, other railroad-building projects adopted similar financing strategies. Indeed, all the major transcontinental railroads were built by some sort of construction company. This company structure helped to insulate investors from some of the risks that speculative railroad projects inevitably involved.

See also Land Grant Railroads.

References and Further Reading

Ames, Oakes Angier. *Oakes Ames and the Credit Mobilier.* Boston: F. Wood, 1880.

Josephson, Matthew. *The Politicos.* New York: Harcourt Brace, 1938.

Crop Lien

To farm in the post–Civil War South, many people, both black and white, obtained supplies at a local general store on credit. There was seldom enough cash to repay these loans, so liens on future crops became the most common alternative. Along with sharecropping, the crop-lien system dominated southern agriculture and retarded the economic recovery of the region well into the twentieth century.

After 1865 a whole new agrarian economic structure was needed to replace the plantation system that had prevailed in many areas before the Civil War. The key change was the existence of millions of landless agricultural workers who, no longer slaves, were responsible for their own livelihoods. A large percentage of them quickly became sharecroppers, obligated to turn over a portion of their annual crop in lieu of cash payments for rent. But land alone was only one factor these freed men and women needed to be able to produce that crop. Seed, fertilizer, draft animals, and food to keep the family going were also essential.

Just as they had to rent the land, they also had to borrow the supplies they needed. Banks were few and underfunded in the postwar South, so conventional loans were rare. Instead, a prospective farmer was likely to establish a credit arrangement with the local general store owner. Unable to promise cash payment, the creditor typically pledged a part of his future crop to the lender. Informal at first, liens on future crops became so common that many state legislatures passed laws to structure the system. Many lenders took advantage of the resulting regulations and registered their crop-lien contracts with local government authorities. Some of these legal arrangements specified interest rates as high as 200 percent in extreme instances.

Sharecroppers who owed substantial portions of their output to both a landlord and a shopkeeper could easily end the year without any surplus at all. Worse yet, when the crop was harvested, it might have insufficient value to pay the current charges. Even if this were not actually the case, illiterate farmers were easy prey to unscrupulous shopkeepers who juggled the books to make it appear that some indebtedness remained. Croppers who, for whatever reason, failed to meet their current obligations were expected to make up any shortfall out of the subsequent year's crop. This situation locked literally millions of southern farmers into a never-ending spiral of shortfalls and penury.

Another major consequence of the crop-lien system was that it discouraged agricultural diversification. Wherever cotton could be grown, landlords and shop owners preferred that their tenants and borrowers plant it. Cotton was planted year after year, draining the soil of nutrients, and creating an almost continual surplus that kept prices very low. The shopkeepers and landlords also suffered from this price deflation causing the rural South to remain sunk in an agricultural depression throughout the late nineteenth century.

See also Cotton; Sharecropping.

References and Further Reading

DeCanio, Stephen J. *Agriculture in the Post Bellum South.* Cambridge, MA: MIT Press, 1975.

Mandle, Jay R. *The Roots of Black Poverty.* Durham, NC: Duke University Press, 1979.

Shannon, Fred A. *The Farmer's Last Frontier: Agriculture, 1860–1897.* New York: Harper and Row, 1945.

Department Store

The department stores established in the United States grew very quickly after the Civil War. The fundamental characteristics of American department stores were extravagant buildings, enormous varieties of goods for sale, intensive advertising, relatively low prices, and a number of customer services before and after a sale. By 1900 mammoth stores operated by Macy's, Wanamakers, Jordan Marsh, and the like had become crucial contributors to urban life and lifestyles.

The concept of selling a wide variety of goods under a single roof had long historical roots. Early in the fourteenth century, Mercer's Bazaar was operating in Paris as *Paradis des Femmes.* By the mid-sixteenth century, Parisians were being invited to buy at the mammoth *Halles Centrales.* Meanwhile Thomas Gresham was constructing the Royal Exchange in London, which opened in 1566 and rented individual stalls to over 150 specialty purveyors. None of these precedents, however, were true department stores because they housed small-volume independent retailers rather than company-owned and operated retail departments.

Another precedent for huge retail emporiums were the thousands of general stores that sprang up throughout the country at rural crossroads. These establishments stocked an assortment of tools, staples, seeds, and other products to sell or barter to local farm families. A general store usually had a single proprietor who lived in or beside his shop and often ran the local post office as well. Although these country stores filled an important economic service in rural America, they were limited in size and in the variety of products they handled.

In the larger towns and cities that blossomed in the United States after the turn of the nineteenth century, general stores quickly gave way to specialty shops. It made good economic sense for a merchant to specialize in one or a related group of product lines. The sales region contained enough potential customers to justify specialty shops, and the merchants who operated them could often obtain very favorable wholesale prices by buying in bulk. The trend toward specialty shops was so strong that by mid-century most city dwellers seldom had occasion to visit a general store.

At that point, technological changes were creating new opportunities for retailers. The expanding rail network tied cities together across the Northeast, allowing merchants to stock up on all sorts of products and commodities. Horse-drawn trams and other forms of public transport enabled potential customers to get downtown to take advantage of the assortment of goods on sale. At the same time, manufacturing advances were producing an expanding array of finished goods that were seeking retail outlets. The Civil War helped accelerate this trend as the Union Army issued orders for thousands and thousands of ready-made uniforms, shoes, and other equipment. By 1865 the industrial revolution had advanced enough, particularly in the northeastern United States, to offer both sellers and buyers a cornucopia of consumer products.

Some of the specialty retailers whose businesses were growing rapidly decided to branch out into related areas. Alexander Turney (A. T.) Stewart, for example, had prospered as a linen and lace importer and seller, but by the late 1840s, he had expanded into many other related dry goods lines. He built an impressive new sales emporium called the Dry-Goods Marble Palace on lower Broadway in New York City. This large store, handling a number of different lines under unified management, is sometimes credited with being the nation's first true department store. The innovations it introduced, however, represented only some of those that would characterize the retailing giants that developed after the Civil War.

A key factor in successful department store operation was the development of departmental expertise in buying and selling. Each major unit within the store would have managers as well as experienced buyers who could anticipate the market and dicker for advantageous prices. A centralized bookkeeping system, financial management, and overall administrative structure coordinated these independent department managers and buyers.

As department stores arose and became more competitive, they generally adopted similar business practices. The one-price system became standard. Buyers no longer bargained individually; they were expected to pay the set price. This policy worked to everyone's advantage. The buying power of a major department store guaranteed low wholesale costs that could be passed to customers. As their business grew, many department stores began manufacturing their own products, further reducing middleman costs.

Another common and very popular feature was the money-back guarantee. The major department stores had the financial size and flexibility to offer guarantees where smaller retailers would be reluctant to make such promises. Although most establishments operated on a cash basis, the more aggressive retailers offered credit to their customers, a service that naturally increased sales within their stores. By the 1890s free home delivery of major purchases had also become widespread, and wagons emblazoned with a particular department store's logo provided inexpensive advertising throughout the city.

To entice customers into their establishments, department stores mounted aggressive advertising campaigns using fliers, billboards, newspapers, and increasingly elaborate window displays. American manufacturers became capable of producing plate glass in large sizes around 1880, and urban stores were quick to install it along busy streets and sidewalks. Electric lighting became feasible at about the same time, and retailers placed it inside their cavernous buildings to enhance the display of goods.

Although John Wanamaker never liked being called a department store owner, his Philadelphia-based empire set many standards. His decision to buy an abandoned freight warehouse from the Pennsylvania Railroad in 1875 was a brilliant move. He refurbished it into a multistory department store that opened as the Grand Depot just in time to take advantage of crowds assembled in the city for the 1876 Centennial Exhibition. The thousands of out-of-town visitors who patronized his store spread his reputation nationwide.

But Wanamaker's enormous emporium was soon eclipsed by the one Rowland Hussey (R. H.) Macy founded. The Massachusetts native had been involved in several more or less successful ventures before he opened a store devoted to dry goods in New York City in 1858. He was a talented and aggressive salesman, and his successful advertising campaigns enabled him to expand his operation continuously. He engulfed a number of neighboring properties as he added new departments and product lines. By the early 1870s Macy's had become a true department store in the modern sense.

A key decision in 1874 was to lease space to an outside firm. Macy's entered into a profit-sharing deal with Lazarus Straus and Sons in which they operated the china and glass department within the store. This set a precedent for other similar internal leases, one that many present-day stores follow by featuring separate showrooms for Ralph Lauren, Tommy Hilfiger, or Liz Claiborne. Even more important for Macy's however, was the connection it established with the talented family that would assume major leadership responsibilities for the company in the 1890s. Under Straus management, Macy's became the world's largest department store.

Even so, a number of successful competitors thrived in New York and other cities. Lord & Taylor began as a specialty shop in the 1820s but it, too, became a diversified department store after the Civil War. B. Altman (1865) and the Bloomingdale Brothers (1872) were early entrants in this growing field as well. Jordan Marsh (1851) and Filene's (1881) became the dominant department stores in Boston. Marshall Field (1858) and Carson, Pirie, Scott (1864) exercised similar influence in Chicago. Atlanta boasted Rich's (1867), San Franciscans shopped at I. Magnin (1876), and Robinson's (1883) served Los Angeles. A relative late-comer was Nieman-Marcus (1906) in Dallas.

Clearly, department stores became a major retail phenomenon in the late nineteenth century. In succeeding decades, the stores these pioneers founded continued to grow, establish branches, and attract a major share of the consumer dollar. They encouraged the development of recreational shopping, set precedents for customer service, and strongly influenced the advertising industry. Perhaps most important, they served as major magnets to attract all kinds of people downtown, thus enlivening the hearts of the nation's cities.

See also Macy, Rowland Hussey (R. H.).; Shopping; Stewart, Alexander Turney (A. T.); Wanamaker, John.

References and Further Reading

Ferry, John William. *A History of the Department Store.* New York: Macmillan, 1960.

Hower, Ralph M. *History of Macy's of New York: 1858–1919.* Cambridge, MA: Harvard University Press, 1943.

Mayfield, Frank M. *The Department Store Story.* New York: Fairchild, 1949.

E. C. Knight and Co. Case

The E. C. Knight and Co. was the target of the first federal prosecution of a business combination under the Sherman Antitrust Act. In 1895 the Supreme Court ruled in favor of the company, in part because it was engaged in manufacturing and not commerce and therefore fell outside of the Sherman Act's prohibition against "restraint of trade or commerce."

The target of this case was the so-called sugar trust that had been created in the late 1880s modeled after the Standard Oil Trust. In part hoping to avoid antitrust litigation, the combination transformed itself into the American Sugar Refining Company, a holding company chartered under the general incorporation laws of New Jersey in 1891. For several years the sugar trust had been criticized for lobbying in favor of high protective tariffs on sugar imports, substantial contributions to sympathetic politicians, and its dominant position in the refining industry. These criticisms had helped fuel the drive that led to the passage of the Sherman Antitrust Act in 1890.

Even so, President Benjamin Harrison's attorney general instituted the case only after the company purchased four Philadelphia refineries that collectively handled about one-third of sugar processing in the United States. The federal government sought to cancel the stock transfers that brought E. C. Knight and Co. and three other refiners under the control of the larger American Sugar Refining Co. At that point, the government's case alleged, the sugar trust controlled 98 percent of all refining capacity in the United States. A change of administration in 1893 brought Democrat Grover Cleveland to the presidency, so his attorney general, Richard Olney, had to decide how to proceed. After both the federal district and appeals courts had failed to sanction the company, Olney appealed the case to the Supreme Court.

Two years later, the justices, with only one dissenting vote, also ruled against the government. The opinion noted that a transfer of stock like the one involved in this acquisition was a common business practice that did not, in itself, violate the provisions of the antitrust legislation. The opinion went further, however, stating that the refineries being acquired simply processed raw materials, a manufacturing activity that did not fall under the Sherman Act's definition of commerce or trade. Finally, the decision noted that the government had presented no evidence of the company's deliberate intention to restrain competition, ignoring its predominant position within the industry.

The decision had several consequences. It reassured those in manufacturing enterprises that they might be immune from antitrust legislation, although subsequent decisions, notably the one in the Addyston Pipe Case in 1899 shattered that precedent. The decision discouraged federal authorities from pursuing antitrust cases against huge combines, causing a seven-year hiatus in active trust-busting. The opinion also raised interesting questions about standard business practices like stock transfers and intent that complicated antitrust cases for many years. Of course, from the perspective of Henry O. Havemeyer, the president of the American Sugar Refining Company, the decision was absolutely correct, allowing his firm to continue dominating this key industry until his death in 1907.

Such a prominent and controversial company could not escape further attention, however. In 1910 the U.S. attorney general once again sued the American Sugar Refining Company for violating the Sherman Act, but, as before, the government failed to make a convincing case. A consent decree reached in 1920 allowed the combination to continue operating.

See also Antitrust Laws; Holding Company; Trust.

References and Further Reading

Eichner, Alfred S. *The Emergence of Oligopoly: Sugar Refining as a Case Study.* Baltimore, MD: Johns Hopkins Press, 1969.

James, Henry. *Richard Olney and His Public Service.* Boston: Houghton, Mifflin, 1923.

Electric Car

In the late nineteenth century, it was not clear that internal combustion engines would dominate the market for personal transportation. Inventors and innovators constructed both steam and electrically powered vehicles and, for a time, the Electric Vehicle Company was the largest manufacturer of automobiles in the United States. The company set up fleets of electrically powered cabs in New York and other cities. Although technological and managerial problems fatally undermined this initiative, New Yorkers continued to ride in electric cars until 1912.

The chief difference among the hundreds of experiments with horseless carriages in the late nineteenth century was the power plant. Steam engines had a long history, but they were heavy and required bulky coal and water reservoirs. Gasoline engines produced very low horsepower and were balky, smelly, and prone to breakdowns. Electric engines, by contrast, operated smoothly and reliably, but they required heavy arrays of batteries to function. Limited battery life shortened the range of electric vehicles, making them far less attractive for touring.

By the mid-1890s, however, electrically powered cars had become feasible. The Electric Storage Battery Company was the leading American manufacturer in its field, and it became a major partner in the Electric Vehicle Company formed in 1899. This company combined the considerable financial talents of William C. Whitney and the manufacturing expertise of Albert Pope, whose New Haven bicycle factory was an industry leader.

Whitney envisioned the enterprise as an element of the comprehensive urban transportation system he hoped would become a national monopoly. He already controlled electric street railways in New York and Philadelphia, and he supplemented them with electric omnibuses. Electric cars would complete the system, providing personal transportation from homes to tram or bus stops. The Electric Vehicle Company quickly established electric cab service in New York, Philadelphia, Washington, Boston, and Chicago.

At that point no mechanized system existed for building cars, so the company essentially cobbled them together using parts from dozens of suppliers. Much of the assembly was done by hand. With no uniformity among the vehicles distributed to local affiliates, servicing and maintaining the fleets was enormously complicated. This problem plagued the company throughout its existence.

The batteries themselves presented major challenges. Even after the introduction of more powerful and reliable Exide batteries in 1901, the range for an electric cab was about 20 miles. Connections with tram and bus lines did give the cabs access to generators, but recharging a battery took upwards of twelve hours. To keep its vehicles in service, local affiliates maintained extensive shop areas where vehicles could get replacement batteries. With a typical battery pack weighing half a ton or more, slipping one set out and installing a freshly charged set was no mean feat. Moreover, the batteries themselves deteriorated over time, adding to the expense of operating the fleet.

Not surprisingly, service quickly deteriorated and was abandoned in most cities. The New York system, however, remained viable for some time. Charging fares similar to those of horse-drawn cabs, the electric fleet earned a profit. Electric cars enjoyed popularity in high society, and some wealthy patrons paid a monthly fee to have a car and driver on call at all times. A drivers' strike in 1906 put strains on the operation, as did the death of Whitney about the time of the business Panic of 1907. Competition from gasoline-powered cabs put the electric cabs out of business for good five years later.

The experiment with electric cars had many unique features. A fleet of company-owned vehicles tied to other forms of public transportation might have succeeded if the technological problems had not been so challenging. Throughout this period, optimists kept expecting that a huge breakthrough in battery technology would occur. If it had, electric cars might well have moved beyond the realm of a controlled, constricted urban environment. But no such breakthrough has yet occurred, and recent experiments with electrically powered cars remain almost as disappointing as the ones that occurred a century ago.

See also Moving Assembly Line; Selden Patent; Whitney, William Collins.

References and Further Reading

Greenleaf, William. *Monopoly on Wheels.* Detroit, MI: Wayne State University Press, 1961.

Kirsch, David A. *The Electric Vehicle and the Burden of History.* New Brunswick, NJ: Rutgers University Press, 2000.

Electric Power

The electric power industry is indelibly associated with Thomas Edison in the late nineteenth century, and he was a pioneer in making electric lighting feasible. He developed the incandescent lightbulb and designed and built power plants and power grids. A committed advocate of direct current (DC) electricity, Edison was slow to recognize the enormous flexibility and potential of alternating current (AC). George Westinghouse took the lead in promoting this system, designing and building massive steam turbine generators to serve a variety of customers, communities, and purposes.

The versatility of electricity encouraged a broad range of experimentation. After the Civil War, inventors, engineers, and entrepreneurs worked cooperatively or competitively to develop practical uses for electricity, some of which aimed to provide opportunities for individuals to obtain great wealth or economic control. It was hardly surprising that the nation's most well-known finance capitalist, J. P. Morgan, was the first to install a comprehensive home electric lighting system in his New York City mansion.

Much of the early experimentation with electricity occurred in Europe. The names of pioneers like Luigi Galvani and Alessandro Volta in Italy, Andre Ampere in France, and Michael Faraday in England became associated with various characteristics of electricity they discovered. Benjamin Franklin was the only early American to earn international repute for his experimentation with lightning and the invention of lightning rods to protect buildings.

Faraday's writings on electromagnetism stimulated the work of American Samuel F. B. Morse in developing the telegraph in the 1830s as well as the work of Alexander Graham Bell in the 1870s that produced the first working telephone. And it was Faraday who conceived of the earliest practical electrical generators that could produce continuous electrical current when driven by waterfalls or steam engines. Best of all, Faraday discovered that applying a current to a reconfigured dynamo reversed the process and created an electric motor.

The first major race to use electric power on a broad scale, however, was as a source of artificial light. Sir Humphrey Davy demonstrated a battery-powered carbon-arc light in 1809, and other experimenters jumped in quickly to exploit this phenomenon. In 1876 Russian engineer Paul Jablochkoff produced a commercial arc-lighting system that used electric current. The carbon sticks that served as terminals for the electrical arc wore down rather quickly. It soon became apparent, however, that they deteriorated much less quickly when subjected to alternating bursts of current rather than the traditional direct current that batteries produced. Generators capable of creating alternating current were already available at that point.

Thomas Alva Edison recognized the limitations of arc lighting and set out to develop an alternative that would send current through a durable filament. Edison encountered a number of hurdles before he managed to complete his showcase system in Manhattan. He and a team of coworkers at his Menlo Park, New Jersey, laboratory designed glass bulbs as well as advanced vacuum pumps to vacate them. After enormous research and experimentation, Edison found that carbonized bamboo fibers could glow incandescently for hundreds of hours in high-vacuum bulbs. Because his financial backers were uninterested in this aspect of the business, Edison independently financed the establishment of a lightbulb factory adjacent to his laboratory.

Transmitting electricity to these bulbs presented its own set of problems. Charles F. Brush drove ahead with a plan to install arc lights along New York City's Broadway Avenue in 1880. His success transformed this famous avenue into the "Great White Way," brilliantly glowing with intense blue-white carbon arc lamps. But Brush's lamps required up to 3,500 volts of alternating current, and high-voltage wires strung along telegraph poles created a substantial safety hazard.

Edison's incandescent bulbs operated just fine on low-voltage, DC power. For additional safety, the inventor favored buried wires. Dirt and moisture wreaked havoc with his primitive insulation systems, and he had to form another company to hire laborers, working mostly at night, to dig "subways" for his wires. Even with large-diameter (and very expensive) copper wires, direct current could not effectively be transmitted beyond about half a mile from where it was generated.

Shortly after the household system flickered on in Morgan's mansion, Edison was ready for his highly anticipated demonstration. A generator located at Pearl Street in lower Manhattan roared into action on September 22, 1882, and lights clicked on along streets and in selected offices. To complete the Pearl Street Station, investors, including Morgan himself, had put up almost half a million dollars. The new technology immediately rendered obsolete the American gas-lighting system, an industry worth some $400 million a year.

Now the true business struggle began. Several companies were formed using Edison's technology and highlighting the name of the inventor. But Edison remained stubbornly attached to his direct current system. To expand electric lighting citywide would require a plethora of generating plants, spaced no more than half a mile apart from one another. Other inventors and entrepreneurs favored a more flexible system using alternating current.

A recent immigrant from Serbia named Nicola Tesla played a key role here. He had devised an electric motor using the principles of induction that operated efficiently and reliably with alternating current. This type of motor could easily be adapted to streetcars, factories, elevators, and other uses that had previously been confined to DC applications. American inventor and entrepreneur George Westinghouse obtained rights to Tesla's ideas and emerged as the leading American advocate for alternating current.

The enormous hydroelectric power potential of Niagara Falls had stimulated a number of different proposals and the creation of several companies in the 1880s. A key stumbling block to raising money for any of these ideas was the fact that only some 5,000 people lived in the immediate vicinity of the falls, far too few to justify the enormous expense of tapping the falls' energy. To make that feasible, the power had to be transmitted at least to Buffalo, 20 miles away, and possibly even further.

High-voltage alternating current can be transmitted with little loss of power over long distances. Simple and relatively inexpensive transformers had been developed as early as the 1830s to step voltage up or down. Regardless of the voltage obtained at the generator, it could be stepped up for transmission and then brought back down to a safe level for users. By the early 1890s, European experimenters had demonstrated that electricity generated more than a 100 miles away could drive motors and light bulbs. Over Edison's continuing and bitter objections, the Cataract Construction Company sided with Westinghouse in moving forward on an AC system.

To avoid spoiling the natural beauty of the setting, the company dug tunnels to carry water from the river above the falls through Westinghouse-built generators 200 feet below. The resulting power was distributed locally in the summer of 1895 and transmitted to Buffalo in November of the following year. The Niagara Falls plant had eight 5,000-horsepower turbines operating by 1899, and convincingly demonstrated that large-scale centralized generating plants could serve customers far more efficiently than Edison's smaller, localized power plants.

In addition to enjoying the vindication of their beliefs, Westinghouse and his collaborators benefited financially from their commitment. Englishman Charles Parsons had demonstrated the first large-scale steam-driven turbine in 1884. Conventional piston-equipped steam engines were incapable of driving electric generators fast enough to produce alternating current, but Parson's turbine reached a speed of 18,000 revolutions per minute. Westinghouse recognized the importance of this development and his company became the leading manufacturer of steam-turbine generators in the United

States. His machines were installed in centralized power stations all over the country.

Fortunately for Edison, his incandescent bulbs worked equally well in either AC or DC systems. By the early twentieth century Edison electric companies had adopted the now proven and versatile AC technology that the inventor had so opposed. At worst, Edison could be criticized for failing to see how extraordinarily flexible electric power would become. The resolve of Westinghouse and his colleagues was essential in taking electricity out of the laboratory and putting it into common usage.

See also Edison, Thomas Alva; Sprague, Frank Julian; Westinghouse, George.

References and Further Reading

Davis, L. J. *Fleet Fire.* New York: Arcade Publishing, 2003.

Jones, Jill. *Empires of Light.* New York: Random House, 2003.

Prout, Henry G. *A Life of George Westinghouse.* New York: American Society of Mechanical Engineers, 1921.

Silverberg, Robert. *Edison and the Power Industry.* Princeton, NJ: Van Nostrand, 1967.

Free List

Tariff laws establish customs duties of various levels on imports. The free list includes commodities or items exempted from taxation. Because tariff legislation and agreements are subject to change, items may be added to or removed from the free list accordingly.

Tariff regulations and import tax levels generated intense political debate throughout the nineteenth century. The rates for individual items might change dramatically depending on which political party or interest group exercised the most influence at a given moment. As general rule, these changes were far more responsive to domestic political and economic trends and relatively less concerned with the consequences for overseas producers.

The tariff on sugar provides a case in point. Because cane sugar was grown in Louisiana and other parts of the Deep South, producers from those areas lobbied for protection from foreign sources. As the nation expanded westward in the late nineteenth century, sugar beet growers in states like Utah and Colorado added their voices to this effort. Production costs in the United States almost always ran higher than those in the Caribbean Islands, so a sugar tariff provided a price cushion for American producers.

In any given year, the demand for sugar in the United States was likely to be far greater than what domestic producers could supply. Growers in Cuba or Hawaii were eager to meet the excess demand, but importers had to pay the tariff. This in turn forced overseas producers to pare their production costs, like wages, to a minimum, and sugar-dependent economies tended to be depressed. The sugar tax rate was so high, however, that in some years the import taxes on sugar alone accounted for 20 percent of all American import revenues.

From time to time, the Hawaiian Kingdom managed to negotiate a reciprocity agreement regarding sugar, allowing its exports to enter the United States tax free. This relationship was a key factor in the revolution that took place on the Islands in the early 1890s and in the desire of the American planters who dominated the Hawaiian economy to encourage annexation to the United States in 1898.

Cuba never fared as well. A Spanish colony, its exports were taxed like those of any other country. In the 1880s as much as 90 percent of the Cuban economy was directly or indirectly related to sugar production, making it highly susceptible to American tariff policy.

In 1890 Ohio Representative William McKinley headed the efforts of the Republican majority in both houses of Congress to draft a new general tariff law that would preserve and even strengthen the principal of protectionism that stood as a cornerstone of his party's doctrine. A major problem, however, was that the relatively high rate schedule currently in force produced substantial unwanted surplus revenue for the federal government. Only by putting sugar on the free list could McKinley justify maintaining high rates for most other commodities.

The McKinley Tariff Act had immediate effects on Cuba. For the next four years, the island's economy boomed as never before. No longer did the island's sugar exporters have to overcome a substantial tariff hurdle to supply the United States. Production costs, including wages, were able to rise, improving the lifestyles of many Cubans.

When Democrat Grover Cleveland recaptured the White House in the 1892 election, he called a special session of Congress to modify the McKinley Act. After tortuous negotiations, the Democratic leadership produced the Wilson-Gorman Bill that lowered many rates to stay in line with Democratic doctrines. But to replace the revenue that would be lost from these changes, the bill removed sugar from the free list and levied a 40 percent tariff on imports.

Once again, U.S. policy had immediate and devastating consequences for Cuba. The economic boom evaporated overnight, rekindling long-standing grievances and resentment against Spanish colonial rule. In 1895 José Marti led a force of rebels into Eastern Cuba, setting off the conflict that would eventually draw the United States into the Spanish-American War three years later. The self-centered domestic political considerations and manipulation of the U.S. free list thus had profound consequences not only for Americans but for the Cuban and Filipino people as well.

See also Protective Tariff; Reciprocity.

References and Further Reading

Dobson, John M. *Two Centuries of Tariffs.* Washington, DC: U.S. International Trade Commission, 1976.

Ellis, Lippert Spring. *The Tariff on Sugar.* Freeport, IL: Rawleigh Foundation, 1933.

Taussig, Frank W. *Tariff History of the United States.* New York: A. M. Kelley, 1967.

Free Silver

The 1896 Democratic Party platform called for the free and unlimited coinage of silver. Its backers believed this proposal would greatly increase the nation's money supply and help stimulate economic recovery. Opponents argued that it would promote unhealthy price inflation, undermine the domestic financial structure, and negatively affect the country's international trading position. A Republican victory in November effectively shut off any possibility that the United States would pursue a free silver strategy.

The 1896 presidential election was the final act in a long-running controversy over what role silver should have in the U.S. monetary system. The federal government had minted silver coins in small denominations from the earliest days of the Republic. Treasury Secretary Alexander Hamilton had proposed that the federal government fix a mint ratio that set the value of 15 ounces of silver equivalent to 1 ounce of gold. This ratio remained somewhat reasonable until the 1830s when the Treasury adjusted it to 16 to 1 to bring it more in line with current market conditions. For the next couple of decades, the 16 to 1 ratio actually undervalued silver because the intrinsic value of the metal in the coins was greater than their minted value.

After the Civil War, new mines in the western states substantially increased the U.S. supply of silver. Its market value soon declined sufficiently to allow the mint to restore the circulation of low-denomination coins. These were part of a complex postwar money supply that included Treasury bonds, national bank notes, greenbacks, and gold coins. By 1873 the market price of silver approached the traditional 16 to1 ratio compared to gold. Even so, conservative attitudes prevailed in Congress, and it passed a bill that year that explicitly prohibited the minting of silver dollar coins.

Critics of this policy branded this demonetization of silver as "The Crime of '73." The nation had tumbled into a deep depression after the Panic of 1873, and many Americans believed it persisted because the U.S. money supply was too small. Price deflation and hard times were convincing arguments for increasing that supply either with more greenbacks or, perhaps, the coinage of silver dollars.

When the Gold Resumption Act of 1875 undermined support for printing more greenbacks, the advocates of an increased money supply focused their attention on silver coinage. Major support for this strategy came from the citizens of mining states who anticipated that expanded federal purchases of silver for coins would support a higher market price for silver. Equally important was the widespread belief among rural Americans that the free coinage of silver would pump more money into circulation, raise prices for agricultural products, and ease their ability to make loan and mortgage payments. This coalition of mining and farming interests became a strident special interest group over the next two decades.

Responding to this pressure, Missouri Democrat Richard Bland shepherded a bill through the House of Representatives that would authorize the free and unlimited coinage of silver. Iowa's conservative Republican Senator, William B. Allison, succeeded in limiting the bill's scope with amendments in the upper house. The resulting 1878 Bland-Allison Silver Purchase Act authorized the minting of silver dollars but limited the number to be coined. It ordered the Treasury secretary to buy between $2 and $4 million worth of silver a month to be converted into dollar coins.

Although the Treasury seldom exceeded the authorized minimum monthly purchase, over the next twelve years the mint stamped out over $300 million silver dollars. These were generally unpopular with the public due to their size and weight, so the Treasury also printed silver certificates. They could be redeemed for silver coins, but most of them circulated widely like other paper currency. The coins and their corresponding certificates definitely increased the nation's money supply in the 1880s.

Meanwhile expanding mine production so glutted the silver market by 1890 that silver's value in nongovernment transactions had declined to a ratio of around 20 to 1 compared to gold. The Treasury therefore found itself in the uncomfortable position of providing an arbitrary price support to the silver-mining industry. Consequently, President Benjamin Harrison's administration proposed that the government stop issuing dollar coins and certificates at the old 16 to1 ratio, and the Sherman Silver Purchase Act of 1890 implemented a new approach. The Treasury would still buy up to 4.5 million ounces of silver a month, but instead of silver certificates it would issue Treasury notes backed by its general reserves. As a policy, the government systematically tried to redeem these notes with gold rather than silver whenever possible, and it minted new silver dollars only if they were necessary to supplement the gold redemption process.

Both elements of the pro-silver movement objected to the Sherman Act. The government was now buying silver at a reduced price that cut the miners' profits, and its restricted coinage policy did not add significantly to the money supply. The newly formed Populist Party fought back by including a free silver plank in its 1892 presidential platform. Not surprisingly, the splinter party's candidates did well in the western mining states and in rural areas where farmers struggled with low prices and high indebtedness.

Fiscal conservatives continued to control the two major parties, however. Democrat Grover Cleveland had already been president from 1885 to 1889. He won election in 1892 to a second term and was an outspoken advocate of an undiluted gold standard. Other gold bugs held key positions in both houses of Congress. The sharp depression that set in after the Panic of 1893 convinced Cleveland and his allies to change the monetary policy once again. With substantial support from Republican legislators, Congress revoked the Sherman Silver Purchase Act in 1894, halting all federal purchases and coinage of silver.

This move encouraged the Populists to focus their attention in the 1896 presidential campaign on their free silver agenda. The Republicans predictably nominated William McKinley for president on a solid gold standard. The chaotic Democratic convention, however, staged a floor debate pitting three gold bugs against three silverites. William Jennings Bryan, a Nebraskan who epitomized the downtrodden western agrarian sector, delivered a spellbinding speech in favor of free silver. It ended dramatically with these words: "We will answer their demand for a gold standard by saying to them: You shall not press down upon the brow of labor this crown of thorns, you shall not crucify mankind upon a cross of gold." This rhetoric so galvanized the party delegates that they adopted a free silver plank and named Bryan their candidate.

Bryan had stolen the Populists' thunder. Convening shortly afterward, they, too, nominated Bryan as their standard-bearer, but named their own vice-presidential candidate. Bryan stumped throughout the nation, calling at every stop for the free and unlimited coinage of silver at the traditional 16 to 1 ratio. But this simplistic formula could not dilute the growing trend toward Republicanism, and McKinley won a comfortable majority in both the popular and electoral votes. The free silver crusade had failed.

The money supply grew without further legislative tinkering around the turn of the twentieth century, in part due to the nation's positive trade balance that boosted an influx of gold. The Republican Party confirmed its position by passing the Gold Standard Act in 1900, effectively demonetizing silver once again and permanently ending the government's price support for silver. Alternatives to silver would be championed and used in later economic crises.

See also Greenbacks; Panic of 1873; Panic of 1893; Shinplasters; Soft Money.

References and Further Reading

Dewey, Davis Rich. *Financial History of the United States.* New York: Longmans Green, 1934.

Hicks, John D. *The Populist Revolt.* Lincoln, NE: University of Nebraska Press, 1961.

Jones, Stanley L. *The Presidential Election of 1896.* Madison, WI: University of Wisconsin Press, 1964.

Shannon, Fred A. *The Centennial Years.* Garden City, NY: Doubleday, 1969.

General Incorporation Laws

Well before the Civil War, state legislatures began passing general incorporation laws as alternatives to issuing charters. These allowed any individual or group to establish a corporation simply by meeting certain conditions. The doors swung open even wider in 1889 when New Jersey passed new general incorporation legislation that allowed corporations within its borders to own property in other states. This change set the stage for an enormous upswing in the creation of enterprises with truly national scope.

Well into the nineteenth century, state-level politicians jealously guarded their power to issue corporation charters. Based on colonial and royal precedents, legislatures retained the right to control those hoping to conduct business within their jurisdictions. While some charters involved minimal politicking, unscrupulous or simply ambitious legislators often demanded bribes or other compensation for their votes. Many a prudent and well-planned incorporation effort could be forestalled entirely or become entrapped in a scandalous influence-pedaling process.

Even in ideal circumstances, the chartering process could be so time-consuming and potentially costly that it discouraged enterprise. Recognizing the desirability of promoting rather than hampering productive businesses, legislators eventually saw merit in simplifying the process. The general incorporation laws they promulgated typically required statements of ownership, capitalization, and purpose. Annual reporting requirements were also common. These stipulations gave state authorities some control over operations and valuable information about enterprises in their states.

While individualized charters remained necessary for some business activities, most could easily comply with general incorporation provisions. Railroads, manufacturing concerns, commercial businesses, and even large-scale farms seized the opportunity to incorporate. By the middle of the nineteenth century, most corporations in America operated under such laws.

A key provision in every state's legislation, however, was that corporations organized under them could not own property or operate in other states. This constraint had been fundamental to the earlier chartering process as it gave state authorities considerable control. While the general incorporation laws made it much easier to start new businesses, the states were initially unwilling to see them reach across their borders.

This ownership restriction underlay John D. Rockefeller's decision to form a trust in the early 1880s. He owned property throughout the Northeast and he collected all his holdings in a given state into a single company, usually under the Standard Oil banner. But the existing corporation laws prevented any of these individual companies from conducting their own operations or those of subsidiaries in adjacent states. Therefore, a controlling interest in each of the state-incorporated companies was transferred to Rockefeller and his associates as trustees. It was the Standard Oil Trust, then, that managed and coordinated the individual companies' activities.

The success of the Standard Oil Trust encouraged other industrialists to use a similar structure, and over 300 trusts came into existence. This burst of entrepreneurial activity attracted the attention of legislators in the state of New Jersey. To encourage companies to establish headquarters in their state, they passed a new general incorporation law, the New Jersey Holding Company Act, in 1889. It permitted a company based in the state to own and operate properties in other jurisdictions.

In short order those interested in doing business on a national scope flocked to incorporate in New Jersey. The holding company format proved to be an ideal mechanism. Many existed solely as *shell operations,* entities whose chief purpose was to own and manage the stocks and operations of other firms located throughout the country. A holding company's board of directors performed the same sort of functions that Rockefeller's board of trustees had in the oil industry.

A holding company had several advantages over a trust. As owner rather than trustee of shares, it could assert even more direct control over operations. Its stock could be bought and sold on the exchanges more easily than trust certificates. Moreover, the 1890 Sherman Antitrust Act articulated the public's concern over trusts, and holding-company organizers hoped they might evade antitrust suits if they operated under an alternative format. As it turned out, the Sherman Act's language was broad enough to apply to any combination restraining interstate commerce, so a number of holding companies were sued and broken up in the early 1900s.

Other states soon followed New Jersey's example. Delaware was one of the first to emulate its neighbor, and the general incorporation legislation it passed proved extraordinarily attractive. Hundreds of corporations chose to establish their head offices, if not their whole management structures, in Wilmington or other Delaware locations. By the turn of the century, however, many other states had joined the trend, allowing holding companies of all sorts to proliferate throughout the United States.

The new formulation proved so popular that it ultimately superceded the trust format completely. Even Standard Oil reorganized as a New Jersey-based corporation in 1899. The word *trust* continued to retain its notoriety, however. Long after the last one had disappeared Americans continued to criticize what they considered to be the monopolistic or unfair behavior of the so-called beef trust, the sugar trust, or the money trust. Antitrust laws have continued to be applied almost exclusively to holding companies and other entities, not to trusts per se.

It should be noted that the passage of these more liberal general incorporation laws had many positive consequences. Businesses increasingly wanted and needed to operate on interstate or even national bases, and the new laws stripped away outmoded, parochial limitations. An alternative in the form of federal chartering or incorporation laws might have served this purpose, but no such legislation appeared. Instead it was left to innovative state governments to create a mechanism that would encourage the development of a truly national marketplace.

See also Antitrust Laws; Charter, State; Morgan, John Pierpont (J. P.); Northern Securities Co. Case; Trust.

References and Further Reading

Josephson, Matthew. *The Robber Barons.* New York: Harcourt, Brace and World, 1962.

Kirkland, Edward C. *Industry Comes of Age.* New York: Holt, Rinehart and Winston, 1961.

Micklethwait, John, and Adrian Wooldridge. *The Company: A Short History of a Revolutionary Idea.* New York: Modern Library, 2003.

Wiebe, Robert. *The Search for Order.* New York: Hill and Wang, 1967.

Gold Corner

In 1869 Jay Gould and Jim Fisk took advantage of the disparity between the value of gold and greenbacks and attempted to control the nation's supply of gold. The scheme peaked with a tumultuous spate of buying and selling on Black Friday, September 24, 1869.

Seven years earlier, the U.S. Treasury had begun issuing greenbacks (U.S. Notes) to help finance the Union government's Civil War campaign. Because these notes lacked any tangible backing, their value fluctuated wildly when compared to gold, falling to one-third of their face value at one point in 1864. A substantial price differential persisted even after the war, creating an active market for speculation in the Gold Room on Broad Street, adjacent to the New York Stock Exchange.

By 1869 the U.S. money supply contained only about $100 million in gold coins or certificates. The federal government held the vast majority of the specie, storing much of it in *subtreasuries.* A local subtreasury's primary function was to receive tax or other revenues and pay federal obligations. Occasionally the subtreasury in a particular city might sell gold for greenbacks or other currency to stabilize the market.

Jay Gould and Jim Fisk had recently captured control of the Erie Railroad from Cornelius Vanderbilt and his cronies. Gould initially used his railroad connections to justify his scheme to drive up the price of gold versus greenbacks. If gold increased in value, it would give overseas agents greater buying power. In Gould's view, this would encourage foreigners to buy more American farm produce—grain and other commodities that would travel on his Erie Railroad from the Midwest to New York City for export. Thus Gould tried to portray his actions as primarily benefiting hardworking American farm families.

Gould's plan to raise the value of gold depended on his ability to engineer a real or apparent shortage of specie. That meant that he had to prevent the New York subtreasury from emptying its vaults. To help him influence the federal government, he ingratiated himself with Abel R. Corbin, an elderly gentleman who had recently married President Ulysses Grant's sister. Gould purchased gold futures in Corbin's name and lavishly entertained him as a means to meet with Grant himself. Gould then urged the president to keep the subtreasury's gold off the market.

Having apparently neutralized the federal government, Gould and Fisk began buying gold futures on a massive scale. In late September 1869, the price of gold hovered around 130 or, essentially, a 30 percent premium compared to greenbacks. On Friday morning, September 24, the bidding began in the mid 130s and eventually topped 160. Gould had secretly learned, however, that Grant had broken with Corbin and ordered the New York subtreasury to flood the market with its gold reserves. Gould immediately reversed course and acted as a bear, selling his future contracts at high prices and reaping a substantial profit.

Fisk meanwhile continued to bid prices up until the news of the subtreasury's plans became public and instantly drove the price down to 138. The collapse apparently did not harm Fisk because he had not personally bought anything. Rather he was acting as an agent for a brokerage firm that was unable to meet its obligations and quickly collapsed. A congressional investigation of the attempted gold corner in 1870 failed to determine the size of Gould's profits or whether Fisk, too, benefited handsomely.

The audacity of this plan and the turmoil it created in the market helped convince federal authorities that they should end the price differential between gold and silver. In 1875 the Resumption Act promised that, as of 1879 the U.S. Treasury would exchange gold for greenbacks at their face value. This action stabilized the market and eventually ended the disparity altogether.

See also Gould, Jay; Greenbacks.

References and Further Reading

Grodinsky, Julius. *Jay Gould.* Philadelphia: University of Pennsylvania Press, 1957.

Klein, Maury. *The Life and Legend of Jay Gould.* Baltimore, MD: Johns Hopkins Press, 1986.

Greenbacks

The term *greenback* is generally applied to many types of federal paper currency because the reverse or back side of each bill is printed in green ink. Greenbacks first became familiar to Americans during the Civil War, and bills with this distinctive green color have circulated ever since.

There was good reason for the introduction of a new type of paper currency during the sectional conflict. The Union war effort's unprecedented expenses quickly stretched well beyond what Abraham Lincoln's government could reasonably collect from the traditional sources of taxes and loans. As an emergency expedient, Congress approved three bills authorizing the Union Treasury to issue a total of $450 million worth of U.S. Notes, but the amount actually distributed fell well short of that upper limit. Americans nicknamed these U.S. Notes greenbacks to distinguish them from other paper currency already in circulation.

As a fiat currency lacking any metallic or even institutional basis, greenbacks were a novelty even though enormous varieties of paper money circulated in the nineteenth century. Private banks had issued most of this paper money, but the federal government had from time to time chartered banks to issue federal bank notes. The Bank War in the 1830s brought a halt to that activity. Instead, the U.S. government relied on specie as the primary means of exchange, minting and circulating gold and silver coins in various denominations. The weight and bulk of gold coins then encouraged the Treasury to issue gold certificates that authorized the bearer to redeem them for the gold held in Treasury vaults. To emphasize the fact that these certificates were backed by gold, the reverse side of each bill was printed in orange (gold) ink. And, because of their guaranteed gold backing, these certificates were much more likely to circulate at face value than other types of paper money.

When Congress took the unprecedented step of approving the issuance of U.S. notes that were not backed by gold, the Treasury printed them with green backing rather than orange, hence the name *greenbacks.* The U.S. notes stated that they were "legal tender for all debts public and private." Federal authorities used them to buy war supplies and pay wages; citizens could pay taxes and other federal obligations with them at face value. But because they could not be exchanged directly for specie, private citizens often considered them risky. Consequently greenbacks tended to fluctuate in value, falling markedly when news from the front lines was discouraging but often recovering some of their value when the Union armies appeared to be moving toward victory. Fluctuations continued after the war so a gold exchange was established in New York City to facilitate trading between gold and greenbacks. This exchange was the focus of the attempted gold corner in 1869.

Uncertainties about the value of greenbacks caused many Americans to avoid them or call for their withdrawal from circulation. When the Panic of 1873 struck, however, the United States suffered severe price deflation that many attributed to an inadequate money supply. To correct this perceived problem, they advocated issuing even more greenbacks. That proposal was unpopular with the fiscally conservative Republicans who had dominated national politics since the war. When the Republicans lost enough seats in the 1874 elections to guarantee Democratic control in the next Congress, the lame-duck Republican majority took defensive action. In January it engineered passage of the Resumption Act of 1875. One of its key provisions legislated an end to the disparity between gold and greenbacks by ordering the Treasury to pay gold for greenbacks at face value beginning in 1879. But the widespread desire to maintain an adequate money supply as the depression worsened encouraged the inclusion of another provision that ordered the circulation of greenbacks to be stabilized at $300 million. Like most political compromises, this one disappointed the extremists on both sides: trenchant hard money advocates and those who hoped for an expansion of the money supply.

The controversy over greenbacks tended to pit debtors against creditors. Creditors were hardly likely to favor inflation that would effectively reduce the value of their loans. Debtors, on the other hand, stridently advocated an increase in the money supply so they could more easily meet their repayment obligations. Not surprisingly, any proposal for expanding the money supply was popular in the agrarian regions of the country. Many farmers had borrowed extensively, only to find themselves mired in an agricultural depression that persisted through the last quarter of the nineteenth century.

To strengthen their call for more greenbacks, some outspoken advocates organized a splinter political party. The Greenback Party fielded candidates for local and federal positions in 1876, but its presidential candidate attracted little support. When the depression plumbed new depths in 1878, however, congressional candidates running under the combined Greenback-Labor banner won over a million votes, primarily in rural districts. This demonstration of popular interest encouraged Congress to order the Treasury to stop withdrawing greenbacks. At that point a total of $346,681,000 remained in circulation. This legislation has never been rescinded, so U.S. notes remained in public circulation through the Second World War, mostly in the form of two-dollar bills. More recently the greenbacks have been held in storage but not destroyed, with Federal Reserve notes serving as the only circulating currency. Figure 3.1 illustrates the relative importance of greenbacks compared to other forms of money in circulation during the the late nineteenth century.

By late 1878, the resumption of gold payments ordered three years earlier was just around the corner, so the disparity in value between gold and greenbacks disappeared. Because the Treasury committed to redeem

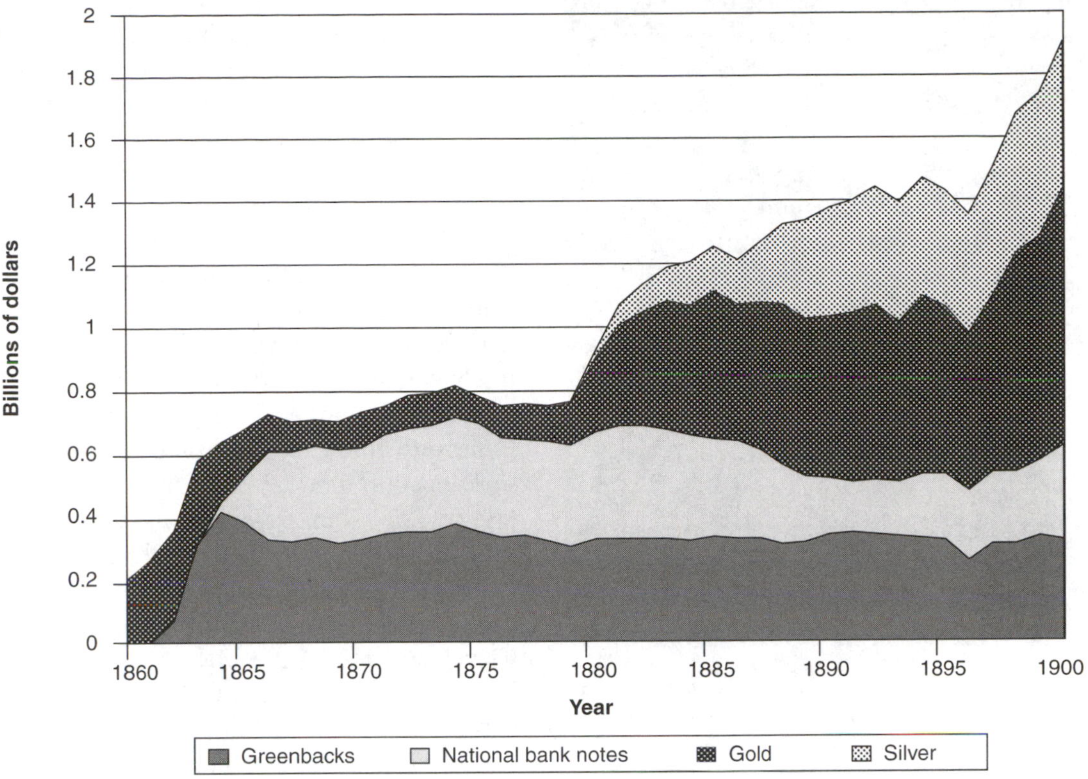

Figure 3.1 U.S. money supply in the Gilded Age, 1860–1900. (Data from Historical Statistics of the United States, Colonial Times to 1970. *Washington, DC: U.S. Bureau of the Census, 1975.)*

greenbacks at face value, they ceased to be considered soft money and lost their attraction to people hoping to use them to inflate the money supply. The committed advocates of a larger money supply switched their attention to the free silver movement, which peaked in 1896.

The stabilized circulation of U.S. notes was completed by 1880, but they were not the only bills with green backs. National bank notes lacked direct gold-backing as well, so when they began appearing during the Civil War, they, too, were printed with green backs. And, because these notes were the forerunners of the Federal Reserve notes in circulation today, the nation's paper currency can still appropriately be referred to as greenbacks.

See also Free Silver; Gold Corner; National Bank Notes; Panic of 1873.

References and Further Reading

Hoogenboom, Ari. *The Presidency of Rutherford B. Hayes.* Lawrence, KS: University Press of Kansas, 1988.

Nugent, Walter T. K. *Money and American Society, 1865–1890.* New York: Free Press, 1968.

Usher, Ellis B. *The Greenback Movement.* Milwaukee, WI: E. B. Usher, 1911.

Horizontal Integration

A company that controls, or nearly controls, one aspect of a production process is said to have achieved horizontal integration. A manufacturing process may, for example, require access to raw materials, transportation of those materials to a factory or mill, raw processing, finished production, distribution, and marketing. Any one of these stages of production could be targeted for horizontal integration. If a particular company or

John D. Rockefeller founded Standard Oil Co. His adoption of horizontal integration in refining and transportation led to Standard Oil's dominance of the industry. (Library of Congress)

group of companies can gain monopoly control over such a production stage, it may well be able to dominate a whole sector.

In the late nineteenth century, some entrepreneurs aggressively attempted to achieve such dominance. At one point, Henry Clay Frick achieved substantial horizontal integration of the Pennsylvania production of coke, a vital raw material for producing steel. That enabled him to charge very high prices, so high, in fact, that Andrew Carnegie decided he must bring Frick into partnership to cut costs. At that point, Frick's coke resources became a key element in the very successful vertical integration scheme that Carnegie exploited to reduce his production costs and enhance efficiencies.

Frick was exceptional in his ability to control a raw material. The U.S. economy had ample natural resources and a long tradition of private landholding and private enterprise. Whether the raw material was a mineral like iron ore or an agricultural commodity like cotton, thousands of individuals could take part in attempting to meet demand, jostling one another in an often brutal competitive struggle.

The burgeoning oil industry is a case in point. Once Canadian geologist Abraham Gesner demonstrated how crude oil could be distilled into clean-burning kerosene, a stampede to develop America's oil fields began. Early attention focused on the relatively easily exploited oil deposits in western Pennsylvania. Reminiscent of the California gold rush, thousands of eager oil seekers poured into the area, buying or leasing land, building boomtowns, and scrapping with one another over rights.

John D. Rockefeller viewed this brawling activity from the relative calm of nearby Cleveland, Ohio. At the end of the Civil War, he had invested some of the profits from his commission agency in an oil refinery. Recognizing that the raw material was too easily obtainable, he decided to expand his control over the refining business, laying the groundwork for horizontal integration. Where he could not buy, he leased; where he could not lease, he coerced. By 1870 Rockefeller and his associates had formed the Standard Oil Co., which controlled about 20 percent of all the refineries in the United States, the first step in his integration scheme.

To achieve this expansion, Rockefeller had negotiated substantial rebates from local railroads. That assured him much lower shipping costs than his rivals. In another five years Standard's very favorable rebates helped it become the nation's leading refiner. Facing a competitive threat from both railroads and shipping interests, Standard created the Central Refiner's Association. Aware of its parent company's size and competitive edge, many independents joined the association. This organizational structure gave Standard considerable control over the whole industry, enabling the company to allocate crude supplies, transportation capacity, and markets for itself and its associates.

Standing in the way of Standard's intention to complete its horizontal integration of refining were those who controlled the eastern transportation network. Both crude and refined oil moved primarily on railroad cars. In the early days, these were flat cars carrying wooden barrels, each holding about 45 gallons. In 1865 Amos Densmore introduced a major innovation: a flat car with two large, round, vertical tanks that could quickly be filled and emptied. Four years later these had evolved into the familiar sausage-shaped single-tank cars that have been the industry standard ever since. The railroads themselves owned and operated many of these tank cars just as they supplied gondola and box cars for other purposes.

The owner of the largest fleet of oil tank cars, however, was neither a railroad nor a refining operation. With the backing of Tom Scott, president of the Pennsylvania Railroad, Joseph Potts had organized the Empire Transportation Co., and it soon became the dominant force. Although Potts negotiated his most favorable deal with Scott, he made his cars available to other railroad operators as well. As Rockefeller's refining capacity grew, he necessarily ended up paying a good deal to Empire to transport his refined oil.

By the mid-1870s industry leaders, and the general public for that matter, recognized that Rockefeller's expanding holdings were threatening to dominate the industry. Potts decided to fight back by having his company move into refining. Rockefeller was outraged at this infringement on what he now considered his personal realm, and he moved ever more quickly and secretly to keep ahead of his competition. In the end, the bloody railroad strike of 1877, not Rockefeller's competition, toppled the Empire Transportation Co. The strike inflicted so much damage on the Pennsylvania Railroad that it simply had to cancel its financial support for the transport company.

Only one potential buyer had enough capital to absorb the pieces. The Standard Oil group purchased much of Empire's equipment at very low cost. As was typical in a Rockefeller takeover, the company's fleet of distinctive green tank cars continued to operate as though it was independent. Meanwhile, another Standard affiliate maintained the Union Tank Line, whose cars sported Standard Oil's bright red paint.

Pipelines offered a final threat to Standard's dominance. Several shorter pipelines had proven to be very efficient at carrying crude oil from fields to refining or reshipment points. In the late 1870s the Tidewater Pipe Co. began laying down a large-diameter pipeline across the Alleghenies, designed to link the oil regions with Atlantic Coast refineries and markets. To offset its potential advantage, Standard began building its own pipeline to the east, simultaneously expanding a network of smaller pipelines to collect crude from the wellheads. In the early 1880s, Rockefeller obtained enough shares in the Tidewater Co. to convince it to sign a quota agreement with its share fixed at 11 $^1/_2$ percent and Standard's affiliates controlling the remaining 88 $^1/_2$ percent.

At that point, Standard had effectively achieved a second level of horizontal integration to layer on top of its refining empire. Rockefeller associate Henry Flagler told a Congressional committee in 1888 that of the 6,132 tank cars in the United States, Standard's affiliated Union Tank Line owned 3,833. What he did not admit was that another 1,800 tank cars were owned by companies that were clandestine Standard affiliates. Thus Standard and its subordinates owned more than 90 percent of the nation's tank car fleet. Combined with its dominance in short and long pipelines, Standard had virtually total monopoly control of the oil transportation capabilities of the United States.

Although Standard companies did engage in some oil exploration and drilling, it was their horizontally integrated refining and transportation systems that enabled Rockefeller and his colleagues to control the oil industry. Another successful example of horizontal integration appeared in sugar refining, where at one point the United Sugar Co. controlled 98 percent of the nation's processing capacity. Although it was exercised by an oligopoly of five major participants, the meatpacking industry also represented an example of horizontal integration leading to full market control.

It is hardly surprising that the activities of these aggressive entrepreneurs came under federal scrutiny. State laws, regulations, and charter restrictions simply were not capable of exercising restraint. Congressional investigations ultimately led to legislative proposals that resulted in the Sherman Antitrust Act in 1890. Even so, Standard Oil and other powerful exploiters of horizontal integration continued to dominate their sectors of the economy for years to come.

See also Antitrust Laws; Dodd, Samuel Calvin Tate; Oligopoly; Rebates; Rockefeller, John Davison; Vertical Integration.

References and Further Reading

Carr, Albert Z. *John D. Rockefeller's Secret Weapon.* New York: McGraw Hill, 1962.

Chernow, Ron. *Titan: The Life of John D. Rockefeller, Sr.* New York: Knopf, 2004.

Hawke, David Freeman. *John D.: The Founding Father of the Rockefellers.* New York: Harper and Row, 1980.

Tarbell, Ida. *The History of the Standard Oil Company.* New York: McClure Phillips, 1904.

Interstate Commerce Commission

The Interstate Commerce Act that Congress approved in 1887 represented the first major implementation of the interstate commerce clause of the Constitution. The act was a response to cutthroat competition among railroads that had alienated many Americans. It created the Interstate Commerce Commission (ICC) and charged it with examining railroad rates and operations to prevent abuse. By 1900 a series of adverse court decisions had stripped away virtually all of the commission's power to regulate trade, however, undermining faith in federal regulation in general.

For almost a century, the interstate commerce clause written into the Constitution in 1787 remained largely neglected. Several cases argued before the Marshall Court called attention to the provision's existence, defending the supremacy of federal over state or local regulation of interstate commerce. But Congress failed to promulgate major federal initiatives to assert this authority. Particularly during the term of Chief Justice Roger Taney, the courts countenanced broad ranging state regulatory legislation even when it affected interstate commerce.

The growing complexity of internal trade and a strong adherence to the laissez-faire doctrine provided a wide field for corporate abuse. Railroads in particular engaged in brutal competition for routes, passengers, and freight. Their owners and managers used kickbacks, rebates, rate reductions, and many other devices to undermine rivals. Public hostility to special treatment for large shippers became particularly pronounced.

States responded to this growing resentment in a number of ways. One of the most effective was the Massachusetts Board of Railroad Commissioners, established in 1872. Headed by Charles Francis Adams, Jr., the commission codified state regulations, collected statistics, developed a model general incorporation act, and encouraged accurate accounting practices. Railroads operating within the state welcomed this impartial panel's recommendations, and the public reports that it issued helped level the playing field among competitors.

Many other state legislatures had long since passed laws regulating business activities within their borders. In the 1870s farmers in rural areas formed Granges, chapters of a broader organization known formally as the Patrons of Husbandry. These groups exercised enough political influence to encourage a whole new slate of "granger laws" that enhanced the scope and extent of state regulation of railroads.

Not surprisingly, these new laws provoked a response from railroad and grain elevator operators opposed to any government regulation of their activities. In its landmark decision in the case of *Munn v. Illinois,* however, the Supreme Court acknowledged the state's right to issue regulations regarding the prices a railroad-owned grain elevator paid to farmers. This decision sparked a new spate of granger laws over the next decade, with state governments aggressively attempting to regulate commerce.

That approach suffered a sharp setback in 1886 when the Supreme Court issued its decision in *Wabash v. Illinois.* In this instance, the state had attempted to set freight rates for the transportation of agricultural goods from Illinois to points east. The Court concluded that this action violated the Constitution's interstate commerce clause. If rate regulation across state lines was to be accomplished, Congress alone had the authority to do so.

While the *Wabash* decision is often credited with triggering the passage of the Interstate Commerce Act in the following year, the concept of federal rate regulation had already attracted a good deal of support. Railroads clearly had to operate across state lines, so state laws simply could not control them. Farmers who saw high freight rates eroding their profits, smaller shippers who could not negotiate a favorable rate, and people in general who could never count on consistent treatment all called for federal action. The idea was even popular among many of the railroad operators themselves because they hoped that a federal initiative might lessen the destructive competition they faced.

Dozens of congressmen had introduced unsuccessful bills calling for federal control of interstate commerce. In 1884 the platforms of both major political parties endorsed the concept. As momentum grew, the House and Senate developed separate approaches. These were so different that lengthy hearings had to be held to sort out a more acceptable approach. The final measure that emerged in 1887 was, not surprisingly, a complex, confusing compromise. As the first major attempt to erect a federal regulatory framework, it was bound to have flaws and inconsistencies.

The Interstate Commerce Act of 1887 prohibited rebates and other special deals for railroad customers. It also outlawed the practice of charging more for a short trip than a long one on the same railroad system, the so-called long-haul-short-haul abuse. The law also made pooling illegal. Although it did not specifically set rates, it called for them to be "reasonable and just" and ordered railroads to publish their rate schedules. Finally, the act called for naming a five-member commission to implement its various provisions.

Within a matter of months, the commission had received over 1,000 complaints and questions. Some of these came from people who wanted clarification of the law's provisions; many others were objections to them. The long-haul-short-haul provision proved especially controversial, and the commission struggled with interpretations and definitions. It also had to grapple with the question of what precisely constituted a "reasonable" rate.

The law was so confusing and open to interpretation that it inevitably provoked litigation. Even after the commission held hearings and made a decision, an aggrieved party could appeal it to the court system. The ICC found itself assailed in an expanding series of cases, some of which dragged on for several years; the courts were slow to abandon their opposition to government regulation of the economy.

Two Supreme Court decisions in 1897 almost completely eviscerated the Interstate Commerce Act. In the *Maximum Rate* case, the Court concluded that Congress had not given the ICC the power to prescribe rates. Shortly afterward, the decision in the *Alabama Midland* case undermined the commission's authority to end the long-haul-short-haul abuse. Having lost the ability to control rates, the ICC was reduced to little more than a data-collection agency.

The federal government's first major effort to regulate interstate commerce had been rendered toothless. New legislation in the twentieth century would restore some of the ICC's regulatory power, but only in response to a general weakening of laissez-faire sentiment during the Progressive Era. Even so, the passage of the Interstate Commerce Act and the early experience of the commission it created provided essential precedents for the much more widespread and pervasive application of the interstate commerce clause in years to come.

See also Antitrust Laws; Interstate Commerce Clause; Interstate Commerce Commission, Reform of; Railroad Consolidation.

References and Further Reading

Faulkner, Harold U. *The Decline of Laissez Faire: 1897–1917.* New York; Rinehart, 1951.

Frankfurter, Felix. *The Commerce Clause.* Chapel Hill, NC: University of North Carolina Press, 1937.

Garraty, John A. *The New Commonwealth: 1877–1890.* New York, Harper and Row, 1968.

Knights of Labor

For a time, the Noble and Holy Order of the Knights of Labor appeared to be a model national organization for all working Americans. Founded in 1869 it grew slowly until it opened its doors to both skilled and unskilled workers. In the 1880s its membership rose dramatically and its affiliates became involved in a number of confrontations with employers. After a few dramatic successes, the Knights suffered one debilitating defeat after another, and the organization shriveled to an ineffective remnant in the early 1890s.

A group of nine tailors founded the first Assembly of the Knights of Labor in Philadelphia in 1869. They adopted a complex ritual and operated as a secret society for nearly a decade. It did admit what it called sojourners from other cities and other crafts, and these, in turn, convinced new members to join. Uriah Stephens became the national organization's first Grand Master Workman, and he emphasized reform and cooperatives over industrial strife. Secrecy was deemed essential to protect members from being summarily fired. This factor certainly seemed wise in light of the virulent antiunion sentiments that flared during and after the railroad strike of 1877.

When Stephens left the organization in 1879 to pursue an unsuccessful political career, Terence V. Powderly picked up the reins. A thoughtful strategist, Powderly constantly emphasized that the organization he led was not a union in the traditional sense. He encouraged the Knights to abandon secrecy and admit members from traditional unions as well as unskilled laborers. The Knights of Labor quickly began to grow as Americans from diverse industries and with a broad range of capabilities signed on.

Powderly was an outspoken opponent of strikes and boycotts. He preferred to direct his efforts at consulting and negotiating with employers and creating cooperatives for the membership. The latter strategy was somewhat successful, but as economic conditions deteriorated generally in the mid-1880s, local units of the Knights resorted to strikes. When these incidents occurred, Powderly reluctantly endorsed them and used the organization's resources to support those out of work.

The most dramatic confrontation involved a strike that began when the Wabash Railroad announced wage cuts in 1885. The Knights imposed a boycott on Wabash equipment that caused major disruptions throughout Jay Gould's extensive railroad empire. The notoriously antiunion magnate conferred with Powderly, and they worked out an agreement that restored wage levels and protected jobs. In a matter of months, the paid membership of the Knights of Labor rose from about 100,000 to over 700,000. Powderly and the central organization had barely managed to maintain control of their sprawling federation of semi-independent local assemblies earlier—it now became completely impossible.

Worse yet, smarting from his embarrassing concessions to the Knights, Jay Gould handled the next strike against his companies with ruthless efficiency. Thousands of strikers lost their jobs in this confrontation, the first in a series of highly publicized failures for the union. Even though the Knights of Labor had opposed a national strike for an eight-hour working day in 1886, the country's most prominent labor organization nevertheless became the target of antiunion and antiradical outrage in the wake of the deadly Haymarket Affair in 1886.

Powderly left the dispirited organization in 1893 when its membership had fallen below 75,000. It dwindled into insignificance in subsequent years, a victim in part of its overblown, hothouse growth. More important, however, was the fact that it simply did not meet the nation's needs at the time. The conservative and carefully organized American Federation of Labor offered a much more effective mechanism for skilled workers to achieve their goals. But that organization refused to enroll the unskilled workers who had briefly found hope in the Noble and Holy Order of the Knights of Labor.

See also American Federation of Labor; National Labor Union; Pool.

References and Further Reading

Dulles, Foster Rhea. *Labor in America.* New York: Crowell, 1966.

Fink, Leon. *Workingmen's Democracy: The Knights of Labor and American Politics.* Urbana, IL: University of Illinois Press, 1996.

Weir, Robert E. *Beyond Labor's Veil: The Culture of the Knights of Labor.* University Park, PA: Pennsylvania State University Press, 1996.

Land Grant Railroads

Between 1850 and 1871 Congress approved a series of bills that transferred public land to various railroad projects. Most of this activity occurred after the outbreak of the Civil War and focused on the construction of six different transcontinental railroads. Financial difficulties, geographic obstacles, and uncertain economic returns dogged all these projects. The first transcontinental connection opened in 1869, and the other tracks succeeded in linking the Midwest and the West Coast over the next three decades. Collectively, the land grants and associated government investment in these endeavors represented the largest peacetime federal business investment.

Railroad construction was already booming in the United States in the 1840s when a visionary named Asa Whitney first proposed that the federal government grant public lands to support construction of a transcontinental line. He had lived in China for a couple of years and was entranced by the concept of linking the eastern United States with the Orient over a landline to the Pacific Coast. He lobbied Congress energetically for years, but sectional politics thwarted his vision. If a railroad across a northern route was proposed, southern congressmen insisted on a similar commitment to build across the southern territories, and no consensus was ever reached.

The first federal railroad land grant avoided this problem by focusing on a route that would link North and South. In 1850 Congress gave tracts of land in Illinois, Mississippi, and Alabama to the promoters of the Illinois Central Railroad. This legislation set a precedent for future grants. The company was assigned the alternate or odd-numbered sections stretching 6 miles on each side of its right of way. Although the government was expected to compensate for the grants by doubling the price of the adjacent public land that remained under its control, historical evidence suggests that this policy failed to achieve the desired objective. Nevertheless, all subsequent land-grants used the same checkerboard system, with later grants providing more land per mile of track completed.

The withdrawal of Southern delegates from Congress in 1861 freed Northern senators and representatives to move ahead on a transcontinental land grant connecting the free states with California. A group of Californians created the first company that lined up to receive a grant. An engineer named Theodore Judah had already convinced four

The first transcontinental railroad was completed in 1869 when the golden spike was hammered into place linking two land grant railroads, the Central Pacific from the West and the Union Pacific from the East. (National Archives)

Sacramento businessmen that he had surveyed a feasible route from Sacramento over the Sierra Nevada Range. Based on Judah's claim, Collis P. Huntington, Leland Stanford, Mark Hopkins, and Charles Crocker—the so-called Big Four—created the Central Pacific Railroad Company in 1861 and sought financial backing from Congress.

Congress responded with the Pacific Railroad Act of 1862, offering 10 square miles or sections of federal land for each mile of track laid. The legislation also included federal loans with thirty-year payouts at 6 percent interest. For each mile of track laid, the company would receive a loan of $16,000, $32,000, or $48,000 depending on whether the route lay through level, hilly, or mountainous terrain. Congress also created a commission charged with raising sufficient capital to begin construction. The Civil War provided plenty of other attractive investment possibilities, however, forcing Congress to sweeten the deal by approving a second Pacific Railroad Act in 1864. It doubled the size of the land grants from ten to twenty sections per mile and allowed the federal loans to be counted as second rather than first mortgages. These more favorable terms satisfied both the Central Pacific's promoters and the group that formed the Union Pacific Railroad Company.

The Central Pacific began laying tracks early in 1864, heading east from Sacramento. The Union Pacific's start was delayed until mid-1865, and its tracks moved slowly westward from Omaha. Lacking the concerted authority and wealth of California's Big Four, the Union Pacific struggled financially until it established a separate company to serve as contractor for the work. Eventually known as the Credit Mobilier, this organization's suspect financial arrangements and multimillion dollar profits became the subject of a political scandal that tainted the Grant administration in the 1870s.

Hoping to earn more land and loans, the two railroads laid out 200 miles of overlapping roadbed in Utah. It took a joint resolution of Congress to force the companies to link their rails with a golden spike at Promontory Point on May 10, 1869. Over the next two decades this first transcontinental route became the heart of two expanding systems. The Union Pacific dominated the nation's midsection with branch lines linking Colorado, Nebraska, and other adjacent states into its central artery. The Big Four continued to dominate West Coast transportation, obtaining an additional land grant for the Southern Pacific route and extending their reach northward into Oregon.

Four other transcontinental railroads received generous federal land grants as well, but none of them benefited from the federal loan programs that had helped finance the Union Pacific and the Central Pacific. Both the Northern Pacific and the Great Northern lines planned to link the upper Midwest with the Pacific Northwest, and each received up to forty sections of land for every mile of track. The Atchison, Topeka, and Santa Fe carved out its main route through the northern reaches of the New Mexico and Arizona Territories. Further south, the Texas and Pacific Railroad was the smallest system that emerged. Chartered in 1871, it received the last major grant of federal land and was repeatedly the target of financial speculation and corporate warfare. Jay Gould finally took control in the early 1880s and used the road as the centerpiece in his expanding southwestern system.

Collectively, the six transcontinental roads received 77 percent of all of the federal land granted. Another 15 percent went to midwestern regionals like the Illinois Central, and the final 8 percent was distributed to southern roads attempting to rebuild during the Reconstruction Era. In addition to these federal grants, a number of states provided land to encourage development of local rail service. The total area thus granted was a just under 180 million acres, of which 130 million came from federal lands and almost 50 million derived from state resources. The 280,000 square miles thus transferred from public to private ownership is greater than the combined areas of the states of California and Nevada.

While this might appear to have been a stupendous gift and subsidy to corporate America, much of the land was either unproductive or rather quickly redistributed to settlers and other users. James J. Hill was perhaps the most energetic of all the promoters, offering substantial tracts to anyone who would agree to settle along his Great Northern route. He mounted elaborate advertising campaigns both in the United States and abroad designed to attract immigrants and emigrants to the Red River Valley. In a sense, then, some of the federal lands had simply been transferred to enthusiastic sales agents. Whether settlement came faster or slower in particular regions as a result of the distribution of land grants to railroads remains a matter of dispute. But there can be little doubt that the process did encourage the completion of a nationwide rail network sooner than would otherwise have been the case.

The Credit Mobilier scandal was only one of the factors that discouraged Congress from distributing further land to railroad construction companies. The six major routes already either constructed or envisioned would provide reasonably comprehensive rail service to the expanding West. Moreover, all of the companies that received land grants encountered a host of finance and capitalization problems throughout the period. The most dramatic was the failure of Jay Cooke's financial house in 1873. This was largely attributable to his overinvestment in the struggling Northern Pacific Railroad.

The railroad land-grant era lasted only two decades, but it encompassed some of the most optimistic and visionary planning in American history. It represented a creative way of converting the nation's land wealth into capital for industry. In that way, it placed the federal government very actively at the heart of the industrial revolution, a major break from the laissez-faire attitudes that generally prevailed in the nineteenth century.

See also Cooke, Jay; Credit Mobilier; Gould, Jay; Railroad Consolidation.

References and Further Reading

Bain, David Haward. *Empire Express: Building the First Transcontinental Railroad.* New York: Penguin Books, 2000.

Eliot, Jane. *The History of the Western Railroads.* New York: Crescent Books, 1995.

Greever, William S. *Arid Domain: The Santa Fe Railway and Its Western Land Grant.* Stanford, CA: Stanford University Press, 1954.

Mercer, Lloyd J. *Railroads and Land Grant Policy.* New York: Academic Press, 1982.

National Bank Notes

During the Civil War, Congress approved issuing national bank charters to private institutions. These banks were then authorized to issue national bank notes based on their holdings. They circulated for many years, eventually to be supplanted by the Federal Reserve notes still in use today.

While the national banking system, established in 1862, had long-term consequences for both banking and finance, it was created primarily to help the U.S. Treasury borrow money to pay for the Union war effort. Once it became clear that the conflict would continue well beyond the optimistic estimates (on both sides) of six months, Treasury Secretary Salmon Chase faced a rapidly escalating demand for federal funds. Tax collections paid for only about 21 percent of the wartime costs, and the issuance of greenbacks accounted for another 13 percent. That meant that over 60 percent of the needed revenue had to be borrowed.

To accomplish that goal, the Treasury issued a variety of government bonds. The fluctuating fortunes of the Union armies and the protracted length of the conflict dampened enthusiasm among potential war-bond buyers. The government had not offered a federal banking charter to any institution since President Andrew Jackson destroyed the central bank in the Bank War in the 1830s. Congress broke that precedent by passing the National Banking Act (1863, revised in 1864) that offered federal charters to interested individuals and institutions. To qualify for such a charter, the bank had to agree to purchase a minimum of $30,000 worth of federal bonds.

Throughout the nineteenth century, institutions had been issuing their own banknotes. The advantage the federal charter granted was the authority to issue national bank notes backed by the federal bonds the banks had purchased. Because these bonds in effect provided a federal guarantee of the value of the notes, they generally circulated at their face value. As it turned out, the federal restrictions and promised stable currency values were not uniformly attractive to those who had profited in the free-wheeling, unregulated private banking environment. Congress therefore imposed a 10 percent annual tax on private banknotes to encourage bankers to apply for a federal charter and, not incidentally, to purchase war bonds. The result was that 1,644 national banks had been formed by October 1866. Figure 3.2 demonstrates that national bank notes completely supplanted the banknotes issued by banks prior to the creation of the national banking system.

At the end of the war, some $300 million in national bank notes were in circulation throughout the United States. The victory at Appomattox sharply reduced the federal government's need to borrow money, however, so it gradually ceased issuing new

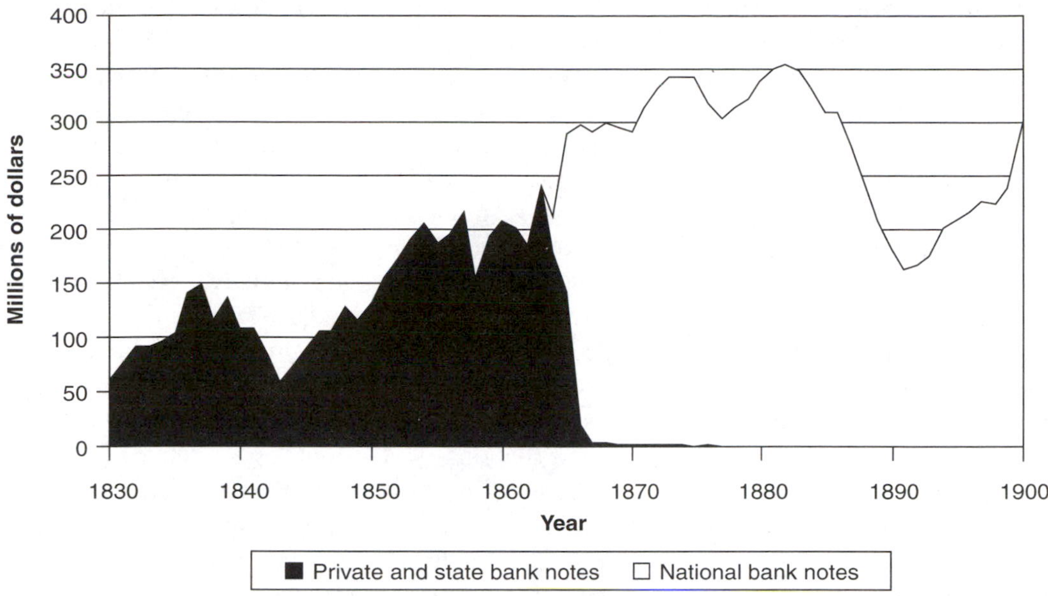

Figure 3.2 Banknotes in nineteenth century America, 1830–1900. (Data from Historical Statistics of the United States, Colonial Times to 1970. *Washington, DC: U.S. Bureau of the Census, 1975.)*

bonds. Moreover, because the war-inspired high tariffs remained equally attractive to postwar Republican politicians, the federal government soon found itself collecting far more in tax (tariff) revenue than it needed to cover current expenses.

The resulting federal surplus allowed the Treasury to retire many of its war bonds far in advance of their anticipated redemption dates. The decline in the number of bonds outstanding led to a corresponding decline in the amount of federal backing available for the national bank notes. By 1891 the total amount in circulation had fallen to $168 million, far below the wartime level. This reduction in the money supply came just at the moment when free silver advocates were insisting that the money supply needed to be expanded dramatically. Even so, the federal government did not seriously consider expanding the circulation of national bank notes.

Additional bonds were issued during the Spanish-American War at the end of the decade, however, and additional borrowing in the twentieth century increased the number of bonds available as backing for national bank notes. In 1913, on the eve of the creation of the Federal Reserve System, the 7,473 national banks had more than $700 million worth of national bank notes in circulation. Gradually Federal Reserve notes, similarly backed by federal securities, ended up taking the place of national bank notes. Today, institutions throughout the United States retain their federal charters and the right to call themselves national banks, but they no longer issue banknotes like their nineteenth and early twentieth century antecedents.

See also Banknotes; Federal Reserve System; Free Silver; Greenbacks.

References and Further Reading

Davis, Andrew M. *Origin of the National Banking System.* New York: Arno Press, 1980.

Hammond, Bray. 1970. *Sovereignty and an Empty Purse: Banks and Politics in the Civil War.* Princeton, NJ: Princeton University Press, 1970.

Nugent, Walter T. K. *Money and American Society, 1865–1890.* New York: Free Press, 1968.

National Labor Union

Throughout the early nineteenth century labor organizers in various industries called for the formation of national organizations to promote workers' causes. Early efforts brought together activists in particular sectors, but most of these were short-lived. A more general approach resulted in the formation of the National Labor Union in 1866. It pursued political solutions to workers' problems, a strategy that received little encouragement in the laissez-faire economy. By tying its fortunes to a failing general political reform movement, the union soon disappeared as well.

Prior to the Civil War, labor union activity focused primarily on improving working conditions and providing social support for workers in specific industries or with particular skills. Most of these initiatives were localized, grappling with economic conditions in the immediate area. Occasional efforts were made to link local activities with those in other cities or towns, but these generally failed to materialize or, if they did, they faded quickly.

The typographers were an exception. For many years local associations of printers had exchanged information about wages, encouraged skilled workers to demand fair pay, and opposed the hiring of unqualified individuals. In 1850 a New York local hosted a convention that drew delegates from five other cities. This led to subsequent meetings, the adoption of a constitution, and the creation of the National Typographical Union in 1852. This organization of highly skilled, literate, and articulate workers became the first national union to survive.

Organizers in other industries attempted to emulate this achievement. Local unions representing iron molders, for example, responded to a call in 1859 for a national organization. William H. Sylvis traveled all across the country, working with local organizers and encouraging cooperation. He was named treasurer of the national group. By 1865 the Iron Molders' International Union was the nation's most prominent labor organization.

But Sylvis had become convinced that strikes and confrontations were far from ideal methods to improve the worker's lot, so he looked for an alternative. He joined other unions' leaders in calling for a meeting in Baltimore in 1866. This assemblage laid the basis for the creation of the National Labor Union. Rather than focusing on the bread and butter issues that dominated local union discussions, the new grouping emphasized political activism. One of its primary goals was to urge passage of laws in favor of an eight-hour work day. It also advocated government action to restrict immigration, especially from the Far East, to outlaw convict labor, and even to establish a federal department of labor. At the same time, the group was sensitive to the needs and desires of women and blacks in the workforce.

Sylvis was elected president of the National Labor Union, and under his leadership it became increasingly politicized. Reformers of all sorts either joined the union or attempted to garner its support for their causes. Concern for the plight of workers lost ground to more general reforms like expanding the money supply and women's suffrage. Some even called for the organization to transform itself into a full-scale political party.

Sylvis died suddenly in 1869, leaving the National Labor Union rudderless. By 1872 it had forged a fatal alliance with Horace Greeley who ran a hopeless presidential campaign against a very popular Ulysses Grant. Many of the political initiatives the union had supported ultimately came to pass, but it signally failed as an effective means for improving working conditions. Other leaders and other approaches were necessary to achieve that goal.

See also American Federation of Labor; Knights of Labor.

References and Further Reading

Dulles, Foster Rhea. *Labor in America.* New York: Crowell, 1966.

Taft, Philip. *Organized Labor in American History.* New York: Harper and Row, 1964.

Office Appliances

During the last quarter of the nineteenth century American inventors and manufacturers produced a cornucopia of mechanical aids designed for business. Typewriters, adding machines, and cash registers quickly became standard in offices and shops all across the country. The concurrent appearance of such machines, generally referred to in those days as office appliances, was hardly surprising. All of them used intricate keyboard, printing, and mechanical devices encouraging rapid evolution and improvement.

A desire to relieve clerks of the tedious process of hand-writing information in ledgers and letters encouraged many American tinkerers to try to mechanize writing. In 1866 Christopher Latham Sholes developed a machine with individual type bars manipulated by keys. Because he relied on gravity to return his type bars to their starting positions, any attempt at speedy typing created a tangle of bars. But Sholes was a printer, well aware of the frequency and location of individual letters in English text. He used that knowledge to lay out his keyboard so letters used frequently in combinations struck the printing surface from different angles. Long after springs and electric motors had eliminated the tangling problem, typists continue to use the QWERTY arrangement of keys that Sholes devised.

Sholes's successful prototypes attracted the attention of E. Remington Sons, a company whose experience included the manufacture of small arms and sewing machines. Sholes signed an agreement with Remington in 1873 to build his typewriters, and they quickly found a market. Five years later Remington introduced machines that could type both capital and lower case letters. A decade later, the company shifted the orientation of the action so the typist could actually read the printed text emerging from a platen facing the keyboard.

E. Remington Sons began manufacturing typewriters such as this 1873 model based upon the invention of printer Christopher Latham Sholes. (Time and Life Pictures/Getty Images)

Hundreds of other companies produced typewriters incorporating these characteristics, and over 100,000 machines were selling each year by the late 1890s. Its early start and continuous innovations allowed Remington to remain the industry leader well into the next century. Electromagnetic relays were introduced by some manufacturers in the 1920s, a technology IBM aggressively marketed in its electric typewriters in the 1940s and 1950s.

Mechanical adding machines appeared as early as the seventeenth century, generally consisting of interlocked wheels that advanced one another to deal with the issue of carrying. By the late nineteenth century, simple, stylus-driven adders had become common even in private households. William Seward Burroughs recognized that businesses would be interested in something more robust than these flimsy devices. He produced his first keyed calculator in the mid-1880s and had incorporated a printed recording tape into it by 1893. The Burroughs company manufactured millions of adding machines, paralleling Remington's success in the typewriter industry.

The standard Burroughs machine had rows of keys running from 9 to 0 pegged to gears inside much like the simpler adding machines they replaced. A major innovation came with the installation of a handle that pushed a lever to record a transaction. It allowed operators to double-check their entries by looking at the depressed keys before pulling the handle. Electric motors replaced the handles in the 1920s. Other companies like Monroe took the technology even further, producing electrically powered calculators that could multiply and divide as well as add and subtract. All of them, however, tended to resemble the multibutton, roll-printing design that Burroughs had pioneered in the 1890s.

Similar features became familiar in cash registers. Two brothers living in Dayton, Ohio, James and John Ritty built a prototype cash register in 1879 and formed the National Manufacturing Co. two years later to build and market their machines. The early standard they set included pop-up number flags so both seller and buyer could observe the transaction. The registers did exactly that: they registered each sale on a paper tape, creating a continuous record of commercial activity.

In 1884 another Dayton resident, coal dealer John Patterson purchased a couple of Ritty cash registers. Soon his company's accounts were in far better order than ever before, leading to efficiencies and reliable records. Patterson was so impressed that he bought a majority interest in the failing National Manufacturing Co. and renamed it National Cash Register (NCR). The new company prospered from the start, often leasing its equipment rather than selling it.

The market for cash registers was enormous, given the number of small businesses in the United States. NCR distributed over a million registers in 1911 alone, and its volume continued to grow. The standard machine maintained an internal record of all transactions on a paper tape, produced a printed receipt for the customer, and contained partitioned drawers for currency and coins. As it had in adding machines and typewriters, electric power replaced the earlier mechanical operation, but the basic functions remained very similar to those of NCR machines perfected in the 1890s.

Office appliances of all kinds had an enormous impact in the United States. They facilitated buying and selling, record keeping, accounting, and communication. They truly qualified as labor-saving machines, enabling clerks, secretaries, and other office workers to be far more efficient. They also laid the groundwork for the development of the information age that would come to fruition in the twentieth century.

See also Computers; Patterson, John Henry; Remington, Philo; Tabulating; Watson, Thomas J.

References and Further Reading

Current, Richard N. *The Typewriter and The Men Who Made It.* Arcadia, CA: Post-Era Books, 1988.

Ifrah, Georges. *The Universal History of Computing.* New York: Wiley, 2000.

Marcosson, Isaac Frederick. *Wherever Men Trade.* New York: Arno Press, 1972.

Oligopoly

An oligopoly exists when a small number of companies or individuals can control or manipulate the market for a particular sector or service. Americans have generally been uncomfortable with oligopoly or, at the extreme level, monopoly control. Antitrust suits and legislation have frequently focused on rooting out or breaking up oligopolies. Even so, oligopolies have developed and persisted in a number of sectors, especially since the end of the Civil War.

The meatpacking industry in the late nineteenth century provides an example of how an industry with literally thousands of independent participants evolved into one in which five major players came to dominate. German-born Nelson Morris profited enormously from supplying food to Union troops during the Civil War. As a buyer, he had few peers in judging the true value of livestock. Unlike his competitors, Morris also invested in western lands to guarantee that he would have access to supplies of high-quality cattle. By the 1870s he was a prominent participant in Chicago's bustling and rapidly expanding meatpacking industry.

A New Englander by birth, Philip Danforth Armour also headed for the Midwest as a young man, working initially with partners in Milwaukee. Armour's first major coup involved selling pork futures short in anticipation of the price decline that would inevitably occur when the Civil War ended. He cleared well over $1 million in that speculation alone, enabling him to expand his interests both in meatpacking and grain. When Armour relocated to Chicago in the mid-1870s, one of his partners, Michael Cudahy headed further west to establish a dominant position at the Omaha stockyards.

Another key player who arrived in Chicago in 1875 was Gustavus Swift, a successful New England butcher and meat seller. At that point the eastern market for beef and pork was fairy limited, but the huge supply of beef on the hoof in Chicago stimulated Swift's entrepreneurial imagination. He was one of the pioneers in adopting both refrigerated rail cars and storage facilities. Swift's packing plants in Chicago used these technological innovations to supply fresh meat to Boston and New York in substantial quantities. The taste and market for Swift's products quickly expanded.

The final element of what would develop into the meatpacking oligopoly was the firm of Schwarzchild and Sulzerger. Founded by German immigrants, it had initially specialized in the kosher meat business. In the 1880s and 1890s, S&S grew quite large, competing with other major meatpacking giants on an equal footing. By the time of the First World War, however, the company was near bankruptcy and its stockholders welcomed a takeover by Thomas E. Wilson. He renamed the company after himself, and Wilson and Co. thrived under his leadership.

During the late nineteenth and early twentieth centuries, the companies these pioneers founded came to exercise enormous control over the meatpacking industry. Swift, Armour, Morris, Cudahy, and S&S (later Wilson) thus constituted the associates of the perceived oligopoly that dominated the industry. Jointly they controlled more than half of all the business in the United States and were major exporters of meat and meat products as well. The extent of the group's influence in some areas was even more pronounced, such as their combined ownership or control of over 90 percent of the nation's refrigerator cars. Other food producers and shippers who needed these specialized railroad cars to preserve their goods helped line the pockets of the meatpacking oligopoly.

From time to time, various members of this meatpacking elite resorted to outright collusion and price fixing. A number of secret arrangements and secret meetings occurred over the years, designed to reduce the destructive competition that might have occurred in an unregulated market. In 1888, for example, Swift, Armour, and Morris formed the Allerton pool, which federal investigators charged with price fixing. There is some evidence that the publicity about these arrangements helped trigger the passage of the Sherman Antitrust Act two years later.

Fear of federal intervention did not seem to concern the oligopolists. In 1893 Cudahy joined the same three firms in sending representatives to weekly meetings at the offices of Henry Veeder. A lawyer who had originally worked with Swift and Co., Veeder oversaw discussions in which the participants divided the market among themselves and agreed to mutually beneficial prices. The popular perception was that when animals arrived at a stockyard four or five bidders would appear representing the major firms. In fact, only one of these would make a serious offer at a relatively low price, and the other company agents would defer to the designated buyer.

Although they benefited from such informal arrangements, the major players also attempted to reduce competition still further through consolidation. In 1902 Swift, Armour, and Morris agreed to a merger that would create a super corporation capable of controlling 60 percent of the market. When that deal fell through due to problems collecting sufficient capital, the companies incorporated a new entity named the National Packing Co. For a time, this shell organization functioned in the same manner that the Veeder pool had done earlier.

Muckrakers and other critics stigmatized these companies as the Beef Trust although no formal consolidation ever took place. Both stock growers, who believed the oligopoly was deflating their income, and consumers, who blamed it for arbitrary price fixing, agitated for government action. Between 1902 and 1910, federal authorities instituted six different antitrust suits against the major players and their associated companies. None of them ended in definitive rulings. By 1916 the so-called Big Five had expanded their control to almost two-thirds of the total market.

Similar oligopolies developed in other industries, although many of the participants remained stubbornly independent of one another. The Big Three automobile manufacturers in the 1930s and 1940s are representative. Ford, General Motors, and Chrysler built and marketed a variety of automobiles at all price levels to compete one-on-one with those of their rivals. Throughout that period, a number of smaller independent automakers continued to survive like Studebaker, Packard, and Nash, building for more specialized segments of the market. The dominance of the Big Three seemed to be growing even more pronounced in the United States until Japanese and European cars began to cut into their sales.

Over time, in part due to the perceived excesses of players like the Big Five meatpackers, the term *oligopoly* assumed a somewhat negative connotation. As the consolidation movements of recent decades have occurred, however, American consumers are increasingly being served by relatively few producers or marketers in a substantial range of goods and services. Whether one considers the major broadcast networks, motion picture studios, or recording labels, for example, a handful of companies provides the major output in each entertainment medium. Thus de facto oligopolies exist on a broad scale in twenty-first century America.

See also Antitrust Laws; Armour, Philip Danforth; Horizontal Integration; Monopoly; Swift, Gustavus Franklin.

References and Further Reading

Corey, Lewis. *Meat and Man.* New York: Viking, 1950.

Fowler, Bertram B. *Men, Meat and Miracles.* New York: Julian Messner, 1952.

Leech, Harper, and John Charles Carroll. *Armour and His Times.* New York: Appleton-Century, 1938.

Swift, Louis F. *The Yankee of the Yards.* Chicago: A. W. Shaw, 1927.

Panic of 1873

Popularly known as Jay Cooke's Panic, a financial crisis that began in September 1873 was the first warning that the American economy was dangerously overheated. Cooke's banking house had issued far too many shares and bonds in the attempt to finance building the Northern Pacific Railroad. Driven into insolvency, the firm abruptly closed. The unexpected failure of the nation's leading brokerage house set off a chain reaction of other financial collapses before the end of the year and ushered in a major depression that lasted through the end of the decade.

The New York Stock Exchange closed on Saturday, September 20th after the collapse of Jay Cooke's financial house triggered the Panic of 1873. (Library of Congress)

The Panic of 1873 was a startling and disquieting end to an industrial and financial upturn that arose during the Civil War and persisted through the postwar years. Investments in manufacturing and transportation appeared to be sure moneymakers in the northern economy. Pent-up international demand raised cotton prices and assured profits to those southerners fortunate enough to harvest new crops. Fueling this economic euphoria were large supplies of greenbacks, national bank notes, and war bonds that were available for capital investments.

Westward expansion blossomed as well. The 1862 Homestead Act encouraged new settlement in public lands, and federal land grants stimulated transcontinental railroad construction. The Union Pacific and Central Pacific railroads joined their tracks in Utah in 1869. Their success encouraged Congress to approve additional land grants for other transcontinental lines.

The Northern Pacific's grant encompassed 47 million acres of public land and attracted thousands of investors. In 1869 the project came under the exclusive control of Jay Cooke and his Philadelphia and New York-based brokerage houses. Capitalizing on his success and fame as the financier of the Union war effort, Cooke mounted a similarly ambitious and energetic fund-raising campaign for the railroad project. Even though construction dawdled, his firm optimistically issued stocks and bonds with a par value of over $100 million, intending to sell half of them in Europe.

By the early 1870s, however, European buyers had grown skeptical of American railroad securities. Publicity about the Credit Mobilier scandal associated with the building of the Union Pacific demonstrated just how questionable, and even criminal, some of these huge funding schemes could be. The 1869 Chicago fire wiped out substantial amounts of investment capital as well. Meanwhile many new investment opportunities competed for the attention of potential investors both in the United States and abroad. There simply was not enough capital available to fuel all of these endeavors even if they had been well managed and prudently structured.

The Northern Pacific was neither. It was true that constructing a railroad through virtually unpopulated territory took immense amounts of capital. But years or even decades of settlement and development would be necessary to begin to pay off this enormous investment. No individual or group of individuals could possibly have made this an immediately profitable enterprise, but the fact that it was the redoubtable Jay Cooke who failed ensured that the panic on Wall Street and throughout the country would be intense.

Cooke's overextended financial empire collapsed quickly once the Northern Pacific project failed. Its tentacles were intertwined with other banking and brokerage operations that also quickly fell into bankruptcy. The negative pressure was so intense that the New York Stock Exchange closed down all operations for ten days. Before the year was out, over 5,000 commercial firms failed. Industries related to railroads suffered particular damage. The anticipation of escalating demand from the railroad-building boom encouraged too much construction of steel mills, for example, and only the most efficient and well-managed plants survived the downturn. Hard times hit industrialized urban areas first, but falling prices, unemployment, and massive financial losses combined to reduce consumer demand for all products. Agricultural prices had begun to soften even before the panic set in; they fell even more quickly when the depression's deflationary effects took hold. Figure 3.3 shows the profound effect both the Panics of 1873 and 1893 had on the nation's gross national product (GNP), a comprehensive measure of all economic activity in a given year.

The depression of the late 1870s was the nation's first full-scale industrial downturn, and it set off the first nationwide labor confrontation. The railroad strike of 1877 shocked and angered an already disheartened populous. Recovery was slow to develop, and the economic outlook only gradually improved by 1879. Henry Villard inherited the Northern Pacific Railroad project and, using watered stock and hype, managed to complete construction of the line in the early 1880s. Then he, too, floundered into bankruptcy, opening the way for James J. Hill to take control and to consolidate the troubled line with his much more successful Great Northern.

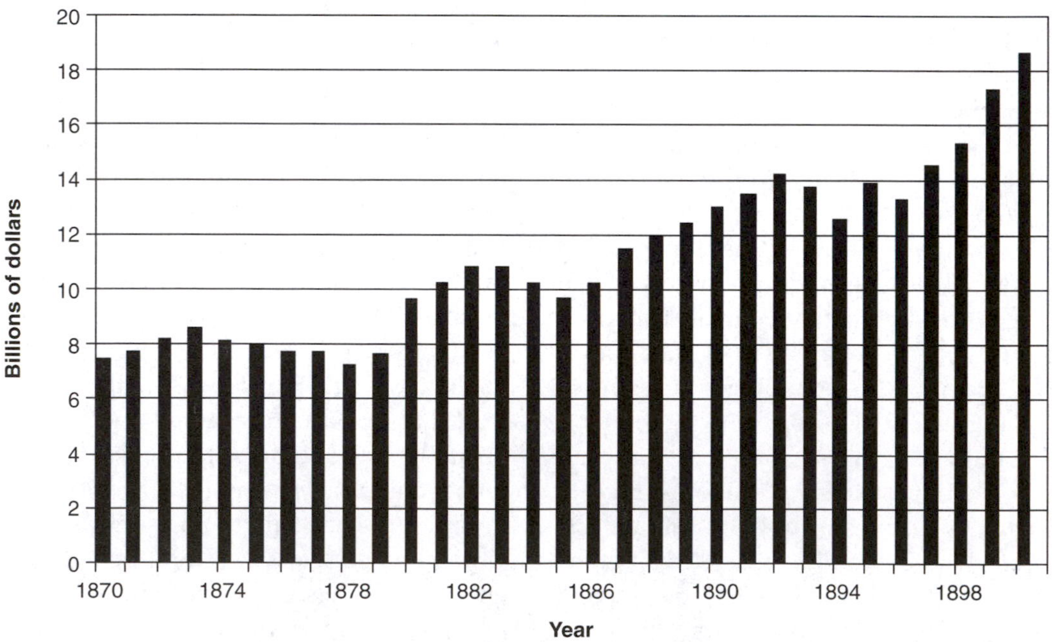

Figure 3.3 Estimated U.S. gross national product (GNP), 1870–1900. (Derived from a regression model from data in Historical Statistics of the United States, Colonial Times to 1970. *Washington, DC: U.S. Bureau of the Census, 1975.)*

See also Cooke, Jay; Pool.

References and Further Reading

Josephson, Matthew. *The Robber Barons.* New York: Harcourt, Brace and World, 1964.

Larson, Henrietta Melia. *Jay Cooke, Private Banker.* Cambridge, MA: Harvard University Press, 1936.

Lewty, Peter J. *Across the Columbia Plain: Railroad Expansion in the Interior Northwest.* Pullman, WA: Washington State University Press, 1995.

Wicker, Elmus. *Banking Panics in the Gilded Age.* New York: Cambridge University Press. 2000.

Panic of 1893

A major financial panic erupted in late June 1893 fueled by concerns that the federal government might not be able to continue redeeming its outstanding certificates and other currency with gold. Within a few months a major economic recession became apparent, one that worsened considerably in the following year.

Some 500 banks and 16,000 other businesses had collapsed by the end of 1893 alone. The Pullman Strike and many other major walkouts and labor confrontations demonstrated the frustration of working class Americans. In retrospect it is clear that several causes played major roles in the downturn. A post–Civil War track-laying spree had created a seriously overbuilt railroad system by the early 1890s. The banks and financiers who had ridden the railroad boom crashed dramatically when the system's overcapacity reduced or eliminated individual railroad company's profitability. Moreover, for twenty years, the nation's farmers had struggled with overproduction and low prices. Their plight worsened considerably when a worldwide depression reduced the overseas markets for American goods.

Unfortunately, the federal government's reaction to the panic and recession did nothing to address these underlying causes. The financial panic began on June 26, 1893, when the government of India abruptly announced that it would no longer mint silver coins. The United States was a major world supplier of silver, so this decision by a major overseas customer immediately undermined the value of American silver stockpiles and simultaneously cut the value of U.S. silver dollars by 10 percent.

The shock to silver set off expanding tremors throughout the complex American financial market. At that point, the U.S. government supported four major types of monetary instruments: gold, silver, greenbacks, and national bank notes. The Sherman Silver Purchase Act of 1890 mandated that the U.S. Treasury buy 4.5 million ounces of silver every month and either mint it as coins or issue silver certificates to represent the unprocessed specie. The Sherman Act also required that the Treasury redeem both silver and gold certificates with gold, and the Resumption Act of 1879 required gold redemption of the nearly $350 million greenbacks also in circulation.

By 1893 the federal government had exhausted its budget surplus and held slightly less than the legislatively mandated minimum $100 million in its gold reserve. In late August Democratic President Grover Cleveland called a special session of Congress to request repeal of the Sherman Silver Purchase Act. Nearly three months of debate ensued due to strenuous objections from Free Silver advocates, most of whom were Democrats, before the Sherman Act was repealed.

While that action halted the government's silver purchases, it failed to relieve the pressure on the specie reserves. To attract additional gold, Treasury Secretary John G. Carlisle began issuing interest-bearing federal bonds. These issues continued through 1894, and many of them were marketed both at home and abroad through a syndicate of banks and financiers headed by J. P. Morgan. The syndicate members profited both from sales commissions and from their ability to sell the bonds at a substantial premium. The so-called Morgan loans further undermined the Cleveland administration's reputation with the farmers and other working-class people who had been the backbone of the Democratic Party's support.

The only other major governmental initiative aimed at restoring the nation's economic health was equally controversial. In his first presidential term in 1887, Cleveland had become an outspoken advocate of reducing U.S. import duties to well below the levels set in the protective tariffs that the Republican Party favored and had maintained largely unmodified since the early days of the Civil War.

West Virginia Representative William Wilson introduced a bill that would reduce many tariffs moderately and generally exempt raw materials from any taxes. With a few minor changes, the House passed the Wilson bill and sent it to the Senate. There a coalition of protectionist Republicans and some Democratic allies led by Senator Arthur Pue Gorman of Maryland, restored most of the existing rates. The Senators on the conference committee would accept no changes. President Cleveland refused to sign the resulting Wilson-Gorman bill of 1894, but he did allow it to go into effect.

In the off-year elections of 1894, the president's party suffered an unprecedented reversal, losing 116 seats in the House of Representatives. The Republican Party thus emerged from the panic and recession in a much stronger position, one that would provide them with an excellent springboard for the 1896 election. By that time, natural economic forces had halted the economic decline and set the nation on the path to over three decades of largely unalloyed prosperity.

See also Free Silver; Morgan, John Pierpont (J. P.); Pullman, George Mortimore; Pullman Strike.

References and Further Reading

Fels, Rendigs. *American Business Cycles, 1865–1897.* Westport, CT: Greenwood, 1959.

Welch, Jr., Richard. 1988. *The Presidencies of Grover Cleveland.* Lawrence, KS: University Press of Kansas, 1988.

Pool

To reduce potentially harmful competition, two or more participants in the same economic activity may decide to pool their resources or profits. A pool arrangement can be as informal as a handshake or as complex as an intricate, formalized agreement that explicitly defines each participant's share of inputs and outcomes. Participants often try to keep the existence and operation of a pool secret to mislead competitors. Antitrust legislation and, later, SEC rules outlawed most pooling arrangements.

Pools were a common feature of nineteenth century American business, cropping up in a number of areas such as land-purchase, stock price manipulation, or market-control schemes. An excellent case in point is the pool formed by the major railroads serving the East Coast in the 1870s. It was in part a response to the persistent depression that settled in after the Panic of 1873, but its existence helped provoke a massive railroad strike in the summer of 1877.

The participants in the pool included the four major eastern trunk railroads: the Pennsylvania, the New York Central, the Erie, and the Baltimore and Ohio. Ordinarily, these companies competed fiercely with one another for shipments from Atlantic ports to the Midwest. But the economic downturn reduced traffic and revenues for all of them. Aware that lowering their labor costs might trigger a walkout, the managers of the four companies agreed in April 1877 to a formula for distributing all revenue they collectively earned from carrying east-west traffic. Because of its relative size and traditional market share, the Pennsylvania Railroad would receive 43 percent of all the revenue this traffic pool generated whether or not it was operating. The two New York lines were each assigned 22 percent, and the much smaller B&O could count on 13 percent of the total.

This arrangement meant that no railroad's bottom line would suffer even if strikers shut it down temporarily. With little fanfare and almost no protest, the Erie led the cost-cutting drive by reducing the wages it paid by 10 percent. The much larger Pennsylvania went next and its operations also continued without major disturbance. But when the B&O announced its 10 percent reduction in July, activists in the small and previously overlooked Trainmen's Union closed the tracks running through Martinsburg, West Virginia. The state's governor attempted to stem the crisis by calling out the local militia, but many of its members also belonged to the striking union. Sympathizers created stoppages and confrontations up and down the road; eventually both state militia and federal troops had to be sent in to suppress the strike.

Meanwhile the Pennsylvania Railroad was instituting additional cost-cutting measures that directly affected its workforce. One example was the "doubleheader" order that assigned only one engineer and crew to a train that needed the pulling power of two or more engines. Strike activity broke out along its route. Pittsburgh, the hub of the railroad's operations, suffered through two weeks of unrestrained violence that destroyed millions of dollars worth of company property and rolling stock. The strike soon spread to the other members of the traffic pool, the New York Central and the Erie, as well as to affiliated railroads as far away as Texas before it burned itself out. Somewhere between 100 and 200 people died in this, the first nationwide strike in U.S. history.

Fortunately, most late nineteenth century pooling arrangements had less catastrophic consequences. Even so, negative publicity was sure to arise whenever it became known that ostensible competitors were actually engaging in collusive practices that negatively affected other business or consumer interests. The pervasiveness of laissez-faire attitudes, however, meant that many years would pass before effective restrictions were erected to discourage or outlaw pools.

See also Laissez-Faire; Panic of 1873.

References and Further Reading

Bruce, Robert V. *1877: Year of Violence.* Indianapolis, IN: Bobbs-Merrill, 1959.

Stowell, David O. *Streets, Railroads, and the Great Strike of 1877.* Chicago: University of Chicago Press, 1999.

Pullman Strike

During the depression year 1894, workers affiliated with the American Railway Union in Pullman, Illinois, went on strike to protest a reduction in wages. Union members staged sympathy actions all across the United States including boycotts of trains pulling Pullman railroad cars. Federal troops eventually broke the strike.

Ironically, the Pullman Strike broke out in what many considered an ideal, almost utopian industrial setting. George Mortimore Pullman was not the first but certainly the most successful innovator of sleeping cars. They contained rows of seats that folded down and converted into sleeping berths for overnight travel. By the 1890s most long-distance passenger railroad service included cars built at the Pullman Palace Car Company.

As a successful businessman and manufacturer, Pullman decided to construct a model modern company town southwest of Chicago. Named after the famous industrialist, Pullman was conceived as a comfortable, controlled, and self-contained community. In addition to modern housing, the town boasted public buildings that included shops, meeting rooms, and even a library. Employees at the railroad car manufacturing plants in the town qualified to rent company-owned housing. Reporters, social commentators, industrialists, visionaries, and many others came to Pullman to assess its success and perhaps adapt some of its characteristics to other settings.

The Panic of 1893 set off an unusually sharp economic decline. By the summer of 1894, no one was in a position to buy any luxurious sleeping cars. To maintain his competitive position in the market, however,

George Pullman decided to continue manufacturing and servicing freight cars at his company town. Because the market for them was also depressed, he claimed to be operating his factories at a loss. Not surprisingly, the manufacturing company laid off nearly one third of its workforce and imposed a 25 percent wage cut on those it continued to employ.

There was no corresponding reduction in the rent charged for company housing. Many workers found themselves in the impossible position of earning too little at the Pullman factory to pay their rent in the Pullman town. Nor could they avoid paying the rent because the employer automatically withheld it from their pay. When this situation was brought to George Pullman's attention, he stated that "The renting of the dwellings and the employment of workmen at Pullman are in no way tied together."

Having held a variety of railroad jobs Eugene Debs had observed many instances of what he considered to be exploitation of workers. A literate, charismatic young man, Debs set out to create an organization to help those interested in improving their working conditions. To attract the largest possible membership, the American Railway Union (ARU) he founded invited anyone who worked on railroads in any capacity to pay the modest membership fee and become a member. At its height, the union had 150,000 members enrolled, some of them employed at the Pullman Palace Car Company. The leaders of the local ARU chapter in Pullman attempted to negotiate either a wage hike or lower rents with the company, but they gave up in frustration on May 10, 1894. The membership went on strike, closing down all manufacturing activity in Pullman.

George Pullman stood firm, refusing to accept Debs's offer to serve as an outside arbitrator. On July 26 the ARU announced a nationwide boycott, urging its members not to service or handle any train that included a Pullman-built car. Because these cars were in widespread use, it would be difficult to assemble a train without one. Moreover, the railroad owners had no intention of even trying. They deliberately included Pullman cars to break the resolve of the union. Confrontations between railroad workers and management spread eventually to twenty-seven states and involved almost 100,000 people.

The Democratic Governor of Illinois, John P. Altgeld, was sympathetic to the plight of the Pullman workforce, and he hoped to negotiate a peaceful resolution. Democratic President Grover Cleveland was not nearly so empathetic, and his attorney general, Richard Olney was even more determined. Congress had passed the Sherman Antitrust Act four years earlier, but it had never been applied. The Sherman Antitrust Act's key provision stated that "A combination in restraint of interstate commerce is illegal." Olney interpreted the ARU's boycott activities as restraining interstate commerce. To ensure that it would become a federal issue, he urged the railroads to include a U.S. mail car in every train as well. When union workers refused to handle a train, they could also be charged with the federal crime of impeding delivery of the mail.

After serious and destructive rioting took place in the Chicago rail yards in early July, a federal judge acted on an omnibus indictment and issued an injunction ordering Debs to halt the union members' illegal actions. It simultaneously barred Debs and other union officials from communicating with their membership. Even if they had been allowed to do so, the strike had spread so broadly that Debs could not possibly have stopped it even if he wanted to. When the strike continued unabated, Debs was arrested and jailed for violating the Sherman Antitrust Act.

Over Governor Altgeld's strenuous objections, Attorney General Olney had already ordered federal troops to enforce the law. Local police, special deputies, and railroad security people working in tandem with U.S. Army troops gradually stifled resistance. The ARU boycott ended on August 2, but not before twelve strikers had been killed and over seventy people had been arrested and jailed under the omnibus indictment.

The failed strike spelled the end of the ARU. Debs was released from jail after six months, but the experience had profoundly changed him. He emerged as an outspoken advocate of socialism. By the turn of the twentieth century, Eugene Debs had become the leading Socialist in the United States, and the Socialist Party nominated him for president in every election from 1904 until his death.

George Pullman reopened his production facilities, only to die of natural causes a couple of years later.

See also Antitrust Laws; Boycott; Panic of 1893; Pullman, George Mortimore.

References and Further Reading

Almont, Lindsey. *The Pullman Strike.* Chicago: University of Chicago Press, 1942.

Carwardine, William H. *The Pullman Strike.* Chicago: Illinois Labor History Society, 1971.

Leyendecker, Liston E. *Palace Car Prince.* Niwot, CO: University of Colorado Press, 1992.

Railroad Consolidation

Large-scale consolidation swept the railroad industry so thoroughly that, by 1906, just seven major entities controlled two-thirds of the track and 85 percent of all railroad revenues in the United States. The methods devised to accomplish this consolidation encouraged similar combinations in other industries. At the same time, consolidation created vast, interstate corporations that seemed capable of monopoly control over particular regions or sectors. This in turn encouraged the development of federal regulatory legislation and agencies that grew more important in the twentieth century

Overbuilding obviously encouraged railroad consolidation. Every community in the United States wanted to be linked to the growing railroad network, and enthusiastic entrepreneurs and government officials joined forces to raise capital. By 1900 some 200,000 miles of track were in operation, actually far more than was reasonable. Railroads with high fixed costs for track, equipment, and maintenance often competed ruthlessly with one another for freight and passenger traffic. Rate-cutting wars, overly generous rebates, and other costly competitive strategies inevitably forced some railroads into bankruptcy.

A shocking example of the industry's frailty came in 1873 when Jay Cooke's financial house collapsed due to its overinvestment in the troubled Northern Pacific Railroad Co. The ensuing panic spread so broadly that over one-fourth of all railroad companies descended into receivership. Reorganization and consolidation seemed essential to restore investor confidence and customer service.

The creation of statewide or regional systems had already demonstrated the benefits of consolidation. The New York Central strung together seven local lines in the early 1850s. The mighty Pennsylvania Railroad ultimately incorporated over 100 smaller lines into what became the dominant system in the Northeast. Sometimes a major system sprouted from a small local line. A 90-mile road that linked two towns in Kansas grew into the huge Atchison, Topeka, and Santa Fe system by 1890 with over 9,300 miles of track serving twelve states.

Those interested in reducing competition through consolidation experimented with a variety of techniques. Perhaps the simplest was to negotiate a lease with either a competitor or a railroad that tapped an adjacent market. Under its president Thomas A. Scott, the Pennsylvania Railroad took full advantage of this approach, locking a number of independent properties into long-term leases. Because lessees were paid out of operating revenues, the leasing approach required relatively little capital. Some leases promised fixed payments; others contained provisions giving one side or the other a percentage of any new profits the expanded system generated. The goal was, of course, to arrange leases that would either reduce costs and competition or increase market share and revenues.

Some of those interested in more reliable consolidation actually bought a controlling interest in a desired property. Cornelius Vanderbilt and his son and heir, William Vanderbilt, used this method to expand the influence of the New York Central system. The senior Vanderbilt's most dramatic failure came when he attempted to seize control of the Erie Railroad in the late 1860s. He learned much from that debacle and pulled off a number of dramatic coups involving other roads. Like leasing, this approach often required less capital than outright ownership because the number of shares needed to control a company varied widely. With a bloc of 10 percent or even less, a Vanderbilt could dominate a board of directors and convince it to cooperate with his other properties.

While some considered the Vanderbilts to be unscrupulous, they did seem interested ultimately in building a stable, profitable system. The same could not always be said of their chief rival in the Erie battle, Jay Gould. Leaving the looted Erie behind, Gould focused his attention on Texas and the Southwest. He bought into a number of railroads, often deliberately using them to create a nuisance for other system-builders who ended up paying Gould a premium to leave them alone.

A third consolidation method promised even more permanent control. It involved outright purchase of desired properties. Sometimes an existing road or system would draw a rival under its direct authority. In other cases, a new entity was created specifically to purchase control of the elements of a system. The leading exponent of that approach was financier J. P. Morgan, and his preferred mechanism was the holding company.

The generous general incorporation laws that emerged in the last decade of the nineteenth century allowed a holding company organized in one state to own properties in other states. Morgan either created or assumed control of such a holding company and arranged substantial financing for it. The company used this capital to buy controlling interests in target corporations. While the Panic of 1893 once again emphasized just how overbuilt the nation's railroad industry had become, it did allow Morgan to pick up failing or bankrupt railroads at bargain prices.

Once he had assembled his stable of companies, Morgan squeezed the water out of their stock, trimmed excesses, streamlined management, and benefited from the economies of scale that the newly combined entity created. To ensure his investment, he insisted that one or more of his associates be included on the holding company's board of directors. Morgan's reputation for astuteness and thoroughness usually generated very positive public images for the companies he formed. Investors rushed to place their funds in a Morgan-organized operation, anticipating that it would be more stable and profitable than other enterprises. At least in the case of the Southern Railway System, their confidence was well placed.

Unfortunately, Morgan's attempt to pull off a similar success in New England was a disaster. He began with the New Haven Railroad, cleaning up its finances and raising additional capital. The company then began buying large and small railroad properties throughout the region as well as urban trolley operations and coastal shipping companies. The goal was a comprehensive transportation system, but the result was a debacle. Ten years after this consolidation attempt began, an Interstate Commerce Commission investigation reported that waste and mismanagement had cost upwards of $90 million and the system never functioned as anticipated.

The consolidation phenomenon not only crossed state lines, it spread well beyond discrete regions. J. J. Hill almost single-handedly punched the Great Northern Railroad from Minneapolis through to Seattle. With Morgan's backing, he then took up the challenge of reorganizing the troubled Northern Pacific and soon controlled all rail service in the Northwest. Meanwhile Edward Henry Harriman and his associates were consolidating the massive Union Pacific and Southern Pacific systems. After a costly speculative battle, the two giants surrendered controlling interests in all their western properties to the newly formed Northern Securities Co. This holding company's control of virtually all rail service in the western United States triggered a federal antitrust suit. In 1904 the Supreme Court ordered that the holding company be broken up, the first successful trust-busting case in U.S. history.

At that point, however, an enormous amount of railroad consolidation had already taken place. Over the next decade, Congress greatly expanded the Interstate Commerce Commission's authority to regulate railroads. These changes enabled the federal government to monitor and control railroad operations effectively, and it used that power far more than its antitrust authority to manage large railroad combines. After all, much of the consolidation had promoted efficiency, cut costs, and even cut shipping rates and passenger fares while improving service. The success of consolidating in these areas encouraged similar integration in other industries and still more consolidation in transportation.

See also Gould, Jay; Holding Company; Interstate Commerce Commission, Reform of; Morgan, John Pierpont (J. P.); Northern Securities Co. Case; Pool; Railroads.

References and Further Reading

Chandler, Jr., Alfred D. *The Railroads.* New York: Harcourt, Brace and World, 1965.

Josephson, Matthew. *The Robber Barons.* New York: Harcourt, Brace and World, 1934.

Kirkland, Edward C. *Industry Comes of Age.* New York: Holt, Rinehart and Winston, 1961.

Nelson, Ralph L. *Merger Movements in American Industry.* Princeton, NJ: Princeton University Press, 1959.

Stover, John F. *American Railroads.* Chicago: University of Chicago Press, 1997.

Rebates

At the basic level, a rebate is a payment returning some of the purchase price to a favored buyer. Rebates may be designed to encourage additional purchases or to reward repeat customers. In the late nineteenth century, rebates that railroad companies provided to favored shippers became the subject of public outrage, criminal investigation, and legislative action. Bulk shippers like the Standard Oil Co. repeatedly negotiated favorable rates that put them at an advantage over their competitors. Federal action in the early twentieth century attempted once and for all to put an end to the use of rebates.

Several factors encouraged railroad operators to provide rebates. Because accurate accounting or assessment of actual operating costs was difficult in the early days, railroad managers frequently altered or adjusted the rates they charged freight customers. A railroad could do little to alter its fixed costs such as building and maintaining tracks, right-of-way, and locomotives, but the marginal costs of running additional cars or trains declined substantially if traffic increased. Shippers who were capable of providing frequent and large loads knew this as well, so they used that knowledge to negotiate lower rates than occasional shippers paid. Rather than reduce rates overall, the railroad frequently left its established rates in place and compensated the bulk shipper with a secret rebate or kickback.

John D. Rockefeller benefited from rebates throughout his career, both before and after he formed the Standard Oil Co. He recognized that the larger his operation, the more effectively he could bargain for favorable treatment. Refiners in Cleveland could send their output east over affiliates of either the Erie and Lakeshore or the New York Central railroads. Rockefeller and his associates played one railroad against the other to obtain the most advantageous rebates.

As Standard Oil expanded in the 1870s, its ability to dictate rates grew correspondingly. Meanwhile, the company became the owner of the nation's largest fleet of oil-tank cars. Railroads wanting a share of the oil-shipping business simply had to meet Standard's demands. Rebates as large as 50 percent of the printed rates were not unusual, and they sometimes were even more substantial.

The competitive advantage of a company effectively paying only half as much to get its product to market was only part of the story. From time to time, the overeager railroads also agreed to pay to Standard some of the money they collected from other shippers. Called a *drawback,* this device effectively gave the recipient the equivalent of a rebate on a competitor's shipment. Rebates and drawbacks were key, but by no means the only factors that enabled the Standard Oil Co. to control nearly 95 percent of all the refining in the United States by the 1880s.

Rebates and drawbacks were common in other industries as well, and virtually every railroad engaged in rate fixing arrangements for preferred customers. In many instances, state legislatures outlawed the practice of granting rebates, but the secrecy of the deals and a general lack of either capability or interest in enforcement allowed the practice to continue. Moreover, because so much of the transportation system spilled over state lines, the issue eventually became a federal concern.

The Interstate Commerce Commission (ICC) was created in 1887 in part to monitor freight rates. But the agency remained largely a fact-finding body until after the turn of the century. In 1903 the Elkins Act finally attacked the issue head on by outlawing all rebates. Special arrangements continued to occur, however, as long as the ICC lacked appropriate access to corporate records and enforcement authority. The Hepburn Act (1906) and the Mann-Elkins Act (1910) considerably strengthened the federal government's ability to curb the practice of granting rebates.

See also Horizontal Integration; Interstate Commerce Commission; Rockefeller, John Davison.

References and Further Reading

Carr, Albert Z. *John D. Rockefeller's Secret Weapon.* New York: McGraw-Hill, 1962.

Chernow, Ron. *Titan: The Life of John D. Rockefeller, Sr.* New York: Knopf, 2004.

Hawke, David Freeman. *John D.: The Founding Father of the Rockefellers.* New York, Harper and Row, 1980.

Sharecropping

Sharecroppers are landless farmers who earn a portion of a farm's output in return for planting, cultivating, and harvesting a crop. Sharecropping or simply "cropping" expanded dramatically in the post–Civil War South. By 1900 some two-thirds of all southern agricultural workers were tenant farmers, most of them sharecroppers. Throughout the United States even today, a substantial amount of land is farmed on a sharecrop basis.

Even though aspiring farmers in the United States had greater opportunities to own land than their counterparts anywhere else in the world, many precedents for the sharecrop system emerged in the colonial and antebellum periods. While the 1862 Homestead Act offered landownership in return for labor, it applied only to unsettled public lands. By the mid-nineteenth century, most of the arable land in the southeastern United States was already privately owned. And, due to President Andrew Jackson's generous pardoning policies and the redemption of the war-ravaged South by Democratic politicians, most southern land was restored to the individuals or families who had owned it prior to the Civil War.

Slaves had farmed much of that property in the 1850s, but the Thirteenth Amendment (1865) outlawed slavery in the United States. The so-called freedmen who had previously worked on plantations often had no other skills. It was quite reasonable, therefore, for them to continue as farmers even though they themselves owned no land.

Immediately after the war, the federal government's Freedman's Bureau attempted to establish a contract labor system for the reconstructed South. Under this plan, landowners would negotiate contracts with potential farmers, outlining the expectations on both sides. But in that unsettled period both landlords and tenants often failed to fulfill their contracts. Owners sometimes threw tenants off their land before the harvest; discouraged laborers often left partway through the year to seek other opportunities. An alternative was needed that gave both sides a tangible incentive to fulfill their contractual obligations.

Sharecropping provided that incentive. To encourage a tenant farmer to work throughout the whole crop cycle, landlords promised a share of the output, often around one-third of the crop produced. No compensation would be paid if no crop was produced.

The promise of a share of the resulting harvest might be expected to encourage a cropper to work harder than those who worked for fixed wages, but sharecropping was hardly ideal from an economic and efficiency perspective. Sharecropping discouraged crop diversification. Cotton was perfect for a sharecropping system because individuals could not consume cotton as they could other farm commodities, and cotton could be stored in the bale for extended periods of time. Unfortunately, cotton prices remained largely depressed in the late nineteenth century, so both landowners and tenant farmers suffered from limited returns. Moreover, cotton cultivation remained hand-labor intensive well into the twentieth century, with the first really successful mechanical cotton pickers being marketed only in the 1920s. The cotton-intensive sharecropping economy failed to share in the agricultural prosperity that occurred elsewhere in the early 1900s.

Even so the system spread well beyond the traditional plantation owners and their ex-slaves because it offered an avenue for landless or land-poor white farmers to survive. As sharecropping became the preeminent system of agricultural activity in large areas of the southern United States, it was natural that it would become more popular in other regions. Today it is quite common in agricultural states like Iowa where the number of people available to operate family farms declines every year. Neighbors or even corporate concerns equipped with expensive, underutilized farm machinery are willing to crop other land for a share of the output.

In one way, sharecropping represents a holdover of the colonial period's barter system. Here workers barter their labor for a commodity and are paid only when they sell their shares of the crop.

See also Cotton; Crop Lien.

References and Further Reading

Donald, Henderson H. *Negro Freedman.* New York: Schuman, 1952.

McPherson, James. *Struggle for Equality.* Princeton, NJ: Princeton University Press, 1964.

Montgomery, David. *Beyond Equality: Labor and Radical Republicans, 1862–1872.* New York: Knopf, 1967.

Shinplasters

From time to time, both the U.S. government and some banks printed bills in denominations smaller than one dollar. This so-called fractional currency was a substitute for coins. A popular, disparaging name for these notes was *shinplasters* because they were of such low value that soldiers reputedly used them to line their worn boots.

The Union government began printing fractional currency during the Civil War when industrial demand sucked silver and copper coins out of circulation and into melting pots. Small-denomination postage stamps facilitated some transactions, and the government sold ungummed stamps specifically for that purpose. Beginning in 1862, the U.S. Treasury also began printing fractional currency with values ranging from three cents to fifty cents. Congress ultimately authorized the issuance of some $50 million worth of these notes, so a substantial number of shinplasters were printed and circulated. Like greenbacks, which also lacked specie backing, fractional bills fluctuated in market value even though the federal government remained committed to accepting them at face value.

After the war ended, the nation's stock of silver gradually became plentiful enough to support coinage. A congressional decision in 1873 prohibited the issuance of silver dollars, but silver coins in smaller denominations were once again minted on a regular basis. By 1876, the stock of metallic coins in circulation had become substantial enough to allow the Treasury to stop printing fractional currency.

See also Free Silver; Greenbacks.

References and Further Reading

Moore, Carl H., and Alvin E. Russell. *Money, Its Origin, Development and Modern Use.* Jefferson, NC: McFarland, 1987.

Shopping

Although Americans bought goods for personal use whenever and wherever they could well into the nineteenth century, shopping as a defined activity came into its own around the time of the Civil War. It coincided with the establishment of department stores and mail-order houses, both of which offered potential customers diverse products and a variety of styles and prices. The concentration of retail stores in downtown shopping districts also tempted undecided potential customers. By the twentieth century shopping was a popular personal activity that stimulated many changes in marketing.

Handmade goods predominated in colonial America, as did homegrown food and homespun clothing. The few goods actually purchased by pioneer subsistence farm families came from itinerant peddlers or, as settlement became more established, rustic general stores. Buyers had limited cash or barter goods to exchange, and the peddlers and storekeepers offered little variety in the types of products they stocked.

The development of towns and then cities expanded the opportunities for both buyers and sellers. But even though Philadelphia was the largest city in Revolutionary America, its population of 30,000 was hardly sufficient to stimulate large-scale retail activity. The major cities existed and thrived because they were ports and exchange points for bulk cargoes.

As cities grew larger in the early nineteenth century, many merchants began to specialize. Some dry goods stores emphasized ribbons and lace; others sold calico or wool cut from bolts. Tailors, seamstresses, and housewives fashioned made-to-measure clothing from these raw materials for men, women, and children. Butcher shops sold dressed meat, greengrocers provided fresh fruits and vegetables, and dairies delivered milk and butter to individual homes. Provisioners filled orders and delivered them to both middle- and upper-class homes throughout the city.

By the 1840s specialty retailers were beginning to concentrate in particular districts. Customers who made their way to these districts might find a dozen or more shops selling similar products clustered together on a single city block. To find the best price or particular items that met their needs, customers might visit a number of retailers before making a selection. This sort of shopping was time-consuming, however, and did not allow for a great deal of variety.

Several technological developments around the time of the Civil War facilitated a move toward more general shopping. Public transportation in the form of horse-drawn trams and, later, electric streetcars enabled customers to travel to and from retail districts. Steam-powered elevators gave way to electric lifts carrying customers to multiple sales floors in multistory shops. Mass-production of clothing to meet the wartime demand for uniforms and footwear persisted and expanded into a thriving ready-to-wear clothing business. Even a basic factor like the introduction of relatively inexpensive plate glass had a key impact as it enabled shopkeepers to bring light into their stores and attract customers with attractive window displays.

These and other factors encouraged the development of department stores that combined the product lines of many different specialty stores under one roof. The new urban retail stores were built on a grand scale, with high ceilings, elevators, light-admitting atriums, and, very soon, extensive electric lighting systems. Visiting A. T. Stewart's Cast-Iron Palace on upper Broadway in New York, or touring John Wanamaker's vast Grand Depot in Philadelphia could be a major outing for the whole family.

By and large, however, retailers targeted their advertising and marketing campaigns to women. The major department stores stocked extensive lines of ready-to-wear clothing, kitchen and household utensils, furniture, and knick-knacks. Even when a prospective customer set out to buy a single item, attractive displays of other goods in the same store encouraged additional purchases. Increasingly shopping became a leisure activity as well as a commercial venture, and many people set out on shopping expeditions without any specific purchase in mind.

Shopping has continued to be a major activity for all Americans. The venues have moved to accommodate the casual customer as well as the dedicated buyer. The development of suburban malls after World War II brought the old shopping district concept to the suburbs. A successful mall not only has major anchor department stores, but also a huge variety of smaller specialty shops designed to lure in the casual shopper. Where the old country general store served as a small-town informal community center, the modern shopping malls have sucked the life out of the traditional downtown shopping districts. Shopping or just hanging out at the mall have become major commercial and social activities for all ages.

See also Department Store; Macy, Rowland Hussey (R. H.); Stewart, Alexander Turney (A. T.); Wanamaker, John.

References and Further Reading

Ferry, John William. *A History of the Department Store.* New York: Macmillan, 1960.

Mayfield, Frank M. *The Department Store Story.* New York: Fairchild, 1949.

Single Tax

Henry George's famous book, *Progress and Poverty,* publicized his belief that a tax on rental income would solve many social problems. This single tax would presumably strip unearned income from landlords and allow the government to redistribute wealth to workers whom George claimed were responsible for creating the wealth in the first place. The single-tax concept became extraordinarily popular both in the United States and abroad but it was never comprehensively applied. In the long run, its chief effect was to help undermine popular faith in and support for laissez-faire and Social Darwinist principles.

Henry George's experience in California was a major influence on his thinking. There he observed that those who had somehow managed to gain possession of land profited enormously when the population in its vicinity increased. George insisted that working people's labor actually made the land more valuable, not any contribution the landowners made. He saw rising rent collections as simply an "unearned increment" that should be taxed away. Carried to an extreme, his plan would result in every landlord in the country receiving the same, limited return on an acre of land.

A skilled typographer, George wrote and then set into type and published *Progress and Poverty* in 1879. It became one of the best-selling books of the era both in the United States and abroad. Support for imposing a single tax on land became very strong in urban areas where those living in poverty resented the wealthy and, particularly, the landlords they had to pay. Single-tax clubs sprang up and single taxers became major political factors. In 1886 Henry George himself ran for mayor of New York City on a single-tax platform. He lost to Democrat Abram Hewitt, but won more votes than the Republican candidate, the youthful Theodore Roosevelt.

The single tax was understandably less attractive in rural areas where millions of Americans actually owned the land they worked. Indeed, many grangers and, later, Populists objected strenuously to the property taxes they already had to pay whether or not their farms made a profit. For them, a tax on income would be far more equitable than raising taxes on land. Even so, millions of people saw the single-tax concept as an ideal way to ameliorate the growing disparity between the wealthy and the poor in the late nineteenth century. But it was far too simplistic to solve such a complex economic and social phenomenon. Support for a single tax faded in the early twentieth century, giving way to more attractive and more rational Progressive proposals. Nevertheless, the single-tax craze had been vital in leading Americans to question the efficacy of laissez-faire and laying the foundation for much more active government regulation and control of enterprise.

See also Laissez-Faire; Social Darwinism.

References and Further Reading

Brown, H. James, ed. *Land Use & Taxation.* Cambridge, MA: Lincoln Institute of Land Policy, 1997.

George, Henry. *Progress and Poverty.* New York: Robert Schalkenback Foundation, 1955.

Social Darwinism

Social Darwinism was a philosophical theory that developed in conjunction with the biological evolutionary theories Charles Darwin advanced in the late the 1850s. His description of natural selection seemed equally applicable to human society. Because Social Darwinists opposed governmental or other arbitrary interference in "natural" economic laws, they were strong proponents of the traditional laissez-faire approach. Industrialists and financiers found justification for their wealth and their strategies in the tenets of Social Darwinism.

Herbert Spencer is usually credited with developing the framework for Social Darwinism. Spencer actually published his pioneering work, *Social Statics,* in 1851, eight years before Darwin's *On the Origin of the Species* appeared. Indeed, it was Spencer who coined the term "survival of the fittest" that Darwin elaborated on in his own work. Once Darwin's theories became famous, Spencer and his colleagues took advantage of his notoriety to publicize their theories about social development.

The fundamental principles of social and biological evolution ran along parallel lines. Darwin described a process of continual modifications in the animal world that culminated in the evolution of human beings—nature's "highest order." Social Darwinists took that process a step further, indicating that the evolutionary struggle should be allowed to continue undisturbed within human society. That would permit some individuals, through natural selection, to emerge as far more successful than others. Social Darwinists considered this a laudable outcome because only through this process would society continue to evolve positively. Artificial or arbitrary interference in either the biological or the social context should be avoided.

The most prominent Social Darwinist was Yale University's William Graham Sumner. He opposed any attempt at state-supported charity. He used the expression "It's root hog or die" to emphasize his belief that everyone was responsible for his or her own advancement. Similarly, he criticized any suggestion that legal or judicial restraints be imposed on those exploiting the laissez-faire economy in the late nineteenth century.

Not surprisingly, one of the most successful American entrepreneurs of all, Andrew Carnegie, was a prominent advocate of Social Darwinism. It allowed him to amass a huge fortune without guilt and to argue against income or inheritance taxes that might confiscate his money. Instead, Carnegie promulgated the concept of the "stewardship of wealth." In this formulation, the individual whose skill, foresight, and ability had earned him money should be permitted to use those same capabilities in deciding how to distribute that money. Carnegie considered himself a benevolent steward of his wealth, selecting worthy charities like building community public libraries or endowing a foundation to promote world peace.

While some might agree that Carnegie had the public's welfare in mind, the ostentatious living of other wealthy magnates in late nineteenth century American society provoked considerable criticism. The industrial revolution that enabled a few to succeed beyond anyone's imagination also kept millions of Americans trapped in abject poverty. Depending on whether one was at the top or the bottom of the socioeconomic heap, laissez-faire and Social Darwinism could look very good or very bad indeed.

A theoretical criticism of Social Darwinism appeared with the 1883 publication of *Dynamic Sociology,* written by a federal bureaucrat named Lester Frank Ward. Rather than allow natural selection alone to distribute wealth, Ward insisted that society could and should redistribute some of the wealth either through taxes or other government intervention. By the 1890s these and other ideas had blossomed into a fully articulated assault on both Social Darwinist and laissez-faire doctrines. By 1900 advocates of such change were being referred to as Progressives. Progressivism grew so strong in both major political parties that by 1912, it represented the dominant political perspective.

Social Darwinism thus had a relatively short shelf life. It comforted the wealthy and the successful because it seemed to give a scientific explanation and justification for their achievements. At the same time, it provoked a growing and ultimately quite effective countervailing philosophy that instituted permanent changes in the way business was conducted and how wealth was retained and redistributed.

See also Carnegie, Andrew; Laissez-Faire; Single Tax.

References and Further Reading

Bannister, Robert C. *Social Darwinism: Science and Myth in Anglo-American Social Thought.* Philadelphia: Temple University Press, 1979.

Hawkins, Mike. *Darwinism in European and American Thought, 1860–1945.* New York: Cambridge University Press, 1997.

Hofstadter, Richard. *Social Darwinism in American Thought.* Boston: Beacon Press, 1955.

Tabulating

Business consolidation and expansion in the late nineteenth century created an increasing demand for information. Simply collecting information was not enough; it had to be analyzed. The experience Herman Hollerith gained in developing an automated tabulating system for the 1890 U.S. Census enabled him to create a general tabulating system with broad applicability. The technology he used became the basis for IBM, the most successful business machines company in the world.

Having worked both for the U.S. Census Bureau and the U.S. Patent Office, Herman Hollerith was well positioned to compete when the Census Bureau sought proposals for a more efficient tabulating system. Hollerith tested his concepts in 1886 with data from the Department of Health in Baltimore. First he entered vital statistics on punched cards. Then each card was laid on a table with dozens of mercury contacts positioned under the hole locations. When a plate with similarly arranged wires was closed down over the card, current flowed through any wire that touched the mercury beneath a hole. Each current detected advanced an electrical counter by one stop, tabulating the data from all of the input cards.

Hollerith was hardly the first person to punch holes in cards. Frenchman Joseph-Marie Jacquard had revolutionized the weaving industry in the early nineteenth century by installing a moving array of punched cards along a belt. The automated loom would lift specific warp threads whenever its sensors encountered a hole in a card, creating regular patterns in the resulting weave. Hollerith's brother was engaged in the textile industry, so he was well aware of the Jacquard technology.

In the 1830s Englishman Charles Babbage designed an elaborate mechanical computing machine that also envisioned cards with holes in them to deliver data. But Babbage never completed a working model, and there is no evidence that Hollerith was aware of this precedent. Instead, he was familiar with telegraphy systems that used paper tapes with holes to activate transmitting keys. Hollerith initially considered using a punched tape in his census machinery, but abandoned it when he concluded that cards could be sorted much more easily into subcategories once they had been read.

Hollerith perfected his technology sufficiently to win the U.S. Census contract in 1889, and the result was a remarkable increase in the speed of analysis. Meanwhile he undertook a carefully planned campaign to obtain patents for his concepts. Unfortunately, a severe depression struck the United States in 1894, just when his census project ended, leaving him without a major client. For the next several years he devoted his attention to expanding the scope of his tabulating capabilities, focusing on the needs of railroads. In 1896 he signed a major contract with the New York Central, the nation's second largest system, and shortly afterward established the Tabulating Machine Co.

Although Hollerith's system was used for the 1900 census, the director of the Census Bureau concluded in 1905 that his process was too expensive. In addition to encouraging his own employees to improve the technology, he also contracted with James Powers to build a competing system. The technology Powers developed became a key element in the success of the Remington Rand Corporation in the 1920s.

Even so, Hollerith remained the industry's leader, and railroads, department stores, and other data-intensive businesses became clients. His own enterprise continued to struggle, however, so he accepted the advice of a successful business consolidator named Charles R. Flint. He assembled a combine that included Hollerith's firm, the International Time Recording Co. and the Computing Scale Co. of America. The new combination began operating in 1911 as the Computing-Tabulating-Recording Co. (CTR).

The tabulating business was by far the most important element in this combine, and Hollerith received over half of the $2.3 million in stock it issued. CTR made its most important personnel decision in 1914 when it named Thomas J. Watson as general manager. In 1924 Watson assumed total control over the very successful company. Having linked up with a Canadian affiliate, Watson decided to rename CTR the International Business Machines Co.

In the first half of the twentieth century IBM cards were ubiquitous, recording data in countless businesses for countless purposes. In addition to producing millions of its standard, eighty-column cards, the company also manufactured and often leased card punching machinery, sorters, and tabulators—all elements Hollerith had used in his census programs. The company continued to benefit from government work, providing the record-keeping and check-issuing machinery for the Social Security System introduced in 1935.

Hollerith had revolutionized data tabulation and his successor company pushed the technology forward. It was inevitable, therefore, that IBM would become a leader in the computer industry in the 1940s and 1950s. The initial purposes of its massive, room-sized computers were in many ways very similar to those that the company's founder had pursued in the 1890s: the tabulation and analysis of data.

See also Computers; Hollerith, Herman; Office Appliances; Watson, Thomas J.

References and Further Reading

Akera, Atsushi, and Frederik Nebeker, eds. *From 0 to 1*. New York: Oxford University Press, 2002.

Chandler, Jr., Alfred D., and James W. Cortada, eds. *A Nation Transformed by Information*. New York: Oxford University Press.

Pugh, Emerson W. *Building IBM*. Cambridge, MA: MIT Press, 1996.

Trademarks

Beginning in 1870s the U.S. Patent Office began to register words and names for specific manufacturers or producers. Known as trademarks, these became useful devices for identifying the output of particular factories or shops. Producers used trademarks in advertising and marketing their goods, and consumers came to trust a trademark as an assurance of consistent quality. The more successful or popular the trademark became, however, the more likely it was to encourage counterfeiters or infringement.

Artists and artisans had been marking their wares with distinctive designs long before trademarks achieved official recognition. Makers of clay pots or even bricks in ancient Egypt stamped their output with carved stone seals. Medieval artisans' guilds developed elaborate systems for indicating the date, metallic content, and makers of utensils, jewelry, and dinnerware. Silversmith Paul Revere fashioned dozens of pieces in a classic design that is still known as a Revere bowl, and clockmaker Seth Thomas perfected a distinctive mantle clock that continues to carry his name.

In 1842 the U.S. Patent Office began issuing design patents to individuals or companies that had developed products with unique characteristics. Although the requirements for obtaining such a patent were far less rigorous than those in place for standard patents, fewer than 1,000 design patents were issued in the nineteenth century. Millions more have appeared since then as manufacturers recognize the importance of registering the creative efforts of their designers.

By 1870 many producers were using specific names or terms associated with their products. Congress recognized the growing interest in some sort of legal recognition for this practice in new legislation based on the patent provision of the Constitution. The Patent Office duly began registering trademarks, issuing the first one to Averill Paints.

In 1879, however, the Supreme Court ruled in three related cases that the 1870 law was unconstitutional. A trademark, the justices insisted, "requires no fancy or imagination, no genius, no laborious thought. It is simply founded on priority of appropriation . . . we are unable to see any such power in the constitutional provision concerning authors and inventors, and their writings and discoveries." New legislation based on the interstate commerce clause had to be developed, and the trademarking process began in earnest only in the 1890s. The registration process carried a twenty-year term, and it could be renewed repeatedly as long as the holder continued to use the mark or brand-name in trade.

Federal registration of trademarks became increasingly essential as the expanding transportation network made nationwide marketing far more common. Signs, labels, and advertisements began featuring the trademark and the legend: "Reg. U.S. Pat. Off." In fact, the Patent Office did just that: register the trademark. It provided no other service or enforcement, but the registration process did allow trademark holders to bring suit in the federal court system against counterfeiters or infringers.

At the restaurant he operated in Poughkeepsie, New York, in the 1840s, James Smith developed a medicated sugar lozenge that seemed to help ease coughs. His sons, William and Andrew, turned their father's product into a nationwide best-seller, using labels and advertisements that included images of their own bearded faces. The label for their cough drops also prominently displayed the words *trade* and *mark* underneath these portraits, however, so several generations of Americans believed that the Smith Brothers were actually named Trade and Mark.

Trademarks for specific brand-names became quite common in the twentieth century. Indeed, some of these names became almost too universally recognized. Aspirin, thermos bottles, nylon, cellophane, and kleenex have slipped into common usage for products that were originally trademarked. Kimberly-Clark still manufactures Kleenex and continues to tout its brand-name in advertising, sincerely hoping that those in need of a kleenex will be pulling it from one of its company's boxes and not a competitor's carton of tissues.

At present, trademarks, logos, and brand-names have become so universal that American consumers have long since lost the ability to keep track of them. Virtually every one of the 40,000 or 50,000 items on sale at a supermarket is packaged in a distinctive way. And, even though generic items often cost much less than an identical brand-name product, buyers typically opt for the package with a familiar name—or even an unfamiliar one in the belief that a trademark or brand name implies a higher quality product. Often, of course, it just means the price includes a hefty increment to offset advertising expenses.

The Smith Brothers would understand. After all, they made a fortune from a patent medicine that was simply a mildly doctored lump of sugar. By using a trademark, they convinced millions of Americans to buy their little drops whenever they felt a cough coming on.

See also Patents.

References and Further Reading

Bugbee, Bruce W. *Genesis of American Patent and Copyright Law.* Washington, DC: Public Affairs Press, 1967.

Campbell, Hannah. *Why Did They Name It . . . ?* New York: Fleet, 1964.

Kursh, Harry. *Inside the U.S. Patent Office.* New York: Norton, 1959.

Trust

A trust is a legal framework that authorizes an individual or a group of trustees to manage assets. A simple trust usually involves the assets of a single individual, but the mechanism can be used to handle the combined assets of several owners. Major trusts developed in the 1880s to manage large interstate business operations.

The most famous business trust was the one that managed the Standard Oil companies in the late nineteenth century. It dictated the operation of companies in several states. John D. Rockefeller personally owned the largest share of the assets controlled by the Standard Oil Trust.

After the Civil War, Rockefeller and his business partners began an aggressive campaign to control oil refining, first in Cleveland, but very quickly in several eastern and midwestern states. By 1880 this group had expanded its reach well beyond refineries to include tank cars, retail agents, pipelines, and storage facilities.

Restrictions in state charters complicated the already difficult task of managing such a diversified and far-flung industrial and commercial empire. To operate within a given state, businessmen had to obtain a charter. At that time, most state charters specifically forbade a company from owning property or operating business ventures outside the boundaries of the state issuing the charter.

Prior to the formation of the trust, therefore, the Rockefeller group had obtained charters for separate companies within all the states where it had operations. But this patchwork of companies and managers simply could not run efficiently. Rockefeller turned to a savvy corporate lawyer, Samuel Calvin Tate Dodd, and asked him to develop a legal method for managing what had become a major interstate business.

Working within the existing structure, Dodd encouraged the consolidation of all properties in a given state into a single company. The result was a series of Standard Oil companies, one each in Ohio, Indiana, New York, and so on. This consolidation of ownership provided the first stage of coordination for the sprawling oil empire.

In 1879 Dodd conceived of the Standard Oil Trust, and it was fully functioning in 1882. To implement the plan, major stockholders of the state-chartered companies had to assign control of their shares to a board of trustees. The board established its headquarters at 39 Broadway in New York City. Rockefeller himself served as one of the nine trustees and, because he personally held the largest bloc of shares in most of the companies, the board was most likely to approve his proposals.

With the authority they had accumulated, the trustees could coordinate the activities of an operating company in one state with those in others. Shipments of crude or refined oil were passed along from one state company to the next. Because much of the trust's activity involved exporting petroleum products, the storage and transshipment facilities of the Eastern Standard Oil Co. (ESSO, later changed to EXXON) in New Jersey were kept very busy.

The financial success of this combine was remarkable. By 1890, the Standard Oil Trust owned or controlled more than 90 percent of the oil business in the United States. And it seemed to be a law unto itself. No single state was powerful enough to control the trust; no federal authority existed to prevent it from doing whatever it pleased. Indeed, the structure appeared so successful that several other major industries copied the format Dodd had developed. Outright trusts controlled some industries like sugar and tobacco. Even the beef packing industry where a group of independent firms formed an oligopoly was often referred to as the Beef Trust.

The power and perceived exploitation that the trust structure permitted generated enormous public criticism. Congress responded to this outcry by passing the Sherman Antitrust Act in 1890, based on its constitutional authority lodged in the interstate commerce clause. Although the Sherman Act was largely unenforced for over a decade, its existence discouraged the formation of new trusts. Even more important than the federal action, however, was the passage of general incorporation laws in certain states like Delaware. The Delaware law allowed a company that established its headquarters in that state to operate freely in other states. That change made the trust formulation unnecessary.

See also Antitrust Laws; Charter, State; Dodd, Samuel Calvin Tate; General Incorporation Laws; Rockefeller, John Davison.

References and Further Reading

Nevins, Allan. *Study in Power: John D. Rockefeller.* New York: Scribner, 1953.

Solberg, Carl. *Oil Power.* New York: Mason/Charter, 1976.

Tarbell, Ida. *History of the Standard Oil Company.* New York: McClure, 1904.

Vertical Integration

To cut production costs, a manufacturer may buy or otherwise gain control over raw material sources or component suppliers. This process is sometimes called *backward integration,* and it can be a step leading to vertical integration. A completely vertically integrated enterprise is one that controls the flow of raw materials, the processing and manufacturing of a product, and a system for marketing it. The goal is to minimize costs to improve one's competitive position.

Andrew Carnegie's steel empire was a classic example of vertical integration in the late nineteenth century. He began by investing $1 million to build the J. Edgar Thomson steel mill near Pittsburgh in 1872. Alexander Kelley helped design the plant that included ten state-of-the-art Bessemer converters. Although the mill opened in the depression that followed the Panic of 1873, it always made money, returning a remarkable 100 percent annual return on its investment. To reduce his costs even further, Carnegie looked to control his suppliers. The Mesabi Range in northern Minnesota contained massive amounts of low-phosphorous iron ore, perfectly suited to his processing system. In addition to buying substantial tracts of ore-bearing land, Carnegie purchased ships to transport his ore across the Great Lakes. He also bought much of the town of Conneaut, Ohio, to serve as the lake port where his ore ships unloaded. These steps cut out middleman costs in mining and shipping, allowing Carnegie to reap all the profits from his endeavors.

Another key raw material was coke, processed bituminous coal that both heated the converters and supplied the carbon needed to convert molten iron to steel. Henry Clay Frick had earned the nickname Coke King by aggressively buying coal-producing properties centered in Connellsville, Pennsylvania. He took advantage of the depressed times in the early 1870s to continue absorbing other producers, building more coke ovens, and expanding his property holdings. The price fell as low as ninety cents a ton during the worst of the hard times, but Frick continued to produce and sell, even at a loss, to maintain his position in the industry. By 1878 he exercised near monopoly control over the highest quality coke in the United States and was able to boost the price as high as five dollars a ton for his product.

Andrew Carnegie bought more coke from Frick than anybody else, and he was naturally concerned as the cost continued to rise. In 1883, therefore, he and his associates bought a half interest in the Frick Coke Co. The purchase made Frick a major partner in the broader steel enterprise. His focused, cost-cutting personality was a perfect match for Carnegie, and six years later, Frick became the general manager of the Carnegie properties.

It was Frick who completed the vertical integration that solidified the position of Carnegie and his associates as the owners of the most efficient and largest steel producing enterprise in the world. Frick controlled every aspect of production from the iron ore and coal mines to the final processing of steel rails, girders, and ingots. This integrated industrial sector generated unprecedented efficiencies in production methods while keeping costs well below those of any competitors. Meanwhile, a high protective tariff artificially propped up the price of steel, allowing Carnegie and his associates to reap enormous profits from their activities.

It should be noted that this group never attempted to monopolize the steel industry, contenting itself instead with being the largest and most cost-effective producers within it. No one else came close to meeting their competition, and it was their very success that encouraged rivals to consider alternatives. Buying Carnegie out emerged as the most attractive strategy, something that J. P. Morgan accomplished in 1901 with the establishment of the United States Steel Corporation.

See also Carnegie, Andrew; Frick, Henry Clay; Horizontal Integration; Morgan, John Pierpont (J. P.).

References and Further Reading

Livesey, Harold. *Andrew Carnegie and the Rise of Big Business*. Boston: Little, Brown, 1975.

Temin, Peter. *Iron and Steel in Nineteenth-Century America*. Cambridge, MA: MIT Press, 1964.

Wall, Joseph F. *Andrew Carnegie*. New York: Oxford University Press, 1970.

Watered Stock

Prior to the establishment of the Securities and Exchange Commission, those who issued stock encountered few constraints. Companies could issue large numbers of shares and were often able to sell them at prices that had little relationship to the value of the assets they represented. The difference between share price and actual value was known as water. Watered stocks proliferated in the nineteenth century, sometimes generating remarkable amounts of capital for those who issued or sold them.

The terminology associated with watering financial stocks arose from a similar practice in the livestock trade. Even today, cattle prices are reported as so many dollars per hundredweight, so it is advantageous for a seller to make sure that the animals weigh as much as possible. An unscrupulous seller could achieve that goal simply by leading a thirsty herd to water. The cattle would gorge themselves, often adding dozens of pounds to their weight. If a naive buyer paid full price for the resulting "watered" stock, he was, indeed, paying for just that, water.

The same principle applied when securities were arbitrarily or artificially overvalued. Although caveat emptor (buyer beware) certainly applied to any stock purchase, buyers could easily be influenced by creative advertising, falsified company records, or rumors. When a new issue was involved, the company had the opportunity to announce its capitalization, but that figure might well have little relationship either to the assets or the prospects of the enterprise.

The capitalization of the nation's first billion-dollar corporation provides a case in point. Financier J. P. Morgan had arranged for a new holding company, the United States Steel Corporation, to purchase Andrew Carnegie's $400 million steel empire as well as another $300 million of related companies, mills, equipment, and inventory. Morgan announced a capitalization for U.S. Steel of $1.4 billion. Shares sold briskly as investors and speculators jumped at the chance to get in on the ground floor of this organization that seemed likely to dominate a key industry. But, because the assets of the company had a realistic value of only $700 million, half of the value of the stock was so-called water. In this particular case, it all worked out because by 1920 the actual value of the combine had risen above its initial capitalization, thus squeezing the water out of its stock.

While the U.S. Steel case raised some eyebrows, it was far less controversial than other examples of watered stock. One of the most famous instances of watering stock occurred in the late 1860s during the so-called Erie War. Cornelius Vanderbilt's New York Central Railroad was determined to eliminate competition by the Erie Railroad whose tracks paralleled its line through New York State. The Vanderbilt group therefore began buying Erie shares with the goal of obtaining a controlling bloc.

At that point the Erie was being managed by three unscrupulous operators, Jay Gould, Jim Fisk, and Daniel Drew. Company procedures allowed management to borrow funds by issuing bonds, so the trio began printing bond certificates by the thousands. These were convertible bonds, however, which a holder could convert to shares of stock. The net result was to vastly increase the number of shares in the Erie Railroad. No matter how many shares Vanderbilt bought, he could never get ahead of the printing presses that churned out additional securities. He finally abandoned this futile effort, but it left the Erie Railroad with millions and millions of dollars worth of watered stock in circulation. No amount of growth or expansion could ever squeeze all the water out of its devalued securities.

Watered railroad stocks were all too common in the late nineteenth century in part because speculators both in the United States and abroad seemed to have had an insatiable desire to buy American shares. Reckless financial practices left many companies in impossible positions. One survey of railroad properties operating in the state of Kansas is illustrative. It noted that the railroads had issued stock capitalized at some $300 million and had borrowed an additional $300 million by issuing bonds. A realistic evaluation of the actual worth of these companies' assets set it at no more than $100 million or one-sixth of the paper value.

The ultimate victims of this sort of overvaluation were the customers whom these railroads served. They had to pay rates and fares far higher than the value of the service they received just to enable the railroads to pay the interest on their outstanding bonds. It was hardly surprising that railroad companies were prime casualties whenever a recession or depression hit. And it is also quite understandable why Populists and Progressives were so critical of unregulated big businesses. The drive for federal regulation that energized the Interstate Commerce Commission after 1900 was seen as a necessary, even inevitable reaction to practices like watering stock.

See also Billion Dollar Corporation; Interstate Commerce Commission.

References and Further Reading

Gordinsky, Julius. *Jay Gould.* Philadelphia: University of Pennsylvania Press, 1957.

Satterlee, Herbert L. *J. Pierpont Morgan.* New York: Macmillan, 1939.

BIOGRAPHIES

Armour, Philip Danforth (1832–1901)

Born in upstate New York, Philip Danforth Armour joined the gold rush to California in the early 1850s. There he made money selling water to miners panning gold. Back east in Milwaukee, he went into partnership in a pork packing operation that boomed filling Civil War orders. After the war he centered his operations in Chicago, coordinating the activities of several of his brothers and other associates in a rapidly expanding meatpacking empire. Armour and Co. was noted for adopting technological advances and exploiting by-products to the extent that Armour could claim that he sold "all but the squeal." Armour's firm became the largest of the oligopolistic Big Five meat packers in the 1890s. His reputation suffered some tarnishing when his firm was accused of selling embalmed beef to American troops during the Spanish-American War even though the official investigation of the allegations proved inconclusive. Jonathan O. Armour superintended the continued growth and influence of the company he inherited from his father.

See also Oligopoly; Swift, Gustavus Franklin.

References and Further Reading

Leech, Harper, and John Charles Carroll. *Armour and His Times.* New York: Appleton-Century, 1938.

Ayer, Francis Wayland (1848–1923)

At the age of twenty-two, Francis Wayland Ayer founded what became one of the first major advertising agencies in the United States. Based in Philadelphia, he began by seeking advertising for publications but quickly switched sides, offering his services to the advertisers themselves. Pioneering techniques that would later become industry standards, he and his partners developed comprehensive campaigns using a variety of media for their clients. In the 1890s Ayer also became prominent in banking and cattle breeding.

See also Thompson, James Walter.

References and Further Reading

Norris, James D. *Advertising and the Transformation of American Society, 1865–1920.* New York: Greenwood, 1990.

Bell, Alexander Graham (1847–1922)

Born and educated in Scotland, Alexander Graham Bell did not become an American citizen until 1884, eight years after he patented the telephone. Bell's family had gained renown as experts in speech and hearing, and his father, Alexander Melville Bell, developed a system called Visible Speech that enabled deaf people to learn to speak. In 1871 Alexander Graham Bell brought the Visible Speech system to Boston where his expertise earned him a position as a professor of vocal physiology at Boston University. Meanwhile, Bell experimented with a number of techniques to transmit messages at different frequencies over telegraph wires, something he called harmonic telegraphy. While this proved less than satisfactory, continued experimentation enabled him to send actual sounds over wire. Bell rushed to patent the concept early in 1876, before he actually succeeded in getting his system to transmit understandable human speech. He demonstrated that capability at the Centennial Exposition in Philadelphia that summer, however, and it generated widespread public interest. Bell's future father-in-law, Gardiner Hubbard, assumed responsibility for creating the Bell Telephone Co. Bell's telephone patent became the most valuable single patent in American history, but the inventor was content to serve as the company's technical advisor and let others like Theodore N. Vail wring huge profits out of his technology. Bell's early sale of the company's stock made him independently wealthy, allowing him to pursue his training of the deaf, to support scientific organizations like the National Geographic Society, and to experiment with metal detectors and primitive aircraft designs.

See also Office Appliances.

References and Further Reading

Bruce, Robert B. *Bell.* Ithaca, NY: Cornell University Press, 1973.

Burroughs, William Seward (1855–1898)

Son of an unsuccessful inventor in Rochester, New York, William Seward Burroughs seemed fated to follow in his father's footsteps. Young William became a bank clerk in Auburn and found the work laborious and unrewarding. In 1882 Burroughs left banking and moved to St. Louis to work in a machine shop. There he convinced a couple of local men to provide start-up funding and then he found a machine shop owner willing to rent him space for his experiments. Over the next several years, Burroughs collected additional funding to perfect his models and created the American Arithmometer Co. in 1886 to market them. Four more years passed before the company began manufacturing a reliable adding machine. The company evolved into the Burroughs Adding Machine Co. in the 1890s, destined to become the world's largest supplier of adding and other mechanical business machines. Burroughs had suffered from tuberculosis since his mid-twenties, however, and the disease claimed his life just when his company was coming into its own.

See also Office Appliances.

References and Further Reading

Burroughs Corporation. *A Better Day's Work at a Less Cost of Time, Work, and Worry to the Man at the Desk.* Detroit: Burroughs Adding Machine Company, 1910.

Busch, Adolphus (1839–1913)

Although their father ran a successful brewer's supply business in Mainz, Germany, young Adolphus Busch and his brother Ulrich decided to emigrate to the United States. They settled in St. Louis, which boasted a large German population and numerous breweries. With their inheritances the Busches established their own brewer's supply business. One of their best customers, Eberhard Anheuser, became their father-in-law when the Busch brothers married his daughters. Anheuser and Adolphus Busch then established their own brewery, and Busch proved to be an outstanding marketer. In 1875 a friend provided the brewers with a recipe he had brought from Budweis, a German community, and Budweiser became the company's primary product, aggressively advertised and distributed widely. After his father-in-law's death, Busch continued to expand the Anheuser-Busch Co., adding a draft-only beer he called Michelob in 1896. Adolphus Busch used the fortune he accumulated for construction projects and charities. The pressures of prohibition and the Great Depression caused Busch's son and heir to commit suicide, but the king of beers rebounded dramatically under the leadership of grandson August Busch, Jr.

See also Coors, Adolph.

References and Further Reading

Robertson, James D. *The Great American Beer Book.* Ottawa, IL: Caroline House, 1978.

Carnegie, Andrew (1835–1919)

Scottish born Andrew Carnegie moved to Pittsburgh in 1848 where he found work in a textile mill, as a furnace stoker, and delivering telegrams The superintendent of the Pittsburgh Division of the Pennsylvania Railroad, Thomas A. Scott, recognized his talent and hired him as a personal secretary. Scott eventually became president of the railroad, leaving Carnegie to take over as superintendent. After the Civil War, Carnegie left the railroad and began building bridges. This led to his involvement in the burgeoning steel industry. In 1872 Carnegie built the J. Edgar Thomson steel plant, the largest in America up to that time. Using vertical integration he became the nation's most efficient and wealthiest steel monger. He bought other properties and brought in Henry C. Frick, a coke supplier, to manage his operations. Carnegie was then able to travel widely, and he even purchased a castle in Scotland. J. P. Morgan headed an investment group that bought Carnegie's holdings in 1901 and used them as the basis for the United States Steel Co. Carnegie spent the rest of his life involved in various philanthropic activities including grants for the construction of public libraries all across the country. He also established several foundations including the Carnegie Endowment for International Peace.

See also Frick, Henry Clay; Vertical Integration.

References and Further Reading

Wall, Joseph F. *Andrew Carnegie.* New York: Oxford University Press, 1970.

Cooke, Jay (1821–1905)

Popularly known as the financier of the Union war effort, Philadelphia-based financier Jay Cooke hired 2,500 agents, advertised broadly, and managed to convince northerners and Europeans of all classes to buy federal bonds. His marketing campaign eventually resulted in the sale of over $1 billion worth of bonds. He continued to buy and sell bonds after the war but became overextended in Northern Pacific Railroad shares. Lack of progress on this transcontinental railroad project caused the collapse of his banking and brokerage operations, which in turn precipitated the Panic of 1873.

See also Land Grant Railroads; Panic of 1873.

References and Further Reading

Larsen, Henrietta Melia. *Jay Cooke.* Cambridge, MA: Harvard University Press, 1936.

Coors, Adolph (1847–1929)

To avoid military conscription in his native Germany, Adolph Coors stowed away on a ship bound for America. He worked for a Denver brewery before starting his own business in nearby Golden, Colorado, in 1873. The "clear, Rocky Mountain spring water" he tapped helped give his beer a lighter taste than the beers of other brewers. Production remained limited for many years, and Coors beer could only be bought locally. In 1914 the Adolph Coors Brewing Co. was incorporated, and the family's patriarch remained its president until his accidental death fifteen years later. The Coors family has always retained strict ownership and control of the company whose major market remained confined to several western states right through the Second World War. Serious labor problems, unpopular political stands, and a reluctance to advertise undermined the company's fortunes in the 1970s and 1980s. Equally damaging was the introduction by other brewers of light beers that competed directly with the Coors product. Only in recent years has the company succeeded in expanding its market nationwide with both conventional and light beer, but it continues to be manufactured in only one plant in Golden, Colorado.

See also Busch, Adolphus.

References and Further Reading

Baum, Dan. *Citizen Coors.* New York: William Morrow, 2000.

Depew, Chauncey Mitchell (1834–1928)

Born into a wealthy family in Westchester County, New York Chauncey Mitchell Depew enjoyed every benefit that status afforded. He attended private schools to prepare for Yale University. After he graduated, he read law for a couple of years and was admitted to the New York State bar in 1858. An enthusiastic recruit to the newly formed Republican Party, Depew was active in politics throughout his long life, eventually serving as a U.S. senator. He made a wise decision in 1866, however, when he gave up a chance to be U.S. minister to Japan for an opportunity to work as a lawyer for Cornelius Vanderbilt's sprawling railroad interests. Vanderbilt relied on Depew to cajole government officials into actions beneficial to his railroads and rewarded Depew with increasingly responsible managerial positions. These culminated in the presidency of the New York Central Railroad, which Depew held until he was elected to the Senate in 1899. Even then, he continued to serve as chairman of the board of this enormously important transportation system, using his political influence to buffer it from federal interference. Chauncey Depew thus personified the strong interrelationship between politics and business that proliferated in the early twentieth century.

See also Railroad Consolidation; Vanderbilt, Cornelius.

References and Further Reading

Depew, Chauncey M. *My Memories of Eighty Years.* New York: Scribners, 1922.

Dodd, Samuel Calvin Tate (1836–1907)

Samuel Calvin Tate Dodd was admitted to the bar in western Pennsylvania in 1859, the same year Colonel E. L. Drake brought in the first gusher in the United States. For the next decade, Dodd represented individuals and firms engaged in the infant oil industry, often in opposition to John D. Rockefeller's interests. The increasingly powerful entrepreneur recognized Dodd's talents and experience and Rockefeller put the lawyer on his payroll as general solicitor for the Standard Oil Co. Dodd remained on salary for the rest of his life, refusing to accept any stock or other equity in the companies he served. In 1882 Dodd created the Standard Oil Trust that enabled a nine-member board of trustees to coordinate the affairs of forty operating companies. A decade later, the Ohio Supreme Court ruled that the trust was illegal so Dodd developed an alternative. His ultimate configuration came in 1899: the massive Standard Oil Co. of New Jersey, a holding company that performed the same integrated managerial functions as the earlier trust. Dodd did not live to see the Sherman Antitrust Act used to dismember his final corporate creation.

See also Rockefeller, John Davison; Trust.

References and Further Reading

Chernow, Ron. *Titan.* New York: Random House, 1998.

Duke, James Buchanan (1856–1925)

Although the Civil War had devastated his home in Durham, North Carolina, young James Buchanan Duke and his brother found economic success by marketing packaged leaf tobacco. Moving into the manufacture of cigarettes in 1881, Duke helped perfect the Bonsack machine that replaced hand labor. This enabled him to lower his prices and, in conjunction with aggressive advertising campaigns, he quickly expanded his market control nationwide. In 1889 his company sold half the cigarettes bought in the United States. Spurning competitors' attempts to buy him out, Duke formed the American Tobacco Co. the next year and became its president. During the subsequent decade he superintended the consolidation of virtually all cigarette manufacturing and related industries and created an overarching holding company to control the combine. In 1911 the Supreme Court ruled that Duke's arrangement violated the Sherman Antitrust Act, and the combine was broken up into several distinct entities. The trust fund he created in 1924 provided substantial funding for Duke University.

See also Antitrust Laws; Rule of Reason.

References and Further Reading

Duke, Maurice. *Tobacco Merchant.* Lexington, KY: University Press of Kentucky, 1995.

Eastman, George (1854–1932)

No one had a greater impact on the photography industry than George Eastman. Born in upstate New York, he completed high school and worked as a bookkeeper. In his spare time he became fascinated by photography. It was a time-consuming hobby in the 1870s involving glass plates that had to be emulsified just prior use. Eastman gladly abandoned this wet-plate process for dry-plate technology and formed the Eastman Dry Plate and Film Co. to market it. He quickly moved on to rolls of paper-backed celluloid film and finally to unbacked roll film. To simplify the process for consumers still further, in 1888 he began selling a preloaded box camera he called a Kodak for $25. After exposing the film, users returned the apparatus to Eastman's processing plant and received their pictures and a reloaded camera in return. He extended his market further by introducing a $1 camera called a Brownie and sales soared. Headquartered at a massive manufacturing and processing center in Rochester, New York, Eastman Kodak dominated the personal photography business in the early twentieth century. His market share and his insistence that customers use his processing plant led to antitrust litigation, but his firm continued to flourish. A life-long bachelor, George Eastman donated more than $100 million to universities and other charities, including establishing the endowment for the Eastman School of Music at the University of Rochester.

References and Further Reading

Brayer, Elizabeth. *George Eastman.* Baltimore, MD: Johns Hopkins University Press, 1996.

Edison, Thomas Alva (1847–1931)

Known as the Wizard of Menlo Park, Thomas Alva Edison received 1,093 patents for his many inventions. These inventions, in turn, established the bases for several business enterprises. Born in Ohio, Edison early found employment as a telegrapher despite his hearing loss. For many years, he moved from one telegraph office to another, often because his employers objected to Edison's unauthorized use of their equipment for experiments. One early result of his tinkering was the development of duplex and, later, quadraplex telegraphy, which allowed a single wire to carry more than one message at a time. Other early innovations included a primitive fax machine, improved stock tickers, and an automated telegraphy sending and receiving system. In the 1870s Edison located his experimental laboratory in Menlo Park, New Jersey, where he and his talented team perfected the incandescent lightbulb. In the early 1880s the inventor organized the Edison Electric Illuminating Co., which lit up Broadway with a direct-current generating plant located on Pearl Street. To meet the demand this successful demonstration created, Edison established a manufacturing headquarters at Schenectady, New York, later in the decade, and it evolved into the General Electric Co. in 1892. In the mid-1880s, he sold rights to the mimeograph duplicating system he had devised to A. B. Dick whose company became the industry leader. Another of Edison's key interests was sound recording and his early phonograph used foil-wrapped, and later wax-coated cylinders. His wise decision to adopt more popular flat discs enabled his phonograph player and record company to profit handsomely. Edison's contributions to the infant film industry included a roll of sprocketted celluloid film that displayed moving pictures. In the early twentieth century, Edison expanded his inventive scope to cement manufacture, storage batteries, and an underwater sound detection mechanism for military purposes that anticipated sonar. While Edison did not maintain a major role in most of the companies and businesses his inventive genius created, his work significantly transformed and expanded the market for consumer products of all types.

See also Electric Power; Movies.

References and Further Reading

Baldwin, Neil. *Edison: Inventing the Century.* New York: Hyperion, 1995.

Frick, Henry Clay (1849–1919)

Born in western Pennsylvania, Henry Clay Frick studied accounting and worked in a family-owned distillery in Connellsville. With his own and borrowed money, Frick bought coal lands in the area and erected ovens to convert the coal to coke, a key raw material for steel production. To cut costs, Andrew Carnegie invited Frick into his steel-producing partnership in 1883 and Frick later became the general manager for the Carnegie Brothers interests. Rabidly anti-union, Frick provoked the bloody Homestead Strike in 1892. He and Carnegie parted company in 1899. Frick continued to be active in the coke and steel industries, and he bought substantial real estate in downtown Pittsburgh. He moved himself and his outstanding art collection to New York City in 1905, participating in charitable activities in later life.

See also Carnegie, Andrew; Vertical Integration.

References and Further Reading

Singer, Martha Frick Symington. *Henry Clay Frick.* New York: Abbeville Press, 1998.

Gompers, Samuel (1850–1924)

Born in London, young Samuel Gompers followed his father's trade, learning to roll cigars at the age of ten. Three years later, his family moved to New York, where Samuel found employment and joined a local of the United Cigar Makers, a craft union. By 1875 Gompers was president of his union local, and ten years later he had become second vice president of the Cigar Makers' International Union. His dedication to craft unionism naturally led him to become a founding leader of the Federation of Organized Trades and Labor Unions in 1881, a group that evolved into the American Federation of Labor (AFL) in 1886. Except for the year 1895, Gompers served as president of the federation from its founding until his death. He was a conservative force in unionism, focusing on wages, hours, and the right to organize. This strategy encouraged growth of his federation from its initial 50,000 members to over 3 million in the mid-1920s. Although Gompers early attempted to be nonpartisan, he became associated with the Democratic Party during the First World War. President Woodrow Wilson appointed him to important coordinating boards, worked with him to protect workers' rights during the conflict,

Samuel Gompers (shown here casting a ballot) helped found the American Federation of Labor. The group initially comprised skilled workers and craftsmen. (Library of Congress)

and sent Gompers to participate in postwar international labor conferences.

See also American Federation of Labor.

References and Further Reading

Livesay, Roger. *Samuel Gompers and Organized Labor in America.* New York: Little, Brown, 1978.

Gould, Jay (1836–1892)

Nicknamed the "Mephistopheles of Wall Street," Jay Gould was the quintessential industrial robber baron of the late nineteenth century. Born and raised in upstate New York, he early began speculating in railroad stocks. By 1868 he and his partners, Jim Fisk and Daniel Drew, had wrested control of the Erie Railroad from Cornelius Vanderbilt and his cronies. Using the railroad as a base, he and Fisk then attempted the Gold Corner of 1869. He worked closely with Tammany Hall's Democratic Party boss, William Marcy Tweed and other influential politicians. For a time he ran the Western Union Telegraph Co., and he eventually controlled several western railroads including the Union Pacific. An implacable enemy of unionization, Gould was instrumental in frustrating the efforts of Terence V. Powderly's Knights of Labor in 1885 and 1886.

See also Gold Corner; Railroad Consolidation; Watered Stock.

References and Further Reading

Klein, Maury. *Life and Legend of Jay Gould.* Baltimore: Johns Hopkins Press, 1986.

Grace, William Russell (1832–1904)

Like thousands of his countrymen, William Russell Grace left his home in Ireland and headed for America at an early age. In this case, however, Grace ended up on the west coast of South America, where he established a shipping supply business for the hundreds of vessels that loaded and transported guano to fertilize worn-out tobacco and cotton plantations in the southern United States. He relocated to New York City in 1866 where he and his relatives became engaged in an enormous variety of enterprises. One of the most successful was the establishment in the 1870s of the Merchants Line that connected New York and Peru by sea. In the early twentieth century this organization had evolved into the W. R. Grace Lines, the most prominent shipping company serving North and South America. Grace was twice elected as a reform mayor of New York City in the 1880s, but he continued to pursue exotic interests. His company built railroads in Central America, dabbled in the rubber business in Brazil, and championed building an Isthmian canal. His successful career could have been the model for a Horatio Alger novel.

References and Further Reading

James, Marquis. *Merchant Adventurer.* Wilmington, DE: SR Books, 1993.

Harriman, Edward Henry (1848–1909)

New Jersey–born Edward Henry Harriman left school at the age of fourteen to become a Wall Street office boy. At twenty-one he borrowed money from an uncle to buy a seat on the New York Stock Exchange. An astute and successful trader, he soon became fascinated by railroads. By 1883 he was a major force on the Illinois Central, and a decade later played a vital role in reviving and reconstructing the Union Pacific, the nation's first transcontinental railroad. A goal of his revitalization campaign was to link the Union Pacific to Chicago and to the Pacific Northwest. That ambition inevitably brought him into conflict with J. J. Hill. After a panic-causing stock battle over the Northern Pacific, Harriman and Hill formed the Northern Securities Co. to manage their combined systems. This holding company was the first to be broken up under the Sherman Antitrust Act in 1904, a result that considerably tarnished Harriman's reputation. He pushed ahead with ambitious plans to extend his transportation empire around the world, sponsoring American penetration into China. His unexpected death in 1909 brought those plans to an abrupt halt.

See also Land Grant Railroads; Northern Securities Co. Case; Railroad Consolidation.

References and Further Reading

Klein, Murray. *The Life and Legend of E. H. Harriman.* Chapel Hill, NC: University of North Carolina Press, 2000.

Hearst, William Randolph (1863–1951)

The son of a successful California mine owner and U.S. senator, William Randolph Hearst had ready access to great wealth. Although he failed to graduate from Harvard University he did polish his journalistic skills there. He also worked briefly for Joseph Pulitzer on *The New York World,* a newspaper that would become his greatest rival in the 1890s. His first independent

William Randolph Hearst typified the aggressive, impulsive journalism of his age. (Library of Congress)

foray into journalism involved the *San Francisco Examiner,* which to this day remains a cornerstone of the Hearst family enterprises. With his father's financial assistance Hearst reinvigorated the *Examiner* and then purchased the *New York Morning Journal,* laying the basis for a national newspaper chain. Hearst's circulation war with Pulitzer encouraged both publishers to resort to sensationalism, and because they both ran tinted cartoon strips on their front pages, they became founders of what is known as yellow journalism. Hearst took great pride and assumed much personal credit for fomenting enthusiasm for American participation in the war in Cuba in 1898. In the early twentieth century, Hearst maintained a publishing philosophy that was highly popular with working-class Americans. A staunch Democrat, he supported other candidates and repeatedly sought high political office. His only success was a couple of terms in the House of Representatives, but Hearst continued to consider himself a king maker throughout his life, ignoring his many failures. A poor business manager, Hearst became disastrously overextended and had to sell much of his extensive art collection to retain control, of his publishing empire. Solid professional managers eventually took control, enabling Hearst to pass on to his son and namesake an extensive publishing empire that included major national magazines and, at times, reached more than 10 percent of all newspaper readers in the United States.

See also Pulitzer, Joseph.

References and Further Reading

Nasaw, David. *The Chief: The Life of William Randolph Hearst*. Boston: Houghton Mifflin, 2000.

Heinz, Henry John (1844–1919)

Young Henry John Heinz began his food marketing career with a garden plot at his western Pennsylvania home. He was selling his produce at the age of eight and in his teens hired several subordinates to help him cultivate and distribute his products. After some business college training, he worked at his father's brickyard, but returned to food production in 1869. Heinz struggled through the depression of the 1870s, but the company he formed with a brother and a cousin had become quite healthy by the end of the decade. He reorganized it into the H. J. Heinz Co. in the late 1880s. Although the company eventually marketed hundreds of different products including sauces, vinegar, and pickles, H. J. Heinz stuck with the slogan "57 Varieties" simply because it sounded good to him. A benevolent employer, Heinz built an attractive manufacturing complex near Pittsburgh and employed a large number of immigrant women. The company provided recreation, education, and other fringe benefits for its employees, and its factory became something of a tourist attraction. Heinz publicly criticized rivals for adulterating or artificially coloring their products and was a leading advocate of the Pure Food and Drug legislation that appeared in 1906. The company he founded remains a major component of the food industry to this day.

References and Further Reading

Alberts, Robert C. *The Good Provider.* Boston: Houghton, Mifflin, 1973.

Hollerith, Herman (1860–1929)

A native of Buffalo, New York, Herman Hollerith attended the College of the City of New York and graduated with perfect grades from the Columbia School of Mines at the age of nineteen. He immediately took a position with the U.S. Census Bureau in Washington, D.C. Encouraged by Census Director Francis Amasa Walker, Hollerith began envisioning an automated process for tabulating results. When Walker became president of MIT, he invited Hollerith to come to Cambridge to teach. But the young man soon returned to Washington to work at the U.S. Patent Office, convinced that knowledge of patent law would be essential to his success as an inventor. He won a competition for designing a tabulating system for the 1890 census, patented his technology, and further developed his punch-card reading system for commercial purposes. He founded the Tabulating Machine Co. in 1896 that merged fifteen years later into the Computing-Tabulating-Recording Co. (CTR). This merger made him a millionaire, and the combination continued to prosper, becoming International Business Machines (IBM) in 1924.

See also Tabulating.

References and Further Reading

Pugh, Emerson W. *Building IBM.* Cambridge, MA: MIT Press, 1996.

Macy, Rowland Hussey (R. H.) (1822–1877)

Born on Nantucket Island, it was hardly surprising that Rowland Hussey Macy shipped out on a whaling ship as a teenager. After four years at sea and several more in the dry goods business in Boston, the adventurous young man headed for California. He returned for another stint in Massachusetts before settling in New York City. There in 1858 he opened a shop selling dry goods. He was such a talented and persuasive advertiser that his business literally grew by leaps and bounds. He was constantly in need of more sales space as he continually added new product lines. He very quickly adopted a departmental organization for his company, and by the early 1870s it had become a prototype department store. Although he had launched a very successful business venture, he was denied the opportunity to enjoy its benefits, due to his rather early death in 1877. He left an estate worth about $300,000, but his major legacy was a business strategy that would eventually create the world's largest department store.

See also Department Store.

References and Further Reading

Hower, Ralph M. *History of Macy's of New York: 1858–1919.* Cambridge, MA: Harvard University Press, 1943.

Patterson, John Henry (1844–1922)

After serving in the Union Army, Ohio-born John Henry Patterson obtained a degree from Dartmouth College in 1867. He returned to Dayton where he worked for a canal company and then as a partner with his brothers in the coal business. That earned him enough money to buy majority control of a struggling office machine manufacturer in 1884. He changed its name to the National Cash Register Co. (NCR), and under his management it became the industry leader. Patterson was one of the first to realize that retailers in a growing consumer economy would eagerly purchase improved cash registers, and both he and his company's engineers introduced a number of innovations. Patterson's leadership presented a number of contrasts, however. He built open, airy workplaces and introduced employee welfare programs and fringe benefits. At the same time he was a tough taskmaster, insisting on absolute obedience to his dictatorial commands. He was also a ruthless marketer. Young Tom Watson, future head of IBM, worked for NCR as a clandestine agent, setting up dummy shops in various cities to undersell the competition. While these tactics helped win NCR a 90 percent share of the market, they also led to the conviction of Patterson and several associates for criminal conspiracy and restraint of trade.

See also Office Appliances; Watson, Thomas J.

References and Further Reading

Marcosson, Isaac Frederick. *Wherever Men Trade.* New York: Dodd, Mead, 1945.

Penney, James Cash (J. C.) (1875–1971)

Missouri-born James Cash Penney suffered through a couple of failed ventures before he opened a general store in the tiny mining town of Kemmerer, Wyoming. His strong religious faith caused him to name his establishment the Golden Rule Store. His only rival was a local company store that sold goods on credit, but Penney insisted on cash purchases. That policy enabled him to cut his costs and, consequently, charge much lower prices than the company store. The cash-only, low-price strategy continued to prevail as Penney opened additional Golden Rule stores. A fundamentalist Christian who refused to allow his employees to smoke or drink, he did provide them with strong motivation by offering his best employees part ownership in the stores they managed. Having incorporated in 1911, he changed the name on his stores to J. C. Penney's, and the chain expanded to almost 1,400 units by 1929. After World War II, Penney's became full-scale department stores and finally accepted credit purchases. J. C. Penney remained actively involved with his retail empire until his death at the age of 95.

See also Chain Stores.

References and Further Reading

Curry, Mary Elizabeth. *Creating an American Institution.* New York: Garland, 1993.

Pillsbury, Charles Alfred (1842–1899)

Charles Alfred Pillsbury obtained a classical education at Dartmouth College in his home state of New Hampshire before heading north to Montreal to work as a commission agent, serving as a wholesaler and supplier of all sorts of goods and collecting commissions for his services. When that business failed in 1869 he moved west to Minneapolis where an uncle, John S. Pillsbury, had established a hardware business. With family financial support, Charles bought a substantial stake in the Minneapolis Flour Milling Company, and it quickly became quite profitable. He formed his own company, C. A. Pillsbury, the following year and subsequently accumulated or built additional mills along the upper Mississippi River. Pillsbury and his family partners were quick to adopt innovations in their facilities like replacing millstones with much more efficient steel rollers. The new technology was particularly useful in processing the hard winter wheat grown in increasing volume in the Red River Valley of northwest Minnesota and North Dakota. The company was an early adopter of steam and electric power, established a chain of grain elevators to assure its supply, and trademarked the name "Pillsbury's Best" and the "XXXX" designation as symbols of quality. In the late 1890s a spin-off company began marketing breakfast cereal and evolved into the General Mills Co. Charles Pillsbury was very active in local affairs and served several terms as a state legislator, but his major contribution lay in helping Minneapolis become the world's leading flour milling center.

References and Further Reading

Powell, William J. *Pillsbury's Best.* Minneapolis, MN: Pillsbury Co., 1985.

Pulitzer, Joseph (1847–1911)

Hungarian-born Joseph Pulitzer was so eager to become a soldier that he visited several European countries before an American recruiter in Germany enlisted him in the Union Army in 1864. Mustered out a year later, Pulitzer made his way to St. Louis hoping to find employment among its substantial immigrant population. Hired as a reporter by Karl Schurz for his German-language paper the *Westliche Post,* Pulitzer quickly developed skill as a crusading investigative reporter and honed his English-language abilities. By 1876 he had been admitted to the bar and become a staunch Democrat. Two years later he bought the nearly defunct *St. Louis Dispatch* and entered a partnership with the owner of the *Evening Post* to create the *St. Louis Post-Dispatch.* The paper remained the cornerstone of his family's publishing empire well into the twentieth century. Eager to broaden his influence, Pulitzer bought another failing paper, the *New York World.* He increased its circulation tenfold in two years by emphasizing solid investigative reporting and sensational stories. William Randolph Hearst purchased the *New York Journal* in 1895 and, jealous of Pultizer's success, hired away at exorbitant salaries many of his staffers, including the cartoonist whose yellow-tinted artwork gave both papers their reputation for yellow journalism. The two moguls engaged in a nasty but often rewarding circulation war with sensational stories about events associated with the Spanish-American War. Disturbed at the depths to which the campaign had sunk, Pulitzer retreated to more intellectual and responsible reporting after the turn of the century. In his final years, Pulitzer provided a substantial endowment to Columbia University's School of Journalism, some of which still funds the prestigious Pulitzer Prizes.

See also Hearst, William Randolph.

References and Further Reading

Brian, Denis. *Pulitzer: A Life.* New York: Wiley, 2001.

Pullman, George Mortimore (1831–1897)

In 1855 George Mortimore Pullman established himself as a building contractor in Chicago, dedicated to improving the urban environment. Having accumulated considerable wealth, he turned his attention to railroad equipment. In 1858 he modified a standard passenger railroad coach by installing seats that could be converted into berths. Seven years later, he produced the first purpose-built sleeping car. Over the next several years his Pullman Palace Car Co. became the leading manufacturer of sleeping cars and other specialized equipment like dining cars. In 1880 he combined his two interests into a single major project: building a model industrial community. Although it was annexed into Chicago in 1888, Pullman, Illinois, continued to function as a company town into the 1890s. Economic troubles in 1894 triggered the Pullman Strike, which began in the town and quickly spread all across the country. Federal intervention halted the strike and associated violence.

See also Panic of 1893; Pullman Strike.

References and Further Reading

Leyendecker, Liston E. *Palace Car Prince.* Niwot, CO: University Press of Colorado, 1992.

Rockefeller, John Davison (1839–1937)

Born in western New York State, John Davison Rockefeller moved with his family to Cleveland, Ohio. There he completed high school and trained in accounting. With a loan from his father, young John and Maurice B. Clark formed a partnership that served as a commission agency. The partners did very well during the Civil War, fulfilling federal contracts. After the war, Rockefeller invested in the largest oil refinery in Cleveland and quickly began to acquire competing properties. Exploiting generous rebates and a dubious charter for the South Improvement Co., he and his partners soon controlled virtually all refining in Cleveland. Over the next several years, he expanded his control to refiners nationwide and purchased thousands of tank cars. In 1879 he asked Samuel Calvin Tate Dodd to develop a mechanism for managing his interstate holdings that came to be known as the Standard Oil Trust. At one point it controlled over 90 percent of the oil refining business in the United States. Rockefeller also participated in many other industrial and business activities including major investments in railroads. While a 1907 antitrust action broke up Standard Oil, he personally retained ownership of the stock in its component companies. He left much of his billion-dollar fortune to the Rockefeller Foundation he endowed in 1913.

See also Dodd, Samuel Calvin Tate; Horizontal Integration; Rebates; Trust.

References and Further Reading

Nevins, Allan. *Study in Power: John D. Rockefeller.* New York: Scribner, 1953.

Scott, Thomas Alexander (1823–1881)

As a boy in rural Pennsylvania, Thomas Alexander Scott left school at the age of ten to work at various jobs including clerking for his brother-in-law, a toll collector for the state's turnpike and canal system. His railroad career began in 1850 as a station agent on a small local line, but two years later he began his life-long affiliation with the Pennsylvania Railroad. By the late 1850s he had moved up to the position of superintendent of its Pittsburgh division and hired Andrew Carnegie as his private secretary, setting the future steel magnate on his road to success. Scott continued to work for the railroad throughout the Civil War, but was frequently called into service as a volunteer officer to plan and carry out major transportation assignments for the Union Army. After the war, Scott's career flourished as the Pennsylvania Railroad developed into the nation's premier system, and he became its president in 1874. He also held top positions in the Union Pacific and the Texas and Pacific Railroads, both of which were transcontinental trunk lines. Perhaps the most dramatic moment in his long career came in 1877 when the Pennsylvania Railroad suffered massive damage during a depression-spawned strike.

See also Carnegie, Andrew; Panic of 1873; Railroad Consolidation.

References and Further Reading

Jacobs, Timothy. *The History of the Pennsylvania Railroad.* Greenwich, CT: Bonanza, 1988.

Sears, Richard Warren (R. W.) (1863–1914)

The unlikely beginning of the most successful catalog-sales enterprise came when someone refused delivery of a package. Richard Warren Sears was the twenty-three-year-old station agent in Minnesota who ended up with the unwanted package full of inexpensive watches. Sears contacted the shipper and obtained permission to market the watches himself. As this business flourished, he took on a partner, Alvah Roebuck, a watchmaker, and they attempted several different company structures before establishing Sears, Roebuck and Co. in 1892. The company continued to feature watches and jewelry but quickly added other items to the catalogs it distributed. When Roebuck sold his interest back to Sears, the master salesman found a new partner in Julius Rosenwald, a men's clothing manufacturer who had supplied Sears. Rosenwald brought order to the haphazardly managed enterprise, greatly expanding the variety of items in its catalogs. After financial difficulties suffered in the wake of the Panic of 1907, Sears became disillusioned with Rosenwald, and he later sold his $10 million share of the company to Goldman Sachs. Rosewnald remained in control and led the company to new heights.

See also Catalog Sales; Ward, Aaron Montgomery.

Richard Sears founded what became the largest mail order business in the United States. (Library of Congress)

References and Further Reading

Worthy, James C. *Shaping an American Institution.* New York: New American Library, 1986.

Sherman, John (1823–1900)

John Sherman was a prominent Ohio politician and brother of Civil War General William Tecumseh Sherman. He worked as an engineer and passed the bar before being elected to the House of Representatives in 1855 as a founding member of the Republican Party. He moved to the Senate in 1861 where he frequently chaired the Committee on Finance. He served as President Hayes' treasury secretary from 1877 to 1881, then returned to the Senate as a replacement for newly elected President James Garfield. Frequently touted as a presidential candidate, he completed his Senate career in 1897 and served one year as President McKinley's secretary of state. His name is associated with two key pieces of business legislation that both appeared in 1890: the Sherman Antitrust Act and the Sherman Silver-Purchase Act.

See also Antitrust Laws; Free Silver.

Reference and Further Reading

Burton, Theodore E. *John Sherman.* Boston: Houghton Mifflin, 1906.

Sprague, Frank Julian (1857–1934)

Connecticut native Frank Julian Sprague won an appointment to the U.S. Naval Academy. Its excellent engineering curriculum and several subsequent assignments gave the young naval officer ample opportunity to experiment with electrical devices. His skill convinced Thomas Edison to hire him to work on his urban electric power systems, but Sprague decided to form his own company, Sprague Electric Railway and Motor Co. in 1884. He had by that time developed a reliable, powerful electric motor that became popular in elevators. Sprague's real interest, however, was in electrifying street railways, so he bid for a contract to construct a major system in Richmond, Virginia. To succeed, Sprague and his associates had to invent or adapt a number of elements, but the result was a very efficient, cost-effective operation. Although it lost money on the Richmond project, Sprague's company soon became the nation's leading trolley builder. The General Electric Co. bought his company in 1889, but Sprague once again broke away to form another company that continued to improve elevators and installed Chicago's famous elevated trolley system. He devoted much of the rest of his life and his considerable fortune to a largely unsuccessful campaign to electrify the nation's intercity railroads.

See also Electric Power.

References and Further Reading

Sandler, Martin W. *Straphanging in the USA.* New York: Oxford University Press, 2003.

Stanford, Leland (1824–1893)

Born and raised in upstate New York, Leland Stanford read law and moved to Wisconsin to establish a practice. When a fire destroyed his office and law library in 1852, Stanford headed west to California where he opened a store that sold supplies to gold miners. When he relocated his burgeoning mercantile business to Sacramento, he formed a partnership with Charles Crocker, Collis P. Huntington, and Mark Hopkins, the so-called Big Four. By 1861 Stanford had become governor of the state, a position that greatly facilitated his lobbying activities in favor of a transcontinental railroad. The Big Four organized the Central Pacific Railroad to take advantage of federal funding. Stanford left the governorship in 1863 to become president of the railroad company that completed its transcontinental link with the Union Pacific in 1869. The Big Four financed feeder lines in central California and then created the Southern Pacific Railroad as a holding company to ensure their control over virtually all rail service in California. Stanford retained his title as president of the Central Pacific while he served as a U.S. senator in the 1880s. After his son died, he founded Leland Stanford Junior University in his honor and contributed over $20 million to its operation.

See also Land Grant Railroads.

References and Further Reading

Tutorow, Norman E. *The Governor.* Spokane, WA: Arthur H. Clark, 2004.

Stewart, Alexander Turney (A. T.) (1803–1876)

After teaching school briefly in New York, Alexander Turney Stewart returned to his native County Lisburn in Ireland to collect an inheritance. He spent the money on Irish linens and lace and returned to New York to sell them. As his dry goods business grew, he constantly moved into larger quarters. In 1848 he constructed a magnificent building called the Marble Dry-Goods Palace on lower Broadway. By that time, he had expanded his operation to include many related product lines and, to handle them, he created internal subdivisions. While he never referred to his enterprise as such, it had many characteristics of the department stores that developed during and after the Civil War. Stewart moved his headquarters further uptown to the Cast Iron Palace in 1862, one of the first major buildings constructed with a metal skeleton. Considered the largest retail store in the world at the time, the building was later sold to John Wanamaker when he wanted to open a branch in New York. Stewart also invested wisely in real estate and textile mills and made millions off wartime contracts. His $50 million estate was the largest fortune accumulated by an American merchant in his time.

See also Department Store; Wanamaker, John.

References and Further Reading

Ferry, John William. *A History of the Department Store.* New York: Macmillan, 1960.

Gustavus Swift pioneered the use of refrigerator cars to ship processed beef all over the United States. (Library of Congress)

Swift, Gustavus Franklin (1839–1903)

A preeminent figure in the meatpacking business, Gustavus Franklin Swift started his career as a wholesale butcher in Massachusetts. By 1875 he had moved to Chicago, the hub of a railroad network that linked western stock-growing regions with eastern urban centers. One of Swift's key contributions was to develop a refrigerated rail car to carry dressed beef from slaughterhouses in Chicago to customers in New York and Boston. The success of the endeavor depended on constructing refrigerated warehouse facilities and developing an aggressive marketing strategy for the products of Swift and Co. The entrepreneur assembled a vertically integrated operation that extended from stockyards to the corner butcher shop. Swift's operation involved functional rather than geographical divisions, with specialized segments of the company handling purchasing, meatpacking, shipping, marketing, and advertising. This organizational structure maximized the benefits of a division of labor, and helped Swift both compete and collaborate with the other members of the so-called Big Five (Armour, Cudahy, Hormel, and Wilson) from a position of strength. His company remained a predominant force long after his death.

See also Armour, Philip Danforth; Oligopoly.

References and Further Reading

Swift, Louis, and Arthur Van Vlissingen, Jr. *Yankee of the Yard.* New York: AMS Press, [1927], 1970.

Thompson, James Walter (1847–1928)

Born in Massachusetts but educated in Ohio, James Walter Thompson served two years in the U.S. Marine Corps before settling in New York City. In 1868 he began working for the Carlton and Smith advertising agency, which bought bulk space in local newspapers and then sold it to advertisers at a profit. This was typical for an agency in those days, but Thompson quickly extended its scope and functions. His first innovation was to place advertisements in the general circulation magazines that were becoming popular in the late nineteenth century, and he is often referred to as the father of American magazine advertising. He also developed outlets for advertisers in rural and local publications, creating the basis for national marketing campaigns. In 1878 he bought the agency and renamed it J. Walter Thompson. When he retired from the business in 1916, his company had grown into the largest advertising agency in the United States and had established many international linkages.

See also Ayer, Francis Wayland.

References and Further Reading

Garvey, Ellen Gruber. *The Adman in the Parlor.* New York: Oxford University Press, 1996.

Wanamaker, John (1838–1922)

John Wanamaker's success made his name a watchword in his native Philadelphia. The haberdashery he opened with his wife's brother did so well that it quickly became the nation's largest retailer of men's clothing. In 1876 Wanamaker dramatically broadened his merchandising by converting an old Pennsylvania Railroad freight facility into the Grand Depot, a huge precursor to the department store empire he developed over the next several years. He was a pioneer in offering a money-back guarantee for his goods and was widely praised for forward-looking personnel policies. While serving as postmaster-general under President Benjamin Harrison, he championed the introduction of rural free delivery. To accommodate a branch in New York City in 1896, Wanamaker bought the enormous Cast Iron Palace that A. T. Stewart had constructed a quarter of a century earlier.

See also Department Store; Stewart, Alexander Turney (A. T.).

References and Further Reading

Appel, Joseph Herbert. *The Business Biography of John Wanamaker.* New York: Macmillan, 1930.

Ward, Aaron Montgomery (1843–1913)

Born in New Jersey, Aaron Montgomery Ward moved with his family to Chicago. He left school at fourteen and briefly apprenticed to a barrel maker and then a brickyard before switching to sales. As a traveling salesman he visited small country stores and concluded that he could undercut their prices by selling products directly by mail. After losing his initial inventory to the great Chicago Fire of 1871, he revived the plan in 1872 and issued his first, one-page catalog. For several years, it remained a family enterprise with his wife and other relatives working long hours to fill the orders that poured in. A key partnership developed with brother-in-law Charles Thorne, a man whose own family remained very much involved in the business well into the twentieth century. In 1899 the company moved into a 385-foot-tall building on Michigan Avenue, at that time the tallest structure west of the Mississippi. A respected civic leader, Montgomery Ward used his influence to champion the preservation of public space along Lake Michigan, ensuring that Grant Park and Lakeshore Drive would remain assets of Chicago's downtown setting. Although he continued to be listed as president of Montgomery Ward and Co., he took no active part in the company's management after 1903.

See also Catalog Sales; Sears, Richard Warren (R. W.).

References and Further Reading

Latham, Frank. *1872–1972: A Century of Serving Customers.* Chicago: Montgomery Ward, 1972.

Westinghouse, George (1846–1914)

Like so many other tinkerers-turned-inventors, George Westinghouse sharpened his skills by working on agricultural machinery. His father had established a shop in Schenectady to build and improve farming implements, and young George was an active participant in the endeavor. Service in both the army and as an engineer in the navy during the Civil War interrupted his civilian pursuits, but did not prevent him from obtaining his first patent in 1865 for a steam engine. Over the next several years Westinghouse invented several railroad-related items, the most important of which was an air-powered braking system. He patented it in 1869 and created the Westinghouse Air Brake Co. to market it. Air brakes became the standard not only for trains in the United States but around the world. The creative genius continued to experiment, developing an electric railroad signaling system and a safe natural-gas pipeline system. It was a natural step, then, for him to turn his attention to electric power. An advocate of alternating current, he formed the Westinghouse Electric Co. in 1886 and immediately became involved in a bitter squabble with Thomas Edison, the chief proponent of direct current systems. A contract to light the Chicago World's Fair in 1893 and the installation of alternating current generators at Niagara Falls later in the decade effectively demonstrated the superiority of Westinghouse's technology. Although his companies struggled in the early 1900s, Westinghouse retained a solid reputation as a foresighted inventor and innovator.

See also Edison, Thomas Alva; Electric Power.

References and Further Reading

Garbedian, H. Gordon. *George Westinghouse.* New York: Dodd, Mead, 1943.

Whitney, William Collins (1841–1904)

Born in Massachusetts and educated at Yale and Harvard Law School, William Collins Whitney had all the characteristics of a blue-blooded aristocrat. It was odd, therefore, that he remained a lifelong Democrat, playing a prominent role in ousting the Tweed Ring from New York City. In 1869 he married Flora Payne, a union that brought him access to great wealth and social influence. His most notable business ventures involved successful partnerships that controlled street railways in New York and the less successful Electric Vehicle Co. Democratic President Grover Cleveland brought him to Washington as secretary of the navy in 1885 where he played a major role in the development of the nation's fleet of all-steel, steam-powered warships. He remained active in Democratic Party politics after his return to New York as well as in social and philanthropic ventures.

See also Electric Car.

References and Further Reading

Hirsch, Mark D. *William C. Whitney, Modern Warwick.* New York: Dodd, Mead, 1948.

Woolworth, Frank Winfield (F. W.) (1852–1919)

Although he ultimately founded a successful retail chain, mistakes and failures plagued many of Frank Winfield Woolworth's early business ventures. Born in rural New York, Woolworth found early employment as a farmhand, a job he hated so much he was willing to try almost anything else. He even worked at no pay for Augsbury and Moore, a Watertown, New York, retailer. By 1877 he had become senior clerk at Moore and Smith, and it was there that he created his five-cent counter. The inexpensive items sold quickly and, better yet, allowed customers to serve themselves, thus reducing labor costs. Two years later he applied this principle on a larger scale by opening the Great 5-Cent Store in Utica, but it quickly failed, as did several of his other early retail attempts. Relying heavily on partners who functioned like modern franchisers, Woolworth was gradually able to create a chain of stores in the 1880s and 1890s. In 1905 he drew his disaggregated holdings together as the F. W.

Woolworth and Co. A frequent victim of ill health, Woolworth spent lengthy sojourns in Europe where he exploited suppliers of high-quality but inexpensive goods. He also established overseas outlets and his chain exceeded 1,000 stores at the time of his death.

See also Chain Stores.

References and Further Reading

Winkler, John K. *Five and Ten: The Fabulous Life of F. W. Woolworth.* Freeport, NY: Books for Libraries Press, 1970.

SECTION 4

BOOM AND BUST, 1900–1940

The United States entered the twentieth century with a fully mature industrial economy. Its driving force was consumer spending so factory owners and business executives focused their attention on serving customers' needs and desires. General prosperity prevailed for the first three decades, much of it stemming from a remarkable rise in workers' productivity. The boom collapsed dramatically in the early 1930s, however, tumbling the nation and the world into the deepest and longest depression in history. The boom and bust cycle was so extreme it left Americans dumbfounded, anxiously seeking explanations and palliatives for the hard times that seemed all the harder coming as they did after such an exhilarating period of prosperity and optimism.

Americans had hardly been complacent in the early years, however. Reform-minded writers nicknamed **muckrakers** helped popularize the Progressive movement's concepts and concerns. As their number increased, Progressives in both major political parties engineered major political changes, many of them aimed at restraining or regulating the industrial and financial behemoths that had arisen in the late nineteenth century. Most of these had adopted a **holding company** format, the structure that J. P. Morgan had selected for the United States Steel Co., the nation's first **billion dollar corporation**. Those who considered such giant combinations dangerous took heart when the Supreme Court in the **Northern Securities Co. Case** used the Sherman Antitrust Act to break up a major business consolidation.

Progressives in Congress meanwhile expanded the federal regulatory apparatus. New legislation led to **reform of the Interstate Commerce Commission**, beefing up its authority over transportation and utility providers. In 1912 the **Pujo Committee** staged a dramatic investigation of what it called the Money Trust. Shortly afterward, Congress extended ICC-style oversight and regulation to most other industries by creating the **Federal Trade Commission**. The substitution of regulation for trust-busting seemed appropriate because the Supreme Court had articulated a **rule of reason** in the Standard Oil case that appeared to weaken the 1890 Sherman Antitrust Act's impact. Democratic Progressives attempted to plug holes in the Sherman Act by writing a series of explicit prohibitions into the **Clayton Antitrust Act** in 1914.

While the passage of the 1900 Gold Standard Act had muted the debate over alternative monetary systems, it did nothing to regulate or restrain financial markets. Progressive politicians who favored federal banking reform finally settled on the creation of the **Federal Reserve System** in 1914. Among its other capabilities, the Fed (i.e., the Federal Reserve Board) began to use **open market operations** to manage both the nation's debt and its **money supply**.

Significant changes took place in manufacturing as well. To increase worker productivity, many factories adopted the principles of

scientific management that Frederick W. Taylor popularized. Although he claimed to have developed his concepts independent of Taylor, Henry Ford's installation of a **moving assembly line** and his successful fight against the **Selden Patent** vastly increased his ability to meet the demand for his popular Model T Ford. To compete more effectively against the industry leader, visionaries like Pierre S. du Pont and Alfred P. Sloan at General Motors exploited **product differentiation** and **built-in obsolescence** to develop a line of cars at different price levels, effectively **bracketing the market**. To achieve greater benefits from product differentiation, many larger firms instituted **brand management** in the 1930s.

Like the auto industry, other sectors also experienced substantial growth. Commercial **radio** networks created a national market for advertisers. **Movies** evolved from five-minute reels in nickelodeons to full color, high-quality sound films in sumptuous theaters. Dramatic technological changes also took place in the field of **commercial aviation**. Retailers increasingly relied on **consumer credit** to stimulate repeat sales, and the growth of **parcel delivery** services also encouraged consumer spending.

The size and complexity of the American economy provided some protection from external disturbances. A long string of positive annual trade balances culminated in 1914 with the United States becoming the world's largest **creditor nation**. When the Great War broke out, Britain, France, and their allies therefore found it difficult to pay for the arms, food, and supplies they desperately needed. Private loans helped offset this disadvantage, but the Entente Powers' growing debt to Americans definitely played a role in convincing the United States to enter the war in 1917. It was hardly ready to do so. Many months passed before the **War Industries Board** became an effective purchasing and regulating authority. To constrain inflation, efforts were made to determine a **just price** for goods in high demand. The board also ordered **standardization** to cut costs and promote efficiency. Secretary of Commerce Herbert Hoover continued to promote standardization in the 1920s in conjunction with his energetic support of **associationalism**. The war debts remained largely unpaid until the **Dawes Plan** created a structure for stimulating increased international exchange in 1924.

A core aspect of the Dawes Plan was its encouragement for Americans to invest in Germany, but the lure of a heady **bull market** at home was hard to resist. Many credulous speculators fell for the **Ponzi Scheme**; others lost big in the **Florida Land Bubble**. Although they seemed much safer, the **leveraged investment trusts** that developed late in the 1920s also put shareholders' money at risk. Many had already become dangerously overextended by taking out low-margin **brokers' loans** and gambling on **call loans**. Even the most savvy average citizen, however, could not offset the advantages available to the insiders included on **preferred lists** of investors.

The bull market mentality so dominated Americans' thinking that few were aware of or interested in Wesley Mitchell's studies of **business cycles**. But even Mitchell did not anticipate the magnitude of the impending stock market **crash**. Historical perspective provides much greater understanding of the **causes of the Great Depression**. One of these clearly was significant **underconsumption** stemming in part from a declining or static growth in real wages in the 1920s. A great many things had to go wrong, however, to create the **character of the Great Depression**.

One response of President Herbert Hoover's administration was to create the **Reconstruction Finance Corporation** to provide federal loans to struggling industries. Despite its failure to trigger any immediate recovery, it remained in operation for a decade. Hoover's support of much higher tariffs threatened to push the United States toward **autarky**. Fortunately, this flawed approach to international trade relations eased in 1934 with the adoption of a **reciprocity** policy.

As the Depression intensified, the electorate took a chance on the New Deal that Franklin Roosevelt promised by electing him president and handing his Democratic Party control of Congress. A sweeping financial crisis caused Roosevelt immediately to announce a national **bank holiday**. Once that crisis had passed, the president began tinkering with the gold standard, even going to the extreme of experimenting with a **commodity dollar**. A far better long-term solution appeared in 1935 legislation that instituted substantial **reform of the Federal Reserve System**. The Fed has functioned much more effectively ever since. In a similar vein, Congress created the **Securities and Exchange Commission** charged with regulating stock and bond sales as well as imposing regulatory controls and reporting requirements on corporate financial operations.

Although these reform efforts were generally appropriate and reasonable, they did not significantly improve the nation's overall economic situation. Neither did the many **relief** programs the Roosevelt administration implemented. Simultaneously, it experimented with a number of programs specifically designed to encourage economic **recovery**. The flawed theory of **induced scarcity** underlay both the National Recovery Administration and the **Agricultural Adjustment Acts**. Neither spawned the positive changes that were anticipated and the Supreme Court declared both of them unconstitutional in the mid-1930s. Subsequent legislation did, however, revive the concept of **parity**, which has remained a fundamental principle of agricultural subsidy programs ever since.

Some advocates of **Keynesian economic** theory called for massive federal **deficit spending,** but Roosevelt refused deliberately to unbalance the budget. The Second World War's demand for materiel quickly scuttled that policy. By 1945 the national debt had ballooned to an all-time high and the U.S. economy was more productive than ever. That suggests that deficit spending might, after all, have fueled recovery in the 1930s had it been done aggressively enough.

KEY CONCEPTS

Agricultural Adjustment Acts

The first Agricultural Adjustment Act of 1933 was designed to ease the farm population's suffering. It hoped to use the induced scarcity principle to raise prices on agricultural commodities to more reasonable levels. When its package of production quotas and price standards was declared unconstitutional in 1936, Congress crafted a second Agricultural Adjustment Act. The new program helped ensure that federal price supports would become a permanent aspect of American agricultural policy.

The agrarian crisis of the 1930s had long roots. After experiencing very good times in the years immediately prior to the First World War, farmers continued to prosper as wartime demand remained strong. While an immediate postwar decline was predictable, throughout the 1920s, conditions simply never improved to the levels they had reached earlier.

The conservative Republican administrations in control during the decade were philosophically opposed to aggressive federal intervention into any economic sector. Consequently a number of proposals for agrarian relief failed, torpedoed either by congressional tactics or presidential opposition. The persistent agricultural depression definitely helped drag the rest of the economy down once the Great Depression began in the early 1930s.

Along with prices for most other goods, agricultural prices had fallen to extremely low levels by 1933. Stories circulated about midwestern farmers burning corn for heat because, at eight cents a bushel, it was far cheaper than coal. Dairy farmers protested the very low prices for their products by dumping milk down sewers to gain public sympathy for their plight. The chief problem was the same one that affected products of all sorts: a lack of purchasing power in the hands of consumers. When federal action finally tried to stem the crisis, however, it focused on other supposed causes of price deflation.

Fundamental to most of these efforts was a conviction that the major problem was overproduction. Therefore the major efforts were to limit production or remove excess commodities from the market. If a scarcity could be induced, policy-makers believed, prices would inevitably rise. Unfortunately, there were major problems with any approach based on inducing scarcity. First of all it was very difficult to accomplish in an industry that had literally millions of producers. Even more discouraging, simply reducing or limiting production in no way solved the general shortage of purchasing power that persisted throughout the Depression.

When the first concerns about overproduction surfaced in the late 1920s, the federal government instituted a policy reminiscent of President Herbert Hoover's term as wartime head of the Food Administration. The plan was to have the government simply buy up the surplus and hold it off the market. The resulting induced scarcity was supposed to force prices up for those commodities still available for sale. Over $350 million was expended on this hopeless program—hopeless because it did nothing to actually limit production or to generate purchasing power.

President Franklin Roosevelt appointed a highly respected Iowan, Henry A. Wallace, to be his secretary of agriculture. Wallace's father had served in that same position in the 1920s, so the new man was well versed in the problem. Literally hundreds of suggestions poured in to his office, many of them completely contradictory. But the crisis demanded quick action, so Congress cobbled together the Agricultural Adjustment Act of 1933 without lengthy consideration of all of its ramifications.

It created an Agricultural Adjustment Administration (AAA) charged with limiting production. The most prominent of its programs was the development of quotas for seven basic commodities: wheat, corn, rice, hogs, tobacco, cotton, and dairy products. The Agriculture Department established national quotas for each, designed to match anticipated demand so that prices would settle in at reasonable or normal levels. Committees at the state, county, and even local levels would receive allocations of production, and individual farmers signed agreements to produce no more than their share of the overall quota.

To encourage compliance, the AAA paid farmers not to produce. For example, it provided compensation to those who left land fallow. A special tax collected from food processors provided the funding for these subsidies. Unfortunately, the elaborate process of defining quotas through all of the regional and local levels took several months. Because many of them were delayed until August or September, some farmers had to plow up grain nearly ready for harvest. Over 6 million hogs were slaughtered to reduce the national output. One of the many ironies of the AAA was the decision to convert much of the slaughtered meat into fertilizer that, when used, increased production of field crops.

Quotas were unpopular, farmers took only their poorest land out of production, and food processors objected to the taxes. Worse still, the program destroyed vast amounts of food at the same time people were literally starving in the cities. In 1936 the Supreme Court concluded that the processing tax was unconstitutional, thereby canceling the source of the subsidies and making the program unworkable. Many farmers and administrators were actually quite relieved at this decision because the program had basically failed to improve conditions.

But the problems persisted, so a chastened Congress drafted a second Agricultural Adjustment Act in 1938, one that survived judicial review. The new legislation established a more reasonable expectation of boosting prices to 75 percent of their optimal or parity level. The processing tax was eliminated, but subsidies for limiting production were included. Indeed, this concept of agricultural subsidies has become institutionalized in the United States ever since.

The second act also expanded the tools the federal government could use to stabilize agricultural price levels. It encouraged cooperative marketing agreements designed to benefit both producers and buyers. Like the Hoover administration's approach, the government purchased surplus commodities to keep them off the market. Rather than simply hold them, however, the government aggressively marketed these surpluses overseas and, in some instances, funneled them into relief programs for hungry Americans who could not afford to buy their own food. Using harvested crops as collateral, the Commodity Credit Corporation loaned money to individual farmers, allowing them to hold their produce off the market until they could obtain favorable prices.

Not surprisingly, the complexities of these new programs made them much more accessible to larger operations. Small holders, tenant farmers, and other marginal operators either lost out completely or obtained very limited help. Wealthier farmers and commercial farming operations took full advantage of the subsidies and the CCC loans to maximize the profitability of their efforts.

The continuation and, indeed, vast expansion of crop subsidies in the decades since the Great Depression have generally failed to alleviate all agricultural distress. In later years programs like the soil bank, which paid farmers to keep land out of production, recalled experiments first attempted in the 1930s. The legacy of the Agricultural Adjustment Acts is one in which the federal government has become deeply and permanently involved in shoring up and regulating the nation's farm community.

See also Great Depression, Character of; Induced Scarcity; Parity.

References and Further Reading

Dubofsky, Melvyn, and Stephen Burwood. *Agriculture During the Great Depression.* New York: Garland, 1990.

Halcrow, Harold G. *The Agricultural Policy of the United States.* New York, Prentice-Hall, 1953.

Saloutos, Theodore. *The American Farmer and the New Deal.* Ames, IA: Iowa State University Press, 1982.

Schapsmeier, Edward L., and Frederick H. Schapsmeier. *Henry A. Wallace of Iowa.* Ames, IA: Iowa State University Press, 1968.

Volanto, Keith J. *Texas, Cotton, and the New Deal.* College Station, TX: Texas A&M University Press, 2005.

Associationalism

In the 1920s Herbert Hoover became the most prominent advocate encouraging trade and other associations to engage in self-regulation. He expected that the associationalism he favored would eliminate waste, improve efficiency, and promote conservation to the betterment of the lives of all Americans. To advance his goals, Hoover criticized antitrust laws and prosecutions, thus cementing his pro-business image. By the 1930s his supportive approach to associationalism had largely given way to intrusive and aggressive governmental intervention designed to revive the depressed economy.

Trade associations of various kinds had existed for decades, some tracing their roots back to medieval guilds of craftsmen. Twentieth century trade associations, however, had come to encompass much larger groups of producers or professionals. Industrialization encouraged this trend, creating highly capitalized firms increasingly competing on a national basis.

At the basic level, members of a trade association benefited from communication and an exchange of ideas about production methods, marketing campaigns, and labor management. Many associations systematically collected data from and about their members. This data in turn helped individual firms set prices and realize efficiencies. In some cases, an association exercised considerable power over its members to the extent of dictating or fixing prices.

Mobilization during the First World War stimulated interest in the benefits of associations. During the conflict, the War Industries Board and the Food Administration among others actively promoted cooperative behavior in many industries. Because these federal agencies also had major purchasing responsibility, they could control prices and inflation. Equally important, to keep production costs down they encouraged standardization, mechanization, elimination of waste, and even consolidation of units locked in wasteful or destructive competition.

Herbert Hoover headed the Food Administration in 1917 and 1918, and that experience definitely influenced his attitudes when he became secretary of commerce in 1921. Hoover saw positive possibilities for a continuation of the industrial and trade associationalism that had paid dividends during the war. His hope was that enlightened businessmen would see the advantages of a cooperative rather than a competitive approach. Associations could be very helpful in promoting that development. They would collect data, exchange information about production techniques and innovations, and might even encourage industry-wide advances.

Some 2,000 trade associations existed in the 1920s, and many of them took actions that went well beyond Hoover's idealistic conception. A key problem was price fixing, made all the more effective if a strong association existed. And price fixing could very easily be considered a violation of the antitrust laws' prohibition on restraint of trade. Hoover faced an uphill battle when he criticized Justice Department efforts to prosecute trade associations.

When the government lost two key Supreme Court cases in the mid-1920s, it cleared the way for cooperative corporate action. Trade associationalism boomed in the latter half of the decade under President Calvin Coolidge's benign administration. Some of these organizations fit nicely with Hoover's plan for self-regulating, community-interested entities. Businessmen who participated in such associations benefited from predictability about pricing, insulation from market invasion, and collaborative colleagues. Many associations went so far as to develop codes for pricing, ethical behavior, and labor relations. In other cases, however, some associations came to resemble exclusive and powerful oligopolies, capable of exerting detrimental market control and price fixing.

The Great Depression that effectively destroyed President Herbert Hoover's reputation dealt devastating blows to associationalism. Many firms abandoned their cooperative stances in an effort to save themselves in the downturn. Those associations that survived lost much of their influence and ability to promote predictability. The concept of cooperative behavior throughout an entire industry did persist in the recovery programs that President Franklin Roosevelt's administration promulgated. The price, production, and ethical codes that the National Recovery Administration hammered out often built on models that trade associations had produced in the previous decade.

Trade associations still function in the American business system. They continue to provide many of the same benefits that were articulated in the 1920s. Advocacy of associationalism as such, however, has declined in recent years as alternative structures and regulatory regimes have played a more prominent role.

See also Recovery; Standardization.

References and Further Reading

Burner, David. *Herbert Hoover: A Public Life.* New York, Knopf, 1979.

Hoover, Herbert. *The Memoirs of Herbert Hoover.* New York: Macmillan, 1952.

Wilson, Joan Hoff. *Herbert Hoover: Forgotten Progressive.* Prospect Heights, IL: Waveland Press, 1992.

Autarky

If a country or government tries to seal itself off from external trade and economic involvement, it is said to be pursuing *autarky*. Being totally insulated from outside influences is impossible, of course, but from time to time, some nations have deliberately tried to achieve that goal. Some accused President Franklin Roosevelt of pursuing a policy of autarky in the early 1930s, pointing to several steps he took regarding trade and financial policy. Whatever Roosevelt's intentions might have been, the United States quickly backed off from autarky and attempted to reestablish its central position as an international trading partner.

From the very beginning, the Europeans who settled in the American colonies remained highly dependent on continuous infusions of money, supplies, and immigrants. This dependency continued up to the Revolution and, as soon as political independence had been achieved, the citizens of the newly created United States fell back into their traditional dependent status. Great Britain remained the major trading partner, providing 90 percent of U.S. imports and absorbing about 75 percent of U.S. exports in the 1790s.

The nation's first encounter with a deliberate policy of autarky came in the early 1800s when Napoleon Bonaparte was emperor of France. Hoping to economically destroy his implacable British enemy, Napoleon issued a decree that established the Continental System. Its objective was to turn France and the other countries that Napoleon's armies had subjugated into a self-sustaining, independent economic unit. Britain's economy could only thrive if it was able actively to trade and ship goods to Europe. If Napoleon succeeded in creating a continental autarky, he could presumably vanquish the enemy that his armies and navies had failed to defeat.

Because Britain was the main focus of Napoleon's policy, the French welcomed trade from the United States. Continental autarky was therefore never even close to being complete. American producers, exporters, and shipowners took advantage of the decline in British shipping to Europe, but in doing so angered the British. This hostility eventually led to the War of 1812. No one revived the Continental System once Napoleon had gone into exile in 1815.

The United States's long tradition as an energetic trading nation made many Americans uncomfortable when the country seemed to be withdrawing from the rest of the world in the early 1930s. One obvious reason for turning inward was that the European economies were falling into deep depressions of their own and were unable to provide financial or other support to the United States. At that point the American economy was by far the world's largest and, because of its size and geographic diversity, the United States was better positioned for self-sufficiency than other nations.

Groundwork for isolation had been laid after the First World War when the United States refused to ratify the Treaty of Versailles or participate in the League of Nations. It handled international economic issues with carefully sanitized approaches like the Dawes Plan of 1924. When the American stock market crashed five years later, it drained investment funds that might otherwise have flowed overseas. An abrupt cessation of American overseas investment appeared to many outsiders to be a symptom of autarky.

President Franklin Roosevelt's initial emergency financial arrangements fed that image. After experimenting with a commodity dollar through the fall of 1933, the United States announced that it would no longer peg the value of its dollar to gold. The president has also been charged with torpedoing the London Economic Conference in 1933 by undermining his own secretary of state, Cordell Hull, who had planned to have the United States shore up international efforts. The deliberate deflation of the dollar to around fifty-nine cents of its former value was designed to boost prices in America, but it had catastrophic effects on the nation's trading partners. The volume of world trade fell to only one-third of the level it had achieved in the late 1920s, further insulating the United States and other nations from each other.

By 1934, however, the Roosevelt Administration turned away from autarky. A key sign of that change came with the passage of the Reciprocal Trade Agreements Act in that year. It encouraged the reduction of tariffs across the board. Negotiations began with dozens of trading partners, seeking mutually beneficial accommodations that would encourage rather than limit exchange. The development of the so-called Good Neighbor Policy for Latin America helped improve trading and diplomatic relations throughout the Western Hemisphere. Long before the Second World War began in Europe in 1939, the United States had reestablished its posture as the world's greatest trading nation, the very antithesis of an autarky.

Although the term is seldom mentioned, some economies could be considered autarkies. An obvious example would be the current regime in North Korea, which, for political reasons, has literally sealed itself off from most external contacts. Even the onslaught of a devastating famine in the late 1990s opened few portholes to the outside. The world economy has become so remarkably integrated and interdependent, however, that autarky simply no longer is a rational policy—if it ever had been.

See also Commodity Dollar; Dawes Plan; Reciprocity.

References and Further Reading

Calvin, Patricia. *The Failure of Economic Diplomacy.* New York: St. Martins, 1996.

Feis, Herbert. *1933: Characters in Crisis.* Boston, Little, Brown. 1966.

Freidel, Frank. *Franklin D. Roosevelt: Launching the New Deal.* Boston: Little, Brown, 1973.

Bank Holiday

Shortly after his inauguration, President Franklin Roosevelt called for a nationwide bank holiday. His executive order was an emergency response to a banking crisis that had grown ever more threatening in the last days of the Hoover administration. Once the banks were closed, Congress passed a comprehensive banking bill designed to eliminate some of the factors that had created the crisis in the first place. Roosevelt's actions, including a reassuring radio broadcast to the nation, allowed most banks to reopen a few days later without fear.

Bank failures were not uncommon even in the prosperous decade of the 1920s. Around 600 institutions closed their doors each year, but the vast majority of them were very small ones serving villages or other rural customers. Over 90 percent of them were capitalized at under $100,000, and they were particularly susceptible to even minor fluctuations or stringencies in their immediate environment.

The real problem lay with larger banks. About 20 percent of those that failed during the decade were members of the Federal Reserve System, and their combined assets amounted to almost $1 billion. After the stock market crash, the number of bank failures rose rapidly, and a much larger portion of them had substantial holdings. Nearly 2,300 institutions folded in 1931 alone, accounting for $1.7 billion in deposits. Though the pace of failure eased somewhat in the next year, collapses came with alarming regularity, further undermining confidence in a population already traumatized by the crash and economic downturn.

Bank runs could materialize in a matter of hours, fed by distrust, rumor, and generalized economic fears. No institution was immune from a run, regardless of how scrupulously managed. Even though member banks could summon reserves from the Federal Reserve System's banks, the general population could never be certain that their deposits would be available for withdrawal. In the fall of 1931, Great Britain abandoned the gold standard, triggering a $700 million shrinkage in the value of U.S. gold holdings, and nervous Americans compounded the problem by withdrawing another $400 million from their deposit accounts.

Drastic action seemed necessary to protect the remaining banks from panic. Nevada was the first state to announce a holiday in October 1932. This action closed the institutions and prevented clients from withdrawing funds and further decimating their holdings. By early 1933 holidays were being instituted in other states. One of the most frightening occurred in Michigan on February 10, a recognition that the Detroit-centered automobile industry had fallen deep into the Great Depression. By the eve of Franklin Roosevelt's inauguration on March 4, bank holidays were in place or had been called in almost half of the states.

Outgoing President Herbert Hoover had accurately pinpointed general fear verging on panic as a major cause for the bank runs, suspensions, and holidays. He had urged Roosevelt to make a strong, reassuring public statement to reverse this phenomenon, but the incoming Democrat refused to do anything that might be construed as either supporting Republican policies or limiting his own freedom to act.

Even before the inauguration, however, Roosevelt's advisors and congressional leaders had been devising a plan to deal with the problem. Using almost forgotten emergency powers dating back to the First World War, the new president announced a national bank holiday on Monday morning, March 6, 1933. Treasury officials and bankers began examining the true state of the nation's financial system, and three days later Congress convened in a special session to pass the Emergency Banking Act to deal with the crisis.

The legislation confirmed Roosevelt's authority to call the holiday in the first place. It also permitted the Federal Reserve system to issue banknotes based on commercial paper and other securities rather than the traditional federal bonds. This resulted in a rapid expansion of the nation's money supply that helped ease fears of a monetary collapse. The emergency legislation also ordered banks to divorce themselves from brokerage houses. Finally, it proposed the institution of a federal insurance program for depositors.

Meanwhile Treasury officials hastily evaluated the nation's banks and sorted them into four categories. About half of the banks with 90 percent of the assets were found to be basically sound and could be reopened immediately. Various restrictions and oversight were imposed on those in the second two categories, those that could be reopened with minor policy revisions and those that would need more heroic recovery programs. The final group of about 1,000 institutions representing 5 percent of the whole appeared unsalvageable and they remained closed permanently.

President Roosevelt established a precedent for talking confidently with the American people. On Sunday, March 12, in the first of his "fireside chat" radio broadcasts, he told his fellow countrymen what steps the administration and Congress had taken to insure the safety of their bank deposits. The result was that more money flowed into the reopened banks the next morning than was withdrawn. The immediate crisis was over. The holiday had achieved its goal.

The emergency legislation that accompanied the holiday was only a first step toward the development of a much broader, more comprehensive reform and restructuring of the nation's banking system. New rules were imposed, the deposit insurance program was made permanent, and the Federal Reserve System as a whole was considerably changed and strengthened in the next few years. For these and other reasons, the 1933 national bank holiday was the only one of its kind in U.S. history. Bank closures in the rest of the Depression averaged around fifty per year, far below the rate that had marred the more prosperous 1920s.

See also Commodity Dollar; Crash; Federal Reserve System, Reform of; Great Depression, Character of.

References and Further Reading

Mitchell, Broadus. *Depression Decade.* New York: Harper and Row, 1947.

Perkins, Dexter. *The New Age of Franklin Roosevelt.* Chicago: University of Chicago Press, 1957.

Billion Dollar Corporation

In 1901 J. P. Morgan superintended the creation of the United States Steel Corporation. This giant company combined Andrew Carnegie's vast industrial empire with those of eight other major holding companies. Collectively, the new combination produced more than half of all the raw and finished steel products in the United States. The final capitalization for this behemoth was $1.4 billion, making it the first billion dollar corporation in U.S. history. Later enterprises also exceeded the billion dollar mark, but the formation of U.S. Steel represented a major milestone in the industrialization of the United States and set many precedents for others to follow.

In one sense, the formation of U.S. Steel was a natural culmination of a consolidation trend that had flourished throughout the 1890s. The American steel industry was huge, disorganized, highly competitive, and ultimately very wasteful. Andrew Carnegie richly deserved his nickname "the Steel King" precisely because of his success in constructing by far the most efficient system for succeeding in this chaotic business. Using vertical integration, he had streamlined the whole manufacturing process from raw materials to finished goods, enabling him to undercut his competitors' prices and profit even in depressed times. A major economic downturn in the early 1890s forced thousands of companies out of business, but Carnegie's annual balance sheets remained comfortably in the black.

During the same decade J. P. Morgan emerged as the nation's leading finance capitalist. The profitability of the business combinations he created only enhanced his ability to attract enormous amounts of capital. He took pride in eliminating waste and destructive competition through organization and top-down control. Morgan considered the internecine warfare that characterized the American steel industry as highly inefficient. Seizing on the newly available mechanism of the holding company, he set out to rationalize the industry by eliminating waste, destructive competition, and a splintered industrial leadership.

Morgan looked favorably on the efforts of Judge Elbert Gary and John W. Gates to consolidate the steel industry in the upper Midwest. In 1898 these two men developed the American Steel and Wire Company of Illinois, which controlled over 80 percent of the nation's wire production. Similar consolidations resulted in holding companies capable of dominating other subsectors like steel tubing, tin plate, and hoops. With solid Morgan backing, Gary played a key role in organizing the Federal Steel Co. in 1899, and the financier insisted that Gary become its president. In many ways Federal Steel copied the Carnegie model, encompassing ore-bearing lands, railroad equipment, pig iron, and finishing mills in a vertically integrated operation. Capitalized at $200 million, it was second in size only to Carnegie's operation.

Carnegie viewed these developments as a threat to his still predominant empire. Reacting in his characteristic fashion to competition, he announced plans for his own state-of-the art tube mill in Conneaut, Ohio, that would easily outperform Morgan's National Tube Co. This sort of competition was precisely what Morgan hoped to avoid, so he opened negotiations with Charles M. Schwab, the president of Carnegie's operation.

Schwab knew Carnegie was seriously considering retirement from the steel business so he could devote the remaining years of his life to philanthropy. Schwab also knew that Carnegie and Morgan disliked each other intensely. His skill as a mediator helped the two adversaries forge an agreement in which Carnegie would sell all of his holdings to

Morgan for some $400 million. As a reward for his services, Morgan had Schwab named as the first president of his newly organized holding company, the United States Steel Corporation.

Chartered on February 23, 1901, the company combined the Federal Steel Co. and the National Steel Co., two diversified basic steel and raw materials concerns with the much larger Carnegie assets. In addition U.S. Steel controlled the operations of five major holding companies devoted to specialized products: American Tin Plate Co., American Steel and Wire Co., National Tube Co., American Steel Hoop Co., and American Sheet Steel Co. Shortly after its formation, two other units, the American Bridge Co. and Shelby Steel Tube Co., were added to the mix.

A realistic valuation of the actual worth of all of these properties would stand at about $700 million. Morgan nevertheless issued stock with a par value of twice that amount, $1.4 billion, feeding the public's perception that U.S. Steel was, indeed, a billion dollar corporation. The watered stock reflected Morgan's belief that the new company would eventually reach that value. After all, the properties he had brought together in 1901 represented 44 percent of the nation's steel ingot capacity, 75 percent of its tin plate capacity, and 80 percent of its wire and tube capacity. By 1920 no one could dispute Morgan's optimism.

The huge company accomplished other key Morgan goals. It eliminated much of the destructive competition that had prevailed before 1900, and it represented a solid, reliable institution in which to invest. At the same time, U.S. Steel tended to be rather conservative in its operations. As president, Charles Schwab had bold, innovative ideas, but the powerful board of directors led by Judge Gary showed little inclination to pursue them. Schwab was too outspoken and controversial to survive in such a situation, so he left the company in 1903. Gary remained the chief architect of the corporation's success until his death in 1927.

With some 150 operating companies under its control, U.S. Steel was able to close inefficient plants and eliminate middleman costs on a grand scale. From a business perspective, therefore, it operated far more efficiently than its rivals, enjoying the benefits of economies of scale simply unavailable to smaller concerns.

This same factor reinforced the corporation's fundamental conservatism, enabling other, more aggressive operators like Bethlehem Steel to develop innovations. Charles Schwab became president of this much smaller concern after leaving U.S. Steel and, over the next decade, his dynamic leadership built Bethlehem into the nation's second largest steel company. It was Bethlehem, for example, that developed a lightweight but very strong wide-flanged H-beam in 1908, something that U.S. Steel was unable to manufacture until the late 1920s.

An organization as large as U.S. Steel naturally raised antitrust concerns. President Theodore Roosevelt agreed not to bring suit against it in return for what he perceived to be J. P. Morgan's assistance in helping the nation weather the business panic of 1907. Roosevelt's successor, William Howard Taft, felt no such obligation, so his attorney general duly instituted antitrust proceedings. This action led to a remarkable moment when ex-President Roosevelt was called to testify in court regarding his attitudes toward the company's behavior. The case dragged on for years, finally ending in 1920 with a decision that left the company intact. This was hardly a surprising result, given the nation's reversion to a more conservative mood tolerant of big business in the wake of the First World War.

The success of the first billion dollar corporation encouraged others to follow its lead. A number of other major business consolidations took place in the early twentieth century that reached or exceeded the billion-dollar capitalization mark. General price inflation over the course of the century further deflated the importance of that milestone.

Even so, the creation of the United States Steel Corporation was momentous, the opening event to three decades of industrial and business prosperity.

See also Carnegie, Andrew; Gary, Elbert Henry; Holding Company; Morgan, John Pierpont (J. P.); Vertical Integration.

References and Further Reading

Hessen, Robert. *Steel Titan: The Life of Charles M. Schwab.* New York: Oxford University Press, 1975.

Misa, Thomas J. *A Nation of Steel.* Baltimore, MD: John's Hopkins University Press, 1995.

Schroeder, Gertrude G. *The Growth of Major Steel Companies, 1900–1950.* Baltimore, MD: John's Hopkins University Press, 1953.

Tarbell, Ida M. *The Life of Elbert H. Gary.* New York: Appleton, 1925.

Bracketing the Market

Some consumers are willing to pay more for a product if they can be convinced it is superior to another. Producers who recognized this variability can bracket the market by offering a range of similar products at several price levels. Their customers make buying decisions on the basis of real or perceived quality enhancements, advertising campaigns, brand-name recognition, and other factors.

The General Motors (GM) Corporation pioneered this practice with one of the most comprehensive plans for bracketing the market in the mid-1920s. GM president Alfred P. Sloan deserves the credit for this successful marketing strategy. Sloan was also instrumental in dramatically reorganizing the administrative structure of the conglomerate. In the process, he not only reoriented a corporate giant, he also fundamentally altered the nature of automobile production and marketing in the United States and around the world.

In developing his Model T, Henry Ford tried to produce the perfect motor car, one he could build and sell forever. This basic automobile was so successful in the second decade of the twentieth century that Ford devoted virtually all of his entrepreneurial energies simply to reducing both the production costs and sales prices of his Model Ts. But by the mid-1920s almost everyone who could afford to buy a car already had one and there was little incentive for someone to buy a new Model T identical to the one already in the garage.

The General Motors Corporation had a much different and initially less successful experience. The chief player here was not an inventor like Ford but rather an accumulator and consolidator. William C. Durant was head of the Buick Motor Car Company in 1908 when he conceived of the General Motors Corporation and began using its stock to acquire various automobile-related enterprises. These included independent auto companies like Cadillac and Oakland as well as parts manufacturers and suppliers. Financial troubles forced Durant out of control for a while, but he returned in 1915 and continued his acquisition strategy. Alfred P. Sloan was the president of one of the parts manufacturing companies Durant brought into GM in 1916. Five years later the postwar depression forced Durant out of control permanently.

Durant had obtained considerable funding from the Du Pont family along the way, and Pierre S. du Pont took charge as president of GM in 1921. He moved Sloan up to the presidency in 1923, in recognition of his remarkable organizational skills. Together they developed a comprehensive reorganization plan to rationalize the components Durant had assembled.

In the mid-1920s new car sales in the United States leveled off at about 4 million units a year. To expand his company's market share, Sloan recognized that current owners would need an incentive to buy new cars instead of being content with the ones they already owned. He also recognized that some individuals were capable of spending a good deal more on a car than the $645 base price for a 1922 Model T Ford. GM was already selling cars at various prices under several different brand names, but these prices and models reflected the historical traditions of the individual companies Durant had added to the corporation, not a coordinated plan.

Sloan rationalized the entire GM product line, creating in his words, "a car for every person and purpose." He bracketed the market with automobiles ranging in price from $525 for the least expensive Chevrolet to $3,045 for the top of the line, a Cadillac Coupe. In between, at ascending price levels were Pontiacs, Oldsmobiles, Oaklands, and a finely differentiated range of Buick models. This strategy proved so successful for GM that other automakers like Chrysler soon developed brackets of their own. Even the recalcitrant Henry Ford eventually sold Fords, Mercurys, and Lincolns to increasingly affluent buyers.

Price bracketing was only one of Sloan's innovations. He devised additional product differentiation by changing models on a yearly basis. The goal was to convince owners to trade in their current cars for new ones, so GM introduced and advertised extensively each year's new models. The basic plan involved a major model change every third year, with an annual facelift to draw customers' attention between major changes. Because of the conglomerate's interconnectedness, GM could implement these annual changes at relatively low cost. For example, an improvement in the higher-priced Buick line one year became the advertised innovation in next year's Chevrolet.

When Sloan took the reins of General Motors in 1923, the corporation controlled only about a 20 percent share of the U.S. auto market, far behind Ford's 50 percent share. Four years later, GM had captured 43 percent of the market. It would remain the dominant automaker for decades to come. Much of this dramatic change came about because of Sloan's organizational skills and his recognition of the importance of bracketing the market.

See also du Pont, Pierre Samuel; Durant, William Crapo; Ford, Henry; Product Differentiation; Sloan, Jr., Alfred Pritchard.

References and Further Reading

Brands, H. W. *Masters of Enterprise.* New York: Free Press, 1999.

Chandler, Jr., Alfred D. *Giant Enterprise.* York: Harcourt, Brace, World, 1964.

Sloan, Jr., Alfred P. *My Years With General Motors.* Garden City, NY: Doubleday, 1963.

Brand Management

In 1931 Procter and Gamble (P&G) was the world's largest producer of household products, marketing soap, cleaners, food, and other products under a variety of brand names. Many of these products faced internal competition from other P&G products. A young go-getter named Neil McElroy wrote a memorandum suggesting that a team be created to focus attention on a particular brand. P&G adopted brand management and the concept quickly spread to other companies that produced a variety of goods.

Product differentiation was fundamental to brand management. Trademarks and brand names had become common in the United States in the twentieth century, and companies jealously defended their brand-named products from competitors and infringers. Neil McElroy's specific problem, however, was that his assignment was to promote Camay soap in a company whose flagship product was Ivory soap.

Ivory had been invented accidentally in the late nineteenth century when a technician left a soap-mixing machine on so long it had beaten air into the product. The resulting bars were light enough to float in water. An aggressive advertising campaign was quickly devised to exploit this unintended feature. The company conducted tests and found that Ivory also had fewer impurities than other bar soaps, so the advertising slogans "99 and 44 one-hundredths percent pure" and "it floats" became familiar to all Americans.

McElroy proposed that he lead a team of marketers responsible for differentiating Camay not only from Ivory but from competitors' products like Colgate's Palmolive soap. With P&G's blessing, Camay became known as a beauty soap, distinct from the more plebeian Ivory. McElroy's timing was crucial because he invented brand management just as the nation fell into the Great Depression. Skillful advertising and devoted concern to brand management enabled companies like Procter and Gamble to survive the hard times with relatively less stress than their competitors.

Brand management has since become a well-recognized and widely used technique in the consumer products industries. Alfred P. Sloan had laid the groundwork for aggressive product differentiation with his market bracketing scheme at General Motors in the 1920s, and many other manufacturers followed his lead. Thoughtful and deliberate brand management definitely enhanced the effectiveness and success of product differentiation.

See also Product Differentiation; Trademarks.

References and Further Reading

Dyer, Davis, et al. *Rising Tide.* Boston: Harvard Business School Press, 2004.

McCraw, Thomas K. *American Business, 1920–2000.* Wheeling, IL: Harlan Davidson, 2000.

Schisgall, Oscar. *Eyes on Tomorrow.* Chicago: Doubleday, 1981.

Brokers' Loans

In the early twentieth century many investors borrowed money from their brokers to supplement their own funds and thus increase the number of shares they could purchase. These brokers' loans were also called borrowing on a margin or margin loans, where the margin was the percentage of money that formed the basis for the investment. Because all the dividends and appreciation in the value of an individual's portfolio accrued to the investor, in a rising or bull market speculators could reap very high returns on the share of the leveraged investment they actually contributed. In a falling or bear market, however, reverse leverage forced brokers to sell stocks at very low prices, wiping out their clients funds and stimulating further declines in market prices.

Margin loans enjoyed a good deal of popularity as stock ownership became more common. Loan interest rates in the late nineteenth and early twentieth centuries remained quite modest, so investors anticipating a steady appreciation in stock values could borrow with confidence. For example, if a company's stock price rose 10 percent in a given year and money could be borrowed at half that rate, a borrower stood to reap a net profit of 5 percent on the loaned money. If he borrowed on a 50 percent margin, the net return on the personal funds he invested was 10 percent plus an extra 5 percent from the broker's loan, yielding this fortunate investor a net 15 percent return on his original investment.

In the heady days of the bull market in the late 1920s, many stocks rose far more than 10 percent annually and many brokers' required far less than a 50 percent margin. While most considered 50 percent a prudent level, optimism on both sides permitted loans on as little as a 20 percent margin. And even as credit became tighter in the months prior to the crash, brokers' loan rates fluctuated around the 6 or 7 percent level, low enough to encourage additional borrowing. In ideal circumstances, it was entirely possible for an investor to rake in over 100 percent profit on his investment in a given year if the stock purchased boomed and he took advantage of low-interest, low-margin loans.

As the bull market advanced, analysts began to view the amount of margin-loan money in the market as an indicator of the health of the system. By August 1929 an estimated $8 billion had been borrowed and invested in the companies listed on the New York Stock Exchange, representing about 10 percent of the paper value of all of those companies' outstanding shares. Because only around $6 billion in margin loans had existed a year earlier, optimists concluded that confidence in the continued rise in the market was growing.

When the market ceased to rise in late 1929, however, the negative aspects of brokers' loans became all too apparent. If the market price of a particular stock began to slip far enough, brokers were obligated to issue "margin calls" to their clients. With stock tickers reporting price fluctuations in real time and telegraph and telephone service widely available, brokers could respond quickly to changing market conditions. As the slide began to occur, thousands of margin calls flashed over the wires to clients throughout the country who were suddenly overextended. A few could divert other assets to the stock market to shore up their margins, but a great many others simply had no resources on which to draw.

If no additional margin was forthcoming and the price approached the point where the broker would lose everything, he had to sell immediately. Even if a timely sale salvaged the broker's funds, a rapid decline in prices could completely wipe out an investor's personal capital. Overnight, both modest and affluent investors saw their holdings reduced to nothing.

Panic sales of leveraged lots of stock had an additional unfortunate consequence. Brokers placing sell orders by the thousands inevitably intensified the downward pressure on prices. Low-margin investors were the first to expire, but as prices continued to slide, even those who had 50 percent margins or who had borrowed years earlier saw their wealth evaporate. In the immediate aftermath of the crash, a good many people concluded that highly leveraged margin loans had been a major cause of the disaster.

This conclusion had important consequences. In many cases, the brokerage houses that bought and sold stock as well as loaning money to their speculative clients were either parts of or closely allied to deposit banks. Astute bankers who might only be able to earn 2 or 3 percent from mortgages and other investment opportunities had been eager to finance brokers' loans at 6 or 7 percent. To that degree, money deposited in banks for safekeeping had been transformed into speculative investments.

The perceived negative consequences of the close connection between banking and brokerage activities led to federal action. The 1933 Glass-Steagall Act hastily pushed through Congress in the early days of the New Deal outlawed direct connections between banks and brokerage houses. This separation was designed specifically to discourage the transfer of supposedly safe bank deposits into the hands of leveraged speculators borrowing from their brokers.

Further federal control stemmed from the Securities Exchange Act, passed in the following year. It placed supervision of margin loans under the control of the Federal Reserve and stipulated uniform procedures for such borrowing. In subsequent years the Fed carefully monitored speculative loan activity, frequently adjusting the margin requirements. From time to time, the central bank raised the margin all the way to 100 percent, as it did in late 1946. Such a requirement effectively stopped any borrowing for investment purposes, forcing buyers to provide cash for the full value of their purchases.

The bad reputation brokers' loans earned during the crash and the subsequent economic decline has persisted. While leveraging investments can in many instances produce positive benefits, the incestuous financial relationship between brokers and their clients has been eliminated.

See also Bull Market; Call Loans; Crash; Leveraged Investment Trust; Securities and Exchange Commission.

References and Further Reading

Bierman, Jr., Harold. *The Causes of the 1929 Stock Market Crash.* Westport, CT: Greenwood Press, 1998.

Geisst, Charles R. *Wall Street: A History.* New York: Oxford, 1997.
Klein, Maury. *Rainbow's End: The Crash of 1929.* New York: Oxford, 2001.

Built-in Obsolescence

As manufacturers increasingly focused their production on meeting consumer demand in the early twentieth century, they adopted more sophisticated marketing strategies. The better one could differentiate one's product from competitors' or even earlier versions of the same product, the more likely one was to make an initial sale and encourage subsequent purchases. One possible strategy was to deliberately or inadvertently build in to a product's design or technical components aspects that would either date it or cause it to cease functioning. The resulting built-in obsolescence could be exploited to increase sales.

One example of built-in obsolescence was a decision to put different versions of a particular product on sale, each tailored to a specific customer. Often the differences or improvements touted in advertising campaigns were cosmetic or minor variations in the standard product. Even so, these changes could be exploited to convince customers to buy the "new and improved" item.

Deliberate planning of such changes occurred in many sectors of the economy. A leading proponent of this strategy was Alfred P. Sloan at General Motors. His strategy of introducing and then aggressively advertising major or minor alterations in his automobiles each year served to date all earlier models. In this instance the obsolescence built into the product line was primarily a result of design and style rather than basic quality. Customers nevertheless responded positively to the announcement of yearly model changes, and many bought new models simply because their existing cars now appeared outdated.

There was nothing underhanded in the General Motors plan to encourage sales of new cars by producing and advertising new models. At the same time, many Americans came to believe that manufacturers were deliberately marketing products with internal flaws, short-lived elements, or shoddy materials. When these built-in flaws caused a product to break down or cease working, the consumer would be likely to buy a replacement.

Over time most products do wear out or cease functioning. Whether or not these failures stem from normal wear and tear or arise from intentional design decisions is debatable. Encouraging repeat sales by building in obsolescence may seem attractive in the short run, but a company's reputation and that of its products is a key factor in attracting buyers. If people become suspicious of the quality of a company's products, sales may plummet.

Product warranties that promise replacement or free repair of "manufacturing defects" have become the norm in recent years. Although these tend to be limited warranties either in time or cost, they do provide some assurance to buyers that a company stands behind its product. They can also mitigate consumer suspicion that obsolescence has deliberately been built in.

See also Bracketing the Market; Product Differentiation; Sloan, Jr., Alfred Pritchard.

References and Further Reading

Beath, John, and Yannis Katsoulacos. *The Economic Theory of Product Differentiation.* New York: Cambridge University Press, 1991.
Chandler, Jr., Alfred D. *Strategy and Structure.* Cambridge, MA: MIT Press, 1962.

Bull Market

In Wall Street parlance, bulls are investors who anticipate continued prosperity and ever higher values for their investments. A bull market is therefore characterized by rising stock prices and general business enthusiasm. When a bull market develops, optimistic investors and speculators bid up the prices of shares on various exchanges, sometimes to artificial or unreasonable levels. If the bull market is not founded on realistic analyses of the nation's true economic health, it can end dramatically in a business panic or stock market crash and may contribute to triggering a depression.

Bull markets developed in the United States from time to time throughout the nineteenth century, but they tended to be rather short-lived. Panics occurred at irregular intervals, undermining speculative enthusiasm and forcing overextended investors into bankruptcy and more conservative financiers into careful reassessments of their positions. General prosperity seemed to have set in by the early 1920s, however, and, as stock prices continued to climb year after year, many Americans concluded that a permanent bull market had come into being. The exciting events of the 1920s remain the most dramatic example of a bull market in American history. Historians, economists, and other analysts have put forth a number of explanations for why this bull market developed and persisted, only to end in a dramatic stock market crash in late 1929. A simplistic notion is that investors and speculators were so swept up in the bull market enthusiasm that they pushed stock prices far above reasonable levels. More thoughtful analysts, however, have concluded that stock price levels were not irrationally high even in 1929 whether compared to earlier levels or to more recent circumstances. To fully understand the 1920s bull market, economic, political, regulatory, and psychological factors must be examined as well as a number of new or changing investment practices and techniques employed in the decade.

The concept of the 1920s as a "prosperity" decade gained wide acceptance. The United States quickly recovered from its postwar depression. The war effort had stimulated expansion of all sorts of commodity production, equipping the country with modern factories and plentiful investment capital. New products like radios, expanded use of electric power, and high demand for automobiles and other consumer products all encouraged economic expansion. New businesses sprang up overnight and profits mushroomed, allowing companies to pay handsome dividends to their stockholders. Over the decade an enormous amount of consolidation took place, creating business combines capable of remarkable efficiencies of production and market control. These economic developments naturally encouraged increased investment, which in turn spurred a rise in share prices across the board.

A benevolent political climate encouraged this economic boom. The conservative, business-oriented Republican Party dominated national politics, and presidents Warren G. Harding and Calvin Coolidge favored expansion. Both presidents ensured that existing Progressive regulatory agencies like the Interstate Commerce Commission and the Federal Trade Commission worked for, rather than against, corporations. Treasury Secretary Andrew Mellon, an extraordinarily wealthy man who had made his fortune in the aluminum industry, devoted his efforts to balancing the federal budget and paying off a substantial portion of the war-generated national debt.

An active Federal Reserve System might have imposed some constraints on explosive business expansion. The Fed, however, was a relatively young organization lacking sufficient power and experience to exercise major restraints on the economy. Its chief tools—the rediscount rate that set national norms for bank interest and open market operations involving the buying and selling of government bonds—were poorly understood and far too weak to stem the raging bull market enthusiasm even if the system's administrators had favored limitations. Meanwhile, the old-line conservative banking establishment also became somewhat marginalized as new entrants participated in the finance capital field, players who had never experienced a business panic. As a result, no solid institutional constraints hindered the bulls.

Every uptick in stock prices added new recruits to the herd. Americans in the 1920s felt their country was on top of the world, insulated from foreign troubles and capable of out-competing any other economic system. Many believed that the United States had entered an unprecedented era that had permanently solved the problems that had caused panics and depressions in earlier years. To a degree, the underlying economic health of the country justified optimism, but not the heedless faith of the most enthusiastic bulls.

Over the course of the decade several financial and investment practices further inflamed the bull market mentality. One key development was consumerism. American manufacturers increasingly focused their attention on consumer products. Advertising budgets soared because ads were designed to provoke more demand. When demand exceeded consumers' ability to pay, corporations, retailers, and bankers stepped forward with loans that allowed consumers to "buy now and pay later." Installment buying rose dramatically in the 1920s, substantially increasing sales, which in turn provided corporations with more profits to turn into dividends. Investors and speculators confidently purchased shares in companies that showed such handsome profits.

Like installment-buying consumers, investors who lacked sufficient funds could turn to brokers or other lenders for help in arranging margin loans. Many of these were "call" loans that carried relatively high interest rates but, as long as stock prices continued to rise, both borrowers and lenders considered these loans safe, sound investments. By 1928 over $6 billion in call money had been loaned to stock buyers, a figure that rose even higher in the subsequent year.

Investment trusts also provided artificial stimulation to stock prices. Introduced in the mid-1920s, these trusts funneled money into stock purchases. Leveraged investment trusts became extremely popular, promising their investors exaggerated returns well beyond the already very attractive growth in overall stock prices. These and other devices encouraged much broader participation in stock speculation, allowing individuals with very limited resources to benefit from the bull market.

As the decade drew to a close, the relatively higher returns on call loans and investment trusts began attracting corporate investment as well. If a particular company had no immediate plans for expansion, it naturally looked for a profitable investment for its surplus capital. By 1929, for example, Bethlehem Steel had distributed nearly $160 million in outstanding brokers' loans, and Standard Oil had loaned just under $100 million to margin investors. Substantial corporate investment in brokers' loans definitely stimulated additional stock purchases that drove up prices—often including those of a lending corporation's own stock. Such activity certainly appeared to place these corporations in a conflict of interest, but no regulations or rules precluded it.

A comparable lack of rules or restraints encouraged widespread manipulation of stock prices. Some firms paid newspaper columnists and radio commentators to tout their shares. "Confidential" newsletters circulated with planted pitches for certain stocks. Many companies maintained "preferred lists" of individuals who were offered blocs of shares at prices well below market levels. Bear pools and bull pools often operated quite openly, attempting to lower or raise the market price of particular stocks. Instead of expressing outrage at these manipulations, many Americans were envious of their success and eager to find ways to benefit from them themselves.

The fundamentally sound American economy in the 1920s justified optimism about the future and a corresponding rise in stock prices. The participation of an ever increasing number of investors and the use of new investment devices added considerably to the bull market mentality. Brokers' loans proliferated, investment trusts offered remarkable profits, installment buying stimulated sales, and corporations diverted their own funds to stock speculation either directly or in the form of call loans. The result was a greatly exaggerated bull market.

A few examples illustrate just how dramatic the bull market's performance was. The percentage increase in measures of general economic conditions between 1923 and 1929 ranged from a low of 22 percent for the nation's gross national product to a high of only 32 percent for manufacturing output per man-hour. In contrast, measures related to the stock market and general business indices over the same period grew a minimum of twice as fast to more than ten times as quickly. Corporate profits, for example, rose 62 percent, and the average prices of common stock rose nearly three times as much, a factor of 178 percent. The most telling indicator of the existence of a bull market, however, was the number of shares traded, which rose 377 percent in the same six-year period.

The bullish rise of stock prices in many corporations far exceeded these average figures. The Radio Corporation of America (RCA), for example, was widely viewed as a bellwether for the modern era. David Sarnoff formed the enterprise in 1919 to exploit the exciting new technology of radio. Five years later some RCA shares sold as high as 66, although the 1924 low was only 42. Lucky speculators could sell those same shares for up to 420 in 1928. At that point the company carried out a five-for-one stock split to make its shares more affordable. Even so, RCA share prices had risen another 36 percent just prior to the stock market crash in late 1929. Many other corporations enjoyed similar success in both real growth and even more spectacular stock price rises. General Motors shares rose from a low of 64 in 1924 to a high of 224 in 1928.

The Dow Jones Industrial Average tracks the prices of shares of carefully selected manufacturing concerns, and it rose throughout the decade, graphically tracking the bull market. The Dow fluctuated around 100 during 1923 and into 1924, and it lingered in the 150 range throughout 1926. The bull market influence really showed up beginning in 1927, causing the Dow to rise pretty smoothly into the low 300s during the first half of 1929. A final bullish burst pushed the average to 381 on the eve of the crash in October. Figure 4.1 illustrates how dramatically the Dow Jones

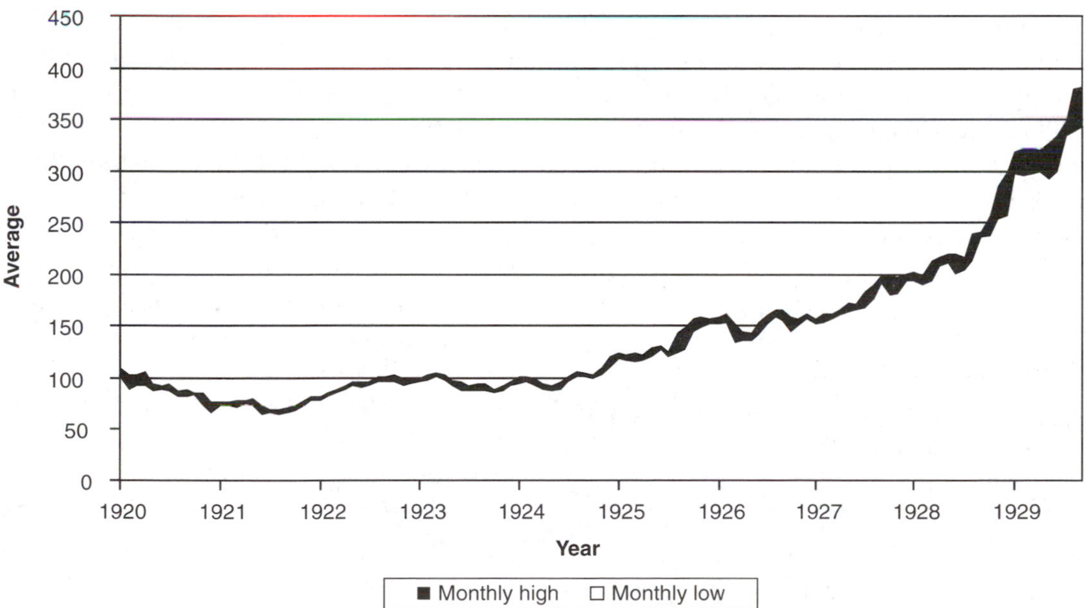

Figure 4.1 Bull market: Dow Jones industrial averages, 1920–1929. (Data from Phyllis S. Pierce, The Dow Jones Averages: 1885–1990. *Homewood, IL: Business One Irwin, 1991.)*

industrial average rose, especially in the late 1920s.

At that point, stock prices had reached truly remarkable levels, levels that could only be sustained if general economic conditions began to catch up with the market's enthusiasm. Even more crucial, however, was confidence that the bull market phenomenon would continue in the future. Call loan investments could only succeed if prices continued to advance at rates higher than interest rates. When price increases fell short of that figure, thousands of speculative investments became unsustainable. Even a slight slow-down or pause in the bull market could thus prove fateful. In September 1929 pauses began to occur; by late October prices began what would become a precipitous fall.

The stock market crash dramatically ended the 1920s bull market. While some adjustment or moderation of the unrealistic expectations was inevitable, sound economic growth justified much of the market optimism. Bull markets are not automatically bad or unjustified. The imposition of much stricter federal regulations through the Securities and Exchange Commission and other mechanisms in the early 1930s have tended to dampen unreasonable optimism and to protect investors and speculators from stock manipulation and fraudulent stock issues. Bull markets in the latter years of the twentieth century therefore have tended to be less risky but also far less exhilarating than the great bull market of the 1920s.

See also Brokers' Loans; Business Cycles; Call Loans; Crash; Leveraged Investment Trust.

References and Further Reading

Allen, Frederic Lewis. *Only Yesterday.* New York: Harper and Row, 1957.

Bierman, Jr., Harold. *The Causes of the 1929 Stock Market Crash.* Westport, CT: Greenwood Press, 1998.

Galbraith, John Kenneth. *The Great Crash.* Boston: Houghton Mifflin, 1961.

Robertson, Robert Trescott. *The Great Boom and Panic.* Chicago: Regenry, 1965.

Sobel, Robert. *The Great Bull Market.* New York: Norton, 1968.

Soule, George. *Prosperity Decade.* New York: Harper and Row, 1947.

Business Cycles

Although the performance of the U.S. economy had always exhibited ups and downs, the phenomenon of business cycles was subjected to scientific analysis only in the early twentieth century. Economists offered widely differing opinions about the causes and consequences of business cycles, but they generally came to recognize four major stages. In the expansion phase, the economy began its *recovery* from bad times and reached a level of *prosperity.* In the contraction phase, the economy experienced a *crisis* that led to a period of *depression.* At some point, recovery from that depression would begin, setting off renewed expansion. Interest and concern over the magnitude and consequences of business cycles naturally peaked during the Great Depression of the 1930s.

While classical economists like David Ricardo had early attempted to analyze the causes of cyclical economic behavior, Wesley Mitchell is generally recognized as the first to systematically study business cycles. He published his early conclusions in 1913 and greatly expanded his analysis in subsequent books, culminating in *Measuring Business Cycles,* coauthored with Arthur Burns in 1946. To systematize his work, Mitchell cofounded the National Bureau of Economic Research (NBER). This nonpartisan organization became widely recognized as an authoritative source for economic and business data collection.

It was Mitchell who clarified the four stages of a business cycle. Capitalistic systems around the world experience the four stages of recovery, prosperity, crisis, and depression that are familiar to Americans. Mitchell was careful to point out, however, that historical data show no regularity in the length of time an economy may remain in a particular stage nor are the magnitudes of the fluctuations necessarily similar from one peak or trough to the next. Indeed, the length of a business cycle might be as short as a year or as long as a decade.

A key aspect of the analysis of business cycles is identifying the turning points where growth or stagnation began to hold sway. A jarring historical event like the business panic of 1873 clearly marked a crisis moment for the American economy. After the panic, depression persisted for most of the 1870s until a slow recovery became apparent. Financial panics were quite a bit easier to identify than the other phase changes in a business cycle, so the NBER assembled enormous amounts of data that could be statistically analyzed. Mitchell and other researchers gradually developed a consensus about the ebb and flow of business cycles.

They identified a series of eleven peaks and troughs in the U.S. business cycle from the Panic of 1893 to the depths of the Great Depression. Over that forty-year period, peaks occurred on average about every three and a half years. The cycle then descended into a trough in a little over a year, only to start a two-year climb to a new peak. Two exceptional bull market periods varied from the norm. The economy sustained a long period of growth beginning in 1914 that faltered only after the conclusion of the First World War. An even longer upswing came in the following decade, a five-year run-up that peaked with the 1929 stock market crash. Not surprisingly, the economy's tumble following that all-time high was long and deep, reaching its trough nearly three and a half years later in the spring of 1933.

Long before Mitchell and his colleagues began systematizing the study of business cycles, various theories and explanations for the recurring ups and downs had emerged. One group, for example, tried unsuccessfully to link business cycles to sunspot activity. In fact, sunspot activity does appear to have somewhat predictable influence over the earth's climate. And weather, in turn, certainly can play a role in boosting or limiting agricultural output. But any explanation that relied on a single causative factor like weather proved inadequate. A modern capitalist economy is too complex an organism to be subject to the vagaries of a single factor.

To help predict economic behavior, therefore, Mitchell's research led him to identify three types of economic indicators. One group he called *leading indicators* and it included data series that appeared to anticipate the overall business cycle. *Coincident indicators* reached their highs or lows just when the cycle peaked or reached its nadir, and *lagging indicators* typically reached maximum or minimum levels sometime after the overall business cycle had done the same. The U.S. Commerce Department routinely tracks these indicators, and the stock market and other business entities pay particular attention to the behavior of the leading economic indicators as a predictor of future economic behavior.

Among the twelve leading indicators tracked are weekly hours of production by workers in industry, weekly unemployment claims, manufacturers' orders, an index of 500 common stock prices, plant and equipment orders, private housing starts, manufacturing and trade inventories, the money supply, and changes in outstanding credit. The coincident indicators include measures of active business exchange like the number employed in nonagricultural sectors, industrial production, and sales. The lagging indicators measure such factors as how long individuals have remained unemployed, commercial and industrial loans outstanding, and banks' average prime rate. Because these lagging indicators reflect business and commercial decisions already made, it is reasonable to expect them to follow rather than lead changing overall economic conditions.

The study of business cycles has become quite sophisticated in recent years, enabling economists to state with certainty that the leading, coincident, and lagging indicators currently used are as valid today as they were in Mitchell's time. What remains impossible, however, is a method for accurately predicting exactly when a cycle will reverse course. If such predictions were possible, shareholders could confidently follow the classic advice to buy low and sell high. Instead, even those who carefully study past cyclical behavior and track the leading indicators assiduously are not able to take full advantage of business opportunities or to avoid costly downturns.

See also Bull Market; Great Depression, Causes of; Mitchell, Wesley Clair; Panic of 1873; Panic of 1893.

References and Further Reading

Adams, Arthur B. *Analyses of Business Cycles.* New York: McGraw-Hill, 1936.
Burns, Arthur, and Wesley Mitchell. *Measuring Business Cycles.* New York: National Bureau of Economic Research, 1946.
Mitchell, Wesley C. *Business Cycles.* New York: National Bureau of Economic Research, 1927.
Sherman, Howard J. *The Business Cycle.* Princeton, NJ: Princeton University Press, 1991.

Call Loans

A *call* or demand loan is one that is typically made on a daily basis as opposed to a longer-term or time loan. A lender agrees to provide funds for a borrower at a call rate that is higher than quarterly or annual rates. Depending on current conditions the call rate can rise or fall each day. While call loans are subject to renegotiation and renewal each day, lenders can demand or "call" for repayment at a moment's notice.

Based on their reading of instantaneous fluctuations in stock prices, speculators tend to jump in and out of the market at unpredictable moments. During and after the First World War, many speculators switched from longer term to call loans to finance their activities. Short-term call loans provided an ideal method for increasing their investment funds while avoiding long-term obligations and rigidity.

Financial institutions found call loans quite profitable because of the frequent refiguring of call rates, rates that almost always exceeded interest charges for more conventional loans. Moreover, they could demand repayment of their loaned funds on short notice should stringencies arise. Because they could be quickly liquidated, lenders were willing to extend call loans on the basis of very little collateral or margin. In the 1920s borrowers might be able to arrange a call loan on as little as a 5 percent margin as compared to the 20 percent or more necessary to arrange a conventional, long-term loan.

Call loans were particularly attractive in times of easy credit, low overall interest rates, and attractive investment opportunities. Those conditions prevailed in the United States during the First World War, and many speculators took advantage of call loans to increase their stock purchases. By 1919 call loans accounted for over $1 billion worth of the money invested in American stocks.

Postwar dislocations undermined confidence in call loans. The Federal Reserve rediscount rate is the government's charge for short-term loans to bankers; the Fed continually raised the rate. Whenever it did, it created consternation among borrowers about what the call-loan rate should be. To make matters worse, the stock market stumbled into a relatively brief postwar decline, but it was sufficient to force lenders into calling in their loans and plunging many speculators into bankruptcy.

The return of prosperity in the early 1920s and a chastened Federal Reserve System's commitment to maintaining stable, relatively low rediscount rates revived interest in call loans. Speculators once again negotiated loans that enabled them to take advantage of short-term growth in stock values. In the absence of any legal restrictions, the overall amount of money available through call loans and other types of margin loans rose substantially, topping $6 billion by

1928, and playing a significant role in fueling the bull market's growth prior to 1929.

The stock market crash and subsequent depression destroyed confidence in the nation's securities and discouraged speculation at all levels. By 1934 the Securities and Exchanges Commission had come into existence with authority to impose limits on margin loans. Call loans can still be negotiated, but federal regulations make them far less attractive to both borrowers and lenders than they were in the heyday of the 1920s bull market.

See also Brokers' Loans; Bulls and Bears.

References and Further Reading

Brooks, John. *Once in Golconda.* New York: Wiley, 1999.

Klein, Murray. *Rainbow's End.* New York: Oxford University Press, 2001.

Sobel, Robert. *The Great Bull Market.* New York: Norton, 1968.

Clayton Antitrust Act

Passed in 1914 the Clayton Act was designed to bring greater precision to the 1890 Sherman Antitrust Act. Critics of the earlier act considered it too general or vague, so the new legislation prohibited a number of specific actions that might lead to monopolistic abuse. It forbid exclusive sales contracts, rebates to favored customers, and cutting prices in one geographical area while maintaining higher prices elsewhere to undermine local competition. It also prohibited interlocking directorships that limited competition. The act also shielded labor unions from antitrust litigation. A number of cases have been brought under the Clayton Act over the years, but many of its supporters were disappointed at how limited its effects appeared to be.

Some of this disappointment arose even before the bill became law. When the Supreme Court promulgated its "rule of reason" in 1911, many Progressives in both political parties concluded that it had taken the teeth out of the Sherman Act. Consequently, they set out to define explicitly what they considered inappropriate or dangerous business practices. If a new act specifically prohibited these actions, its sponsors believed that it would limit judicial flexibility and result in more effective federal control over large business combinations.

In his 1912 presidential campaign, Woodrow Wilson developed a platform called the New Freedom. One of its key planks was a commitment to trust-busting by using the federal government's authority to outlaw monopolistic or oligopolistic business combinations. When Wilson won the presidency and his Democratic colleagues took control of both houses of Congress, many expected that the government would adopt an aggressive antitrust stance. The original bill Alabama Congressman Henry De Lamar Clayton drafted appeared to head in that direction.

At the same time, Wilson and many other Progressive Democrats had become convinced that a new federal regulatory agency should be created as well. Rather than confining the resulting Federal Trade Commission in a legislative straitjacket, Congress chose to weaken the language in Clayton's bill. Because the commission was given greater flexibility and broader powers to ameliorate corporate abuses, the final list of prohibitions in the Clayton Act was shorter and less proscriptive than had originally been anticipated.

The act focuses a good deal of its attention on discriminatory pricing policies. It outlaws rebates and certain types of targeted price-cutting that might undermine or eliminate competition. It also prohibits interlocking directorships in which directors or principals of one company sit on the boards of competitors. The goal of these provisions is to prevent unfair competition and encourage free enterprise.

One somewhat anomalous provision in the act is its statement that labor unions have the right to strike, boycott, and picket. The law specifically states that courts may not issue injunctions against unions for such behavior. Judicial rulings in subsequent years considerably undermined the protections that the Clayton Act had presumably given, however, and union advocates had to lobby for additional federal support.

Having emerged in a much less aggressive format than anticipated, the Clayton Act did not trigger a large-scale trust-busting campaign. Even so, it has continued to serve as the authority for antitrust litigation. In 1936 the Robinson-Patman Act strengthened the price-fixing provisions, and in 1950 the Celler-Kefauver Act did the same for the prohibitions regarding interlocking controls in competing companies. In many ways, however, the nearly simultaneous creation of the Federal Trade Commission set the nation's antitrust policies off in a much different direction.

See also Antitrust Laws; Federal Trade Commission; Rule of Reason.

References and Further Reading

James, Scott C. *Presidents, Parties, and the State.* Cambridge: Cambridge University Press, 2000.

Kolko, Gabriel. *The Triumph of Conservatism.* Glencoe, IL: The Free Press, 1963.

Commercial Aviation

The use of aircraft to carry passengers and freight became feasible in the 1930s. Four major manufacturers dominated the industry, and each company attempted to provide commercial air service. By the end of the decade, however, service providers had separated from manufacturers, and independent airlines were competing for passengers and routes across the United States and around the world.

The Wright Brothers' twelve seconds in the air in 1903 demonstrated the feasibility of flight, but until the outbreak of the World War a decade later, airplanes remained in a primitive stage of development. Biplanes with wooden frames and cloth skins carried only a pilot and occasionally a single passenger. They were limited to short ranges and to demonstration or exhibition use. Although substantial progress occurred in aeronautical engineering during the First World War, few commercial uses for airplanes emerged in the 1920s.

Daredevil barnstormers thrilled audiences at country fairs, and occasional newspaper stories recorded more adventurous exploits. Cross-country air races and long solo flights were particularly popular. Charles Lindbergh pulled off the most outstanding feat in 1927 when he piloted his *Spirit of St. Louis* across the Atlantic. His flight did more to stimulate public interest in aviation than any previous event. Capitalists responded to this interest by pouring more than $400 million into the industry, enabling several manufacturers to emerge as leaders.

One was William E. Boeing whose inherited wealth from a family timber business allowed him to dabble in aviation. In 1928 he created a new company named United Aircraft and Transport Corporation and established assembly operations in Seattle. His holding company used capital from the National City Bank to buy controlling interests in other firms including Pratt and Whitney, the nation's leading aircraft engine maker. A rival holding company, North American Aviation, made a similar move, acquiring control of Curtiss-Wright, the only other major engine maker. In 1929 General Motors expanded into aviation in partnership with Fokker. The fourth major player was Aviation Corporation (AVCO), closely associated with the dominant Republican Party leadership.

All four of these firms obtained military and naval contracts as well as postal agreements to deliver airmail. Military pilots carried the mail on many of these routes. When the Democratic Party swept into control of the federal government in the early 1930s, however, President Franklin Roosevelt's administration cancelled all mail routes. Deeply suspicious of big business and opposed to oligopolistic control, the government also demanded that manufacturing operations be divorced from air-service activities.

In the major reorganization that followed, the United Air and Transport Corporation split into three separate entities: Boeing to manufacture airplanes, Pratt and Whitney to make engines, and United Airlines to carry passengers and mail. North American became an independent manufacturer, and its service components coalesced into Transcontinental and Western Airlines. AVCO spun off its service arm into a separate entity named American Airlines.

Douglas Aircraft Corporation had always focused on the manufacturing end of the business, and it produced an industry-transforming product in 1935. The third model to be developed in the Douglas Commercial line, the DC-3 was a monoplane with two engines and an aluminum frame and skin. The company subsequently produced thousands of these remarkably versatile workhorses, fitting them for both passenger and military cargo use. The Army Air Corp flew them as C-47 Sky Trains, and Britain's Royal Air Force called them Dakotas.

The DC-3 proved to be an excellent, reliable passenger carrier, and it quickly became the mainstay of several airlines. Uniformed stewardesses, meal service, and other accoutrements made air travel both comfortable and glamorous. Douglas continued to innovate, building larger aircraft like the DC-6, a four engine, longer range airplane that joined commercial fleets after the Second World War.

A major problem in the late 1930s, however, was a lack of major landing strips. Whereas a DC-3 could take off and land almost anywhere, larger passenger planes needed extended runways. A temporary solution came in the form of large, four-engine "flying boats" to carry passengers to and from port cities. Boeing and Sikorsky were the industry leaders here, building what came to be called *clippers* in tribute to the long, lean sailing ships of the nineteenth century. Like those earlier clippers, flying boats flourished for only a few years. Modern airport facilities were built by municipal authorities and, particularly during the war years, for military use. By the late 1940s large commercial airplanes like double-deck Boeing Stratocruisers, and graceful, triple-rudder Lockheed Constellations were providing air service to all major American cities.

International air travel blossomed as well. Juan Trippe took full advantage of the advent of the clippers, introducing air service between Key West and Havana. The success of this venture prompted him to extend service to a number of other Caribbean and Latin American destinations as the Pan-American Airways System. He even developed links to China and Africa, which proved particularly useful during the Second World War. Transcontinental and Western evolved along similar lines, adding international linkages and changing its name to Trans-World Airlines.

Commercial aviation was thus firmly established by 1939 when the Second World War broke out in Europe. The pioneering technologies, airport construction, and international flight experience all proved very useful when the United States was drawn into the conflict. Like the automobile industry, aircraft companies became totally focused on wartime production. Commercial aviation enjoyed a resurgence after 1945 with bigger, faster, longer range aircraft that built on and incorporated military innovations.

See also Boeing, William Edward; Douglas, Donald Wills; Military Aviation; Trippe, Juan.

References and Further Reading

Freudenthal, Elsbeth E. *The Aviation Business.* New York: Vanguard, 1940.

Rae, John B. *Climb to Greatness.* Cambridge, MA: MIT Press, 1968.

Simonsen, R. G., ed. *The History of the American Aircraft Industry.* Cambridge, MA: MIT Press, 1968.

Commodity Dollar

The United States briefly experimented with a commodity dollar when President

Franklin Roosevelt set a price for the dollar based on the value of a commodity or set of commodities rather than a metal standard like gold.

In 1933 the United States resorted to the use of a commodity dollar as one of many strategies for dealing with the financial crises of the Great Depression. The Gold Standard Act of 1900 had set a price of $20 for one ounce of gold, and that remained the official U.S. Treasury rate through April 1933. Then in a series of steps, Roosevelt's New Deal government took the United States off the international gold standard despite protests from international critics as well as many Americans. In the late spring, an amendment to the bill that became the Agricultural Adjustment Act of 1933 gave the president wide latitude in dealing with the country's persistent price deflation, including authority to manipulate the dollar price of gold.

Some of his advisors advocated using a commodity dollar whose value would be continuously adjusted to remain linked to commodity prices in the United States. In his fourth Fireside Chat in late October 1933, Roosevelt announced that the government would begin buying gold at inflated prices, well above the $20 figure that had previously prevailed. The goal was to drag the dollar's value down relative to commodity prices. Acting as the government's purchasing agency, the Reconstruction Finance Corporation began buying newly minted gold at a price of $31.36 per ounce.

For the next several weeks, the president met with his financial advisors every morning to decide what price the government should pay for gold that day. They deliberately made arbitrary decisions to prevent anyone from benefiting from insider knowledge about the price changes. Some days no change occurred, but each succeeding alteration moved the price upward. This strategy was in line with Roosevelt's goal of gradually inflating the price of the dollar compared to gold and thereby encouraging a corresponding rise in commodity prices.

The unpredictable changes dismayed many people. Attempting to restore fiscal stability, Congress passed the Gold Reserve Act in late January 1934. It authorized the president to set a new fixed government price of $35 per ounce of gold. While this action realigned U.S. currency with the international monetary community, it stabilized the dollar's value at just fifty-nine cents compared to its pre-Depression value. Meanwhile, the Treasury recalled all gold coins and certificates, permanently severing the domestic link between dollars and gold. Federal Reserve notes became the standard currency of the United States, which never again experimented with commodity dollars.

See also Agricultural Adjustment Acts; Recovery.

References and Further Reading

Crawford, Arthur W. *Monetary Management Under the New Deal.* New York: De Capo Press, 1972.

Friedman, Milton, and Anna J. Schwartz. *Monetary History of the United States.* Princeton, NJ: Princeton University Press, 1963.

Johnson, Jr., G. Griffith. *The Treasury and Monetary Policy, 1933–1939.* New York: Russell and Russell, 1939.

Consumer Credit

Although Americans had begun buying some items on time early in the nineteenth century, credit for general purchases became common only after 1900. Major department stores were happy to offer reliable customers open credit accounts hoping they would become repeat buyers. Consumer credit arrangements flourished in the prosperous years that followed, but the Great Depression dampened enthusiasm on both sides. The early experience with consumer credit did, however, set the stage for the explosive growth in credit-card usage after the Second World War.

Manufacturers of relatively expensive products were offering time-payment schemes even before the Civil War. Cyrus

McCormick personally financed buyers of his reapers and provided backup credit for his network of dealers. Isaac Merritt Singer did the same for those who wanted to purchase his sewing machines. A buyer would make a downpayment of five dollars and then pay a similar amount for several months to complete the purchase.

Credit arrangements also facilitated more routine purchases. Many a local grocer maintained a supply of order forms with carbon copies for trusted customers. The forms listed items purchased and their costs. The merchant then submitted a monthly bill based on the total of all purchases during the preceding period, allowing a customer to settle accounts with a single check or cash payment. Informal systems like this persisted in some areas well into the 1950s.

Merchants extended credit to build customer loyalty and repeat business. Those same goals motivated department stores, hotels, and oil companies to issue identifying cards to their best customers. Such cards became common around the time of the First World War and their initial purpose was simply to identify people with credit accounts. Beginning in 1928 many stores adopted a new technology called a "charge-plate," a metal plate embossed with a customer's name, address, and account information. The retailer placed these plates in a roller stamp that printed the information on bills and receipts.

Store and oil company cards were unashamedly designed to encourage additional purchases. They were particularly useful to the companies selling gasoline and other auto-related products, and services that were largely indistinguishable from those of their competitors. The possessor of a Shell or Standard Oil card was presumed to be more likely to patronize that company's stations.

As the popularity of these accounts grew, issuing companies developed nuances and improvements. For example, many offered customers a thirty-day grace period to clear their accounts, and some went so far as to establish a minimum payment for those suffering from temporary shortages. Finance charges were often imposed on the unpaid balance. In many cases companies offering these credit arrangements actually lost money on them but could justify credit account losses as simply another of the many costs of doing business in a competitive environment.

Consumer credit was well established by 1950 with many features that would be adapted to the credit-card business. Department store and oil company cards continued to circulate, offering alternatives to the more universally accepted credit cards. Indeed, they are still available today, although they account for only a small fraction of overall consumer purchases.

See also Credit Cards; Electronic Fund Transfers; Shopping.

References and Further Reading

Evans, David S., and Richard Schmalensee. *Paying with Plastic.* Cambridge, MA: MIT Press, 2005.

Mandell, Lewis. *The Credit Card Industry.* Boston: Twayne Publishers, 1990.

Crash

Stock market crashes have occurred periodically. They involve a rapid, precipitous decline in stock prices and can lead to business panics or other emotional behavior on the part of investors and speculators. The most dramatic crash in American history began in late October 1929. By mid-November stock prices had lost half the value they had reached in the previous month. Some of the causes for the great crash resembled those for earlier and later readjustments, but many unique circumstances contributed to the enormity of this financial disaster.

To a degree, stock market readjustments are a natural phenomenon, occurring at more or less regular intervals. Major financial panics perturbed Americans in the United States in 1819, 1837, 1857, 1873, 1893, and 1907. Prior to the 1929 crash, the markets had also experienced less severe readjustments, including downturns in 1911,

Distressed investors and speculators mobbed the New York Stock Exchange in 1929 in the wake of the great stock market crash. (Library of Congress)

1914, 1919, 1921, and 1924. Each of these events occurred in part because bullish enthusiasm had pushed stock prices to levels somewhat higher than the overall economic health of the nation's corporations justified. A similar overvaluation of share prices developed as a result of the long-running bull market that developed in the mid-1920s.

Sometimes a particular event can trigger a crash. In 1873, for example, Jay Cooke's investment house collapsed after it became overextended in questionable railroad stocks, setting off a domino effect among other financial institutions, railroads, and corporations. The 1919 decline was directly related to a predictable readjustment from a booming wartime economy to less dynamic peacetime conditions. No such signal event or underlying economic cause appears to have precipitated the 1929 crash, however. Instead the crash was the result of a combination of factors, some related to underlying economic conditions, others to financial and investment strategies, and, not incidentally, to major changes in investor psychology.

There is no question that the bull market of the late 1920s was a major factor. Bullish enthusiasm stimulated exuberant buying of corporate stocks on an unprecedented scale. This enthusiasm naturally led to bidding up prices. Unlike investors, speculators hope to reap short-term profits by buying securities they believe will rise quickly in price. By 1929 the bull market had attracted an enormous number of speculators either ignorant of, or disinterested in, the real value of the corporations whose shares they purchased.

The speculative fervor pushed stock prices higher than underlying economic conditions warranted. At high levels, the market value of the outstanding shares of a particular company often greatly exceeded the value of that company's assets and market share. Under normal circumstances, market forces would tend to moderate share prices until they better reflected real conditions. But the bull market mentality overwhelmed any such rational reassessment. As long as everyone thought prices would continue to rise, there was little incentive to adjust them downward.

Enormous amounts of money were flowing into, rather than away from, the markets by late 1929. The amount invested in brokers' loans increased dramatically in 1928 and 1929, reaching almost $8.4 billion on the eve of the crash. Most brokers' loans were call loans carrying relatively high interest rates, but that did little to discourage either lenders or borrowers. In the year prior to the crash, the interest rate for call loans had averaged around 12 percent on an annual basis. But the Federal Reserve rediscount rate during that period never exceeded 5 percent, so banks could earn handsome profits by borrowing money from the Fed and lending it to speculators.

Investment trusts proliferated as well, with 265 new trusts formed in 1929 alone. Many of these were leveraged investment trusts that only made financial sense if prices continued to rise. If they began to drop or even to level off for an extended period, the leverage that had made them so popular would work in the opposite direction, causing the value of their shares to fall much more rapidly than non-leveraged investments. The same was true with margin loans that were essentially leveraged at a minimum of 50 percent or more.

The first disconcerting tremors hit the market on September 3, and share prices fell rather alarmingly for the next two days. As had been the case so many times before, however, this stutter-step was short lived, and prices recovered and advanced for the next several weeks. The initial shock apparently did convince some investors and speculators that the bull market was nearing its climax, and they began to sell their holdings in anticipation of a major downturn.

By late October share prices had risen to all-time highs across the board. Shortly before the exchange was to close on Wednesday, October 23, a sudden rush of sell orders reached the floor traders. A phenomenal 2.6 million shares changed hands in the last hour, more than twice the average number of shares traded on the exchange's previous busy days. The wave of frenetic selling continued even more furiously the next morning. By market close on "Black Thursday" a staggering 12.9 million shares had been traded.

A lack of timely information spurred growing panic among speculators. The system simply could not keep up with such a high number of trades, and the stock ticker ran minutes and eventually more than an hour behind. Brokers and their clients had to make buy and sell decisions with outdated information. Prudent brokers sent out calls for more margin and issued stop-loss orders that would automatically sell shares if prices fell to unacceptable levels. Many of the clients who were contacted for more margin simply did not have access to additional cash or credit, so their investments had to be sold at whatever price was currently available.

A panicked mind-set naturally developed in these circumstances. For a time, rumors circulated that there would be organized support for prices, though it was unclear who would organize it. A group of leading bankers met Thursday afternoon, and some of them subsequently issued dramatic buy orders at prices well above the current levels. The steep decline had actually ended around noon, and these gestures seemed to buoy confidence.

Trading continued at a less frenetic pace and without major price declines on Friday into Saturday morning, and the following Monday. A widely respected optimist, Yale Professor Irving Fisher explained that the previous slide had only shaken out "the lunatic fringe," those naive speculators who should never have been in the market at all. But much more was involved. Many of the banking and corporate entities that had been participating in the call market now withdrew their funds from New York, crimping the margin loan business. Other major players strategically sold their holdings too, so the huge influx of funding that had crested in the bull market wave began to ebb even before the final catastrophe.

The cataclysmic event took place on "Black Tuesday," October 29, 1929. An unprecedented 16.4 million shares were offered for sale, often at whatever price they could bring. The stock ticker ran more than two hours behind the activity on the trading floor, fueling even more margin calls, stop-loss orders, and widespread panic. Two different bankers' meetings that day failed to generate any coherent action. Without support, organized or otherwise, stock prices fell disastrously, effectively wiping out all of the gains that had occurred in the preceding twelve months of bull market buoyancy.

The great stock market crash of 1929 was only beginning. Despite shortened trading days and deliberate closures, the New York Stock Exchange continued to record daily losses right through November 13. At that point the slide essentially ended, but price levels averaged no more than half of what they had been at their peak. The bull market was over; it collapsed as effectively as any of the historical speculative bubbles. Figure 4.2 illustrates the sharp decline in share prices that occurred during the 1929 stock market crash, and the continuing slide that set in shortly afterward.

Hundreds of thousands of investors lost everything. Among them were individuals who had sold early, before the crash, but had then jumped back in when prices dropped to unexpectedly low levels. These people took some satisfaction from the fact that a mild recovery took place during the first three months of 1930, but it stalled in April. By June prices began another slide that continued pretty much unchecked for the next two years. At that point, the nation was immersed in the abyss of the Great De-

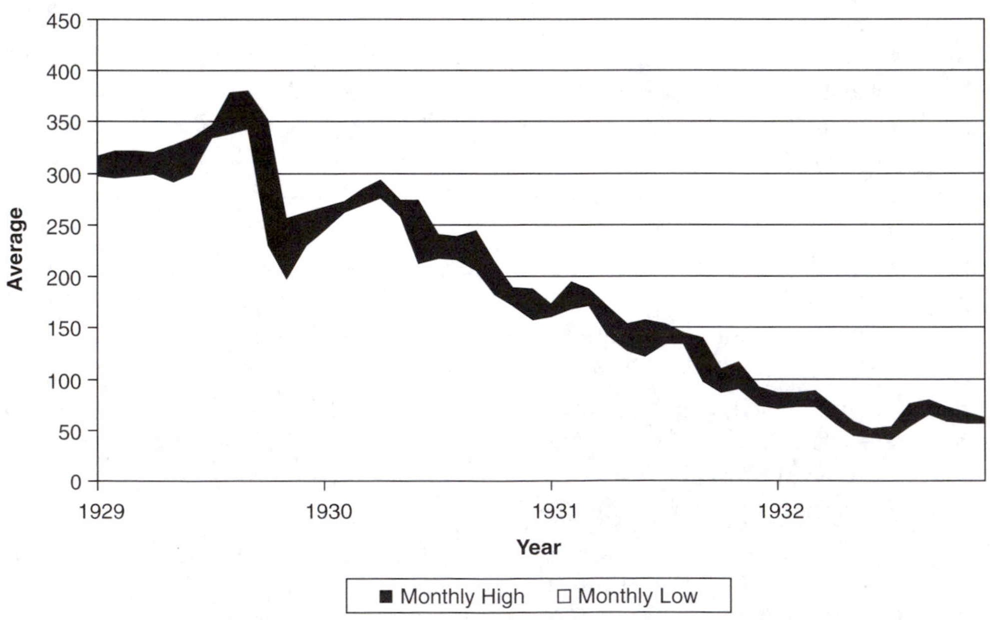

Figure 4.2 Crash and depression: Dow Jones industrial averages, 1929–1933. (Data from Phyllis S. Pierce, The Dow Jones Averages: 1885–1990. *Homewood, IL: Business One Irwin, 1991.)*

pression, with stocks of major corporations selling at only a tenth or even a twentieth of their pre-crash highs.

Most economists and historians do not consider the stock market crash to have triggered the Great Depression, citing a variety of other tangible causes for that economic disaster. At the same time, the emotional shockwaves of the crash certainly played a part in convincing the American people that the country was in crisis. The overweening faith in the bull market, in bankers, in stocks, even in the future, cascaded away during and after the great crash.

The survivors were more than ready to accept substantial changes, spearheaded by the creation of the Securities and Exchange Commission (1934) and major revisions to the Federal Reserve System (1935.) New federal regulations severely restricted access to low-margin loans, severed the relationship between banks and brokerage houses, and demanded full, honest disclosure of corporate performance. Although these and other crisis-inspired policies have not eliminated the possibility of future crashes, no subsequent stock-market readjustment has ever approached the magnitude and devastation of the 1929 crash.

See also Brokers' Loans; Bull Market; Call Loans; Great Depression, Causes of; Leveraged Investment Trust.

References and Further Reading

Bierman, Jr., Harold. *The Causes of the 1929 Stock Market Crash.* Westport, CT: Greenwood Press, 1998.

Galbraith, John Kenneth. *The Great Crash.* Boston: Houghton Mifflin, 1961.

Klein, Maury. *Rainbow's End.* New York: Oxford University Press, 2001.

Thomas, Dana L. *The Plungers and the Peacocks.* New York: Texere, 2001.

Creditor Nation

Shortly after the outbreak of the First World War the United States became a creditor nation. The key factor that had brought about that circumstance was a long-running favorable trade balance. For several decades Americans had been exporting goods and services with higher value than they imported. Well into the twentieth century, this phenomenon continued to draw wealth from other nations to the United States. These favorable trade balances represented a historic reversal that had important consequences for Americans and the world. When they ended in the late twentieth century, the United States entered a new and disconcerting era.

A nation's international trade balance depends on the relationship between its imports and its exports. If imports exceed exports, the balance is unfavorable. The British colonists in North America ran up trade deficits every year, buying far more goods from the mother country than they could offset with their largely agrarian exports. After the Revolution, trade fell back into previous patterns as Americans continued to rely on British sources for manufactured goods. Right through the Civil War, the United States annually ran an unfavorable trade balance.

The U.S. industrial revolution helped Americans wean themselves from British manufactured goods at the same time that western expansion and farm mechanization vastly increased U.S. agricultural production. The trade balance finally shifted in the 1870s in what appeared to be a permanent change. Through the last decades of the nineteenth century and into the new one, Americans consistently exported far more than they imported.

During those years, the nation gradually paid off nearly two centuries worth of accumulated indebtedness. Gold transfers made up the difference between commodity imports and exports, so the nation's gold supply rose markedly. The favorable balance of trade thus eased concerns about the money supply, allowing the dominant Republican politicians to tie it firmly to the gold standard in 1900.

The accounts were finally settled in 1914, turning the United States into the world's most influential creditor nation, owed more by foreigners than the U.S. population owed them. The timing of this change had important consequences because it meant that neither France nor Great Britain could draw on reserves to purchase American food, manufactured goods, and, most crucially, war materiel. President Woodrow Wilson recognized that the U.S. economy would suffer if foreign purchases dried up, so he approved credits and then outright loans to the Entente Powers to enable them to continue buying. Critics later claimed that these decisions made it seem essential that the United States go to war to protect its investment in an Entente victory.

In the 1920s the American economy only grew stronger in comparison to that of war-ravaged Europe. The Dawes Plan of 1924 acknowledged that situation by promising private U.S. investment in Germany's economy to get it back on its feet. American productivity continued to churn out far more than was needed at home, so the favorable trade balances continued until the global economy tottered into the Great Depression.

In the 1940s the United States gave away or shot away billions of dollars to fight fascism and then gave away additional billions through the Marshall Plan to rebuild war-torn Europe. The Cold War put additional drains on U.S. productivity and the Vietnam conflict absorbed billions more. By the 1970s the United States had lost its trading edge, and unfavorable balances became the norm.

As the nation's economy evolved into its current postindustrial status, it has become ever more difficult to reverse the trend. U.S. trade deficits with Japan and Korea are persistent and growing. Dependence on massive oil imports shows no sign of slackening. More recently, an unfavorable trade relationship with the People's Republic of China has been adding tens of billions of dollars in foreign indebtedness every year. The only bright spot is that foreign nations have invested many of their surplus dollars in American securities and Treasury bills.

Policy makers, economists, and diplomats are all keenly aware of the growing international debt, but no effective remedies have been devised. Tinkering with tariff levels has become virtually impossible in the era of the World Trade Organization. Charges of unfair competition and price supports in other countries do no good. Worse yet, American corporations have sent millions of jobs offshore, seeking inexpensive labor and lower production costs. At this point it appears that the United States is locked in a permanent unfavorable trade balance that will have unpredictable consequences for future generations.

See also Dawes Plan; GATT; Protective Tariff; Trade Balance.

References and Further Reading

Aubrey, Henry G. *United States Imports and World Trade.* Oxford: Clarendon Press, 1957.

Bonker, Don. *America's Trade Crisis.* Boston: Houghton Mifflin, 1988.

Evans, John T. *From Trade Surplus to Deficit.* New York: Garland, 1995.

Dawes Plan

To help restore Europe's economic balance in the mid-1920s, American bankers and others met to devise a recovery strategy. Charles Dawes headed the group, so the arrangements became known as the Dawes Plan. Among other provisions, it included a promise that American investment funds would flow to Germany. Germany's economy recovered, enabling it to pay reparations that stabilized Britain and France. The Young Plan replaced the Dawes Plan in 1929.

The effect of these two plans had some resemblance to the Marshall Plan's impact after the Second World War. In the latter case, however, reconstruction funding came directly from the U.S. government. The political situation in the 1920s made direct federal intervention impossible. A key factor was the conservative Republican mentality in both Congress and the White House, based on a set of beliefs that favored private enterprise rather than intrusive government action.

Even more crucial was the awkward relationship the United States had with the League of Nations and the Versailles Treaty that had created the tension. President Woodrow Wilson had been the main advocate of these complex postwar agreements, but they had proven so unpopular at home that the U.S. Senate never ratified the treaty. American statesmen therefore had to devise diplomatic methods that operated outside the treaty structure.

A treaty provision that culminated in a crisis in 1923 was a requirement that Germany pay reparations to Britain and its allies for costs they had incurred during the First World War. But the war-wracked German economy was barely sputtering along in the early 1920s, providing no surplus funding from which to pay its reparations. When it defaulted in 1923, France and Belgium seized control of the Ruhr Valley, planning to extract the money they were due from that rich industrial region.

This crisis convinced Secretary of State Charles E. Hughes to convene a group of American businessmen and financiers to seek a solution. Charles Dawes, a Chicago banker and later vice president, headed the committee. It examined Germany's economic situation and proposed a less rigorous payment scheme. The Americans also pledged to invest in German industries to help boost recovery and reduce the burden of the reparations payments.

Between 1924 and 1928, American investors sent over $2 billion to Germany, money that played a major role in the so-called economic miracle that reinvigorated the economy. Germany paid nearly $3 billion in reparations over the same period, and Britain and France made some $2 billion in payments to the United States to offset their own war loan indebtedness. Conditions had improved so markedly by 1929 that another American committee headed by Owen D. Young developed a revised plan. The Young Plan substantially reduced the overall German obligation.

The whole system broke down completely in the early 1930s. Huge amounts of American investment money had evaporated in the 1929 crash, drying up the lifeline of funding to Europe. Germany once again defaulted on its obligations. President Herbert Hoover imposed a temporary moratorium on all international payments, hoping for conditions to improve. Although the moratorium expired, no additional reparations payments or war loan repayments occurred in the 1930s.

The Dawes Plan seemed like an excellent solution to the problem when it first appeared. In the long run, however, its success depended on a continuous flow of investment money overseas. When that flow ended, the underlying weaknesses of the European economies rapidly became apparent. Those weaknesses, in turn, contributed substantially to the worldwide downturn that became the Great Depression.

See also Autarky; Creditor Nation; Great Depression, Character of.

References and Further Reading

Case, Josephine, and Everett Case. *Owen D. Young and American Enterprise.* Boston: D. R. Godine, 1982.

Dawes, Charles G. *A Journal of Reparations.* London: Macmillan, 1939.

Deficit Spending

From time to time, government expenditures exceed revenues and therefore create a deficit. To make up the difference, the government may borrow to continue its deficit spending. Although government officials usually try to avoid deficit spending, during the 1930s some advocated doing it deliberately as a strategy for lifting the United States out of the Great Depression. The leading academic advocate of this policy was

John Maynard Keynes, and the use of deficit spending is a primary element of what is often called *Keynesian* economics.

Balancing income and expenditures is difficult enough for individuals, and the constraints, regulations, and circumstances facing governments demand even greater efforts. Even so, deficit spending at the federal level has frequently occurred. Indeed, it began at the very birth of the United States when the Continental Congress issued unbacked promissory notes to pay its debts. Once the Constitution granted the federal government the right to levy taxes, it took advantage of that income stream to pay its expenses and fund the national debt.

Large deficits cropped up over the years, sometimes resulting from forces beyond the government's control. During the War of 1812, the Civil War, and the First World War, government expenses rose far higher than its income from taxes. Much of the money used to pay for these conflicts came from selling bonds. Because bonds may represent debt accumulated in earlier years, the existence of government bonds does not necessarily mean that the account involves deficit spending. But federal authorities generally try to balance the books in each fiscal year so that no further indebtedness occurs and any surplus can be applied to retiring earlier bond issues.

Conservative Republican administrators in the 1920s did a very good job of controlling federal spending. That enabled Treasury Secretary Andrew Mellon to reduce the public debt by almost half. In other words, the United States essentially paid for half of the costs it had incurred in the First World War by astute financial actions in the subsequent decade.

When the Great Depression began to exert its influence, however, President Herbert Hoover's administration found itself spending more than it earned. Although the deficits that accumulated during Hoover's last years in office were minor, they became a political embarrassment. It was all the more humiliating because of the pride the Republicans had expressed in their earlier sound fiscal management.

During his campaign for the presidency, Franklin Roosevelt criticized Hoover's deficit spending and pledged to balance the federal budget if elected. Like so many other campaign promises before and since, this one proved very difficult to fulfill. The nation's economy was almost completely stalled in 1933 when Roosevelt was inaugurated, and he was an old-line Progressive who believed the government had a responsibility to step in. Fifteen major bills passed through Congress during his first hundred days in office and they embodied his New Deal philosophy.

Not surprisingly, this massive set of initiatives was costly, and it provoked continued deficit spending. Over the next several years, however, Roosevelt never abandoned his intention to restore balance to the federal budget. Although his conservative critics would never have admitted it, Roosevelt often imposed constraints and restraint on his enthusiastic supporters in an effort to avoid deeper annual deficits.

Many New Dealers were not convinced that fiscal restraint was the best idea. A widely respected British economist, John Maynard Keynes, disagreed as well. Having studied the economic downturn in his own country as well as the one across the Atlantic, Keynes concluded that the government had an obligation to replace the lost purchasing power of the consumer economy. In the depths of the Depression, underconsumption was a key problem. As long as the general population either could not or would not spend, the economy remained stalled.

The Keynesian call for deficit spending found many supporters in the United States, but Roosevelt was not one of them. He and Keynes met briefly at one point and instantly disliked each other. The president stoutly refused to be characterized as a Keynesian. Moreover he really did believe that balanced budgets were desirable and, for that matter, most Americans agreed. Any deliberate policy of unbalancing the budget in the absence of major relief or recovery programs would have met with widespread public criticism.

Throughout the late 1930s, deliberate deficit spending to solve economic woes was never used. Once he had superintended the creation of his welfare programs like Social Security and the Works Progress Administration, Roosevelt throttled back and waited for them and the many New Deal reforms to turn the economy around. Conditions worsened in 1937 and 1938, however, so additional action seemed prudent. Even so Roosevelt never proposed deficit spending per se as a solution to the continuing economic troubles.

Would it have worked? A couple of experiments suggest that it well might have. In Germany in the late 1930s the government of Adolph Hitler abandoned all pretense of balanced budgets in a frenetic rearmament campaign. By 1939 deficit spending for military goods had so stimulated the German economy that it had become one of the healthiest in the world. Unfortunately, Hitler's armies then used this awesome array of materiel to invade Poland and much of Europe.

That international crisis shocked other countries and the United States into massive war preparations of their own. A flurry of procurement, training, and overseas assistance programs overwhelmed any concern about balancing the budget. Deficit spending increased after the Japanese attack on Pearl Harbor. When the conflict ended in 1945, the U.S. government had spent over $280 billion on its war effort. Tax revenues paid for less than half of that cost; the rest had been borrowed. Ironically, this massive, unplanned deficit spending did exactly what Keynes had predicted. The American economy recovered from the Depression and reached unprecedented heights of industrial and agricultural productivity. Although severe strains and dislocations occurred in the years immediately after the war, the American people never again suffered from anything approaching the doldrums of the Great Depression.

In more recent times, deficit spending has continued to occur from time to time, but almost always as an inadvertent or unplanned result of broader policy decisions. When a recession threatens, one occasionally hears calls for deliberate deficit spending to jump-start the economy. Fortunately, the nation has avoided an economic meltdown on the scale of the Great Depression, so heroic fiscal policies have not been needed. At the same time, persistent deficit spending is unsettling, particularly during peacetime. One can only hope that the economy will not have built up a tolerance or immunity to it if deficit spending is ever needed to offset a major depression.

See also Great Depression, Causes of; Keynesian Economics; Underconsumption.

References and Further Reading

Clarke, Peter. *The Keynesian Revolution in the Making*. New York: Oxford University Press, 1990.

Gilbert, J. C. *Keynes's Impact on Monetary Economics*. London: Butterworth Scientific, 1982.

Temin, Peter. *Did Monetary Forces Cause the Great Depression?* New York: Norton, 1976.

Federal Reserve System, Creation of

Congress approved the Federal Reserve Act in late 1913, but it took some time for the resulting twelve-member banking system to be established. Among the act's many goals was the creation of a lender of last resort for the nation's banks and the establishment of a national clearinghouse for checks. Another objective was to create an elastic currency that would match the nation's overall business needs, and Federal Reserve notes have subsequently become the chief U.S. medium of exchange. Not incidentally, the system was expected to provide some federal government influence over the nation's private banking and commerce. While many of these objectives had been achieved in the 1920s, the system failed to stave off the 1929 stock market crash and subsequent Depression. Consequently significant changes were instituted in the management and operation of the system in the early 1930s.

Americans had been debating the benefits and drawbacks of a central bank ever since Alexander Hamilton created the first Bank of the United States in 1791. President Andrew Jackson effectively ended the possibility of a Hamiltonian institution in the Bank War of the 1830s, leaving the nation to make do with independent treasuries and a highly dispersed national banking system through the end of the nineteenth century. By the turn of the twentieth century, however, even conservative financiers and politicians had concluded that something more was needed.

The business panic of 1907 shocked the Republican Party into action. Senator Nelson Aldrich, a Republican representing Rhode Island, was the powerful chair of the Senate Banking and Finance Committee, and he took the lead in sorting through various proposals. In 1908 Congress passed the Aldrich-Vreeland Act that called for establishing a national clearinghouse. Aldrich subsequently prepared a bill to do just that by creating a Federal Reserve Association that would be headquartered in Washington, D.C., but have fifteen regional branches. The association was to be a privately owned and managed operation with no direct government participation.

Progressive spokesmen were meanwhile championing government by experts and direct federal intervention in economic and financial matters. The Democratic Party swept the 1912 elections, giving it control of both houses of Congress and the White House, a takeover that halted progress on Aldrich's plans and set the stage for a much different approach. The Pujo Committee's report critical of the activities of the nation's leading finance capitalists and investment bankers appeared early in 1913, and it helped reinforce the Progressive belief that governmental authority needed to be included in any new banking legislation.

Virginia Representative Carter Glass became chair of the House Committee on Banking and Currency, and he took the lead in developing the ultimately successful approach. President Woodrow Wilson exercised considerable influence as well. Responding to pleas from rural and regional constituents, both Democratic leaders resolved to prevent the close-knit and powerful New York financial community from dominating the new structure. To that end, the Federal Reserve Act called for the creation of between eight and twelve regional banks, each with an independent and locally based board of directors. The existing national banks within each Federal Reserve District were expected to help capitalize the bank in their regions.

Equally important was the act's provision for the creation of a Federal Reserve Board to set policy and oversee the operations of these regional institutions. The secretary of the treasury and the comptroller of the currency would be ex officio members of this board, assuring direct and meaningful federal participation. The president was authorized to appoint the other five members of the board. During the early years of the Federal Reserve System, the regional banks and the central board constantly jockeyed for power, preventing either entity from exerting total control.

A key responsibility of the resulting twelve Federal Reserve banks was to maintain substantial funds in their vaults. This money would be immediately available for national banks and other financial institutions in their districts to draw on whenever their holdings threatened to become overdrawn. The law required each national bank to transfer an amount equal to 3 percent of its capitalization to the reserve bank, and an additional 3 percent could be called up if needed. In practice, the Federal Reserve System functioned so effectively as the holder of 3 percent of the nation's bank capital that it never collected the additional funds.

With its nationwide locations, the Federal Reserve System served as a clearinghouse for checks and other interbank transactions. In doing so, it recalled the banknote redemption activities of the First and Second Banks of the United States. Just as the earlier federally chartered institutions had discouraged fly-by-night banking activities, the Federal Reserve System's check-clearing activities helped promote responsible financial behavior throughout the country. Because it adhered to strict rules of accountability, it only handled about one-third of the clearings in the 1920s, leaving the remainder to the private clearinghouse system that had developed over the years.

In addition to facilitating transfers, the existence of the reserve funds enabled the Federal Reserve banks to act as lenders of last resort. Even a well-managed bank might from time to time need to access these reserves to avoid having to call in loans or take other steps to avoid temporary insolvency. The Federal Reserve system supplemented and strengthened the already well established practice of sharing reserves among existing banks, but its operating procedures discouraged it from making risky investments. In particular, it was specifically forbidden to lend money for the purpose of buying stocks or corporate bonds.

Instead the new institutions were to deal primarily in what were called *real bills,* loans for which collateral consisted of property, inventories of goods, or other tangible, as opposed to speculative, assets. As initially conceived, the real bill doctrine meant the Federal Reserve's activities did not encourage inflation or artificially promote or discourage enterprises. It provided a relatively safe place for bankers to transfer assets and to obtain loans at reasonable discounts.

Managing reserves, providing low-cost loans to banks, and facilitating interbank transfers were relatively noncontroversial functions compared to the system's currency operations. Throughout the nineteenth century, many Americans believed that an inadequate money supply had stymied growth and prosperity. The Progressives who helped formulate the Federal Reserve system hoped that it would be able to increase or decrease the money supply in accordance with the needs of the nation's economy. An elastic rather than a fixed currency was desired.

The legislation equipped the new system with two types of tools to manage the money supply. One was authority to manipulate its own discount rates to offset seasonal demand. Farmers needed to sell their harvested produce every fall, and this activity required the transfer of money from urban to rural districts. Typically, this transfer put a strain on the money supply, momentarily raising interest rates. The Federal Reserve System's resources were substantial enough to enable it to offset this periodic stringency and presumably create a more predictable and balanced flow of funds.

Even more important in the long run were the provisions that allowed Federal Reserve banks to issue notes. National banks had always been able to issue notes based on their holdings of federal bonds. But that requirement set an arbitrary limit on the number of national bank notes in circulation, and it fluctuated not according to the demands of the economy but rather on surpluses or deficits in the federal budget.

The Federal Reserve Act gave the banks it created authority to issue notes based on the real bills it handled on a daily basis. If it discounted more real bills in a given period, it could issue more Federal Reserve notes tied to these resources. Similarly, if economic activity waned and the Fed's holdings of real bills declined, it had to withdraw notes from circulation. Ideally, this process would cause the money supply to expand or contract in conjunction with the expansion or contraction of actual business activity. The goal was to reduce inflationary or deflationary pressures on prices by matching the available currency to the need for it.

In the early years, Federal Reserve notes were seen as a supplement to the gold, silver, national bank notes, and greenbacks already circulating. By 1920, however, Federal Reserve notes had become the most important element in the nation's money supply, accounting for over 60 percent of the money in circulation. Although their influence declined somewhat in the subsequent decade, Federal Reserve notes continued to play a very essential part in facilitating exchanges and promoting economic activities.

No one in 1913 anticipated that this influence would rise so quickly or be so pervasive. When the First World War broke out in August 1914, it immediately subjected the American economy to enormous strains. The Federal Reserve System thus faced unexpected pressures from the very beginning. Even before the United States entered the conflict, wartime demands threw off all calculations. Very quickly the Federal Reserve System began to include substantial holdings of federal bonds in its reserves, and the system assumed responsibility for selling government securities on a broader and broader scale. Wartime adjustments led the system to take on new responsibilities and undercut the influence and effectiveness of some of its prewar expectations.

How the Federal Reserve System would have developed in the absence of the wartime dislocations cannot be determined. Many of the Progressive concepts that had helped shape its original structure were no longer in vogue in the 1920s. Instead, conservative Republicans allowed private entrepreneurs considerable latitude in finance and speculation, further undercutting the influence of the central banking system. The weakened system was no match for the unanticipated and violent dislocations associated with the 1929 stock market crash and the onset of the Great Depression. The Banking Act of 1935, based on President Franklin Roosevelt's New Deal philosophy, substantially reconfigured the Federal Reserve System and established it as a much more prominent and effective institution.

See also Banknotes; Federal Reserve System, Reform of; National Bank Notes.

References and Further Reading

Meltzer, Allan H. *A History of the Federal Reserve.* Chicago: University of Chicago Press, 2003.

Moore, Carl H. *The Federal Reserve System.* Jefferson, NC: McFarland, 1990.

White, Eugene Nelson. *The Regulation and Reform of the American Banking System, 1900–1929.* Princeton, NJ: Princeton University Press, 1983.

Federal Reserve System, Reform of

The Federal Reserve System came under severe criticism for failing to stave off the 1929 stock market crash and the subsequent decline into depression. Emergency banking legislation in 1933 attempted to apply a fix to some of the system's supposed inadequacies, and a comprehensive Banking Act of 1935 further modified the nation's banking community. This process centralized control over the Federal Reserve System and strengthened the authority of its increasingly independent board of governors.

Sorting through the financial rubble that accumulated in the early 1930s, many analysts concluded that the Federal Reserve System had not acted responsibly. Brian Strong, governor of the New York Federal Reserve Bank, was singled out for particular criticism. Responding to European requests, his bank had kept interest rates unrealistically low. Moreover, his institution had played a central role in facilitating the flow of funding to speculators boosting the bull market. On a broader basis, critics charged that the central banking system had done too little to shore up prices and encourage recovery. Finally, the spate of bank runs and bankruptcies that blossomed in 1932 and early 1933 called into question the system's ability to maintain a sound financial structure.

President Roosevelt's intervention into the banking crisis in March 1933 provoked the first round of changes. The hastily drafted Banking Act of 1933 ordered the separation of banks from brokerage houses. It solidified support for the federally backed insurance on deposits that the Emergency Banking Act had mandated during the bank holiday. It also assigned more authority to the Federal Reserve Board over the regulation of loans that might be used for stock speculation as well as the foreign operations of member banks.

These steps were only the beginning. Over the next two years a number of additional changes were suggested, many of them in clear contradiction to one another. The Treasury Department and the president collaborated in manipulating prices, in taking the United States off the gold standard, and in developing spending plans. The Fed remained somewhat marginalized in the circumstances until Mariner Eccles began making his influence felt. Roosevelt had brought the successful Utah banker to Washington and soon determined that he should take charge of the Federal Reserve System.

Eccles offered a number of proposals for change, some of which were politically unpopular. On several occasions, he found himself at odds with Senator Carter Glass, the Virginian who had personally structured the 1913 bill that had created the Fed. Glass remained a powerful force in the negotiations that resulted in the comprehensive Banking Act of 1935. A key constraint was continuing opposition to creating too strong a central bank. Harking back to Andrew Jackson's war on the Bank of the United States in the 1830s, many politicians remained convinced that localized, distributed authority would be safer than centralized control. Equally important was concern that an incumbent president might have too much influence if control lodged in Washington rather than in regional banks.

More centralized control seemed inevitable, however, and the new legislation altered the structure with a name change. The new organization established the Board of Governors of the Federal Reserve System, headed by a chairman. To no one's surprise, Eccles became the first chairman of the board, a position he held until 1948. To insulate this board from direct political influence, the law stipulated that the seven governors would serve fourteen-year terms after being appointed by the president and confirmed by the senate. The treasury secretary and comptroller of the currency were removed from the board.

The board exercised increased control in several areas. It had the power to approve or disapprove of the choice of the regional bank's elected leaders, now called presidents. It also held majority control over the Open Market Committee. The committee included all seven governors and five presidents of regional banks in rotating slots. Moreover, all reserve banks had to participate in this activity that had been optional under earlier procedures. The new rules also authorized the board to dictate changes in the reserves member banks held. The 1935 act made the Federal Deposit Insurance Corporation (FDIC) a permanent feature and raised the limit from $2,500 to $5,000 per account.

The impact of the new rules varied. The FDIC program appears to have been a great success as the number of bank failures declined to almost nothing. During the late 1930s, however, the Federal Reserve Board operated quite conservatively in the realm of open market operations and setting discount rates. It played a more forceful role during the Second World War in the 1940s, and has become a major independent force in managing the nation's banking and financial affairs in recent times.

Although born out of the crises of the Great Depression, the reforms instituted in the early 1930s essentially completed the process of developing a strong central banking system for the United States. The more centralized and powerful governors of the Federal Reserve Board thus serve as heirs to the concepts Alexander Hamilton promulgated in his service as the nation's first treasury secretary.

See also Bank Holiday; Federal Reserve System, Creation of; Money Supply; Open Market Operations.

References and Further Reading

Groseclose, Elgin. *Fifty Years of Managed Money.* New York: Books, Inc. 1965.

Meltzer, Allan H. *A History of the Federal Reserve.* Chicago: University of Chicago Press, 2003.

Moore, Carl H. *The Federal Reserve System.* Jefferson, NC: McFarland, 1990.

Federal Trade Commission

Hoping to create a less confrontational regulatory mechanism, Congress created the Federal Trade Commission (FTC) in 1914. It absorbed the responsibilities of the existing Bureau of Corporations and was assigned responsibility for administering and enforcing the Clayton Antitrust Act. Over the years the authority of the FTC has ebbed and flowed, and subsequent legislation has armed it with a changing set of tools. Throughout its history, however, the commission has served as a major avenue of communication between business and government.

Many individuals and organizations expressed interest in the creation of a federal agency that would manage relations between business and government. The trust-busting agendas under Presidents Theodore Roosevelt and William Howard Taft further stimulated interest in an alternative. Roosevelt himself recognized that a lawsuit under the Sherman Antitrust Act was a crude instrument for regulating and moderating corporate behavior. With his strong support, Congress created a new entity, the Department of Commerce, in 1903. A key element in this department was its Bureau of Corporations.

The bureau's primary responsibility was to collect data and publish reports on aspects of corporate activity in the United States. Although it had no enforcement authority under the antitrust laws, many corporate leaders sought advice from the bureau regarding their existing or planned operations. The new agency thus fit the progressive model of government by experts, with businessmen using the expert advice they received to modify or shape their initiatives.

In his strident presidential campaign in 1912, Roosevelt promoted a platform called the New Nationalism. One of its key planks was a call for a cooperative rather than antagonistic relationship between business and government. Instead of suing business combinations with the goal of breaking them up, Roosevelt now favored the creation of a government agency that would head off or discourage unfair practices.

Democratic presidential candidate Woodrow Wilson initially seemed to favor the more traditional trust-busting approach. Once he and his party won control of the executive and legislative branches, however, they considered alternatives. One of their legislative initiatives led to the Clayton Act of 1914 that outlawed specific corporate practices. Simultaneously the Democratic majorities proposed the creation of a regulatory body that would promote cooperation.

The Federal Trade Commission Act of 1914 implemented this strategy. The five-member commission was to serve as a bridge between business and government. A key responsibility of the new commission was to absorb the substance of the Bureau of Corporations and continue its data-collecting and related activities. The FTC also assumed responsibility for investigating and enforcing the provisions of the Clayton Act that was signed shortly afterward. The commission could issue cease-and-desist orders to companies or combinations that appeared to be violating the price control and management strictures of the Clayton Act.

Once in operation, however, the Federal Trade Commission began to expand its impact well beyond these narrow confines. Business leaders generally welcomed the creation of an agency they could consult. A firm could request advice from the commission about whether or not it could or should engage in a particular business strategy. The FTC thus acted as a sounding board for government's attitudes. There was no guarantee, of course, that a corporation would not be subject to antitrust litigation if it overstepped the bounds, but it could avoid major pitfalls by following commission advice.

As was the case with every other agency, the First World War profoundly affected the Federal Trade Commission. President Wilson sought its expert advice regarding manufacturing costs and product pricing, even though the War Industries Board and the Food Administration made the actual purchases. It also assumed direct responsibility for enforcing the 1917 Trading with the Enemy Act, which allowed the president to impose restrictions on exports to countries with which the United States was at war. The FTC also administered the 1918 Webb-Pomerene Act that relaxed some antitust regulations for companies assisting in the war effort.

Serving as a clearinghouse for corporate information and an advisor on business practices, the FTC stimulated cooperative action among competing manufacturers. This function found particular favor in the 1920s when secretary of commerce and later President Herbert Hoover became an energetic proponent of associationalism. The FTC further stimulated this initiative by sponsoring what were called trade practice conferences devoted to various industries. The commission's sponsorship was especially important because it was responsible for evaluating the legality of any cooperative agreements that business associations formulated.

The Great Depression forced the FTC once again to adapt to new conditions. New Deal legislation created the National Recovery Administration, which took over some of the commission's responsibilities in drafting business codes for various economic sectors. The stock market collapse encouraged the formation of the Securities and Exchange Commission, which assumed other responsibilities that the FTC had formerly handled.

Subsequent legislation expanded the scope and authority of the Federal Trade Commission. The 1938 Wheeler-Lea Act modified the Clayton Act and, in doing so, authorized the FTC to impose civil penalties on entities that violated federal guidelines. The 1950 Celler-Kefauver Act focused on mergers and assigned the FTC authority in that area. Over time, the commission became increasingly active in the consumer protection arena. Perhaps its most popular recent initiative was the establishment of the National Do Not Call Registry, a program that it based on the 1994 Telemarketing and Consumer Fraud and Abuse Prevention Act.

Internal conflict among commissioners and external political jockeying and criticism have often limited the effectiveness of the Federal Trade Commission. It proved a disappointment to the more radical progressives dedicated to restoring competition by destroying large business combinations. At the same time, some criticized it for not being sufficiently pro-business. Such conflicting views are no doubt unavoidable in an agency that was designed and continues to be simultaneously a buffer and a conduit between business and government. Yet it persists as an enduring legacy of the early twentieth century Progressive drive to impose federal regulation and control over private enterprise.

See also Antitrust Laws; Clayton Antitrust Act; Recovery; War Industries Board.

References and Further Reading

Blum, John Morton. *The Progressive Presidents.* New York: Norton, 1980.

James, Scott C. *Presidents, Parties, and the State.* Cambridge: Cambridge University Press, 2000.

Peritz, Rudolph J. R. *Competition Policy in America, 1888–1992.* New York: Oxford University Press, 1996.

Weinstein, James. *The Corporate Ideal in the Liberal State: 1900–1918.* Boston: Beacon Press, 1968.

Florida Land Bubble

In the mid-1920s, land speculation spiraled out of control in Florida. In a matter of months, eager investors found they had vastly overestimated the number of people who intended to take up residence, and the Florida land bubble burst.

Transportation to southern and western Florida improved markedly after World War I, stimulating a rise in the number of people vacationing there. The Seaboard Air Line Railroad connected northern industrial cities with Miami and, like many other railroad projects, the company actively promoted interests in the area it served. Simultaneously, the rise in private ownership of automobiles provided many other people with the means to visit Florida.

Once they had sampled the mild climate and semitropical environment, many Americans were expected to move there permanently. To exploit this anticipated major migration, real estate promoters and speculators began staking out housing developments and commercial districts to meet the demand. By the summer of 1925, Miami alone supported an estimated 2,000 real estate offices employing a sales force of 25,000.

Some of the developments were well planned and reasonably well financed. George Edgar Merrick's father had roofed his house with native coral stone, and the younger Merrick exploited this characteristic in planning the community of Coral Gables. He mounted extensive advertising campaigns and encouraged development. By 1926 the bustling suburb contained 2,000 houses and a vibrant business district.

Other developers were less scrupulous. As demand for Florida property began to boom, they marked out subdivisions in swamp lands, in inaccessible interior regions, and along fragile coastlines. That hardly mattered because a vast number of purchases were made sight unseen by people who had no intention of actually living in Florida. Instead, they bought a lot or a tract with a small down payment, intending to sell it in a rapidly inflating market before they had to make any other payments.

It often worked out that way. Depending on location, prices rose dramatically. A plot of land that sold for $25 in 1896 brought $150,000 in 1925. Huge increases occurred in much shorter time frames. One man sold a plot for $2,500 and then bought it back a few months later for $35,000 after it had been resold three times at huge mark-ups. Prices for downtown plots naturally increased at much higher percentages than did suburban house lots, but for a brief period you almost literally could not lose money on a Florida land investment.

The boom began to crest in the spring of 1926. At that point the number of residential plots available outnumbered the potential buyers by a factor of ten to one. Prices began to slide, and that slide became increasingly pronounced because so many people had bought on margins of 10 percent or less. Further greasing the slide, two major hurricanes struck Florida's Gold Coast in September, killing more than 400 people, injuring 6,300 others, and wreaking substantial property damage.

The Florida land bubble burst, leaving thousands of speculators destitute and millions of acres of "developments" anything but that. The speculative fever that had swept through Florida had helped stimulate real estate booms in other parts of the country as well, but by the late 1920s, land speculation had definitely lost its attraction. It was left to the raging bull market on Wall Street to step in and distract the losers and fleece the winners in the Florida land bubble.

See also Bubble; Bull Market.

References and Further Reading

Allen, Frederick Lewis. *Only Yesterday.* New York: Harper, 1931.

Frazer, William, and John J. Guthrie, Jr. *Florida Land Boom: Speculation, Money and the Banks.* Gainesville, FL: University of Florida Press, 1998.

Great Depression, Causes of

The United States has suffered through a number of depressions, but the economic hard times that persisted throughout the 1930s justifiably qualify as the Great Depression. At no time before or since has such a large percentage of the population been so profoundly affected for so long. A number of factors combined to plunge the economy into a seemingly limitless downturn, one that was all the more disconcerting since it came on the heels of an unusually prosperous decade. And despite extensive and expensive measures, neither public nor private efforts had substantial success in relieving the misery.

Many contemporaries blamed the 1929 stock market crash for bringing on the hard times. More thoughtful analysts, equipped with more data and more distance from the events, have tended to downplay the crash as a cause. It may instead have been an advance warning or symptom of underlying economic weaknesses rather than a major precipitating event. The immediate post-crash performance of share prices does show a rather substantial recovery in the early months of 1930 before they plunged again, this time very much in conjunction with economic and business distress. At the very least, the psychological impact of the stock market crash persisted long afterwards, guaranteeing that the American people would be far more cautious and more emotionally depressed in their views of the future.

At least four major categories of troubles played significant roles in generating the Great Depression and ensuring that it would persist. Several economic sectors had weakened substantially in the 1920s, and they only got worse in subsequent years. Consumer spending, the chief engine of the American capitalist system, fell off markedly and, for a variety of reasons, remained limited. Banks and businesses created in the flush of a bull market were poorly structured to weather bad times. Finally, international economic conditions deteriorated as quickly or even more profoundly than they did in the United States, pulling the American economy ever downward. Each of these factors deserves consideration.

General prosperity and bullish attitudes in the 1920s effectively masked the fact that some industries were doing poorly. Agriculture, for example, never approached the heady excitement that had characterized its prewar golden era or the stimulus of the war itself. War-torn Europe quickly reestablished its agricultural productivity, and European governments worked hard to encourage agricultural self-sufficiency. American farmers thus suffered a permanent loss of their best overseas customers. Commodity prices remained relatively low throughout the decade, preventing millions of independent farmers and agricultural workers from participating in the rising income levels that buoyed spirits in other industries. As the nation descended into the Great Depression, trouble on the farm only worsened as prices plummeted to unprecedented low levels.

Several other economic sectors experienced weakness as the 1930s approached. The American textile industry, for example, suffered from fashion changes. The popularity of much lighter, skimpier women's attire, often made out of artificial fibers, substantially undermined the traditional cotton and wool textile industries. Railroads, formerly the nation's major engine of economic expansion and power, lost passengers and freight to private automobiles and trucking firms. Oil and hydroelectric power cut deeply into the coal industry. Even in the apparently booming automobile industry, signs of market saturation and declining profits were apparent by 1929. Simultaneously, the construction industry, always subject to cyclical forces, slid into a lull having overbuilt homes and commercial buildings.

Energetic, rising consumer demand could have had very positive effects on all of these weak sectors, but it simply was not there. Between 1929 and the depths of the depression in 1933, overall consumer spending declined

The Great Depression affected everyone from the nation's wealthiest business leaders to the members of destitute farm families like these unfortunate Oklahomans captured in Dorothea Lange's famous photograph. (Library of Congress)

a full 40 percent. The stock market crash clearly shook consumer confidence in the early stages of this decline. By the early 1930s, however, preferences alone were far less important than the fact that literally millions of Americans had lost their jobs and were no longer capable of making purchases.

Ironically wealthy Americans as well as poorer ones contributed to the underconsumption phenomenon. In the prosperous decade of the 1920s, the distribution of wealth in the United States grew increasingly attenuated with the rich getting richer far faster than the poor were getting less poor. Factory workers' wage increases fell further behind workers' productivity, so real wages actually declined. Meanwhile, those shareholders and managers who benefited from this rising productivity piled up larger and larger fortunes. Many of these increasingly wealthy individuals failed to spend their new money on consumer goods. They were far more likely to invest it or save it, behavior that led to underconsumption just as surely as did falling wages.

As it turned out, supply and demand, the forces that were traditionally expected to self-correct a declining economy, failed to work. American farms and factories were capable of producing consumer products in great abundance, creating a supply that should have driven prices downward. And prices did decline markedly in the early years of the decade. But the underconsumption problem had by then become so widespread that fewer and fewer consumers were capable of buying no matter how low the prices.

A natural consequence of this failure was for producers to reduce their output, a tactic that inevitably laid off workers by the hundreds of thousands. And so it became a self-perpetuating problem. A smaller employed workforce may have produced fewer products, but the growing army of unemployed had no money to buy them in any case. Several New Deal programs were based on the idea of inducing scarcity in the hope that such a policy would push up prices. But whether goods were scarce or plentiful, too few buyers were willing or able to buy, so prices remained inordinately low.

Economist Milton Friedman dismisses underconsumption as a major cause for the collapse. Instead he adopts what is known as a monetarist approach, focused on the behavior of the nation's banks. Friedman is particularly critical of the Federal Reserve System's behavior when it attempted to shrink the money supply just when price deflation and bank failures were becoming common. The Fed stepped in momentarily with open market operations designed to put more money in circulation in the late spring of 1932, but then abandoned the economy to the fates. It is questionable, however, that conditions would have improved even if the Fed had pursued the activist approach that monetarists favor. Its tools, adjusting the rediscount rate and open market operations, were wholly inadequate to the task of reversing such a pervasive and profound collapse.

By 1932 banks all across the country were failing. The poorly structured Federal Reserve System was incapable of saving them, especially since many of them were parts of complex and ill-planned business combinations. One obvious flaw was the connection between banks and brokerage houses that had lost and would continue to lose in the ever-declining stock market. The wave of consolidation that had crested in the 1920s had created a number of strange economic bedfellows, some of whose parts dragged otherwise sound divisions into the abyss.

The utilities industry provided a particularly appalling example of bad corporate structure. Sam Insull had moved aggressively and recklessly in the 1920s, assembling a huge, multilevel pyramid of holding companies in the electric power industry. Lacking both a coherent structural plan and enlightened management, this empire collapsed in 1932, wiping out over $700 million in assets. As the largest corporate collapse that had occurred up to that point, the dramatic fall of the Insull empire overshadowed thousands of other corporate and banking wrecks. Until more rational business planning could be implemented, the economy was bound to continue in its depression.

Suffering from myriad internal and structural problems, Americans could not count on help from abroad. Throughout the 1920s the United States had been the leader, a tower of strength from which other countries had drawn inspiration and significant transfusions of economic sustenance. In 1931 Austria's central bank, the *Kreditanstalt,* caved in dramatically, exerting downward pressure felt all around the world. Nor was Austria an isolated case. American investment had kept the German economy afloat, artificially breathing life into a moribund postwar economy. When the New York stock market crash absorbed vast amounts of investment capital, it also cut off Germany's financial lifeline. Soon Germany halted its reparations payments to France and Britain, subjecting their already weak economies to additional stress. In a very real sense, the Great Depression in the United States represented a long-delayed recognition that the First World War had truly devastated the world economy.

While weak sectors, underconsumption, faulty corporate structures, and international financial woes were major causes of the Great Depression, countless other mistakes, frailties, and insolvencies pushed the decline along and contributed to its depth. The fact that the modern economy had become so thoroughly interconnected meant that failure in one region or sector inevitably pulled others down with it. A kind of domino effect occurred, undermining and toppling otherwise sound or stable elements. Once the downward slide became steep enough, as it certainly had by 1931, literally everything was caught up in the slump.

This broad economic collapse also triggered emotional depression. A growing army of laid-off factory workers, impoverished farmers, redundant white-collar employees, and bankrupt investors bemoaned their fates. Newspaper reports of stress and distress compounded the extensive emotional miasma. Perhaps the only comfort anyone could take was that the depression engulfed people from all classes and walks of life. Unfortunately, a key greatness of the Great Depression was its pervasive negative influence on every individual, every industry, and every region of the country.

See also Bull Market; Crash; Federal Reserve System, Creation of; Great Depression, Character of; Underconsumption.

References and Further Reading

Bernstein, Michael A. *The Great Depression.* New York: Cambridge University Press, 1987.

Friedman, Milton. *The Great Contraction.* Princeton, NJ: Princeton University Press, 1965.

Garraty, John A. *The Great Depression.* New York: Anchor/Doubleday, 1987.

McIlvaine, Robert S. *The Great Depression.* New York: Times Books, 1984.

Watkins, T. H. *The Great Depression.* Boston: Little, Brown, 1993.

Great Depression, Character of

The Great Depression began to be felt shortly after the stock market crash of 1929, and it bottomed out in 1933. Despite strenuous efforts on the part of politicians, businessmen, and financiers, hard times continued with relatively little relief right through the end of the decade. High unemployment, low stock prices, bank closings, deflation, agrarian misery, and stalled industries persisted year after year. The Great Depression remains the longest and most severe period of economic hardship in the history of the United States.

Economists define depression as a period in which a nation's gross domestic product has declined for two or more consecutive quarters. In the early 1930s, declines occurred with disheartening effects in each successive quarter through the summer of 1933. After that, occasional upticks generated momentary optimism, but not until 1941 did the U.S. economy recover to the level it had reached in 1929. In that sense, the Great Depression ran for a full decade.

The behavior of national indicators sketch the portrait of an economy and a nation in deep distress. One measure of economic health is the amount of money devoted to investment. In the peak year of 1929, over $16 billion flowed into investments of all types. Three years later in 1932 a scant $1 billion found its way into investments. Another vital index of the health of a modern capitalist economy is the amount of money expended for consumer goods and services. At the height of the bull market in 1929, Americans spent over $77 billion. When the Depression bottomed out in 1932, consumption expenditures had fallen to only $46 billion, a decline of more than 40 percent. Throughout the entire decade of the 1930s, neither consumption expenditures nor investments rose to the levels they had achieved just prior to the stock market crash.

A measure of the country's overall economic activity, the gross national product (GNP), had fallen to just over half: $55.6 billion in 1933, down from $103.1 billion in 1929. Figure 4.3 illustrates the remarkable decline and very slow recovery in the nation's GNP during the depression decade. It should be noted, however, that considerable financial deflation occurred during the same period. If that deflation had not occurred, the 1933 GNP would have been

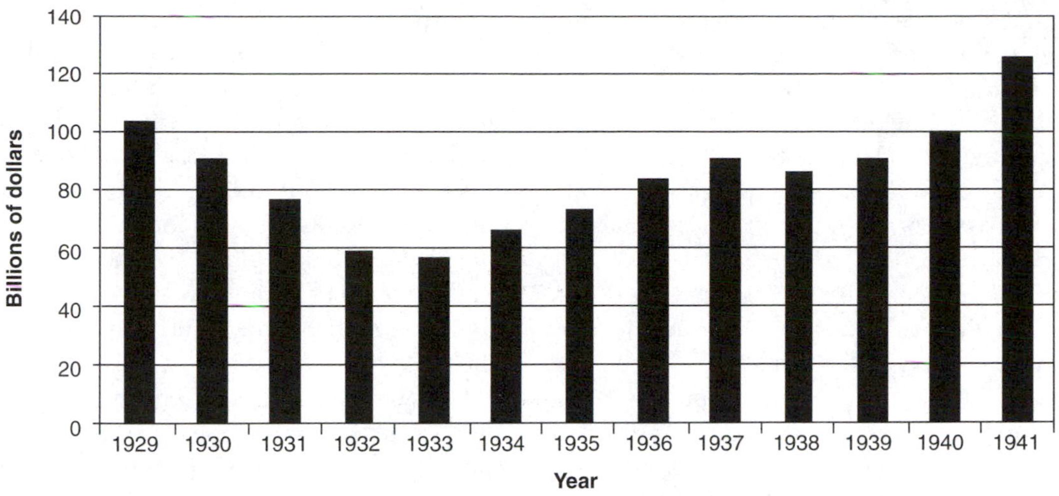

Figure 4.3 Estimated U.S. gross national product (GNP), 1929–1940. (Data from Economic Report of the President. *Washington, DC: United States Government Printing Office, 1990.)*

around $72 billion in adjusted, 1929 dollars. Still, that represents a decline of almost a third. Moreover, most Americans were slow to adjust their mind-sets to accommodate the deflation, so they saw the drop as very steep indeed.

The consumption figures graphically illustrate the decline in consumer spending, an indispensable component of the mass consumption economy the United States had become in the twentieth century. These figures support the contention that underconsumption was a major precipitating factor for the Depression. To raise the economy to its former level, either consumer buying had to recover or an alternative like federal spending on war materiel had to replace missing consumer demand.

Investment activity remained weak as well. With little or no new money flowing into the market in 1931 and 1932, it is hardly surprising that stock prices plummeted well below the already low levels they had reached during the 1929 stock market crash. The Dow Jones industrial average in July 1932 stood at 41, down 80 percent from its October 1929 level. Many corporations suffered an even more disastrous meltdown. Shares of Montgomery Ward were offered for sale at 4, down from 138, and United States Steel stock stood at 22, well below the 262 it had achieved three years before.

Banks were particularly hard hit. Links to failing brokerage firms in the wake of the stock market crash dragged some banks down early in the Depression. Once financial stringencies began to occur, poor organization and a lack of association or government controls destroyed others. Bank runs arose instantly among the psychologically depressed population, capable of driving otherwise sound and conservative institutions into bankruptcy. Throughout the 1920s bank failures occurred at a rate of fewer than 600 per year. In 1930 that figure more than doubled to 1,352, and it rose to a high of 4,004 in 1933. These closures affected millions of Americans from banking moguls to small-time village depositors.

The human trauma of the Great Depression extended far beyond lost savings. By 1929 the federal government had begun systematically collecting information about unemployment. At the nadir of the Depression in 1933, the official unemployment rate stood at 24.9 percent, representing nearly 13 million individuals. Then as now, the government's official figures undercount those actually out of work because the unemployment rate includes only those who are actively seeking work. By 1933 millions more had given up all hope of finding jobs and had thus dropped out of the active labor pool.

While New Deal relief programs began hiring workers in 1933, their effect remained modest. The unemployment rate had improved relatively to 14.3 percent by 1937, but it ballooned again to 19 percent the following year. It did not fall below 5 percent until wartime demand developed in 1942. Figure 4.4 illustrates how profoundly the Depression affected individual workers.

Industrial and commercial slowdowns and shutdowns stranded a sizable number of jobless people in the nation's cities. One study of a Philadelphia neighborhood in 1932 found many families literally living on bread and water—and local charities were supplying the bread. Racial and ethnic minority communities were especially hard hit as their residents were almost always the first to be laid off and those still working earned very low wages.

The only protection many rural Americans had was that farm families could still produce some of their own food. By the mid-1930s, however, even that became problematic when a severe drought settled in on the Great Plains. Persistent hot winds dried up the land and created huge dust storms that made farming and living nearly impossible. Unemployed farmers and their families from Oklahoma and Arkansas migrated by the thousands to California, seeking employment opportunities that turned out to be all too rare. Other able-bodied men left their families behind and became itinerant hobos, seeking any kind of work anywhere they could find it.

Hastily assembled relief efforts morphed into comprehensive, long-term programs. The Civilian Conservation Corps paid young men a dollar a day to reforest land, build irrigation and flood control projects, and perform other public works. Most sent the dollar home to their destitute families. The Works Progress Administration (WPA) had hired 11 million people by 1942. Some performed specialized work based on their training and talents, like writers, artists, and actors. Others simply showed up for work to do boondoggle projects. Still others labored on substantial infrastructure projects like bridges, post offices, highways, and recreation areas. The WPA's National Youth Authority paid students to stay in school to keep them off the breadlines and joining the millions of Americans unemployed.

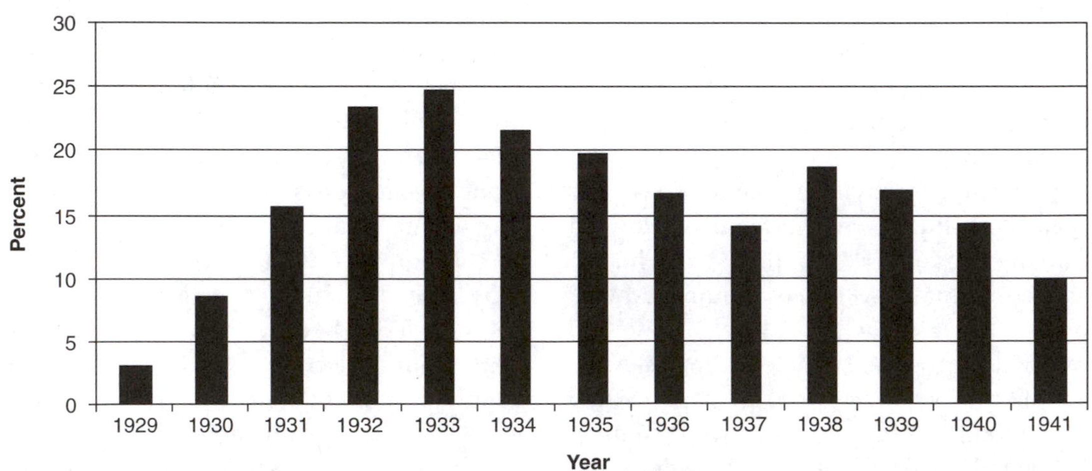

Figure 4.4 Percent of workforce unemployed, 1929–1940. (Data from Economic Report of the President. *Washington, DC: United States Government Printing Office, 1990.)*

Industrial and agricultural recovery programs were far less effective. Based on the induced scarcity principle, they failed to raise prices and promote consumer spending even as their restrictions and rules alienated businessmen, workers, and farmers. Meanwhile substantial reforms of banking, stock exchanges, and tariff policies were instituted. While many had relatively minor immediate effects, most have remained in place ever since.

As the Depression decade drew to a close, organized labor gained strength from its own recruiting efforts and a friendlier attitude in Washington. The National Labor Relations Act of 1935 provided the first major boost, and favorable court decisions in the next couple of years further strengthened their movement. Social security, including both old age pensions and unemployment insurance, began to ease the human anguish, and a minimum wage program in 1938 benefited those fortunate enough to have jobs.

The Depression was so long and so deep that it stimulated an enormous number of experimental solutions. Many failed immediately and others stumbled along for a year or two before being abandonded as ineffective. Even the more widely accepted and popular approaches seemed incapable of truly turning the economy around. The flurry of programs that appeared between 1933 and 1935 ensured strong support for Democratic President Franklin Roosevelt and his New Deal approach. But when he eased off and waited for the programs to promulgate recovery, the economic hard times intensified once again. Few new ideas were available when unemployment rose and economic activity slowed again in 1936 and 1937.

The most important factor in finally ending the Great Depression came at considerable cost. It took American economic support for, and eventual military involvement with the allies in World War II, to revive demand and, with it, employment. U.S. factories converted to war work as soon as the European conflict began in the fall of 1939. In addition to exporting war materiel to Britain and France, in 1940 the U.S. government instituted its own major military rearmament program. Expanded foreign and domestic demand for war materiel proved to be an effective substitute for the missing consumer spending that had helped bring on the Great Depression. By 1941 the Gross National Product finally topped its 1929 high, and unemployment fell to normal levels in the following year.

A debate has raged since that time about what was done and what else might have been done to pull the nation out of the Great Depression. Some advocated much more extensive deficit spending on the part of the federal government. Others criticized New Deal administrators for pursuing fruitless or naive approaches. In the long run, however, the crisis was so intense and so protracted that it seemed capable of defying all human efforts to end it. Fortunately, the Great Depression finally did disappear in the war years, and no similar economic disaster has ever again befallen the United States.

See also Crash; Deficit Spending; Great Depression, Causes of; Induced Scarcity.

References and Further Reading

Bernstein, Michael A. *The Great Depression.* New York: Cambridge University Press, 1987.

Garraty, John A. *The Great Depression.* New York: Anchor/Doubleday, 1987.

Leuchtenberg, William E. *Franklin D. Roosevelt and the New Deal.* New York: Harper and Row, 1963.

McIlvaine, Robert S. *The Great Depression.* New York: Times Books, 1984.

Turkel, Studs. *Hard Times.* New York: Pantheon, 1970.

Watkins, T. H. *The Great Depression.* Boston: Little, Brown, 1993.

Holding Company

Using the more liberal general incorporation laws that emerged in the late nineteenth century, financiers began organizing companies capable of operating on a regional or national basis. Many states permitted corporations based within their borders to own shares of companies located in other states. In many instances these new structures existed solely to own stock in other firms, relying on the industrial and business activities of their subordinate operations to generate profits for the overarching organization. Because they held controlling blocs of stock in operating companies, these mega corporations were called holding companies.

Because a holding company was a simpler, more straightforward structure than a trust, most large-scale businesses abandoned the trust format in favor of a holding company. Such a change did not exempt the newer organizations from the antitrust laws, however, as its fundamental principle was that any "combination in restraint of interstate commerce" was illegal. The combination could be a trust, holding company, or alternative. Moreover, well into the twentieth century, the public and the press continued to refer to large business combines as trusts regardless of their actual managerial structure. For example, the United States Steel Co. was popularly known as the Steel Trust even though J. P. Morgan had created it specifically as a New Jersey–based holding company.

Like U.S. Steel, some larger holding companies owned controlling interests in smaller holding companies. These, in turn, might themselves control subsidiary holding companies as well as operating companies. Sometimes waves of consolidation took place beginning when local or regional organizers created a holding company, only to see the resulting firm bought out or taken over as a subordinate of a larger company. Repeated instances of this process created a holding company pyramid, with the capstone company perched atop several layers of subsidiary holding and operating companies.

Perhaps the most famous and certainly the most notorious pyramid developed in the late 1920s when Sam Insull assembled a monumental utility holding company structure with eight distinct levels. A key drawback of this type of attenuated organization was that top-level managers were primarily interested in the profitability of the whole rather than concerned about the immediate or long-term health of individual operating companies. Managers at subsidiary levels found themselves under the gun to produce profits as well, and customer service often suffered as a result.

At the same time, a holding company could benefit enormously from the goodwill and solid reputations that its subsidiaries had developed. The holding company often remained primarily a financial and management structure, leaving subsidiary companies' names and trademarks unchanged. The subsidiary could continue operating in much the same way it always had while benefiting from the stability that could come from its position as a division of a well-capitalized, overarching holding company. A good many modern corporate giants like Time Warner are essentially holding companies.

The holding company format spurred business mergers and consolidation. It is flexible enough to function in any economic sector, and it can accommodate mergers of widely diversified operating companies. Some of the major holding companies like U.S. Steel remain largely confined to a single industrial sector; others branch out to encompass a broad array of operating segments. The term *conglomerate* came into vogue in the mid-twentieth century to describe such highly diversified holding companies.

In some cases, in fact, there seems to be no inherent logic to the types and extent of diversification that has occurred. Defenders argue that a highly diversified operation is an ideal mechanism to weather difficult economic times. If recession hits a particular sector, a diversified holding company can shift resources to and from its operations in healthier sectors to offset any losses in its focused subsidiaries. In part to achieve this sort of benefit, the general trend in recent years has been away from highly specialized firms to broader, more diversified business combinations.

Another consequence of the rise of holding companies is the opportunity they create for individuals with generalized financial and business expertise. Such business people may have almost no direct experience whatsoever with the day-to-day issues industrial operating companies face. But executives and managers can shuttle from one holding company to another, confident in their ability to deal with the problems they will encounter in the upper reaches of a complex business organization. Industrial experts who have fundamental expertise and experience in a particular sector of the economy may find themselves taking orders from executives with only limited understanding of the intricacies of their sectors.

See also Antitrust Laws; Billion Dollar Corporation; Conglomerates; General Incorporation Laws.

References and Further Reading

Faulkner, Harold U. *The Decline of Laissez Faire.* New York: Rinehart, 1951.

Kolko, Gabriel. *The Triumph of Conservatism.* New York: The Free Press, 1963.

Sklar, Martin J. *Corporate Reconstruction of American Capitalism, 1890–1916.* New York: Cambridge University Press, 1988.

Wiebe, Robert H. *Businessmen and Reform.* Cambridge, MA: Harvard University Press, 1962.

Induced Scarcity

In the depths of the Great Depression, some economists suggested that the government induce a scarcity of particular commodities, expecting that policy to raise their prices. Two key New Deal programs, the Industrial Recovery Act and the first Agricultural Adjustment Act incorporated induced scarcity initiatives.

By the spring of 1933, the American economy was in a steep decline, with too few consumers available to buy what appeared to be surpluses of goods. The natural supply and demand curves led to severe price reductions for particular commodities and monetary deflation throughout the economy.

While President Franklin D. Roosevelt had little formal academic training about, or understanding of, economic forces, he was blessed with an abundance of advice from his so-called Brain Trust and many other widely recognized or self-identified experts. Many of these people simplistically blamed the declining prices on a mismatch between the inventory of goods and the number of consumers capable of buying them. To reverse the deflation, they urged the use of mechanisms aimed at reducing the stockpile of goods available by artificially inducing a scarcity. According to classical economy theory, limiting the supply of goods should automatically raise their market prices.

The induced scarcity approach was a cornerstone of the National Industrial Recovery Act of 1933. The act created the National Recovery Administration (NRA). Headed by Hugh Johnson, it was charged with stimulating rebound in ten industrial sectors including steel, coal, autos, and so on. The NRA convened industrial boards of experts including manufacturers and labor representatives to draft comprehensive production codes. The codes designated quotas for particular goods. These quotas were subdivided among code-adhering manufacturers, limiting their output to fixed levels, usually substantially lower than the unregulated production that had occurred in earlier periods. The advantages to the producers included protection from competition from excessive production and more predictable manufacturing costs.

The Agricultural Adjustment Act of 1933 established similar quotas. In this instance, Agriculture Secretary Henry A. Wallace developed production regulation mechanisms for seven key commodities such as cotton, sugar, and beef. Developing reasonable quotas took several months and involved literally thousands of participants including county-level extension boards. As a result most farmers did not receive individual quotas until late summer, well into the growing season. To meet these newly defined quotas, millions of acres of field crops were plowed under and some 6 million baby pigs were slaughtered to meet the AAA pork production limitations.

This dramatic intrusion of federal control was extraordinarily unpopular, particularly among independent-minded farmers. The manufacturing controls also generated vocal opposition. Worse still, the enormous effort to induce scarcities of both manufactured and agricultural products had very little perceptible effect on price levels. A fundamental flaw in the induced scarcity initiative was its failure to recognize that many American consumers in 1933 simply did not have any money to buy goods regardless of their cost. To that extent some analysts see underconsumption rather than overproduction as a major contributing factor to the Great Depression. Cutting the output of items no one could afford to purchase at any price could not promote recovery.

So many other problems arose in the operation of the National Recovery Administration's multiple programs that few complained when the Supreme Court declared in 1935 that its key provisions were an unconstitutional extension of the interstate commerce clause. A similar fate befell the Agricultural Adjustment Act the following year.

Even though these comprehensive attempts at price manipulation failed, the induced scarcity concept has survived in modified form in a number of different initiatives including the varied and changing agricultural price-support programs.

See also Agricultural Adjustment Acts; Recovery; Underconsumption.

References and Further Reading

Hawley, Ellis W. *The New Deal and the Problem of Monopoly.* Princeton, NJ: Princeton University Press, 1966.

Johnson, Hugh S. *Blue Eagle.* Garden City, NY: Doubleday, Doran, 1935.

Perkins, Van L. *Crisis in Agriculture.* Berkeley, CA: University of California Press, 1969.

Interstate Commerce Commission, Reform of

Adverse court decisions had severely undermined the authority of the Interstate Commerce Commission (ICC) by 1900. In the ensuing decade and a half, however, a series of congressional acts revitalized the commission, transforming it into the nation's first truly effective federal regulatory agency. By 1913 it had undisputed authority to set passenger and freight rates based on comprehensive knowledge of a railroad's operating costs. The development of this powerful commission represented the full implementation of the Constitution's interstate commerce clause.

Many railroad owners and managers cheered this change. When the twentieth century began, more than 200,000 miles of track were in operation, providing the nation with far more capacity than was prudent. Competition among parallel lines and in busy markets had always been fierce, and heedless overbuilding only intensified that rivalry. To lessen its impact people like J. P. Morgan and Jay Gould pulled several railroads together into regional systems. Other railroad men began to believe that federal regulation might be a more palatable way of protecting their profits and reducing destructive competition.

Politics played a most important role in the development of more authoritative regulation of interstate commerce. The Republican Party (GOP) routinely supported the development and consolidation of big business, and a number of powerful conservative members of the GOP held key positions in both houses of Congress. Until they were either convinced or outvoted, no antibusiness changes would be possible.

Meanwhile, many Republicans and Democrats alike began to espouse progressive concepts. Among Progressivism's basic tenets as it developed into a powerful political force was a conviction that the government could and should take greater responsibility for the U.S. economy. Literally thousands of Progressive proposals were floated, many of them suggesting the use of experts or government commissions to investigate and, even more important, actually to regulate and control certain industrial and financial activities. Railroads at that point constituted the leading industrial and financial sector of the country, so it was only natural they would become the target of Progressive legislation.

The first hint of change came with the passage of the Elkins Act in 1903. Stephen Elkins was a senator from West Virginia and one of the most partisan and outspoken advocates of the railroads in Congress. Yet even he was willing to sponsor a bill that would outlaw rebate payments. The 1887 Interstate Commerce Act had included the same prohibition, but adverse court rulings and the ICC's inherent weakness failed to prevent the continuing use of kickbacks for major shippers. The Elkins Act alone was not sufficient to guarantee a change in practice, however, so Progressives and other critics of the current system lobbied for broader and more effective action.

President Theodore Roosevelt took up the cry, particularly after he had won election in his own right in the fall of 1904. A master politician, Roosevelt recognized that the conservative Republican leadership in the Senate had to be cajoled into cooperating or nothing would happen. Senator Nelson Aldrich of Rhode Island chaired the Senate Interstate Commerce Committee, and he and Iowa Senator William B. Allison had devoted much of their long careers to protecting the railroad industry from federal interference. By 1906, however, they had become increasingly aware of the public's disgust with railroad policies and knew something had to be done to counter it.

Early that year the House of Representatives approved the Hepburn Bill designed to restore authority to and strengthen the Interstate Commerce Commission. Specifically, it gave the ICC responsibility for setting railroad rates and for enforcing the Elkins Act's prohibition against rebates. Progressive senators on both sides of the aisle enthusiastically favored this proposal. Robert M. LaFollette of Wisconsin felt it did not go far enough, however, and he proposed an amendment to the Senate version that would give the ICC access to full information about railroad operating costs and capital values so that it could, in fact, set "just and reasonable rates." This proposal was too advanced for the moment, and LaFollette's amendment failed.

Meanwhile, conservatives were proposing amendments of their own. Senator Allison's was the most important, calling for a very broad court review of any disputes that might occur. If the ICC set a rate and a railroad disagreed, he argued, the company should be able to seek judicial review. President Roosevelt objected to this suggestion, wanting any court review to be confined only to procedural questions. Otherwise, in his view, the ICC would not actually have the regulatory authority that he considered essential.

The final decision on this issue was unresolved when the Hepburn Act won Senate approval with only three votes against it. The legislation expanded the size of the ICC from five to seven members, extended its authority beyond railroads themselves to include pipeline and sleeping car companies, and strengthened its power to prevent rebates. The key provision was its assignment to the ICC of authority to set rates. A weakness was the provision that the ICC could only investigate rates if it received a complaint. An even more serious problem was that if a railroad took the matter to court, the existing rate would remain in force until the court had ruled.

Some anticipated concerns failed to materialize, but others ultimately weakened the Hepburn Act's impact. Though it failed to specify how broadly the courts could interpret their responsibilities, in practice the judiciary conducted narrow reviews focused on procedural matters only. And for a time the ICC's rate-setting activities provoked few complaints. It did not take long, however, before more and more railroads demanded court review of ICC decisions, creating a logjam of cases. And, as long as their rates were in dispute, the railroads could continue collecting what they had charged all along.

By 1910 the Progressive wing of the Republican party had grown considerably stronger and its initiatives found strong support from the Progressive Democrats. The ICC's weaknesses stirred a new round of debate that ended with the passage of the Mann-Elkins Act. It greatly strengthened the ICC's hand, assuring that the commission-determined rates would go into effect immediately even if there was a court challenge. The legislation also discouraged challenges by placing the burden of proof on the railroad, not the ICC, to prove its case. The ICC also won the right to investigate rate levels without waiting for a complaint. Finally, the Mann-Elkins Act expanded the commission's span of control to include telegraph and telephone service providers.

By that point, the United States had developed a strong and effective regulatory agency, but it still lacked one essential element. Recalling LaFollette's earlier proposed amendment, Congress attempted to remedy this omission with another act in 1913. It gave ICC investigators full access to a railroad's books so that the commission could appropriately evaluate the company's actual operating costs. The rates the commission then imposed should therefore have been able to benefit the public without driving a railroad into insolvency.

The long process of creating and strengthening the Interstate Commerce Commission appeared complete. Even so, the railroad industry continued to suffer both from what it considered arbitrary or flawed ICC rulings and from the inherently competitive nature of the business. One persistent problem was that the government had not abandoned its traditional faith in competition even though transportation systems were more inclined to function as natural monopolies. In the long run consolidation of railroads often served the public interest better than the maintenance of smaller, less efficient rivals.

Dramatic support for that strategy appeared during the wartime emergency in 1917 and 1918. The hastily created U.S. Railroad Administration assumed centralized control of virtually all rail service in the nation, streamlining operations and ultimately making the whole system more profitable. Some owners and operators hoped the centralized system would continue, but it was quickly abandoned once the war ended.

Conservative Republican control of the federal government returned in the 1920s, and commitment to central regulation faded quickly. Although the ICC continued to operate, conservative appointees to the commission gradually took over, reducing its energy and aggressiveness. Worse yet, the overbuilt railroad structure faced rising competition from trucks and passenger cars. The increasingly diffuse nature of interstate transportation and commerce also limited the regulatory power of agencies like the ICC.

See also Federal Trade Commission; Interstate Commerce Commission; Railroad Consolidation.

References and Further Reading

Faulkner, Harold U. *The Decline of Laissez Faire.* New York: Rinehart, 1951.

Sklar, Martin J. *The Corporate Reconstruction of American Capitalism.* New York: Cambridge University Press, 1988.

Wiebe, Robert. *The Search for Order.* New York: Hill and Wang, 1967.

Just Price

People often attempt to determine a just price for a commodity or service, but such efforts draw special attention during wartime or other periods of economic stress. Rather than let free enterprise or the workings of supply and demand curves set a price, governments may wish to set or regulate prices in a deliberate and fair manner.

While the concept of a just price has a long history, it became particularly prominent during the First World War as the United States grappled with monumental mobilization and supply problems. During the twenty-month period of American participation in the conflict, scarcities, profiteering, and massive government purchases nearly doubled the nation's cost of living.

Inflationary pressures had already become evident by July 1917, just four months after President Woodrow Wilson sent his war message to Congress. The inflation caused military purchases to cost more, complicating the government's efforts to arm and supply its own armed forces and to support its allies. Price increases affected both finished goods and raw materials. On July 11 Wilson threatened to nationalize the nation's steel industry if the government could not get steel at a "just price." The next day, he publicly explained what that meant. A just price would be a level that enabled producers to sustain production, pay reasonable wages, and even be encouraged to expand production as needed. This definition provided fairly wide latitude for American industrialists and farmers even as it worked to discourage profiteering.

Determining a just price was only part of the problem. Government agencies or other mechanisms had to be developed to enforce the president's desires. Over the next year agencies like the Food Administration and the War Industries Board became increasingly adept at controlling prices. One factor that helped these agencies exercise control was that they placed such huge orders for certain goods that they effectively set the market price for all buyers. A subsidiary of the Food Administration called the Sugar Equalization Board went a step further, essentially buying all sugar available and then reselling it at a fixed price. The board recognized that different producers had widely varying production costs, so it paid more for beet sugar than for imported cane sugar. In this way, it was acting in line with the just price concept.

More recent programs like parity price supports in agriculture or subsidies for crucial war materials are also manifestations of the just price phenomenon. As a general rule, however, American businessmen have opposed governmental efforts to set or control prices.

See also Parity; Rationing; War Industries Board.

References and Further Reading

Cuff, Robert D. *The War Industries Board.* Baltimore, MD: Johns Hopkins University Press, 1973.

Keynesian Economics

In the depths of the Great Depression, British economist John Maynard Keynes published a book that proposed innovative remedies for the economic downturn. One of its most controversial recommendations was that governments vastly increase their expenditures to generate new demand. This demand should, in turn, stimulate production that would open factories, employ destitute workers, and ultimately jump start economic recovery. This call for the use of fiscal policies aroused both enthusiastic support and bitter criticism. By the mid-twentieth century, however, Keynesian economics had become widely accepted.

In contrast to classical economic theory, Keynes insisted that the most important factor in any economic system was aggregate demand. He examined three different factors to assess this demand. The first was *consumer* desire for goods and services. The second area of demand arose from those businessmen who wanted to build factories and buy machinery, making the sort of *investments* that would enable them to meet consumer demand. The third major player in this formulation was *government spending,* which in the twentieth century represented a substantial percentage of all demand. The resulting combination of consumer, investment, and government expenditures (C + I + G) added up to the nation's total or aggregate demand.

When the economy lapsed into recession, aggregate demand fell as well. Regardless of what had caused the decline, Keynes insisted that recovery would occur only if aggregate demand revived. Generating changes in consumer or investment demand would be very difficult to achieve indeed, far more than bumping up government spending. In a major break from classical economists who believed that natural forces should to be allowed to iron out economic disparities, Keynes advocated substantial government spending.

The tools available to governments like that of the United States were either to increase purchases or reduce taxes. These actions are called fiscal policies and either would fulfill Keynes's objective. Obviously if the government initiated a major buying spree, it would directly increase the government's demand for goods and, by extension, raise the value of G in the C + I + G formula. On the other hand, if the government reduced taxes, it would effectively leave more money in the hands of taxpayers. When they spent this money, they would be raising the value of C in the formula and, likewise, increase aggregate demand.

Keynes's proposals were considered quite radical when first articulated. The United States still harbored a traditional adherence to the laissez-faire doctrine, and many viewed greater government intervention in the economy as tantamount to socialism. Even if the philosophical hurdles could be overcome, there was considerable concern that massive increases in government spending or substantial tax reductions would unbalance the federal budget. The result would be deficit spending, an abhorrent result in a generally conservative era.

Keynesians were willing to accept these negative consequences if the result was economic recovery. Once that recovery occurred, after all, the government could reduce expenditures and, possibly restore higher taxes, reducing the artificial inflation of the G factor. Although many Americans considered Franklin Roosevelt far too liberal a president, he deliberately chose not to pursue a Keynesian approach in the 1930s. Indeed, he repeatedly spoke in favor of and took actions to restore balance to the federal budget. And, as the Keynesians were quick to point out, the U.S. economy really did not recover despite all of the New Deal programming.

When the United States was drawn into the Second World War, the focus switched from fiscal conservatism to all-out national defense. During the conflict, government expenditures for military goods rose meteorically and federal deficits ballooned. By V-J Day the country was enjoying a war-induced prosperity that persisted long after the fighting ceased. Perhaps Keynes had been correct all along. Massive deficit spending appeared to have so dramatically increased aggregate demand that the economy permanently shucked off its depression doldrums.

By the early 1960s Keynesian economics had achieved widespread acceptance. Government leaders systematically tinkered with fiscal policies hoping thereby to achieve stability and healthy economic growth. But in 1963 Milton Friedman proposed an alternative in the form of monetarist theory. He insisted that monetary, not fiscal, policy was the key to future prosperity. Nevertheless, Keynes's theories fundamentally altered economic thinking in the United States and around the world, and fiscal policy remains a major focus of attention in Washington, D.C.

See also Deficit Spending; Monetarism; Recovery; Underconsumption.

References and Further Reading

Felix, David. *Keynes: A Critical Life.* Westport, CT: Greenwood Press, 1999.

Kahn, Richard F. *The Making of Keynes' General Theory.* New York: Cambridge University Press, 1984.

Keynes, John Maynard. *The General Theory of Employment, Interest and Money.* New York: Harcourt, Brace, 1936.

Pasinetti, Luigi L., and Bertram Schefold, eds. *The Impact of Keynes on Economics in the 20th*

Century. Northampton, MA: Edward Elgar, 1999.

Leveraged Investment Trust

In the mid-1920s a new business form appeared called a leveraged investment trust. These trusts sold stocks and bonds to investors and used the capital thus generated to purchase a broad range of securities. They were particularly attractive to stockholders, however, because they used leverage to pay substantially higher dividends than were available on other investments. Unfortunately, they only worked well in a rising market, and they collapsed quickly and devastatingly when share prices began to level off and then fall in 1929. Leveraged investment trusts thus played a significant role in encouraging overoptimism among investors early on, and then dragging the market down when it began to decline.

Long before the decade of the 1920s, people had established investment trusts to create attractive, diversified investment opportunities. Like industrial corporations, these trusts sold both stocks and bonds to investors. With the capital thus accumulated, the trust managers bought stocks and bonds of various types, much like a present-day mutual fund. Investors in a trust received dividends on their stock and interest on their bonds corresponding to the success of the trust's portfolio.

In 1924 the United States and Foreign Securities Co. introduced an additional wrinkle in the form of leveraging. The leveraged investment trust operated like a regular investment trust in that it bought and sold securities and issued its own stock and bonds to those interested in participating. Some trusts sold bonds with a market value equal to that of their stocks. For example, a trust might collect $2 million in capital, half from selling bonds and the other half from stock sales.

Bonds in this era seldom produced more than a 5 percent annual return, so the trust would be obligated to pay out no more than $50,000 each year in interest. In the bull market that flourished in the late 1920s, it was not at all unusual for a trust's overall investment portfolio to earn at least a 10 percent profit in a given year, or $200,000. After paying its bond interest, the trust had $150,000 to distribute as dividends to its stockholders. The 15 percent return from this hypothetical leveraged trust would be considerably higher than what would accrue to owners of non-leveraged investments.

The better the market performed, the higher the value of the leveraged investment. In the earlier example, a 20 percent gain for the trust would translate into a 35 percent annual stock dividend. It was hardly surprising that leveraged investment trusts became extraordinarily popular in the late 1920s. Many were listed on the stock exchange, selling their shares at premium prices to buyers anticipating very high profits.

And for several years buyers did very well with their leveraged investment trust holdings. The problem with leverage, of course, is that even a slight decline in profits has an exaggerated negative effect. In the prior example, if the trust's overall performance netted only 2.5 percent in a given year, all of that would have to go to the bondholders, leaving the stockholders with no profits whatsoever. As soon as the stock index stopped rising, savvy investors rushed to sell their leveraged shares, an action that hastened the decline in share values and encouraged broader sell-outs. The collapse was so abrupt that even the bondholders lost out.

In the aftermath of the stock market crash, the Securities and Exchanges Commission stepped in with a number of new regulations including a prohibition against leveraged investment trusts.

See also Bull Market.

References and Further Reading

Klein, Maury. *Rainbow's End: The Crash of 1929.* New York: Oxford University Press, 2001.
Mitchell, Broadus. *Depression Decade.* New York: Rinehart, 1947.

Sobel, Robert. *Panic on Wall Street.* New York: Truman Talley Books/Dutton, 1988.
Steiner, William Howard. *Investment Trusts, American Experience.* New York: Adelphi, 1929.

Money Supply

In the twentieth century Americans began to pay a great deal of attention to the overall supply of money in their economy. Recognizing that bills and coins represented only a small fraction of the nation's purchasing power, calculations expanded to include factors like bank accounts, short-term bonds, and money market investments. These could easily be accessed and used for expenditures of all sorts. Tracking the growth or decline of the money supply enabled planners, politicians, and businessmen to adjust their conduct to complement the behavior of the capitalist economy.

Politicians had been debating the issue of how much and what types of money should circulate since the Revolution. The presidential election of 1896, for example, had pitted an articulate advocate of free silver, Democrat William Jennings Bryan, against a conservative Republican, William McKinley, whose platform favored adherence to the gold standard. McKinley won and superintended the passage of the Gold Standard Act of 1900, a move that seemed to represent a definitive rejection of the century-long struggle over soft money.

Several factors helped make the gold standard work in the early decades of the twentieth century. During that period, the United States enjoyed an extraordinarily favorable international trade balance that annually brought millions of dollars worth of gold into the country in exchange for its exports. Equally important was the establishment of the Federal Reserve System in 1913, which created a conservative central banking structure. With minor setbacks, prosperity prevailed, generating more bank deposits, federal and corporate bonds, and improving the country's general welfare.

The 1929 stock market crash and the ensuing Depression appeared to invalidate earlier monetary assumptions. President Franklin Roosevelt introduced a variety of financial schemes to halt the decline and stabilize the economy. Announcing a federal bank holiday, experimenting with a commodity dollar, and abandoning the gold standard were all designed to pump up the money supply. The Great Depression also encouraged much more sophisticated measurement of economic data and more attention to historical trends.

The data collectors settled on two measures of the money supply: M1 and M2. M1 counts all of the funds instantly available to the public. These funds include currency (notes and coins), travelers' checks, and demand deposits. The latter are more familiarly known as checking accounts. Demand deposits represent money that can be withdrawn at any moment (on demand) and so represent money that can be spent immediately. In 1999 the value of M1 stood at a little over $1 trillion.

While M1 measures immediately available spending power, the public can also convert or draw on substantial additional monetary resources. They include savings deposits and money market accounts that, though they may not include check-writing privileges, can still be withdrawn pretty much on demand. Small-denomination time deposits with short terms and retail money market mutual funds also represent public money readily available to consumers. In 1999 the aggregate total of these funds was about $3.4 trillion or three times the value of M1.

To provide a better assessment of the overall money supply, the balances of all of these funds are combined with those in M1 into another measure known as M2. Because M2 includes all funds either at hand or that can be drawn on in short order, it represents a more comprehensive evaluation of the people's ability to buy. Moreover, M1 is far more susceptible to fluctuations and short-term economic factors than the more stable deposits in savings and money market fund accounts. Tracking M2 damps out temporary shifts and provides a more stable assessment of the money supply.

Freed from a linkage to finite reserves of gold or silver, the money supply has been able to expand in conjunction with the growth of the U.S. economy. But there is never a perfect correspondence between these factors, and serious consequences can occur when they get out of alignment. Substantial price inflation can occur if the money supply increases more rapidly than the economy expands. On the other hand, a relative reduction in the money supply can discourage investment, cut consumer spending, and ultimately throw the economy into recession.

The Federal Reserve Board is well aware of these possibilities and has used both its open market operations and discount rate adjustments to stimulate or limit growth in the money supply. Tinkering with such a substantial factor is not easy and may or may not have the expected consequences. Even more frustrating is the fact that an enormous and unpredictable variety of domestic and international developments can influence the money supply. A dramatic increase in world oil prices in the 1970s, for example, invalidated all projections about the money supply.

An ongoing academic debate about the importance of the money supply has further complicated the matter. In the 1960s a new economic theory called *monetarism* concluded that the behavior of the money supply was more important than any other factor in promoting economic growth. Other economists insisted that the money supply was an effect rather than a cause for economic fluctuations. The experts at the Fed and the U.S. Treasury continue to experiment with various tools and policies in attempting to adjust the money supply to match the real needs of both its private and public users.

See also Federal Reserve System, Reform of; Monetarism; Open Market Operations.

References and Further Reading

Boorman, John T., and Thomas M. Havrilesky. *Money Supply, Money Demand, and Macroeconomic Models.* Boston: Allyn and Bacon, 1972.

Fisher, Douglas. *Money Demand and Monetary Policy.* Ann Arbor, MI: University of Michigan Press, 1989.

Kennedy, Paul E. *Macroeconomic Essentials.* Cambridge, MA: MIT Press, 2000.

Visser, H. *The Quantity of Money.* New York: Wiley, 1975.

Movies

One bright spot in the otherwise bleak Depression era was the development of a dynamic and creative film industry. The introduction of sound movies in the late 1920s opened new vistas and attracted huge audiences to theaters all across the country and around the world. The golden era of Hollywood in the 1930s involved business consolidation, oligopoly, organized labor, high finance, and bitter competition. In these respects, the film industry resembled other sectors of the economy engaged in turning out a popular consumer product.

A number of technological hurdles had to be overcome before the movie industry could mature. A great many people both in the United States and in Europe laid claim to inventing motion pictures. One was Thomas Edison whose chief innovation was to punch holes along the edge of a roll of celluloid film so it would pass smoothly over sprocketed wheels in both cameras and projectors. Edison put his invention to work producing short films for peep shows that drew crowds into tiny screening rooms. The standard admission for a viewing was five cents, so these theaters became known as nickelodeons.

As with so many other innovations, the early pioneers attempted to control all aspects of the nascent film industry. In 1908 Edison and other inventors formed the Motion Picture Patents Co., and it began demanding royalty payments from anyone who used the technology. William Fox and others objected to this attempt at control.

Protesting that the company violated antitrust laws, they won a favorable decision from the Supreme Court in 1917.

To reach an audience, early filmmakers had to have access to production facilities, a distribution mechanism, and exhibition halls. This three-part system provided many opportunities for entrepreneurs. Independent producers often found themselves at the mercy of distributors and exhibitors. One successful distribution company decided to extend its control to both the source and the marketing aspects of the industry. Eventually known as Paramount, it implemented a vertical integration plan by putting filmmakers like Cecil B. DeMille on its payroll, but it ran into stiff opposition from Marcus Loew, the owner of a chain of theaters. Loew decided to fight fire with fire by rolling his holdings into a production company called Metro-Goldwyn-Mayer (MGM). MGM and Paramount thus became rivals, both vertically integrated, both producing films, distributing them, and exhibiting them in their own theater chains. These two organizations emerged as the first major studios located in Hollywood.

Some of the most creative people in the fledgling industry were unwilling to bend to studio dictates. D. W. Griffith, a pioneering director, and three popular actors, Mary Pickford, Douglas Fairbanks, and Charlie Chaplin, formed their own production company named United Artists in 1919. By the mid-1920s, the Warner brothers had become involved in movie-making as well, and they needed a gimmick to set their efforts apart from those of their competitors. They found it in a sound technology that used discs like phonograph records. They set up the Vitaphone Co. to use the system and produced the first talkie, a phenomenally popular film called *The Jazz Singer* in 1927. After a period of competitive innovation, the industry dropped the Vitaphone system in favor of an optical sound system the Radio Corporation of America (RCA) had developed.

The growing popularity of sound movies attracted the attention of finance capitalists, and the industry received large infusions of capital in the late 1920s, just in time to pay for the much more elaborate and expensive soundstages and advanced equipment needed to produce sound movies. When the onset of the Great Depression strained finances, however, it aided the larger studios in their efforts to dominate the industry. They enhanced their influence by putting actors and technicians on a payroll so they could churn out movies in an almost assembly-line fashion. Although some of their output was of marginal quality, audiences responded positively anyway, finding that movies helped them escape from the despair of the Depression.

By the mid-1930s a few major studios exercised oligopoly control. Warner Brothers and MGM remained leaders. RCA had combined with the Keith-Orpheum theater chain to promote its sound system, and the resulting RKO studio prospered as well. Paramount declared bankruptcy in the early 1930s, but a new infusion of capital revived it. William Fox had always been a maverick independent, and he, too, fell on hard times. The Chase Manhattan Bank came to the rescue this time, assembling a new combination by merging Fox with the Twentieth-Century studio. United Artists, Columbia, and Universal rounded out the Hollywood leadership.

When the National Recovery Administration drafted a code for the movie industry in 1933, the studio chiefs maneuvered it into giving them very favorable treatment. To fight back, actors and writers took advantage of the New Deal's support for organized labor. The Screen Actors Guild and the Screen Writers Guild led the way in bargaining for better treatment for the artistic members of the industry. Technicians, craftsmen, and even directors followed suit with their own organizations.

The movie industry thus emerged from the Great Depression as a fully mature enterprise. Its prominence gave actors recognition as stars and directors prestige as creators. Color brightened the screens in the late 1930s drawing ever larger audiences; elaborate musical soundtracks were spun off onto records that sold separately. Not surprisingly, the industry made a lot of money. But unexpected competition was just around the corner. RCA's primitive television system demonstrated at the 1939 Chicago World's Fair would grow into the movie industry's greatest marketing challenge in the postwar years.

See also Television.

References and Further Reading

Kindem, Gorham. *The American Movie Industry.* Carbondale, IL: Southern Illinois University Press, 1982.

Lees, David, and Stan Berkowitz. *The Movie Business.* New York: Vintage, 1981.

Stanley, Robert H. *The Celluloid Empire.* New York: Hastings House, 1978.

Moving Assembly Line

The Ford Motor Co. created the world's first moving assembly line in early 1913 and quickly adapted the system to its entire production process. The speed and efficiency of the system enabled Ford to produce automobiles far more quickly to meet the enormous demand for its popular Model T cars. Other manufacturers soon adopted moving assembly lines, and they have now become a standard production technique around the world.

It is hardly surprising Ford would be the first to develop this manufacturing process. Henry Ford had initially focused all of his considerable skill and attention on creating a tough, uncomplicated automobile in the Model T. One of his chief collaborators, James Couzens, then established a nationwide sales network of some 7,000 individual dealerships to sell and service them. The combination of a very affordable, reliable vehicle handled by dealers throughout the country created a huge demand for the product.

Like other early automakers, Ford and his associates had begun by hand-building their first models. As demand for their product grew, however, the company continually, indeed, incessantly, experimented with methods for speeding production. This encouraged them to break down a particular procedure into smaller, simpler steps that individual workers could perform with a maximum of efficiency. It also meant that the Ford factory was constantly evaluating machinery and adopting or developing new machines and machine tools to handle particular, specialized functions.

The pursuit of speed crowded the manufacturing space. Even after the operation moved to a huge new plant in Highland Park, Michigan, bottlenecks and excessive or unnecessary movement hindered output. By early 1913, a series of lines had been laid out on the factory floor so that workers could move from one station to the next to do their specialized tasks. It was a logical next step to eliminate the wasteful movement of workers and move the assembly line instead.

The first fully automated line produced flywheel magnetos (a type of electrical alternator), and it reduced the manufacturing time for one magneto every twenty minutes to one every thirteen minutes. Simplifying procedures and further tinkering with the speed of the moving line cut that to just five minutes. The same technique was then adapted for other parts lines.

In August the plant set up its first moving assembly line for automobile chassis, with moving assembly lines for parts feeding into it. Within a few weeks, the manufacturing time for a completed car had dropped from an average of fourteen hours to about one and a half. That represented a giant step toward fulfilling Henry Ford's life-long goal of producing a car every minute. Managers sped up the moving belts, instituted better control of side assemblies, and simplified

Rows of completed Model Ts roll off the Ford Motor Co. assembly line in the United States, ca. 1917. (Library of Congress)

individual worker functions to minimal levels. On October 31, 1925, one of Ford's assembly lines produced over 9,000 completed cars in a single 24-hour day, a rate of six cars per minute.

The ever increasing speed of the moving assembly line forced workers at the Ford plant to do simpler, repetitive tasks at faster and faster rates. Although Ford was not a student of Frederick W. Taylor, the automaker conducted numerous time and motion studies, clearly in line with the increasingly popular theories of scientific management. Many experts studied the company's procedures and encouraged other manufacturers to adopt them as well. The spread of this system went well beyond the automobile industry, as it was adaptable to a mass production process in any industry.

The system was not, however, universally popular. Its most outspoken critics were labor organizers who branded it as dehumanizing. Even without the encouragement of rabble-rousers, laborers found working conditions very uncomfortable at Ford. In some months the company suffered a labor turnover rate as high as 60 percent. Henry Ford had devised the most efficient manufacturing system the world had yet seen, but he could barely keep enough workers on the job to exploit it.

He decided to buy them. Early in 1914 the Ford Motor Co. announced that it would pay workers $5 per day, an astronomical increase above the Detroit area automobile industry's current top wage level of $2.34. Thousands of workers mobbed the Ford plant, eager to more than double their daily wages. To qualify for that top wage, however, workers had to stay on the job for a considerable period and to abide by the very strict moral codes that Henry Ford personally dictated.

Even so, the $5 per day policy was a huge success. It enabled the company to select the most energetic and capable workers from virtually the entire nation's industrial labor force. When these motivated workers stepped up to the line, they could work at a faster pace, allowing the speed of the moving assembly line to be cranked up as well. That meant that the actual labor costs per unit dropped so significantly that they offset the cost of the higher wage package. The combination of ever more sophisticated machinery, highly adept workers, and the increasing speed of the moving assembly line enabled the Ford Motor Co. to produce 20 million Model Ts and account for more than half of the annual automobile sales in the United States well into the 1920s.

See also Ford, Henry; Scientific Management.

References and Further Reading

Simonds, William Adam. *Henry Ford: A Biography.* London: Michael Joseph, 1946.

Sward, Keith. *The Legend of Henry Ford.* New York: Rinehart, 1948.

Muckrakers

When writers and journalists began criticizing big business practices in the early twentieth century, President Theodore Roosevelt referred to them as *muckrakers.* He based this on characters in *The Pilgrim's Progress,* a popular book by John Bunyan. Muckrackers were downtrodden people who spent their days raking through mud at their feet, never looking up and appreciating the glory of the world around them. Despite its initial negative connotation, the name gained instant popularity with both the public and the writers to whom it was applied. Muckraking books and articles exposed predatory corporate behavior, unfair competition, exploitation of workers, unsanitary production methods, corrupt city government, and countless other questionable practices. The Progressive political movement cited muckrakers' findings and proposed legislative remedies to the injustices these writers exposed.

As the nineteenth century drew to a close, larger and larger business combinations came into being, developing oligopolistic or near monopolistic control over various sectors of the economy. Negative comments about these combinations, their tactics, and their dominance arose from a range of critics. At one extreme were outspoken socialists and Marxists who advocated a complete overthrow of the existing capitalistic system. At the other end were mainstream reformers who, while appreciative of the progress that technology and entrepreneurial talent had given society, spoke out against what they perceived to be unethical or harmful behavior.

These critics of the system took advantage of the development of new mass media outlets. Samuel McClure began publishing his magazine in 1893. Priced at fifteen cents a copy, *McClure's Magazine* included illustrated fiction and nonfiction pitched to attract a broad readership. With a circulation of around 500,000, *McClure's* did reach a wide audience. Recognizing the growing public interest in big business and government, he commissioned articles from writers like Ida Tarbell, Lincoln Steffens, and Ray Stannard Baker.

Tarbell's series of articles was later published in book form as *A History of the Standard Oil Company.* Less polemical than Henry Demarest Lloyd's *Wealth Against Commonwealth* (1894), Tarbell described the questionable tactics that John D. Rockefeller and his colleagues had used to build an oil refining and transportation empire that controlled more than 90 percent of the U.S. market. Tarbell was well positioned to write such an exposé because her father had been an executive of the Pure Oil Co. that the Standard Oil juggernaut had engulfed. Tarbell's work stimulated popular resentment against Rockefeller and encouraged the federal government to institute antitrust proceedings.

Lincoln Steffens focused his *McClure's* series on corruption in city and state governments. As with Tarbell, his articles were collected and published as *The Shame of the Cities* in 1904. In addition to describing raw political corruption, Steffens exposed questionable connections between those who supplied utilities and other services to urban populations. The impact of his muckraking crusade came in the form of Progressive reforms that created new forms of city government and encouraged public ownership and management of utilities and transportation systems.

Fictional accounts also had an impact. Frank Norris earned acclaim by writing novels that criticized big business practices. *The Octopus* (1901) told of struggling wheat farmers victimized by an uncaring railroad combination. Published posthumously, *The Pit* (1903) portrayed unscrupulous behavior among those who conducted futures trading in the Chicago grain market.

Perhaps the most notorious muckraking novelist was Upton Sinclair. His book *The Jungle* (1906) told the story of an immigrant family's experiences working in the brawling Chicago stockyards. A committed socialist, Sinclair hoped his book would encourage protests or even revolt among downtrodden workers. But many readers overlooked the ideology to focus on the novel's graphic descriptions of the unsanitary conditions that prevailed in the meatpacking industry. President Roosevelt himself read the book and encouraged passage of the federal Meat Inspection Act and the Pure Food and Drugs Act of 1906.

Although the heyday of the early muckrakers coincided with the Progressive political movement prior to the First World War, investigative reporting and crusading writing has continued to expose corporate and government corruption. More recent muckraking tracts have often generated considerable public interest, but few have triggered as direct responses and regulatory action as did those of Tarbell and Sinclair. Even so, journalists and book authors find a ready audience as they continue to shed light on corporate misbehavior, carrying on the proud tradition of the early muckrakers.

See also Rockefeller, John Davison; Trust.

References and Further Reading

Filler, Louis. *The Muckrakers.* University Park, PA: Pennsylvania State University Press, 1976.

Jensen, Carl. *Stories That Changed America: Muckrakers of the 20th Century.* New York: Seven Stories Press, 2000.

Wilson, Harold S. *McClure's Magazine and the Muckrakers.* Princeton, NJ: Princeton University Press, 1970.

Northern Securities Co. Case

In 1902 President Theodore Roosevelt's Attorney General shocked the U.S. business community by bringing an antitrust suit against the Northern Securities Co., a recently formed holding company that controlled virtually all railroad traffic west of the Mississippi. The Supreme Court ruled in favor of the government in 1904, and ordered that the company be dissolved. As the first successful litigation under the Sherman Antitrust Act of 1890, it earned Roosevelt the title *trustbuster* and set a precedent for dozens of similar cases during the Progressive Era.

Although the Sherman Antitrust Act had enjoyed wide popular support when it was passed in 1890, it had little impact over the next dozen years. Except for being applied against a labor union during the 1894 Pullman Strike, the only major case had been the government's unsuccessful suit against the sugar trust in the 1895 *E. C. Knight Co.* case. That outcome had reassured businessmen that the Sherman Act would not be used against them. Financiers and industrialists therefore engaged in a major round of business consolidation, much of it using the recently developed holding company mechanism.

A holding company seemed to offer an ideal way to resolve a dramatic conflict between two major railroad investment groups. James J. Hill had almost single-handedly built the Great Northern Railway connecting Minnesota to Seattle. By 1900 he had allied himself with J. P. Morgan in a consolidation scheme that brought the Northern Pacific Railroad into his fold. At that point Hill and Morgan were eager to connect their combined system through to Chicago, the rail hub of the United States. They focused their attention on the Chicago, Burlington, and Quincy Railroad (CB&Q), and in the spring of 1901, they convinced Burlington shareholders to sell virtually all of their holdings to the Morgan-Hill group. The final distribution left the Northern Pacific and the Great Northern companies with almost equal shares of the CB&Q.

During these negotiations, two rival railroad magnates, E. H. Harriman and Jacob Schiff had attempted to become co-shareholders on behalf of the Union Pacific Railroad. Morgan and Hill rejected this move. The thwarted financial warriors decided to stage an encircling movement by secretly obtaining a controlling interest in the Northern Pacific. The Union Pacific raiders began buying substantial blocs of Northern Pacific stock, only to foment a buying frenzy on the part of the Morgan-Hill group. The resulting bidding war drove the market price for a share of Northern Pacific stock from around $100 to over $1,000 at its peak. This dramatic battle unsettled markets all around the world, rousing criticism from all quarters.

The combatants themselves realized how destructive this raid had been even to their own interests, so they agreed to abandon their hostile moves and consolidate control in an overarching holding company. After an extensive review, the company's organizers chose New Jersey as the location of their incorporation because of the liberality of its general incorporation laws. They founded the Northern Securities Co. with an initial capitalization of $30,000, but its charter allowed for up to $400 million in capitalized stock.

In relatively short order the former adversaries had transferred to the Northern Securities Co. 76 percent of the Great Northern shares and 96 percent of those for the Northern Pacific. The new company's board of directors contained six from the Northern Pacific, four from the Great Northern, three from the Union Pacific, and two others. Its structure enabled it to control all of the rail traffic in the northwestern United States in close coordination with the Union Pacific. Collectively the combine operated the major railways in eighteen states and its reach stretched from Seattle to St. Louis and from Duluth to San Francisco.

The prominence of the individuals involved and the magnitude of the control the company stood to exercise set off a flurry of action in state courts, but a federal antitrust case quickly grabbed the headlines. President Theodore Roosevelt personally urged U.S. Attorney General Philander C. Knox to investigate whether the Northern Securities Co. violated the Sherman Act. On February 19, 1902, Knox issued a statement indicating his belief that it did. Consequently, he brought suit against the holding company in the U.S. circuit court in St. Paul. When the lower courts decided in favor of the government, the company's lawyers lodged an appeal with the Supreme Court.

In a five to four vote, the higher court ruled against the company. The majority based its decision on the language of the Sherman Antitrust Act that the Northern Securities Co. was truly a "combination in restraint of trade." The company's lawyers had argued that its purpose had been to reduce inefficiency and wasteful competition for the benefit of those the railroads served. But the court concluded that the 1890 legislation was designed to preserve competition as the best way to protect the public's interests, and it ordered the company to be dissolved.

That proved rather difficult because the Northern Securities Co. shares had essentially replaced the Great Northern and Northern Pacific stock certificates. Complex legal and financial steps were necessary to restore the preexisting situation. Even when these steps complying with the court's decision were completed, there was little change in the way the railroad systems operated. Hill, Morgan, Schiff, and Harriman still held controlling blocs of shares in the now separated companies, so they could continue to run them cooperatively rather than competitively even without the overarching holding company.

The Northern Securities case had far more important consequences for other holding companies. The success of the litigation encouraged both the Roosevelt and the succeeding Taft administrations to assail other powerful business combinations. And the precedent the Supreme Court had set assured that the government would win many of these cases.

Equally important, Roosevelt's decision to institute the suit in 1902 brought a halt to the rampant consolidation that the earlier antigovernment *E. C. Knight Co.* decision had encouraged. Corporate managers and financiers were far less likely to consider major consolidation during the Progressive Era. Not until conservative Republican Party dominance returned in the 1920s did another burst of consolidation take place.

See also Antitrust Laws; E. C. Knight Co. Case; Holding Company.

References and Further Reading

Abrams, Richard M. *The Issue of Federal Regulation in the Progressive Era.* Chicago: Rand McNally, 1963.

Ely, Jr., James W. *Railroads and American Law.* Lawrence, KS: University Press of Kansas, 2001.

Hidy, Ralph W. *The Great Northern Railway.* Boston: Harvard Business School Press, 1988.

Klein, Maury. *The Life & Legend of E. H. Harriman.* Chapel Hill, NC: University of North Carolina Press, 2000.

Open Market Operations

Since the early 1920s Federal Reserve banks have bought and sold federal bonds. These transactions are called open market operations because the Fed bids for these bonds along with other potential purchasers on the open market. The effect of these operations is to increase or decrease the amount of cash in circulation, so open market operations provide the system with an alternative to manipulating the rediscount rate for managing the nation's money supply.

The 1913 legislation that established the Federal Reserve System did not envision the use of open market operations to influence the money supply. Subsequent to that legislation, however, the federal government conducted seven war bond drives and a postwar victory bond campaign to help finance its military and diplomatic activities. A substantial reservoir of federal debt in the form of various bonds remained after the war.

In the early 1920s several Federal Reserve banks developed large cash surpluses, money for which they could find no reasonable private investment opportunities. Consequently, they decided to purchase interest-paying federal bonds, bidding against private banks and investors. Beginning in October 1921 and continuing for another six months, the Fed more than tripled its holdings of government securities to a total of more than $600 million. Once purchased, the bonds in the Federal Reserve System remained basically inert investments, but the cash paid for them circulated as part of an enhanced money supply that tended to encourage economic growth and, potentially, price inflation.

Recognizing the important influence their open market operations had on the money supply, the Fed created an Open Market Investment Committee in April 1923 to coordinate the various member banks' activities. As a result, the system began to buy or sell federal bonds on the basis of a deliberately planned strategy. If the banks bought bonds, they increased the money supply. Selling bonds had the opposite effect. As private individuals or entities bought them, they returned cash to the system's vaults. If the banks then held this cash, it remained out of circulation, unavailable for other purposes.

As the decade advanced, the Fed found open market operations to be as effective a method for manipulating the money supply as the interest or rediscount rate it charged for its loans to other banks. Some criticized the Fed for failing to do more to limit the money supply during the last stages of the great bull market. In fact, its ability to use open market operations for that purpose was increasingly limited. Treasury Secretary Andrew Mellon's conservative management of federal finances had enabled him to pay off a substantial portion of the national debt. That meant that millions of dollars worth of bonds were withdrawn, leaving fewer of them available for purchase or sale by the Federal Reserve banks.

For better or worse, no such stringency has existed since the Second World War. Indeed, in an era of persistent budget shortfalls, the Treasury is constantly forced to issue additional bonds. The Federal Reserve System therefore currently has ample opportunity to use open market operations as a powerful tool for managing the money supply.

See also Bull Market; Federal Reserve System, Reform of; Money Supply.

References and Further Reading

Galbraith, John Kenneth. *The Great Crash.* Boston: Houghton Mifflin, 1961.

Sobel, Robert. *The Great Bull Market.* New York: Norton, 1968.
Wells, Donald R. *The Federal Reserve System.* Jefferson, NC: McFarland, 2004.

Parcel Delivery

In the 1920s, the first of the major parcel delivery companies, United Parcel Service (UPS), expanded its operations to eastern cities. Previously, major department stores had maintained in-house services to handle customer deliveries in their market areas. The efficiencies of turning this expensive business over to a firm that could handle deliveries for many different stores gave the fledgling delivery company its start. In succeeding decades, UPS and its rivals like FedEx and DHL established national and worldwide services.

As early department stores expanded their lines well beyond dry goods and clothing, they needed to distribute purchases to their customers' homes. Macy's, Gimbels, and other New York City merchants bought wagons and hired drivers to carry purchases throughout the five boroughs. After the turn of the century, gasoline-powered trucks replaced the wagons, and New Yorkers became accustomed to seeing their distinctively colored vans on the city's streets.

In 1907 James E. Casey led a group of Seattle associates in creating the American Messenger Service. It started small, just a couple of boys riding bicycles, but quickly grew into a major service in West Coast cities. Within a few years, it adopted the name Merchants Parcel Delivery, which accurately described its chief function. The name changed again in 1919 to the United Parcel Service, and UPS has remained in operation ever since.

Ten years later, Casey himself moved to Manhattan, hoping to take advantage of the busiest and most lucrative market. The Associated Dry Goods Corporation, parent company of Lord & Taylor, was Casey's first client, and within a year he had signed up over one hundred other stores. Brown UPS trucks soon became familiar throughout the city, although some well-established companies held out. Macy's finally abandoned its fleet of delivery trucks shortly after the Second World War, the last of the major New York companies to maintain an independent service.

It was far more efficient for a single company to handle deliveries for multiple stores, developing standard routes, regular delivery schedules, and massive warehouse capacity. Personal delivery service became less important when suburban shopping malls began to spring up in the postwar years. With customers carting most of their purchases home in private automobiles, UPS increasingly emphasized intercity delivery as well as company-to-company service. The company's success encouraged competitors like Federal Express, Airborne, and DHL to create and expand their own delivery networks.

These services gradually came to dominate long-distance transportation of smaller packages. The United States Postal Service was perhaps most affected, as these private companies competed directly with its long established parcel post service. In recent years, the rise of Internet shopping has greatly expanded the importance of and the clients for all types of parcel service, and the traditional brown UPS trucks prowl cities, suburbs, and small towns every day.

See also Department Store.

References and Further Reading

Ferry, John William. *A History of the Department Store.* New York: MacMillan, 1960.

Parity

In the 1930s the federal government attempted to manipulate prices of agricultural commodities so they would match those of earlier times. The objective was to bring prices up to parity, a level comparable to prices in the 1910s. Several New Deal programs were designed to bring about parity, but they fell far short of that goal during most of the Great Depression. Even so, the concept that farmers should get a fair return for their efforts continued through and after the Second World War and to a degree still serves as a justification for the current crop subsidy payment programs.

In trying to determine just what a fair price for a given commodity was, both farmers' advocates and many policy makers harked back to the so-called golden era of American agriculture as a proper baseline. The golden era ran from 1910 to 1914, a period when steady or increasing demand meant that agricultural produce sold at relatively high prices. The concept of parity, however, involved more than higher prices. Fair market value meant looking beyond agriculture to compare returns to overall purchasing power. George N. Peek, administrator of the Agricultural Adjustment Administration, explained the policy as one in which agricultural commodities would sell for prices that would enable farmers to afford the same industrial products they had been able to buy during the golden era.

Several aspects of this search for parity were questionable. First, agricultural prices during the golden era were relatively higher than they had been during any previous period of peacetime. Parity goals were thus set at unrealistic levels. A second consideration was that high prices paid to farmers would inevitably mean higher cost foods and other necessities for all Americans regardless of their income or wealth. Why farmers should be singled out for preferential price supports at the cost of society in general was a question never effectively answered. Finally, a most unfortunate aspect of aspiring to guarantee parity was that no program or approach seemed very effective. American farmers ended up being even more disappointed than they might have been if this unrealistic goal had never been promised.

The 1933 Agricultural Adjustment Act outlined several approaches, the most important being production limitations that were expected to induce a scarcity of goods that would inevitably raise prices. But the implementation of limitation programs was deeply flawed, and millions of potential consumers simply did not have the wherewithal to bid prices up even for necessities. The second Agricultural Adjustment Act in 1938 proposed a more reasonable goal of bringing price levels up to 75 percent of parity. A combination of cooperative marketing mechanisms, federal loans to farmers desiring to hold their produce off the market until prices improved, government purchases of surpluses, and federal encouragement of conservation finally did succeed in elevating agricultural prices after years of stagnation.

The outbreak of the Second World War rendered many of the restrictions on agricultural production irrelevant. To a degree, federal officials had to cope with the opposite problem of controlling potentially runaway prices. The government used 110 percent of parity as a yardstick to evaluate its controls, and shortages and rationing became the order of the day rather than production limitations.

As in the 1920s, however, the restoration of peace knocked the market props out from under the agricultural sectors. Variations of the New Deal approaches were revived, many of which continue in force to the present. The primary goal may no longer be to achieve specific adherence to parity goals, but a greatly expanded and pervasive price support structure still characterizes an economic sector that pure market conditions have seldom rewarded to the degree that its members and advocates believe reasonable.

See also Agricultural Adjustment Acts; Great Depression, Character of; Induced Scarcity.

References and Further Reading

Bonnifield, Paul. *The Dust Bowl.* Albuquerque, NM: University of New Mexico Press, 1979.

Perkins, Dexter. *The New Age of Franklin Roosevelt.* Chicago: University of Chicago Press, 1957.

Ponzi Scheme

Also known as a pyramid scheme, a Ponzi scheme involves selling promissory notes to early buyers and then paying the promised dividends with money collected from later buyers. Pyramid schemes advertise huge potential profits and, because early buyers appear to be benefiting enormously, many more people are encouraged to buy. The scheme collapses when no new buyers can be found to keep money flowing into the system.

The most famous American pyramid scheme is named for the unrepentant rogue Charles Ponzi. Operating in Boston in 1920, he claimed to have found a way to make enormous profits off the exchange of international postal coupons; he promised investors a 50 percent bonus in only ninety days. To stimulate even more investment, he paid some early plungers the promised premium in just forty-five days, a policy that only intensified the buying frenzy. Over a period of a few months, thousands of gullible citizens invested nearly $10 million in his get-rich-quick scheme.

Bank regulators and local and federal investigators quickly began questioning his ability to continue redeeming his promissory notes. Their doubts were confirmed when the whole edifice inevitably collapsed. Convicted of postal fraud, Ponzi spent many years languishing in prison and fighting off additional charges both from disappointed investors and various government jurisdictions.

See also Bull Market; Florida Land Bubble.

Reference and Further Reading

Weisman, Stewart L. *Need and Greed.* Syracuse, NY: Syracuse University Press, 1999.

Preferred List

In the 1920s select groups of people took advantage of opportunities to buy shares at below-market prices. Names of favored buyers were often maintained on what was called a *preferred list.* The investigations of the Pecora committee in 1933 exposed this practice, and they led to legislation that outlawed preferred lists.

Prominent people in a number of fields benefited from inclusion on preferred lists. Some of the more predictable were officers and directors of banks, corporations, brokerage houses, and others directly involved in issuing and trading securities. But the benefits of these deals spread well beyond those circles.

A particularly egregious example was the Allegheny Corporation. J. P. Morgan and Co. offered blocs of shares to those on its preferred list at the price of $20 per share. The chairman of the National Democratic Committee, John J. Raskob bought 2,000 shares at that price when the market price had already risen to 33. Within a few months it had reached 57 or almost three times what Raskob paid. Other buyers at the $20 level included the treasurer of the Republican National Committee, the secretary of the U.S. Navy, the speaker of the New York Assembly, and the presidents of the U.S. Chamber of Commerce and the American Bar Association. It is difficult to believe that the corporation did not expect political favors in return for including such influential individuals on its preferred list.

The creation of the Securities and Exchange Commission in 1934 and naming Ferdinand Pecora as one of the first commissioners ensured that preferred lists as such would no longer be tolerated. While the blatancy of creating preferred lists may have disappeared, other methods and types of insider trading have persisted in the years since even though the practice has been made illegal.

See also Bull Market; Securities and Exchange Commission.

References and Further Reading

Broadus, Mitchell. *Depression Decade.* New York: Harper and Row, 1947.

Product Differentiation

To thrive in a market with dozens or hundreds of competitors, a seller must convince potential buyers of the difference or superiority of his product as compared to those of his rivals. This product differentiation can be accomplished either by making major or minor modifications or improvements in the product or simply by mounting an advertising campaign that convinces buyers of the merits or desirability of a particular item.

Brand-name advertising is a common strategy for differentiating one line of goods from others even in the absence of real differences. Nineteenth century manufacturers, distributors, and retailers increasingly used this method to boost sales. By the twentieth century many brand names like aspirin, cellophane, Kleenex, and thermos had become household words and, to that extent, no longer identified a particular manufacturer's product.

Another popular way to differentiate one product from another was to introduce periodic changes. Many of these changes served no other purpose than to create the impression among consumers that a product was superior. General Motors President Alfred P. Sloan elevated this marketing strategy to a new level in the 1920s. Many of the automobiles General Motors sold under one brand name had only minor or inconsequential differences from those in an alternative line. Putting a Buick nameplate on a basic vehicle, however, encouraged customers to pay more for it than for essentially the same car at the Chevrolet dealership down the street.

Creating real or imagined differences in complex products like automobiles is quite easy, but the more basic the product, the more creative the advertising strategy must be. In the 1940s and 1950s, for example, many customers were urged to buy "Blue Coal" to fire their home heating plants. The Blue Coal Co. sent coal through huge breakers that crushed it into standard sized chunks, then actually sprayed the resulting lumps with blue paint. Not surprisingly it burned just like "regular" coal, but the company was able to charge premium prices for its product to consumers who would only settle for "the best."

See also Bracketing the Market; Brand Management; Patents; Sloan, Jr., Alfred Pritchard; Trademarks.

References and Further Reading

Beath, John, and Yannis Katsoulacos. *The Economic Theory of Product Differentiation.* New York: Cambridge University Press, 1991.

Ireland, Norman J. *Product Differentiation and Non-Price Competition.* New York: Blackwell, 1987.

Pujo Committee (Money Trust)

Revelations coming out of antitrust cases in the early 1900s convinced many Americans that a "money trust" existed, controlling financial markets and dictating corporate behavior. A congressional investigation of this possibility took place in late 1912 and early 1913 under the auspices of a subcommittee chaired by Arsène Pujo. The Pujo Committee's hearings shed considerable light on the nation's financial system, but it failed to prove that a money trust per se existed.

As political Progressives became increasingly assertive in the early twentieth century, they examined fundamental American institutions with an eye to imposing governmental regulation or control. The behavior of industrial and banking leaders came under particular scrutiny. Republican President Theodore Roosevelt initiated a trust-busting campaign that his successor, William Howard Taft, pursued even more energetically. Testimony at antitrust trials described special favors, interlocking management arrangements, and what were perceived to be anticompetitive business practices. Although a variety of organizational structures existed, Americans tended to refer to any large-scale, anticompetitive institution as a *trust.*

The names of a few prominent bankers and financial enterprises turned up frequently in reports of antitrust litigation. A belief began to spread that an overarching trust or combination exercised significant control over the nation's financial system. Critics complained that a money trust had come into being, capable of denying capital and credit to newcomers at the same time it supported and strengthened the power and authority of those industries and railroads it favored.

The Progressive movement had gained influence in both political parties by 1910 and, in the elections that year, the Democratic Party gained control of the House of Representatives. Progressive Democrats immediately cranked up the level of congressional concern over business arrangements. They favored a return to a more competitive business environment that would open opportunities to new entrepreneurs and enterprises. To the extent that they believed a business elite was stifling free enterprise, they were willing to propose federal initiatives to restore competition.

It was in this environment that the House Banking and Currency Committee established a subcommittee to investigate "the concentration of money and credit." Louisiana Representative Arsène Pujo chaired the subcommittee, and public interest in the Pujo Committee's activities ran high. The hearings it held in late 1912 and early 1913 included testimony from the nation's leading bankers and financiers. Committee counsel Samuel Untermeyer actually framed the investigation and questioned the witnesses. A wealthy corporate lawyer himself, Untermeyer was well aware of corporate finance mechanisms and his questions put many of his witnesses on the spot.

The inquiry focused on the nation's investment bankers. The subcommittee's report concluded that a small number of individuals and firms had inordinate influence and control over the financing of the nation's railroads and industries. Moreover, these financiers typically insisted on naming one or more members to the boards of directors of the corporations they helped finance, assuring continuing influence over their operations. The committee report noted that 180 bankers associated with the leading houses served as directors of 341 corporations who possessed a total of $25 billion in resources or about one-fifth of all of the corporate wealth in the country.

When J. P. Morgan was called to testify, however, he was unrepentant. He stubbornly insisted that investment bankers like himself actually exercised very little if any influence over the plans and operations of the corporations they financed. He also dismissed concerns about the lack of competitive bidding among the major banks, claiming that familiarity with and confidence in known associates had led to interlocking directorates and other connections.

Not surprisingly Morgan's testimony failed to reassure Untermeyer and the other Democratic members of the subcommittee. The report they issued provided many details about the strong links among various investment firms and generally criticized the system as one that discouraged potential entrepreneurs. At the same time, the investigation failed to find evidence of a deliberately planned or organized collusive structure. The money trust as such did not exist. The absence of such an entity denied the Progressives a specific target for their concerns, and no major legislation arose from the Pujo Committee's findings. In the succeeding months, however, considerable effort was expended on creating the Federal Reserve System, which was designed to exercise greater federal control over financial affairs generally.

See also Federal Reserve System, Creation of; Morgan, John Pierpont (J. P.); Trust.

References and Further Reading

Allen, Frederick Lewis. *The Great Pierpont Morgan.* New York: Harper, 1949.

Carosso, Vincent P. *Investment Banking in America.* Cambridge, MA: Harvard University Press, 1970.

Radio

Commercial broadcasting began in the early 1920s and by the end of the decade over 7 million American homes were equipped with radios. The most dramatic communications development in the decade, radio encouraged scientific and engineering research and development, advertising, and entertainment. It also competed with long-established print media as a news outlet. The network structure radio broadcasters established also served as the prototype for television in later years.

The scientific underpinnings for wireless electronic communication included Thomas Edison's experimentation with vacuum tubes in the late nineteenth century. In 1904 Englishman John A. Fleming crafted a modified vacuum tube that could detect electromagnetic waves. Three years later American Lee De Forest took the process one step further by developing a more sophisticated vacuum tube called a triode, capable of significantly amplifying an electrical signal. Amplification of the very weak signals carried on electromagnetic waves was essential to the building of radio receivers.

An Italian inventor, Guglielmo Marconi, assembled the pieces into an effective radio transmission and reception system. Because it seemed most applicable to maritime uses, British investors took the lead in establishing a company to exploit Marconi's concepts. With the world's largest navy and merchant fleet, Great Britain was interested in ship-to-shore or ship-to-ship communication, neither of which was possible with wires or cables. The Marconi system got its first dramatic publicity when the *Titanic* sent out a distress signal after striking an iceberg in the North Atlantic.

A young Russian immigrant in New York named David Sarnoff was working for General Electric (GE) in 1912, and he picked up these signals on a primitive apparatus. Three years later, he drafted a proposal for his company to create a "radio music box" that consumers would purchase to receive broadcasts from a central location. Sarnoff's concept was premature and, even if GE had been interested, the U.S. Navy seized control of all radio developments once the First World War broke out.

The Navy used radio primarily for ship-to-ship communication through the war, delaying commercial development in the United States. Owen Young, a GE vice president, took the lead in urging the federal government to allow private exploitation, and he played a key role in the formation of a GE subsidiary called the Radio Corporation of America. The name was chosen specifically to emphasize that it was not under foreign influence. The Navy and other companies contributed a pool of patents to encourage the new enterprise.

Still in his twenties, David Sarnoff became head of RCA, and he vigorously pursued his radio music box concept. To his chagrin, a Westinghouse engineer created the first broadcast station, KDKA, in Philadelphia in 1920 to transmit returns from the presidential election that year. Sarnoff countered this competitive threat by setting up broadcast facilities in several cities for a heavyweight boxing championship fight in 1921, and some 300,000 listeners, many of them sitting in specially wired movie theaters, heard the blow-by-blow report.

Realizing he needed a network of broadcasters to reach a wider audience, Sarnoff spent several years identifying affiliates and establishing landlines to enable them to air programming simultaneously. Complex negotiations involving GE, Westinghouse, AT&T, and others eventually led to the establishment of two networks in 1926 both bearing the name National Broadcasting Company. NBC Red was wholly controlled by RCA; NBC Blue belonged to a consortium of owners. In a 1941 divestiture agreement arranged to avoid antitrust litigation, RCA withdrew from NBC Blue and it became known as the American Broadcasting Company (ABC). Several other networks were established in the 1920s, but the Columbia Broadcasting System (CBS) formed by William Paley in 1928 emerged as RCA's chief competitor.

Hundreds of companies jumped in to manufacture radio sets to receive the broadcast programming, and the price for a set ranged from $25 to $400 in the 1920s. The low-cost instruments were well within reach for most Americans, and 7.5 million sets had been sold by 1930. At that point some 500 stations nationwide were on the air. Radios continued to sell well even during the Great Depression because they provided relatively inexpensive access to entertainment.

While some of the programming followed Sarnoff's music box concept, the broadcast industry moved in directions he had not anticipated. Where he had envisioned a subscription system like the one that finances the BBC in Great Britain, American broadcasters relied on advertisers to fund their operations. Commercial radio was just that, with music, news, and dramatic programming constantly interrupted for a word from the sponsor.

One of the most aggressive advertisers was Procter and Gamble (P&G), a company that distributed a broad range of products for the home. In the 1920s some of P&G's programming resembled present-day infomercials, with experts touting the use of their products. In 1933, however, the company sponsored the first of what came to be called soap operas. *Ma Perkins* aired every day for fifteen minutes, and it was so popular that P&G and other sponsors paid for homey programs on all the networks. Most of them played during the workday hours and were specifically targeted at housewives, the most likely buyers of the products advertised.

News reporting also became a major aspect of network broadcasting. President Franklin Roosevelt made very effective use of this communication system. He broadcast the first of his fireside chats a few days after his inauguration, explaining his plans for dealing with the nation's banking crisis. Live broadcasts of sporting events were also popular with listeners and sponsors.

While he was proud of his success at fathering the commercial radio industry, David Sarnoff remained unsatisfied. Throughout the 1930s he aggressively pursued an even greater challenge, but the Second World War interfered with his goal of establishing commercial television. Even so, the network structure, programming, financing, and many other aspects of radio provided useful experience and models for the future.

See also Paley, William Samuel; Sarnoff, David; Television.

References and Further Reading

Albarran, Alan B., and Gregory G. Pitts. *The Radio Broadcasting Industry.* Boston: Allyn and Bacon, 2001.

Barfield, Ray E. *Listening to Radio, 1920–1950.* Westport, CT: Praeger, 1996.

Lyons, Eugene. *David Sarnoff: A Biography.* New York: Harper and Row, 1966.

McCraw, Thomas K. *American Business, 1920–2000.* Wheeling, IL: Harlan Davidson, 2000.

Paper, Lewis J. *Empire: William S. Paley and the Making of CBS.* New York: St. Martin's Press, 1987.

Reciprocity

When one trading nation offers to reduce the duty charged on a particular import, the exporting country may make a similar concession on something it imports from the first country. Worked out on a reciprocal basis, such reductions typically lead to lower tariff rates on both sides. While many had advocated reciprocity for years, it did not become the primary approach to American trade policy until the United States implemented the Reciprocal Trade Agreements Act of 1934.

Throughout the nineteenth century, the United States pursued a unilateral tariff policy characterized by politically inspired trade barriers. A series of tariff acts erected those barriers. The customs duties levied in these acts fluctuated over time, with the

Whigs and their Republican successors generally favoring higher "protective" rates. These often reflected the successful lobbying efforts of American manufacturers who maintained that their production costs were higher than those in other countries. Ostensibly to foster domestic industry and promote national self-sufficiency, high tariff rates were maintained to discourage imports or, at the very least, raise the price of imported goods to match the level of those produced in the United States.

Occasionally certain American industrialists requested reductions in the tariff levels for particular imports that served as raw materials for their operations. Other American manufacturers complained that the high import duties other countries levied on their products limited their ability to sell overseas. Locked as they were in a tariff structure dictated by domestic political considerations, critics of protective tariffs often found it easier to convince government officials to consider individualized, targeted reductions. These in turn became prime subjects for reciprocal trade negotiations.

As has so often been the case in American history, sugar tariffs provide an interesting case in point. Responsive to southern cane growers and western sugar beet producers, the U.S. Congress stipulated high duties on sugar imported from abroad. Spain's colony Cuba was the most prolific potential exporter, but American planters who had settled in Hawaii saw themselves as victims of excessive protectionism on the part of the United States. Simultaneously, domestic manufacturers and exporters increasingly viewed Hawaii as a potentially profitable market for American goods. To satisfy both groups, the United States worked out a reciprocal trade agreement that reduced the American duty on Hawaiian sugar and, simultaneously, the Hawaiian kingdom's levies on goods imported from the United States. This arrangement became moot, of course, when the United States annexed Hawaii as a colony in 1898.

In 1922 the Republican-controlled Congress raised protective rates in the Fordney-McCumber Act of 1922, but included a flexible tariff provision. Although it had been added to allow American trade policy to be more responsive to changing global economic conditions, procedural complications prevented all but a few changes. The United States Tariff Commission could not even recommend a change without conducting a thorough background study and then holding public hearings. In 1924 the commission finally recommended a reduction in the tariff on Cuban sugar from 1.76 cents per pound to 1.23 cents. President Coolidge refused to take any action in an election year; in 1925 he rejected the recommendation outright.

Advocates of reciprocity suffered an even worse defeat in 1930 when the Hawley-Smoot Act raised rates even higher than the 1922 levels. The Republican sponsors of the bill claimed that higher tariffs would protect the American economy from external threats. Shortly thereafter, the United States and all of its trading partners plunged into a devastating worldwide depression. Many other nations responded like the Hoover administration, pursuing strategies that promoted autarky, a policy designed to make their national economies self-sufficient. International trade declined precipitously, intensifying the global depression.

Many of the advisors President Franklin Roosevelt gathered around him were either old-line Democratic advocates of free trade or, at least, of developing mutually beneficial reciprocal trade arrangements. Focused as he was on domestic crises in banking, industry, and agriculture, Roosevelt was slow to adopt a trade policy. A former Democratic congressman from Tennessee who had long advocated reciprocity, Secretary of State Cordell Hull led the assault on protectionism. The Democrats who controlled Congress responded by passing the Reciprocal Trade Agreements Act of 1934 with large majorities in both houses. Some critics complained that the new policy transferred tariff rate setting from Congress to the State Department, but the plan withstood a constitutional challenge.

The law allowed the president to reduce the duty on a particular commodity up to 50 percent in return for reciprocal tariff reductions by a trading partner. In the next several years, the United States negotiated reciprocal trade agreements with dozens of other nations, and the effect was a general decline in American tariff rates. Negotiators frequently identified the nation that was the principal supplier of a particular import and worked out reciprocal concessions with that nation. Because the United States already had most-favored-nation agreements in place with many nations around the world, it had to extend to them the same concessions it had given the principal supplier. In this way, tariff reductions on particular commodities quickly took effect for virtually all of the country's trading partners. The protectionism that had traditionally characterized American international trade gradually began to fade away.

Reciprocity became the cornerstone of all U.S. international trade policy. During the Second World War and afterwards, the United States used this mechanism to energetically push for lower trade barriers. Reciprocity lies at the heart of the General Agreement on Tariffs and Trade (GATT) that the United States negotiated along with twenty-two other nations beginning in 1946. In 1994 the World Trade Organization (WTO) came into existence, replacing the GATT but retaining reciprocity as a major mechanism for promoting world trade.

See also Autarky; Creditor Nation; Free List; GATT; Protective Tariff; Trade Balance.

References and Further Reading

Bayard, Thomas O. 1994. *Reciprocity and Retaliation in U.S. Trade Policy.* Washington, DC: Institute for International Economics, 1994.

Dobson, John M. *Two Centuries of Tariffs.* Washington, DC: U.S. International Trade Commission, 1976.

Tate, Merze. *Hawaii: Reciprocity or Annexation.* East Lansing, MI: Michigan State University Press, 1968.

Reconstruction Finance Corporation

In 1932 President Hoover called for the creation of the Reconstruction Finance Corporation (RFC) to provide short-term loans primarily to banks to increase their credit liquidity. These loans were expected to cause a trickle-down phenomenon to reinvigorate the economy on the verge of the Great Depression. The RFC loaned over $1.5 billion, but it failed to stem the economic decline. It remained in existence until 1953 as a federal lending agency for a variety of purposes.

The Reconstruction Finance Corporation was a bridge between the Republican Party's limited government approach and the mixed economy of the New Deal. Throughout his years as secretary of commerce and president, Herbert Hoover consistently advocated organized efforts to deal with economic issues. Until 1932, however, he relied on private or volunteer groups to supply the needed organization. When the stock market tumbled in 1929, for example, bankers and investment houses attempted to counter the trend, but the Hoover administration remained largely on the sidelines.

By late 1931 the president had apparently become convinced that softness in the nation's credit system was a major factor causing the economic downturn. In line with his traditional views, he urged the nation's banking community to create a private lending agency called the National Credit Corporation (NCC). This organization would pool resources to make loans to banks suffering from temporary insolvency. The NCC did come into existence and make some loans, but it never had enough resources to meet the need. It quickly closed down when the federally financed and controlled Reconstruction Finance Corporation became operational.

The model for the RFC was the War Finance Commission (WFC) created in 1918 to lend money to industries engaged in war work. It expanded its mission to include loans to exporters, agricultural enterprises, and other sectors. In 1924 Congress ordered it to begin liquidation, and it closed its doors five years later, just prior to the stock market crash.

Hoover reluctantly concluded that the economic decline in the early 1930s posed such a serious threat to the nation's well-being that a federal rather than a private agency needed to step in. His purpose was to restore confidence in the economy by having the government make short-term loans to banks and other entities that were suffering temporary cash or credit shortages. He hoped these loans would restart stalled sectors and the benefits would trickle down or percolate through the whole economy. Representative Fiorello La Guardia (D-NY) dismissed the proposal as "a millionaire's dole . . . a reward for speculation and unscrupulous bond pluggers."

Even so, substantial majorities in both houses approved the bill in January 1932 along with an authorization of half a billion dollars. The RFC immediately began processing loan applications, but many recipients used the funds to offset prior obligations or to stabilize their own credit. Very little money trickled down to consumers. By the end of the year, the RFC had increased its outstanding loans to $1.5 billion and given them to a much broader array of industries. Except for a relatively brief pause early in 1932, however, the economic slide continued.

The RFC was the Hoover administration's only substantial federal initiative aimed at halting the deflationary tide. When Franklin Roosevelt became president, he and his New Dealers introduced a number of relief, recovery, and reform programs designed to restart the economy. Interestingly enough, they also retained the RFC as a useful vehicle for managing federal loan programs. It operated throughout the 1930s and the 1940s, focusing its activities first on anti-Depression and later wartime projects. It finally closed in 1953.

See also Crash; Great Depression, Character of.

References and Further Reading

Fausold, Martin L. *The Presidency of Herbert Hoover.* Lawrence, KS: University Press of Kansas, 1985.

Olson, James Stuart. *Herbert Hoover and the Reconstruction Finance Corporation, 1931–1933.* Ames, IA: Iowa State University Press, 1977.

Recovery

Although the National Industrial Recovery Act of 1933 authorized the largest peacetime government involvement in business affairs in American history, it failed in its chief objective. Recovery from the Great Depression apparently could not be dictated from above. Countless modifications, adjustments, changes, and, most of all, time were needed to reinvigorate the shell-shocked economy. Massive deficit spending and wartime demand ultimately brought about the recovery that the New Deal programs failed to accomplish.

The economy was almost completely stalled by the time of Franklin Roosevelt's inauguration as president in March 1933. In his first hundred days in office, he sponsored fifteen major legislative initiatives, each focused on particular problem areas. The nation had become highly industrialized so it was only natural that one of the key New Deal programs was the passage of the National Industrial Recovery Act (NIRA).

Dozens of often contradictory concepts were crammed into the hastily written bill. Like the agricultural recovery program that was passed almost simultaneously, the primary goal of the NIRA was to manage production with the somewhat incompatible goals of raising prices and stimulating consumer demand. To do so, the new industrial recovery program relied on inducing scarcities across the board. This unfortunate reliance on induced scarcity was only one of a number of flaws in the recovery program.

Precedents set by the War Industries Board during the First World War convinced policy makers that they could accomplish their goals. Another key historical factor was the associationalism that had received considerable attention and federal encouragement in the 1920s. The codes of ethical behavior and fair practices that trade associations had developed provided a basis for the more comprehensive codes the NIRA envisioned.

Administrative leadership for the initiative fell to Hugh Johnson, a veteran of the War Industries Board and a vigorous advocate of national planning. President Roosevelt appointed him head of the National Recovery Administration (NRA). This agency had a number of responsibilities including helping industries draft codes of behavior, reviewing and approving their efforts, and monitoring the operation of resulting industrial processes. Not incidentally, the NRA also aggressively publicized its work, developed a distinctive logo with a blue eagle, and encouraged both producers and consumers to support the program.

To earn the right to fly the blue eagle flag, members of an industrial sector had to abide by the appropriate NRA code. In those industries where effective trade associations existed, the NRA code often closely resembled the association's previously developed set of standards. In other sectors, drafting a reasonable code was far more time-consuming and complex. In all instances, the drafting body was supposed to include representatives of producers, the relevant labor force, and consumers. In practice, producers exercised the major influence. Except for adhering to the NIRA's provisions for recognizing the right of organized labor to bargain collectively and outlining minimum wage levels and reasonable working conditions, the codes focused on production and pricing.

To induce scarcity or at least discourage overproduction in a given sector, many of the industrial codes attempted to set production limits. Once national output goals had been specified, each participant was assigned a production quota. These inevitably discouraged expansion and innovation as well as prevented new entrants from joining the industry. Price setting accompanied the production limits. Reflecting the power of the manufacturers and producers who dominated the writing of the codes, prices were pegged to provide reasonable profits regardless of their impact on consumer demand or ability to pay.

Factories that operated in accordance with the NRA code for their industry could advertise their adherence. Consumers placed blue eagle decals on their windows, signifying their commitment to buy only items produced in compliance with the codes. The major sanction available to Hugh Johnson's staff was its ability to deny a manufacturer the right to display the NRA symbol.

An enormous wave of positive sentiment on all sides greeted the implementation of the NRA program. But the complexities of developing detailed codes for hundreds of sectors and subsectors quickly undermined the initial enthusiasm. And almost immediately, some firms and, indeed, some whole sectors began exploiting loopholes or delaying implementation of the constrictive codes. Worse still, few positive results seemed to arise from this complex structure. Industrial recovery simply did not occur.

Disillusionment with the whole scheme had therefore become widespread long before the *Schecter* case reached the Supreme Court in 1935. The Schecter Brothers Co. processed poultry on Long Island and claimed that because its products sold almost exclusively across the East River in New York City, it was not engaged in interstate commerce. The court agreed, striking down the chief justification for federal regulation of industrial behavior. The decision overturned the National Industrial Recovery Act and, with it, the entire administrative structure it had spawned.

Hardly anyone mourned its demise. Many of the industries continued to operate generally within the parameters of the NRA codes, but on a voluntary basis and only if it benefited them directly. Consumer prices bounced around, buffeted by the natural forces of competition. New entrants and new industries could more easily arise.

Only organized labor felt aggrieved. Because the ruling Democratic Party was beholden to and supportive of labor, Congress and the president did rescue the labor provisions contained in Section 7(a) of the NIRA. The National Labor Relations Act of 1935 contained much of the same language as the earlier law, assuring workers the right to organize and to bargain collectively. The American Federation of Labor and the Congress of Industrial Organization made substantial gains in major industries like steel and automobiles in the late 1930s with backing from the National Labor Relations Board.

Ironically, despite the rather humiliating collapse of the NRA system in 1935, a similar and even more elaborate apparatus reappeared a few years later. In the early 1940s, mobilization for the Second World War necessitated the revival or reinstitution of many aspects of a national economic planning strategy. The Supplies, Planning and Allocation Board, the Office of Price Administration, and dozens of other federal agencies ultimately controlled production, pricing, and distribution of the nation's industrial output far more thoroughly than the NRA ever would or could have.

See also Agricultural Adjustment Acts; Induced Scarcity; Johnson, Hugh; War Industries Board.

References and Further Reading

Bernstein, Michael A. *The Great Depression*. New York: Cambridge University Press, 1987.

Fine, Sidney. *The Automobile under the Blue Eagle*. Ann Arbor, MI: University of Michigan Press, 1963.

Hawley, Ellis. *The New Deal and the Problem of Monopoly*. New York: Fordham University Press, 1995.

Relief

Massive unemployment overwhelmed private and local efforts to assist the destitute in the depths of the Great Depression. The federal government eventually assumed responsibility for providing relief to those without work. So many different kinds of people were suffering that no single approach seemed appropriate. As a result, President Franklin Roosevelt's administration cobbled together a variety of programs, each aimed at a particular segment of the population in need. Although initially conceived as short-term solutions, many of these programs persisted into the early 1940s.

As governor of New York, Roosevelt had won acclaim for using state funds to relieve economic distress. In his campaign for the presidency in 1932, his reputation as a "reliefer" contrasted sharply with that of his opponent, incumbent Republican President Herbert Hoover. While no clear plans had been articulated by the time of Roosevelt's inauguration in March 1933, his advisors were considering literally dozens of ideas.

Many of these advisors had Progressive credentials, and they were quite willing to have the government step in when the private economy failed to do so. Progressives also favored conservation. These two factors came together in the first major relief program: the Civilian Conservation Corps (CCC). The CCC focused on young men without job prospects. They were enrolled in the Corps, often sent far from home, and housed in camps run by military officers. CCC boys were trained to do outdoor projects like building flood-control dams and levees, replanting forests, clearing brush, and other projects designed to improve or preserve the environment. Paid a dollar a day, most shipped that dollar home to their destitute families. Over two million men had served in the CCC by the time it closed down in the early 1940s.

Several other relief programs focused on public works projects. The Public Works Administration (PWA) also created in 1933 got off to a slow start because its administrator, Secretary of the Interior Harold Ickes, insisted on personally approving the plans for every project. In 1935 a much more ambitious program called the Works Progress Administration (WPA) hired millions of unemployed people and set them to work on all sorts of projects. Many of these were public works projects the PWA had failed to take on such as building post offices, bridges, and highways. These projects significantly improved the nation's infrastructure.

The WPA inevitably ended up hiring many people with special skills that the private economy simply could not absorb. The administration therefore created specialized initiatives to exploit their talents. Actors in the Federal Theater Project took live drama to communities all across the country. The Federal Writers Project dispatched historians and others throughout the country where they researched local records and wrote town and county histories. The National Youth Administration paid students a stipend to stay in school either to complete their degrees or pursue graduate studies. That kept them out of the ranks of the unemployed. Eleven million people participated in WPA programs over the course of its existence.

Older Americans were far less likely to enroll in these often demanding programs, however. To make matters worse, very few people had pensions. Company retirement programs were almost nonexistent. Only the most fortunate workers had been able to accumulate savings, and the onset of the Great Depression quickly ate into those resources. To help the destitute cope, Congress passed the Social Security Act in 1935. It provided retired people with monthly relief checks, funded by mandatory contributions from workers and their employers. From the very first, Social Security was a transfer rather than a pension program, shifting money directly from the employed to the retired. A companion program set aside funding for people thrown out of work through no fault of their own.

Whether these relief programs focused on jobless teenagers, unemployed artists and intellectuals, surplus industrial workers, or superannuated retirees, they all had a common impact. They distributed federal money to people very likely to spend it immediately. To that extent, they directly responded to the underconsumption problem that had helped trigger the Great Depression. Because of the multiplier effect, every dollar spent on these programs generated a cascading effect that flowed through the economy.

Several factors ultimately limited the impact of these programs and of the money they put into circulation. The government never felt comfortable competing with private enterprise, so it restricted its support to projects that no one else would have tackled. Federal authorities were also loath to pour too much funding into the relief programs, concerned as they were to avoid deficit spending. At the same time, many Americans were equally uncomfortable having to resort to the federal "dole." In those years the work ethic was strongly ingrained in American society, and people were embarrassed to have to rely on government charity.

But for the millions who overcame such qualms, the New Deal relief programs were a godsend. They may have done little to end the Depression, but they definitely helped people survive its vicissitudes. Most of these programs were shelved when a wartime boom developed in the 1940s. Social Security, however, has remained a fundamental safety net for older Americans and others in need ever since. It deserves recognition along with the many New Deal reforms as a creditable benefit drawn from the nation's most severe economic crises.

See also Recovery; Underconsumption.

References and Further Reading

Rose, Nancy Ellen. *Put to Work: Relief Programs in the Great Depression.* New York: Monthly Review Press, 1994.

Schieber, Sylvester J., and John B. Shoven. *The Real Deal.* New Haven, CT: Yale University Press, 1999.

Singleton, Jeff. *The American Dole.* Westport, CT: Greenwood, 2000.

Rule of Reason

In two landmark antitrust cases in 1911 the U.S. Supreme Court promulgated a *rule of reason* regarding large-scale business combinations. In both cases, the justices noted that neither size nor market share alone was enough to compel the dissolution of a combination. Instead, the entity had to have engaged in unreasonable behavior that limited competition or otherwise impeded fair trade. This conclusion provided some comfort to corporate leaders at the same time it roused resentment from dedicated Progressive reformers. Even so, the rule of reason has continued to be a factor in antitrust cases ever since.

The justices decided that the rule of reason was, in itself, something they should consider when handling a case brought under the Sherman Antitrust Act of 1890. The key provision in that legislation's first section states that "every contract, combination in the form of trust or otherwise, or conspiracy, in restraint of trade or commerce is . . . declared to be illegal." When the law finally began being applied in the early 1900s, a literal interpretation of that provision suggested that any arrangement that seemed to limit competition was illegal. Some of the first dissolution decisions appeared to apply that standard to the corporation or business combination being sued.

During that same period, however, a number of Progressive thinkers including President Theodore Roosevelt became convinced that many large-scale business combinations were ultimately beneficial. They might reduce production costs, enhance efficiencies of mass production, eliminate waste, and even reduce consumer prices. Moreover, the development of larger and larger combinations seemed a natural outgrowth of an expanding nation and the application of modern technologies. Many public and private figures urged the government to moderate or even abandon its assault on big business.

Simultaneously, the courts were grappling with the apparent conflict between the rights of individuals to buy and manage their property in any way they chose and the expectations or needs of society as a whole. The United States had a long-standing tradition of supporting and protecting individual property rights. The judges and justices who considered antitrust cases were naturally sensitive to this tradition.

In 1911 two major antitrust cases reached the Supreme Court. One was a suit against the Standard Oil Trust; the other involved the American Tobacco Co. Both of these sprawling and powerful entities exercised near monopoly control over the processing and distribution of petroleum and tobacco products in the United States. If the justices chose to apply a literal interpretation of the Sherman Act, both these trusts would be illegal and should be dismantled.

At that point, however, a majority of the court had become convinced that size or market share alone were not appropriate measures for determining whether or not a combination should be broken up. They chose instead to investigate the question of whether the combination had behaved properly or improperly. In both instances, a majority of the justices concluded that both Standard Oil and the American Tobacco Co. had behaved unscrupulously and, thus, had exercised unreasonable restraint of trade.

The reaction to these two decisions was understandably mixed. Those who wished to promote ethical behavior welcomed the Court's orders to dissolve the combinations. At the same time, businessmen interested in promulgating ever larger combinations were reassured that as long as they behaved "reasonably" they could avoid litigation under the antitrust act. When the antitrust case against the United States Steel Corporation eventually reached the Supreme Court in 1920, the justices concluded that it did not violate the Sherman Act. Even though it controlled upwards of 80 percent of all steel production in the United States at that point, it had not used "unreasonable" methods and therefore should be allowed to continue operating.

The promulgation of the rule of reason shocked and outraged literalists and a good many outspoken Progressive reformers. For many of them, bigness alone gave the combinations an inherent ability to constrain competition. Worse yet, the Supreme Court did not at that time, or in the future, carefully define just where the line lay between what it would consider reasonable and unreasonable behavior. This inexact, fuzzy principle allowed for broad, subjective determination and decisions.

It was hardly surprising, therefore, that disappointed critics mounted an energetic campaign to revise the antitrust laws. Their goal was to state explicitly just what kinds of behavior they considered unacceptable. Explicit definitions would eliminate the discretion of the federal court system, a system that the reformers considered hopelessly conservative and pro-business. The Democratically controlled Congress developed just such a bill in 1914, and Progressive Democratic President Woodrow Wilson signed the resulting Clayton Act into law.

Although the strictures of the Clayton Act did somewhat limit judicial discretion, the rule of reason continued to serve as a precedent for many subsequent rulings. It encouraged further combinations during the First World War and, especially, during the 1920s. In the long run, both the Sherman Act and the Clayton Act were far less effective reform measures due to the repeated use of the rule of reason.

See also Antitrust Laws; Clayton Antitrust Act; Northern Securities Co. Case; Trust.

References and Further Reading

Peritz, Rudolph J. R. *Competition Policy in America, 1888–1992.* New York: Oxford University Press, 1996.

Shenefield, John H., and Irwin M. Stelzer. *The Antitrust Laws.* Washington, DC: AEI Press, 2001.

Sullivan, E. Thomas. *The Political Economy of the Sherman Act.* New York: Oxford University Press, 1991.

Scientific Management

The goal of scientific management was to arrange factory layouts and simplify each worker's task to promote increased industrial productivity. Popularized by Frederick W. Taylor, scientific management was also known as *Taylorism,* and it stimulated considerable change in both manufacturing techniques and labor utilization in the early twentieth century.

As the nineteenth century drew to a close, many American industrial enterprises were consolidating into larger and larger units. Plant managers and foremen operating in behemoth factories faced unprecedented problems in organizing production flow and motivating workers. While many changes developed through natural evolution, a few visionaries believed that the same sort of scientific and technical thinking that helped foster these industrial giants could be applied to the task of making them more efficient.

The leading exponent of this scientific management approach was Frederick W. Taylor. As a teenager, he had worked as an apprentice pattern maker at the Enterprise Hydraulic Works in Philadelphia. Pattern making required very precise drafting and modeling skills, both of which matched Taylor's talents. When he moved on to the Midvale Tool Co. he became intrigued with improving the performance of tool steel implements.

In the early 1880s he began using a stopwatch to evaluate workers' behaviors. Much of his subsequent work was in line with that of a developing group of professionals who used time and motion studies to increase worker productivity. Indeed, Taylor collaborated closely with two of the most well-known time-and-motion experts, Frank

Gilbreth and Ernestine Gilbreth Carey. This couple put their professional skills into practice in raising a family of twelve children. Their book *Cheaper by the Dozen* became a bestseller and was made into a popular film.

Taylor was an outspoken advocate of a piecework wage system to encourage individual workers. His goal was to break each job into small steps, simplifying the task and eliminating wasted motions. This process also encouraged hiring unskilled workers as opposed to skilled craftsmen. He conducted "scientific" studies to determine an optimum output for each job and then proposed higher pay scales for those workers who exceeded these quotas on a daily basis. Not surprisingly many workers found these quotas difficult to maintain and resented being reduced to "cogs in the machinery."

Managing the activities of individual workers required new supervisory skills as well. Taylor pioneered the concept of "functional foremen" whose duties like those of the workers they managed were also simplified and focused. Specialists like speed bosses, quality inspectors, and other narrowly focused functionaries replaced the highly skilled generalists who had previously overseen factory operations.

On a broader level, reorganizing the flow of work on a factory floor was also seen as an essential factor in increasing productivity. To meet Taylor's quotas, workers had to have ready and continuing access to the tools, parts, and supplies needed for each task. While Taylor had no direct role in the factory-wide moving assembly line that Henry Ford and his colleagues established in 1913, the new system exploited many principles of Taylorism.

Scientific management became very popular with industrialists and plant managers. It even won some support among the Progressives, a political movement that lauded the participation of experts in government. At the same time, Taylorism roused strenuous opposition from labor organizers who ran the gamut from the highly skilled craft-union spokesmen of the American Federation of Labor to the committed socialists of the International Workers of the World.

Although Taylor died in 1915, the concepts and techniques he advocated continued to win converts. The remarkable increase in workers' productivity that helped fuel the bull market of the 1920s stemmed in large measure from the application of scientific management principles. Industrialists around the world adopted Taylorism to increase their factory efficiency as well. All modern manufacturing enterprises contain some elements of the scientific management doctrine.

See also Ford, Henry; Moving Assembly Line; Taylor, Frederick Winslow.

References and Further Reading

Gabor, Andrea. *Capitalist Philosophers.* New York: Times Business, 2000.

Kanigel, Robert. *The One Best Way.* New York: Viking, 1997.

Wrege, Charles D., and Ronald G. Greenwood. *Frederick W. Taylor, the Father of Scientific Management.* Homewood, IL: Business One Irwin, 1991.

Securities and Exchange Commission

The creation of the Securities and Exchange Commission (SEC) in the summer of 1934 was a predictable response to the manipulation and lack of regulation that had bedeviled the stock exchanges during the 1920s. The commission's five members were charged with overseeing the very core of the nation's capitalist system: buying and selling stocks and bonds. Unlike many of the emergency New Deal programs, the commission has remained a primary federal watchdog ever since with increasing authority and scope.

Although many critics believed that federal intervention into the unregulated and unregimented stock exchanges was long overdue, the development of an appropriate oversight mechanism required exhaustive investigation and careful deliberation. Early

New Deal legislation had outlawed some practices such as direct links between banking and brokerage houses, but the extent and depth of unjustifiable behavior required more aggressive measures.

The most persuasive investigation took place over nearly two years in a subcommittee of the Senate Committee on Banking and Currency. Ferdinand Pecora became this group's lead counsel in 1933, and revelations from the Pecora Committee often shocked an already jaded and cynical public. Witnesses described the use of preferred lists of powerful individuals who bought stocks at prices well below those available to the general public. Stock exchange officials seemed unperturbed by the formation of bull or bear pools that, often through selling shares among their members, artificially raised or lowered stock prices. Investment trusts and public utility holding companies came in for particular criticism, and the committee's thousands of pages of testimony clearly illustrated that a great many corporations systematically disseminated false or misleading information to enhance the values of their shares.

The Securities Act of 1933 and the Securities Exchange Act of 1934 stipulated a number of rules and requirements for those engaged in marketing stocks. The legislation assigned the Securities and Exchange Commission responsibility for implementing the bolder and some would say more intrusive federal policy. Pecora himself was one of the five commissioners the president appointed, and the SEC began operations on June 30, 1934.

A primary focus in the commission's early days was ensuring honesty and full disclosure. Corporations had to register with the SEC and publish accurate prospectuses prior to offering shares for sale. Each potential investor had to be supplied with a prospectus. A company's annual reports had to reflect its true financial status. The SEC lacked authority to prosecute those who violated its rules, but it worked closely with the attorney general who could sue malefactors for criminal behavior. It was to everyone's advantage to abide by the commission's requirements, especially in face of the widespread public disillusionment and fear that the stock market crash had engendered.

In subsequent years additional legislation expanded the scope of the SEC's actions. For example, the commissioners played the central role in enforcing the Public Utilities Holding Company Act of 1935. It was triggered by the dramatic collapse of rickety holding company pyramids like the one Sam Insull had created. The SEC was charged with tearing down the pyramids by insisting that intervening layers of holding companies be abolished. A single, overarching holding company was still permissible, coordinating the activities of a series of operating companies. But the prohibition against intervening layers meant that the managers of a public utility holding company inevitably remained much more involved with and sensitive to the needs of both the operating companies and their customers.

By 1937 the SEC was deeply involved in sorting through the elaborate jungle of investment trusts that had sprung up in the heady days of the bull market. Like other investment opportunities, the trusts were obligated to provide full disclosure, and countless examples of deception and outright fraud were exposed. The commission also studied the behavior of financial advisors who had frequently misled their clients. Recommendations based on the SEC's exhaustive survey heavily influenced the strictures included in the 1940 Investment Company Act and the Investment Advisors Act.

Much of what the SEC handled in its early years were past abuses. Its full disclosure rules for corporations combined with the numerous guidelines and regulations it imposed on the stock exchanges themselves helped restore public confidence in the system. Potential buyers had access to much better information in making their investment decisions. Inevitably, however, inventive financiers and speculators continued to create new challenges for the commission. In the late twentieth century, for example, the SEC came under fire for its failure to monitor the misleading auditing techniques and other strategies corporations like Enron used to convince people to bid up their stocks. Even so, the commission remains a vital federal watchdog, one that no one would seriously consider abolishing.

See also Brokers' Loans; Bull Market; Crash; Leveraged Investment Trust; Preferred List.

References and Further Reading

Mitchell, Broadus. *Depression Decade.* New York: Harper and Row, 1947.

Pecora, Ferdinand. *Wall Street Under Oath.* New York: A. M. Kelley, 1968.

Selden Patent

In 1895 George B. Selden obtained a U.S. patent for a gasoline-powered automobile. The description of the vehicle was broad enough to encompass virtually any car manufactured. Over the next decade and a half, auto manufacturers either took out a license under the Selden patent or fought against it. In 1911 Henry Ford won a long legal battle that effectively ended this attempt to reap royalties from every automobile in America.

George Selden was a classic American type—the inveterate tinkerer. During the daytime he worked as an attorney specializing in patent law. In his spare time he worked in a basement in Rochester, New York, experimenting with steam and gasoline engines that he hoped would power a self-propelled carriage. By 1879 he had a partially completed three-cylinder gasoline engine, but that was as close as he ever came to actually building an automobile.

In that same year, however, he filed preliminary papers for a patent describing a mechanical road carriage powered by a gasoline engine. Although the U.S. Patent Office issued hundreds of other patents related to automobile parts and techniques, Selden's was the first application that brought together all of the elements of a basic vehicle. Typically, a working model was submitted to the patent office, but Selden had never completed a vehicle, and he was determined to pursue his patent on the basis of descriptions and diagrams alone.

For the next sixteen years, Selden and Patent Office officials exchanged correspondence about his pending patent. The office's procedures gave an applicant up to two years to respond to its queries, and Selden took maximum advantage of that delay, providing answers at the last possible moment, answers that triggered additional queries. Enormous progress had been made around the world in the development of automobiles by 1895 when Selden completed his final modifications and received his patent.

Having derived virtually no benefit from the patent on his own, Selden assigned it to what became the Electric Vehicle Co. in 1900. This company eventually failed in its main goal of creating electric cab fleets for eastern cities. To generate capital to offset its huge losses, the company began serving notice on manufacturers of gasoline-powered automobiles that they were infringing on the Selden patent.

Some car makers agreed to pay royalties to the company, but others either ignored it or fought back. One prominent target was Alexander Winton, whose company resisted for some time and at great cost before agreeing. A group of independent automakers hoping at least to exercise some control created the Association of Licensed Automobile Manufacturers (ALAM) in 1903. It collected a 1.25 percent royalty from all of its licensees on each car built, retaining .5 percent for itself and paying the remaining .75 percent to the Electric Vehicle Co., holder of the Selden patent.

The ALAM mounted aggressive advertising campaigns and harassed companies that were reluctant to take out licenses. Those who had paid their royalties could use ALAM certification in their advertisements to reassure customers that their products were "legitimate." As the number of automobiles manufactured rose exponentially each year, the ALAM generated increasing funds for its publicity and enforcement campaigns. By 1910 it was powerful enough to restrict some of its licensees to the manufacture of particular types of vehicles or to impose quotas on their output.

Henry Ford developed his classic Model T car in 1908 and devoted the next several years to streamlining its production. A skilled mechanic, inventor, and innovator, Ford had no intention of paying royalties to someone for concocting a vaguely worded description that was now long out of date. Being told that his basic cars might not be sophisticated enough to qualify for an ALAM stamp of approval only intensified his determination to break its power.

The conflict between Ford and the ALAM reached its first conclusion in a federal district court decision in 1909 that upheld the Selden patent and made the association even more intrusive. Ford appealed the case, however, and won a favorable ruling in January 1911. The decision questioned whether such a vague patent should ever have been issued in the first place. Moreover, automotive technology had made enormous progress since 1879, and current production techniques and cars were far different from those envisioned in Selden's patent.

The decision destroyed the ALAM and made Ford a hero among auto manufacturers. It also enhanced his reputation among the American people. He had taken on and defeated what appeared to be little more than a power-hungry attempt to monopolize and control a major industrial sector. Its defeat fit right in with the antitrust sentiments that prevailed in the Progressive Era.

See also Electric Car; Ford, Henry; Patents.

References and Further Reading

Brinkley, Douglas. *Wheels for the World.* New York: Viking, 2003.

Flink, James J. *The Car Culture.* Cambridge, MA: MIT Press, 1975.

Greenleaf, William. *Monopoly on Wheels.* Detroit, MI: Wayne State University Press, 1961.

Standardization

In the 1920s the Commerce Department became an effective advocate for standardization and simplification. Secretary of Commerce Herbert Hoover was a strong proponent of eliminating waste of all sorts, and he believed that issuing standards for products and component parts would accomplish that goal. Many of the standards developed in the 1920s remain in use today.

American inventiveness spawned an enormous number and variety of products and methods. In many instances individual manufacturers produced items that were so unique that they could not be interchanged with those of other producers. Replacement parts only worked in proprietary products, forcing repair shops and wholesalers to maintain huge inventories. This proliferation of types and models was a predictable outcome of the laissez-faire approach that prevailed in the United States through the early 1900s.

When the United States began gearing up for and eventually participating in the First World War, the diversity of products compounded enormously the government's attempt to supply its own and its allies' troops. Although it only operated for a few months, the War Industries Board made a substantial start at encouraging standardization of products and parts. And because it became the major consumer of manufactured goods during the latter stages of the conflict, its impact permeated the whole industrial system. The Food Administration had a somewhat similar impact on agricultural production.

Wartime controls abruptly vanished after the signing of the armistice in 1918, but the wartime experience deeply affected the retired head of the Food Administration, Herbert Hoover. In 1921 President Warren G. Harding appointed Hoover to be secretary of commerce, and he turned that previously marginal department into one of the most active and influential entities in Washington. An engineer who became a successful businessman, Hoover was very interested in eliminating waste and promoting efficiency wherever possible.

Sensitive to public opinion, he insisted on thorough consultation. The Department of Commerce contacted the major manufacturers or producers of a given product line and sought recommendations for standardization. Preliminary suggestions were circulated to both producers and consumers for comment. When a general consensus emerged, the Commerce Department publicized the proposed standards.

Some of these involved simplification. Rather than dozens of different sizes of automobile wheels, the Commerce Department encouraged manufacturers to produce only three standard sizes. This change simplified the manufacture of tires as well. Simplification worked best in cases like wheels where style mattered little or not at all. Auto manufacturers were free to install any sort of chassis and body on the interchangeable wheels.

Standardization of parts or components also occurred. A typical example was the development of standardized threading for pipes, bolts, nuts, and other connectors. Here again, style played no role, and the standardization of threading simplified manufacturing processes, facilitated repairs, and reduced the need for huge inventories of specialized parts. Thus standardization worked hand-in-hand with simplification and promoted the elimination of waste.

By the end the decade, the Commerce Department had promulgated standards for over 3,000 articles ranging from the tiniest screws to office furniture. Almost anything might become a subject for standardization. Building materials like bricks, doors, windows, and hardware were produced in common sizes, making them interchangeable. Mattresses, springs, and the associated sheets and blankets were standardized. The size and threading for lightbulbs and sockets were defined and present-day standard-socket American fixtures still match those developed in the 1920s.

The Commerce Department continued to provide guidance, with its National Bureau of Standards playing a primary role. The bureau recently became part of the National Institute of Standards and Technology (NIST). Both NIST and its predecessor engaged in research and development in a wide range of fields to develop reasonable standards and to devise new methods or products. In the long run, the standardization and simplification campaign initiated in the 1920s achieved Hoover's larger goal of promoting efficiency and reducing waste.

See also Associationalism; War Industries Board.

References and Further Reading

Hoover, Herbert. *The Memoirs of Herbert Hoover.* New York: Macmillan, 1952.

Wilson, Joan Hoff. *Herbert Hoover: Forgotten Progressive.* Prospect Heights, IL: Waveland Press, 1992.

Underconsumption

In an ideal capitalistic economy, purchases of consumer goods would exactly balance the production of those goods. This equation can become unbalanced if too many goods are produced (overproduction) or if consumers will not or cannot purchase all of the goods available (underconsumption).

While either phenomenon can occur at any time, the conditions that prevailed in the late 1920s and early 1930s were particularly conducive to creating an underconsumption problem. Throughout the decade of the 1920s, improving management structures, cost-accounting practices, and manufacturing technologies all contributed to a remarkable growth in worker productivity. But while productivity was rising at a rate of approximately 3 percent a year, industrial wage levels did not.

Some industrialists recognized that their employees might be potential consumers of their products. For example, one of Henry Ford's motives in introducing the $5 day in

1913 was to pay his top workers enough so that they could buy the Model Ts they were building. In the 1920s, however, too few manufacturers followed this pattern, and that failure contributed to the relative decline in industrial workers' purchasing power.

Instead, much of the added wealth that the rising productivity generated flowed into the hands of owners and stockholders. Throughout the 1920s this process had the effect of transferring wealth the working class generated to investors, causing the nation's distribution of wealth to become increasingly skewed. The wealthy got richer at a much faster rate than the poor became less poor. But increased purchasing power in the hands of the wealthy does not necessarily translate into increased consumer buying because much of the surplus is invested or saved.

The stock market crash in 1929 resulted from a variety of factors, only some of them related to broader economic conditions. After the crash, however, many producers and retailers found themselves with growing inventories of unsold goods. Simultaneously, distressed manufacturers laid off some or all of their labor forces. Neither the relatively underpaid workers still on the job nor, certainly, the newly unemployed had the wherewithal to continue buying. Nor did wealthy Americans suddenly begin purchasing more basic consumer goods. A downward spiral of underconsumption ensued.

People frequently misinterpreted this problem as one of overproduction. But many potential consumers wanted or needed the goods that appeared to be available in surplus; they just lacked the resources to buy them no matter how low prices fell. The national distribution system fell apart, with literally starving people in one location unable to purchase food stockpiled and going to waste in other areas.

Almost nothing was done deliberately to relieve the underconsumption problem. Early New Deal recovery programs like the National Recovery Administration (NRA) and the Agricultural Adjustment Act were aimed at controlling production to induce scarcities and, presumably, to raise prices. With no one capable or willing to buy, however, upward pressure on prices failed to occur.

Fortunately, some of the New Deal's relief programs inadvertently eased the underconsumption problem. The Works Progress Administration (WPA) eventually hired some 11 million unemployed people who were highly likely to spend whatever they earned immediately. Similarly, Civilian Conservation Corps members earned $1 a day—but typically that dollar was sent back to the CCC boys' families in the cities where it was promptly spent on consumer goods.

In the long run the full-employment economy the Second World War created also cured the underconsumption problem. Not only did unemployment fall to unprecedented lows, but many people held second or even third jobs in the wartime crisis. Price controls and rationing held down consumer expenditures during the conflict, so that plenty of pent-up consumer demand was available to assist the nation navigate the economic shoals of a postwar economy.

See also Crash; Great Depression, Causes of; Moving Assembly Line; Induced Scarcity.

References and Further Reading

Himmelberg, Robert F. *The Great Depression and the New Deal.* Westport, CT: Greenwood, 2001.

Nash, Gary D. *The Crucial Era.* Prospect Heights, IL: Waveland, 1998.

Wheeler, Mark, ed. *The Economics of the Great Depression.* Kalamazoo, MI: Upjohn Institute for Employment Research, 1998.

War Industries Board

Created in the summer of 1917, the War Industries Board (WIB) gradually assumed control over industrial production in the United States. To accomplish its primary goal of supplying essential supplies for the war effort, it extended its influence throughout the economy, affecting every stage of production from raw materials through finished goods. The board represented the nearest the U.S. government had yet come to managing a fully planned economy.

President Woodrow Wilson announced that the United States would remain "neutral in thought, word and deed," shortly after the Great War began in Europe in the late summer of 1914. This statement did not, however, protect the American economy from being immediately and profoundly affected by events overseas, especially a strident demand from Britain and France for supplies. While Wilson steadfastly tried to avoid direct American participation in the conflict, both he and Congress recognized the need to be prepared for possible U.S. involvement.

As part of its preparedness legislation in 1916, Congress created the Council of National Defense. Its main prewar achievement was to inventory the nation's productive capacities, identifying its strengths and weaknesses. Once the United States entered the war in April 1917, the council assumed larger coordination responsibilities. It lacked sufficient authority, however, to play a major role in the acquisition and distribution of military supplies.

By the end of April the council had formed the General Munitions Board to help standardize production and serve as the chief purchasing agent for the Army and the Navy. It quickly became apparent that fighting a world war required much more than munitions. At the end of July the council abolished the Munitions Board and replaced it with the much broader ranging WIB.

The evolutionary process continued over the next several months as the board struggled to find its proper role and gain the respect and support it needed to function effectively. New legislation in the spring of 1918 finally reconstituted the WIB into an authoritative agency. Prominent Wall Street speculator Bernard Baruch had served on the earlier boards, and he now took over as director of the WIB. Through executive orders, President Wilson gave Baruch emergency powers to coordinate virtually all aspects of the industrial war effort. The board's reach encompassed a broad range of industries, although other specialized federal agencies regulated key areas like food, fuel, shipping, and railroads.

One of the board's major achievements was to develop standards for various commodities that promoted efficiency of production and utilization. The varieties of automobile tires, typewriter ribbons, and even steel plows declined markedly at the urging of the WIB. This not only promoted far more compatibility among parts but it also helped the board standardize prices. When he became secretary of commerce in the 1920s, Herbert Hoover carried this standardization process forward and applied it to countless civilian goods.

One effective tool the WIB had to control prices was its responsibility for making massive purchases for the U.S. government and its allies. Because cooperation with the two military services was essential, the board included representatives from the Army and the Navy. Further efficiencies came from the board's efforts to convince various manufacturers to consolidate their activities. While productivity in some sectors increased dramatically during the war as a result of the WIB's efforts, other areas, particularly those involving raw materials like steel and copper, were far more difficult to expand.

Throughout its evolution, the WIB's goal had been to collaborate with, rather than coerce, the nation's industrialists and businessmen. A businessman himself, Baruch had great credibility with his peers, enabling him to co-opt their participation with a minimum of pressure. In some sectors this approach was quite successful. Government officials and industrial representatives jointly worked out reasonable production quotas, pricing structures, and distribution mechanisms.

In other instances cooperation was less evident and sometimes downright nonexistent. Baruch triggered an uproar in the automobile industry when he called for a major reduction in output for the year 1918. In fact, he felt his requests were quite reasonable because the WIB controlled the nation's steel production at that point, and it was fully capable of shutting down the automobile industry altogether. In general, however, Baruch and his fellow board members tried to avoid such confrontations even though the president had given them substantial authority.

Perhaps the board's most conspicuous failure was its lack of any comprehensive planning for the postwar period. As it turned out, though, any planning it might have accomplished could well have been irrelevant in any case. Less than three weeks after the November 11, 1918, armistice, Baruch and Wilson agreed to close down the WIB. It ceased operations almost immediately, leaving many industrialists and businessmen disappointed and confused. They might very well have benefited from a more thoughtful and planned industrial demobilization.

To an extent, the carefully cultivated image of the government cooperating with businessmen and vice versa was as important as the actual details of the WIB's operations. Baruch personally received very favorable reviews for his government service and many people believed that the board had played an essential role in the successful war effort. Its real or perceived experiences served as precedents for later government-industry cooperation such as the National Recovery Administration in the 1930s.

See also Baruch, Bernard Mannes; Johnson, Hugh; Rationing; Recovery; Standardization.

References and Further Reading

Cuff, Robert D. *The War Industries Board.* Baltimore, MD: Johns Hopkins University Press, 1973.

Kirkland, Edward C. *American Economic History Since 1860.* Northbrook, IL: AHM Publishing, 1971.

BIOGRAPHIES

Aldrich, Nelson Wilmarth (1841–1915)

No other U.S. senator better exemplifies the businessman in politics than Nelson Wilmarth Aldrich. He was born in Rhode Island, the state he represented in the House and Senate. Aldrich began working in the wholesale grocery business, earning a partnership and establishing the basis of a very successful and rewarding business career. After serving in local and state government positions and two terms in the U.S. House of Representatives, he began an extended career in the U.S. Senate in 1891. He unashamedly used his political position to the advantage of his continuing business activities, supporting high protective tariffs and the gold standard. As one of the Senate's most powerful conservative Republicans, he was able to influence and limit the impact of such regulatory legislation as the 1906 Hepburn Act. His position as chair of the Senate Banking and Finance Committee inevitably fed his interest in designing a more effective banking system. He became an articulate advocate for a central reserve function but favored private rather than government control. Although he had retired from the Senate by 1913, many of the features he had advocated were included in the legislation that created the Federal Reserve System.

See also Federal Reserve System, Creation of.

References and Further Reading

Stephenson, Nathaniel W. *Nelson W. Aldrich.* New York: Scribners, 1930.

Arden, Elizabeth (1884–1966)

Florence Nightingale Graham was born in Canada but migrated to New York as a teenager. She held several secretarial jobs, including one for Eleanor Adair, a British-based cosmetics firm. In 1910 she borrowed $6,000 from a relative and opened her own salon named Elizabeth Arden. The young entrepreneur soon changed her name to match that of her company. In addition to selling cosmetics, her salons offered massage, diet, and exercise programs. She expanded to other American locations before the First World War and established her first overseas Red Door Salon in Paris in 1922. Elizabeth Arden's expanding commercial empire eventually included health spas and a line of clothing. On her death, Eli Lilly and Co. bought her assets and continue to market products under the Elizabeth Arden trademark.

See also Lauder, Estée; Rubinstein, Helena.

References and Further Reading

Shuker, Nancy. *Elizabeth Arden.* Englewood Cliffs, NJ: Silver Burdett, 1989.

Baruch, Bernard Mannes (1870–1965)

Born into a wealthy Jewish family in South Carolina, Bernard Mannes Baruch retained a southern viewpoint throughout his long life. His family moved to New York City in 1881 where Baruch completed his education at the College of the City of New York. He then joined a brokerage firm as a bond salesman and excelled at profiting from short-selling in bear markets. He was a millionaire at the age of 30, and he established his own firm in 1903. A strong believer in Progressivism, he became well-known in Democratic Party circles. Fellow southerner Woodrow Wilson exercised the most important political influence on Baruch's long career. The president gave him very broad powers as director of the War Industries Board in 1918 and then included him on the team that participated in the Versailles Peace Conference. Baruch remained an important Democratic advisor through the New Deal period but never held as powerful a position as he had exercised on the War Industries Board. He continued to influence party leaders during the Second World War and afterwards, retiring from public life only after the end of the Korean War.

See also Standardization; War Industries Board.

References and Further Reading

Grant, James. *Bernard M. Baruch.* New York: Simon and Schuster, 1983.

Birdseye, Clarence (1886–1956)

Clarence Birdseye was born in Brooklyn but lived in New Jersey as a child. Lacking the money to complete his education, he dropped out of Amherst College but pursued his interest in natural history as a summer employee of the U.S. Biological Survey. This experience introduced him to the fur trade, and for five years he lived in Labrador pursuing that interest. There he observed that when fish were reeled in, they often froze very quickly in the region's subzero temperatures, and Birdseye became convinced that many other foods could be fast-frozen and preserved successfully. The First World War and subsequent government employment delayed his experimentation, but in 1924 he and three partners established the General Seafoods Co. in Gloucester, Massachusetts, to process quick-frozen seafood. Financial problems forced him to sell all of his interest in the company, which was reorganized as General Foods Corporation. In the early 1930s the inventive entrepreneur established the Birds Eye Frosted Foods Co. to market a wide range of frozen foods including vegetables. In his later years Clarence Birdseye experimented with other products and processes, but his name is most closely associated with the development of the U.S. frozen food industry.

References and Further Reading

Williams, E. W. *Frozen Foods.* Boston: Cahners, 1970.

Boeing, William Edward (1881–1956)

Born into a wealthy family, William Edward Boeing left his Detroit home for Yale University where he studied engineering but failed to graduate. With profits from a brilliant land investment he had made near Taconite, Minnesota, he moved west and invested in timberland and other speculative ventures in the Seattle area. First attracted to flying as a hobby, in 1916 Boeing invested $100,000 to create the Pacific Aero Products Co. It obtained a major federal contract in World War I and continued to fill military orders in the 1920s. In addition to winning mail contracts and sometimes piloting the planes himself, Boeing began assembling an integrated aircraft manufacturing operation centered around his Boeing Air Transport Co. Called United Aircraft and Transport Corporation, it included subsidiaries like engine-maker Pratt and Whitney and boasted the design talents of visionaries like Igor Sikorsky and Chance Vought. United Airlines emerged as the transport company from this consolidation. During the Depression, however, aircraft companies came in for bitter condemnation, often focused on the enormous profits they had generated before the stock market crash. After defending his actions before a congressional committee, Boeing sold all of his aircraft-related interests and spent the remainder of his life pursuing ranching and other interests. He lived long enough to see the company he had founded become the nation's major airframe manufacturer.

See also Commercial Aviation; Military Aviation.

References and Further Reading

Bauer, Eugene E. *Boeing: The First Century.* Enumclaw, WA: TABA, 2000.

Carrier, Willis Haviland (1876–1950)

Like so many other American inventors, Willis Haviland Carrier spent much of his childhood tinkering with the machinery at his upper New York State farm home. The 1893 depression delayed his education, but he eventually studied electrical engineering at Cornell University. While working at the Buffalo Forge Co., Carrier developed a humidity-controlling system for a publishing company that cooled air in the plant as a side benefit. Carrier Air Conditioning Co. emerged as a subsidiary of Buffalo Forge in 1907, but Carrier and several partners established the independent Carrier Engineering Corporation eight years later. Willis Carrier was the inventive genius for this enterprise, adapting or inventing a number of technological advances including novel compressors and safer, cheaper refrigerants. His early customers were the owners of tobacco factories and other processing plants, but he scored a major public relations coup by air-conditioning the Hudson department store in downtown Detroit in 1924. Carrier systems received even more enthusiastic publicity in subsequent years when they were installed in movie theaters all across the country. In the 1930s his company expanded to include other firms, and the Carrier Corporation became the nation's leading supplier of cooling systems for stores, skyscrapers, railroad cars, and, particularly after World War II, private homes.

References and Further Reading

Ingels, Margaret. *Willis Haviland Carrier.* New York: Arno Press, 1952.

Chrysler, Walter Percy (1875–1940)

Son of a Kansas railroad engineer, Walter Percy Chrysler spent four years as an apprentice mechanic with the Union Pacific Railroad. He then worked in other railroad shops before moving up to management. His last railroad-related position was as a plant manager for a locomotive manufacturer. Recognizing Chrysler's mechanical and managerial skills, Charles Nash put him in charge of production at Buick, encouraging him to revolutionize production along lines similar to those Henry Ford was adopting. When Charles Durant recaptured control of General Motors in 1916, Chrysler continued to work for the auto-making giant until he became disillusioned with Durant's leadership style. By 1923 Chrysler had taken over as president of the Maxwell Motor Co., a position he exploited to develop a sleek, advanced vehicle he named the Chrysler Six. It sold so well that it eclipsed the Maxwell line thereby allowing Chrysler to rename the company after himself. In the late 1920s the Chrysler Corporation bought the Dodge Motor Co. and added its lower-priced models to its increasingly diversified line. At about the same time, Chrysler began construction of the New York skyscraper that still bears his name. He remained active in his auto company until his death.

See also Product Differentiation; Scientific Management.

References and Further Reading

Curcio, Vincent. *Chrysler.* New York: Oxford University Press, 2000.

Disney, Walter Elias (1901–1966)

Walter Elias Disney was only seven years old when he began selling cartoon drawings to neighbors in Marceline, Missouri. He continued to study art and drawing, interrupted only by a year in France as a World War I ambulance driver. In the early 1920s he moved to California to join his brother Roy in setting up a studio in a garage. After a few minor successes, in 1928 Walt Disney introduced Mickey Mouse in *Steamboat Willie,* the first film cartoon with a sound track. By 1937 he had greatly expanded his stable of artists. With a $1.5 million budget, his studio was able to produce the millions of hand-drawn and colored cels that constituted the world's first feature length cartoon movie, *Snow White and the Seven Dwarfs.* For the next couple of decades, Walt Disney studios dominated the animated film industry, expanding into television in the 1950s and live movie production under the name of Buena Vista Films. Disney exploited his active artistic vision in creating the world's first major theme amusement park, Disneyland, in 1955. His plans for an even more elaborate Magic Kingdom came to fruition after his death in the form of Florida's Walt Disney World in 1971 and Epcot Center ten years later. Walt Disney remains a major entertainment company, and it exercised its influence in urging Congress to extend copyright protection well beyond seventy-five years. The urgency arose because its most famous creation, Mickey Mouse, was fast approaching that milestone.

See also Movies; Television.

References and Further Reading

Smith, Dave, and Steven Clark. *Disney: The First 100 Years.* New York: Hyperion, 1999.

Dodge, John Francis (1864–1920), and Horace Elgin Dodge (1868–1920)

The Dodge brothers cut their teeth working at the machine shop their father operated in Niles, Michigan. After relatively brief stints working for other employers, John Francis and Horace Elgin Dodge established their own shop in Detroit in 1897. The high quality of their work won them a contract from automaker Ransom Olds to build transmissions for his cars. The brothers switched allegiance to Henry Ford in 1902, however, and their design and manufacturing capabilities were key factors in the production of his first Model A. Short of cash, Ford had to compensate them with shares in his fledgling company. Over the years the Dodge brothers' holdings of Ford Motor Co. stock became extremely valuable, and they used the dividends from it to finance expansion. Worried that Henry Ford might cease relying on them for parts, the brothers decided to build their own automobile. The Dodge that rolled off their assembly line in 1914 was an instant success. The brothers constantly improved their vehicles, enabling the Dodge Co. to become the second largest U.S. automaker after Ford. A messy legal battle between Ford and the Dodge brothers led to Ford buying out their interest completely in 1919, proving that their earlier decision to go it alone had been wise. John Dodge died of the flu early in 1920, and Horace seemed to lose the will to live, passing away less than a year later. The booming company they left behind was badly mismanaged until Walter Chrysler took it over in 1928. The Chrysler Corporation continues to market popular lines of Dodge cars and trucks.

See also Chrysler, Walter Percy; Ford, Henry.

References and Further Reading

Hyde, Charles K. *The Dodge Brothers.* Detroit: Wayne State University Press, 2005.

du Pont, Pierre Samuel (1870–1954)

The Du Pont family built its first gunpowder mill in Wilmington, Delaware, in 1799. It was natural then for Pierre Samuel du Pont to take a chemistry degree at MIT to prepare for work in his family's firm. He and cousins Alfred and Coleman were restless in the hidebound firm, however, and they welcomed an opportunity to buy control in 1902. Pierre du Pont introduced modern cost accounting techniques, a research facility, and vertical integration. He became president in 1915 and superintended the company's highly profitable war production as well as its diversification into plastics, dyes, and other products. He invested some of his personal fortune in General Motors Corporation (GM) stock, emerging with a 37 percent ownership share in 1920. He retired from Dupont and devoted the next eight years to GM, making the key decision to promote Alfred P. Sloan, Jr. into the presidency and helping build it into the world's largest corporation.

See also Product Differentiation; Sloan, Jr., Alfred Pritchard.

References and Further Reading

Chandler, Jr., Alfred D., and Stephen Salsbury. *Pierre S. du Pont and the Making of the Modern Corporation.* New York: Harper and Row, 1971.

Durant, William Crapo (1861–1947)

A flamboyant and energetic entrepreneur, "Billy" Durant went into the carriage manufacturing business with Josiah Dort in 1886 in Flint, Michigan. Four year's later their Durant-Dort Carriage Co. had become the leading carriage maker in the United States. In 1904 Durant signed on with the Buick Co., serving as its president until 1908 when he formed the General Motors Corporation (GM). This holding company acquired all sorts of automobile and related parts and accessories companies. Durant became overextended and lost control of GM in 1910 but continued to found and acquire auto-related firms including the Chevrolet Motor Co. He then used Chevrolet as a base to

William C. Durant founded General Motors Corporation in 1908, but lost control of it after World War I. (Library of Congress)

reacquire control of GM, which he headed until 1920. His presence as a major player in the auto industry ended at that point, but the diversified conglomerate he had assembled eventually became the leading automaker in the United States.

See also Chrysler, Walter Percy; du Pont, Pierre Samuel; Olds, Ransom Eli; Sloan, Jr., Alfred Pritchard.

References and Further Reading

Madsen, Axel. *The Deal Maker.* New York: Wiley, 1999.

Firestone, Harvey Samuel (1868–1938)

Ohio native Harvey Samuel Firestone was fortunate in being in the right location and the right industry to benefit from growth in the U.S. auto industry. In the late 1890s he was working in the carriage industry where his particular interest was solid-rubber carriage tires. Firestone and his associates developed an alternative method for attaching tires to wheels that enabled them to sell their tires more cheaply. Throughout his career Firestone exploited low prices to expand his market share, and he spurned attempts to be drawn into consolidation. After the turn of the century, Firestone's company became adept at manufacturing pneumatic tires and, largely due to its low-price policy, Henry Ford awarded the company a contract for his Model N cars in 1906. That naturally led to a succeeding association with Ford's hugely popular Model T. In the 1920s Firestone established retail outlets and dealers for his tires that helped maintain his firm's competitive edge. Although it represented only a minor part of his company's operations, Firestone earned notoriety for developing rubber plantations in Liberia that exploited low labor costs and played a dominant role in that African nation's economy. Harvey Firestone always retained a substantial bloc of shares in his company and accumulated a large fortune.

See also Ford, Henry.

References and Further Reading

Leif, Alder. *The Firestone Story.* New York: Whittlesey House, 1951.

Ford, Henry (1863–1947)

Although he became incredibly wealthy, Henry Ford never abandoned his image as a homespun, working-class American. Born on a Michigan farm near Detroit, young Henry so disliked farmwork that he found escape by becoming a mechanic. He first worked on farm implements and later as an engineer for the Detroit Edison Co. There his monthly salary of $100 was sufficient to finance his experimentation with horseless carriages in his garage. His first successful car hit the street in 1896, and within a couple of years he was building cars especially designed for racing. His favorite driver, Barney Oldfield, set numerous speed records, and Ford's racing successes encouraged backers to finance the creation of the Ford Motor Co. in 1903. After turning out a number of prototypes, the company introduced its Model T five years later. The car sold for less than $1,000 and proved to be so remarkably reliable and rugged that some 20 million rolled off the assembly line before production ended in 1927. To fill a seemingly inexhaustible consumer demand, Henry Ford devoted much of his ingenuity in the middle years to refining and speeding up the manufacturing process with moving assembly lines and other innovations. He also collected subsidiaries to produce the parts he needed, creating an extraordinarily efficient, vertically integrated company. By 1919 he had bought out all of his partners including the Dodge brothers but struggled through the early 1920s due to recession and indebtedness. Even so, Henry Ford decided to make a foray into aviation and his company built the successful Ford Tri-Motor airplane. By the mid-1920s the diversified products of competitors like General Motors and Chrysler had undermined Ford's market po-

Henry Ford built the most successful automobile of all time, the Model T, and in the proces revolutionized the American automobile industry. (Ford Motor Company)

sition, so he fought back with the Model A that featured a V-8 engine. He also began bracketing the market with top-of-the-line Lincolns and mid-market Mercurys. Although he had won acclaim for his announcement of the $5 day in 1914, his intrusive attempts to regiment his workers' lives and lifestyles hurt his reputation as an employer. He bitterly resisted the organizing efforts of the United Auto Workers in the late 1930s but finally accepted unionization in 1941. His most dramatic wartime effort involved an only marginally successful attempt to mass-produce aircraft. To avoid paying huge income and estate tax levies, he endowed the Ford Foundation late in life, a decision that enabled his heirs to remain major shareholders in the sprawling empire he had founded.

See also Moving Assembly Line.

References and Further Reading

Bak, Richard. *Henry and Edsel.* Hoboken, NJ: Wiley, 2003.

Nevins, Allan. *Ford.* 3 vols. New York: Scribner, 1954–1963.

Gary, Elbert Henry (1846–1927)

Although he was a talented corporate lawyer, no one anticipated that Elbert Henry Gary would be plucked from relative obscurity to head the first billion-dollar corporation. Born near Wheaton, Illinois, he lived there into his fifties. Gary completed his studies at the Union College of Law in 1868, and settled into an active practice that led to his election as DuPage County judge in 1884. Long after he left the bench, he continued to be known as Judge Gary. In 1892 John Gates asked Gary to help him organize a combine of five competing barbed wire companies, and he was so successful that Gates sought his assistance five years later in pulling together eighty wire companies. To finance the resulting American Steel and Wire Co., Gates introduced Gary to J. P. Morgan. Shortly afterward, the astute finance capitalist asked Judge Gary to become president of Federal Steel, a large, integrated corporation he was creating. That move put the transplanted Illinois lawyer in line to chair the board of directors of Morgan's billion-dollar holding company, United States Steel, in 1901. Within a couple of years, Gary replaced Charles Schwab as CEO, a position he retained until his death. When U.S. Steel decided to build a massive new plant on the shores of Lake Michigan, it created the town named Gary, Indiana. Judge Gary remained a life-long opponent of organized labor, but he managed to guide his embattled company through strikes and antitrust assaults.

See also Billion Dollar Corporation.

References and Further Reading

Warren, Kenneth. *Big Steel.* Pittsburgh: University of Pittsburgh Press, 2001.

Giannini, Amadeo Peter (A. P.) (1870–1949)

Amadeo Peter Giannini's family were Italian immigrants engaged in farming in San Jose, California, but his first business success came when he moved to San Francisco as a teenager. There he worked himself up to a partnership in his stepfather's produce business. He retired in 1901 but was almost immediately drawn back into business when he inherited a directorship in a local bank. Frustrated by its elitist policies, Giannini and several other directors formed a new institution called the Bank of Italy. The young banker personally rounded up depositors and approved small loans to serve a largely immigrant population in San Francisco's North Beach district. When the 1906 earthquake hit, he carted $80,000 in coins and bills to his suburban home, a move that enabled the Bank of Italy to reopen almost immediately. Three years later Giannini took advantage of California legislation permitting the establishment of branches and quickly created a statewide system. In the late 1920s he obtained a national banking charter and stretched his empire, now named Bank of America, well beyond California. Once again he retired, only to dive into a contentious proxy battle in 1933 to regain control of Transamerica, the system's holding company. Giannini retained the position as chairman of what had become the world's largest commercial bank until his death.

References and Further Reading

Bonadio, Felice A. *A. P. Giannini: Banker of America.* Berkeley, CA: University of California Press, 1994.

Hershey, Milton Snavely (1857–1945)

Milton Snavely Hershey was born in a rural Pennsylvania community named Derry Church, but his family moved often. Young Milton left school after the fourth grade, briefly apprenticed to a printer, and then found his true calling as an apprentice in a confectioner's shop. He made several unsuccessful forays into the candy business with his own shops. Not until 1886 did he hit his stride by mixing fresh milk with caramel. He set up a production company in Lancaster, Pennsylvania, but was intrigued by a display of German chocolate-making machinery at the 1993 Chicago World's Fair. Shortly afterward he founded the Hershey Chocolate Company as a subsidiary of his caramel operation. In 1900 he sold the caramel division and devoted his full attention to manufacturing milk chocolate bars under the Hershey brand name. He never felt he had to advertise his very popular product, and he used the profits from its sales to return to his birthplace of Derry Church, rename it after himself, and build a model community much like the one George Pullman had constructed south of Chicago. And, as had happened at Pullman, Illinois, low wages and company restrictiveness triggered a series of labor revolts in Hershey, Pennsylvania, in the late 1930s. After World War II, the enterprise Milton Hershey left behind suffered intense competition from companies like Mars that advertised broadly, so Hershey reluctantly did too beginning in 1970.

References and Further Reading

Brenner, Joël Glenn. *The Emperors of Chocolate.* New York: Random House, 1999.

Hill, James Jerome (J. J.) (1838–1916)

James Jerome Hill fully justified his reputation as "The Empire Builder." Born in Canada, he moved in his teens to St. Paul, Minnesota, where he lived for the rest of his life. An energetic and versatile businessman, Hill dealt in lumber, coal, fur, and land in addition to developing a keen interest in railroad building. As president of the St. Paul, Minneapolis, and Manitoba Railway, he forged linkages that whetted his interest in the wheat-growing potential of the Red River Valley. In 1889 he founded the Great Northern Railway and stretched its reach all the way to Seattle four years later. In addition to laying tracks, Hill actively advertised the agricultural potential of the road's hinterland and provided those who settled it with up-to-date farming information and community-building support. In 1896 Hill collaborated with J. P. Morgan to acquire control of the Great Northern's rival, the Northern Pacific. Five years later they purchased the Chicago, Burlington, and Quincy Railway to complete the connection of their western properties with Chicago. Edward H. Harriman attempted to gain control of this valuable combine, but agreed to cooperate with Morgan and Hill to establish an overarching holding company called the Northern Securities Co. It was the first combine to be broken up under the Sherman Antitrust Act, but Hill personally retained effective control of all three railroads even after the holding company was disbanded. He was a highly respected member of the St. Paul community and seldom roused the sort of criticism that other railroad barons engendered.

See also Northern Securities Co. Case; Railroad Consolidation.

References and Further Reading

Malone, Michael P. *James J. Hill*. Norman, OK: University of Oklahoma Press, 1996.

Hilton, Conrad Nicholson (1887–1979)

Conrad Nicholson Hilton spent his early years in the New Mexico Territory where his father engaged in a number of businesses including, at one point, operating a hotel in Socorro. Young Conrad dropped in and out of several schools, including a stint at the New Mexico School of Mines. His most successful early business activity involved banking but he abandoned that to serve in the American Expeditionary Force in France during the First World War. After leaving the army, he headed to Texas and bought a couple of deteriorating hotels in the Ft. Worth area. Through the early 1920s he expanded his chain by renovating and redecorating other existing hotels and, later in the decade, building new structures. Severely overextended during the Great Depression, Hilton barely managed to retain control of his Texas holdings, but had recovered sufficiently to buy the Sir Francis Drake Hotel in San Francisco in 1938. The next few years were devoted to the acquisition of prominent landmarks like Chicago's Palmer House and culminated with his purchase of the Waldorf-Astoria in New York City. The Hilton Hotel Corporation he formed in 1946 became the first hotel operation listed on the New York Stock Exchange. The chain expanded overseas and engulfed the Statler Hotel chain, always maintaining a reputation for elegant, comfortable accommodations. Conrad Hilton retired in 1966 and turned over control to his son Barron Hilton.

References and Further Reading

Dabney, Thomas Ewing. *The Man Who Bought the Waldorf*. New York: Duell, Sloan and Pearce, 1950.

Hughes, Howard Robard (1905–1976)

One of the most erratic and eccentric businessmen the United States has produced, Howard Robard Hughes inherited a huge fortune at the age of eighteen. His father, Howard Robard Hughes, Sr., had invented a revolutionary drill bit that made his Hughes Tool Co. a giant in the booming oil industry. His son retained total ownership of the tool company until 1972, and it provided much of the funding for his other ventures. Fascinated by Hollywood, Hughes produced a number of movies as an independent, but many of them lost money. His final movie fling came after the Second World War when he owned RKO Studios for five years. Meanwhile he was winning renown for flying exploits that included record-breaking transcontinental and round-the-world flights. In 1933 he founded Hughes Aircraft Co. and six years later became a major stockholder in what would become Trans World Airlines. Less successful than other entrepreneurs in obtaining and fulfilling wartime orders, Hughes drew much criticism for unrealistic projects like his wooden flying boat ridiculed as the Spruce Goose. Even so, Hughes Aircraft flourished and, after Howard's death, became a major player in the space exploration business. A life-long hypochondriac, the billionaire endowed the Howard Hughes Medical Institute in Florida. Despite several marriages, Hughes was a loner who spent the last years of his life living in seclusion in a series of hotel suites.

See also Commercial Aviation; Movies.

References and Further Reading

Barlett, Donald L., and James B. Steele. *Howard Hughes*. New York: Norton, 2004.

Insull, Samuel (1859–1938)

Born in England, Samuel Insull became Thomas Edison's private secretary. Later he managed and acquired several electric generating companies based on Edison's technology. In the 1920s he began assembling multilevel holding company pyramids that provided utility service for millions of customers. While these appeared to be highly profitable business ventures prior to the 1929 stock market crash, they relied on a continuous influx of investment. In essence, Insull's empire was a massive Ponzi scheme that could only thrive in a continuing bull market. In the inevitable meltdown of Insull's empire in the 1930s, some $750 million in paper investments evaporated, generating the most colossal American business failure up to that point.

References and Further Reading

McDonald, Forrest. *Insull*. Chicago: University of Chicago Press, 1962.

Johnson, Howard Deering (1896?–1972)

Long before Ray Kroc wandered into the McDonald brothers hamburger stand in California, Howard Dearing Johnson had established a very successful franchise restaurant chain. Son of a Boston cigar wholesaler, Howard Johnson worked for his father both before and after army service in the First World War. When his father died, however, Johnson discovered that the business was deeply in debt. While digging himself out of the red, Johnson bought a combination drugstore and newsstand that he was able to turn into a very successful venture. Finding that ice cream was the most profitable product he sold, Johnson bought the recipe for a tasty, high fat-content ice cream and went into production. He opened his first restaurant in 1929 but, along with all other Americans, struggled through hard times. In the mid-1930s, however, he found he could expand his reach by offering franchises to people capable of financing their own operations. By the end of the decade more than a hundred Howard Johnson's restaurants were in operation, with their namesake providing high-quality food, design, and quality control. The ice-cream business remained at the heart of the chain's success with its widely advertised "28 Flavors" available in outlets strategically located along the nation's highways. When Johnson retired in 1959 his chain included 550 restaurants and motels.

See also Franchises; Kroc, Ray.

References and Further Reading

Editors of Nation's Business. *Lessons of Leadership*. Garden City, NY: Doubleday, 1968.

Johnson, Hugh (1888–1979)

Hugh Johnson was an old-school cavalryman who rose to the rank of brigadier general in the First World War. Toward the close of that conflict he served as the Army's representative on the War Industries Board and, as a civilian, he continued his association with the board's founder Bernard Baruch in the 1920s. Widely perceived as an industrial management expert, he was a natural choice for Franklin Roosevelt's Brain Trust. After the

1932 election, the president named Johnson to head the National Recovery Administration (NRA). The NRA attempted to manipulate and control industrial production, hoping to exploit the induced scarcity principle to stimulate a rise in prices. The NRA was declared unconstitutional in 1935, and Johnson's influence in the New Deal waned quickly.

See also Recovery; War Industries Board.

References and Further Reading

Johnson, V. *Blue Eagle.* Garden City, NY: Doubleday, Doran, 1935.

Kellogg, John Harvey (1852–1943)

Although he is most remembered for the corn flakes that bear his name, John Harvey Kellogg invented them almost by accident. Born in Michigan and reared in the Seventh Day Adventist Church headquartered in Battle Creek, the young man enthusiastically subscribed to Adventist tenets related to health reform. After attending school erratically he managed to complete a doctorate at New York's Bellevue Hospital Medical College. An outstanding surgeon, he donated his fees to a variety of causes including an Adventist-founded health reform institute. When he became its head in 1876, he renamed it the Battle Creek Sanitarium and spent the next several decades developing a wide-ranging health program that involved diet, exercise, water treatments, and other novel procedures. In the sanitarium's experimental food laboratory, Kellogg invented granola and, later, his popular flaked cereal by extruding cooked grain through rollers. It was his younger brother, Will Kellogg, who developed the marketing plan and eventually ran the Kellogg food company, leaving John to pursue his extraordinarily active writing, lecturing, educational, and charitable pursuits.

References and Further Reading

Schwarz, Richard W. *John Harvey Kellogg, M.D.* Nashville, TN: Southern Publishing Assn., 1970.

Knox, Rose (1857–1950)

Ohio-born Rose Markward moved to Gloversville, New York, as a child and, not surprisingly, began her career working in a glove factory. There she met a successful glove salesman named Charles Briggs Knox. They were married in 1883 and saved enough to buy a gelatine factory in Johnson, New York. The couple's holdings expanded into other industries, but when Charles died in 1906, Rose sold everything but the gelatine business. She then set out to make Knox Gelatine an absolutely essential ingredient for millions of homemakers. She set up an experimental kitchen to test recipes, printed the successful ones on the side of her product's boxes and in recipe books, and wrote advertising copy to promote the product. Rose Knox remained associated with her very successful company throughout her life, serving as chair of the board until her death at the age of ninety-three.

References and Further Reading

Rutledge Books. *The Knox Gelatine Cookbook.* New York: Benjamin Co., 1977.

Land, Edwin Herbert (1909–1991)

A visit to the brightly lit Great White Way on Broadway stimulated Edwin Herbert Land's interest in finding a way to reduce glare. He dropped out of Harvard, conducted his own research, and founded the Polaroid Corporation in 1937. It produced polarized glass and plastic sheets that found many uses during the Second World War, boosting the company's profits and profile. Land exploited both to continue experimenting and inventing. He claimed to have conceived of an instant-developing camera in 1943 and to have solved the chemical and mechanical problems within six months. Even so, commercial sale of his Polaroid Land Camera was delayed until 1948, but it was an immediate hit. Within a few years, his company had become second only to Eastman Kodak in the consumer photography business. Land's vision remained unfilled so he spent half a billion dollars to develop a color instant printing camera, the SX-70, another marketing triumph. His plans for instant developing movies, however, fell victim to television and video cameras. Over the course of his busy career, Land received over 500 patents, second only to Thomas Edison's total.

See also Eastman, George.

References and Further Reading

McElheny, Victor K. *Insisting on the Impossible: The Life of Edwin Land.* Reading, MA: Perseus Books, 1998.

Mayer, Louis Burt (1885–1957)

Although his name came last in MGM, Louis Burt Mayer was a key personality in vaulting the film studio to the top of the Hollywood heap. Born Lazar Meir in Central Europe, he accompanied his family when it emigrated first to New York and then to Canada. L. B. Mayer moved to Boston in his late teens to work in the scrap metal business like his father, but found his true calling by converting a burlesque hall into a movie house in 1907, the first of a profitable chain of theaters. Seven years later Mayer established a distribution company to supply films for his chain, as well as Metro Pictures Corporation and then his own Hollywood-based company to produce them. His obvious success in all three aspects of the film industry—production, distribution, and exhibition—convinced Marcus Loew to put him in charge of the combine he created out of Metro Pictures and Samuel Goldwyn's operation. Mayer headed production at the resulting Metro-Goldwyn-Mayer for two decades, although his success derived in part from the brilliance of Irving Thalberg and the astuteness of Loew's financial manager, Nicholas Schenck. MGM studios dominated Culver City, employed over 4,000 people, and produced almost 50 movies a year in the late 1930s. Autocratic, energetic, and opinionated, Mayer remained a powerful force in the industry until his resignation from MGM in 1951, at about the same time the studio system itself gave way to a more diversified business model.

See also Movies.

References and Further Reading

Crowther, Bosley. *Hollywood Rajah.* New York: Holt, 1960.

Maytag, Frederick (1857–1937)

It was natural for a farm boy from Illinois to become a farm implement salesman. Frederick Maytag began working for McKinley and Bergman in Newton, Iowa, and did so well that he was able to buy the dealership a year later. He took a brief respite from the business to sell lumber in the early 1890s but then became general manager of another implement dealer in Newton. Unhappy with the business's cyclical nature, Maytag decided in 1907 to produce and sell washing machines with wooden tubs in the off season. Two years later he formed the Maytag Co. to handle his rapidly growing business, which boomed even more when it began attaching electric motors to its machines. By the 1920s the Maytag Co. was devoted exclusively to producing washing machines, and its manufacturing facility in Newton became the world's largest. From the very beginning the Maytag brand promised high quality and reliability, characteristics that all of the company's products embodied as it expanded into other household equipment, eventually becoming the third largest appliance maker in the United States.

References and Further Reading

Funk, A. B. *Fred L. Maytag.* Cedar Rapids, IA: Torch Press, 1936.

Mellon, Andrew William (1855–1937)

Andrew William Mellon's father, Thomas Mellon, was a respected Pittsburgh lawyer and judge, whose dealings with Henry Clay

Frick and Andrew Carnegie introduced young Mellon to the exciting world of speculative investment and art collecting. Mellon stopped short of graduating from a university to dive into banking and speculation. In 1887 he and a younger brother founded the T. Mellon and Sons Bank. The Mellon Bank remained a major factor in his success for the rest of his life. He invested in new technologies including those used to refine bauxite into aluminum, an interest that paved the way for his rise to leadership in the Aluminum Corporation of America (ALCOA). He also was a founder of the Gulf Oil Co., a major participant in the merger that created United States Steel, and a participant in several major construction projects including Panama Canal locks and the George Washington Bridge. As a wealthy and influential supporter of the Republican Party, he was a logical choice to become secretary of the treasury in 1921, a position he held through the Harding, Coolidge, and Hoover administrations. His greatest success in that position was to cut the war-swollen national debt almost in half. In the 1930s he announced his intention to donate his huge art collection to the United States and provide funding for the construction of the National Gallery of Art on Washington's Mall to house it. That gift alone was valued at $65 million.

See also Dawes Plan.

References and Further Reading

O'Connor, Harvey. *Mellon's Millions.* New York: John Day, 1933.

Mitchell, Wesley Clair (1874–1948)

Illinois native Wesley Clair Mitchell earned a doctorate at the University of Chicago in 1899. There he had ample opportunity to absorb the ideas of Thorsten Veblen and John Dewey who were leading economic theorists bridging the gap between classical economic ideas and more modern concepts. A life-long academic, Mitchell taught at the University of California and other institutions before settling at Columbia University. There he became an early director of the New School for Social Research. He also helped found the National Bureau of Economic Research and served as its director. He wrote a number of books and articles on economic and social scientific topics, but he became most famous for his insightful statistical analyses of business cycles. He was invited to serve on a number of governmental panels and commissions because of his reputation as an authority on business and economic change.

See also Business Cycles.

References and Further Reading

Burns, Arthur F. *Wesley Clair Mitchell: The Economic Scientist.* New York: National Bureau of Economic Research, 1952.

Morgan, John Pierpont (J. P.) (1837–1913)

Because his father moved from Connecticut to England to pursue a career in international finance, young John Pierpont Morgan attended school in Geneva and college in Göttingen. Back in the United States, he served for many years as agent for his father's interests even as he pursued his own successful speculations during and after the Civil War. He consciously adopted a conservative approach to capital formation and finance and earned a reputation as an astute negotiator during the turbulent years of railroad consolidation. He used his resources and persuasiveness to create effective and efficient railroad combinations, some of which grew into major regional systems. During the Panic of 1893 President Grover Cleveland beseeched him to market federal gold bonds abroad, and his success simultaneously generated respect and also concern that he was too powerful. His creation of the United States Steel Corporation in 1901 reinforced both views. Some of his later consolidation attempts like his New England railroad scheme and an even more ambitious ocean shipping combine badly miscarried. Even so, he retained such enormous respect in the banking community that he was able to cobble together a major investment pool that eased the impact of the Panic of 1907. His influence was so pervasive that he was seen as a principal player in the so-called Money Trust, and he was called to testify before the Pujo Committee shortly before his death. Although he left a relatively modest fortune of $77 million, he remains the chief personification of the successful, powerful, and often ruthless finance capitalists of the Gilded Age.

See also Billion Dollar Corporation; Northern Securities Co. Case; Pujo Committee; Railroad Consolidation.

References and Further Reading

Strouse, Jean. *Morgan: American Financier.* New York: Random House, 1999.

Olds, Ransom Eli (1864–1950)

Ransom Eli Olds' family moved from his Ohio birthplace to Lansing, Michigan in 1880 where his father, Pliny Fisk Olds, established a machine shop. Young Ransom was so competent in working for his father that he quickly emerged as the dominant force in the business. Under his management the shop moved beyond repair and service to manufacturing a gasoline-fired steam engine that sold very well. Olds installed one of these engines on a carriage body but soon became convinced that internal-combustion gasoline engines offered much greater potential. With substantial funding from Samuel L. Smith, Olds established a manufacturing plant in Detroit that delivered the first Oldsmobile in 1900. It was enormously popular, and the 5,000 vehicles the Olds Motor Vehicle Co. produced in 1904 made it the largest auto manufacturer in the world. To meet the demand, Ransom Olds introduced many innovative mass production techniques including a slowly moving assembly line. The entrepreneur insisted on spending much of his time at the Lansing engine works, however, so the Smith family ousted Olds from the company and eventually sold out to William C. Durant who incorporated it into General Motors. Meanwhile, Olds formed a new enterprise of his own called Reo Motor Car Co., and it produced another very popular car called a Reo and, in 1911, a line of trucks. Having twice pulled off brilliant automotive successes, Olds gradually turned his attention to other interests, retaining only a marginal interest in the industry he had done so much to advance.

See also Durant, William Crapo.

References and Further Reading

May, George S. *R. E. Olds, Auto Industry Pioneer.* Grand Rapids, MI: Eerdmans, 1977.

Paley, William Samuel (1901–1990)

Although he often began a step or two behind his leading rival, David Sarnoff, William Samuel Paley's skill and perceptiveness enabled his CBS network to routinely forge ahead of Sarnoff's NBC. Born to wealthy immigrant parents in Chicago, William Paley joined his father's cigar manufacturing company after graduating from the Wharton School of Business. While managing the company's radio advertising campaign in the mid-1920s, he became so fascinated with the medium that he convinced his father to help him buy the struggling United Independent network. Paley added dozens of affiliates and renamed it the Columbia Broadcasting System in 1929. He proved to be a master at programming, turning CBS into the nation's leading radio network with particular strength in news reporting. He was slow to acknowledge the rise of television but then moved quickly to establish CBS as the industry leader in the 1950s. Again, the network's news coverage with anchor Walter Cronkite consistently drew the largest audience. Paley also established successful spinoffs like Columbia Records and unsuccessful experiments like a mechanical color-separation system for television and videodiscs that quickly lost out to videotapes. He frustrated his hand-picked successor, Frank Stanton, by refusing to step down as CEO for more than a decade and serving as chairman of the board off and on until his death.

See also Radio; Sarnoff, David; Television.

References and Further Reading

Paper, Lewis J. *Empire: William S. Paley and the Making of CBS.* New York: St. Martin's Press, 1987.

Phillips, Frank (1873–1950)

Although he was born in Nebraska, Frank Phillips spent his childhood in Creston, Iowa. He left school at the age of fourteen and worked as a farm- and ranch hand until he married the daughter of a banker. Financed in part by the bank, Frank Phillips moved to Bartlesville, Oklahoma, in 1903, intending to strike it rich in the oil business. A string of dry wells nearly bankrupted the venture he and his brother Lee Elder Phillips had begun, but they brought in a gusher in 1905. The Phillips brothers never looked back, eventually incorporating the Phillips Petroleum Co. in 1917 with Frank as its president. In the 1920s the company began selling its trademarked Phillips 66 gasoline, which became a popular brand with consumers across the United States. Frank Phillips also operated a highly successful banking concern in Bartlesville, in part to generate funds for his oil exploration. In the 1930s he donated huge acreage in northern New Mexico to the Boy Scouts of America, and it has operated as the Philmont Scout Ranch ever since. Long after Frank Phillips passed away, the company he headed remained a major player in the oil industry, merging with the Continental Oil Co. in the early twentieth century to become Conoco-Phillips.

See also Rockefeller, John Davison; Sinclair, Harry Ford.

References and Further Reading

Wallis, Michael. *Oil Man.* New York: St. Martin's Griffin, 1995.

Reynolds, Richard Joshua (R. J.) (1850–1918)

The son of a wealthy Virginia slave owner and planter, Richard Joshua Reynolds could hardly avoid becoming involved in the tobacco business. While working in his father's plug tobacco operation, Reynolds decided to set up on his own at a location with better transportation service. In 1874 he began operating in what would become Winston-Salem, North Carolina, a location with good railroad connections as well as ready access to flue-cured tobacco. To develop a popular chewing tobacco with this ingredient, Reynolds was one of the first to use saccharin to sweeten his plugs. With the support of relatives, his enterprise became the R. J. Reynolds Tobacco Co. in 1890, but it encountered cutthroat competition from James B. Duke's American Tobacco Co. Reynolds bowed to the inevitable by joining Duke's tobacco trust in 1899, though he retained control of his own company as the trust's preeminent producer of plug tobacco. A federal antitrust suit in 1907 emboldened Reynolds to introduce Prince Albert brand smoking tobacco, which soon dominated the pipe market. After a 1911 court decision broke up the tobacco trust, Reynold's company began producing Camel cigarettes using a tobacco blend that Reynolds himself had devised. At the time of his death, Camels accounted for one-third of the lucrative cigarette market. Reynolds' company survives as part of the RJR Nabisco combine, a critical development that has facilitated broad diversification away from the increasingly unpopular cigarette business.

See also Duke, James Buchanan.

References and Further Reading

Reynolds, Patrick, and Tom Shachtman. *The Gilded Leaf.* Boston: Little, Brown, 1989.

Rubinstein, Helena (1871–1965)

Born into a large family in Krakow, Poland, Helena Rubinstein at first considered a career in medicine. She abandoned that goal in 1902 and traveled to Australia. She carried with her seven jars of Polish face cream and used them as the basis for opening a salon to sell various skin creams to counter the effects of the sunny climate. She returned to Europe to study dermatology and opened another salon in London in 1908. She is often credited with popularizing cosmetics for the general public. By 1916 Rubinstein was opening salons in major U.S. cities. That brought her into direct competition with Elizabeth Arden, and their rivalry continued for many years. With some reluctance, Rubinstein decided to market her products in department stores as well, but only if they agreed to hire her trained cosmetologists as sales staff. Her products eventually sold worldwide, allowing her to accumulate a fortune of over $150 million and an extensive art collection.

See also Arden, Elizabeth.

References and Further Reading

O'Higgins, Patrick. *Madame: An Intimate Biography of Helena Rubinstein.* New York: Viking, 1971.

Rudkin, Margaret (1897–1967)

Betty Crocker of General Mills and Ann Page of the A&P grocery chain were fictional, but Pepperidge Farm's Margaret Rudkin was the real thing. Margaret Fogarty grew up in Manhattan. After high school she worked as a bookkeeper and planned a career in business, but cut it short when she married wealthy broker Henry Albert Rudkin. His fortunes blossomed in the bull market era, enabling the family to establish an extensive estate called Pepperidge Farm in Fairfield County. But the Depression caught up with the family, forcing it to cut back its lavish lifestyle. When one of Margaret Rudkin's sons suffered acute asthma, a doctor suggested that she prepare homemade bread without the additives or preservatives that might be exacerbating his condition. At the age of forty Margaret Rudkin set about learning how to bake bread in the kitchen at Pepperidge Farm. By the late 1930s her preservative-free, home-style bread was selling throughout New York. In 1940 Rudkin expanded to a Connecticut factory and broadened her product line to include cakes, melba toast, and, with stale unsold bread, croutons and stuffing mix. Under Margaret Rudkin's astute leadership, Pepperidge Farms became the nation's largest independent bakery until she sold out to Campbell Soup in 1962.

References and Further Reading

Collins, Douglas. *America's Favorite Food.* New York: H. N. Abrams, 1994.

Sarnoff, David (1891–1971)

Acclaimed as the "father of television," David Sarnoff made many other contributions to the broadcast industry. Born in Russia, he moved with his family to New York while still a child. He left school after the eighth grade and began working for the American Marconi Co. An extremely capable young man who made himself known to Marconi himself, he rose quickly in the company, which General Electric (GE) incorporated into the Radio Corporation of America (RCA) in 1919. With the support of GE executive Own D. Young, Sarnoff soon became RCA's chief executive. He energetically pursued his concept of commercial radio broadcasting, establishing the NBC network and promoting technical advances. In the 1930s he turned his considerable energies toward doing the same for television, but the war intervened. He obtained a commission in the army where he served as a communications advisor to General Eisenhower, leaving the service as a brigadier general. By the late 1940s "General Sarnoff" had begun to see success in his drive for commercial television, though it took longer to sweep the nation than he had anticipated. He was a hard-driving, egotistical man but one with great vision.

David Sarnoff was the nation's leading media entrepreneur, forming both the radio and television arms of the National Broadcasting Corporation (NBC). (Hulton Archive/Getty Images)

See also Paley, William Samuel; Radio; Television.

References and Further Reading

Lyons, Eugene. *David Sarnoff: A Biography.* New York: Harper and Row, 1966.

Sinclair, Harry Ford (1876–1956)

Born in West Virginia, Harry Ford Sinclair moved to Kansas at an early age and earned a pharmacist's certificate at the University of Kansas. When his father's drugstore failed, young Harry obtained financial backing from J. M. Cudahy, a major Chicago meat packer, to purchase oil drilling rights in southern Kansas and Oklahoma. An ambitious and energetic independent oil man, Sinclair drilled dozens of wells, bought refineries, constructed pipelines, and eventually created a vertically integrated operation he named the Sinclair Consolidated Oil Corporation in 1917. Sinclair personally served on federal boards during the First World War, service that cemented his ties to major political figures. In 1923 congressional investigators found that one of his subsidiaries, the Mammoth Oil Co., had illegally obtained leases to naval oil reserves located at Teapot Dome, California, and Elk Hills, Wyoming. Several government officials were convicted of fraud, and, while Sinclair avoided that charge, he did serve six months for contempt of Congress and other questionable actions. Sinclair sold a half interest in Sinclair Consolidated to Standard Oil in the early 1930s, and spent the rest of the decade bailing out or reorganizing other oil-related businesses. Sinclair Consolidated was a major supplier of 100-octane aviation fuel in the Second World War, and it expanded its auto service stations nationwide in the late 1940s.

See also Phillips, Frank; Rockefeller, John Davison.

References and Further Reading

Connelly, William L. *The Oil Business as I Saw It: Half a Century with Sinclair.* Norman, OK: University of Oklahoma Press, 1954.

Sloan, Alfred Pritchard, Jr. (1875–1966)

The son of a machinist, Alfred Pritchard Sloan, Jr., was a brilliant student who completed an electrical engineering degree at MIT in just three years. Even so, the most attractive job he could find in the depressed 1890s was as a draftsman at the Hyatt Roller Bearing Co. in Newark, New Jersey. Within a few years, Sloan had risen to the presidency of the company, which produced quality bearings for the burgeoning automobile industry. When his company was acquired by General Motors Corporation (GM), Sloan became an executive in the larger corporation. He worked first with William Durant and later with Pierre du Pont on an extraordinarily effective management plan for the diversified auto-making conglomerate. Elected GM president in 1923, he developed the corporation's successful market-bracketing strategy and introduced the annual model change policy. He remained associated with GM for the rest of his life, serving as its chief executive officer for twenty-three years. The Sloan Foundation he endowed held over $1 billion in assets in the early twenty-first century.

See also Bracketing the Market; Built-in Obsolescence; du Pont, Pierre Samuel.

References and Further Reading

Farber, David. *Sloan Rules.* Chicago: University of Chicago Press, 2002.

Taylor, Frederick Winslow (1856–1915)

Born into a prosperous Pennsylvania Quaker family, Frederick Winslow Taylor was expected to attend Harvard. But severe astigmatism made it difficult for him to read, so he apprenticed himself as a pattern maker at a Philadelphia hydraulic machinery manufacturer. Soon he was working at Midvale Steel Co. where he devoted many years to studying manufacturing processes. An early experimenter with time and motion studies, Taylor also proposed incentive-based piecework wages. After 1900 he became an independent consultant on scientific management, sometimes also known as Taylorism. His advocacy of breaking industrial jobs into basic movements and rearranging the factory work-floor to promote efficiency had widespread and long-lasting influences in the United States and around the world.

See also Scientific Management.

References and Further Reading

Copley, Frank Barkley. *Frederick W. Taylor.* New York: A. M. Kelley, 1969.

Trippe, Juan (1899–1981)

Juan Trippe left Yale in 1917 to join the Navy and learn how to fly. Although he later returned to Yale to complete his degree, his fascination with airplanes dominated his life. He opened an air taxi service in Long Island in the 1920s and won an airmail contract between Boston and New York. Soon he was off to Florida where he founded a new company that linked Caribbean islands with the mainland. By the late 1930s his enterprise had evolved into Pan-American Airways, an early adopter of the amphibian flying boats he called clippers. Trippe's long-range clippers enabled him to extend Pan-Am's routes to South America, China, and Africa. After the Second World War, he fought the rest of the airline industry to expand his customer base by offering "tourist class" fares. Trippe eagerly switched to jet-

Juan Trippe was one of the most colorful aviation entrepreneurs, expanding what had begun as a local air mail delivery service into the giant Pan American Airways. (AP/Wide World Photos)

powered Boeing 707s in the 1950s and played a major role in convincing the airframe giant to construct 747 jumbo jets with hundreds of seats for tourist-class passengers. Some suggest that his overinvestment in the very expensive jumbo jets fatally injured Pan-American, which went bankrupt ten years after Trippe's death. During his lifetime, Juan Trippe was an air travel icon, rivaled only by his bitter competitor, Howard Hughes and his TWA venture.

See also Commercial Aviation; Hughes, Howard Robard.

References and Further Reading

Daly, Robert. *An American Saga, Juan Trippe and His Pan Am Empire.* New York: Random House, 1980.

Vail, Theodore Newton (1845–1920)

Born in Ohio, Theodore Newton Vail grew up in New Jersey but found his first job in New York City as a telegraph operator. Over the next few years he tried his hand at several careers before landing a position with the U.S. postal system in Omaha. There he devised a more efficient sorting system that attracted the attention of the railway mail superintendent, a position Vail himself assumed in 1876. It was a short step from there to general manager of the new telephone company Alexander Graham Bell and his associates formed in Boston. For seven years Vail headed American Bell, focusing his energies on building a nationwide long-distance capability. In 1885 Vail assumed the presidency of a spin-off company named American Telephone and Telegraph Co. (AT&T) whose sole business was long-distance telephone service. The company's financial backers disagreed with Vail's business strategy, however, and forced him out in 1887. Twenty years later, J. P. Morgan took control of AT&T and reappointed Vail as its president. For the next thirteen years, Vail brilliantly outmaneuvered competitors and so astutely managed relations with the federal government that AT&T never faced antitrust litigation even as it assumed virtual monopoly control over the nation's long-distance communication system.

See also Bell, Alexander Graham.

References and Further Reading

Paine, Albert Bigelow. *Theodore N. Vail.* New York: Harper, 1929.

Wallace, Henry Agard (1888–1965)

The Iowa-based Wallace family was highly influential in a variety of agrarian enterprises. They published *Wallace's Farmer,* the most widely circulated agrarian journal, and pioneered the development of hybrid crops. Henry Cantwell Wallace, served as secretary of agriculture in the Harding and Coolidge administrations in the 1920s, but his son, Henry Agard Wallace became a prominent Democrat. He served as secretary of agriculture and subsequently vice president under Franklin Roosevelt. Wallace is most widely known for his association with the Agricultural Adjustment Acts with their emphases on price controls and supports for agricultural commodities. Popular with the liberal Democrats, Wallace unsuccessfully ran for the presidency in 1948 as the Progressive Party candidate.

See also Agricultural Adjustment Acts; Induced Scarcity.

References and Further Reading

Culver, John C., and Joan Hyde. *American Dreamer.* New York: Norton, 2000.

Watson, Thomas J. (1874–1956)

The conservatively dressed, highly educated white-collar workforce at IBM epitomized mid-twentieth century American business, and it in turn personified Thomas J. Watson's vision. He started out selling pianos and organs on the road, but found more stable work at National Cash Register. Its dynamic president, John Henry Patterson, not only introduced Watson to the world of business machines but was an inspirational leader and an aggressive competitor. When Tom Watson became general manager of the Control-Tabulating-Recording Co. (CTR) in 1914, he applied the lessons he had learned from Patterson. He created a central research department and personally conducted motivational seminars for his salespeople. When Watson assumed full control as president of CTR in 1924, it had expanded its operations overseas, so he changed its name to International Business Machines (IBM). Building on CTR's historic links to Herman Hollerith's tabulating technology, IBM marketed punched cards that became the universal means for entering and tabulating data. Although Watson was no scientist, he was an astute businessman who invested half a million dollars and donated expensive equipment to Howard Aiken's Harvard project that created the Mark I computer. After a falling out, Watson exhorted his own researchers to outdo Aiken, and they succeeded in developing a premier line of large-scale computers. Tom Watson's motto was "Think!" and it motivated a whole generation of IBM engineers, scientists, and salesmen at the world's largest supplier of business machines.

See also Computers; Patterson, John Henry; Tabulating.

References and Further Reading

Maney, Kevin. *The Maverick and His Machine: Thomas Watson, Sr., and the Making of IBM.* New York: Wiley, 2003.

Section 5

Recent America, 1940 to the Present

The Second World War did far more than all the New Deal programs combined to pull the United States out of the Great Depression. Even before the attack on Pearl Harbor, the global conflict had generated enormous demand for American material goods. Factories reopened, millions of unemployed workers found jobs, and international trade revived. The demand for goods became even more intense after the United States entered the war, producing shortages and stringencies that caused the federal government to impose price controls and **rationing**. Consumer production took a distant back seat to war-related industries like **military aviation**, and defense contracts stimulated the development of **computers**. Postwar involvement in the Cold War, Korea, and Vietnam helped raise concerns about the growing influence of what was called the **military-industrial complex**.

Meanwhile the revival of a strong postwar consumer focus in the U.S. economy had a number of consequences. By the 1950s manufacturers were systematically analyzing consumer desires through the use of the **marketing concept**. People fled to the suburbs where **malls** provided an alternative to shopping downtown. This sprawl also encouraged the spread of very diversified **franchise** opportunities.

Exciting technological innovations fueled consumerism. In addition to creating a huge market for receiving sets, **television** provided an extraordinarily effective means of advertising. In the 1950s vacuum tubes in TV sets gave way to **transistors** and they, in turn, evolved into **microchips** for literally thousands of uses. Chips became essential elements in the **personal computers** that proliferated in the last two decades of the twentieth century.

The technological revolution affected how and what people bought. Microchips and laser technology combined to make the **universal product code** system feasible. **Credit cards** replaced cash in many consumer purchases, and **electronic fund transfers** handled many other monetary exchanges. The postwar housing boom spurred adoption of **adjustable rate mortgages**, but even these more flexible loan instruments did not prevent a massive, nationwide **savings and loan crisis** in the 1980s and 1990s.

Changing and growing consumer demand encouraged parallel changes and growth in various industries. In the 1950s entrepreneurs began cobbling together giant **conglomerates** that cut across traditional industrial sectors. Many of these resulted from **leveraged buyouts**, some of which were funded with **arbitrage** and **junk bonds**. Developing industries that lacked traditional corporate structures or marketing records relied on **venture capital** to get started. New companies often compensated their most creative employees with **stock options** as a substitute for or supplement to salaries and bonuses.

By the 1980s many conglomerates had proven to be unmanageable or unprofitable, and a number of them became victims of **hostile takeovers**. To defend themselves, corporate executives either sought rescue by a **white knight** or swallowed a **poison pill** to make their companies less attractive to corporate raiders. Some raiders were bought off with **greenmail** payments, but if a takeover succeeded, the ousted managers often resorted to **golden parachutes** to cushion their fall from power.

The relationship of government to business in the late twentieth century presented some marked contrasts to earlier periods. Shortly after the Second World War, the United States took aggressive steps to convince other nations they should adopt freer trade principles. U.S. leadership in drafting the **General Agreement on Tariffs and Trade (GATT)** signaled a permanent abandonment of protectionism. The economy continued to experience cyclical behavior, however, until it settled into **stagflation** in the 1970s. This condition seemed to defy classical economic thinking and neither of the newer macroeconomic theories, **monetarism** and **supply-side economics,** seemed to offer relief. In the end a conscious decision to promote **deregulation** may have been the most important federal initiative, reversing decades of Progressive and New Deal reforms.

As the twentieth century drew to a close, many Americans subscribed to a 1920s-style belief that the United States had entered a permanent boom period. The end of the Cold War lessened the nation's focus on weapons and deterrence that had raised concerns about the military-industrial complex. Simultaneously the seemingly limitless possibilities of the computer revolution spawned thousands of dot-com start-ups. Unfortunately, as Wesley Mitchell's cyclical theories would have predicted, a disheartening bust followed the boom, leaving Americans in the dawn of a new century unsure of where their nation's economy and businesses were headed.

KEY CONCEPTS

Adjustable Rate Mortgages

New legislation in the 1980s allowed federally chartered savings and loan associations (S&Ls) to offer mortgages with variable or adjustable rates of interest. Over time the lender could adjust the rates up or down to correspond with the rise or fall of interest rates in general. Adjustable rate mortgages (ARMs) became so popular that by the end of the decade more than half of all new mortgages involved variable rather than fixed interest rates.

Variable rate mortgages had become common in Great Britain by the end of the nineteenth century, but American lending institutions were slow to seek their advantages. Both federally and state chartered savings and loan institutions functioned successfully by issuing long-term, usually thirty-year mortgages with a fixed rate of interest. As long as the U.S. economy avoided sharp or persistent inflation, fixed-rate mortgages represented a fair and equitable arrangement for both borrowers and lenders.

The massive costs of the Vietnam War fueled inflation during the late 1960s, however, and it became even more intense in the 1970s. An Arab oil embargo in 1973 and OPEC policies later in the decade combined with other forces to drive general interest rates to historic levels. They eventually topped 20 percent in the early 1980s. The S&Ls simply could not remain solvent paying the high interest rates depositors demanded and earning substantially lower returns from their portfolios of low-interest, fixed-rate thirty-year mortgages.

In the late 1970s some states permitted the S&Ls they chartered to offer adjustable rate mortgages. The 1982 Depository Institutions Deregulation and Monetary Control Act extended this opportunity to the thousands of S&Ls that operated under federal charters. This legislation recognized the impossible financial bind facing S&Ls, and it encouraged them to issue mortgages with rates that would climb if and when general interest rates and other economic indicators rose.

To encourage borrowers to accept the new instruments, S&Ls often set low initial rates, even lower than they would have for a fixed-rate mortgage. Once the borrower had signed up, interest rates could be adjusted upward in the out years, although the change in a single year was often limited to no more than a percent or two. Fortunately for borrowers, inflation eased in the late 1980s, lessening the pressure on S&Ls to bump up mortgage interest rates. Even so, ARMs remained very popular, so much so that by the end of the decade over half of all S&L mortgages involved adjustable rates.

ARMs continued to be popular in subsequent years. A significant and seemingly persistent inflation in the prices for domestic real estate in the 1990s and early twenty-first century convinced many borrowers that the increasing equity value of their homes would more than offset any costs. By the early 2000s, therefore, interest-only mortgages had become very common. In these, borrowers made no principal payments in the early years. When payments became necessary, the buyer could either increase his or her monthly payment or simply sell the house at a substantial profit. On average Americans move every seven to ten years, so selling out and buying a different home is something of a norm.

Both variable-rate and interest-only mortgages work best in a market where real estate prices continue to escalate. Because the annual inflation in home prices in many communities has exceeded 10 percent in recent years, both types of loans have proved relatively safe for borrowers and lenders. Yet should the housing price boom begin to taper off or, worse, end or decline, those locked into long-term mortgage contracts with adjustable payment schedules may find themselves in very awkward situations.

See also Savings and Loan Crisis.

References and Further Reading

Friedman, Jack P. *Adjustable-rate Mortgages.* Hauppauge, NY: Barron's, 2004.

Irwin, Robert. *The New Mortgage Game.* New York: McGraw-Hill, 1982.

White, Lawrence J. *The S&L Debacle.* New York: Oxford University Press, 1991.

Arbitrage

Arbitrage takes many forms. In essence an arbitrager's goal is to buy securities at one price and sell those same securities or their equivalent at a higher price either immediately or very quickly. Because arbitrage can create an instant market for new securities and otherwise serve as short-term bridge funding to facilitate selling and buying stocks and bonds, it can smooth the transfer of securities. As the pace of corporate mergers and reorganization dramatically quickened in the 1980s, however, the role of arbitrage and arbitragers became much more prominent.

The classic form of arbitrage involved a person buying in one market or exchange and immediately selling that same item in another venue at a higher price. The price differentials that created opportunities for arbitrage might occur when the markets were in different countries and communication between them was slow. International currency exchange frequently took place at differing prices in different countries. In recent years instantaneous, computer-enhanced information transmission has made this type of arbitrage almost impossible.

Arbitragers therefore began to exploit different tactics. Most U.S. securities transactions took place in New York City, so arbitragers sought out particular financial instruments that allowed for minor price differentials. One favorite was the convertible bond. A company seeking additional capital might issue bonds that included a provision to enable the holder to convert or trade them in for a certain number of shares of company stock. Convertible bonds provided arbitragers with relatively risk-free opportunities. Market forces usually allowed them to purchase a particular bond at a price somewhat below its equivalent value in shares of stock. An immediate profit could be realized by converting the bonds. If the company's prospects look good, however, the arbitrager might hold the bonds for a time in anticipation of a rise in the share prices that would net an even higher return.

Arbitrage involving stock-for-stock transactions is sometimes called risk arbitrage and it became more common in the 1980s. A proposed corporate merger or leveraged buyout typically began with an offer to purchase the target firm's shares at a premium price. The premium could be 20 percent or higher than the shares' current market price. Arbitragers jumped in with attractive offers for blocs of shares at prices lower than the merger proposal but higher than the market price. Cautious or dubious shareholders were happy to sell their stock to an arbitrager if they were interested in locking in gains without having to wait for the merger process to grind to a conclusion or possibly fail completely.

Sometimes arbitragers ended up holding huge percentages of a target company's stock, making them increasingly committed to ensuring that the reorganization or takeover went through. Major brokerage houses were often involved. Goldman Sachs and Salomon Brothers, who had added arbitrage to their financial services, were naturally eager to do what they could to facilitate the conclusion of a proposed merger.

The takeover shakeout eased in the 1990s, however, and arbitrage reverted to more stable and predictable functions. Nevertheless, arbitrage continues to perform an important role facilitating stock transfers and making markets for new issues in advance of their popular acceptance. But as the risks have declined, so have the potential gains from this type of activity.

See also Boesky, Ivan; Hostile Takeovers; Leveraged Buyout.

References and Further Reading

Eades, Simon. *Options, Hedging and Arbitrage.* Chicago: Probus, 1992.

Evans, Jr., Morgan D. *Arbitrage in Domestic Securities in the United States.* New York: Parker, 1965.

Computers

A number of experimental data-processing systems were devised to meet military needs during the Second World War. Army and Navy contracts financed most of the developments in the early computer industry, and dozens of ideas and prototypes appeared. Wartime secrecy tended to limit collaboration, but nationwide and worldwide interest blossomed in the late 1940s. Within a few years literally hundreds of new computing systems were being marketed.

No single person invented the computer; it was the product of an assembly of scientific and engineering concepts. For example, the systems operating in the 1950s used the same punch card input system that Herman Hollerith had developed for tabulating census data in the 1890s. Englishman Alan Turing's thinking in the 1930s was vital in that it encouraged users to break complex computations into a series of easily programmable steps. Turing applied his ideas to practical problems while working on code-breaking machinery at England's Bletchly Park facility.

John Vincent Atanasoff constructed a working model of a digital computer that used mechanical and vacuum tube relays in 1939 at Iowa State College (later University). John Mauchly visited Ames and discussed the project with Atanasoff and his graduate student collaborator Clifford Berry. Back at the University of Pennsylvania, Mauchly and an associate, J. Presper Eckert, accepted a challenge from the U.S. Army Ordnance Department's Ballistic Research Laboratory to produce a machine ca-

The world's first all-purpose electronic computer, a 30-ton behemoth of steel, wire, and tubes, known as the Electronic Numerical Integrator and Computer (ENIAC), is shown in an undated photo. ENIAC was launched at the University of Pennsylvania in February 1946. (Hulton Archive/Getty Images)

pable of calculating shell trajectories. Completion of their Electronic Numerical Integrator and Computer (ENIAC) was delayed until 1946, but it found immediate use in analyzing data related to atomic weaponry.

ENIAC did more to popularize digital computers than any previous machine, but it was hardly unique. Howard Aiken at Harvard had earlier contacted Thomas J. Watson, head of IBM, with plans for his own system. IBM provided money and equipment that Aiken incorporated into his Mark series of computers. This type of linkage between industry and university researchers was quite common during the next few years, and it provided IBM with a significant advantage when the company began developing its own machines for commercial use.

Throughout the first decade most of the enormous computing systems were built for specific purposes. Racks of vacuum tubes, switching equipment, and input-output devices filled large rooms and were far too expensive for routine work. IBM and other makers generally leased rather than sold their equipment, provided competent technical support, and adopted time-sharing capabilities to allow many users to participate.

Magnetic memory drums and data tapes introduced in the early 1950s broadened the capabilities of these early computers. Even more essential was the incorporation first of transistors and then integrated circuitry that sped up computation processes at the same time they reduced the size of the machines. After successfully marketing its 700 and 600 series computing systems for specific purposes, IBM created the 360 series in 1964. This was a new concept: a system that could be programmed to perform almost any computational process. Even more attractive was the fact that it used a standard operating system that enabled programs from one model to run equally well on another.

Meanwhile, a number of other manufacturers were exploiting the expanding computer market. One company that pioneered a different approach was Digital Equipment Corporation (DEC) founded by Ken Olson in Massachusetts. DEC took full advantage of the miniaturization of components and introduced its PDP-8 model, the nation's first minicomputer. Although minicomputers often weighed more that 200 pounds, they were far less expensive than IBM machines and were quite versatile. They proliferated in university settings where students and faculty across campus could tap into the mainframe to run their own programs. Meanwhile, individuals like Seymour Cray moved in the opposite direction, concocting supercomputers capable of unprecedented computational feats.

Remarkable progress in miniaturization of components allowed the industry to speed up computing processes and increase the size of batches that could be analyzed. At the same time, software developers worked to simplify the programming process itself. FORTRAN was introduced in 1956, a language primarily suited to scientific purposes, and COBAL appeared three years later, destined to become the most common programming language for business applications.

By the early 1970s computers had become common in business and academic settings. They enabled companies to track and analyze business data in much greater detail and with much more sophistication than ever before. University researchers and students could tackle research problems that would have been impossible earlier. Both private and public users encouraged continual improvements. The introduction of personal computers in the 1970s represented the culmination of this trend. While mainframe computers still function in many settings, the development of widely affordable personal computers touched off a new revolution in information technology.

See also Microchips; Olsen, Kenneth; Personal Computers; Wang, An; Watson, Thomas J.

References and Further Reading

Akera, Atsushi, and Frederik Nebeker. *From 0 to 1*. New York: Oxford University Press, 2002.

Burks, Alice Rowe. *Who Invented the Computer?* Amherst, NY: Prometheus, 2003.

Chandler, Jr., Alfred D., and James W. Cortada, eds. *A Nation Transformed by Information*. New York: Oxford University Press, 2000.

Ifrah, Georges. *The Universal History of Computing*. New York: Wiley, 2001.

Conglomerates

A new form of big business organization called a conglomerate became very popular in the 1950s and triggered a full-scale boom in the following decade. A conglomerate grew through aggressive acquisitions of existing companies. Unlike most earlier business consolidations, however, conglomerates expanded in a variety of directions, often collecting firms in unrelated industries. A good many conglomerates, including some of the largest, ran into severe financial trouble in the 1970s leading many to question just how wise the conglomerate strategy had been.

Nineteenth century Americans used two types of business consolidation: vertical and horizontal integration. Vertical integration involved the acquisition of firms that had buy-and-sell relationships with one another, such as a supplier of raw materials and a manufacturing concern. Horizontal integration occurred when an industrialist sought mergers with other firms in the same industry or that occupied a similar market niche. Conglomerates pursued neither of these strategies; instead they drew under centralized management firms engaged in diverse businesses.

Although many saw little sense to such acquisitions, closer analysis reveals three distinct types of conglomerates. One group engaged in *market extension,* acquiring companies or product lines that sold similar products but in different geographical areas. A second strategy was to pursue *product extension,* drawing together companies in related industries like food and beverages. But many of the most successful and notorious examples were "pure" conglomerates, assembling components with no obvious relationship whatsoever.

Several presumed benefits motivated conglomerators. Tax advantages played a key role in some instances. In assembling the collection of firms that constituted Textron, for example, Royal Little deliberately sought to match profitable companies with others running in the red. This reduced his conglomerate's overall tax obligations since he could charge the profits in one component against another's losses.

Avoiding antitrust actions was another motivation. A highly diversified conglomerate might have enormous capitalization and extensive market penetration yet control only a small percentage of sales in any given sector. Ironically the passage of the Celler-Kefauver Act of 1950 encouraged businessmen to expand in unrelated areas. With horizontal and vertical consolidation clearly in mind, the act discouraged mergers that would lessen competition. Federal authorities had a difficult time making a case against a highly diversified conglomerate.

Something called *synergy* also drew attention in this period. Pulling together a variety of business ventures would ideally create opportunities for cooperation, reduce wasteful duplication, and perhaps open doors to creativity. Except for a few isolated cases, it is difficult to conclude that most conglomerates actually engendered synergy. Indeed, some of the major players deliberately chose to buy companies that had already originated innovative products rather than fund research and development on their own. To some extent, conglomerates may well have stifled creativity rather than promoted it.

Another aspect of this new wave of consolidations was a popular belief that the issues managers faced were quite similar regardless of the product or service a modern company produced. This belief led to a proliferation of graduate programs in business administration. The holder of an MBA was presumed capable of dealing with corporate finance, personnel management, and even general marketing strategies that would be applicable in any company. In fact, many of those either heading up or drawn into conglomerates lacked the specialized production, product, or market knowledge they needed to function effectively as managers.

The experience of the earliest major conglomerate, Textron, illustrates the flaws in some of these assumptions. Royal Little had started out in the textile industry, becoming an early advocate of rayon. During the Second World War, demand for rayon skyrocketed because it was used in parachutes. After the war Little's core business was generating such high profits he was able to acquire other firms like Nashua Manufacturing, a major New England textile operation. At that point he seemed to be pursuing a product extension strategy, but his decision to acquire an airplane strut manufacturer, Cleveland Pneumatic Tool Co. had no such obvious relationship to his other holdings. Over the course of several years, Little bought a number of subsidiaries, many of which failed to prosper as elements of his conglomerate. He was far better at acquiring properties than he was at managing them.

The same could be said for other notable conglomerators. Harold Geneen shaped International Telephone and Telegraph (ITT) into the world's largest conglomerate, but it never functioned as a coherent whole. ITT stock reached an all-time high price of $124 a share in 1967 but had fallen to only $12 in 1974. Tex Thornton had a similar experience with Litton Industries, another highly diversified conglomerate. Over the same period Litton stock fell from $104 a share to less than $3. Whether lacking synergy or simply the victims of poor management, many other high-flying conglomerates crash-landed in the recession-plagued 1970s.

It was hardly surprising, then, that many of the leveraged buyouts and hostile takeovers in the more prosperous 1980s involved breaking up clumsy, unprofitable conglomerates. A corporate raider who captured control of a diversified holding company could sell off its unrelated or struggling components and leave behind a cleaner, more focused and healthier firm.

Many conglomerates have continued to exist, though many go through periodic restructuring and shuck off less productive elements. Government officials have become more sophisticated in dealing with these combinations, causing potential conglomerators to be more cautious and thoughtful than those who thrived in the 1960s. But the frenetic mixing and reshuffling of ownership and control that occurred in that period has made it difficult in many cases to understand or even know what product or company is a division of some other, more anonymous concern.

See also Geneen, Harold; Horizontal Integration; Hostile Takeovers; Kravis, Henry; Leveraged Buyout; Ling, James J.; Simon, Norton; Vertical Integration.

References and Further Reading

Adams, Walter, ed. *The Structure of American Industry.* New York: Macmillan, 1990.

Sobel, Robert. *The Rise and Fall of the Conglomerate Kings.* New York: Stein and Day, 1984.

Winslow, John F. *Conglomerates Unlimited.* Bloomington, IN: Indiana University Press, 1973.

Credit Cards

The modern credit-card industry dawned in 1949 with the issuance of the first Diners Club cards. Ironically, Diners Club accounted for only 0.5 percent of all credit-card transactions in the United States by 2005. The two major competitors, VISA and MasterCard, on the other hand, processed over 70 percent of the $1.4 trillion credit-card purchases Americans made that year. The growth of the credit-card industry was so phenomenal, in fact, that some predicted that plastic would completely supplant cash. Although that has not occurred, credit cards have become an indispensable feature of the nation's consumer economy.

A variety of consumer credit arrangements had developed in earlier years, but they tended to focus either on single items like automobiles and houses, or purchases from particular stores and companies. The revolutionary change that occurred in the early 1950s was the extension of consumer credit through cards that could be used for large and small purchases at many retail outlets.

It might never have happened if Frank McNamara had not discovered he had left his wallet at home while lunching at a Manhattan restaurant in 1949. The president of a New York credit company, McNamara thought many professionals would like to have instant credit at a variety of eating places. In association with Alfred Bloomingdale and Ralph Snyder, he formed a company that enrolled hundreds of members in his "Diner's Club," each of whom paid an $18 annual fee. Simultaneously he tried to convince restaurant owners to pay him 7 percent of their take from customers who presented the card. That fee financed tracking and billing procedures for his new venture.

One obstacle to the growth of the Diners Club was reluctance on the part of potential customers to pay a fee unless they could use the card everywhere. Equally difficult was enrolling merchants who had to surrender such a large percentage of their profits. The Club thus grew rather slowly, enabling other companies to initiate their own schemes. It was hardly surprising that two major travel-oriented companies, American Express and Hilton Hotels, were among the first to issue cards in 1958. The Carte Blanch cards Hilton distributed were designed to be universally acceptable not only at its own chain but at other hotels and restaurants.

It was a short step from these travel- and entertainment-focused programs to more ambitious operations. Two of the largest banks in the United States jumped in almost immediately. The Bank of America issued its BankAmericard, and Chase Manhattan established the foundation for what would become Master Charge. Growth was slow until the late 1960s when the major players engaged in aggressive advertising and mass-mailing campaigns that induced millions of Americans to sign up. That, in turn, convinced skeptical merchants to sign contracts as well.

A number of hurdles had to be overcome. Mass-mailings provoked government restrictions. State usury laws limited the interest that could be charged on unpaid balances. Even so, hundreds of other banks and companies jumped in, issuing their own cards. The advantages of size and merchant accessibility soon convinced many of these to affiliate with the two major networks. Name changes helped. BankAmericard became VISA in 1976, and Master Charge adopted the more streamlined MasterCard image four years later.

While both prospered, VISA outstripped MasterCard during this period. Many banks insisted on the right to issue either or both of these familiar and popular cards, blurring the distinction between the systems. But their head-to-head competition benefited customers by discouraging charging annual fees and helped merchants who often enjoyed discounts of no more than 2 percent. American Express and other companies that continued to impose annual fees and higher discounts retained loyal customer bases, but expanded more slowly than the giants.

Another popular credit card, Discover, drew its initial clients from the huge Sears, Roebuck customer base. As part of its expansion into the finance area, Sears launched the Discover card in 1986. One of its appeals was a 1 percent rebate to customers on all purchases they made. Similar inducements became common, with cards racking up airline miles, points for various benefits, and even discounts on major purchases like cars. Affinity cards were also popular, with links and sometimes contributions to universities or charities.

Relaxation of usury laws in the 1980s cleared the way for credit-card companies to levy ever higher finance charges on outstanding balances. The majority of credit-card holders avoid these charges by paying in full each month, but a substantial number routinely pay only the minimum charge. That has led to a huge and growing volume of credit-card debt that averaged around $9,000 per family in 2005. Credit-card offers continue to clog customers' mailboxes, however, because finance charges set at 5 or 10 percent over the prime rate provide banks with much higher returns than they can reap from other investments.

Technological innovations have had substantial impacts. The computer revolution has enabled merchants and card-issuers to track purchases and payments instantaneously. These transactions have increasingly relied on electronic fund transfers, a development that has blossomed in recent years. Verbal authorization has given way to automatic checks. Indeed, a customer may never interact with a merchant in person at all if he or she is buying "pay-at-the-pump" gasoline. The vast expansion of credit-card customers has also stimulated enormous growth in the credit-checking industry.

In the end, however, the individual customer has probably benefited most from the credit-card revolution. It simplifies both buying directly and through electronic means. It extends both short- and long-term credit yet allows prudent buyers to delay payment without penalty. Because the systems have long since crossed international borders, it also facilitates travel and commerce abroad. Like Frank McNamara, it allows us all to leave our cash at home and still take full advantage of the consumer economy.

See also Consumer Credit; Electronic Fund Transfers.

References and Further Reading

Evans, David S., and Richard Schmalensee. *Paying with Plastic.* Cambridge, MA: MIT Press, 2005.
Mandell, Lewis. *The Credit Card Industry.* Boston: Twayne Publishers, 1990.
Manning, Robert D. *Credit Card Nation.* New York: Basic Books, 2000.

Deregulation

Ronald Reagan made deregulation a centerpiece of his presidential agenda. Although some restraints and limitations had taken place in the previous decade, the 1980s saw a concerted and pervasive rollback of federal regulation. As a result, many industries like electric power and airlines operated in new, presumably more competitive environments. Some of this deregulation was reversed in the 1990s, but just how the government should influence and control businesses and the economy remain matters of debate.

The Interstate Commerce Act in 1887 was the first major federal regulatory move, and during the next quarter century Progressive politicians erected a number of independent regulatory agencies. The Federal Trade Commission, the Federal Reserve System, the Pure Food and Drug Act, and similar initiatives were responses to public concern that privately owned corporations were becoming too powerful and needed to be restrained.

The federal role expanded enormously during the First World War, raising fears of too intrusive a government. The return to what President Warren G. Harding called "normalcy" in the 1920s included widespread support for retrenchment. Existing regulatory agencies remained in operation, but conservative appointees throttled back their activities, helping clear the way for a comparatively unconstrained bull market. The Great Depression once again reversed public perceptions. President Franklin Roosevelt's experimentation with a number of potential government remedies included a healthy dose of regulation. The 1934 Securities and Exchanges Commission, for example, was modeled after the Progressive agencies that dealt with other activities early in the twentieth century.

Much of the regulatory structure was designed to constrain corporate greed and malfeasance in pursuit of fair competition that would presumably benefit all. The civil rights and antiwar movements in the 1960s also roused concerns related to consumer and worker protection and safety. New regulatory entities like the Environmental Protection Agency and the Consumer Product Safety Commission reflected these concerns and demanded additional layers of compliance reporting from corporations. In 1970 the Occupational Safety and Health Administration (OSHA) threatened even more federal intrusion into the workplace. Social regulation thus joined economic regulation in an ongoing effort to improve the American way of life.

Instead Americans suffered a series of reverses in the 1970s. Shortages of key items like oil, sugar, and paper suggested that the economy was being mismanaged. By the middle of the decade unnerving stagflation had set in. Nothing that presidents Gerald Ford and Jimmy Carter tried seemed effective. In this discouraging environment, many began to blame the federal government for overregulating the economy, citing the high costs of economic and social policies with their flood of restrictions and paperwork.

President Carter responded with a few efforts to cut back on these restraints. Regulatory agencies were increasingly required to conduct cost-benefit analyses, assessing the probable impact of new or existing regulations. The Office of Management and Budget (OMB) became a major player in this process, evaluating the impact of regulations not only on the federal budget but on society at large.

These changes apparently failed to reassure American voters, especially when Carter's Republican challenger, Ronald Reagan promised much more. President Reagan immediately began issuing executive orders that demanded widespread review and accountability from the regulatory agencies. He also imposed a sixty-day freeze on the promulgation of new regulations, providing time for public comment and administrative review. Cost-benefit analyses like those Carter had instituted continued to be required. The result of these policies was a remarkable slackening of the pace of regulation.

In addition Reagan fundamentally shifted the ground under the agencies. Regulatory agencies suffered the full effects of his plan to curtail federal expenditures. Agencies' budgets were cut and they had to provide much more in the form of justifications for the funds they did receive. And, just as Harding had done in the 1920s, Reagan appointed industry-friendly conservatives to head both the economic and social regulatory activities. The effects of these measures became evident almost immediately in a measurable decline in new rules and a general weakening of existing constraints.

George H. W. Bush had headed Reagan's Task Force on Regulatory Relief while he was vice president, and Republicans expected him to do nothing to hinder the deregulation bandwagon when he became president in 1989. Bush did establish a Council of Competitiveness and asked his vice president, Dan Quayle, to chair it. But overall President Bush was much less successful than his predecessor in curbing regulation. Indeed, two landmark pieces of legislation he signed in 1990 had the opposite effect. The Americans with Disabilities Act and the Clean Air Act both triggered a massive new round of regulations and rules.

President Clinton's record regarding deregulation was equally ambiguous. Although he spoke in favor of the social regulations that applied to the environment, workplace safety, and consumer protection, he retained the cost-benefit ratio assessments and many other aspects of the Reagan era. The election of Republican majorities in both houses of Congress in 1994 further dampened any chance of reviving broad-scale regulation. There is no reason to expect that the struggle to find the proper balance between regulation and free enterprise will end anytime soon.

See also Antitrust Laws; Interstate Commerce Clause; Recovery; Savings and Loan Crisis; Stagflation.

References and Further Reading

Eisner, Marc Allen, et al. *Contemporary Regulatory Policy.* Boulder, CO: Lynne Reinner, 2000.

Meeropol, Michael. *Surrender: How the Clinton Administration Completed the Reagan Revolution.* Ann Arbor, MI: University of Michigan Press, 1998.

Parzych, Kenneth M. *Public Policy and the Regulatory Environment.* Lanham, MD: University Press of America, 1993.

Electronic Fund Transfers

The computer revolution that dramatically altered the credit-card industry also opened new pathways for the transfer of funds electronically. One example of an electronic fund transfer (EFT) is the use of a debit card rather than a credit card. An expenditure conducted with a debit card instantly deducts funds from the buyer's account. In more sophisticated systems the same transaction can instantaneously add funds to a seller's account. The EFT networks in place today can also be used for telephone, Web-based, and other financial transfers without cumbersome checks, cash, or credit-card billing.

Once the concept of electronically transferring funds caught on, advanced technology for it quickly developed. The most familiar equipment used in EFTs is the automated teller machine (ATM) installed in banks, stores, gas stations, and sometimes even in blank walls. Englishman John Shepard-Barron was the first to propose such a system in 1965, and within a matter of months, ATMs cropped up in Europe. Texas-based Docutel was formed in 1967 to develop baggage-handling systems, but it quickly added cash dispensing machines to its product line.

Docutel coding in a card's magnetic stripe enabled it to access an ATM. Additional security was provided by the use of personal identification numbers or PINs. The heart of the operation, however, was the delivery of cash to the customer and the simultaneous deduction of a like amount from his or her bank account. Unlike credit cards, a debit card does not permit delayed or minimum balance payments. An electronic transfer of funds is instantaneous.

Banks adopted ATMs for several reasons. They could achieve cost savings by replacing human tellers, and they offered service outside normal business hours. Sophisticated ATMs can do much more than deliver cash—they can accept deposits, provide immediate account information, and sell stamps. And because the transactions are carried out electronically and instantly, they do not involve paper checks or require complex billing procedures.

Today debit cards can be used like credit cards for purchases at retail outlets and gas stations. But because debit-card users essentially operate on a pay-as-you-go basis, there are no outstanding balances on which banks can charge interest. As a result, many debit-card issuers collect annual or transaction fees from their customers to fund the costs of the relatively expensive machinery and networks involved.

Although it has taken longer than many anticipated, the use of electronic fund transfers in other transactions is becoming more widespread. Bill payments can be made by telephone, computer linkages, or websites. Banks offer direct payment of recurring utility bills or other charges, using electronic means to transfer funds directly from a depositor's account to that of the payee. Some futurists confidently believed that EFTs would ultimately supplant all other forms of payment, making cash and even credit cards obsolete. There is some irony in the fact, however, that a significant number of EFTs involve dispensing cash. In that sense, the ATM revolution has retarded the disappearance of old-fashioned paper currency.

See also Consumer Credit; Credit Cards.

References and Further Reading

Kirkman, Patrick R. A. *Electronic Funds Transfer Systems.* New York: Blackwell, 1987.

Mandell, Lewis. *The Credit Card Industry: A History.* Boston: Twayne Publishers, 1990.

Turner, Paul S. *Managing the Risks of Payment Systems.* Hoboken, NJ: Wiley, 2003.

Franchises

In 1980 the cash registers of local businesses operating under franchise agreements rang up almost one-third of all retail sales in the United States. National companies with extensive advertising campaigns and popular brand names encouraged local entrepreneurs to join with them in opening outlets offering services, clothing, fast food, and countless other consumer products. These franchising opportunities offered options to local business people, but in many cases, they supplanted neighborhood stores and businesses with long histories.

The franchise phenomenon that blossomed after the Second World War had long roots in the traditional dealership system. Cyrus McCormick had essentially franchised the machine shops and distributors that constituted his dealer network in the 1850s. When the automobile age arrived, local entrepreneurs established themselves as owners of dealerships offering sales, financing, and service. The auto industry also encouraged the growth of franchised gasoline stations. Many other businesses used franchising to expand. For example, Howard Johnson found himself short of capital during the Great Depression, so he signed franchise agreements with others who were capable of funding new restaurants that featured his ice cream and popular menu to traveling Americans. These businesses continue to operate, of course, but the franchise or dealer explosion that occurred in the second half of the twentieth century encompasses a remarkable variety of goods and services.

Several factors can help convince someone to sign a franchise agreement. The central organization provides branded prod-

Ray Kroc opened his first McDonald's outlet in Des Plaines, Illinois, in 1955. (Getty Images)

ucts, serves as a reliable wholesaler, and often offers management training programs. It also conducts market surveys to identify potentially profitable new features. The franchiser generally strives to limit competition among its local units by assigning them reasonable, exclusive sales areas. Best of all, the successful franchised operation has usually ironed out the basic business risks associated with its products or services. And not incidentally its national advertising campaigns build continuing customer loyalty.

Franchises also benefit consumers. They trust the central organization to impose quality control on local operators to protect its brand identification. As Americans became increasingly mobile, traveling either for business or pleasure, they were reassured by the appearance of familiar franchise logos on the road. They knew what to expect.

In the 1960s the nation experienced a franchise boom when hundreds of new national franchises entered the market and opened thousands of new outlets. Recessions in the 1970s put the brakes on expansion, however, and highlighted the inherent dangers in the system. Franchise fees could be excessive, performance goals set by the central organization could be difficult or impossible to meet in some locations, and some franchisers required their agents to buy directly from them at elevated prices. If the central organization itself went bankrupt, franchise holders could be stranded with specialized inventory, equipment, and even distinctive buildings unsuitable for alternative uses. Overall, however, a franchise offered an aspiring proprietor less risk than attempting to start up a unique business.

No other corporation has been so successful in this realm than McDonalds. In the 1950s Ray Kroc bought the rights to the brand name of a very successful southern California drive-in hamburger restaurant. While he was signing up franchise dealers all across the country, Kroc revolutionized what came to be known as the fast-food business by applying what an earlier generation would have called scientific management. By restricting the menu to a few standard items, he was able to simplify and streamline the food preparation process by using specialized equipment and imposing strict guidelines. The result resembled an industrial assembly line, and it allowed his franchisees to hire unskilled workers like high school students at very low wages.

Meanwhile the corporation mounted an aggressive advertising campaign whose budget exceeded $200 million in 1980. In the early days the golden arches supported a red sign that announced a specific number of millions of hamburgers sold. That slogan gave way to "billions and billions" as the number of franchises grew meteorically in the United States and abroad. Unlike most franchisers, the McDonalds Corporation itself bought land and built outlets, owning about three-fourths of the property it then leased to local operators.

Dozens of other fast-food chains copied this success, enrolling franchisees who erected Wendy's, Burger King, Kentucky Fried Chicken, and Subway signs along highways and in strip malls across the country. Service outlets for laundries, telephones, auto parts, and hundreds of other consumer needs have established franchises. They have also proliferated in major suburban shopping malls. To a large degree they have supplanted the "mom and pop" stores that formerly served small towns and urban neighborhoods. The franchise phenomenon is perhaps the most visible and ubiquitous sign of the growth in national and international marketing opportunities in recent decades.

See also Johnson, Howard Deering; Kroc, Ray; Malls; Scientific Management.

References and Further Reading

Birkland, Peter M. *Franchising Dreams.* Chicago: University of Chicago Press, 2002.

Bradach, Jeffrey L. *Franchise Organizations.* Boston: Harvard Business School Press, 1998.

Kroc, Ray. *Grinding It Out.* Chicago: Henry Regenery, 1977.

Love, John F. *McDonald's: Behind the Arches.* New York: Bantam, 1986.

GATT

Although the General Agreement on Tariffs and Trade, more familiarly known as GATT, was signed in 1948, it represented the culmination of literally years of negotiations. The multinational agreement reduced tariffs on thousands of items in an effort to promote increased international trade. U.S. participation was based on the reciprocal trade agreement procedures it had adopted in 1934. The general agreement was subject to continuous review and modification in subsequent years, almost always in the direction of freer trade.

The concept of a general agreement on tariffs and trade became popular as an adjunct to the creation of the United Nations in 1945. The onset of the Cold War shortly thereafter further stimulated interest in improving trade relations among the countries that constituted the so-called free world. Many internationalists hoped that a general reduction in trade barriers would not only strengthen those arrayed against Communism but would simultaneously promote prosperity around the world.

The U.S. legislative authority to engage in the creation of GATT was an extension of the 1934 Reciprocal Trade Act. Both before and during the Second World War, American diplomats and statesmen had taken full advantage of that authority to reduce U.S. tariffs to 50 percent below those stipulated in the 1930 Smoot-Hawley Tariff Act. More reductions seemed desirable, so Congress passed the Trade Agreements Extension Act of 1945, authorizing the president to cut any existing rate in half again.

A flurry of bilateral negotiations immediately took place. They largely followed the *principal supplier* approach, in which the United States focused its attention on the overseas trading partner that supplied the most imports of a particular item. Once a reciprocal trade agreement with a principal supplier had been worked out, it was safe to extend that same reduced rate to all other trading partners through the most-favored-nation policy.

As each participating country completed its bilateral negotiations, it created a consolidated list of all concessions. These lists were then appended to the General Agreement on Tariffs and Trade signed in Geneva in 1948. The huge document stipulated tariff rates for some 45,000 items and represented the culmination of the largest multinational trade negotiation in history. Fortunately, the general reduction in trade barriers all around the world had the desired effects, promoting additional international exchange and domestic prosperity.

Political considerations within the United States tended to stymie further negotiations, however. The Republican-controlled Congress was loath to allow Democratic President Harry Truman much additional leeway. At the same time, Congress took pains to legislate protections for American firms that might suffer negative effects. American agreement to the GATT included an escape clause that permitted the United States to cancel a concession if an American firm could demonstrate it had been harmed. The concept of *peril points* emerged, levels below which domestic producers and workers might be imperiled. The U.S. Tariff Commission, later transformed into the U.S. International Trade Commission, became mired in a slew of investigations to evaluate whether peril points had been breached or the escape clause should be applied.

International pressures for continued progress remained strong throughout the 1950s. The administration of President Dwight Eisenhower continued to participate in additional rounds of negotiations, still focused on exhaustive studies of individual rates. In the early 1960s President John Kennedy sponsored yet another round of negotiations. Congress agreed to a modified strategy for the so-called Kennedy Round. Unlike earlier negotiations, the various nations came to the table with proposals for across-the-board cuts. Here again, the U.S. commission was supposed to identify products or industries that should be excluded from the general cuts, but the negotiations were much easier to conduct.

GATT remained the predominant instrument for the encouragement and regulation of international trade through the end of the Cold War. In the 1990s the World Trade Organization supplanted the complexities of the general agreement. Its primary focus is on supporting freer trade around the world, a goal for which GATT had laid important and enduring groundwork.

See also Protective Tariff; Reciprocity.

References and Further Reading

Bagwell, Kyle, and Robert W. Staiger. *The Economics of the World Trading System.* Cambridge, MA: MIT Press, 2002.

Dobson, John M. *Two Centuries of Tariffs.* Washington, DC: U.S. Printing Office, 1977.

Zeiler, Thomas W. *Free Trade, Free World: The Advent of GATT.* Chapel Hill, NC: University of North Carolina Press, 1999.

Golden Parachute

As the spate of hostile takeover bids became a flood in the 1980s, corporate executives developed a number of defensive strategies to prevent or discourage an unfriendly takeover. Because none of these strategies guaranteed protection, astute executives also considered their personal vulnerabilities. Boards of directors therefore began approving what were called golden parachutes: financial compensation packages for executives who might be ousted or choose to resign rather than work under a takeover regime.

A golden parachute might come into play whenever a major change in the corporation's control occurred or was imminent. The arrangements usually applied to a relatively small number of top executives—those most likely to be fired or to be uncomfortable working under the new management. A typical golden parachute would consist of a lump-sum payment to a departing executive based on a multiple of his annual compensation.

Because executive compensation was rising dramatically in this era, a golden parachute could, indeed, consist of a lot of gold. In 1989 F. Ross Johnson was serving as CEO of RJR Nabisco. To the shareholders' surprise, he proposed a "management buyout" in which the current directors offered to buy a controlling bloc of shares in the company. This offer attracted other bidders, most notably a proposal from Kohlberg Kravis Roberts (KKR). In the end the board decided to accept the KKR deal, and Johnson was sidelined. He deployed his golden parachute and collected over $50 million.

The existence of golden parachutes or other expensive compensation schemes for those forced out of a company could deter potential takeovers. The severance pay, after all, came right out of the company's resources, reducing its value to buyers. Not surprisingly, when other employees and shareholders became aware of these high-cost payout arrangements, they provoked considerable criticism. In some instances the directors attempted to defuse public outcry by extending the severance program to more employees. If the package applied to a much larger group of executives it might be downgraded to a "silver parachute," and a "tin parachute" might be designed to cover all of a company's employees.

By the late 1980s these arrangements had become so notorious that they provoked special federal tax treatment. A company could no longer deduct the cost of a golden parachute deemed excessive from its tax obligations, and the recipient of such an inflated payment was assessed a 20 percent excise tax on top of his or her income tax responsibility. In practice, however, a payout had to be greater than three-years' worth of salary and benefits to be considered excessive, so substantial severance compensation continues to be paid.

See also Greenmail; Hostile Takeovers; Leveraged Buyout; Poison Pill.

References and Further Reading

Wasserstein, Bruce. *Big Deal: The Battle for Control of America's Leading Corporations.* New York: Warner Books, 1998.

Greenmail

To prevent hostile takeovers, some corporations in the 1980s paid exorbitant prices to buy back shares from potential raiders. This process became known as greenmail, an obvious reference to the criminal act of blackmail. Although it was not technically illegal, greenmail drew widespread criticism both for those who paid and those who took greenmail payments. Federal legislation late in the decade imposed high taxes on greenmail profits, discouraging the use of this tactic.

Outsiders had attempted to capture control of companies for decades. Cornelius Vanderbilt quit trying to take over the Erie Railroad in the late 1860s only when the Erie directors agreed to pay him over $4 million to leave them alone. Similar deals were struck during the period of intensive railroad consolidation around the turn of the twentieth century, but several highly publicized instances in the 1980s focused public attention on the practice.

Although he stoutly denies he ever intended to extract greenmail payments, many consider T. Boone Pickens to be one of the chief beneficiaries of this tactic. In the early 1980s Pickens and his associates at the Mesa Petroleum Co. obtained a substantial bloc of shares in the Phillips Petroleum Co. They then demanded that the company's executives agree to a major management restructuring. Instead, Phillips offered Pickens $53 for each share he had bought for $45. While Pickens made a substantial profit on the deal, he was disappointed at the failure of his takeover bid.

After fending off Pickens, Phillips attempted to recapitalize its shares to ensure that all stockholders enjoyed the same $53 he had received, but Carl Icahn stepped in with a takeover offer pegged at $55 a share. Phillips frantically cobbled together an even more ambitious recapitalization to offset Icahn's offer and sealed the deal with a $25 million payment to compensate him for "expenses." This sort of greenmail payment to a corporate raider who attempts to benefit from an earlier failed coup is known as *double dipping*. It also illustrates a major problem for corporations. Even if management can round up enough money to finance a greenmail payment, the effort may leave the company vulnerable, inviting further rounds of assault.

Among several high-profile greenmail campaigns in the 1980s, Saul Steinberg's run at the Walt Disney Co. generated considerable notoriety. In return for accepting $325 million for his stock and another $28 million for expenses, Steinberg signed a *standstill* agreement. Standstill agreements typically include promises by potential raiders that they will limit the size of their holdings in the company and often preclude them from voting their proxies. All of these provisions are designed to protect the current management from assault.

Public outcry against greenmail combined with corporate lobbying convinced Congress to take action. Its most effective move came in the 1987 Tax Reform Act. It imposed a nondeductible excise tax on the profits from any greenmail collected. At the same time new accounting rules, corporate policies, and public and shareholder objections discouraged companies from paying greenmail. The virtual disappearance of greenmail, however, has not halted interest in mergers and takeovers.

See also Icahn, Carl; Leveraged Buyout; Pickens, T. Boone; Poison Pill; White Knight.

References and Further Reading

Pickens, T. Boone. *Boone.* New York: Houghton Mifflin, 1987.

Smith, Roy C. *The Money Wars.* New York: Dutton, 1990.

Wasserstein, Bruce. *Big Deal: The Battle for Control of America's Leading Corporations.* New York: Warner Books, 1998.

Hostile Takeovers

The craze for conglomerates in the 1950s and 1960s included a number of mergers that distressed some participants. Characterized as hostile takeovers, these changes disrupted old-line firms, ousted existing managers, shook up financial markets, and generated negative publicity. None of that seemed to concern the corporate raiders intent on building empires or squeezing profits out of the resulting combines. A second wave of hostile takeovers crested in the 1980s, exploiting novel financial arrangements like junk bonds. Interestingly enough, these later moves often split up the very conglomerates that had been assembled in the earlier period.

Mergers of businesses and industries had, of course, occurred throughout the late nineteenth and into the twentieth centuries. When a committed entrepreneur like John D. Rockefeller or J. P. Morgan set his sights on particular targets, the current owners and managers often opposed the action. The rationales for these earlier forced mergers included market consolidation, horizontal or vertical integration, and production efficiency. In the years after World War II, however, many takeover efforts seemed motivated by simple greed.

A basic first step in the 1950s was the announcement of a tender offer, usually made directly to a company's stockholders rather than its management. The takeover group would commit to buying a controlling bloc of shares at a substantial premium over the current trading price. Not surprisingly a good many shareholders jumped at the chance to cash out their holdings at premiums that could be as high as 30 or 40 percent. The buyout proposal typically came with a deadline, and some states like New York even issued guidelines that prevented a tender offer from extending for more than two weeks.

Creative financing schemes enabled corporate raiders to assail targets that were much larger than the entities they controlled. James Ling was one of the most successful. He established his first company by selling his house for $2,000. To expand he raised money by personally peddling shares at the Texas State Fair. Between 1955 and 1965 he transformed his tiny electrical contracting firm into a giant conglomerate. Many of his assaults were hostile takeovers, including the acquisitions of Temco Electronics and Missiles and airframe manufacturer Chance Vought.

Reincorporated in 1963, Ling-Temco-Vought (LTV) continued to expand. It picked up Okonite, a cable manufacturer, Wilson Co., one of the Big Five meat packers, and Greatamerica, a widely diversified conglomerate in its own right. In 1968 Ling staged a takeover of the nation's sixth largest steel producer, Jones & Laughlin. In that year LTV rose to fourteenth position in the Fortune list of the 500 top industrial corporations, but it was a step too far. An antitrust suit, an economic downturn, and poor performance by the steel company combined to undermine LTV's position, forcing Ling to step down as its CEO.

A new generation of corporate raiders arose in the 1980s. T. Boone Pickens engineered hostile takeover attempts on Cities Service, Phillips Petroleum, and Union Oil Co. None of them succeeded, but they earned Pickens a reputation as a ruthless predator. He also collected a lot of money in greenmail payments. He remained unrepentant, however, claiming that his chief goal was to force lazy or incompetent oil company executives to maximize the value of their enterprises. Shareholders benefited enormously from these raids because they ultimately resulted in consolidation or comprehensive restructuring that significantly enhanced the value of the target company's shares.

A successful hostile takeover did not guarantee future prosperity. Ron Perlman's aggressive assault on Revlon won him control of the company. He quickly shucked off almost everything but its core cosmetics business and has continued to manage the corporation into the twenty-first century. On the other hand, corporate raider Carl Icahn captured control of a reluctant Trans World Airlines in the late 1980s and it stumbled badly under his leadership, finally lapsing into bankruptcy in the mid-1990s.

Corporate managers used a number of tactics to stave off hostile takeovers. They might adopt a poison pill defense that bloated the number of shares in circulation and thereby reduced their value in an acquisition. Or they summoned a white knight, another company or group whom they trusted to carry out a friendly merger. Lawsuits and injunctions were frequently deployed to delay or discourage a raider. By the late 1980s SEC rules and government monitoring of the merger process made a truly hostile takeover much harder to achieve.

It should be noted that only a small number of the many mergers that occurred in this period could be described as hostile takeovers. Various estimates based on differing assessments of the level of hostility involved suggest that the percentage of successful hostile takeovers in any given year was in the single digits. At the same time, many assaults by corporate raiders triggered defensive plans and alternative merger outcomes that might never have been considered otherwise. Corporate executives in those years thus had good reason to fear hostile takeover attempts even when they ultimately failed.

See also Greenmail; Leveraged Buyout; Ling, James J.; Pickens, T. Boone; Poison Pill; Revson, Charles; White Knight.

References and Further Reading

Aurback, Alan J. *Corporate Takeovers: Causes and Consequences.* Chicago: University of Chicago Press, 1988.

Coffee, Jr., John C., et al. *Knights, Raiders and Targets.* New York: Oxford University Press, 1988.

Sobel, Robert. *Dangerous Dreamers.* New York: Wiley, 1993.

Junk Bonds

In recent decades investors have become quite sophisticated in assessing the quality of corporate bonds. Those that rating services give AAA ratings are considered much safer investments than others pegged at BBB or lower. The services make their calls on the perceived stability and creditworthiness of the corporation issuing a bond. When these matters are in question, they may dismiss a particular bond as not being of industrial grade. Bonds in that category are often referred to as *junk bonds,* alerting potential buyers they may be risky investments.

Given the apparent riskiness, why would anyone purchase junk bonds? One attraction is that they usually carry higher interest rates than industrial-grade bonds. Moreover market forces affect the cost of all bonds, and junk bonds often sell at prices well below their face value. This in turn increases their effective yield over the long term. At the height of the junk bond craze, high interest rates and fear of continuing inflation caused many individual and corporate investors to include high-yield junk bonds in their portfolios.

The most persuasive advocate of junk bonds, Michael Milken, worked at what became Drexel Burnham in the 1970s. He had immersed himself in academic and historical studies of high-yield bonds and concluded that they offered remarkable opportunities. He eventually convinced Drexel to allow him to relocate his junk-bond peddling operation to Beverly Hills where it operated almost completely independent of the company's more staid East Coast offices. Milken's operation proved remarkably successful, often generating more than half of Drexel's entire profits in a given year.

Milken's pitch included a number of points. Obviously the higher interest associated with these below-grade bonds was attractive in and of itself. While historical surveys demonstrated that high-yield bonds defaulted more frequently than other issues, their default rate remained rather low, averaging no more than 1 or 2 percent in a given year. A buyer who diversified his holdings of junk bonds could expect most of them to remain sound. The higher yield on those that survived could more than offset the losses of the few that proved worthless.

When Milken first entered the business in a big way, he relied on "fallen angels" as his primary source of supply. These were bonds that had been issued in good faith with reasonable ratings by companies that had subsequently encountered financial difficulties. As the bonds' value fell in the market and agencies stripped them of their ratings, they settled into junk bond status.

But Milken was hardly content with just rescuing fallen angels. As his sales pitch became more sophisticated and convincing, it encouraged companies to issue bonds that never qualified for ratings at all. The par value of junk bonds issued rose from just under $7 billion in 1970 to $210 billion in 1990. This boom helped Drexel Burnham rise from a comparatively small financial house to the leading underwriter and marketer of junk bonds.

In the public mind, junk bonds were linked with leveraged buyouts, and junk bonds did help finance a number of takeovers. The company making the takeover bid would combine capital from the sale of junk bonds with other monies to create the funds it needed to purchase a controlling interest in the takeover target. Corporate raiders like T. Boone Pickens, Carl Icahn, and Ron Perlman all turned to Milken's Drexel operation for junk bond financing.

While their dramatic corporate raids made for exciting headlines, less than one-quarter of the junk bonds issued in the 1980s were devoted to such purposes. In that financially unsettling and unsettled decade, many junk bonds were issued for more conventional purposes as corporations struggled to raise capital for their projects. And for a time they found ready buyers. Savings and loan associations and insurance companies in particular had become overinvested in long-term, fixed interest instruments, so adding a diversified portfolio of high-yield junk bonds to their investment holdings seemed a sound strategy as long as default rates followed historical trends.

By the late 1980s that no longer held true. Failed or foolishly overoptimistic corporate takeovers led to devaluation and defaults in the junk bonds associated with them. The stock market suffered a major setback in 1987, undermining investor confidence and encouraging reallocation of holdings away from riskier junk bonds into more stable instruments. To make matters worse, a major insider trading scandal erupted shortly thereafter that eventually led to a plea bargain and imprisonment for the godfather of junk bonds, Michael Milken. Swamped with unsalable junk bonds in a declining market and lacking its financial genius, Drexel Burnham tottered into bankruptcy and dissolution.

Despite this dramatic collapse, junk bonds remain a reasonable alternative for some purposes. Their higher yields will always be attractive. In a rising market like the one that characterized the late 1990s, general corporate expansion provides some insurance against default. Some speculators will always be willing to accept the risks of owning junk bonds in return for reaping a higher financial gain.

See also Hostile Takeovers; Leveraged Buyout; Milken, Michael Robert.

References and Further Reading

Platt, Harlan D. *The First Junk Bond.* Armonk, NY: M. E. Sharpe, 1994.

Stein, Benjamin J. *A License to Steal.* New York: Simon and Schuster, 1992.

Zey, Mary. *Banking on Fraud: Drexel, Junk Bonds, and Buyouts.* New York: Aldine de Gruyter, 1993.

Leveraged Buyout

An enormous amount of attention in the 1970s and 1980s was focused on leveraged buyouts (LBOs). Some firms came into existence solely to assemble funding to purchase other companies or parts of conglomerates. Because these firms relied extensively on borrowed funds, they were able to leverage their investments in dramatic ways. The apparent rewards of such efforts increased the magnitude of LBO transactions from a total of about $2 billion in 1980 to over $80 billion at the end of the decade.

The heart of an LBO is using someone else's money to help finance a purchase. An individual or group interested in buying a company seldom has enough ready cash to complete the transaction, so it must borrow. Because the borrower only has to pay fixed interest on the resulting loans, it can apply any additional profit to its original cash investment. If the deal is well conceived, the resulting return to equity can be much larger (highly leveraged) than other types of investments.

A personal home mortgage is one kind of leveraged purchase, but buying a company requires considerably more money and often a number of layers or components of indebtedness. When J. P. Morgan carried out his complex machinations to consolidate railroad systems in the 1890s, he drew funds from a number of sources. The basic concept of an LBO thus has a long tradition in American business history.

Activities in the 1970s and 1980s, however, involved new motivations and creative methods. Underlying conditions helped stimulate the rise in LBOs during those years. Many older, privately held companies with solid records were poised for a change in leadership. An LBO offered an attractive way for an individual or a family to capitalize on assets. At the same time many of the hastily assembled conglomerates that had arisen in previous decades were performing less dynamically than anticipated. An LBO that shook up management and, in many cases, provoked divestiture of subordinate units might appear to be an attractive way for shareholders to realize greater gains.

An early example of a modern LBO occurred in 1965 when an employee of Bear Stearns named Jerome Kohlberg bought Stern Metals from its family owners. The private owners welcomed Kohlberg's LBO, and his intercession proved both wise and profitable. Bear Stearns carried out other relatively small-scale LBOs, but Kohlberg decided to team up with two younger financiers, Henry Kravis and George Roberts. The resulting firm was named Kohlberg, Kravis, and Roberts, or KKR. Although Kohlberg left the firm in the late 1980s, KKR has remained the nation's major LBO operation.

An LBO in the 1980s typically involved several tiers of financing. The takeover group usually put up a relatively small amount of cash. The banks and other conservative lending agencies that supplied the first layer of borrowed funds insisted that their debts receive priority for interest payments and redemption. The middle layer or *mezzanine* financing frequently came from other lenders like insurance companies or pension funds. Startling success stories from the early LBOs reassured both banks and mezzanine financiers of the soundness of such investments. If additional funding was necessary, the bottom layer might well be raised by selling junk bonds.

The sponsor of an LBO would then approach the target company with a tender offer for shares at a premium over their current market price. The announcement of a bid could stimulate other potential buyers to develop their own LBO packages or encourage company executives to attempt an internal LBO in their own interest. If the original bidder had done its homework well, it could put forth a very attractive bid with a short time limit. This was sometimes referred to as a bear hug, because it left little room for either executives or other potential bidders to maneuver.

A key factor in determining an appropriate bid price for an LBO was the target company's anticipated ability to fund the resulting debt. Bank interest rates were often reasonable, however, and junk bond obligations were limited, so a prudent LBO could easily succeed. Once the takeover had occurred, the new team could restructure the company's management, streamline operations, and promote efficiencies that may not previously have been considered. Reducing bank obligations took first priority, but the other layers of funding often had much longer time horizons.

The leverage in a successful LBO could provide very handsome returns on the initial investment. Firms like KKR typically charged transaction fees and commissions for their services, so the LBO might well triple or quadruple its payout. Moreover, many LBOs were deliberately designed to reap short-term gains. In the case of a privately held company, once the initial profits of the LBO had been achieved and the company's market position enhanced, it was often put up for sale. Many investors were likely to buy stock in companies whose management had been stimulated and whose operations had been streamlined.

When an LBO involved a conglomerate, this resale process might begin immediately. The new management would assess the various elements in the combine and sell off units to other corporations or market them to shareholders as stand-alone entities. The money from these sales could be used for purposes such as paying off bank loans and redeeming junk bonds. A debt-free core or residual firm with sound market prospects might emerge from this process.

Hundreds of leveraged buyouts occurred in the 1980s. Although public attention focused on those portrayed as hostile takeovers, they represented a relatively small percentage of the total. Company executives themselves often initiated friendly takeovers, either in the form of an internal LBO or in conjunction with a trusted outside entity. The positive stories about what had begun as a relatively limited process aimed at smaller targets encouraged a rapid escalation in the number of LBO participants and the size of their targets.

KKR executed the largest LBO to date in 1985 when it offered $5.6 billion for Beatrice. The offer was so attractive it caught the corporation's executives in a bear hug they could not escape. A series of divestitures took place under the leadership of Donald P. Kelly who had inspired the takeover. Its component units like Avis, Playtex, and Tropicana found ready buyers. In 1990 ConAgra purchased the remaining elements. After dealing with outstanding debts and expenses, KKR and its partners netted $2.2 billion, a handsome return on their initial $400 million equity investment.

As the pace of the LBO phenomenon became more frenetic, bidding wars pushed purchase prices up. The complexities of managing or disposing of a target's assets reduced the attractiveness of LBOs. By the late 1980s Drexel Burnham's bankruptcy had severely limited the availability of junk bonds. Federal officials were increasingly concerned about the excesses of the LBO boom. While leveraged buyouts continue to occur, they have receded in importance and in the public consciousness in recent years.

See also Hostile Takeovers; Junk Bonds; Kravis, Henry.

References and Further Reading

Anders, George. *Merchants of Debt.* New York: Basic Books, 1992.

Baker, George P., and George David Smith. *The New Financial Capitalists.* New York: Cambridge University Press, 1998.

Bierman, Jr., Harold. *Private Equity.* New York: Wiley, 2003.

Davidson, Kenneth M. *Mega-Mergers.* Cambridge, MA: Ballinger, 1985.

Smith, Roy C. *The Money Wars.* New York: Dutton, 1990.

Malls

As Americans migrated to the suburbs after the Second World War, retailers decamped as well, building or renting new stores on the fringes of cities. These often clumped together in shopping centers or malls, surrounded by acres of parking space for increasingly mobile American motorists. Major retailers established anchor stores at these locations that helped attract smaller satellite retailers. Malls rapidly became the nation's major shopping centers, sucking customers and consumer spending out of traditional downtown shopping districts.

As early as the 1930s some visionaries were planning and building retail space away from the city center. County Club Plaza, for example, was located well south of downtown Kansas City. It was a carefully planned, architecturally pleasing development covering several blocks and providing plenty of parking. High-end retailers quickly signed up for space in this attractive area, convinced that it would attract both focused and casual shoppers in large numbers. The Plaza remains a desirable shopping destination to this day.

Similar shopping centers spread out from other cities in the postwar years. A key development occurred in 1956 when Southdale, the nation's first enclosed shopping center, opened for business in Edina, a suburb of Minneapolis. The location was hardly accidental. The fully air-conditioned and heated mall provided a welcome relief from Minnesota's harsh winters and humid summers. Other enclosed malls sprang up all across the country, creating inviting and comfortable shopping environments.

Most mall business plans envisioned locking in one or two major retail giants like Sears, Bloomingdales, or Montgomery Ward, and installing them as anchors at each end of the facility. Smaller volume, more specialized shops were strung between the anchors, recreating the same opportunities for shoppers that diversified downtown districts had offered. All of the retailers benefited from walk-in shoppers and impulse buying.

In recognition of the increasingly busy lives their customers led, malls extended their hours of operation to include evenings and Sundays. The artificiality of an enclosed, lighted mall presented the appearance of a safe, welcoming area at any time of day. That in turn meant that restaurants, video arcades, and multiplex movie houses could benefit from mall locations. Many people considered a trip to the mall as an entertainment expedition even if all they did was window shopping.

The early malls did so well they encouraged the development of store formats specifically designed for suburban shopping centers. The Kresge Corporation expanded well beyond its five-and-dime origins by creating a "big box" group of K-Mart stores. Minneapolis department store giant Dayton's did the same with its Target chain. These were sometimes referred to as discount stores, but they carried full lines of clothing, household goods, hardware, auto parts, and gardening supplies. More specialized big box chains prospered as well like Home Depot, Best Buy, and Bed, Bath, and Beyond.

While most of the mall and discount store growth occurred in urban and suburban locations, Sam Walton set out to serve rural customers. He opened the Wal-Mart Discount City store in Rogers, Arkansas, in 1962, the first of a chain of twenty-five Wal-Marts that opened within a decade. Walton continued to expand the size of his chain and the scope of individual stores. Walton's early adoption of sophisticated computerized inventory and sales-tracking technology enabled him to assure his customers of "everyday low prices." In the 1980s Wal-Marts began moving into prime suburban locations, often undermining the market base for K-Marts and Targets. Wal-Mart Superstores began selling groceries as well, with low prices that cut into the sales of established grocery chains.

Traditional shopping malls are hardly obsolete. The Mall of America opened its doors in 1992 in another Minneapolis suburb, Bloomington. It covered 4.2 million square feet, boasted four major anchors, 500 shops, restaurants, and entertainment centers, and parking space for 13,000 cars. Designed to be a full-service facility, it also houses a theme park with rides and an 18-hole miniature golf course. It remains the largest shopping mall in the world and has become so famous that bus companies conduct tours to it from distant towns and cities.

Some malls have suffered from deterioration or aggressive competition in recent years, but the shopping center concept continues to attract capital and customers. In 2003 over 45,000 malls existed in the United States encompassing almost 6 billion square feet of retail space. Some downtown shopping districts like Chicago's Miracle Mile have continued to thrive. But many major cities resemble ghost towns in the evening and weekends as customers flock to the suburban malls.

See also Department Store; Kresge, Sebastian Spering (S. S.); Shopping.

References and Further Reading

Berger, Arthur Asa. *Shop 'til You Drop*. New York: Rowman and Littlefield, 2005.

Cross, Gary. *An All-consuming Century*. New York: Columbia University Press, 2000.

Underhill, Paco. *Call of the Mall*. New York: Simon and Schuster, 2004.

Marketing Concept

In the 1950s many corporations began using advanced research methods to develop more sophisticated marketing strategies. The marketing concept emphasized determining consumer preferences and needs prior to the design and manufacture of products. If the process was successful, manufacturers could eliminate waste and inefficiency by targeting consumers' actual desires. Producers of all types recognized the advantage of the marketing concept and quickly adopted it.

Postwar and post-Depression circumstances influenced the evolution of the marketing concept. During the 1930s demand for standard consumer goods had persisted, but purchasing power was limited, so manufacturers tended to tailor their production to meet traditional needs. Wartime controls and priorities dictated what and how much the nation produced in the early 1940s. Once these restraints began to lift, pent-up consumer demand ensured that virtually anything and everything produced would sell immediately.

Pent-up demand began to wane in the early 1950s, however, forcing producers to consider more rational planning. Although elements of the marketing concept had been used for some time, Ralph J. Cordiner, chairman of General Electric, is usually credited with popularizing the new approach. In the corporation's 1952 annual report, he advocated the use of research to determine consumer desires. His stated goal was to "introduce the marketing man at the beginning rather than at the end of the production cycle and [to] integrate marketing into each phase of the business."

Cordiner was responding to advancements in *cybernetics* or operations research techniques that had proved vital to the war effort. The initial step was to conduct extensive surveys of potential customers aimed at determining their needs and preferences. Once this survey information had been analyzed, designers and engineers were given the task of creating consumer products that would match those needs and desires.

Advertising played a key role in the process. In addition to claiming to be sensitive to consumer preferences, General Electric could begin targeted advertising campaigns during the development process. Feedback from these efforts influenced the final production and distribution of newer, "improved" models or wholly innovative products, all of which should find ready markets. In contrast to the "selling concept" where companies hyped products they had no assurance would be popular, the marketing concept limited waste and overproduction at the same time it streamlined advertising and sales.

Market research has become increasingly influential in the consumer economy. Computers have vastly simplified both survey and analysis. Expanded national databases are widely accessible, and analytical techniques have improved. The marketing concept has become so common and entrenched in American society that most consumers are not even aware of it. Every time a customer fills out the questionnaire appended to a product registration card on a newly purchased item, he or she is participating as a subject in the marketing research process.

See also Bracketing the Market; Brand Management.

References and Further Reading

Cox, James A. *A Century of Light.* New York: Benjamin, 1979.

Webster, Frederick E. *Market-driven Management.* New York: Wiley, 1994.

Microchips

In 1959 Texas Instruments produced a silicon chip with a printed circuit, a major advance over the single-function transistors it had exploited to become a world leader in the electronics business. Designers quickly began packing more and more circuits onto their chips, starting with self-contained calculators and moving ahead to increasingly complex functions that included advanced computational capabilities as well as memory. Microchips fundamentally altered the whole realm of communications and information technology.

The Cold War provided the context that encouraged this new technology. The United States led all nations in the manufacture and use of transistors in the 1950s. When the Soviet Union sent Sputnik into orbit in 1957, however, it exposed a major weakness in American technology. While the Soviets had been building huge rockets with enormous thrust, the United States had focused on smaller ballistic rockets incapable of putting large payloads into orbit. One way to catch up was to miniaturize electronic components. Multifunctional chips were ideal for this purpose.

Existing facilities could not initially manufacture such complex devices. Robert Noyce and George Moore, working at a start-up named Fairchild, solved the problem by designing layered chips with pathways etched directly into the silicon to guide the flow of electrons. This process allowed integrated circuits to become much more complex even as it reduced production costs. Texas Instruments, Fairchild, and Motorola seized on this innovative procedure to become industry leaders.

In addition to their military uses, integrated circuits could also serve as the brains of hearing aids, digital watches, and home appliances. By the early 1960s the technology had advanced to the point that a single chip could replace a full-size calculator. Handheld calculators became best sellers, and calculator chips were also incorporated into the burgeoning computer industry. Progress came so quickly that George Moore announced "Moore's Law" stating that the number of transistors on a chip would double every twenty-four months. His prediction quickly proved to be too conservative, so within a few years he revised his law to state that capacity would double every eighteen months. Moore's Law held true right through the turn of the twenty-first century.

In the late 1960s new production possibilities appeared in the form of metal-oxide semiconductors (MOS), but established industrial leaders were reluctant to adopt it. Noyce took the lead in convincing Moore and newly hired Fairchild employee Andrew Grove to start a new venture to exploit MOS capabilities. Their firm came together in 1968 as Intel.

Using a process developed by Italian Federico Faggin, Intel began constructing chips that contained enough circuitry to function as self-contained microprocessors, the heart of modern computers. A related breakthrough came a few years later when Intel began manufacturing computer memory chips using MOS technology. Spurred by rival National Semiconductor's success, Intel produced its 8086 chip, capable of 16-bit processing. The 8086 became the workhorse of the burgeoning personal computer industry.

As Moore's law predicted, advances continued to accelerate. Intel marketed an 80286 chip in 1982, followed by its 80386 three years later and its 80486 in 1989. The 486 version was the first microprocessor to crowd more than a million transistors onto a single chip. Intel's Pentium series introduced in 1993 became the computer industry's standard, operating at speeds more than 100 times faster than the 286 had achieved just a decade earlier.

While Intel remained the industry leader, it was not without rivals. Advanced Micro Devices (AMD) was its major American competitor. As the twentieth century drew to a close, companies in other countries used the same technology to produce their own processor and memory chips. Some American firms actively participated in this growing trend, establishing their own offshore facilities to take advantage of lower wage levels, foreign capital, and government favors.

Consumers benefited from all of these trends. The rapid increase in processing speed, the steep decline in the costs of chips, and international trade rivalry brought unprecedented computational power into the hands of individual users. Highly sophisticated microprocessors became common in home appliances, digital cameras, cellular telephones, automobiles, and dozens of unexpected uses as microchips truly revolutionized modern life.

See also Computers; Kilby, Jack; Noyce, Robert; Transistors.

References and Further Reading

Chandler, Jr., Alfred D., and James W. Cortada, eds. *A Nation Transformed by Information*. New York: Oxford, 2000.

Ifrah, Georges. *The Universal History of Computing*. New York: Wiley, 2001.

Young, Jeffrey. *Forbes Greatest Technology Stories.* New York: Wiley, 1998.

Military Aviation

In 1940 the aircraft industry ranked forty-fourth among all American industries in the dollar value of its output, but it had undeniably moved up to first place when World War II ended in 1945. It had built hundreds of thousands of airplanes during the war years, absorbed enormous amounts of capital, and laid the groundwork for what was later called the military-industrial complex. This phenomenal growth in size and influence involved remarkable technological and production advances.

Prior to the First World War aviation was little more than an avocation for inventors and enthusiasts. The wood and fabric, single-engine biplanes on hand in 1914 were ill-suited to military action. French and British designers had been leaders in the field, however, and their German counterparts quickly caught up. Because the conflict dragged on for over four years, engineers and visionaries had ample opportunity to develop and put into use all sorts of advances. For example, a machine gun was created whose shots fired at coordinated intervals so its bullets would avoid hitting the spinning propeller on the aircraft's nose. Dramatic air-to-air duels between aces got plenty of press coverage, but battlefield surveillance and bombing runs had more direct impacts on the ground fighting in the late stages of the war.

American pilots flew in European aircraft for the most part, but they brought home a great deal of enthusiasm and innovative ideas. General Billy Mitchell had headed the U.S. Army Air Corps during the war, and the experience convinced him that airplanes would be even more crucial in future conflicts. In dramatic demonstrations, he bombed decommissioned naval vessels and easily sank them. Neither the Army nor the Navy was immediately ready to abandon centuries of tradition, however, and Mitchell was eventually convicted by a court martial for his outspoken opinions.

By the mid-1930s both Army and Navy planners had come around to believing in air power. The Army Air Corps incorporated land-based fighters and bombers; carrier-based aircraft were developed for the Navy. The evolution from wood to aluminum allowed designers to vastly improve the maneuverability, speed, and range of military aircraft. Experience building larger commercial aircraft in the late 1930s also proved vital when wartime demand developed.

Production facilities were hardly adequate. The American industry employed only about 50,000 skilled and semiskilled workers in 1939, and they collectively built fewer than 6,000 aircraft. Airplanes were assembled by hand, one at a time, in a labor-intensive fashion. In some ways aircraft assembly plants resembled nineteenth century artisan's workshops more than they did modern automated factories.

The federal government played a crucial role in stimulating the industry. It issued thousands of contracts, stimulated rapid design evolution, and constantly upgraded its specifications and expectations. Private contractors were often unwilling to expand their facilities to meet the demand, worried that they would be saddled with overcapacity when the war ended. Consequently, the government itself ended up building whole factories from scratch.

The massive expansion of the industry did not completely alter the traditional manufacturing process, however. Unit-by-unit assembly remained the norm, but efficiencies in subsidiaries and suppliers helped speed output. Only a tenth of the components used in aircraft had come from outside suppliers in 1940 but nearly 40 percent were flowing into assembly plants from more efficient external factories five years later.

When the federal government ordered the automobile industry to convert to war production, some expected it to apply assembly-line methods to aircraft, and it did help produce specific items like engines. Buick, Packard, Dodge, and other divisions turned out aircraft engines by the thousands. Typically, Henry Ford thought he had a better idea. With a $200 million Army Air Corps grant, he constructed the world's largest factory at Willow Run, near Detroit. His attempt to replicate his Model T success by building airplanes in this enormous facility failed to meet anyone's expectations. When it finally got up and running, the Willow Run plant did manage to turn out 8,685 bombers, but most of them were B-24s, a design that had already been superceded by the larger B-29 superfortresses Boeing was producing.

The final wartime tally was truly impressive. The industry as a whole manufactured 300,000 airplanes, 800,000 engines, and 700,000 propellers. The U.S. government funneled some $45 billion into the industry, some of which survived the war in the form of greatly expanded plant capacity. The U.S. aircraft industry was thus positioned in 1945 to dominate the world market for many years to come. Continual evolution, improvement, and modifications of military aircraft matched similar changes in the commercial aviation field. Industry leaders like Boeing, Douglas, and Lockheed remained preeminent contractors in the military-industrial complex through the Cold War decades.

See also Commercial Aviation; Boeing, William Edward; Douglas, Donald Wills; Military-Industrial Complex.

References and Further Reading

Bilstein, Roger E. *The American Aerospace Industry.* New York: Twayne, 1996.

Loening, Grover Cleveland. *Takeoff into Greatness.* New York: Putnam, 1968.

Lorell, Mark A. *The U.S. Combat Aircraft Industry.* Santa Monica, CA: Rand, 2003.

Rae, John B. *Climb to Greatness.* Cambridge, MA: MIT Press, 1968.

Military-Industrial Complex

In his 1961 farewell address President Dwight Eisenhower warned the American people to "guard against the acquisition of unwarranted influence . . . by the military industrial complex." In so doing, the retiring president gave explicit recognition to a widespread concern over the influence and power of industries feeding off pervasive Cold War fears. Literally dozens of commentators, historians, and social scientists responded to this warning by identifying the participants and assessing the (usually) negative aspects of collaboration between military, political, and industrial participants.

Like so many phenomena, the concept of a military-industrial complex was hardly new. During the Civil War northern industrialists benefited enormously from Union contracts for weapons, clothing, and supplies. In the First World War the federal government stumbled through a number of alternatives before establishing the War Industries Board. The board had extensive authority not only to purchase war materials and supplies, but also to encourage private industrial development as well as finance government-owned production facilities.

In the 1930s, however, Senator Gerald Nye headed a committee that blamed arms manufacturers and suppliers, the so-called merchants of death, for not only initiating the conflict but profiting from its continuation. Simultaneously, historians and others contributed to the negative attitudes toward the arms industries. These complicated the regeneration of an effective military procurement system when the United States entered the much more costly and demanding Second World War.

As it had after previous conflicts, however, the federal government rapidly demobilized, and American industries rushed to produce consumer goods for the Depression-starved and war-restricted population. Meanwhile President Harry Truman devoted his efforts to reducing all federal expenditures. Military spending fell to less than 5 percent of the nation's gross national product (GNP) in the late 1940s.

Cold War anxiety soon overwhelmed all thoughts of economy. In response to recommendations from the Hoover Commission, an integrated Defense Department emerged in 1947. Yet within this overarching organization, the Army, the Navy, and a newly independent Air Force competed for resources. The Air Force easily came out ahead. It favored expanding atomic weaponry, which its aircraft would deliver. One selling point for this strategy was that it would presumably cost less than maintaining a huge conventional armed force.

When Russia exploded its own atomic bomb in 1949 and North Korean armies invaded South Korea the following summer, the United States found itself facing strong and diverse threats. Defense expenditures quickly rose to over 10 percent of the nation's rising GNP, and they have remained in that range ever since. This massive increase in spending inevitably stimulated the growth of defense-related industries, setting the stage for President Eisenhower's comments about the influence of the military-industrial complex.

Substantial elements of the aircraft and aerospace industries became locked into dependent roles. With the notable exception of Boeing, which managed to serve both military and commercial customers, the major American aerospace corporations became heavily invested in military production. Between 1961and 1967, for example, Lockheed collected over $10 billion worth of federal contracts, representing nearly 90 percent of its total sales. Among the other corporations that derived more than half of their sales from military funding were General Dynamics, McDonnell Douglas, North-American Rockwell, and Martin-Marietta.

The microelectronics industry also profited from military contracts. Defense Department funding stimulated the invention of both transistors and integrated circuits. Military buyers constantly urged the industry to reduce the size of components and increase their capability. In this instance, unlike the aerospace industry, the microelectronics companies simultaneously developed very popular civilian uses for their products. Although the industry benefited enormously from federal research support, the major manufacturers generally sold less than a fifth of their output to Pentagon buyers.

In the 1950s sociologist C. Wright Mills set off an animated scholarly debate by criticizing what he saw as an incestuous collaboration of politicians, military officers, and defense contractors. Reminiscent of the reaction to the Nye Committee's pronouncements, many raised alarms about the dangers the military-industrial complex posed to democracy and to personal freedom. At the same time researchers in the very universities that produced critical analyses were exploiting defense-related funding for a huge variety of projects, many of which had only tangential relationship to military uses.

The waning of the Cold War in the 1980s significantly reduced public concern about the phenomenon known as the military-industrial complex. Defense spending remains a major component of the federal budget, however, and many firms continue to depend heavily on Pentagon contracts. Even so, the public's awareness of and sense of foreboding about the military-industrial complex that emerged in the 1960s has lessened considerably. In the twenty-first century, Americans appear willing to continue to support government-industrial collaboration in the name of defense.

See also Microchips; Military Aviation; War Industries Board.

References and Further Reading

Hooks, Gregory. *Forging the Military-Industrial Complex.* Urbana, IL: University of Illinois Press, 1991.

Markusen, Ann, and Joel Yudken. *Dismantling the Cold War Economy.* New York: Basic Books, 1992.

Pursell, Jr., Carroll W. *The Military-Industrial Complex*. New York: Harper and Row, 1972.
Tirman, John, ed. *The Militarization of High Technology*. Cambridge, MA: Ballinger, 1984.

Monetarism

In the early 1960s economists Milton Friedman and Anna Schwarz published a book that established the basis for monetarism. They noted the importance of money in the economy and went so far as to insist that manipulating the nation's money supply was the key to managing U.S. economic growth and well-being. Monetarism became a popular alternative to Keynesian theory, and many Americans continue to believe that monetarist policies are the best way to promote prosperity.

The heart of monetarism is a conviction that the size of the money supply determines the level of economic activity. If more money is available, for example, monetarists believe that individuals will end up with more money than they really desire. They will therefore spend the surplus on goods and services. This spending will, in turn, stimulate production and other economic activities that lead to a general increase in overall economic growth. Similarly, a decline or shrinkage in the money supply will naturally put a brake on expenditures and slow or even halt economic growth.

An important monetarist corollary is that even a slight increase or decrease in the money supply can have major effects. This stems from the so-called multiplier effect. If a consumer spends a dollar, the merchant receiving the money is likely to spend most of it on goods. His supplier will, in turn, spend most of that money for raw materials or labor, and the process continues repeatedly. Conservative estimates suggest that the impact of spending a single dollar will be multiplied at least five times, greatly enhancing the effect of the original expenditure.

Friedman and Schwarz titled their book *A Monetary History of the United States, 1867–1960,* and it analyzed historical trends. Their research led them to conclude that depressions and recessions occurred largely because the nation's money supply either shrank or became inadequate to sustain growth. They were particularly critical of central banking policies in the early 1930s, maintaining that if the Federal Reserve Banks had taken aggressive steps to pump new funds into the money supply, the Great Depression might never have occurred at all or at least would have been much milder than it was.

The Fed does have several tools to do just what the monetarists advocated. Through its open market operations, the central bank buys and sells federal bonds. To increase the amount of money in circulation it buys bonds from their holders and thus transfers more cash to individuals. Selling bonds has the opposite effect: withdrawing cash and therefore shrinking the money supply. The Fed also manipulates its discount rate, that is, the interest it charges to those who borrow money from its reserves. If it raises the discount rate, it makes borrowing more expensive and discourages it. That can reduce the amount of money in circulation and thus shrink the money supply.

The ideal monetarist prescription would have the money supply automatically grow at a fixed pace established to promote modest, healthy economic expansion without inflation. In practice, of course, the Fed is constantly adjusting its monetary policies on the basis of changing economic and business conditions. The board tries to set discount rates that encourage growth but that simultaneously discourage inflation. Its open market operations are heavily influenced by government needs for funding and the size of the federal budget deficit or surplus. As a result, a pure monetarist approach has never been instituted even though a number of prominent politicians, industrial leaders, and even Federal Reserve Board members subscribe to its tenets.

Critics of monetarism reject its simplistic, single-factor approach. Keynesians consider factors like aggregate demand far more important than the size of the money supply in promoting or retarding economic growth. Their remedies call for governmental policies that will affect demand, an approach that many monetarists consider irrelevant or, worse yet, dangerous. As with all macroeconomic theories, it is safe to assume that both approaches have merit. Monetarism's focus on the impact of a single factor, the money supply, has, however, lessened its appeal and perhaps its overall effectiveness in the face of the extraordinary complexities of a modern post-industrial economy.

See also Keynesian Economics; Money Supply; Supply-Side Economics.

References and Further Reading

Frazer, William. *The Legacy of Keynes and Friedman.* Westport, CT: Praeger, 1994.

Friedman, Milton. *Monetarist Economics.* Cambridge, MA: Blackwell, 1991.

Friedman, Milton, and Anna Schwarz. *A Monetary History of the United States, 1867–1960.* Princeton, NJ: Princeton University Press, 1963.

Kennedy, Peter E. *Macroeconomic Essentials.* Cambridge, MA: MIT Press, 2000.

Macesich, George. *Monetarism, Theory and Policy.* New York: Praeger, 1983.

Personal Computers

Personal computers made a splashy debut in the late 1970s when Steve Jobs and Steve Wozniak demonstrated the first models of their Apple computer line. Their prominence faded quickly when IBM introduced its personal computer (PC) in 1981. By the middle of the decade PCs and PC clones had infiltrated offices, private homes, and universities by the millions. Rapid technological advances in microchips, printers, memory storage devices, and, ultimately, the development of the Internet significantly transformed business, communication, and even social life in the United States.

The essential change was the ability to install advanced microchips into typewriter-size housings that sold for thousands of dollars. At that price, millions of Americans could afford to streamline business and personal computational activities. An early inkling of the attractiveness of the new computational capabilities came with Atari's invention of the game Pong. Nolan Bushnell had formed the company to produce both arcade games and primitive video games displayed on home TV screens. As enthusiasm for Pong waned, Atari produced consoles with interchangeable cartridges that contained more complex games.

Young Steve Jobs worked briefly at Atari in what would become Silicon Valley. He invited a friend, electronics whiz Steve Wozniak, to work alongside him on the night shift, and the two men gradually mapped out a scheme for a personal computer. It would be based on a microprocessor and peripherals, use a standard typewriter-style keyboard for entering information and programming, and a TV-type screen for display. Wozniak provided most of the engineering advances but Jobs turned out to excel in vision and marketing. Reminiscent of Henry Ford, they assembled the first working Apple computers in a garage at the Jobs home.

The original customers for Apple computers were hobbyists, but when the entrepreneurs added a spreadsheet capability to their Apple II machines, businesses began snapping them up by the thousands. The program was called VISICALC, and, like Apple's operating system, had been developed by others. After its exhilarating takeoff, the company stumbled badly with its poor-performing Apple III series, a failed minicomputer called Lisa, and an initially unpopular Macintosh. Only the development of the IMAC in the 1990s revived the original company's fortunes.

IBM's introduction of its PC in 1981 proved to be Apple's most damaging rival. Hidebound and conservative, IBM had been slow to recognize the potential of personal computing. Jealousy of Apple's early success finally stimulated internal development of an alternative. Unlike other IBM products, the original personal computer was cobbled together out of readily available parts. It had an Intel processing chip, an operating system from a recent start-up called Microsoft, and many other off-the-shelf components.

Ready access to such components enabled IBM to rush its product to market, but it also opened the way for other manufacturers to produce IBM clones. COMPAQ became a major competitor, producing its first inexpensive knock-off in 1985. For a time IBM's quality control and respected brand name kept it in the lead, dominating more than half of the market in the early years. It also tried to keep ahead by adding hard drives in its PC XT line and a much more powerful 386 chip in its PC AT models. But competitors quickly caught up.

Unlike Apple, which tried to keep its hardware and software proprietary, IBM encouraged outsiders to develop programs compatible with its architecture. Lotus 1–2–3, for example, supplanted VISICALC as the industry standard, and hundreds of other programs written expressly for IBM turned out to be just as useful for the many clones.

The Macintosh line exploited a new visual control program, operated through a mouse. It was based in turn on a concept that Xerox had experimented with at its California research park in the 1970s. Steve Jobs was not alone in adopting it, however. Microsoft Corporation founder Bill Gates soon came to appreciate the potential of a friendlier user interface. Extensive and stormy negotiations with Jobs delayed the premier of Microsoft's first Windows software until 1985. It then took some time to work out bugs and encourage other programs to become compatible with Windows. By the early 1990s Microsoft's system had become the global standard for personal computer software.

As had occurred in the television industry, much of the manufacturing of personal computers, peripherals, and components migrated to other countries during the 1990s. Companies like Sony, particularly with its laptops, gained prominence. Two American companies, Dell and Gateway fought back by offering to assemble custom-designed machines in the United States, although they, too, were heavily reliant on foreign sources for chips, displays, and the like.

By the late 1990s personal computers were in use throughout the business world and in nearly 40 percent of the private homes in the United States. This vast user base fueled interest in interconnectivity through the Internet. It began with a Defense Department initiative designated ARPANET. The project interlinked four universities in 1971, the first of many such steps that gradually connected government, educational, and eventually private users. The term *Internet* was coined in 1984.

The National Science Foundation's willingness to manage the backbone of the Internet in 1987 encouraged even more connectivity. The World Wide Web became a reality in 1990, linking PC users to an astonishing array of information. The development of hypertext markup language (HTML) the following year enabled almost anyone to establish a website. Two years later the first Web browser appeared to facilitate user access to all parts of the Internet.

The Internet in turn spawned a whole range of e-functions. E-mail had its roots in the original ARPANET configuration, enabling scientists to exchange information instantly. e-Bay emerged in the late 1990s as a worldwide marketplace. Amazon.com had a similar splash, serving as an inexpensive but highly accessible source for virtually any book in print and an enormous number that have long since been remaindered. E-trading allows speculators to buy and sell shares of stock instantaneously from their home computers. In short, the Internet allows anyone to conduct almost any sort of business conveniently and inexpensively.

The progression from the plodding room-size IBM 701 in 1950 to the sleek laptop personal computer in 1990 is one of the most remarkable in human history. It is even more astounding to realize that a laptop can perform virtually all the computational functions of the 701 in milliseconds. In addition, it serves as an electronic gateway to the whole world, a true key to the growing global consciousness and interconnectivity of our current lives.

See also Gates, Bill; Hewlett, William Redington; Jobs, Steven Paul; Microchips; Packard, David; Tandy, Charles.

References and Further Reading

Chandler, Jr., Alfred D., and James W. Cortada, eds. *A Nation Transformed by Information.* New York: Oxford, 2000.

Ifrah, Georges. *The Universal History of Computing.* New York: Wiley, 2001.

Young, Jeffrey. *Forbes Greatest Technology Stories.* New York: Wiley, 1998.

Poison Pill

Poison pills proved popular and often quite effective in discouraging or preventing hostile takeover attempts in the 1980s. In essence, a poison-pill provision gave shareholders the right to purchase additional shares in a company at very low cost. This would increase the number of shares issued, making it more difficult and expensive for an outside buyer to establish a controlling interest.

As with so many other modern business tactics, rapidly expanding the number of shares in circulation to discourage takeovers was not new. In the so-called Erie Wars just after the Civil War, Jay Gould and Jim Fisk used the Erie Railroad Company's printing presses to flood the market with convertible bonds. When holders of these bonds converted them to stocks, it vastly increased the number of shares that Cornelius Vanderbilt's group needed to gain control. In the end, Vanderbilt accepted what amounted to a greenmail payment to abandon his takeover attempt.

While much of the merger mania that swept the United States in the 1980s represented positive, friendly consolidation, many companies became targets of hostile takeover bids. There is some irony in the fact that Martin Lipton is credited with inventing the poison-pill defense. A senior partner in a New York law firm, he specialized in facilitating takeovers. But he developed the poison-pill strategy in 1984 even though it could be used effectively against his major clients' interests.

A company's decision to adopt a poison-pill defense did not come without risks. Many stockholders disagreed with management's fear of a potential takeover and did not want to see the value of their shares diluted. Nevertheless, poison pills became so common that by the end of the decade over 1,000 major corporations had resorted to them.

The poison pill remained inert until a particular threshold was crossed. That might occur when an individual or group obtained a major portion, typically 30 percent, of the outstanding shares or made an over-market bid for outstanding shares. If that happened, the company would issue thousands of new shares and sell them to its stockholders at prices well below either the market price or the takeover bid level. To complete the takeover, the potential acquirer would have to round up substantially more funding than it had anticipated, a circumstance that could end the takeover threat altogether.

Nuances were quickly added to the basic poison-pill strategy. A "flip-over" provision might be included, stipulating that if a takeover did succeed, current stockholders were guaranteed an opportunity to buy shares in the new company at prices well below market. Because flip-over provisions threatened to undermine or dilute the value of the takeover company's assets, they too discouraged hostile takeovers.

Recognizing that an outside offer might be so attractive that shareholders would favor its acceptance, many poison-pill arrangements included redemption provisions. In the event of a very favorable offer, company executives could activate the redemption provision, cancelling the authorization for shareholders to buy additional stock. The complexities of these provisions frequently led to litigation initiated by the takeover group, the existing management, or even groups of stockholders dissatisfied with their company's behavior. In the long run, of course, a determined campaigner could swallow the poison pill and complete the hostile takeover regardless of the ultimate costs.

See also Golden Parachute; Greenmail; Hostile Takeovers.

References and Further Reading

Smith, Roy C. *The Money Wars.* New York: Dutton, 1990.

Wasserstein, Bruce. *Big Deal: The Battle for Control of America's Leading Corporations.* New York: Warner Books, 1998.

Rationing

To preserve stocks of scarce goods or those needed for wartime use, a national government may decide to limit consumer purchases. Rationing is one method of controlling consumption. During the Second World War, the Office of Price Administration rationed food and other commodities through price controls and coupon books. Rationing is generally seen as an extreme policy, to be imposed only when other methods of persuasion have failed to limit consumption.

Although the federal government had previously used price manipulations and production controls to manage the distribution of scarce goods, comprehensive rationing in the United States began only after the bombing at Pearl Harbor. The European nations had plenty of experience with rationing by that point, but it was a novel phenomenon for U.S. citizens.

While patriotism and aggressive government publicity campaigns promoted acceptance of the program, many Americans had difficulty understanding why it was necessary. Voluntary programs like "meatless Friday" had developed during World War I, but the major government efforts of agencies like the Food Administration and War Industries Board were aimed at stimulating production of all kinds. Boosting output certainly was a goal in the Second World War, but there was never enough to meet the demand from higher paid workers in war industries and the many members of the military alliance.

Rubber was the first commodity to be rationed. Japanese expansion in eastern and southern Asia cut off almost all access to the traditional sources of natural rubber. Initial orders rationing tires appeared on December 29, 1941. As the limitations were enforced, many private automobiles were simply put up on blocks. Meanwhile, the government poured substantial resources into the creation of a synthetic rubber industry that reached full production by 1944. Even so, rubber continued to be rationed right through the end of the war.

Rationing eventually affected sugar, coffee, shoes, gasoline, butter, canned goods, and red meat consumption. Different classes of consumers were defined for some commodities like tires and gasoline. Doctors and others whose effectiveness depended on automobile transportation received substantially higher monthly quotas than those in other classes. Private citizens whose livelihoods did not depend on car travel fell into the bottom category and were allocated as few as five gallons of gasoline a month.

The Office of Price Administration (OPA) assumed responsibility for administering the rationing program, and it ultimately developed some coherence between its pricing and rationing policies. Americans became accustomed to receiving a monthly allocation of ration stamps with point values. OPA citizen advisory boards met frequently to assess supplies and demand. They recommended adjustments in the number of points necessary to purchase rationed goods. This system allowed consumers greater latitude in making choices than were available in the more rigid schemes other nations' governments imposed.

Not surprisingly, a widespread black market developed during the conflict, and, as had occurred during Prohibition, many otherwise respectable citizens bought restricted goods. At the same time, most Americans accepted rationing as a wartime necessity, one that affected all citizens fairly and reasonably. No one was sorry to see the end of rationing, however, even though it had helped prevent substantial price inflation during the war.

See also Just Price; War Industries Board.

References and Further Reading

Bentley, Amy. *Eating for Victory: Food Rationing and the Politics of Domesticity.* Urbana: University of Illinois Press, 1998.

Lingeman, Richard R. *Don't You Know There's a War On? The American Homefront, 1941–1945.* New York: Putnam, 1970.

Saving and Loan Crisis

When several American savings and loan institutions suddenly failed in the mid-1980s, it set off a massive collapse that ultimately affected thousands of individual institutions. Because most of these institutions operated under the umbrella of the Federal Savings and Loan Insurance Corporation (FSLIC), the government eventually found itself diverting tens of billions of dollars to clean up the financial wreckage. While many Americans believed that fraudulent or criminal activities had triggered the collapse, a number of institutional and environmental factors played a much larger role in this shocking financial fiasco.

The first mutually funded American building society issued its initial home mortgage in Philadelphia in 1831. Even though the borrower soon defaulted on that loan, similar institutions sprang up all across the country, based on the model of British building societies that had first appeared in the late eighteenth century. From the very beginning, these institutions operated on a somewhat risky basis in which they accepted short-term, interest-paying deposits and loaned out the resulting capital for long-term, fixed-interest home mortgages. Until rather late in the twentieth century, savings and loan associations focused their attention on the two functions identified in their designation: savings and loans. While banks also offered savings accounts and made real estate loans, they freely engaged in many other financial services like business and commercial loans, issuing banknotes, and handling checking accounts.

Under normal conditions, the more focused savings and loan institutions' strategy worked reasonably well. For long periods, interest rates remained fairly stable in the United States, and borrowers were reluctant to risk foreclosure by not paying monthly mortgage obligations on the homes in which they lived. The overall default rate on these private loans typically remained below 2 percent.

Inflation, financial panics, commercial bank failures, and other external factors inevitably affected hundreds of relatively small, localized savings and loan associations. The Panic of 1893 proved particularly damaging, but not surprisingly the onset of the Great Depression in the early 1930s presented a much greater challenge. The popular movie "A Wonderful Life" dramatically portrayed the problem. In it, actor Jimmy Stewart's character operated a hometown savings and loan association that barely managed to survive a devastating run from panicked depositors.

Even though the failure rate for savings and loan institutions remained well below that for the nation's banks, reforms still seemed prudent. In 1932 the Federal Home Loan Bank Act created a regulatory structure that resembled the Federal Reserve System. Many S&Ls operated with federal charters, and they were assessed to help finance the Home Loan Banks in their districts. Two years later the Federal Savings and Loan Insurance Corporation (FSLIC) was created to provide protection similar to the FDIC insurance of bank deposits.

These reforms and a relatively stable interest environment through the early 1960s enabled S&Ls to flourish. Home ownership was a popular goal for Americans after the Second World War, and the Servicemen's Readjustment Act (GI Bill) encouraged it with federal guarantees for mortgages taken out by veterans. A nationwide building boom spurred corresponding growth in the S&L industry.

The spiraling costs of the Vietnam War in the late 1960s fueled inflation that put the S&Ls under intense strain. Their typical thirty-year mortgages generated fixed returns, even as traditional depositors sought higher paying investment opportunities. The industry received some help when Congress passed the Interest Rate Control Act in 1966. Under its "Regulation Q," the Federal Reserve allowed S&Ls to pay slightly higher interest rates on deposits than did banks.

This minor advantage encouraged depositors to keep their savings in S&Ls, but they lost their appeal when interest rates spiraled upward in the late 1970s. By the early 1980s the federal government was engaged in a widespread deregulation effort that included the S&Ls. Both state and federally chartered institutions were granted much greater freedoms, including the right to make shorter term loans to private and commercial customers, to offer checking accounts and certificates of deposit, and to participate in a number of other activities that had formerly been confined to banks.

While the industry welcomed this freedom, it caused several problems. S&Ls generally lacked the expertise and experience necessary for prudent management of these new banking procedures and instruments. Even scrupulous directors made poor decisions. At the same time the newly granted freedom attracted first-time participants or freed existing ones who deliberately set out to milk the system for quick profits. By the 1990s hundreds of criminal indictments had been issued for S&L executives, and new examples of unprincipled behavior were revealed on an almost daily basis.

Even so, only a small percentage of the industry's difficulties resulted from outright criminal or dishonest behavior. Deregulation of the industry left S&L managers at the mercy of market or environmental forces they simply could not overcome. Much of the trouble occurred in the Southwest, with institutions in Texas undergoing some of the most dramatic collapses. Steep increases in oil prices had fueled much of the inflation in the 1970s, encouraging ambitious drilling in the southwestern oil regions. Optimism about continually escalating oil profits triggered a huge increase in real estate speculation, with S&Ls lending money to developers and expanding businesses.

Oil reached a peak price of $34 a barrel in 1981 but fell to less than $10 in 1986. In downtown Houston, the nation's oil capital, blocks and blocks of office skyscrapers sat empty. Both white and blue collar workers who had taken out mortgages in expectation of rising wages lost their homes. The S&Ls inevitably suffered because of their heavy investment in private and commercial mortgages.

Sloppy accounting methods caused many institutions to hide their losses even from themselves for many months. By the late 1980s, however, the FSLIC was strained beyond its limits as it tried to compensate all those who had maintained deposit accounts in failed or failing companies. The overworked employees of the FSLIC attempted to promote mergers or takeovers of insolvent institutions, but hundreds of them simply could not be saved.

Congress acknowledged the magnitude of the crisis by passing the Financial Institutions Reform, Recovery, and Enforcement Act (FIRREA) in 1989. It granted the FSLIC authority to borrow up to $50 billion to supplement its own overdrawn funding. Over the next few years, the amount needed rose well beyond even that remarkable level. Although it is popularly referred to as the "S&L Bailout," most of the money expended went to depositors and other victims of the general collapse. The concept of federal insurance for depositors that had motivated New Deal legislators in the 1930s received its most dramatic and costly implementation in the meltdown of the nation's savings and loan industry.

See also Deregulation; Federal Reserve System, Reform of.

References and Further Reading

Pilzer, Paul Zane. *Other People's Money.* New York: Simon and Schuster, 1989.

Robinson, Michael A. *Overdrawn.* New York: Dutton, 1990.

Waldman, Michael. *Who Robbed America?* New York: Random House, 1990.

White, Lawrence J. *The S&L Debacle.* New York: Oxford University Press, 1991.

Stagflation

In the 1970s the U.S. economy began exhibiting an unprecedented combination of rising inflation and rising unemployment. This unemployment developed during periods of economic recession or stagnation. The combination of a stagnant economy and high inflation became known as *stagflation.* Nothing that presidents Gerald Ford and Jimmy Carter did seemed capable of alleviating or ending stagflation. By the mid-1980s, however, the pressures on inflation and unemployment had eased, and stagflation has not recurred.

A key difficulty the government faced in trying to deal with stagflation was that the phenomenon seemed to violate classical economic theory. In previous recessions, for example, when large numbers of workers lost their jobs, they also lost their buying power and thus reduced the demand for goods. Classical economic theory expects prices to be set at the intersection of the supply and demand curves. When rising unemployment weakened demand, price levels were expected to fall. Falling prices, in turn, should lead to deflation.

Struggling to readjust to reduced federal expenditures and other changes as the war in Vietnam wound down, the U.S. economy stumbled into a series of recessions in the 1970s. As each of these downturns cost workers their jobs, unemployment rates naturally went up. At that point a 3 percent rate was presumed to represent full employment, but the rate never fell below 5 percent in the decade and reached as high as 9 percent in 1975. The economy was clearly stagnant at best, but price levels failed to decline. Instead, prices often rose during these recessions, indicating that forces other than consumer demand were at work.

A perceived energy shortage provided one convenient scapegoat for higher prices. During and after the 1973 Yom Kippur War between Israel and its neighbors, many oil-producing Arab countries announced reductions or embargoes on the amount of oil they supplied to the United States and other customers. American drivers parked in long lines waiting to buy gasoline at the few stations with supplies and were willing to pay much more per gallon. Inflation of gasoline prices in conjunction with parallel increases in costs for oil, gas, and other energy sources raised production and distribution prices for many other commodities as well.

Solid historical evidence indicates that much of the energy crisis resulted from deliberate practices like closing some U.S. refineries, withholding products from market, and even diverting oil into the nation's strategic reserve storage complex. Oil companies enjoyed very high profit margins during this period, evidence that some of the higher costs were unrelated to true shortages.

Similar behavior characterized other industries in the 1970s. Corporations or groups of corporations with controlling shares of a particular market could earn a profit by selling fewer goods at higher costs. Many therefore did not automatically cut prices when demand weakened. Meanwhile, some manufacturers benefited from the fact that the recession or stagnation actually lowered their costs for raw materials because they are generally less subject to monopoly control.

Stagflation presented serious challenges to the federal government. If it resorted to deficit spending to offset the recession, it would likely increase inflationary pressures even more. If it expanded its support for unemployed workers, it might discourage job seeking. One novel solution was to propose peace-time price and wage controls. Ironically, it was the conservative administration of President Richard Nixon that effectively used this tool in 1971 and 1972, imposing short-term limits that helped ease the economic pressures that potentially threatened to undermine the president's chances for reelection.

Neither of Nixon's successors found an effective weapon. President Gerald Ford shied away from direct meddling in the economy, proposing instead a psychological and motivational campaign to "Whip Inflation Now." When Jimmy Carter assumed office, stagflation continued to dog the economy. Carter's proposals for voluntary wage and price controls were no more effective than Ford's publicity campaign.

By 1980 the annual inflation rate had jumped to 18 percent, and unemployment continued its inexorable rise, topping out at 9.4 percent two years later. Figure 5.1 illustrates the crux of the problem: prices rising higher than growth of the gross national product. The persistent unemployment pressures and continuing recession that characterized the first two years of President Ronald Reagan's term finally moderated price increases. Stagflation has failed to redevelop since that time, which is quite fortunate given the absence of effective tools available to combat it.

See also Business Cycles; Great Depression, Causes of; Supply-Side Economics.

References and Further Reading

Blair, John, ed. *The Roots of Inflation.* New York: Franklin, 1975.

Sherman, Howard J. *Stagflation.* New York: Harper and Row, 1983.

Stock Options

Although speculators had dealt with options to buy or sell stock at various exchanges for decades, stock options found a new use in the 1960s. Companies began granting stock options to their executives to supplement salaries and bonuses. These options remained popular until the stock market flattened out in the 1970s, but they revived when economic conditions improved.

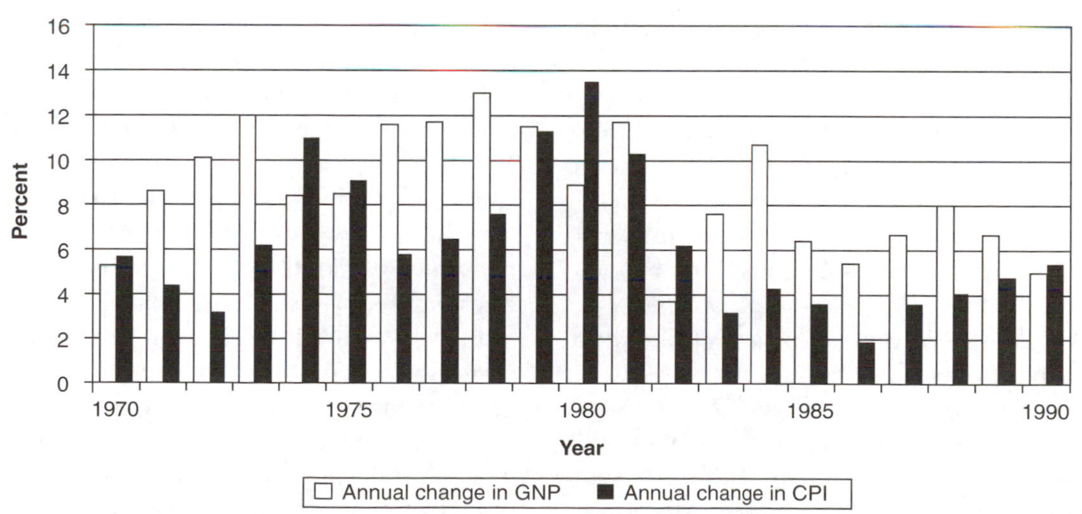

Figure 5.1 Stagflation, 1970–1990. (Data from Economic Report of the President. *Washington, DC: United States Government Printing Office, 1990.)*

Stock options helped fuel the dot-com boom, but lavish distribution of them created accounting nightmares that played into the dramatic collapse of high-flying corporations after 2000.

A stock option is a guarantee or promise that the holder can purchase shares at a future date. Anticipating future increases, bullish speculators use call options to lock in current or *strike* prices. No money need change hands until the option is exercised. The holder then pays the strike price for shares whose current market value is presumably well above that earlier value.

In the 1960s some companies decided to issue stock options to valued employees, usually executives. These options were attractive because they actually cost the company nothing in the short run but provided the favored employee with a potential future bonus. And if the executive did exercise his options, he received stock in the company. Presumably this gave managers an added incentive to promote profits and growth in the companies they ran.

Elaborate tax regulations quickly came into play regarding stock options. In the early days they received relatively favorable treatment, but even as rules became more stringent they retained advantages for both the company and the beneficiary. Because they did not represent an immediate expenditure, a company was not required to include the options in its balance sheet. When an option was exercised, the company had to sell stock at below market value but the difference could be written off as an operating loss.

To exercise an option, the holder had to come up with enough money to buy the stock at the strike price. In many cases, however, the stock was immediately sold at the current market price, generating an instant profit taxed as a capital gain. Many executives in Silicon Valley cashed in their options and bought expensive cars and other symbols of success that their salaries alone would never have justified. Some companies took the process a step further by loaning money to top executives with stock options to enable them to buy the stock. These seemed like reasonable transactions because company stock served as collateral for the loans.

An enormous variety of plans and distributions appeared in the 1980s. Although Lee Iacocca agreed to work for a dollar a year when the Chrysler Corporation hired him to head the company, he did demand substantial stock options. His dynamic leadership turned a struggling enterprise into a very profitable one, allowing him to cash in his options for millions. For a time, the rule of thumb was that an option package should be worth no more than three times an executive's salary, but some CEOs in the late 1990s were collecting eight or ten times as much in options as they received in cash compensation.

Because stock options gave individuals a stake in the success of a company, many corporations distributed them broadly. The Kroger grocery chain offered them as an incentive to all of its regular employees in the mid-1980s, and by 1990 employees owned 35 percent of the company's stock. This policy was a variation of another trend often referred to as an employee stock ownership plan or ESOP. Some of these plans were so extensive that a company like United Airlines could honestly advertise itself as an employee-owned enterprise. Supposedly the ESOP gave its workers an added incentive to provide outstanding customer service.

The dark side of stock options became all too apparent in the early 2000s. The dot-com bubble burst leaving thousands of former employees with options for stock in companies that no longer existed. Even if a company survived, options on its now devalued stock were considered *underwater,* incapable of being exercised except at a loss. Meanwhile the public became aware of outrageous examples of executive compensation in which some CEOs were granted millions in stock options and were loaned millions from company coffers to finance them at low or no interest. Because some accountants failed to properly assess the costs of these excessive packages, shareholders and even the SEC were unaware of them until the company collapsed.

Despite such abuses, the fundamental principle underlying stock options is sound. They certainly can motivate employees. Even more important, they can be used as carrots to workers in underfunded start-up companies. When venture capital is scarce and initial capitalization is limited, ambitious and talented people can still be attracted to a company if it offers them stock options in addition to or in lieu of direct salary.

See also Venture Capital.

References and Further Reading

Crystal, Graef S. *Executive Compensation.* New York: AMACIM, 1978.

Delves, Donald P. *Stock Options and the New Rules of Corporate Accountability.* New York: McGraw-Hill, 2004.

McWhirter, Darien A. *Sharing Ownership.* New York: Wiley, 1993.

Supply-Side Economics

When Ronald Reagan campaigned for the presidency in 1980, he advocated policies based on supply-side economics. Public attention tended to focus on Reagan's proposal for rapid and substantial reductions in tax rates, but the supply-side approach contained a number of other elements. Reagan's popularity combined with widespread disillusion about more conventional economic policies enabled him to implement several changes. Differing assessments of the effectiveness and wisdom of "Reaganomics" continues to be the subject of emotional partisan debate.

No one could claim that the U.S. economy was performing well in 1980. Persistent stagflation had dogged both presidents Gerald Ford and Jimmy Carter. High inflation, unemployment, rising energy prices, and elevated interest rates discouraged American workers and frustrated business leaders.

These unhealthy conditions seemed immune to standard economic remedies. Classical economic theory emphasized the close relationship between supply and demand. If demand increased, prices should rise and stimulate increased production. The Keynesian approach suggested that increased government spending could be used to step up demand. Monetarists, on the other hand, focused on policies designed to manipulate the nation's money supply, hoping to prevent price inflation but maintain interest rates that would encourage investment.

A small group of iconoclastic economists rejected both of these standard approaches, insisting that the focus should be on the supply side. Instead of trying to pump up demand, they believed that increasing the supply of goods and services would do much more to stimulate economic growth and national well-being. Tax reductions would free funds for productive investment on the supply side. Deregulating industries would similarly release them from artificial restrictions and encourage production. Lowering tariffs, increasing investment tax credits, and accelerating depreciation allowances were also expected to have beneficial consequences. Perhaps the most appealing feature of the supply-side theory was its contention that reducing taxes and encouraging production would so stimulate the economy that government revenues would actually rise in the long run.

Within a matter of months, the Reagan administration had guided the Tax Reduction Act of 1981 through Congress. It mandated a three-phase reduction in income taxes totaling 25 percent. Meanwhile the administration aggressively continued the federal deregulation program President Jimmy Carter had begun. A number of related changes also occurred including many other supply-side proposals. Despite the tax cuts, Reagan insisted on a massive build-up of the nation's defense capabilities. He also urged cutting expenditures on domestic and social support initiatives, but he was far less successful than his conservative supporters had anticipated in this area. Reagan

President Ronald Reagan did more than any other individual to popularize the concept of supply-side economics. Here he congratulates Alan Greenspan on his appointment to the Federal Reserve Board. (AP/Wide World Photos)

projected that his policies would lead to a balanced federal budget by the end of his first term.

The immediate impact was hardly encouraging. The economy stumbled into the worst two-year recession the nation had suffered since the 1930s. The annual budget deficit in 1984 was three times as large as the worst yearly figure in the Carter administration. Much of this trouble, of course, stemmed from deep-seated economic problems Reagan had inherited. As the decade wore on, the economy slowly mended itself, and the defenders of Reaganomics claimed it was a success after all.

A dispassionate analysis suggests that the ultimate influence of the supply-side approach was far less than either its critics or advocates had anticipated. Some supporters argued it had never been fully implemented, and that the $749 billion tax cut over five years was not large enough to have the desired impact. It is difficult to accept this contention, however, given that the national debt had risen to more than $4 trillion by 1992. Although largely discredited, the supply-side theory has had residual impacts, as illustrated by the tax cuts that President George H. W. Bush pushed through in his first term.

See also Keynesian Economics; Monetarism; Stagflation.

References and Further Reading

Evans, Michael K. *The Truth About Supply-Side Economics.* New York: Basic Books, 1983.

Kennedy, Peter E. *Macroeconomic Essentials.* Cambridge, MA: MIT Press, 2000.

Krugman, Paul. *Peddling Prosperity.* New York: Norton, 1994.

Sloan, John W. *The Reagan Effect.* Lawrence, KS: University Press of Kansas, 1999.

Television

RCA chief David Sarnoff was proud to be called the "Father of Television," and it represented deserved recognition for the person most responsible for creating the new medium. The Second World War interrupted experimental efforts to broadcast pictures over the airwaves, but television became a leading consumer industry in the late 1940s. Color broadcasting appeared in the next decade, and Sarnoff's drive had catapulted television into the premier American entertainment medium by 1960.

Television broadcasting drew technology from a variety of sources. Russian inventor Boris Rozing patented a cathode ray tube receiver in 1907. A fellow countryman, Vladimir Zworykin, emigrated to the United States and produced a camera tube in 1923 while working for Westinghouse. RCA acquired this project soon afterwards, and Zworykin told David Sarnoff he could develop a complete broadcast and reception system with a $10,000 grant. Some $10 million and a dozen years later, RCA finally managed to demonstrate its system at the 1939 Chicago World's Fair.

RCA's radio affiliate, NBC, began regular television broadcasting in the summer of 1941, but the federal government imposed a moratorium on all television development after the bombing of Pearl Harbor. Even so, thousands of servicemen and engineers got relevant experience during the war with CRT radar screens and other mechanisms that were easily adaptable to television.

Sarnoff eagerly pursued his goal once peace returned. William Paley at CBS was also working along similar lines, but federal authorities chose to set industry standards based on RCA's technology. One key decision was the stipulation that all television cameras and receivers should use a 525-line screen-scanning array. That decision, made in the early 1940s long before commercial television was at all feasible, is still in place. Only very recently has movement toward high-definition television with many more scanning lines capable of generating crisper pictures gained momentum.

An astute businessman who realized that revenues from broadcasting could equal if not exceed those from selling TV sets, Sarnoff insisted that RCA share its designs and technology with other manufactures like Zenith, Philco, and General Electric. His strategy proved wise, as more than 100 manufacturers entered the business, selling over 7 million sets in 1950 alone. NBC, ABC, and CBS had been the nation's leading radio networks, and they quickly assumed the same prominence in television broadcasting.

Sarnoff remained unsatisfied. He wanted to move immediately to color, and his engineers labored to develop an electronic process that would be compatible with the millions of black and white receivers already in place. CBS meanwhile attempted to seize the potential color market with an alternative system that employed spinning color-separation wheels in both cameras and receivers. To Sarnoff's amazement, the Federal Communications Commission adopted this clumsy mechanical system as the industry standard. Fortunately the commission reversed itself a couple of years later, and NBC's brightly colored Peacock logo invaded homes across the country.

As it had with its radio and monochrome TV technology, RCA continued to encourage other firms to take out licenses. At the same time it virtually controlled the supply of color CRTs, so third-party manufacturers had to buy them from RCA, generating a profit of $35 on every tube. In the long run, however, RCA's strategy fatally undermined its business, especially when it shared its technology with Japanese, Taiwanese, and Korean firms. By the mid-1970s Far Eastern suppliers were flooding the American market with low-cost but high-quality products that effectively destroyed the U.S. manufacturing enterprise.

Even so, the American television entertainment industry thrived. Hollywood producers had feared the development of an alternative to motion pictures, but discovered that television had an almost insatiable need for programming. The major studios sold the broadcasters old movies by the thousands, and actors, directors, writers, and technical staffers found ample employment churning out TV series and made-for-TV movies. Like American movies, U.S. television programs drew worldwide audiences with shows like the soap opera "Santa Barbara" becoming one of the most popular shows in Spain in the 1980s.

The inexorable advance of technology included the development of magnetic tape video recorders in the late 1970s, DVDs in the 1990s, and TiVo in the early twenty-first century. To make matters worse for the major networks, they had to struggle to hold audiences both on prime time and during the day when cable channels began to offer dozens and then hundreds of programming alternatives.

In the long run, however, Sarnoff's vision of a color picture receiver in every American household has largely been fulfilled. The signals fed into these receivers now come from many sources, but they all provide news, sports coverage, drama, comedy, and music on a scale far beyond even the Father of Television's most optimistic vision.

See also Movies; Paley, William Samuel; Radio; Sarnoff, David; Turner, Ted.

References and Further Reading

Chandler Jr., Alfred D., and James W. Cortada, eds. *A Nation Transformed by Information.* New York: Oxford University Press, 2000.

Dreher, Carl. *Sarnoff: An American Success.* New York: Quadrangle, 1977.

Greenfield, Jeff. *Television: The First Fifty Years.* New York: H. N. Abrams, 1977.

Watson, Mary Ann. *The Expanding Vista.* Durham, NC: Duke University Press, 1994.

Transistors

Researchers at Bell Laboratories tested the world's first transistor in 1947. It became the prototype for a remarkable burst of innovation involving both germanium and silicon solid-state devices that could switch and amplify electric currents. Transistors quickly began replacing vacuum tubes in radios and calculating machines and encouraged the development of faster and more energy efficient computers. They also evolved into the microchips that served as the heart of the computers and control devices that proliferated in the late twentieth century.

Bell Laboratories was a logical incubator for transistor technology. It had been created as the primary research arm for AT&T, the huge corporation that had evolved from Alexander Graham Bell's telephone patent in the late nineteenth century. Telephone service was so popular that the number of phones installed and the number of calls per day expanded at a remarkable rate. AT&T therefore constantly experimented with techniques that would provide faster, more efficient switching and control.

Thousands of scientists and engineers at Bell Labs participated in this endeavor, but three men were primarily responsible for developing the transistor. William Shockley, John Bardeen, and Walter H. Brattain won the Nobel Prize for physics in 1956, nine years after they had tested a carefully adulterated germanium slab with three wires sticking out of it. By selectively doctoring the germanium, the researchers could make their tiny devices switch electric current on or off or serve as amplifiers of tiny current variations.

Transistors could thus perform the same functions that cumbersome vacuum tubes had been handling for decades. But transistors were far smaller, more reliable, less breakable, and did not generate vast amounts of heat. Because Bell Labs was a research and not a production facility, AT&T made the remarkable decision to license its technology to other companies. In the spring of 1952 company representatives paid $25,000 to attend a week-long seminar at Bell Labs to learn about the technology. Dozens of companies took out licenses even though the market prospects for transistors were far from clear.

One of the licensees was Texas Instruments (TI), a relatively small firm headed by visionary Frank Kilby. By 1954 TI had perfected manufacturing silicon rather than germanium transistors, an advance that reduced costs and produced devices that operated better at normal temperatures. To showcase its technology, TI produced thousands of small, portable radio sets. Although the company lost money on them, the publicity they generated established TI's reputation as the industry leader in the manufacture of transistors.

Some vacuum tube manufacturers chose not to jump on the transistor bandwagon. Within a decade the market for tubes had all but disappeared, and Philco, Sylvania, and RCA had suffered serious reverses. Literally hundreds of new companies sprang up to manufacture transistors in the United States and abroad. The market for transistors boomed as they were incorporated into radios, television sets, telephones, industrial control mechanisms, and hundreds of other electronic devices for domestic and military use.

Transistors also played a major part in making computers more efficient. Early models like the ENIAC and the room-size computers IBM produced contained panels with hundreds of vacuum tubes. By the mid-1950s, these had disappeared, replaced by banks of tiny, reliable transistors. The success of this evolution encouraged researchers and manufacturers to install several transistor-like interfaces on a single piece of silicon. Texas Instruments led the industry in producing the first commercial integrated circuits etched onto a chip of silicon in 1959. Integrated circuits on microchips superseded individual transistors in the 1960s just as they had made vacuum tubes obsolete.

The transistor revolution rose and declined within a period of a dozen years, but it had long-range consequences. It encouraged miniaturization of electronic devices, created a vibrant industry capable of exploiting new advances in electronics, and stimulated collecting and processing data on an unprecedented scale. In short, the transistor was a key element in the emergence of the Information Age.

See also Computers; Kilby, Jack; Microchips; Noyce, Robert.

References and Further Reading

Chandler, Jr., Alfred D., and James W. Cortada, eds. *A Nation Transformed by Information.* New York: Oxford University Press, 2000.

Cortada, James W. *The Computer in the United States.* Armonk, NY: M. E. Sharpe, 1993.

Young, Jeffrey. *Forbes Greatest Technology Stories.* New York: Wiley, 1998.

Universal Product Code

First used in a consumer sale in 1974, the universal product coding system has pervaded not only retailing but manufacturing, wholesaling, inventorying, and hundreds of specialized uses. Adoption of the familiar universal product code (UPC) with its black and white bars came at a very auspicious moment. Use of UPCs requires laser scanning technology and computerized data processing capability that became available just in time to ensure that the system would expand well beyond the retail grocery business where it originated.

A punched-card process for inventorying groceries had been proposed early in the 1930s, but development of a visual coding system was delayed for twenty years. Joseph Woodland was a graduate student at the Drexel Institute of Technology when a colleague suggested that he devise a system for automating the grocery check-out process. Woodland came up with a binary code using thick and thin black and white bars to represent numbers. He obtained a patent for his bar code and a primitive optical scanner in 1952.

Another twenty years passed before an ad hoc committee of grocery executives and technical experts agreed to adopt this innovation and establish it as a universal product code in 1973. The concept quickly caught on as retailers and wholesalers recognized the benefits and efficiencies such a system would provide. The Uniform Code Council came into being to manage the system, monitoring its operation and serving as the authority for assigning UPCs to manufacturers.

The standard American UPC includes twelve numbers. The first and last represent control numbers to ensure accurate scanning. The heart of the code is a five-digit number that identifies a particular manufacturer or distributor. These users in turn assign additional five-digit codes to identify specific products in their lines. The bar code for an individual digit actually consists of seven narrow spaces that are either filled (black) or empty (white). This creates a binary code that, in the case of the number five, for example, consists of a narrow white bar, a black bar filling two spaces, a white bar filling three spaces, and a single-space black bar.

Bar codes are easily read by laser-equipped scanners that instantaneously compare the pattern to those in a computerized database. It contains information about manufacturer and product designators as well as prices for individual items. It records that information on both the customer's printed receipt and in whatever inventory database the store uses. Scanner technology has advanced rapidly since the early 1970s, and bar codes can be read with virtually no errors in either direction and at almost any angle by countertop or portable instruments.

The grocery industry, which handles tens of thousands of products every day, provided the initial impetus for the adoption of UPCs. They enabled a retail clerk to total a customer's purchases rapidly and at the same time produce a record of each item sold. The retailer could then use that information to restock inventories.

UPCs quickly spread to other product lines. The Wal-Mart retail chain was a pioneer in using UPC technology to stock its huge stores efficiently. Centralized inventory information allowed the chain to distribute to each outlet the products its own customers were likely to buy. The result was just-in-time delivery of products that freed the central organization from maintaining large or slow-selling stocks of goods. This strategy was a key factor in Wal-Mart's ability to maintain lower prices than its competitors.

UPCs or other bar code systems have become pervasive. Libraries bar code their books, manufacturer's bar code supplies and materials, and airlines bar code luggage to ensure accurate distribution and tracking. Major shipping companies like DHL and UPS use bar codes to track their deliveries from shipper to recipient. The U.S. Postal Service has adopted its own postcode system for routing mail through automated gateways, speeding sorting and delivery.

In the early 2000s, a successor technology called Radio Frequency Identification (RFID) appeared. Pioneered by Texas Instruments, this system is designed to give every single item in an inventory a unique, radio-readable chip designation and seems capable of making the UPC system obsolete. It is quite clear, however, that RFID experimentation has been encouraged by the enormous benefits to control, inventory, and distribution the universal product code system originally provided. Various studies of its effectiveness have suggested that the widespread use of UPC technology may well have reduced grocery cost inflation by as much as one half since its introduction.

See also Chain Stores; Computers.

References and Further Reading

Erdei, William H. *Bar Codes.* New York: McGraw-Hill, 1993.

Harrell, Gilbert D. *Universal Product Code.* East Lansing, MI: Michigan State University Press, 1976.

Venture Capital

In recent years venture capital groups have become vital sources of start-up funding for people working independently of established companies. After careful analyses, venture capitalists decide which new ideas, innovative technologies, or ambitious individuals to support. Venture capital was particularly crucial to the development of high-tech firms in Silicon Valley and elsewhere during the 1980s.

Raising investment capital for a new enterprise has always been difficult. In the past many aspiring entrepreneurs had to depend on their own resources or those of families and personal friends to get started. Loans might also be arranged, but a company had to be relatively stable before it could borrow extensively. The banks and finance capitalists that had arisen in the late nineteenth century tended to be rather conservative and risk averse.

As the computer revolution gained momentum, no one could be sure just what direction it might take or what functions or peripherals might thrive. Some credit Robert Noyce with being a major force in encouraging investment in innovative ideas. The early venture capitalists he attracted to Silicon Valley had relatively limited knowledge of the rapidly changing field or what the prospects for any given development might be.

By the 1980s, however, venture capitalists had become much more astute. Their fundamental goal was to get in on the ground floor of a start-up company that would blossom into an industry giant. Venture capitalists supplied the money needed to rent or build space, hire talented staff, and fund the time-consuming process of product development. In return they demanded a healthy allocation of new firm's shares, usually in the form of preferred stock that could account for 30 or 40 percent of the start-up's total equity.

To spread the unpredictable risks of funding new endeavors, venture capitalists distribute their funding among several enterprises. Out of ten investments, the general expectation based on experience is that three or four of the firms will fail quickly and completely. Another three or four may survive but barely break even over the long term. But if the remaining one or two start-ups really hit their stride, the returns to investment can reach remarkable levels, ten or even a hundred times greater than their original capitalization. Ideally, profits from successful firms more than offset losses encountered in others.

In addition to providing seed money, venture capitalists typically play a very active role in managing their clients. After all, they are major stockholders in the firms they finance. Seats on the company's board of directors or even the position of CEO will ensure that the start-up firm is responsive to its backers. That means, of course, that if a firm appears to be faltering, the venture capitalists have the authority to close it down immediately to curtail further losses. At the same time, their knowledge of markets and trends can assist them in providing useful and timely advice to an inventor or innovator engrossed in the details of his or her technology.

Venture capitalists typically focus their attention on ideas or innovations that have somehow been overlooked or discarded by established companies. A mature corporation naturally tends to be more conservative in its strategies than start-ups, but the latter often have the greatest potential for exponential growth. Venture capital played a major part in launching such computer industry giants as Apple Computers, Oracle, Sun Microsystems, and Intel. Meanwhile, companies like Genentech in the biotechnology sector have also absorbed vast amounts of venture capital.

Venture capitalists usually plan to cash out of their investments rather quickly even if they are successful so they can recycle their profits and their original capital into new ventures. If a firm thrives, it may execute an initial public offering (IPO) to sell shares to the public. After a company has gone public, venture capitalists can more easily sell their own shares and move on to new projects. In other instances, successful start-ups that occupy specialized or niche positions in their industries are very likely to be bought or merged with other start-ups or absorbed into major corporations. Such buyouts provide ideal opportunities for venture capitalists to exit as well.

Venture capitalists tend to be optimists. A substantial number of the start-up companies that participated in the so-called dot-com boom in the 1990s were fueled by venture capital. The collapse of that boom and the subsequent recession substantially cooled the venture capital market. It has begun to revive, however, and appears to have become a consistent ingredient in promoting creativity and business initiative in the United States.

See also Stock Options.

References and Further Reading

Kaplan, Jerry. *Startup: A Silicon Valley Adventure.* Boston: Houghton Mifflin, 1994.

Lynskey, Michael J., and Seiichireo Yonekura, eds. *Entrepreneurship and Organization.* New York: Oxford University Press, 2002.

White Knight

Threatened with what it considers a hostile takeover, a company may respond by seeking rescue from a so-called white knight. To avoid being absorbed, and possibly replaced by an unfriendly external group, some managers attempt to throw their companies into the arms of whoever they hope will be more compatible and empathetic leaders. Such friendly entities became known as white knights, riding to the rescue of distressed companies besieged by external enemies.

Although hostile takeovers had succeeded in earlier periods, a renewed spate of aggressive assaults in the late 1970s and into the 1980s put company management under intense pressure. At that point a clear separation occurred between a company's managers and its owners (stockholders and speculators). Shareholders' primary interest was in protecting and enhancing their investments; managers often seemed primarily concerned with retaining their high-paying positions.

When an outside individual or group assembled a war chest or a substantial percentage of a company's outstanding shares, it could attempt a takeover. This typically began with a tender offer to buy a great deal more stock at a price considerably higher than its current market value. Stockholders interested in immediate profits were understandably attracted by such offers, which might be 20 or 30 percent more than they could get selling their shares on the open market.

SEC rules stemming from the 1968 Williams Act required anyone with a 5 percent ownership position to make that fact public. The SEC also imposed a delay from that point before a tender offer could be implemented. The delay enabled a company's management to develop a defensive strategy or, if that seemed impossible, to encourage another company to serve as a white knight by making its own tender offer, usually higher than the original bid.

Any number of motivations might underlay an appeal to a white knight. In some instances the hostile takeover attempt came from people with no experience in the industry involved. In such cases management could appeal to stockholders not to sell out or, perhaps more accurately, not to sell off the company's assets to outsiders. Seeking a white knight from within the company's industrial sector would also protect its market position. Often management had less noble motivations. Executives could not trust a hostile takeover group to keep them in their jobs. If they could find a white knight, its management might be more friendly and sympathetic to their situation so its takeover could preserve and even strengthen their individual positions within the company hierarchy.

Major respected corporations were the most likely candidates to serve as white knights. So-called corporate raiders, on the other hand, were often smaller corporations or groups led by aggressive individuals. The announcement of a tender offer by any entity was said to put the target company "into play." And, due to the SEC time lines, once a company was in play, offers and counteroffers had to be developed very quickly.

The Conoco situation illustrates that the chain of events could be quite complex. In May 1981 a small Canadian company, Dome Petroleum, set off a bidding war by making a tender offer for 20 percent of the stock in the Continental Oil Co. (Conoco). That offer put Conoco in play, and Edgar Bronfman, chairman of Seagram Industries, quickly issued a hostile tender offer of his own for 41 percent of Conoco's stock. Conoco chairman Ralph Bailey failed to convince Cities Service, another major player in the oil industry, to step up as a white knight. He then turned to the giant Dupont Co. and convinced it to make a tender offer for all of Conoco's stock. At almost the same moment Mobil Corporation weighed in with its own, much higher tender offer. Even so, the Conoco management was able to convince its stockholders that both the company and their investments would be safer under the aegis of white knight Dupont.

As this convoluted process suggests, not all decisions made in haste are sound. Some successful white knights ended up forsaking chivalry and looting their clients ruthlessly. That might leave the company no better off than it would have been if it had acceded to a hostile takeover in the first place. Moreover, as the takeover mania expanded in the 1980s, major corporations that might earlier have waited on the sidelines for a request to serve as a white knight joined the ranks of those initiating takeovers on their own behalf.

The complexities of arranging a white knight rescue, the very short time available to negotiate it, and the uncertainty of how it might turn out encouraged companies to seek other defensive methods. The invention of poison pills in the mid-1980s made takeover targets less palatable; the development of golden parachutes for ousted executives made them less fearful of being removed. The white knight defense thus became far less popular.

See also Golden Parachute; Greenmail; Leveraged Buyout; Poison Pill.

References and Further Reading

Sobel, Robert. *Dangerous Dreamers.* New York: Wiley, 1993.

Wasserstein, Bruce. *Big Deal: The Battle for Control of America's Leading Corporations.* New York: Warner Books, 1998.

BIOGRAPHIES

Andersen, Arthur (1885–1947)

Although he was born in Illinois, young Arthur Andersen returned with his family to their native Norway for a time before returning to settle in Chicago. There Andersen became an office boy, but he studied accounting at night school. He then enrolled at Northwestern University where he did so well he was asked to join its accounting faculty. Andersen taught at the university until 1922 and wrote highly regarded research and theoretical articles as well. Meanwhile, the private consulting firm, Arthur Andersen and Co. he founded in 1918 prospered, building its reputation as an acknowledged expert in utility issues. To complement the company's accounting activities, Andersen added business consulting expertise, enabling his firm to provide clients with a broad array of services. Arthur Andersen's prestigious academic reputation added weight to his calls for improved, standardized accountancy practices in a rapidly growing service industry. The company he established became one of the so-called Big Four accounting firms, and it continued to expand after his death. Andersen Consulting spun off as an independent entity in 1989 and is now known as Accenture. Unfortunately, Arthur Andersen's accounting reputation suffered fateful damage due to its association with Enron Corporation's collapse in the early twenty-first century, something that would have been unthinkable to the company's strictly ethical founder.

References and Further Reading

Arthur Andersen and Co. *The First Sixty Years.* Chicago: A. Andersen, 1974.

Ash, Mary Kay (1918–2001)

When Mary Kay Wagner's father contracted tuberculosis, her mother had to support the family, leaving her twelve-year-old daughter to care for her siblings and her ailing father. Mary Kay managed to complete high school in her native Texas but had no opportunity for college. Her first marriage produced three children but ended in desertion. To make ends meet, she worked first for Stanley Home Products and then for World Gift Co., two successful direct sales organizations. Frustrated at being passed over and even demoted largely because of her gender, she retired in 1963 but quickly decided to start her own company. She had previously bought proprietary rights to a skin cream formula and used it as the basis for her direct sales operation. Committed to treating her almost exclusively female sales staff far better than she had been treated, Mary Kay offered high sales commissions, thorough training, and annual motivational conventions complete with hundreds of prizes to recognize successful agents. The ultimate Mary Kay reward was a pink Cadillac. Mary Kay Cosmetics are currently sold in dozens of countries and the company controls the largest direct-sale market for skin care products in the United States.

See also Lauder, Estée; Rubinstein, Helena.

References and Further Reading

Ash, Mary Kay. *Mary Kay.* New York: Harper and Row, 1981.

Boesky, Ivan (1937–)

The son of Russian immigrants living in Detroit, Ivan Boesky early established a reputation for cutthroat business dealings. He married the daughter of the owner of the Beverly Hills Hotel and then moved to New York in 1966 aiming to make his fortune as an arbitrager. With funding from both his wife and his stepfather, he founded his own investment firm in 1975 but left it to establish Ivan Boesky Inc., six years later. Boesky never thought small, and his various speculations won big or lost big. His reputation as a sharp operator was already well established when he was charged with insider trading. Lower-level employees at major Wall Street firms had been recruited to pass information up through a complex transmission system, providing Boesky with advance notice of trades, mergers, and other events from which he could profit. He implicated junk bond wizard Michael Milken in a plea bargain that netted him a three-year prison term and a $100 million fine. For better or worse, Ivan Boesky emerged as the most notorious of the pack of corporate raiders that preyed on Wall Street in the 1980s.

See also Arbitrage; Milkin, Michael Robert.

References and Further Reading

Boesky, Ivan F. *Merger Mania.* New York: Holt, Rinehart, and Winston, 1985.

Buffet, Warren Edward (1930–)

Warren Edward Buffet became one of the world's wealthiest men primarily because of his astute investment decisions. Although he lived in Washington, D.C., as a child and later New York, he has maintained his headquarters in Nebraska, earning the nickname "the Wizard of Omaha." While a graduate student at Columbia University's School of Business, he studied under Benjamin Graham, coauthor of *Security Analysis.* Published in the depths of the Depression in 1934, it recommended buying undervalued stocks and holding onto them for the long term. Applying this principle, Buffet formed a partnership in 1956 and began implementing Graham's strategy, increasing his personal share of the partnership from $5,000 to $25 million by 1969. Along the way he purchased Berkshire Hathaway, a Massachusetts textile manufacturing company. Although it continued to struggle for years, Buffet dissolved his earlier partnership and used Berkshire Hathaway as the base for his continuing investment ventures. He never participated in hostile takeovers but controlled so much capital that he became a dominant investor in media (ABC and the Washington Post), financial services (American Express and Salomon Brothers), and insurance (GEICO). His influence continues to expand, even though the undervalued stock opportunities he exploited earlier have become rarer.

References and Further Reading

Hagstrom, Robert G., and Peter Lynch. *The Warren Buffett Way.* New York: Wiley, 1994.

Claiborne, Elisabeth (1929–)

Although she was born in Belgium, Elisabeth Claiborne was the daughter of an American banker and lived in several cities during her childhood. The frequent moves prevented Liz from completing high school, but she did study painting in Europe before winning a *Harper's Bazaar* design contest. In her twenties she worked as an artist and model in New York until Arthur Ortenberg hired her as a designer for a women's sportswear company. Claiborne and Ortenberg soon divorced their spouses and married each other. In 1975 the couple and two other partners formed Liz Claiborne, Inc., to manufacture and market clothing that Liz designed. Her strategy was to produce apparel for working women, a rapidly growing population that other manufacturers had largely ignored. Liz Claiborne styles caught on quickly, and the company was an overnight success due to Liz's comfortable and affordable designs and her husband's astute business management. Initially sold through department stores, the company's products were so popular that the stores often made twice or three times their normal revenue from the space they devoted to Liz Claiborne styles. The company went public in 1981 and achieved Fortune 500 ranking five years later. Liz Claiborne and her husband retired from active involvement in the company in 1991.

See also Lauren, Ralph.

References and Further Reading

Ingham, John N., and Lynne B. Feldman. *Contemporary American Business Leaders.* New York: Greenwood, 1990.

Douglas, Donald Wills (1892–1981)

As a cadet at the U.S. Naval Academy, Brooklyn-born Donald Wills Douglas became discouraged when his Navy colleagues failed to share his fascination with aviation. He therefore left Annapolis and completed aeronautical engineering studies at MIT. His first job was as chief engineer for Glenn L. Martin's aircraft company, but Douglas wanted to run his own operation. With backing from other aviation enthusiasts, he established his first company in Southern California. It produced the Cloudster, a model that won his first government contract. In the 1920s his reorganized Douglas Aircraft Co. worked almost exclusively filling military and naval orders. In the early 1930s, however, the company developed its Douglas Commercial line with the DC-1 rapidly evolving into the extraordinarily innovative and popular DC-3. It became the mainstay of burgeoning airlines around the world, and the company delivered over 10,000 C-47s, the transport version, during the Second World War. Although the company produced thousands of other military aircraft during the conflict, Douglas eagerly reentered the commercial market in the late 1940s with his four-engine DC-4s, DC-6s, and DC-7s. His focus on these propeller-driven aircraft caused him to discount jet propulsion that rival Boeing exploited. In 1967 Douglas reluctantly agreed to a merger with McDonnell, a primarily military aircraft manufacturer. The McDonnell-Douglas Aircraft Co. remained a major industry player, but Donald Douglas never recaptured the spirit and enthusiasm that had helped him transform the industry in the 1930s.

See also Commercial Aviation; Military Aviation.

References and Further Reading

Morrison, Wilbur H. *Donald W. Douglas.* Ames, IA: Iowa State University Press, 1991.

Forbes, Malcolm Stevenson (1919–1990)

Malcolm Stevenson Forbes grew up in New York and New Jersey and eventually earned a degree in political science from Princeton University. Service in the U.S. Army cut short a budding publishing career, but he rekindled it in 1946 when he became a staffer on *Forbes,* a magazine his father had founded. For the next several years, Malcolm Forbes spent much of his energy on politics, serving in the New Jersey legislature and unsuccessfully seeking higher office. By 1964 he had inherited full ownership and control over *Forbes,* however, and he focused his attention on converting it into one of the nation's leading business periodicals. Simultaneously he engaged in ballooning, motorcycle racing, and other adventurous pursuits that kept his name before the public and promoted the popularity of his magazine. A millionaire many times over, Malcolm Forbes bought lavish homes in several locations, hosted parties packed with celebrities, and generally behaved like a nineteenth-century mogul. Even so, his success as a business writer and publisher remained the center of his professional life, and he bequeathed his publishing empire and a huge fortune to his son, Steven Forbes.

References and Further Reading

Winans, Christopher. *Malcolm Forbes.* New York: St. Martin's, 1990.

Gates, Bill (1955–)

Bill Gates's wealthy Seattle parents decided to send their precocious son to a private school. There he met Paul Allen in a programming class. The two teenagers devel-

Bill Gates founded Microsoft, a company that dominates the global software business and that made Gates the wealthiest person in the world. (Waggener Edstrom/PR Newswire)

oped a computerized system for monitoring traffic and formed Traf-O-Data to market it. Their company had earned $20,000 before Gates graduated from high school. He attended Harvard for a couple of years before Allen lured him to Albuquerque to develop an operating system for the Altair 8800, a pioneering microcomputer. Altair soon disappeared, but the programming wizards' company, Microsoft, went on to write operating systems for a number of other experimental computers. The company had moved to the Seattle area when IBM secretly contracted with it to design an operating system for the IBM PC. The Microsoft Disk Operating System (MS-DOS) was bundled with all IBM machines sold, as well as bundled with the IBM clones that proliferated soon afterward. In the 1980s Microsoft expanded its product line to include word processors, spreadsheets, and the Windows operating system to compete directly with Apple Computer's popular user interface. Microsoft went public in 1986, and both Gates and Allen became billionaires within a matter of months. Although a lengthy antitrust suit and charges of unfair competition have dogged Microsoft in recent years, Bill Gates has continued to prosper, becoming the world's richest person.

See also Personal Computers.

References and Further Reading

Wallace, James, and Jim Erickson. *Bill Gates and the Making of the Microsoft Empire.* New York: Wiley, 1992.

Geneen, Harold (1910–1997)

Harold Geneen moved to the United States from England with his mother. She was a vaudeville performer, so young Harold spent his early years in private boarding schools. Geneen held a number of low-paying jobs while completing a night school degree at New York University. A skilled accountant, he worked his way up the corporate ladder in several different companies before landing a top executive position at Raytheon Corporation. His leadership and organizational flair at Raytheon convinced International Telephone and Telegraph Company (ITT) to hire Geneen as its president in 1959. For several years he devoted his energies to rationalizing and reorganizing this global communications firm. Concerned that expropriation or other nationalistic actions might undermine the company's many foreign subsidiaries, Geneen decided to strengthen his firm's core by accumulating American properties in the late 1960s. Early acquisition targets included insurance, publishing, and finance companies, Avis Rental Cars, and vocational schools. Geneen's biggest disappointment came when federal authorities blocked his attempted merger with the American Broadcasting Co. By the late 1960s he had become a committed advocate of conglomeration, drawing under the ITT umbrella diverse properties like homebuilder Levitt and Co, the Sheraton Hotel chain, and the Hartford Insurance Co. Along the way Geneen earned a reputation as a master at assembling and managing his enormous conglomerate. In the early 1970s, however, charges that his company had bribed Nixon administration officials and that one of its South American subsidiaries had a role in the assassination of Chile's Marxist president seriously undermined his credibility. ITT continued to prosper under Geneen's leadership until his retirement from the firm in 1979, long after the conglomerate phenomenon had lost its luster.

See also Conglomerates; Levitt, William Jaird.

References and Further Reading

Schoenberg, Robert J. *Geneen.* New York: Warner, 1985.

Graham, Katharine (1917–2001)

Although she was born in New York City, Katharine Graham's life and influence centered in Washington, D.C. Her father, Eugene Meyer, bought the *Washington Post* in

1933 and Katharine Meyer worked there after graduating from the University of Chicago. She married Philip Graham in 1940, and he became the *Post's* publisher after the Second World War. In 1948 Katharine's father sold his interests to the couple, leaving Philip Graham in complete charge. He expanded his holdings to include *Newsweek* magazine and television stations, but suffered mental deterioration and committed suicide in 1963. Katharine Graham was suddenly thrust into leadership of this media empire but took it in stride, making astute decisions like hiring Benjamin Bradlee to be the *Post's* managing editor. The paper's reputation soared when it published the *Pentagon Papers* and later vigorously pursued the Watergate story that ultimately led to President Richard Nixon's resignation. Graham won the Pulitzer Prize in 1998 for her autobiography, a fitting honor for a remarkable media personage.

See also Hearst, William Randolph; Pulitzer, Joseph.

References and Further Reading

Davis, Deborah. *Katharine the Great*. New York: Sheridan Square Press, 1991.

David Packard (left) and William Hewlett founded their enormously successful electronics company in this Palo Alto, California, garage. (AP/Wide World Photos)

Hewlett, William Redington (1913–2001)

The first name in the most prominent producer of computer printers, William Redington Hewlett was born in Michigan, but spent his childhood in Palo Alto, California. His father taught at Stanford University where William studied electrical engineering under Frederick Terman. After obtaining a graduate degree at MIT, Hewlett returned to Stanford on a fellowship. Terman convinced him and a friend, David Packard, to form a company that developed a number of electronic devices. Walt Disney bought some of the radio oscillators Hewlett devised to use for his film *Fantasia*, and their company, Hewlett-Packard, expanded into the Stanford Research Park that Terman was promoting in what became Silicon Valley. Hewlett left the company to serve as an Army officer in the Second World War but returned in 1946. He provided the engineering creativity for the rapidly growing company. The two entrepreneurs pursued a comparatively conservative approach, refusing to borrow long-term and using company profits to fund their research and development. After limited success in the minicomputer business, the company's fortunes rose dramatically in 1972 when it introduced the H-P 35 scientific calculator. Although Hewlett retired from active involvement in Hewlett-Packard in 1978, his engineering genius and creativity continued to inspire his successors.

See also Packard, David; Personal Computers.

References and Further Reading

Anders, George. *Perfect Enough.* New York: Portfolio, 2003.

Icahn, Carl (1936–)

Carl Icahn's schoolteacher mother provided the stability in their Queens home, enabling the young man to excel in school and graduate from Princeton. Icahn attended medical school for a time and served in the army before becoming a stockbroker. He quickly developed a specialization in options, and his success convinced an uncle to lend him $400,000 to buy his own seat on the New York Stock Exchange. Icahn and Co. traded options and moved into arbitrage as well. In 1978 Icahn executed his first corporate raid almost by accident when he purchased undervalued stock in the Tappan Co. and shortly managed to sell it for twice what he had paid.

Carl Icahn became known in the late 1970s as a savvy and sometimes ruthless corporate raider. (Ricardo Watson/Archive Photos)

He quickly gained a reputation as a ruthless corporate raider, buying into a company and then typically negotiating greenmail payments to get out. In 1983 one of these gambles resulted in his actually capturing control of ACF Industries, a struggling railroad car manufacturer. To everyone's surprise but Icahn's, he turned it around and sold out at a huge profit a couple of years later. He then made a highly controversial run on Trans-World Airlines. When the company attempted to find a white knight, the unions backed Icahn and once again he ended up controlling the company. By buying feeder lines and streamlining operations Icahn improved the company's balance sheet so much that he earned a $2 billion profit when he sold out in 1989. Despite the negative publicity his activities provoked, Icahn's wealth and influence have enabled him to remain a major player. He has recently become involved in a major purchase of General Motors stock, a move with unknown outcomes at the time this book was written.

See also Greenmail; Hostile Takeovers; Junk Bonds.

References and Further Reading

Stevens, Mark. *King Icahn.* New York: Dutton, 1993.

Jobs, Steven Paul (1955–)

Adopted by a family living in Mountain View, California, Steven Paul Jobs grew up in the heart of what was to become Silicon Valley. In high school, he palled around with the "nerds," one of whom was Steven Wozniak, a remarkably creative electronics tinkerer. After attending ultra-liberal Reed College for a semester, Jobs remained immersed in the counterculture, smoking marijuana, working in an apple orchard, traveling to India, and even taking training in primal scream therapy. He worked briefly with computer game manufacturer Atari before returning to Silicon Valley to team up with his high school buddy. Steve Wozniak cobbled together a basic computer in the form of a circuit board that needed peripherals to function. At Jobs' insistence, they called it an Apple I computer and formed the Apple Computer Co. to manufacture it in the garage at the Jobs' family home. While Steve Jobs' technical skills were no match for those of his partner, he was a master at understanding marketing and consumer behavior. It was he who conceived of the Apple II, an attractively cased unit with a keyboard that incorporated Wozniak's circuit boards and attached to a TV set. The Apple II was the world's first successful personal computer, soon accounting for over 80 percent of U.S. sales. Jobs sought financing and management help from A. C. Markkula and eventually hired John Sculley to head the rapidly growing company. Brash, arrogant, and opinionated, Jobs was forced out of Apple after the initial failure of his pet project, a smaller but much more versatile machine called the Macintosh. He formed a new company to build the less-than-successful NeXt computers, owned the Pixar animation studio for a time, but returned to Apple in the late 1990s. Under his aegis, Apple brought out the iPod music/storage device, an instant marketing success that once again confirmed Jobs' insight into consumer desires.

See also Noyce, Robert; Personal Computers.

References and Further Reading

Young, Jeffrey S., and William L. Simon. *iCon: Steve Jobs, the Greatest Second Act in the History of Business.* Hoboken, NJ: Wiley, 2005.

Johnson, John Harold (1918–2005)

Son of an Arkansas mill worker, John Harold Johnson attended segregated schools before his widowed mother relocated to Chicago. He won a scholarship to the University of Chicago where he developed his writing skills. In 1938 he joined Liberty Life Insurance Co. as editor of its house organ. Convinced that black Americans would support magazines focused on their interests, Johnson began publishing *Negro Digest* in 1942 and introduced his flagship publication, *Ebony,* three years later. It aped the format of popular magazines like *Life* and *Look,* but its articles and stories focused on black Americans. Over time the Johnson Publishing Co. introduced other magazines and published books aimed at the same audience. Meanwhile, Johnson branched out into insurance, cosmetics, and broadcasting, emerging as one of the nation's leading businessmen of any race.

References and Further Reading

Johnson, John H. *Succeeding Against the Odds.* New York: Warner Books, 1989.

Kaiser, Henry John (1882–1967)

Production of Kaiser automobiles lasted only a few years, but it was one of Henry John Kaiser's few entrepreneurial failures. Born into a poor family in upper New York State, he apprenticed as a photographer but abandoned that career to pursue an interest in road building. By 1921 he had established himself as a major contractor based in Oakland, California. In addition to underbidding competitors for highway projects, his company also participated in bridge and dam construction. When Kaiser's bid to build Shasta Dam failed, he determined to subcontract the work by making an extremely low bid to supply concrete even though he had no facilities to produce it at that point. When he won the contract, he built the giant Permanente Concrete plant in Los Gatos and bought cargo ships to ferry the concrete northward. Once World War II broke out, Kaiser combined his construction and shipping knowledge into a shipbuilding venture in San Francisco Bay. Using assembly line and scientific management techniques, his firm built over 1,500 liberty ships, constructing one of the 10,000-ton vessels from start to finish in just eight days. After the war he teamed with Joseph Frazer, hoping to fill the pent-up demand for cars, but the Kaiser-Frazer company lost out to the Big Three. Known for his benevolent labor policies, Kaiser worked out an attractive insurance, hospital, and treatment plan for his workers.

This developed into a pioneering health maintenance organization (HMO) that set standards for the nation's health care industry. Kaiser-Permanente continues to offer its members comprehensive medical service, a surviving legacy of a remarkably creative businessman.

See also Military-Industrial Complex.

References and Further Reading

Foster, Mark S. *Henry J. Kaiser.* Austin, TX: University of Texas Press, 1989.

Kilby, Jack (1923–2005)

Jack Kilby grew up in Great Bend, Kansas, where his father operated an electrical company that encouraged the young man to pursue a career in electrical engineering. He earned a bachelor's degree in that field at the University of Illinois and began working for an electronics manufacturer in Milwaukee. Because the transistor had just been invented, Kilby realized he needed training beyond the vacuum-tube technology he had studied earlier, so he earned a graduate degree at the University of Wisconsin. Dallas-based Texas Instruments (TI) hired Kilby in 1958 and allowed him considerable latitude in his research on miniaturization. By September he had created the world's first monolithic integrated circuit, a microchip packed with transistors, resistors, and capacitors capable of independent operation. Fairchild researchers Robert Noyce and Gordon Moore were independently moving in the same direction, but Kilby patented his technology five months earlier than his rivals. Interest in TI's microchips was relatively slow to develop, however, so the company president challenged Kilby to create a tiny calculator to demonstrate their capabilities. Kilby is credited with coinventing the handheld calculator that became an enormously successful product for the company. Kilby left TI in 1970 for a prestigious position at Texas A&M University where he continued exploring electronics and solar power. Over his long career Kilby's work earned him sixty patents and the 2000 Nobel Prize in physics.

See also Microchips; Transistors.

References and Further Reading

Riordan, Michael, and Lillian Hoddeson. *Crystal Fire.* New York: Norton, 1997.

Kravis, Henry (1944–)

Henry Kravis left his childhood home in Tulsa, Oklahoma, to enroll at Claremont College in California. There he became better acquainted with a cousin, George R. Roberts, who was also a student. Kravis subsequently earned a law degree at the University of California and Roberts took an MBA at Columbia. The two switched coasts, however, when they began working at branches of Bear Sterns, a brokerage house. Jerome Kohlberg headed the firm's investment department and became both a mentor and partner of the two younger men. Kohlberg was already engaged in relatively modest leveraged buyouts before the three formed Kohlberg, Kravis, and Roberts (KKR) to devote full attention to corporate takeovers. In the early years, KKR took pride in only handling friendly takeovers. Over time KKR developed larger and larger equity pools on which to base its operations. As the leveraged buyout phenomenon spread, a rule of thumb suggested that a takeover group could support a buy-out ten times larger than the value of its equity pool. In 1983 KKR controlled a billion dollars thereby enabling it to move in on some of the largest firms in existence. At that point the aggressive Kravis began promoting what many considered hostile takeovers, and Kohlberg resigned from active participation in KKR. By 1987 KKR's equity pool exceeded \$5 billion, and shortly afterward Kravis engineered a stunning takeover of RJR Nabisco. By the early 1990s, however, it was clear that many targets of KKR moves had stumbled badly once the dust had settled, and public awe of Henry Kravis gave way to resentment at what appeared to be heedless corporate raiding.

See also Conglomerates; Hostile Takeovers; Leveraged Buyout.

References and Further Reading

Ingham, John N., and Lynne B. Feldman. *Contemporary American Business Leaders.* New York: Greenwood, 1990.

Kresge, Sebastian Spering (S. S.) (1867–1966)

Because he almost reached the century mark, Sebastian Spering Kresge lived through an enormous number of changes in the retail business. Born into a poor Pennsylvania farm family, young Sebastian took every advantage of his limited opportunities for education including attending a business college. In the early 1890s his job as a traveling salesman introduced him to F. W. Woolworth and John G. McCrory, both of whom had created successful dime-store chains. Kresge negotiated a kind of apprenticeship with McCrory and his cousin, George C. Murphy, another dime-store mogul. By 1900 Kresge had established his own retail operation, which he incorporated as the S. S. Kresge Co. in 1912. It began with dime-stores but adopted a variety-store format offering a broader range of products and prices. A frugal, hardworking, and shrewd businessman, Kresge saw his chain expand to nearly 600 outlets by 1930. Like all businessmen, he struggled through the Great Depression but adjusted to changing postwar consumer preferences by establishing suburban outlets. To compete in that environment, Kresge invested heavily in big box discount stores called K-Marts. This move proved to be the company's salvation, although the K-Mart chain underwent bankruptcy reorganization early in the twenty-first century. It revived sufficiently to buy control of the long-established Sears chain in 2005.

See also Chain Stores; Malls.

References and Further Reading

Kresge, Stanley S. *The S. S. Kresge Story.* Racine, WI: Western Publishing Co., 1979.

Kroc, Ray (1902–1984)

In 1922 Ray Kroc became a sales agent for the Lily Tulip Cup Co., a position he held for fifteen years. He then switched product lines by negotiating an exclusive sales agreement with Earl Prince who had invented the "multimixer," a machine that stirred up to five milkshakes at a time and, not incidentally, filled a lot of Lily cups. Kroc traversed the country peddling multimixers, a pursuit that in 1954 led him to a hamburger restaurant that Dick and Mac McDonald operated in San Bernardino, California. Kroc was impressed by the efficiency and profitability of the McDonalds' operation that featured a menu focused on burgers, French fries, and shakes whipped up by multimixers. Kroc negotiated a deal with the brothers to open similar fast-food restaurants all across the country, and he eventually bought them out in 1961. Kroc's innovations included industrial-style machinery and efficiencies that further reduced costs, but never at the expense of his motto: quality, service, cleanliness, and value. By 1963 his largely franchise-operated chain had sold over a billion hamburgers, even before it introduced an enormously successful advertising campaign featuring the clown Ronald McDonald two years later. Serving in executive positions in his corporation until his death, Kroc saw his empire grow into the largest food service purveyor in the world.

See also Franchises.

References and Further Reading

Love, John F. *McDonald's: Behind the Arches.* New York: Bantam, 1986.

Lauder, Estée (1908?–2004)

Although she carefully cultivated an elegant, sophisticated image, Estée Lauder was born Josephine Ester Mentzer in the Borough of Queens to Hungarian immigrant parents. While still a teenager she learned the secrets of concocting a face cream from an uncle. She shortened her name and married Joseph Lauter (later Lauder) and together they began selling her products to local beauty salons. The couple formed Estée Lauder, Inc., in 1946, just in time for a key marketing breakthrough when Bonwit Teller and Saks Fifth Avenue agreed to feature its products. Lauder's company chose to merchandise only through high-end retailers and major department stores, a strategy that reinforced its reputation for sophisticated elegance. Over time Estée Lauder introduced perfume (Youth Dew), men's cosmetics (Aramis), and a hypoallergenic line (Clinique). Some of these product lines lost money for years, but the privately held company could afford long gestation periods. By the late 1980s the company's products accounted for more than one-third of all department store cosmetics sales. Estée Lauder relinquished active management of her company to her son in 1973 but continued to experiment with and market new fragrances.

See also Ash, Mary Kay; Rubinstein, Helena.

References and Further Reading

Israel, Lee. *Estée Lauder: Beyond the Magic.* New York: Macmillan, 1985.

Lauren, Ralph (1939–)

When New Yorker Ralph Lifshitz changed his last name to Lauren in the 1950s, it was only one in a series of decisions he made to tailor a more sophisticated image for himself and his products. He began working as a clerk in a clothing store while still in high school and, after dropping out of New York City College and serving a stint in the U.S. Army, he returned to the haberdashery business. His first success was designing very wide ties for the Beau Brummel Company, and their popularity proved that men would abandon staid, conservative business clothing for more intriguing styles. In 1968 he created his own company, Polo Fashions, to market his growing wardrobe. He introduced a line of women's clothing three years later. Ralph Lauren and Polo became associated in consumers' minds with well-designed, relatively expensive yet conservative sportswear. For a time Lauren drew inspiration from the American West, barely altering the blue jeans style that Levi Strauss had been producing for a century, yet selling them for twice or three times the price of Levis. After enduring a few early business problems, Lauren hired responsible subordinates and expanded his marketing to include licensees, boutique-style space in major department stores, and stand-alone Ralph Lauren stores. He also applied his discerning eye to home fashions like sheets and towels, all of which bear the distinctive Polo player logo. Along with designers like Tommy Hilfiger and Perry Ellis, Ralph Lauren created extraordinarily popular clothing choices to match the sports and leisure lifestyles that many Americans enjoyed or aspired to in the late twentieth century.

See also Claiborne, Elisabeth.

References and Further Reading

Trachtenberg, Jeffrey A. *Ralph Lauren.* New York: Little, Brown, 1988.

Levitt, William Jaird (1907–1994)

Acres and acres of prefabricated homes in Levittowns after the Second World War were the handiwork of William Jaird Levitt and his talented father and brother. The Brooklyn-based family had formed a construction company named Levitt & Sons, Inc. in 1929. William's father Abraham was an attorney and expert in real estate law, his brother Alfred was a building designer, and William himself headed the company, providing financial and management expertise. Despite having been formed just prior to the stock market crash, the construction company did reasonably well during the 1930s building and selling low-cost homes. During the Second World War, William Levitt served in the U.S. Navy Seabees while the company fulfilled government construction contracts back home. Anticipating the tremendous demand for housing that GI-Bill financing would fuel, Levitt and Sons adopted assembly-line techniques and prefabricated components to fill huge suburban tracts with virtually identical homes. Completed on Long Island in 1951, the first Levittown contained 17,500 two-bedroom Cape Cod style houses that sold quickly for around $7,000 each. It was the first of numerous Levitt and Sons projects that literally transformed the landscape and lifestyles of middle-class America. William Levitt's personal fortune may have topped $100 million by the time he sold the company to the International Telephone and Telegraph Corporation in 1968. He subsequently lost most of his huge fortune in unsuccessful foreign construction ventures and judgments against him for misappropriating funds from the Levitt Foundation.

Reference and Further Reading

Gans, Herbert J. *The Levittowners*. New York: Pantheon, 1967.

Ling, James J. (1922–)

Born in Oklahoma and orphaned in his teens, James J. Ling pulled himself up by his bootstraps. He worked briefly for an electrical contractor before enlisting in the Navy where he took advantage of its electrical engineering training programs. In 1947 Ling established his contracting business in Dallas with minimal capitalization. Creative financing including issuing junk bonds as well as his driving ambition enabled him to use that tiny firm as the basis for assembling one of the nation's first highly diversified conglomerates. By 1961 it had engulfed two military contractors, Temco Aircraft and Chance Vought, and Ling combined his properties into a new organization called Ling-Temco-Vought or simply LTV. To generate even more capital, he distributed his holdings into three separate companies under the LTV umbrella and acquired Braniff Airlines, Avis Rental Cars, and Bethlehem Steel among many others. In 1969 LTV had grown so large it triggered a federal antitrust suit. Ling surrendered his leadership position when LTV lost its case, and he eventually left the company entirely. He started up and participated in a number of other investment and industrial operations in later years, but none came close to matching the meteoritic rise and decline of LTV.

See also Conglomerates; Leveraged Buyout.

References and Further Reading

Brown, Stanley H. *Ling*. New York: Atheneum, 1972.

Milken, Michael Robert (1946–)

Born in Van Nuys, California, Michael Robert Milken graduated from the University of California at Berkeley. While engaged in graduate work at the Wharton School, however, he became fixated on junk bonds. These corporate debt instruments had to offer high interest rates because bond rating agencies like Standard & Poor's refused to assign them investment grade ratings of at least BB. Milken's study of the historical performance of these bonds convinced him they were only slightly more risky than higher rated corporate securities. Portraying himself as the champion of start-ups and worthy smaller ventures, he used his position at Drexel Burnham to become far and away the most successful trader in junk bonds. He amassed a personal fortune of well over $1 billion by collecting hefty brokerage commissions and investing wisely—often in junk bonds. From his headquarters in Beverly Hills, he hosted what came to be called the Predators Ball, an annual convention for anyone interested in using junk bonds. He developed financing for corporate raiders like T. Boone Pickens, Carl Icahn, and Henry Kravis engaged in leveraged buyout attempts. When Ivan Boesky was charged with insider trading, however, he implicated Drexel Burnham and Michael Milken. Milken eventually pleaded guilty to a number of counts, served a prison term, and was barred for life from the brokerage business. Even so, he remains a major investor and is universally credited with making junk bond financing both credible and attractive.

See also Junk Bonds; Leveraged Buyout.

References and Further Reading

Bruck, Connie. *The Predators' Ball.* New York: Penguin, 1989.

Noyce, Robert (1927–1990)

During Robert Noyce's formative years in Iowa he tinkered with electronics and other technologies and even built a small glider. He completed his education with a doctorate from MIT before joining transistor inventor William Shockley's start-up company in California. Although Noyce played a major role in the development of integrated circuits, he and seven colleagues concluded they could not work effectively with the demanding and moody Shockley. The so-called Traitorous Eight founded their own company, Fairchild Semiconductor Corporation, as a subsidiary to an East Coast camera and instrument manufacturer. Hampered by its conservative policies, Noyce teamed with Gordon Moore to found Intel in 1968. Intel not only became the world's leading computer chip manufacturer, but under Noyce's innovative management, it was a major factor in developing the technology-intensive community that became known as Silicon Valley. Among Noyce's many acolytes was young Steve Jobs, future entrepreneur of Apple Computers. Noyce was thus instrumental in the development of the integrated circuit, the founding of the leading computer-processor manufacturing concern, and a key participant in the rapid growth of the semiconductor industry in California.

See also Microchips; Transistors.

References and Further Reading

Berlin, Leslie. *The Man Behind the Microchip.* New York: Oxford University Press, 2005.

Olsen, Kenneth (1926–)

Kenneth Olsen's Digital Equipment Corporation (DEC) dominated the profitable minicomputer market niche for many years. Olsen grew up in Connecticut and spent a couple of years in the U.S. Navy before enrolling at MIT. There he came into contact with state-of-the-art developments in computing, and one of his graduate school professors detailed him to work at IBM for a couple of years. Olsen found that company's environment stultifying, so when he and Harlan Anderson established their own company in Maynard, Massachusetts, they determined to encourage an open, creative atmosphere. Funded in part by venture capital, DEC pursued a strategy of building minicomputers that were smaller, much less expensive, but often just as powerful as the IBM machines that dominated the industry. The most successful early DEC products were a series of PDP machines, "programmed data processors." AT&T eagerly snapped up PDP-1s, and the PDP-4 introduced in 1963 was a runaway success. A dozen years later, DEC's sales of PDP-11s assured it more than a third of the minicomputer market. Equally profitable was the development of the VAX (Virtual Address Extension) machines that proliferated in university and business settings, linking users to one another and to mainframe processing power. In the early 1980s DEC had to alter its strategy in face of the microcomputer challenge, but Olsen and his company's creative energies triggered new profitability later in the decade. The company has done less well in recent years, however, a fate it shares with many other high-tech concerns.

See also Computers.

References and Further Reading

Rifkin, Glen, and George Harrar. *The Ultimate Entrepreneur.* Rocklin, CA: Prima Publishing Co., 1990.

Packard, David (1912–1996)

David Packard's decision to leave his native Colorado to attend Stanford University set him on the path to prominence in Silicon Valley. At the university he befriended a fellow student, William Hewlett, and studied under Frederick Terman, the man whose vision created the Stanford Research Park. Both Terman and Hewlett encouraged Packard to return to California after a stint at General Electric, and the two younger men established a start-up company capitalized at $538 in the garage of Packard's house. They developed a number of electronic devices, gaining experience that would prove very useful in the war effort. Packard ran the company on his own while Hewlett served in the U.S. Army. Military orders dried up so quickly in 1946 when Hewlett returned to the company that it had to lay off half of its employees. The two entrepreneurs vowed never to get overextended again and to diversify their product line to avoid being dependent on government contracts. While Hewlett took the lead in research and engineering, Packard devoted his attention to management. He was largely responsible for developing the "H-P Way," a business and organizational philosophy that emphasized good employee relations. Both Hewlett and Packard interacted informally with their workers, provided outstanding benefit programs, and promised long-term employment for all. The company built a strong reputation for sound engineering and high quality in the calculators and printers it produced. Packard served as deputy secretary of defense in the Nixon administration. He retired from HP in the late 1970s but stepped in to guide the company through difficult times in the early 1990s. He and his wife endowed the David and Lucille Packard Foundation with more than $2 billion.

See also Hewlett, William Redington; Personal Computers.

References and Further Reading

Packard, David. *The HP Way.* New York: HarperBusiness, 1995.

Perdue, Frank (1920–2005)

As a child Frank Perdue worked for his father, Arthur Perdue, a local egg producer living on Maryland's Eastern Shore. When disease decimated their laying flock of Leghorn chickens in 1940, the Perdues switched to raising and selling chickens, a move that was timed perfectly to benefit from wartime orders. When Frank Perdue inherited Perdue Farms Incorporated in 1953, it had grown into a substantial operation, earning $8 million annually. Frank pushed it to new heights by taking advantage of technology and advertising. He borrowed extensively to install up-to-date automated incubators, chicken houses, and processing equipment. As production boomed, the company initiated a massive advertising campaign that featured homespun Frank Perdue himself serving as the company's chief spokesperson. Sales in New York City and other eastern markets soared and encouraged competitors to institute their own advertising barrages. Even so, Perdue Farms climbed into the ranks of the nation's leading privately held companies and was the third largest poultry distributor in the United States in the 1980s. When Frank Perdue retired in 1988, his personal fortune was estimated to exceed $350 million, and, as the saying goes, that ain't chicken feed!

References and Further Reading

Law-Yone, Wendy. *Company Information: A Model Investigation.* Washington: Washington Researchers, 1980.

Perot, Henry Ross (1930–)

Long after he became a billionaire, Henry Ross Perot continued to cultivate an image as a humble country boy from Texarkana, Texas. As a child he succeeded at a variety of small business ventures, but achieved a lifelong ambition when he entered the U.S. Naval Academy. He was commissioned in time to participate in the late stages of the Korean War but resigned from the peacetime

Navy in 1957 to become an IBM sales representative. Bored and frustrated with the company's policies, Perot quit to found his own firm, Electronic Data Services (EDS). It provided specialized computer support and sometimes assumed complete control of a company's data-processing systems. When Congress created Medicare three years later, EDS won a massive and lucrative federal contract to handle the program's record-keeping responsibilities. EDS went public in 1968, but Perot retained a hefty majority of its stock personally, and the market value of his shares quickly exceeded $1 billion. In 1984 Perot sold his company to General Motors (GM) for $2.5 billion, much of it in stock, a transaction that made the Texan GM's chief stockholder. For the next two years, Perot drove the staid GM management crazy with calls for responsiveness, openness, and corporate restructuring. The auto giant finally repurchased Perot's shares at a huge premium but retained EDS as a subsidiary. Perot fought back by forming Perot Systems Corporation and competed with EDS for public and private contracts. Although this latter venture was less successful than his earlier ones, Perot's considerable personal fortune enabled him to become deeply involved in politics in the early 1990s. He won 19 percent of the popular vote in the 1992 presidential election, the pinnacle of his political career.

References and Further Reading

Gross, Ken. *Ross Perot.* New York: Random House, 1992.

Pickens, T. Boone (1928–)

Trained as a geologist at Oklahoma A&M College (now Oklahoma State University), T. Boone Pickens worked briefly for the Phillips Petroleum Co. before striking out as an independent oil man. By the mid-1960s his Mesa Petroleum Co. had emerged as a dynamic exploration, drilling, and production operation. In the late 1970s Pickens began attempting a series of what many considered hostile takeovers of major oil companies like Cities Service, Gulf, and Phillips. While critics accused him of demanding greenmail payaments to enrich himself, Pickens steadfastly claimed only to be interested in rationalizing a mismanaged industry. Although he was thwarted in all of his major takeover efforts, he and his associates profited enormously from their ventures. In recent years he has focused his attention on natural gas and water resources.

See also Greenmail; Hostile Takeovers; Junk Bonds.

References and Further Reading

Pickens, Boone. *The Luckiest Guy in the World.* Washington, D.C.: BeardBooks, 2000.

Revson, Charles (1906–1975)

Born in Boston, Charles Revson moved to New York where he worked in a women's clothing store and then a small firm that produced inexpensive fingernail polish. In 1932 he and his brother formed a company with chemist Charles Lachman (the L in Revlon) who had devised a superior nail enamel. Charles Revson's determination was crucial in making the struggling firm a winner. He personally visited beauty salons throughout the city to demonstrate the product, and that experience convinced him that selling quality products to higher-end customers would lead to success. Over the years the Revlon line broadened to include lipstick, perfume, and even health care products that the company advertised aggressively. It drew unprecedented attention from its 1951 "Fire and Ice" campaign that appealed to women's sexuality. Another brilliant move was its sponsorship of the enormously popular TV quiz show "The $64,000 Question," which quadrupled Revlon's sales before the show was defrocked for cheating. To compete with "Estée," the perfume of his bitter rival Estée Lauder, Revlon introduced a scent named for himself, and "Charlie" became the best-selling perfume in the world. Revson maintained tight, dictatorial control over his company, firing or driving off literally hundreds of talented managers over the course of his career. After Revson's death, his company stumbled along until Ron Perlman staged a hostile takeover of Revlon in 1985 and executed a major reorganization that stripped it of losing lines and unprofitable components.

See also Hostile Takeovers.

References and Further Reading

Tobias, Andrew. *Fire and Ice.* New York: Morrow, 1976.

Schwab, Charles (1938–)

Although he was not related to the man of the same name who headed several major steel companies in the early twentieth century, Charles Schwab, the broker, became enormously influential in his own right. After earning both an undergraduate degree and an MBA at Stanford University, Schwab joined Investment Indicators in 1961. It was an advisory service that gave Schwab excellent training in the investment business. In 1971 the young go-getter established his own small investment firm, Charles Schwab and Co. Four years later the SEC cancelled its rules regarding brokers' commissions, so Schwab decided to have his company buy and sell stock for its customers and charge commissions well below those of other brokers. His discount brokerage kept its costs down by stripping off the advisory and other service functions traditional brokers offered. The Schwab customer was presumed to be capable of making his or her own decisions regarding investments; the brokerage acted solely as a buying and selling agent. To extend its customer base, Schwab opened dozens of branches throughout the United States, a strategy that generated additional sales but strained the firm's capital resources. In 1981 Charles Schwab reluctantly sold a huge block of shares to the Bank of America to obtain its backing for continued expansion. It was a troubled relationship, however, and Schwab managed to buy back control in 1987. The business has continued to evolve with Schwab constantly revising his approach to keep ahead of the many competitors who adopted the discount brokerage strategy he had pioneered.

References and Further Reading

Kador, John. *Charles Schwab.* Hoboken, NJ: Wiley, 2002.

Simon, Norton (1907–1993)

Norton Simon is remembered most for his magnificent art collection. The money that financed that collection came from a series of astute and daring investments that began in the food processing business. Born in Oregon, Norton Winfred Simon laid the basis for his business empire by founding a steel distributing company in Los Angeles. In the early 1930s he expanded into food processing by heading up Val Vita Foods, a base from which he began investing in the Hunt Brothers Packing Co. Simon dramatically reformulated this modest company by integrating can-fabrication into its packing operation, mechanizing process, and advertising aggressively. Hunt Tomato products soon enjoyed a strong national reputation and expanding sales. Using profits from the food company, Simon diversified into matches, magazine publication, canning, plywood, and steel. His precipitous attempt to control Wheeling Steel and some other hostile takeovers in the 1960s did not go well, however, so the entrepreneur retreated in 1968, consolidating his varied holdings into Norton Simon, Inc. From then on he focused his attention almost exclusively on his art collection, leaving David Mahoney to run the corporation. Like Simon before him, Mahoney made many changes, some of which, like the purchase of Max Factor cosmetics, proved to be disastrous. Eventually Norton Simon, Inc. itself became the target of numerous takeover attempts, perhaps a fitting destiny for the empire that one of the nation's first corporate raiders had created.

See also Conglomerates; Hostile Takeovers.

References and Further Reading

Ingham, John N., and Lynne B. Feldman. *Contemporary American Business Leaders.* New York: Greenwood, 1990.

Tandy, Charles (1918–1978)

Texan Charles Tandy attended Rice University, graduated from Texas Christian University, and spent a year at the Harvard Business School before joining the U.S. Navy. During the Second World War he noted that rehabilitation programs for injured sailors often featured leather crafting, so he convinced his father to produce handicraft kits at the basic leather supply company he operated in Ft. Worth. Charles bought his father out in 1950, formed the Tandy Leather Co., and greatly expanded its line of mail-order kits. Soon the company added hobby kits of all sorts and opened small retail outlets to market them. Tandy's company struggled through the decade but found a more promising opportunity in the early 1960s when it obtained a controlling interest in a small Boston-based chain called Radio Shack. Within a couple of years Tandy had completely reorganized and restructured the chain and was adding hundreds of new outlets annually. To supply some of the electronics items the chain specialized in, Tandy established major manufacturing facilities in Ft. Worth and elsewhere. In the mid-1970s Radio Shack was the nation's premier supplier of citizen-band radio equipment. When the CB craze faded, it began selling the TR-80, a basic personal computer before either Apple or IBM had completed their own models. The Radio Shack chain suffered stiff competition in the decades after Tandy's death, despite making some recovery with its IBM-clone Tandy computer line. It has, however, remained the nation's most recognized retailer of basic electronic equipment as well as handling computers, cell phones, and other electronic devices.

See also Malls; Personal Computers.

References and Further Reading

Farman, Irvin. *Tandy's Money Machine.* Chicago: Mobium Press, 1992.

Turner, Ted (1938–)

Ohio-born Robert Edward Turner III inherited the remnants of a billboard business when his father committed suicide in 1963. Young Ted demonstrated drive and business acumen in restructuring his father's holdings and, in 1970, buying an Atlanta UHF TV station. In short order, he negotiated broadcast rights with cable companies to give his WTBS "Superstation" a national audience. He then bought the Atlanta Braves and other sports franchises as well as MGM's movie archive to generate programming for the station. His most dramatic move came in 1980 when he used $50 million in profits from WTBS to subsidize the creation of Cable News Network. The ultimate success of CNN and other cable enterprises enabled him to make an unsuccessful bid for CBS in 1985 and arrange a successful merger with Time-Warner in 1996. Turner owned 10 percent of the stock in what was at that point the world's leading entertainment, information, and media company. He has donated over $1 billion to various charities.

See also Television.

References and Further Reading

Auletta, Ken. *Media Man.* New York: Norton, 2004.

Wang, An (1920–1990)

An Wang studied electrical engineering in his native Shanghai and became a teacher after graduating. During the Second World War Wang helped develop communication systems for the Chinese government locked in its war with Japan. Wang came to the United States in 1945 and began graduate work at

Harvard University where he obtained his doctorate in applied physics in 1950. Unwilling to return to a country now under Communist control, he took a postdoctoral position in Howard Aiken's computer laboratory. There Wang developed a magnetic core memory that was widely adopted in the years before microprocessors came on the market. In 1951 he left Harvard to found Wang Laboratories to conduct research. He funded it by manufacturing his memory device before selling his patent rights to IBM. His laboratory moved on to other projects including the production of a remarkably advanced scientific desk calculator in 1964. In the early 1970s Wang turned his attention to word processing, and the Wang system outperformed any other during that decade. The company suffered reverses in the 1980s, however, when microcomputers became capable of word processing and other data manipulation at far less cost than the Wang system. The entrepreneur had retired by that point, though he did reassume leadership of the company briefly in the mid-1980s. An Wang made major contributions to the arts and other charities in his adopted country before his death.

See also Computers.

References and Further Reading

Kenney, Charles. *Riding the Runaway Horse: The Rise and Decline of Wang Laboratories.* Boson: Little, Brown, 1992.

Appendix 1

Key Concepts and Biographies by Section

Key Concepts

2 Abominations, Tariff of
5 Adjustable Rate Mortgages
4 Agricultural Adjustment Acts
3 American Federation of Labor
2 American System
3 Antitrust Laws
1 Apprenticeship
5 Arbitrage
4 Associationism
4 Autarky
4 Bank Holiday
2 Banknotes
2 Bank of the United States
2 Bank War
4 Billion Dollar Corporation
3 Bonanza Farms
1 Book Credit
3 Boycott
4 Bracketing the Market
4 Brand Management
4 Brokers' Loans
1 Bubble
4 Built-in Obsolescence
4 Bull Market
3 Bulls and Bears
4 Business Cycles
4 Call Loans
2 Canal Era
2 Carrying Trade
3 Catalog Sales
3 Chain Stores
1 Charter, Royal
2 Charter, State
2 Checks
2 China Market
4 Clayton Antitrust Act
2 Clipper Ships
4 Commercial Aviation
4 Commodity Dollar
1 Commodity Money
5 Computers
5 Conglomerates
4 Consumer Credit
2 Continental Currency
2 Corn Law
2 Corporations
2 Cotton
2 Cotton Factorage
2 Cotton Gin
4 Crash
5 Credit Cards
3 Credit Mobilier
4 Creditor Nation
3 Crop Lien
4 Dawes Plan
2 Dealership
4 Deficit Spending
3 Department Store
5 Deregulation
2 Division of Labor
1 Dollar
2 Dollar, American
3 E. C. Knight and Co. Case
3 Electric Car
3 Electric Power
5 Electronic Fund Transfers
2 Embargo
1 Enclosure
1 Factor

4 Federal Reserve System, Creation of
4 Federal Reserve System, Reform of
4 Federal Trade Commission
1 Fisheries
4 Florida Land Bubble
5 Franchises
2 Free Banking
3 Free List
3 Free Silver
1 Fur Trade
5 GATT
3 General Incorporation Laws
3 Gold Corner
2 Gold Rush
5 Golden Parachute
4 Great Depression, Causes of
4 Great Depression, Character of
3 Greenbacks
5 Greenmail
1 Guilds
1 Head Rights
4 Holding Company
3 Horizontal Integration
5 Hostile Takeovers
1 Indenture
4 Induced Scarcity
2 Industrial Revolution
2 Integrated Mill
2 Interchangeable Parts
2 Interstate Commerce Clause
3 Interstate Commerce Commission
4 Interstate Commerce Commission, Reform of
2 Japan, Opening of
1 Joint-Stock Company
5 Junk Bonds
4 Just Price
4 Keynesian Economics
3 Knights of Labor
2 Labor Unions, Early
2 Laissez-Faire
2 Land Companies
3 Land Grant Railroads
5 Leveraged Buyout
4 Leveraged Investment Trust
1 Lottery
5 Malls
1 Manufacturing Acts
5 Marketing Concept
2 *McCulloch v. Maryland*
1 Mercantilism
5 Microchips
5 Military Aviation
5 Military-Industrial Complex
1 Molasses Act
5 Monetarism
4 Money Supply
2 Monopoly
4 Movies
4 Moving Assembly Line
4 Muckrakers
3 National Bank Notes
3 National Labor Union
1 Naval Stores
1 Navigation Acts
2 New York Stock and Exchange Board
2 Nonimportation
4 Northern Securities Co. Case
3 Office Appliances
3 Oligopoly
4 Open Market Operations
2 Packet Ships
2 Panic of 1819
3 Panic of 1873
3 Panic of 1893
1 Paper Currency
4 Parcel Delivery
4 Parity
2 Patent Pool
2 Patents
5 Personal Computers
1 Pine Tree Shilling
1 Plantation
5 Poison Pill
4 Ponzi Scheme
3 Pool
4 Preferred List
2 Privateering
4 Product Differentiation
1 Proprietary Colonies
2 Protective Tariff
2 Public Credit, Report on the
4 Pujo Committee (Money Trust)
3 Pullman Strike
4 Radio

3 Railroad Consolidation
2 Railroads
5 Rationing
3 Rebates
4 Reciprocity
4 Reconstruction Finance Corporation
4 Recovery
4 Relief
4 Rule of Reason
5 Savings and Loan Crisis
4 Scientific Management
4 Securities and Exchange Commission
4 Selden Patent
3 Sharecropping
3 Shinplasters
1 Shipbuilding
3 Shopping
3 Single Tax
1 Slavery
3 Social Darwinism
2 Soft Money
2 Specie Circular
5 Stagflation
2 Stamp Act
4 Standardization
1 Staples
2 Steamboats
5 Stock Options
2 Sugar Act
5 Supply-Side Economics
3 Tabulating
5 Television
1 Tobacco
1 Trade Balance
3 Trademarks
5 Transistors
1 Triangular Trade
3 Trust
4 Underconsumption
5 Universal Product Code
5 Venture Capital
3 Vertical Integration
1 Wage Codes
1 Wall Street
4 War Industries Board
3 Watered Stock
5 White Knight

BIOGRAPHIES

2 Adams, Samuel
4 Aldrich, Nelson Wilmarth
5 Andersen, Arthur
4 Arden, Elizabeth
3 Armour, Philip Danforth
5 Ash, Mary Kay
2 Astor, John Jacob
3 Ayer, Francis Wayland
4 Baruch, Bernard Mannes
3 Bell, Alexander Graham
2 Belmont, August
2 Biddle, Nicholas
4 Birdseye, Clarence
4 Boeing, William Edward
5 Boesky, Ivan
2 Borden, Gail
5 Buffet, Warren Edward
3 Burroughs, William Seward
3 Busch, Adolphus
1 Byrd, William, II
1 Calvert, George
3 Carnegie, Andrew
4 Carrier, Willis Haviland
4 Chrysler, Walter Percy
5 Claiborne, Elisabeth
2 Clay, Henry
2 Colt, Samuel
3 Cooke, Jay
3 Coors, Adolph
2 Corning, Erastus
2 Deere, John
3 Depew, Chauncey Mitchell
4 Disney, Walter Elias
3 Dodd, Samuel Calvin Tate
4 Dodge, John Francis, and Horace Elgin Dodge
5 Douglas, Donald Wills
2 du Pont de Nemours, Éleuthère Irénée
4 du Pont, Pierre Samuel
2 Duer, William
3 Duke, James Buchanan
4 Durant, William Crapo
3 Eastman, George
3 Edison, Thomas Alva
2 Evans, Oliver

4 Firestone, Harvey Samuel
5 Forbes, Malcolm Stevenson
4 Ford, Henry
1 Franklin, Benjamin
3 Frick, Henry Clay
2 Fulton, Robert
4 Gary, Elbert Henry
5 Gates, Bill
5 Geneen, Harold
4 Giannini, Amadeo Peter (A. P.)
2 Girard, Stephen
3 Gompers, Samuel
2 Goodyear, Charles
3 Gould, Jay
3 Grace, William Russell
5 Graham, Katharine
2 Hamilton, Alexander
2 Hancock, John
3 Harriman, Edward Henry
3 Hearst, William Randolph
3 Heinz, Henry John
4 Hershey, Milton Snavely
5 Hewlett, William Redington
4 Hill, James Jerome (J. J.)
4 Hilton, Conrad Nicholson
3 Hollerith, Herman
2 Howe, Elias
4 Hughes, Howard Robard
5 Icahn, Carl
4 Insull, Samuel
2 Jackson, Andrew
5 Jobs, Steven Paul
4 Johnson, Howard Deering
4 Johnson, Hugh
5 Johnson, John Harold
5 Kaiser, Henry John
4 Kellogg, John Harvey
5 Kilby, Jack
4 Knox, Rose
5 Kravis, Henry
5 Kresge, Sebastian Spering (S. S.)
5 Kroc, Ray
4 Land, Edwin Herbert
5 Lauder, Estée
5 Lauren, Ralph
5 Levitt, William Jaird
5 Ling, James J.
2 Lowell, Francis Cabot
3 Macy, Rowland Hussey (R. H.)
4 Mayer, Louis Burt
4 Maytag, Frederick
2 McCormick, Cyrus Hall
4 Mellon, Andrew William
5 Milken, Michael Robert
4 Mitchell, Wesley Clair
4 Morgan, John Pierpont (J. P.)
2 Morse, Samuel Finley Breese
5 Noyce, Robert
4 Olds, Ransom Eli
5 Olsen, Kenneth
2 Otis, Elisha Graves
5 Packard, David
4 Paley, William Samuel
3 Patterson, John Henry
1 Penn, William
3 Penney, James Cash (J. C.)
5 Perdue, Frank
5 Perot, Henry Ross
4 Phillips, Frank
5 Pickens, T. Boone
3 Pillsbury, Charles Alfred
3 Pulitzer, Joseph
3 Pullman, George Mortimore
1 Raleigh, Sir Walter
2 Remington, Philo
5 Revson, Charles
4 Reynolds, Richard Joshua (R. J.)
3 Rockefeller, John Davison
1 Rolfe, John
4 Rubinstein, Helena
4 Rudkin, Margaret
4 Sarnoff, David
5 Schwab, Charles
3 Scott, Thomas Alexander
3 Sears, Richard Warren (R. W.)
3 Sherman, John
5 Simon, Norton
4 Sinclair, Harry Ford
2 Singer, Isaac Merritt
2 Slater, Samuel
4 Sloan, Alfred Pritchard, Jr.
2 Smith, Adam
3 Sprague, Frank Julian
3 Stanford, Leland
3 Stewart, Alexander Turney (A. T.)
2 Strauss, Levi

Appendix 2

Key Concepts by Section and Subject

Agriculture

3 Bonanza Farms
2 Cotton
2 Cotton Factorage
2 Cotton Gin
3 Crop Lien
1 Enclosure
1 Factor
1 Fisheries
1 Fur Trade
1 Head Rights
2 Land Companies
1 Naval Stores
1 Plantation
1 Proprietary Colonies
3 Sharecropping
1 Staples
1 Tobacco

Antitrust

3 Antitrust Laws
4 Clayton Antitrust Act
3 E. C. Knight and Co. Case
4 Northern Securities Co. Case
4 Pujo Committee (Money Trust)
4 Rule of Reason
3 Trust

Banking

5 Adjustable Rate Mortgages
4 Bank Holiday
2 Bank of the United States
2 Bank War
4 Federal Reserve System, Creation of
4 Federal Reserve System, Reform of
2 Free Banking
2 *McCulloch v. Maryland*
4 Open Market Operations
5 Saving and Loan Crisis

Business Cycles

4 Bull Market
4 Business Cycles
4 Crash
4 Great Depression, Causes of
4 Great Depression, Character of
2 Panic of 1819
3 Panic of 1873
3 Panic of 1893
5 Stagflation

Capital

5 Arbitrage
5 Junk Bonds
1 Lottery
2 New York Stock and Exchange Board
5 Stock Options
5 Venture Capital
1 Wall Street
3 Watered Stock

Electronics

5 Computers
5 Microchips
5 Personal Computers
3 Tabulating
5 Transistors

ENTERTAINMENT

4 Movies
4 Radio
5 Television

GOVERNMENT

2 Abominations, Tariff of
4 Agricultural Adjustment Acts
2 American System
4 Associationalism
4 Autarky
1 Charter, Royal
2 Charter, State
4 Deficit Spending
4 Just Price
5 Military-Industrial Complex
1 Molasses Act
2 Monopoly
4 Parity
2 Public Credit, Report on the
4 Reconstruction Finance Corporation
4 Recovery
4 Relief
2 Stamp Act
2 Sugar Act
4 War Industries Board

INDUSTRY

2 Division of Labor
3 Electric Power
2 Industrial Revolution
2 Integrated Mill
2 Interchangeable Parts
4 Moving Assembly Line
3 Office Appliances

INTELLECTUAL PROPERTY

2 Patent Pool
2 Patents
4 Selden Patent
3 Trademarks

INTERNATIONAL

2 China Market
2 Corn Law
4 Creditor Nation
4 Dawes Plan
2 Embargo
3 Free List
5 GATT
2 Japan, Opening of
2 Nonimportation
2 Privateering
2 Protective Tariff
4 Reciprocity
1 Trade Balance

LABOR

3 American Federation of Labor
1 Apprenticeship
3 Boycott
1 Guilds
1 Indenture
3 Knights of Labor
2 Labor Unions, Early
3 National Labor Union
3 Pullman Strike
1 Slavery
1 Wage Codes

MERCHANDISING

3 Catalog Sales
3 Chain Store
3 Department Store
5 Franchises
5 Malls
4 Parcel Delivery
3 Shopping
5 Universal Product Code

MONEY

2 Banknotes
1 Book Credit
2 Checks
4 Commodity Dollar
1 Commodity Money
4 Consumer Credit
2 Continental Currency
5 Credit Cards

1 Dollar
2 Dollar, American
5 Electronic Fund Transfers
3 Free Silver
2 Gold Rush
3 Greenbacks
4 Money Supply
3 National Bank Notes
1 Paper Currency
1 Pine Tree Shilling
3 Shinplasters
2 Soft Money
2 Specie Circular

ORGANIZATION

4 Billion Dollar Corporation
5 Conglomerates
2 Corporations
3 General Incorporation Laws
5 Golden Parachute
4 Holding Company
3 Horizontal Integration
5 Hostile Takeovers
1 Joint-Stock Company
5 Leveraged Buyout
3 Oligopoly
5 Poison Pill
3 Pool
3 Vertical Integration
5 White Knight

RAILROADS

3 Credit Mobilier
3 Land Grant Railroads
3 Railroad Consolidation
2 Railroads

REGULATION

5 Deregulation
4 Federal Trade Commission
2 Interstate Commerce Clause
3 Interstate Commerce Commission
4 Interstate Commerce Commission, Reform of
1 Manufacturing Acts
1 Navigation Acts
5 Rationing
4 Securities and Exchange Commission

SPECULATION

4 Brokers' Loans
1 Bubble
3 Bulls and Bears
4 Call Loans
4 Florida Land Bubble
3 Gold Corner
5 Greenmail
4 Leveraged Investment Trust
4 Ponzi Scheme
4 Preferred List

STRATEGY

4 Bracketing the Market
4 Brand Management
4 Built-in Obsolescence
2 Dealership
5 Marketing Concept
4 Product Differentiation
3 Rebates
4 Scientific Management
4 Standardization

THEORY

4 Keynesian Economics
2 Laissez-Faire
1 Mercantilism
5 Monetarism
4 Muckrakers
3 Single Tax
3 Social Darwinism
5 Supply-Side Economics
4 Underconsumption
4 Induced Scarcity

TRANSPORTATION

2 Canal Era
2 Carrying Trade

2 Clipper Ships
4 Commercial Aviation
3 Electric Car
5 Military Aviation
2 Packet Ships
1 Shipbuilding
2 Steamboats
1 Triangular Trade

Appendix 3

Biographies by Section and Subject

Agriculture

2 Astor, John Jacob
1 Byrd, William, II
1 Calvert, George
3 Duke, James Buchanan
1 Penn, William
1 Raleigh, Sir Walter
1 Rolfe, John
2 Symmes, John Cleves

Aircraft

4 Boeing, William Edward
5 Douglas, Donald Wills
4 Hughes, Howard Robard
4 Trippe, Juan

Automobiles

4 Chrysler, Walter Percy
4 Dodge, John Francis, and Horace Elgin Dodge
4 du Pont, Pierre Samuel
4 Durant, William Crapo
4 Firestone, Harvey Samuel
4 Ford, Henry
5 Kaiser, Henry John
4 Olds, Ransom Eli
4 Sloan, Alfred Pritchard, Jr.

Banking

2 Belmont, August
2 Biddle, Nicholas
2 Duer, William
4 Giannini, Amadeo Peter (A. P.)
2 Girard, Stephen
4 Morgan, John Pierpont (J. P.)

Business

2 Adams, Samuel
1 Franklin, Benjamin
2 Hancock, John

Clothing

5 Claiborne, Elisabeth
5 Lauren, Ralph
2 Strauss, Levi

Conglomerates

5 Geneen, Harold
5 Ling, James J.
5 Simon, Norton

Cosmetics

4 Arden, Elizabeth
5 Ash, Mary Kay
5 Lauder, Estée
5 Revson, Charles
4 Rubinstein, Helena

Electronics

5 Gates, Bill
5 Hewlett, William Redington
5 Jobs, Steven Paul
5 Kilby, Jack
5 Noyce, Robert
5 Olsen, Kenneth

5 Packard, David
5 Perot, Henry Ross
5 Wang, An
4 Watson, Thomas J.

ENTERTAINMENT

4 Disney, Walter Elias
4 Mayer, Louis Burt
4 Paley, William Samuel
4 Sarnoff, David
5 Turner, Ted

FOOD

3 Armour, Philip Danforth
4 Birdseye, Clarence
2 Borden, Gail
3 Busch, Adolphus
3 Coors, Adolph
3 Heinz, Henry John
4 Hershey, Milton Snavely
4 Kellogg, John Harvey
4 Knox, Rose
5 Kroc, Ray
5 Perdue, Frank
3 Pillsbury, Charles Alfred
4 Rudkin, Margaret
3 Swift, Gustavus Franklin

GOVERNMENT

4 Aldrich, Nelson Wilmarth
4 Baruch, Bernard Mannes
2 Clay, Henry
2 Hamilton, Alexander
2 Jackson, Andrew
4 Johnson, Hugh
4 Mellon, Andrew William
3 Sherman, John
4 Wallace, Henry Agard

INDUSTRY

3 Carnegie, Andrew
3 Dodd, Samuel Calvin Tate
2 du Pont de Nemours, Éleuthère Irénée (E. I.)
3 Frick, Henry Clay
4 Gary, Elbert Henry
3 Grace, William Russell
5 Levitt, William Jaird
2 Lowell, Francis Cabot
4 Maytag, Frederick
3 Patterson, John Henry
4 Phillips, Frank
2 Remington, Philo
4 Reynolds, Richard Joshua (R. J.)
3 Rockefeller, John Davison
4 Sinclair, Harry Ford
2 Singer, Isaac Merritt
2 Slater, Samuel
3 Sprague, Frank Julian
2 Thomas, Seth
4 Vail, Theodore Newton
3 Whitney, William Collins
2 Winchester, Oliver Fisher

INVENTIONS

3 Bell, Alexander Graham
3 Burroughs, William Seward
4 Carrier, Willis Haviland
2 Colt, Samuel
2 Deere, John
3 Eastman, George
3 Edison, Thomas Alva
2 Evans, Oliver
2 Fulton, Robert
2 Goodyear, Charles
3 Hollerith, Herman
2 Howe, Elias
4 Land, Edwin Herbert
2 McCormick, Cyrus Hall
2 Morse, Samuel Finley Breese
2 Otis, Elisha Graves
3 Westinghouse, George
2 Whitney, Eli

MERCHANDISING

5 Kresge, Sebastian Spering (S. S.)
3 Macy, Rowland Hussey (R. H.)
3 Penney, James Cash (J.C.)
3 Sears, Richard Warren (R. W.)
3 Stewart, Alexander Turney (A. T.)
5 Tandy, Charles

3 Wanamaker, John
3 Ward, Aaron Montgomery
3 Woolworth, Frank Winfield (F. W.)

PUBLISHING

5 Graham, Katharine
3 Hearst, William Randolph
5 Johnson, John Harold
3 Pulitzer, Joseph

RAILROADS

2 Corning, Erastus
3 Depew, Chauncey Mitchell
3 Gould, Jay
3 Harriman, Edward Henry
4 Hill, James Jerome (J. J.)
3 Pullman, George Mortimore
3 Scott, Thomas Alexander
3 Stanford, Leland
2 Vanderbilt, Cornelius

SERVICE

5 Andersen, Arthur
3 Ayer, Francis Wayland
5 Forbes, Malcolm Stevenson
3 Gompers, Samuel
4 Hilton, Conrad Nicholson
4 Johnson, Howard Deering
5 Schwab, Charles
3 Thompson, James Walter

SPECULATION

5 Boesky, Ivan
5 Buffet, Warren Edward
3 Cooke, Jay
5 Icahn, Carl
4 Insull, Samuel
5 Kravis, Henry
5 Milken, Michael Robert
5 Pickens, T. Boone

THEORY

4 Mitchell, Wesley Clair
2 Smith, Adam
4 Taylor, Frederick Winslow

Index